The Peoples Of Canada

J. M. Bumsted

The
Peoples
Of
Canada

A Post-Confederation
History

Toronto
OXFORD
UNIVERSITY
PRESS
1992

Oxford University Press, 70 Wynford Drive, Don Mills, Ontario M3C 1J9

Toronto   Oxford   New York
Delhi   Bombay   Calcutta   Madras   Karachi   Kuala Lumpur
Singapore   Hong Kong   Tokyo   Nairobi   Dar es Salaam
Cape Town   Melbourne   Auckland   Madrid

and associated companies in
Berlin   Ibadan

This book is printed on permanent (acid-free) paper ∞.

Canadian Cataloguing in Publication Data

Bumsted, J. M., 1938-
    The peoples of Canada : a post-Confederation
history

Includes bibliographical references and index.
ISBN 0-19-540914-0

1. Canada - History - 1867-   . I. Title.

FC500.B86 1992   971.05   C92-094548-1
F1033.B86 1992

Design by Marie Bartholomew

1 2 3 4 - 96 95 94 93 92

Printed in Canada by Tri-Graphic

To my children

Contents

Maps

Preface

My Preface to the pre-Confederation volume of this survey of Canadian history, *The Canadian Peoples,* outlined my departure from the traditional progressive nation-building approach. Though the old approach would have provided a comfortable and secure means of organization in the context of prime ministers' tenures, or of the political parties they led, I have chosen to respond to the new scholarship by taking into account new perspectives and new emphases, while by no means disregarding key events in the traditional framework, or the values of traditional historiography. This post-Confederation volume—like the volume that precedes it—is mainly about the peoples of Canada and their society: politics is only one of many aspects of historical development discussed.

The division of history into periods, though always a bit artificial, provides some shape and structure to historical analyses. But it becomes problematical in any attempt to synthesize the new scholarship, because the subject matter often requires time-frames, stretching over lengthy periods, that are only slightly related to political events. It is my view that the most significant turning-point in Canada's development is not the year of Confederation, 1867—since the nation as we know it did not begin to take its present geographical form until the 1870s—but 1885, a year that saw three crucial events: the opening of the Canadian Pacific Railway and the suppression of the Northwest Rebellion in Saskatchewan, which had a long-standing dele-terious effect on French-English relations in central Canada, and the first legislative exclusion of Orientals in Canada. The two volumes of this work, therefore, end and begin respectively with a chapter covering the period 1867-1885—a repetition that is intended to provide continuity for readers who think of 1867 as the critical dividing point. The discussion that follows in this volume is divided into four periods: 1885-1919, 1921-1945, 1945-1972, and 1972 to the present.

The period 1885-1919 was one of economic (especially industrial, but also agricultural) expansion, combined with a great wave of social reform connected with industrialization and its partner, urbanization. It also saw the development of provincial balances to federal authority, the growth of an imperial sentiment in English-speaking Canada (and its rejection in Quebec), the feeling in rural Canada that it was being threatened by the urban concentration of wealth and power, a shift in the nature of immigration, and a quest for equal rights for women. The Great War helped bring many of the disparate threads temporarily together, for better or for worse, but in the exhausted aftermath of that war they all once again separated.

The period 1921-1945 can be characterized by an underlying concern that Stephen Leacock labelled at its outset 'The Unsolved Riddle of Social Justice'. Following the Great War, the peoples of Canada tried unsuccessfully to find ways of responding to demands for social justice; but they soon found themselves facing the Great Depression, which sits like an enormous albatross over the middle of the period. The Depression demonstrated the relative impotence of the central government in dealing with economic and social crises, despite new rhetoric and new strategies. Ironically, it was the Second World War that made possible the beginnings of the modern welfare state in Canada. This period also saw advances on the cultural front—which became more sophisticated and more nationalistic—and the trappings of national sovereignty as Canada moved from under the British to the American military and economic umbrella as a place of shelter from international pressures.

The period from the end of the Second World War to 1972 was coloured by the apparently successful workings of twentieth-century liberalism (and Liberalism), which had a clear centralist-nationalist thrust. At the same time, this was being challenged by the wave of Quebec nationalism that took hold in the 1960s, of which the FLQ crisis of October 1970 was a key event. In spite of internal nationalistic pressures, this period was considered to be one of optimism and affluence, and of unlimited growth (which was brought into question by the oil crisis of 1972). It was characterized by a baby boom and the development of a suburban way of life, as well as by a cultural flowering that was greatly assisted by the public purse (federal, provincial, and municipal). Collective minorities, for so long largely silent, gained some voice. Bilingualism and biculturalism became official national policy, and the nation gained new symbols of sovereignty, including a flag and a national anthem. Internationally, Canada rose and fell as a 'Middle Power', while at the same time becoming integrated into a continental military-industrial system dominated by the United States. Canadians worried about American influence, and not everyone shared in the affluence.

The years since 1972 have witnessed the unravelling of a variety of understandings that had been created in the wake of the Second World War. Liberalism—and its underlying Keynesian economic theory—seemed suddenly to collapse, to be replaced by a private-enterprise mentality. Centralism—under attack from both the provinces and the collective minorities—

also floundered. And nationalism, especially economic nationalism, was replaced by the Free Trade Agreement and a new spirit of continentalism in Ottawa. The baby boomers made their way into the work force, and their needs and desires influenced the economy, helping to produce the frantic consumerism of the 1980s. Canadians were finally forced to confront some of their most cherished assumptions, such as the notion that they were a peaceable, non-violent people, or that the Canadian mosaic was more tolerant of racial minorities than the American melting-pot. The post-1972 period was also characterized by the official development of multiculturalism and of the protection for collective minorities provided in the Charter of Rights—but also by much evidence of continued racism. A major post-1972 development was the emergence of cultural policy, though this was often expressed in economic rather than aesthetic terms. Over the latter part of this period Quebec's future relationship to the rest of the country was like an incubus—with the possibilities of sovereignty-association or the province's separation lurking in the background of increasingly tense rounds of discussion—that was not removed by the overwhelming rejection, in the referendum of October 1992, of the constitutional reforms contained in the Charlottetown accord.

Summarized thus, the periodic structure of this post-Confederation volume makes it sound neater than it really is. The history and aspirations of its central subject—the peoples of Canada—cannot easily be stuffed into tidy chronological compartments. And as I noted in my Preface to the previous volume, I am fully conscious of the fact that virtually every word I write carries heavy political freight; that inclusions, exclusions, and connections can all be seen in a political light. I believe the risk of criticism is well worth running, however, in relating a history of the Canadian peoples that attempts to transcend, while never disregarding, matters that have traditionally been associated with it.

As is true of most works of synthesis, this one literally stands on the shoulders of hundreds of other scholars whose work I have gratefully employed in gaining my own understanding. I repeat the acknowledgements of the first volume, beginning by thanking my students over twenty-five years for their stimulation. My editor, William Toye, has had an essential part in developing this history, constantly challenging me and keeping me lucid. In this regard Sally Livingston, who read the proofs, made many astute suggestions in the interests of clarification and precision. My wife, Wendy Owen, has assisted me in all sorts of ways—most tangibly by sharing the fruits of her unpublished research on Canadian Imperialism that resonates throughout Chapter Five. The librarians at the Government Documents section of the University of Manitoba's Dafoe Library have performed great feats of locating material; and at the Library of St John's College, Pat Wright and his colleagues have been very helpful. Friends and colleagues who have read parts of this manuscript include Kerry Abel, Doug Cole, Barry Ferguson, Robin Fisher, John Kendle, Allan Levine, Larry McCann, Terry Murphy, John Reid, Andy Robb, John Thompson, and Paul Voisey. While their comments have resulted in great improvements in the text, I alone am responsible for the final product, including all errors of commission and omission.

JMB
St John's College, Winnipeg
October 1992

chapter one

The Completion of Confederation

In 1881 the chief clerk of the House of Commons, John Bourinot (1837-1902), published a book entitled *The Intellectual Development of the Canadian People: An Historical Review*, the first of his many books on history and Canadian government. Born in Sydney, Nova Scotia, he was educated at the University of Toronto and then founded the Halifax *Herald* in 1860, becoming chief reporter of the Nova Scotia Assembly in 1861. He had moved to Ottawa in 1868 to join the *Hansard* staff of the House of Commons, attracted—like many other intellectuals—by the economic opportunities and wider horizons that seemed to beckon there after Confederation. In his book Bourinot sought to correct the deprecation of the intellectual efforts of Canadians at home and abroad. Canada, he insisted, had moved 'beyond the state of mere colonial pupilage', and, he implied, the cultural products of the new nation were entitled to a better press to match its political achievements.

Bourinot argued chiefly from advances in education and literacy. He began by writing glowingly of the system of public education—free and accessible—available in most provinces, and of the country's twenty-one colleges and universities. He pointed out that $64,000,000 had been spent on public schools across the Dominion since 1867, adding that in 1839 about one in thirteen young British North Americans had been attending school, while in 1881 the proportion was one in four. Newspapers were another sign of intellectual development, increasing from 65 in all British North America in 1840 to 465—56 of them dailies—in 1880. Fond of arguing from sheer numbers, Bourinot wrote that in 1879, 4,085,454 pounds of newspapers at one cent per pound 'passed through the post offices of the Dominion', and over 30 million copies of newspapers were circulated annually in Canada through the mails.* He concluded with a chapter on literature, which catalogued a number of French-Canadian historians and poets—including Léon-Pamphile Lemay (1837-1918), Octave Crémazie (1827-79), Benjamin Sulte (1841-1923), and Louis Fréchette (1839-1908), whose elegy 'Les Morts' he compared favourably to Victor Hugo's work—and offered a handful of English-Canadian writers, chiefly from the Maritimes. The 'firm, broad basis of general education', Bourinot concluded, meant 'a future as full of promise for literature as for industry.'

Some of Bourinot's comments, especially about French Canada, sound extremely patronizing to the modern ear. He wrote of the 'greater impulsiveness and vivacity of the French Canadians', and was pleased to remind his readers that French Canadians were descendants of Normans and Bretons, 'whose people have much that is akin with the people of the British Islands.' Although such ideas were in common circulation in the Canada of his time, colouring many of the efforts to define the new Canadian identity after Confederation, Bourinot also insisted that in Quebec 'there exists a national French Canadian sentiment, which has produced no mean intellectual feats', and maintained that

> . . . in the essential elements of intellectual development, Canada is making not a rapid but certainly at least a steady and encouraging progress, which proves that her people have not lost, in consequence of the decided disadvantages of their colonial situation, any of the characteristics of the races to whom they owe their origin. [p. 3]

While the work was characterized by a strong underpinning of that great Victorian concept, progress, the very fact that someone in 1881 made an attempt to deal with such a subject as the intellectual development of the Canadian people indicates some of the changes that had been brought about in what the author himself saw as the movement from raw frontier colonies to civilized nation. That development, however, was hardly the simple progression that John Bourinot sought to document.

---

*The federal power that probably touched most Canadians immediately was control of the postal service. In 1867 the Dominion took over the running of 3,477 post offices, which became 13,811 by the Great War in 1914, and almost immediately lowered rates from 5.5 cents to 3 cents per half-ounce on letters; by 1899 the rate was 2 cents per ounce. Post-office patronage greased the wheels of party politics, and Canadians saved their money in the postal savings banks. Throughout the first fifty years of Confederation the Canadian post office made profits, while providing efficient public services that affected every inhabitant of the Dominion. The fact that the postal service was a major federal power in the nineteenth century suggests how much times could change by the twentieth.

Completing the Union

Although 1 July 1867 was obviously a beginning in the development of a Canadian Confederation, in the larger sense it was only an interim point. The new union consisted of four provinces—Ontario, Quebec, Nova Scotia, and New Brunswick—carved from the three that had created it, and Macdonald's government was conscious that a lot of British territory on the continent had been excluded. The new government was also quite obviously the old Canadian coalition, with a few Maritime faces, organized into the old Canadian departments and using buildings erected in Ottawa for the old Union of the Canadas. If the new administration seemed familiar, so did its policies. The malcontents in Nova Scotia were bought off with 'better terms' that were entirely financial, and the Intercolonial Railway was set a-building along the eastern coast of New Brunswick. Much energy was devoted to rounding up the strays.

Manitoba

In 1868 a ministerial delegation was sent to London to arrange the transfer of the Northwest to Canada by the Hudson's Bay Company. While complex negotiations continued, the Canadian government began building a road from Fort Garry to Lake of the Woods—as part of the road and water system connecting Red River with Canada—and establishing informal connections with Dr John Christian Schultz (1840-96), a doctor, the owner of a general store, and the influential leader of the local faction in Red River that had for years been agitating for Canadian annexation. As had been the case with Lord Selkirk fifty years earlier, nobody paid any attention to the Métis, the mixed-bloods who constituted the bulk of the local population of Red River. The Canadian delegation in London finally worked out a deal for the transfer, with the British government receiving Rupert's Land from the Hudson's Bay Company (the Canadian government put up £300,000 and agreed to substantial land grants for the Company) and subsequently transferring it intact to Canada.

Since all of the arrangements for Rupert's Land were made without bothering to inform the Red River people of their import, it was hardly surprising that they were suspicious and easily roused to protest. The Métis were concerned on several counts. A Canadian roadbuilding party had been involved in a number of incidents that had racist overtones, and the transparent haste of the Canadian government to build a road and send in men to survey land suggested, quite reasonably, that Canadian settlement would inundate the colony with no regard for its Métis inhabitants. Furthermore, some of the road-builders were discovered buying land cheaply from the Indians—land the Métis thought was theirs. The Canadians were now seen as a threat not only to the land, but also to the language and religion of the Métis—perhaps to their very existence. The Canadian government was warned in 1869 that trouble was brewing—by the Anglican archbishop of Rupert's Land, Robert Machray (1831-1904); by the governor of the Hudson's Bay Company, William Mactavish (1815-70); and by Bishop Alexandre Taché (1823-94), the Catholic Bishop of St Boniface—but it received all reports with little or no interest.

At this point a leader of the Métis appeared in the person of Louis Riel (1844-85), a member of a respected family in the community; his father, for whom he was named, had successfully led a Métis protest in 1849 against the Hudson's Bay Company over many grievances, including the right to trade freely in furs. The young Riel spoke out publicly against the surveys. In October 1869, while the surveyors were running their line south of Fort Garry through the land of André Nault, his neighbours, led by Riel, rushed to the farm. They stood on the surveyors' chain and told them to stop. This act was Riel's first resistance to Canada's acquisition of the Northwest.

In the meantime William McDougall (1822-1905) was on his way from Canada to assume office as lieutenant-governor of the Northwest. A newly formed National Committee of the Métis resolved that McDougall should not be allowed into the country. They drafted a message to McDougall, who was approaching Pembina on the American border: 'The National Committee of the Métis orders William McDougall not to enter the Territory of the North West without special permission of the above-mentioned committee.'

The town of Winnipeg as shown in the *Canadian Illustrated News* , 18 December 1869: 'To the right, and the most prominent building in the picture, is the building occupied by Dr Schultz as a residence and drug store. Adjoining that is the office of the *Nor'Wester* newspaper; while on the left is shown one of the HB Company's stores.' Metropolitan Toronto Reference Library.

This warning was signed 'Louis Riel, Secretary'.[1] It was his second act of resistance to Canada.

The Council of Assiniboia—which had been appointed by the Hudson's Bay Company to govern the settlement—summoned Riel to explain his action. Riel made quite clear that the Métis were 'perfectly satisfied with the present Government and wanted no other'; that they 'objected to any Government coming from Canada without their being consulted in the matter'; that they 'would never admit any Governor no matter by whom he might be appointed, if not by the Hudson's Bay Company, unless Delegates were previously sent, with whom they might negotiate as to the terms and conditions under which they would acknowledge him'. Finally, Riel insisted that his compatriots were 'simply acting in defence of their own liberty' and 'did not anticipate any opposition from their English-speaking fellow countrymen, and only wished them to join and aid in securing their common rights.'[2]

In early November Riel and a large group of his men, accompanied by sympathizers, walked into Fort Garry, the Hudson's Bay Company fort, and took possession of it. On 7 December he and his men surrounded Dr Schultz's store, taking Schultz and forty-eight Canadians—including Thomas Scott (c.1841-70), one of the road-builders—to Fort Garry as prisoners. The next day Riel issued a 'Declaration of the People', announcing

Louis Riel and his councillors, 1869-70. National Archives of Canada, 12854.

a Provisional Government to replace the Council of Assiniboia. He, as President, offered to negotiate with Canada on the terms for Red River's entry into Confederation. Riel thus declared that what the Métis sought was to be allowed to become a part of the Confederation process. On 18 December McDougall left Pembina and returned to Canada.

On 27 December Donald A. Smith (1820-1914)—the head of the Hudson's Bay Company in Canada, who had been appointed by Sir John A. Macdonald to explain to the people of Red River how Canada intended to govern the country, and to report on the disturbances—arrived at the settlement and suggested a mass meeting.* Two were held, on 19 and 20 January 1870. Smith won the crowd's confidence, particularly among the anglophone mixed bloods, with his assurances that Canada would not interfere with the property, language or religion of the people of Red River. On the second day Riel proposed a convention of 40 representatives, equally divided between the two language groups, and at these meetings a 'List of Rights' was debated, Riel's Provisional Government was endorsed, the Canadian prisoners (many had already escaped) were released, and three delegates were appointed to go to Ottawa to negotiate provincial status within Confederation.

Meanwhile on 12 February 1870 a force of Canadian settlers, led by Major C.A. Boulton (1841-99), a surveyor—and including Charles Mair (1838-1927) and Thomas Scott, both of whom had escaped imprisonment in Fort Garry—left Portage la Prairie to join a party led by John Schultz (another escapee) at Kildonan, near Fort Garry. The plan was to overthrow the Provisional Government. But on 17 February a small force of Riel's men arrested and imprisoned most of these guerillas, except for Schultz, who managed to return to Ontario. Up to this point Riel's strategy and tactics were little short of brilliant. Although bordering on the illegal, the Provisional Government was arguably necessary to maintain order in the settlement, and despite some talk about negotiations with the Americans, Riel and the Métis clearly wanted Red River to be admitted to Confederation. But Riel permitted his men to vent their spleen on Thomas Scott, an Orangeman who hated 'halfbreeds' and was an unruly bully-boy. A Métis jury summarily sentenced Scott to death, and Riel accepted the sentence, commenting 'We must make Canada respect us.' On his way to his execution, just before noon on 4 March 1870, Scott said to the Methodist minister, Thomas Young, who accompanied him: 'This is horrible! This is cold-blooded murder! Be sure to make a true statement!'[3] Scott's eyes were bandaged and he was placed before a firing squad and shot; as his body moved, one man's revolver delivered the *coup de grâce*. Riel stood silently in the background throughout the execution,

---

*Smith later became the largest shareholder of the Company (he provided financial backing for the Canadian Pacific Railway) and in 1889 its chief executive officer. In 1897 he was elevated to the peerage as Lord Strathcona.

This illustration — which appeared in the *Canadian Illustrated News* on 23 April 1870 over the caption 'The Tragedy at Fort Garry' — suggests that Riel himself administered the *coup de grâce* to Thomas Scott, which was certainly not the case. Metropolitan Toronto Reference Library.

and apparently never thought much about it. But this treatment of Thomas Scott would have enormous repercussions in Orange Ontario, which was looking desperately for an excuse to condemn the Red River resistance.

Of the three-man delegation that went to Ottawa with the List of Rights, Abbé Ritchot (1825-1905) was the chief spokesman. A formidable negotiator, he gained concessions from the Canadian government that would guarantee some protection for the original inhabitants of Red River against the expected later influx of settlers and land speculators. At what the Canadian government of Macdonald always regarded as the point of a gun, the Métis extorted the Manitoba Act of 1870, which granted provincial status to Manitoba (a name favoured by Riel), a province of only 1,000 square miles, with 1,400,000 acres set aside for the Métis and bilingual services guaranteed.

In May 1870 the Canadian government sent a so-called peaceful military expedition to Red River, made up of imperial troops and militia units that included many Orangemen eager to kill Riel. A few hours before their arrival at Fort Garry, Riel and several of his associates fled across the American border—that favourite sanctuary for those who defied the Canadian government.

The Scott execution provided the Canadian government with the excuse to deny Riel and his lieutenants an official amnesty for all acts committed during the 'uprising', although those who negotiated with Canada always insisted that such an amnesty had been unofficially guaranteed. The result was that Louis Riel went into long-term exile instead of becoming premier of the province he had created.* Whether the government would keep better faith over its land guarantees to the Métis was another matter.

British Columbia

While the question of Rupert's Land dragged slowly to its conclusion, the Canadian government was presented with the unexpected (although not totally unsolicited) gift of a request from British Columbia—to which Vancouver Island had been annexed in 1866—for admission to the new union. The initiative from the Pacific colony had originated with the Nova Scotia-born journalist Amor De Cosmos (William Alexander Smith, 1825-97), who was a member of the colony's legislative council. In March 1867 he had introduced a motion that the British North America Act, then about to be passed by the British Parliament, allow for the eventual admission of British Columbia. Its entry into Confederation would bring about the introduction of responsible government, as well as resolving the colony's serious financial difficulties resulting partly from the interest on debts incurred for road-building during the gold rushes. One-third of British Columbia's annual revenue was required to service its debt, and office-holders had been forced to take salary reductions. Confederation with Canada received an additional impetus when—coterminously with the passage of the British North America Act but quite separate from it—the American government purchased Alaska from the Russians, touching off expected howls for the annexation of British Columbia. Officially the colony was notified in November 1867 that no action could be taken until Rupert's Land had been duly incorporated into Canada.

While union was put on hold, the colonists played hard to get, some of them even organizing a petition for annexation to the United States. But in early 1870 the British Columbia legislature passed a motion calling for union, providing satisfactory financial terms could be arranged. The legislature wanted to eliminate the debt and to undertake a vast program of public

---

*An amnesty was granted Riel in 1875, conditional on his being banished for five years.

improvements. It did not at first insist as a non-negotiable demand on the building of a transcontinental railroad, an undertaking that British businessmen had long supported, although Governor Anthony Musgrave (1828-88) reported to Britain, 'If a Railway could be promised, scarcely any other question would be allowed to be a difficulty'.[4] However, the British Columbia delegates to Ottawa came equipped with maps and proposed routes.

The negotiations between British Columbia and Canada took place in the late spring of 1870, just as the Canadian government was sending a military expedition to Red River to occupy that territory. The Canadians were generous to a fault. Of course British Columbia could have responsible government. Of course the debt could be wiped out. Of course there would be subsidies and grants, as well as federal support for the naval station at Esquimalt. And of course British Columbia could have a rail link with Canada—which was begun within two years and completed within fifteen.

Governor Musgrave was astounded. The terms were so much better than expected, 'And then the Railway, Credat Judaeus! is *guaranteed* without a reservation! Sir George Cartier says they will do that, or "burst".'[5] The promise was certainly audacious, although hardly surprising. For a variety of reasons, some of them political and some economic, Canada needed a transcontinental railroad to match the lines rapidly being constructed across the United States. As predicted, the railway guarantee virtually wiped out hesitancy in British Columbia, which had to promise in the end that it would not insist on the terms to the letter. On 20 July 1871 British Columbia entered Confederation as the sixth province, and while at the last moment a few lamented the event, one official commenting, 'We are a conquered country & the Canucks take possession tomorrow', most of the Pacific colonists seemed satisfied with their bargain.

While in most respects the new province remained until after 1885 too isolated from Canada to be much influenced by the union, Confederation encouraged and facilitated the gradual development of a new land policy for British Columbia, which opened the lands of the province to massive pre-emption and free land grants.[6] The government of British Columbia would exceed the federal government in its generosity to new settlers.

Prince Edward Island

Prince Edward Island's acceptance of 'terms' in 1873—given the vehemence of its initial rejection of union in 1866—was anti-climactic. The tiny province had been warned by the British to expect little favour outside Confederation, and it was actively wooed by both the Americans and the Canadians, who sent a series of formal proposals to the Island late in 1869. They were rejected on the grounds that they did not resolve the land question. But this was not the decisive factor in the end. In 1871 the Island entered on a profligate policy of railroad construction. Many saw the railway as a scheme to lure the Island into union, and between contracting overruns and the

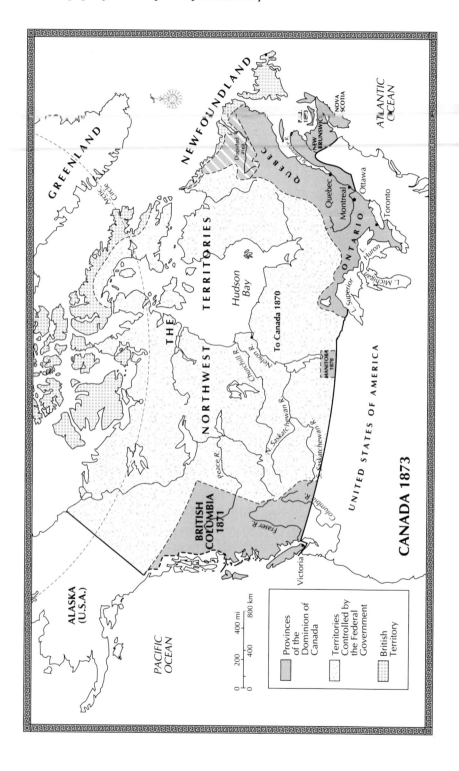

CANADA 1873

Provinces of the Dominion of Canada

Territories Controlled by the Federal Government

British Territory

demands of every village for service, the province quickly found its debentures unacceptable on the London market. Union with Canada was the only way to maintain the public credit, and the Dominion quickly made an offer the Island could not refuse. As well as taking over the debt and the railway, Canada offered to guarantee continuous communication with the mainland and to help buy out the last of the old proprietors. As Sir Leonard Tilley disingenuously explained to the Canadian House of Commons: 'The great local works there having been now completed, there could never be any large local expenditure in the future, and it was in consideration of this fact that the Dominion Government had granted such liberal terms.'[7] Once admitted, the Island would come cheap. Only one Island MLA, the crusty farmer Cornelius Howatt, refused to vote for the Canadian offer.

Newfoundland

Canada was not always successful in convincing latecomers to join the union. Although Newfoundland had sent delegates to the Quebec Conference in 1864, their enthusiasm for union was never matched by two of the colony's major groups: the Protestant merchants and the Irish Roman Catholics. The former feared the economic consequences of intercontinental integration, the latter opposed political unions out of a historical sense that in Ireland they had represented 'a conquest, in which the relationship must always be that of master and slave' and involve the destruction 'of the Irish people as a nation'.[8] Deteriorating economic prospects for the colony in the late 1860s seemed to bode well for an election to be held on the issue of union with Canada in 1869, fulfilling an understanding of popular consultation agreed to in the Newfoundland legislature in 1865. The economy improved, however, while opponents of Confederation employed every argument in their rhetorical arsenal, including rumours that Newfoundland children would be used as wads for Canadian cannon. The 1869 election went decisively against the pro-Confederates. Both the British and Canadian governments acquiesced in Newfoundland's maintaining the automony that continued—despite occasional union discussions, as in 1887 and 1895—until 1949.

✐ The Quest for National Policies

As well as completing the take-over of the northern part of the continent, the Macdonald government gradually improvised some national policies with which to govern the new Dominion. Most of them were left over from the earlier Canadian system, occasionally writ larger to accommodate the other provinces. Sometimes, of course, the interests of the constituent parts had to be sacrificed to larger concerns—one of which was Anglo-American *détente*. The imperial government was most unhappy about efforts by both Nova Scotia and the new Canadian government to keep American fishermen outside a three-mile limit off Canadien shores after the abrogation of reciprocity, particularly given a number of other outstanding issues involving the Americans. These included the *Alabama* claims (the *Alabama* was a Confederate raider built by Britain for the Southern States; the Americans, half-seriously, demanded the cession of British American territory in compensation for the losses it inflicted on northern shipping) and the Fenian claims. In 1871 the British government made Macdonald a member of an international joint commission set up in 1870 to deal with the fisheries question. It advised the Canadians to cede its claims to a three-mile limit only 'in return for an adequate consideration'. Sir Charles Tupper, representing Nova Scotian interests, insisted that fishing rights could not be sold only for a 'money consideration', but the British were willing to surrender Canadian (really Maritime) interests, eager as they were to settle outstanding Anglo-American differences or have them brought to international arbitration. These views prevailed, and Macdonald signed the resulting Treaty of Washington, seeing his signature as some recognition of Canadian diplomatic autonomy and the treaty as a recognition by the United States of the Canadian presence on the continent.

On the domestic front, the banking system of the new nation grew rapidly after Confederation, from 123 chartered bank branches in 1868 to 279 in 1879 and 426 by 1890. There were two major pieces of national legislation: the Dominion Notes Act of 1870 and the Bank Act of 1871. The former allowed the government to issue circulating notes of small denominations, only partly backed by specie, while the latter exerted control over the banking system. The Bank Act specified capital requirements for banks, prohibited new foreign-owned banks, and supplied general regulation, including standards for bank-note issue. Canada was integrated into the international gold standard, but the government would share the issuance of currency (and control of the creation of money) with the banks well into the twentieth century.

Confederation suggested an economic future for Canada that was generally encouraging to foreign investment. From its inception, Canada was able to import large amounts of capital to help create its economic infrastructure, including $166,000,000 (or 7 per cent of the Gross National Product) in the years 1871-5.[9] Between 1865 and 1869 Canada raised $16.5 million in Great Britain, a figure that rose to $94.6 million in 1870-74, $74.7 million in 1875-9, and $69.8 in 1880-4.[10]

The opportunity for further railway expansion was one of the principal economic arguments for Confederation—and railroads were a prime target of foreign investors. Nevertheless, despite the beginning of the Intercolonial Railway through New Brunswick, the Macdonald government was slow to move on that greatest of all railroads, an intercontinental line, chiefly because of the enormous expense involved in building so much ahead of population needs. To some extent the offer to British Columbia was intended to cast the die, and was followed by the usual unseemly scuffling over a charter, which was awarded in 1873 by Parliament to Sir Hugh Allan's Canada Pacific

Railway Company.* Then the Pacific Scandal broke. Allan had provided the government with money—more than $350,000—for its 1872 election campaign, and Macdonald was unable to step clear of this patronage. In November 1873 the government resigned, and was replaced by a Liberal government headed by a former stonemason, Alexander Mackenzie (1822-92), who sought to build a transcontinental line more gradually, using public funds. He was also prepared to encourage private interests to hook up with American western lines, and trains began running from Minnesota to Winnipeg late in 1878. By that time Mackenzie's earnestness had worn thin with the voters, and the probity of his government was not sufficient to save it in the 1878 election.

On his return to power Macdonald recognized the temper of the times and worked very hard to restore in the public mind a sense of total identity between his party and the process of nation-building, in which a certain decisiveness and flamboyance were part of the image. Even before the election he had his platform, introducing into the House of Commons a resolution 'That this House is of the opinion that the welfare of Canada requires the adoption of a National Policy, which, by a judicious readjustment of the Tariff, will benefit and foster the agricultural, the mining, the manufacturing and other interests of this Dominion.'[11] Macdonald invented neither the policy nor the term used to describe it. Both went well back into the development of economic policy for the Province of Canada, which had begun using a tariff as an instrument of both protection and revenue in the late 1840s. Nor did John A. ever articulate a version of the National Policy as it was later described by economic historians and textbook writers, although they have often suggested that he did. He certainly recognized a relationship involving tariffs, manufacturing, employment, and 'national prosperity'. He also wanted a transcontinental railroad and the accompanying western settlement necessary to make it a reality. But all this was a traditional part of Canadian economic expansionism.

What Macdonald achieved was masterful, however. He succeeded in persuading a large number of Canadians that policies strongly driven by the economic self-interest of some of the people in some of its constituent parts were in the best interest of the nation as a whole, and in identifying the party he led with the successful building of that nation. The fact that the opposition party had a different version of the meaning of Confederation helped in this identification.

◢ *Seeking National Identity*

Politicians were not alone in endeavouring to create a sense of nationality to accompany Confederation. No guarantees came with the British North America Act that political unification would inevitably create a nation,

---

*Allan had been knighted by Queen Victoria in 1871.

particularly given the competing interpretations of the meaning of Confederation. Intellectuals and artists played their part as well, both in terms of rhetorical flourishes and in the more mundane business of creating national institutions in which the arts could operate.

Act or Pact?

The development of nationhood in the years after 1867 should not obscure the fact that not all Canadians shared in the same vision (or version) of the meaning of the nation. Put most simply, was Canada an indissoluble new creation or was it the product of a compact among the provinces that they could either modify or even withdraw from? Since the time of the debate over Confederation in the 1860s, people had disagreed over the nature of the union. While most Canadians in 1867 saw Confederation as creating a strong central government, the legislatures of the provinces had certainly not been eliminated, and they would quickly reassert more than a mere 'local power'. An arch-critic of Confederation, Christopher Dunkin, had prophesied in 1865:

> In the times to come, when men shall begin to feel strongly on those questions that appeal to national preferences, prejudices and passions, all talk of your new nationality will sound but strangely. Some older nationality will then be found to hold the first place in most people's hearts.[12]

Even John A. Macdonald had admitted in Parliament in 1868: '. . .a conflict may, ere long, arise between the Dominion and the States Rights people.'[13]

The emergence of a states'-rights (or provincial-rights) interpretation of the new union was initially spearheaded by Ontario rather than by Quebec, although such a movement was inherent in the constitutional arrangements and could have begun anywhere. The arguments of Nova Scotia's repealers in and after the 1867 elections could have become part of such a position, but their failure and surrender seemed not to qualify. In any event, as early as 1869 Ontario became distressed at 'the assumption by the Parliament of Canada of the power to disturb the financial relations established by the British North America Act (1867), as between Canada and the several provinces.'[14] Not surprisingly, it was the old Reform party of Canada West, in the persons of George Brown, Edward Blake (1833-1912), and Oliver Mowat (1820-1903), that took the lead in demanding, in Blake's words of 1871, 'that each government [dominion and provincial] should be absolutely independent of the other in its management of its own affairs.'[15] The *Rouges* of Quebec soon joined in the same call, adding the identification of French-Canadian 'national' rights to Quebec's 'provincial' ones. Before long, Liberals in most provinces—many of whom had opposed Confederation or had been lukewarm about it—had embraced provincial rights.

Provincial rights often seemed interchangeable with Ottawa-bashing for local political advantage, lacking in any other principle than the desire to pressure Ottawa into fiscal concessions. In its early years, the movement was neither dominated by Quebec nor by arguments of a cultural deal between two distinct societies. In 1884, for example, the Honourable Honoré Mercier (1840-94) tabled resolutions in the Quebec legislature that insisted merely that 'the frequent enroachments of the Federal Parliament upon the prerogatives of the Provinces are a permanent menace to the latter.'[16] The ensuing debate did not involve any more cultural nationalism than one backbencher's assertion that '*le Québec n'est pas une province comme les autres*.'[17] Although the Riel business of 1885 (discussed later) pushed Quebec towards arguments of cultural distinctiveness, when Mercier—by this time premier of Quebec— invited the provinces to the Interprovincial Conference in 1887 to re-examine the federal compact, broad agreement could be reached on demands for better terms and constitutional change by the five provinces attending without the need for such clauses.

Canada First

The identification of emerging cultural nationalism in Canada, in the years immediately after 1867, with the movement that called itself 'Canada First' is an unfortunate one, for the Canada Firsters had neither a monopoly on national sentiment nor a very attractive version of it. The original Canada First movement was founded by a small group of intellectuals in Ottawa in 1868, to perpetuate the memory and sentiments of the late lamented D'Arcy McGee.* The founders were not a very prepossessing group of young men. Their ranks included Charles Mair (1838-1927), who had been publicly horsewhipped in Red River for his disparaging remarks about mixed-blood women; Robert G. Haliburton(1831-1901), the son of T.C. Haliburton and lobbyist for the Nova Scotia Coal Owners' Association; and George Denison (1839-1925) of Toronto, a militia officer who had long advocated military preparedness and would later boast of his part in arousing Ontario sentiment against Louis Riel over the 'murder' of Thomas Scott.

Indeed, turning the Canadian public against the Métis was Canada First's chief accomplishment. Its nationalism was in several senses racist. Haliburton was one of the earliest exponents of the notion of Canadians as the heirs of 'Aryan' northmen of the old world and their glorious destiny. 'We are the Northmen of the New World,' he trumpeted in an address to the Montreal Literary Club in March 1869—a new nationality comprising 'the Celtic, the Teutonic, and the Scandinavian elements' and embracing 'the Celt, the Norman French, the Saxon and the Swede'.[18] The group looked down their noses at Indians and Métis, seeing the French as the great 'bar to progress, and to the extension of a great Anglo-Saxon Dominion across the Continent' (the Toronto *Globe*, 4 August 1870). While these notions went together, to some extent, with Canadian westward expansion, they were fortunately not

---

*As a Member of Parliament, McGee had spoken out strongly against the Fenians and was assassinated by one (James Patrick Whelan) in Ottawa on 7 April 1868.

totally typical of the conscious development of Canadian nationalism. The French-Canadian poet Octave Crémazie, for example, lamented ironically that Canada's major literary languages were of European origin, arguing that '...if we spoke Huron or Iroquois, the works of our writers would attract the attention of the old world... One would be overwhelmed by a novel or a poem translated from the Iroquois, while one does not take the trouble to read a book written in French by a native of Quebec or Montreal.'[19]

The search for an essential 'Canadian-ness' went on in many corners of the new Dominion, but was nowhere so crowned with success as in that somewhat remote New Brunswick town, Fredericton, home of the University of New Brunswick. There the rectory of St Anne's Parish (Anglican) produced Charles G.D. Roberts (1860-1943), while not far down the road lived his cousin Bliss Carman (1861-1929). Along with Ottawa's Archibald Lampman (1861-99) and Duncan Campbell Scott (1862-1947), Roberts and Carman comprised the 'Confederation Poets', a designation invented by modern literary critics for the first school of Canadian poets who wrestled with Canadian themes, notably the local or regional landscape, with any degree of skill and sensitivity.

While many intellectuals and artists sought creative ways to express Canadian distinctiveness in their work, others took a more prosaic route in expressing a Canadian national identity. Curiously enough it was the painters who took the lead in organizing national groups to maintain professional standards and publicize Canadian art. The Ontario Society of Artists, formed in 1872 and incorporated in 1877, took the lead in this effort, becoming instrumental in the formation of the Royal Canadian Academy of Arts in 1880—in collaboration with the Governor General, Lord Lorne—and in the establishment that same year of the National Gallery of Canada. The Academy not only held an opening exhibition in Ottawa, but planned others in Toronto, Montreal, Halifax, and Saint John. As one of the founding academicians wrote, '*We are bound to try to civilize the Dominion a little.*'[20] The year 1880 was doubly important in art circles, for it was in that year that the Canadian Society of Graphic Art was also founded.

The Royal Society of Canada was founded in 1882 to promote research and learning in the arts and sciences. Lord Lorne again provided much of the impetus in replicating a British institution to establish the importance of cultural accomplishments in creating a sense of national pride and self-confidence. The first president, J.W. Dawson (1820-99), principal of McGill University—another Nova Scotian transported to central Canada—emphasized in his presidential address a sense of national purpose, especially 'the establishment of a bond of union between the scattered workers now widely separated in different parts of the Dominion.' Thomas Sterry Hunt (1826-92), a charter member and later president, observed that 'The occasion which brings us together is one which should mark a new departure in the intellectual history of Canada,' adding that 'the brightest glories and the most enduring honours of a country are those which come from its thinkers and its scholars.'[21] However romantic that statement may be, what is important is Hunt's emphasis on the country as a whole. Like the Royal Canadian Academy, the Royal Society had its headquarters in Ottawa.

The first president of the Royal Canadian Academy, the painter Lucius O'Brien (1832-99), was art director of an elaborate literary and artistic celebration of the young nation, *Picturesque Canada* (1882), which was based on the highly successful *Picturesque America* and *Picturesque Europe* and was the idea of two Americans, the Belden brothers, who had established themselves in Toronto. The editor of the project—George Monro Grant (1835-1902), Principal of Queen's University—stated in the Preface: 'I believed that

One of the illustrations in *Picturesque Canada*, this engraving shows the three Parliament Buildings in downtown Ottawa as they looked in the early 1880s. The East, West, and Centre Blocks (including the Library of Parliament), were erected in 1860-6. The Centre Block, except for the Library, was destroyed by fire on 3 February 1916, and was rebuilt in 1916-24 to designs by John A. Pearson, who also designed the soaring Peace Tower (1919-27) that stands in front of it today.

a work that would represent its characteristic scenery and the history and life of its people would not only make us better known to ourselves and to strangers, but would also stimulate national sentiment and contribute to the rightful development of the nation.' The two large volumes of *Picturesque Canada* contained some 540 illustrations—wood-engravings based on paintings and, for the West, photo-engravings of photographs—of serene vistas that fulfilled the promise of the title. The descriptive texts by Grant, Charles G.D. Roberts, and others presented an idealized, complacent view of the cities, towns, and regions of Canada, praising the present and pointing to their glorious future. *Picturesque Canada* was a monument to the optimism of the time.[22]

Education

As John Bourinot's comments at the beginning of this chapter indicate, Canadians of his time—if asked to comment on their cultural achievements—would have responded with pride about their school systems, particularly for their accessibility and universality. British North America's first Free Education Act, under which schools were fully financed by the state, was passed in Prince Edward Island in 1852, but the progress of Canadian education in the mid-Victorian age in all provinces observed a pattern of passage from private to public financial support at the same time that schooling became increasingly universal. The movement to public financing permitted the colonial governments and their provincial successors to provide centralized control over education, and small bureaucracies emerged after 1870 in all provinces. Attempts by these centralized agencies to regulate denominational schools in the same way that they controlled public ones would lead to much controversy.

Not all provinces moved at the same pace or in exactly the same way, of course. Education was left in the hands of the provinces by section 92 of the British North America Act, and it is almost impossible to talk about any integrated national movements. Indeed, education would become one of the most central and divisive issues in the new nation, and educational diversity was still the norm. Canada East had been somewhat slower than Canada West to move towards universality, and most of its schools continued to be—as they always had been—dominated by both clerical teachers and clerical values, although Protestants were able to establish their own institutions, particularly after education was reorganized in 1875. In Canada West, rudimentary common schools had always received some state support, but under Egerton Ryerson (1803-82), who served as chief superintendant of education from 1844 to 1876, a series of landmark School Acts gradually moved Ontario education towards state support and universality, at increasingly higher levels of educational attainment. Most western provinces would eventually emulate Ontario.

As early as 1868, a Canadian National Series of Readers was introduced into Ontario based on the Irish National Readers, but 'greatly improved and Canadianized'.[23] An emphasis on using material published in Canada and adapted to its uses was not the same thing as promulgation of a strident or even standard Canadian chauvinism in the schools. In the short run, English-Canadian educators tended to Canadianize by emphasizing 'the rich heritage of British history … reflected in our national escutcheon.'[24]

Other Cultural Activities

Not all cultural activity in Canada after Confederation was greatly affected by the creation of a nation. Indeed, most culture in Canada existed quite apart from national considerations. Despite their self-consciousness about the need for cultural achievements to match their new political accomplishments, in documenting progress Canadians would probably have ignored some of the most interesting arenas for culture, such as the various elements of popular culture. Only a brief sampling of other cultural activity in Canada — focusing on music and organized sport — can be included here.

Music

Although the occasional trained musician existed in colonial British North America, the mid-Victorian era saw the development of a widespread musical life that transcended the singing of hymns and folk songs. Most of the skilled musicians were immigrants who had learned their musical skills abroad, and much of the early advance involved garrison bands and choral groups. The bands often provided the musicians, and choral singing was something that could be done with a minimum of musical knowledge and training.

In Montreal the band of the 23rd Regiment, considered one of the best in the country, was heard with enthusiasm by Charles Dickens in 1842. On the West Coast the band of the Royal Engineers brought· new standards of musical performance when it arrived in the colony in 1859, and from that year until 1863 — when it was reposted to Britain — it entertained in various guises in New Westminister. It was in turns a militia band, a fire-brigade band, a brass band, and even a dance band. Some of its members remained in the province after it was reposted. In British Columbia, as elsewhere, brass bands were the most common and popular forms of instrumental ensembles throughout the nineteenth century. Bands were formed in Victoria in 1864, in Nanaimo in 1872, and in Kamloops in 1886. Moreover, a number of brass bands were organized in native communities and residential schools, at least 33 between 1864 (when the Oblates founded the St Mary's Mission Band near Mission City) and the end of the century. One famous community band made up of native musicians, 21 members strong, was established in 1875 by

William Duncan at Metlakatla, a major missionary station and school on Vancouver Island.[25]

By the time of Confederation, larger cities were producing substantial numbers of musical societies, chiefly choral in their orientation. In 1864, for example, the Montreal Oratorio Society was joined by the Mendelssohn Choir and the Société Musicale des Montagnards Canadiens and Les Orphéonistes de Montréal. The Philharmonic Society of Montreal, founded in 1877, performed many large-scale works, particularly under conductor Guillaume Couture (1851-1915), who had studied in Paris with Franck and Saint-Saens. Couture led a chorus of over 200 voices. Montreal also helped produce the first prominent Canadian composer, Calixa Lavallée (1842-91), who is best known today for the music to 'O Canada' (the words having been composed by a series of political committees). Lavallée made his début at the piano in Montreal at age 13, and spent much time in the United States until he was sent by supporters to Paris in 1873. He returned to settle in Quebec, writing a grand cantata for the reception of Governor General Lord Lorne and his royal wife, which concluded with a stirring contrapuntal intramixture of 'God Save the Queen' and 'Comin' thro' the Rye'. The cantata was acclaimed, but the composer lost money, complaining: '*Le gouvernement Joly [Joly de Lotbinière, premier of Quebec, 1878-9] a reçu la Princesse. Mais c'est moi qui ai payé le violon* [But it is I who paid the piper].'[26] Lavallée spent the last years of his life in exile in the United States.

Sports and Games

The mid-Victorian period saw a continued development of organized sports and games in British North America/Canada. Most were imported, although some—like lacrosse—had local origins. Lacrosse had begun life as a native game called variously 'baggataway' or 'tewaarathon', and was played by many tribes under different rules. In 1833 it was played by the First Nations near Montreal, and in 1856 the Montreal Lacrosse Club was organized, joined by two others before 1860. The game was codified in Montreal and was promoted across Canada by a Montreal dentist, William George Beers (1843-1900), who by October 1867 had brought to life 80 lacrosse clubs with 2,000 members across the new Dominion. The game flourished between 1868 and 1885, achieving great success as a spectator sport. Snowshoeing, which became very popular as an organized winter activity in the 1860s, often among the summer lacrosse crowd, was another obviously Canadian development. The Montreal Snow Shoe Club was organized in 1843, and in Winnipeg a snowshoe club, begun in 1878, was by the early 1880s the major winter diversion for members of the city's élite.

The formulation of rules for these and other sports occurred in most cases between 1840 and 1880, although precise dates are very contentious, with many communities advancing their own claims for 'firsts'. Certainly by 1880 most sports and games familiar to us today had reached a stage of rule development that a modern Canadian could understand. What is important about the development of sport is not simply the introduction of new rules, techniques, and equipment, but the sheer scope and ubiquity of sporting activity, on the part of both participants and spectators. The development of any of the major games followed roughly the same path. Baseball is perhaps one of the most important, for in this period it and lacrosse were probably the closest to a 'national' game in Canada, greatly exceeding in popularity ice-hockey, which required more equipment, special skills (skating), and indoor facilities (arenas) in order to become a true spectator sport.

A composite photograph of a baseball game in Tecumseh Park, London, Ontario, between the London Tecumsehs and Syracuse in 1871. The Middlesex County Court House can be seen in the background. National Archives of Canada, PA 31482.

Baseball was extremely popular in British North America, particularly in Upper Canada, and it spread rapidly both east and west after 1870. By the mid-1850s there were organized teams that gradually came to play American rules. There was an unofficial Canadian championship by the early 1860s, and in the year of Confederation a team from Ingersoll, Ontario, won the junior championship at an American 'world' tournament. By 1876 a Canadian league had been formed, with teams in Kingston, Toronto, Hamilton, Guelph, and London. Its players were for the most part amateurs or semi-professionals, although American players were imported and paid. During this era the Americans organized a professional league, and in 1886 a Toronto team joined one of the American feeder (or minor) leagues. Although initially Upper Canadian in origin, baseball became a major sport in the

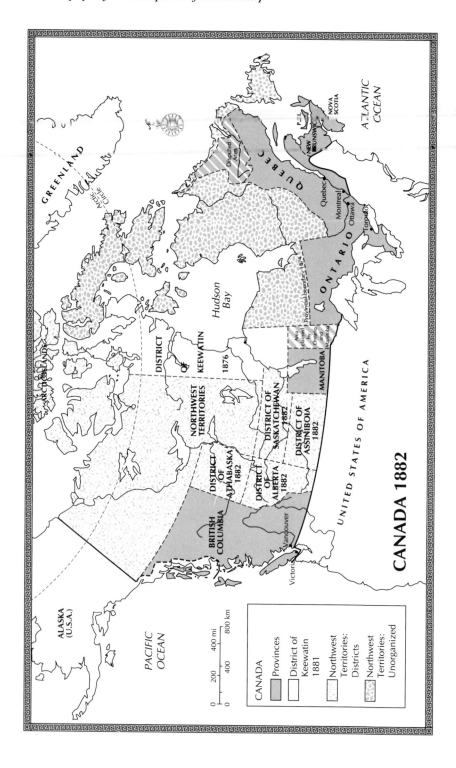

CANADA 1882

CANADA
- Provinces
- District of Keewatin 1881
- Northwest Territories: Districts
- Northwest Territories: Unorganized

0   200   400 mi
0   400   800 km

PACIFIC OCEAN

ALASKA (U.S.A.)

ARCTIC CIRCLE

GREENLAND

Hudson Bay

DISTRICT OF KEEWATIN 1876

NORTHWEST TERRITORIES

DISTRICT

DISTRICT OF ATHABASKA 1882

DISTRICT OF ALBERTA 1882

DISTRICT OF SASKATCHEWAN 1882

DISTRICT OF ASSINIBOIA 1882

BRITISH COLUMBIA

Victoria

Vancouver

MANITOBA

Provincial boundary 1874

Area claimed by Ontario and Manitoba

Disputed Area

QUEBEC

ONTARIO

Quebec

Montreal

Ottawa

Toronto

NEW BRUNSWICK

P.E.I.

NOVA SCOTIA

ATLANTIC OCEAN

UNITED STATES OF AMERICA

Maritimes and in the West, where it was played by farmboys on fields across the Prairies. By the 1870s large crowds would assemble to watch a game between two local teams, and massive crowds paid admission fees to observe the finest semi-professional and professional teams. Hockey and football followed a similar organizational pattern, the latter sport in both Canada and the United States being particularly associated with university teams, which began playing each other in the 1870s.[27]

By 1885 two aspects of sport in Canada had evolved: participation and spectacle. It still had not achieved a political meaning, through the creation of either national leagues or national teams to play in international competitions. But its expansion, sophistication, and growing organization matched the development of the nation. The mobility of the population moved various sports and games around the country and made the interchange of rules possible. Both the development of 'official' rules and growing hierarchies of teams and players anticipated the future.

✐ Confederation and the Less-Visible Minorities

Despite sincere efforts on the part of many in the new Dominion to encourage a sense of nationhood that transcended the linguistic differences between French and English, and the geographical barriers of the provinces and the regions, the fact remains that the new Canadian nationality remained fragile, more than a bit artificial, and very racist. In addition, at least outside French Canada it mainly expressed the prejudices and beliefs of British Ontario writ large. The crucible for the new Canadian nationality, many believed, was in that vast expanse of territory west of the Great Lakes. But here its limitations were most clearly evident.

The interests of the Canadian government in the Northwest, especially under Sir John A. Macdonald, were focused on agricultural settlement, both as an outlet for excess eastern population and as a means of encouraging the development of a truly transcontinental nation. In the process the native inhabitants of the region were pushed aside as quickly as possible. A series of treaties was negotiated with the Indians that extinguished native titles in exchange for reserves on the most marginal and least attractive land. In August 1876, for example, the Indians of central Saskatchewan foregathered at Fort Carlton to consider the terms of the government's Treaty no. 6. The Plains Cree chief Poundmaker (Pitikwahanapiwiyin, *c*.1842-86) objected, saying that the government should be prepared to train the Indians as farmers and assist them in other ways after the buffalo disappeared. This suggestion was not well received by the lieutenant-governor, who presented the terms. Nevertheless, Poundmaker signed the Treaty, and three years later accepted a reserve on the Battle River. Another important Plains Cree chief, Big Bear (Mistahimaskwa, *c*.1825-88), refused to sign for six years. On 8 December 1882, he signed when his people were starving and he wished to provide

Poundmaker. National Archives
of Canada, PA 28853.

Big Bear trading at Fort Pitt, a Hudson's Bay Company post on the North Saskatchewan River until
1884, when it was taken over by the North West Mounted Police. In April 1885 Big Bear and his band
attacked it; it was evacuated, and then burned by Big Bear's Cree followers. National Archives of
Canada, PA 118768.

them with food. The next July his small band was moved north to a reservation near Fort Pitt.

The North-West Mounted Police, based on the Irish constabulary, were established in 1873 to act as a quasi-military agent of the Canadian government in the West. Its officers, drawn from the élites of eastern Canada, were committed to the notion of public stability that associated crime and violence with the 'lower orders' and the native peoples. The 'Mounties' moved ahead of settlement and have always been seen as the chief instruments of a more peaceful western expansion than was true in the neighbouring United States. Certainly in Canada there was less individual violence, but this was often owing to the exertion of state intervention and control.

Like the First Nations, the Métis were systematically driven to the margins. Macdonald's government had created Manitoba as a province only under duress, and the Prime Minister regarded the mixed-bloods as a people to be 'kept down by a strong hand until they are swamped by the influx of settlers.'[28] And swamped they were. As thousands of new settlers, mainly from Ontario, arrived in the province, guarantees of land rights to the Métis were gradually whittled away, and the land itself—about 2 million of the two-and-a-half-million acres promised the Métis in 1870—ended up in the hands of speculators. By 1885 Ontario-born settlers outnumbered Métis 5-to-1 in Manitoba, and only seven per cent of the population of the province was of mixed-blood origin. Many Métis drifted further west, to the Saskatchewan Valley, forming several small mission settlements, including Qu'Appelle, Batoche, and Duck Lake. But the buffalo were becoming scarce. French, English, and Scottish mixed-bloods demanded grants similar to those given to the mixed-bloods of Manitoba under the Manitoba Act. Government surveyors caused uncertainty and fear, as they had done in Manitoba a decade earlier. In addition, the Indians were unable to provide for themselves. The winter of 1883-4 was particularly severe and many were starving. Indian agents complained to Ottawa, but nothing was done. In June 1884 Big Bear and his followers, with many other Indians, travelled to Poundmaker's reserve to hold a big meeting. They discussed the serious state of affairs, after which some 2,000 Indians put on a Thirst Dance, a religious ritual. The Métis, in despair, turned to their old leader Louis Riel.

Riel had apparently put his life back together after years of exile in the United States and hospitalization in 1876-8 for mental disturbance at Longue Pointe, Quebec. He had become an American citizen and was teaching in St Peter's, Montana (where he had married), when a delegation from the Saskatchewan country visited him on 4 June 1884. They told him of all the grievances that were burdening the peoples of the Saskatchewan region, explained that agitation was developing against the Canadian government, and pled with him to return to Canada to lead them. Why Riel agreed to do so is one of the many mysteries surrounding his life. But within a month he and his family were in Batoche.

By December 1884, Riel and W. H. Jackson (secretary of the Settler's Union) had finished drafting a long petition, with 25 sections, which they sent to Ottawa. It concluded by requesting that the petitioners 'be allowed as in [1870] to send Delegates to Ottawa with their Bill of rights; whereby an understanding may be arrived at as to their entry into confederation, with the constitution of a free province.'[29] The petition was acknowledged, but no other response was vouchsafed by Ottawa.

In March 1885 events took a menacing turn. On the 18th Riel and some of his men strode into the Walters and Baker store in Batoche. Riel announced: 'Well, gentlemen, it has commenced.' 'What has commenced?' asked Walters. 'Oh, this movement for the rights of the country,' was the reply.[30] The visitors then helped themselves to ammunition and provisions. On 21 March, Riel sent a letter to Superintendent Crozier of the North-West Mounted Police at Fort Carlton, which was manned by a force of Mounted Police and volunteers. The missive demanded Fort Carlton's surrender, or it would be attacked by Riel and his men. Crozier refused. On 26 March, Gabriel Dumont (1836-1906), Riel's military leader, intercepted a small detachment from Fort Carlton near Duck Lake. When Crozier heard of this action he left the fort with as many men as he could muster. This force met Riel and 300 Métis on horseback before it could reach Duke Lake. Startled, Crozier gave the order to fire. Thirty minutes of gunfire exchanges followed, during which lives were lost on both sides.

The Métis, who outnumbered Crozier's men, forced them to retreat. Gabriel Dumont later recalled this confrontation in vivid detail:

> They had to go through a clearing so I lay in wait for them, saying to my men: 'Courage, I'm going to make the red coats jump in their carts with some rifle shots.' And then I laughed, not because I took any pleasure in killing but to give courage to my men.
>
> Since I was eager to knock off some of the red coats, I never thought to keep under cover and a shot came and gashed the top of my head, where a deep scar can still be seen. I fell down on the ground and my horse, which was also wounded, went right over me as it tried to get away.... When Joseph Delorme saw me fall again, he cried out that I was killed. I said to him: 'Courage! As long as you haven't lost your head, you're not dead!'....
>
> While we were fighting, Riel was on horseback, exposed to the gunfire, and with no weapon but the crucifix which he held in his hand.[31]

Riel wrote a letter to Crozier blaming him for the battle. 'A calamity has fallen upon the country yesterday,' he insisted. 'You are responsible for it before God and man....'[32] He then appealed to the Indians to assist him. Poundmaker's Indians broke into buildings in Battleford, terrifying settlers, and the Cree warrior Wandering Spirit (Kapapamahchakwew, c.1845-85) led a band that attacked Frog Lake, killing nine.

Prime Minister Macdonald was determined to crush this rebellion quickly, sending a force under Major-General Frederick Middleton (1825-98)—by

These men of the Winnipeg Field Battery are having a snooze in a special railway car taking Louis Riel from Swift Current to Regina to stand trial for treason, 22 May 1885. Photographed by O.B. Buell. Saskatchewan Archives photograph, B2298.

way of the new Canadian Pacific Railway—to put it down. Lieutenant-Colonel William Otter (1843-1929) relieved Battleford, but was fired on by Indians at Cut Knife Hill and had to withdraw. Middleton battled with Métis at Fish Creek, which delayed his march on Batoche, where he intended to confront Riel. The Canadian force of 800 men arrived there on 9 May, and quickly defeated Riel and about 200 Métis. The uprising was over by 12 May. Dumont fled to the United States and Riel was arrested.

A formal charge of high treason, carrying the death penalty, was laid against Riel on 6 July.* The trial began on 28 July at Regina, where feelings against him were heated. It was a political trial, infamously coloured in many ways by Macdonald's determination to have Riel found guilty and executed. Riel passionately denied a plea of insanity introduced by his lawyers, and the jury recommended mercy. Ottawa dismissed two appeals, and Riel was hanged on 16 November.**

This execution had a lasting impact on Canada, particularly in Quebec, where French-Canadian nationalism was strengthened and voters were

---

*Despite the fact that Riel was an American citizen, the Canadian government held with the British government that he was also a British subject—that British citizenship could never be renounced.

**Poundmaker stood trial for treason and was sentenced to three years in prison. Released after a year, he died four months later. Big Bear received a similar sentence, but was released after a year and a half. Wandering Spirit was hanged.

Riel in the prisoner's box. He addressed the court twice during his trial: once after all the evidence had been presented, when he spoke for over an hour, and once before sentence was pronounced. National Archives of Canada, C-1879.

Wilfrid Laurier, c.1882. A member of Parliament in 1885, he became leader of the Liberal party in 1887 and the first French-Canadian prime minister in 1896. National Archives of Canada, PA 13133.

turned away from the Conservative party. On 22 November 1885, at a huge gathering in the public square in Montreal called the Champ de Mars, Honoré Mercier, the Liberal leader in Quebec, joined Wilfrid Laurier in denouncing the government action. Mercier insisted: 'In killing Riel, Sir John has not only struck at the heart of our race but especially at the cause of justice and humanity which ... demanded mercy for the prisoner of Regina, our poor friend of the North-West.'[33] Wilfrid Laurier added: 'Had I been born on the banks of the Saskatchewan...I would myself have shouldered a musket to fight against the neglect of governments and the shameless greed of speculators.' The two leaders disagreed over Mercier's proposal that French Canadians leave the two major parties and form one of their own. 'We are a new nation,' said Laurier, 'we are attempting to unite the different conflicting elements which we have into a nation. Shall we ever succeed if the bond of union is to be revenge?'[34] Laurier argued that Mercier's proposal would destroy Confederation.

The military defeat of the Métis and the public execution of Louis Riel in November 1885 for treason were only half the reason why that year (and that month) was so significant, not only in the history of the West but in the history of Canada. For in November 1885 the last spike was driven at Craigellachie in eastern British Columbia to mark the completion of the Canadian Pacific Railway. The CPR had been resurrected in 1881 as a hybrid corporation controlled by private capitalists and financed largely by the state—which, along with public subsidies, gave it about 25 million acres of land along its right-of-way, and other concessions. The question of building in advance of settlement—what T.C. Keefer had called 'colonization lines'—was actively debated at the time, particularly given the inducements needed to convince hard-headed businessmen to proceed with construction; but the Macdonald government defended the railroad on the grounds of national interest. Since this concept is not measurable in quantitative terms, it is impossible to know whether the price was too high. What we can say with certainty is that the construction of the CPR was a spectacular feat of engineering, partly thanks to the managerial skills of William Van Horne (1843-1915). The CPR was executed, however, chiefly on the backs of 6,500 Chinese coolie labourers specially imported for the job. Many died, and those who survived were summarily discharged when the work was completed. Macdonald had defended Chinese immigration in 1883, arguing that 'it will be all very well to exclude Chinese labour, when we can replace it with white labour, but until that is done, it is better to have Chinese labour than no labour at all.'[35] With the completion of the CPR, the Canadian government moved swiftly to limit Chinese immigration.

The West was to be an anglophone colony of Canada. Not only were Indians, Métis, and Chinese cast aside as quickly as possible, but French Canadians were not expected to move there in any substantial numbers. Most Québécois in the years after Confederation saw the West as important mainly

A CPR construction crew at Malakwa, BC. National Archives of Canada, C-1602.

Arrival of the first transcontinental passenger train at the foot of Howe Street, Vancouver, 23 May 1887. City of Vancouver Archives, CAN. P.78, N.52.

in commercial terms, or at best as a better destination for determined Quebec migrants than the United States. Certainly by 1879 the die appeared to have been cast. As *L'Opinion Publique* (Montreal) stated: 'For five years English emigration has flooded Manitoba, and French emigration has been pretty well nil...The North-West, founded and settled by the French, is destined, like the rest of North America, to be English.'[36] The French-Canadian response to the execution of Louis Riel, however, was hardly so fatalistic. By 1885 Quebec public opinion was prepared to believe in theories of anti-French conspiracies, and was convinced that Riel had died because he was French. Certainly a major factor in Riel's execution was the vehemence of Ontario opinion against him; Thomas Scott was still not forgotten. National consolidation was arguably completed in 1885, but much Canadian 'nationalism' still bore the distinctive sting of the Ontario WASP; and two cultures, French and English, were firmly set in opposition to each other. Trying to satisfy the country's two main components was the most challenging political task facing the Canadian government.

chapter two

The First Triumph of Industrialism, 1885-1919

Sir William Mackenzie (1849-1923), if he is remembered at all by Canadians, is associated with his partner Sir Donald Mann (1853-1934) with the building of the Canadian Northern Railway. This line was Canada's second transcontinental, taken over by the Canadian government in 1918 and turned into the Canadian National Railways. Born at Kirkfield, Canada West, the son of Scottish immigrants from the Highlands, Mackenzie became a successful railroad contractor and in the early 1890s was a pioneer in street-railway electrification in Winnipeg and Toronto. Mackenzie's most successful operation was not in Canada, however, but in Brazil, where his Ontario-based São Paulo Railway, Light and Power Company Limited, had the concession to build a street-railway system and to supply electricity to Brazil's second-largest city. The company was so successful that it went on to a repeat performance in Rio de Janeiro through the Rio de Janeiro Tramway, Light and Power Company (1904). In 1912 Mackenzie's various Brazilian utility companies were consolidated in one great holding company, Brazilian Traction Limited, the largest single corporation in Brazil.*

Mackenzie and his various associates in Brazil were not the only Canadian entrepreneurs active in Latin America. William Van Horne, the man largely responsible for Canada's first transcontinental railway, the Canadian Pacific, led Canadian investors and promoters into Cuba after that island's conquest by the United States in 1898. Finally coming to terms in 1900 with a rival group of American entrepreneurs, some of whom were involved in the Brazil operations, Van Horne led a syndicate of 160 capitalists from the United States and Canada who invested $50,000 each to found the Cuba Company, which intended to build a railway between Santiago and Havana, a ten-day

---

*Now Brascan, Ltd, which in 1983 controlled assets of $3.3 billion from its headquarters in Toronto.

ride by horseback.¹ This little venture was centred in a company incorporated in New Jersey (a state with little regulation and supervision of its corporate citizens, and hence a popular place to incorporate in this period) under Van Horne's presidency. Other Canadians, including New Brunswicker Max Aitken (1879-1964, later Lord Beaverbrook), were active in utility development in Cuba, Puerto Rico, and in various British colonies in the Caribbean. What seems most striking, however, is that Mackenzie and Van Horne—the men behind Canada's two great transcontinental railroads—were also active in the creation of utilities in less-developed parts of the Americas.

All things are relative. Despite the seeming inadequacies and weaknesses of the economy of British North America, particularly when compared with the economies of the United States and Britain, Canada in the years after Confederation was one of the richest nations in the world when measured in terms of gross national product and per-capita income.* According to one listing it was number eight in the world table of industrial development. From the late 1870s to the end of the First World War, Canada managed to maintain a privileged position of wealth, if not power, despite the industrial emergence of such nations as Japan and Germany, and the substantial economic growth of many other countries. The relative extent of Canada's technological and financial expertise was reflected in the ability of Canadian businessmen to invest successfully in Latin America and the Caribbean. However weak the Canadian economy often appeared to those at home, from the standpoint of most of the world Canada was rich, powerful, highly industrialized, and 'progressive'. Though the country was well endowed in agricultural and natural-resource production, much of the key to its success nevertheless lay in its industrial development, and the extent to which it was able to create a self-sustaining internal economy and a dynamic foreign trade. Canada was not only able to build upon historic patterns, but to export its entrepreneurial expertise to less-developed neighbours.

Continued industrialization—for the process had begun at mid-century—involved considerably more than the simple construction of new and larger factories. Transportation facilities had to be extended and rationalized, investment had to be mobilized, resources exploited, and a labour force recruited. Despite the 'National Policy' and the introduction of the protective tariff, Canada did not succeed in retaining total control over, or ownership in, its economy. Its emergence on the international scene increased the

---

*Argentinian scholar Domingo Cavallo, in his book *La Argentina que pudo ser* (What Argentina Could Have Become, 1989), insisted that Canada and Argentina remained very similar economically until 1930, after which Argentina turned to protectionism—and stagnated—while Canada profited from American foreign investment—and flourished.

tendency for that economy to be directly affected by world economic conditions and economic cycles. Thus Canada's growth-rate was limited by flat economic conditions around the world from the late 1870s to the mid-1890s, and benefited from an international boom period between 1900 and 1913. Moreover, industrial development was distinctly uneven, with industrial growth above the national average only in Ontario. Throughout the period before 1914, Quebec remained steady at the national average, but the Maritimes fell further and further below it, and the West never became a serious player. If some of the larger Canadian geopolitical regions displayed serious industrial disparities measured against one another, so too were there differences developing within provinces. Between 1880 and 1920, industrial growth in such larger urban centres as Montreal and Toronto expanded constantly, while smaller communities—particularly in central Canada—fell steadily behind.

❧ *Foreign Investment*

One of the keys to Canadian economic growth in this period—in all sectors, but particularly in the industrial sector—was the influx of foreign investment. Few nations have relied so heavily on foreign capital in order to fuel economic growth as Canada has throughout its history, and investment in this era—particularly in the boom years from 1900 to 1913—was significant. Like other countries, Canada used much of its imported capital to finance large development projects, such as railroads and hydroelectric generation. In the grossest terms, Canada's imports of capital came in the two forms of indirect (portfolio) investment and direct investment, which could be roughly identified with Canada's two largest financial partners. Much of the portfolio investment came from Great Britain, while much of the direct investment came from the United States. In terms of the extent of foreign domination of the economy that resulted, the two types produced quite different results. Direct investment implied far more control. But at the time few Canadians agonized overmuch about the extent or the origin of foreign investment. (Foreign control did not become a serious issue in Canadian economic theory or public life until the late 1950s.) Throughout this period almost all Canadians might have agreed with American entrepreneur Frank Clergue, who declared in 1901 that 'foreign money injected into the circulating medium of Canada' would 'remain forever to the everlasting blessing of thousands of its inhabitants.'[2]

Indirect Investment

If contemporaries did not make fine distinctions or worry about implications, we can still appreciate the important differences between indirect and direct investment, particularly as symbols of the different economic strategies pursued by the two imperial powers with which Canada had most direct contact. Portfolio investment represents money borrowed against securities, in this period mainly bonds. Most bonds are issued for limited durations and do not carry the same management involvement as stocks, although they are regarded as 'safer' because they have first claim on the assets of any company and pay a predetermined interest off the top of revenue. That the British by and large chose portfolio investment in Canada reflected no particular willingness to allow Canadians to retain management control, but rather responded to British economic needs. Growing prosperity in Britain had produced thousands of middle-class citizens eager to 'clip coupons' in their old age, and Canada was a relatively secure place in which to invest. Most of Canada's borrowing in Britain was done by government (federal, provincial, and municipal) and by the railroads. The money went to finance transportation networks and public works; little was available for private enterprise, almost none for 'venture capital'. Canada was one of the major borrowers in the British money market; the sale of its securities between 1865 and 1914 represented about ten per cent of foreign issues in London. Some British capital came with immigrants or was subsequently sent to them, such as the investments in fruit growing in the Okanagan Valley of British Columbia, but only a relatively small percentage of British investment was direct, and an even smaller percentage (less than ten per cent) of British direct investment was in manufacturing. More typical British direct investments were in the Hudson's Bay Company as it moved into retailing operations, and in the British Columbia Street Railway Company, which operated the tramlines in the lower mainland of the province. British management of these enterprises was often charged with conservatism, and indeed they were paternally run.

In the years immediately before the First World War the complexities of the British investment market were exploited in new ways by Canadian entrepreneurs, chiefly through the promotion of bond issues by industrial giants created from the merger of smaller companies. In this period such mergers were both fashionable and profitable in most of the industrialized world, as successful companies sought to reduce competition and rationalize an industry. In Canada, no one was more successful at merging than William Maxwell Aitken, son of a New Brunswick Presbyterian minister, who used his success as a securities broker as the basis for consolidating Canadian manufacturing. His greatest success came with the Steel Company of Canada (1910), the bonds of which his Royal Securities firm sold in London on the pre-war boom market. 'I created all the big trusts in Canada,' Aitkin boasted after he had moved to England in 1910 in search of greater challenges, a statement that was a typical exaggeration, for he was only the most visible and sharpest operator in a movement that saw 58 giant corporations created in Canada between 1909 and 1912.

Direct Investment

Throughout most of the period of the First World War, the United States was itself a major importer of British capital, and hence had little available for portfolio investment. The Americans always tended to direct investment as part of an aggressive strategy to gain access to Canadian raw materials and the Canadian market. Much of American investment in Canada was in the resource sector of the economy, either to take advantage of potential profits in newly developing areas (such as mining) or to control supply and prices of raw materials necessary for American industry (such as pulp and paper to supply newsprint for American newspapers). The other major American strategy was to invest in the Canadian manufacturing sector in order to gain maximum access to the Canadian market. Less than half of American direct investment was in Canadian manufacturing, but the total amounts involved here were impressive, well over $100 million by 1910. The protective tariff of the National Policy played an important role in encouraging American 'branch-plant' investment.

What is important to remember about the tariff and the American branch plant is that such American involvement was almost universally regarded as a desirable consequence of protectionism in the years before the Great War. If tariffs on manufactured goods are set sufficiently high, of course, foreign firms cannot compete with domestic ones. But early protectionism was really not concerned so much with the ownership question as with that of employment. As one protectionist Liberal argued in the Reciprocity debate of 1911: 'I want the American manufacturers to be forced to establish plants on this side of the line and provide work for our Canadian workmen if they want to have the advantage of supplying our home markets.'[3] Supporters of the tariff boasted in 1913 that 450 American branch plants represented a total investment of $135 million. Protectionism was therefore not anti-American before 1914, but rather a form of mercantilism that in part encouraged investment. There was no concern about the outflow of profits or the influx of foreign managers. 'That a portion of the profits made on the development of our latent resources has to be paid out in interest is no hardship,' commented one business magazine in 1908, 'since without the capital there would have been no profits at all.'[4]

All Canadians, including Quebeckers, understood that American investment meant prosperity. Far from endangering the Canadian—or French-Canadian—identity, American investment fostered it, for the alternative was immigration to the United States. As one letter-writer to a Montreal weekly insisted in 1903, she supported the tariff as a mother with two boys in the United States. 'I want my boys to come home', she wrote, 'because I think Canada is a purer and better country. They will be better men here. I don't mean that they are not good now. They are both good boys, but I am afraid for the future.'[5] Since American manufacturers had few incentives based on intrinsic cost of production to encourage them to locate their operations in Canada, the tariff was regarded as a necessary step to force most of them to open their doors in this country. The Americans preferred southern Ontario as a location for their branch plants, perhaps because they were more active in the heavy industries of Ontario than in the lighter ones (such as food processing and textiles) located in Quebec. Not until the 1920s was any attention at all paid to the extent of foreign ownership of Canadian industry, and it would be another generation before its implications were seriously considered.

Industrialization and the Growth of Regional Disparity

If few Canadians gave much consideration to the dangers of foreign investment, a good many more were concerned to attract it, particularly in regions that were perceived to be falling behind in the industrial sweepstakes. One of the more revealing economic statistics for this period is the following index of the manufacturing value added per capita in three regions relative to Canada as a whole (expressed as 1):[6]

REGION	YEAR						
	1870	1880	1890	1900	1910	1915	1926
Quebec	0.97	1.03	0.98	1.06	1.03	1.04	1.11
Ontario	1.11	1.16	1.18	1.20	1.45	1.53	1.52
Rest of Canada	0.92	0.81	0.84	0.74	0.52	0.43	0.37

Another related index, outlining per-capita manufacturing output of regions as a percentage of the Canadian average, provides a more detailed regional breakdown:[7]

REGION	1870	1880	1900	1915
Ontario	112	115	123	153
Quebec	101	107	103	100
Maritimes	69	65	59	61
Prairies	—	40	40	38
BC	—	80	132	86

What these tables best illustrate is the growing disparity in manufacturing between central Canada (especially Ontario) and the remainder of the country. While Quebec remained near the national average, Ontario gradually gained at the expense of everywhere else.

Central Canada

Central Canada's industrial growth after 1881 is one of the great success stories of Canadian history, and also one of the most controversial. Much of the political conflict in the nation since Confederation has its origins in that growth, which really accelerated in the late nineteenth century. Central Canada has chosen to explain the development as a product of the region's rich resources of goods and people, while the rest of Canada has insisted that it came at its expense, ascribing much of that growth to government policies and private actions headed by central Canadians. After 1881 manufacturing replaced commerce as the chief propellant of urban growth in Ontario and to a lesser extent in Quebec, and much of that industrial plant involved sophisticated technological applications.

Ontario was the centre of iron and steel production, as well as of the secondary manufacturing of iron and steel (i.e., for the machine-tool industry), which played such an important role in transferring technology from one industry to another. The transformation of the iron industry into the steel industry was symptomatic of the process that was occurring. Coke replaced charcoal as the source of heat, but the big changes did not involve the blast furnace so much as the way in which pig iron was refined into wrought iron. The refining process was turned into two steps, involving first open-hearth furnaces and then a steam-driven rolling mill; the result was a product with a slightly higher carbon content called steel. Then mechanization was added to every step in the manufacturing process. Raw materials were unloaded and moved by machinery; coke was prepared without being touched by human hand; the blast furnace was loaded by machinery that quadrupled output. 'Gigantic automation' was the watchword at huge installations like Stelco's Hamilton plant or Algoma's Sault Ste Marie operation. In the years before the Great War, the major Canadian steelmakers also expanded to control their own raw materials and to diversify their output. Nevertheless, mechanization worked best when a standard product could be manufactured for a steady demand, and in this period steel rails were the most popular order of this type.[8]

Quebec manufacturing relied far less on heavy industry (and vast capitalization) than Ontario, and far more on industry that depended on labour and fussy mechanization, such as clothing, wood products, textiles, and food processing. Part of the explanation for the difference may reside in labour availability, and part—especially after 1900—in cheap hydroelectric power available to Quebec. Ontario's marginal early advantage in secondary over primary manufacturing (the province had over 42 per cent of its total manufacturing in the secondary sector in 1870, while Quebec had only 29 per cent) was eliminated by 1915, when Quebec's secondary percentage was 77.5 and Ontario's 74.6 per cent. While Ontario's manufacturing continued to grow in a number of smaller urban centres, much of Quebec's was concentrated in Montreal, which by 1900 employed about half the manufacturing workers in the province. Nevertheless, it is easy to overemphasize the notorious 'lag' between the two central-Canadian provinces, which were more like one another than they were like the remainder of the country. Certainly the financial power of Montreal was critical, particularly for the Maritime region.

The Maritimes

While before the First World War the Canadian West was for the most part too recently settled to move into an active industrial phase, this condition did not apply to the Maritime Provinces. In that region, the haemorrhaging of population that had begun in the 1860s as a result of rural stagnation was joined in the 1870s by a crisis in the shipbuilding industry, which had represented a substantial proportion of the region's export production. Part of the problem for shipbuilding was the growth of new technologies that rendered the wooden sailing ship obsolescent, if not quite obsolete. The real failure, however—in terms of the future development of the region—was the responsibility of the Maritime shippers, who suffered a collective entrepreneurial failure of will as the sailing vessel went into decline. They had always seen their ships as little more than instruments of trade, and instead of re-investing their capital in a modern shipbuilding industry, they and the business community of the region finally broke with their transatlantic mentality and turned inward to the continent for markets for industrial production. As a result, the region accepted the National Policy and made increasingly serious efforts to work within it, although the competition from central Canada was tough and all the Maritime experience and connections were transatlantic in nature.[9] These attempts at continentalism were initially successful in the 1880s, but rapidly turned to failure. Maritime businessmen expected particularly to be able to develop textile and iron-and-steel industries, the latter based on regionally available deposits of iron. They were successful in the short run, and in some other industries as well, competing up to 1885 with Canadian and other producers.

The reasons for the ultimate Maritime failure remain uncertain. But Maritime entrepreneurs seemed to lack the financial resources to withstand falls in the economic cycle, and by 1886 they were blaming many of their problems on high railroad freight rates. 'How can the National Policy succeed in Canada where such great distances exist between the provinces,' wrote one businessman, 'unless the Government who controls the National Railway meets the requirements of trade?'[10] At the same time that the region's business community was complaining unsuccessfully about railway rates, outside capital moved in and began buying up locally based companies. Much of the damage was done by Montreal capital, which took over and dismantled a good many burgeoning industries. Maritime entrepreneurs, convinced that they were at a geographical disadvantage in competing with central Canada, ceased trying in most sectors after 1895.

Instead the region turned to iron and steel, believing that the presence of local raw materials would make this industry a competitive one. In the short run the strategy appeared successful, with the emergence of the Nova Scotia Steel and Coal Corporation (Scotia) as a major industrial player, to be joined in 1899 by the Dominion Iron and Steel Corporation (Disco). Disco was the creation of New England-born Henry Melville Whitney (1839-1923), who had begun rationalizing the Nova Scotia coalfields in the 1890s and moved on to create a new steel company, financed partly by Nova Scotia interests but chiefly with Toronto and Montreal capital. Its new plant at Sydney opened in 1902 at a cost of $15 million, and was supposed to put Canada into the big leagues of steelmaking. The *Canadian Mining Review* complained in 1903 of the company's 'kaleidoscopic changes, of extravagance, vacillation and blundering', not least of all in its labour relations. The company survived, and was merged by Max Aitken in 1910 with the Dominion Coal Company as the Dominion Steel Corporation.

But spin-off industries—such as the Rhodes, Curry Company of Amherst, which manufactured railroad cars—were subject to buy-ups and mergers by Montreal interests. The conflict between local and outside capitalists reached its peak in 1910, when Max Aitken attempted to include the Nova Scotia Steel company in his Dominion Coal and Steel merger, and was only just beaten off. Nevertheless, Montreal owned or dominated much of the region's industrial enterprise by 1911, replacing Halifax as its dominant financial city. If Montreal attempted to control manufacturing establishments, Toronto—particularly after 1911—moved into the Maritime region in wholesale and retail marketing. Between 1901 and 1921 the number of regional businesses that were branches of central-Canadian enterprise—based in both Montreal and Toronto—more than doubled from 416 to 950. The net result of both sorts of takeovers was a regional loss of industrial, financial, and commercial autonomy that would siphon capital away from the Maritimes—and, when times got tough, result in closures of stores and factories. The region was systematically de-industrialized and de-commercialized, and would never recover its economic vitality.

Banking and Financial Services

In 1914 American 'muckraker' Gustavus Myers, in *A History of Canadian Wealth,* argued that the process of centralization of wealth and capital was a major component of Canadian economic development, particularly since 1879, when railway amalgamation had begun. Canadian banking had always been highly centralized, Myers added, and 'perhaps nowhere in the world can be found so intensive a degree of close organization as among the bank interests in Canada.'[11] He contrasted the situation in the United States, where there were 18,000 banking institutions, with its Canadian counterpart, where 26 banks had 2,888 branches and some of the larger banks (the Royal Bank, the Bank of Commerce) had more than 300 branches each, extending over vast territories. Certainly the control of capital through chartered banks headquartered chiefly in central Canada was one of Canada's great advantages.

How the banks had come to be controlled in Toronto and Montreal was an interesting question. Part of the answer was to be found in the Canadian

The Canadian Bank of Commerce building at 25 King Street West, Toronto—designed by R.A.Waite and erected in 1889-90—was one of several new office buildings in the city that had some claim to architectural distinction and even grandeur. At seven-and-a-half storeys—soaring over neighbouring three- and four-storey buildings—it was influenced by the first skyscrapers in New York and Chicago. Demolished in 1928, it was replaced in 1929-31 by the building that—with 34 office floors above a seven-storey base—was for some years the tallest in the British Empire. City of Toronto Archives, Micklethwaite Collections, SC 497 #21.

banking system's origins, which transferred the centralized commercialism of English banking to British North America. The chief task of the Canadian chartered banks was originally not to serve local customers or provide local credit, but to facilitate the transfer of commodities and funds from one place to another. The first Canadian Bank Act of 1871 guaranteed that banks everywhere in the nation would observe this model. Banks had to be chartered by Parliament. They were allowed to issue notes (i.e., paper money) in larger denominations (the government issued the smaller ones). But unlike American banks, which could issue currency backed by minimal reserve requirements, Canadian chartered banks could not issue notes in excess of their paid-up capital plus reserves, and a failed bank's notes were paid up before any other liabilities. The result was a constraint on the extension of credit in the outlying regions of the nation. In order for banks to increase their currency, they needed to increase their capital.

According to the general manager of the Bank of Toronto, the 1871 Banking Act had been written by the bankers in close co-operation with members of Parliament. Representatives of the chartered banks, he wrote,

> ...sat in conference, day by day discussing the clauses of the proposed act one by one...Many of the directors of the banks and several of their presidents were members of Parliament, some in the Senate, some in the House of Commons. These, of course, sat with us from time to time, so that, though not formally constituted as such, we were really a joint committee of Parliament and banks.[12]

In 1913 Sir Edmund Walker (1848-1924), president of the Bank of Commerce, insisted that no major changes in banking legislation had ever occurred since 1871 that had not been instituted by the industry itself. In an earlier speech to the Canadian Bankers' Association in 1901, Walker had taken a stand similar to that of Gustavus Myers, observing that the American Bankers' Association was a 'great convention' attended by thousands of bankers, while its Canadian counterpart consisted of '40 to 50 men'.[13] In the early years of the twentieth century, the Bank of Nova Scotia was highly critical of the Bankers' Association, and the president of La Banque Provinciale complained that it was 'a tool in the hands of three or four men who today control the whole of the finance of the country.'[14] Although in 1913, Montreal-headquartered banks held almost half the assets of all Canadian banks ($788 million of $1,551 million), Quebec at the time had considerably fewer branch banks per capita than the remainder of Canada. The result was the founding by Alphonse Desjardins (1854-1920) of the *caisses populaires*, often run by *curés* in association with Catholic parishes. Quebec Catholicism could be quite innovative in some areas of economic activity.

Despite sporadic efforts to create competing financial institutions—such as government savings banks, *caisses populaires*, local savings banks, and mortgage companies—a combination of the financial power of the chartered banks and their control over banking legislation ensured that the chartered banks continued to grow. They often opened branches after the collapse of the competition, and were able to drain deposits from local branches, particularly in the Maritimes. Banks with head offices in central Canada refused to make local loans and set local interest rates (including those in Halifax) at higher levels. The chartered banks expanded not only by opening new branches, but by controlling subsidiary financial institutions such as trust companies. Complaints to the Bank of Commerce from the Maritimes about abuse were dismissed by President Walker as 'local grievances against what we regard as the interests of the country as a whole.'[15]

Natural Resources

While the growth in financial centralization and in industrial capacity, particularly the shift from the processing of primary goods into secondary manufacturing of finished goods, were major economic developments in Canada in the years 1880-1919, there were others. As manufacturing occurred mainly for the domestic market (occasionally, in certain primary industries, for the American one), it did not alone propel the nation into the international marketplace. If Canada was to avoid eternal international balance-of-payments deficits (which have plagued Third World countries in our own century) it obviously needed commodities to export, and found many of these in the natural-resource sector. To a considerable extent Canada's resources were the old mainstays of the colonial staple economy, produced in different places, under different conditions, and often in different guises. Not only did they earn money abroad, but they also encouraged manufacturing, for those who produced them needed finished goods, such as farm implements, which they could not make themselves.

Western Agriculture

The traditional Canadian agricultural resource had been grain, chiefly wheat, although before Confederation farmers in the Canadas were shifting out of grain production. But, as if on some master schedule, once the western prairies were opened to agricultural settlement, the wheat economy continued almost without a pause as fields of operation merely moved from southwestern Ontario to Manitoba, and slightly later to the Northwest Territories (which became the provinces of Saskatchewan and Alberta in 1905). Between 1870 and 1890 thousands of farmers, mainly from Ontario, poured into the West, and the number of acres of occupied land went from 2.5 million to over 6 million in the years 1881-91, while the acres of improved land under cultivation went from 279,000 to 1,429,000 in the same ten-year period. Not until the opening of the CPR, and the subsequent building of branch-lines north and south, could the production of western wheat really take off. The early years saw considerable experimentation with new wheat strains particularly suitable to maturation in the short prairie growing season. Red Fife, planted earlier in Upper Canada, was the most popular strain, although it was frost-susceptible.

Breaking the Prairie with oxen on a farm near Lloydminster (Alberta), *c.* 1900. Provincial Archives of Alberta, H. Pullard Collection.

Binders cut the grain and placed it in swaths, to be gathered, tied in sheaves, and stooked by women. National Archives of Canada, C-8893.

Mr Rogerson's old and new homesteads, 21 miles north of Morden, Manitoba, September 1905. National Archives of Canada, PA-11445.

Before the mid-1890s the typical prairie settler was an Ontario-born experienced farmer who felt thwarted by shrinking productivity and/or limited access to land. Often a younger son of a farm family, he came west alone or with wife and young children to make a new start on virgin prairie land. Despite the availability of considerable homestead land—the first Dominion Land Act was passed in 1872—most farmers preferred to purchase land from companies set up by the great corporate benefactors of government policy, particularly the Hudson's Bay Company, and later the CPR and other railroads. Homestead land was commonly believed to be less likely to acquire nearby rail transportation than was land owned and being sold by the railway itself. Nearly all settlement was within a few miles of a railroad, for carrying crops by wagon over long distances was difficult and expensive. Even on homestead land that was free to the male settler, except for the small legal costs of registration (married women were not allowed to apply for homesteads), successful farming on virgin land could not begin without considerable capital investment. Houses and barns had to be built, wells dug, fences strung, and livestock acquired. Conservative estimates of the costs of 'farm-making' ranged from a minimum of $300 to in excess of $1,000, in an age when the former represented a year's wage for an unskilled labourer. Most of the early farmers brought money with them, from the sale of land and other property at home.

Although mechanized harvesting equipment became common by 1890, until well after the turn of the century the farmer still used animals—horses and oxen—to do most of the ploughing and cultivation. Like his earlier Upper Canadian ancestors, he was plainly and uncategorically a market-oriented farmer. The family usually tried to grow as many foodstuffs as possible for personal consumption in the farmyard and in kitchen gardens, but the farmer's instinct was to increase constantly his acreage under production. This drive was limited only by the size of his labour force, and some substantial results were achieved. Thus, with very limited mechanization, Ontario-born A. J. Cotton (1857-1942) harvested in 1898 at Treherne, Manitoba, a crop of over 17,000 bushels of top-grade wheat.

The front cover of a pamphlet from the Manitoba Department of Agriculture and Immigration, *c.* 1892. Manitoba Archives.

The interior of a CPR colonist railway car, as drawn by Melton Prior for the *Illustrated London News*, 24 November 1888. Glenbow Foundation, NA-978-4.

Beginning in the 1890s an open and aggressive Canadian immigration policy, conducted by both the federal government and the various provincial governments, succeeded in bringing a host of new settlers to the Prairies. They were no longer recruited exclusively in the older favoured nations of western Europe, but came in large numbers from various parts of eastern Europe, where there was a long tradition of grain culture. While many moved into western cities, especially Winnipeg, others took up homestead land on the Prairies. By 1900 the older areas of southern Manitoba were already experiencing population pressure, and the new immigrants moved further north in Manitoba and onto the great dry-belt area of Saskatchewan and southern Alberta, where they initially experienced some very good luck with rain and moisture. By 1921 over 44 million acres of the Prairies were under cultivation. According to one set of calculations, the wheat economy between 1901 and 1911 contributed over twenty per cent of the growth in per-capita income in Canada, with other estimates running as high as thirty per cent.[16]

Wheat, of course, was the big prairie crop, although under certain conditions others were possible. Almost every wheat farmer before the Great War cultivated extensive crops of oats, chiefly to feed his draft animals and other livestock. Before the arrival of farmers, much of southern Alberta (and southwestern Saskatchewan) was the domain of ranchers, who grazed thousands of head of cattle on open range leased from the federal govern-ment. Capital costs ran high—with the cost of establishing a herd of cattle rising to $125,000—but so did profits, estimated at 33.3 per cent per annum upon investment. At the height of the cattle boom, in 1898, ranchers exported 213,000 live head. After the turn of the century the industry was greatly constrained by the influx of farmers, and by new restrictions in the primary markets in the United Kingdom. Although ranchers insisted that much of the range land was unsuited for farming because of water shortages, their obvious self-interest in an open range negated much of their argument. Nevertheless, water was a major potential problem in much of the West.

Mineral Extraction

Despite sporadic mineral production in Canada throughout much of the nineteenth century, the fact that in 1890 Nova Scotia—which had rich coal resources and considerable surface gold—was the leading mining province in Canada says a good deal about the relative lack of development. After that year three factors hastened a great shift in mineral extraction. One was the development of new technologies, in terms both of the production of new metals containing minerals that Canada had in good supply and of new methods of extracting ores. Iron ore was not something Canada had in abundance, but nickel, which could harden steel, was commonly available. So was copper, increasingly favoured for electrical uses because of its conduc-tive properties. Another important factor in mining, as in agriculture and almost every other resource enterprise, was the increasing availability of railway transportation to open remote areas to exploitation. But most crucial of all was the international market, which pushed up mineral and precious metal prices just before the turn of the century.

Almost overnight, Ontario and British Columbia replaced Nova Scotia as the leading mineral producers. In both provinces the focus before 1919 was on the extraction of high-grade ores at minimal cost and offering great return to investors. Although the most famous mining 'rush' of the period was to the Yukon's Klondike district for gold, more important was the series of mining towns that suddenly sprang up and closed equally rapidly in British Columbia's Kootenay Mountains over a few years after 1896, when the international price of silver was at its peak. Like most Canadian mines, these required machinery and expertise to exploit, and although not intended to last, they were well beyond the resources of the individual miner to establish. They were opened by well-capitalized corporations.

In most provinces, much of the capital and technology used in mining was American in origin, and certainly the largest mine owners in most places came from the United States. In Quebec, the most buoyant segment of the mineral industry in 1900-20 was in asbestos fibre, chiefly used in construc-tion material consumed in the United States. The mining industry naturally benefited greatly from the military requirements of the First World War.

Klondikers' camp at
slin Lake, BC, June
98. National Archives
Canada, PA-16141.

log jam on the Miramichi River, New Brunswick, 1895. Provincial Archives of New Brunswick.

Forestry

In forestry, the harvesting of eastern white pine reached its peak in 1881, and then declined rapidly with the permanent depletion of the white pine forests, much of the production from which had been sold to Britain as squared timber. The centre of the timbering industry shifted rapidly from the East to British Columbia, with its millions of acres of Douglas fir and cedar. As eastern Canada had done earlier, British Columbia concentrated first on harvesting in the coastal regions close to water. But the province was vast, and the increase in production enormous. From 350 million board feet in the period 1871-80, British Columbia produced in the years 1901-10 over 4.5 billion board feet, most of it destined for the American and Canadian markets. Some use was also found for the eastern forests, including the massive stands of softwood in New Brunswick. Wood products remained a significant part of Quebec's manufacturing output, but changed in nature and location: timbering shifted from the pine forests of the Ottawa Valley to the spruce and fir stands in the St Maurice and Saguenay regions, where cheap hydroelectricity existed. The softwood forests of northern New Brunswick became much more important. In the early 1900s a previously non-existent pulp-and-paper industry burgeoned rapidly, driven by an insatiable American demand for inexpensive newsprint. By 1915 wood pulp and paper represented one-third of the value of Canadian exports, virtually equal to wheat and grain in the overseas markets. Quebec produced nearly half of Canada's wood pulp and paper.

Railroad Expansion

Transportation was of course an essential ingredient for resource development in this period. As in the age of the first railway boom of the 1850s, railroads were viewed in the subsequent boom periods of the 1880s and the 1910s as both means of development and fields for investment. Substantial railroad construction was a constant of this era; but no railroad was built without substantial public subsidy, often in the form of land grants along the right of way, and the costs were high. The debate over costs still rages in Canadian academic journals, centring on the economic profitability of railroads and the necessity/cost of the subsidies provided by the public sector to get them built quickly. The CPR, for example, was given by the federal government the completed line from Fort William to Selkirk, as well as from Kamloops to Port Moody. In addition it received a cash payment of $25,000,000, plus 25 million acres 'fairly fit for settlement', and various tax exemptions on its land as well as protection of its monopoly. The land concessions, which were typically taken in a chequered pattern along the CPR's right of way, helped disrupt prairie settlement for years, as well as limiting the tax base for many prairie communities. Either cash subsidies or public construction, which the Liberals under Alexander Mackenzie had undertaken, would probably have been both less expensive and less disruptive. But such policies would have resulted in a much slower rate of construction, and hence a slower rate of western settlement.

Nor was the Canadian Pacific the only railroad to be so favoured. Literally dozens of railroads were projected and incorporated in Canada during these years—mainly, although not exclusively, in Western Canada. Seeking provincial-government charters was a major industry for prairie entrepreneurs, and some of the railroads were never built, often because they infringed on the CPR monopoly. Many of these railroads were promoted by 'boomers' for speculative purposes, a process well described by Stephen Leacock (1869-1944) in his sketch 'My Favourite Uncle'. (Uncle E.P. Leacock was involved in several dubious promotions.) But it must be recalled that local communities fought desperately for railroads, occasionally projecting the roads themselves. Any town knew that its future depended on its relationship to ribbons of steel: failure to be located on a line was disastrous. Thus the Canadian Northern Railway of Sir William Mackenzie and Sir Donald Mann, amalgamating several spur lines, passed considerably north of the CPR, which Mackenzie and Mann insisted had failed the more northern part of the Prairies. Thus, in 1897, the government of Newfoundland—admittedly not part of Canada—tried to exchange substantial land and resource rights that mortgaged its future in return for the completion of the Newfoundland Railway across the island.[17] Both westerners and easterners objected to differential freight rates, and western farmers complained about the railroads' failure to supply enough freight cars and their efforts to monopolize grain-loading and handling facilities. But everyone relied on the railroad, which was in its heyday in the years preceding the First World War. Passenger travel was swift, with higher hourly mileages achieved than has been the Canadian experience for several generations.

Energy

If transportation was one essential, energy was another. Canada was always richly endowed with potential energy resources, although it did not always take full advantage of them. Coal, essential for the iron and steel industry as well as for domestic heating, was one. In 1914, 44 per cent of Canada's coal production came from Cape Breton alone and 57 per cent from Nova Scotia. But the province nevertheless had difficulty in utilizing this fact to full advantage. That very year Canada imported 57 per cent of its coal from the United States: Pennsylvania anthracite was much closer and cheaper to get to the homes and factories of central Canada. Coal from British Columbia could never compete in central-Canadian markets. The Ontario iron-and-steel industry, ironically, flourished on imported iron and imported coal.

Central Canada may have lacked coal, but it did have abundant water power, which had been used to run grist and saw mills since colonial days. Again, changing technology came to the fore at the end of the nineteenth century, and the result was the harnessing of major natural waterfalls and the creation of others through dams. Shawinigan Dam at the falls in Shawinigan, Quebec, was begun in 1899 by the Shawinigan Water and Power Company, first supplying Montreal with electricity in 1903, Niagara Falls was first developed for hydroelectric purposes in 1905 and 1906. The heavy and rapid flow of the Winnipeg River in northwestern Ontario and eastern Manitoba was initially dammed for hydroelectric power in 1892, with its first hydro-electric station constructed at Pinawa Falls in 1902 to supply Winnipeg. No province was better placed for hydroelectricity than Quebec, which thereby found a use for hitherto wasted water resources along the St Lawrence River system. Six private companies gained most of the province's water rights, and were able to keep domestic rates higher than in Ontario.

The process of harnessing electricity, both for lighting and for motive power, was one of the great technological developments of the age. When technical problems in the transmission of electric energy were resolved early in the twentieth century, water power could be used as an alternative to fossil fuel to generate large volumes of electrical power, at extremely low cost, that could be transmitted over great distances. The engineer T.C. Keefer was one of the early prophets, as he had been with railroads, telling the Royal Society of Canada in his 1899 presidential address that the future belonged to hydroelectricity. Cheap hydroelectric power rapidly became one of the few advantages Canadian industry possessed. One Toronto journalist described his excitement in discovering that 'a source of energy as vast as the entire soft coal deposits of Pennsylvania had by some miraculous process been transferred to Canadian soil and by another miracle made not only clean but inexhaustible as the widow's cruse.'[18] Hydroelectric power also lit Canadian homes at relatively low cost (though electrical appliances did not become common until after the Great War), and fostered the growth of electric-powered public transportation in the form of the trams and trolleys that connected city centre and suburbs in all of the larger urban conglomerations in Canada. Electric transit was cheap and efficient, and cities were never so well served by mass transportation as they were before 1920—when the gasoline engine began to overtake the trolley car.

The Politics of Resource Development

Resource development in Canada, between 1880 and 1920, had its own set of agendas. In the first place, provinces fought very hard to prevent their natural resources from becoming controlled and regulated by the federal government. A major western grievance was that western provinces did not have control over Crown lands (this was not actually achieved until 1930).

And that same Ontario that had led the way to Confederation and an integrated national economic pattern also defended desperately its right to regulate its own resources against federal pretensions; a large portion of Ontario's pioneering defence of provincial rights came in the context of the protection of its right to control its own natural resources.

The development process that took place in Ontario between 1880 and 1914 was both the most highly articulated and the most complex of all the provinces'. It was based on the assumption that the northern wilderness territory of the province could not only provide a frontier for farmers but also help create a new industrial economy. Although Ontario constantly promoted northern Ontario as a settlement area, resource developers pointed out that most homesteaders failed, with fewer than 25 per cent actually proving their patent. 'Where the land is fitted for timber growing, and for that only,' they insisted, 'timber is what should be grown upon it, and properly managed, would be much the most valuable use to which the land could be put.'[19] Certainly Ontarians were easily persuaded by the silver-tongued orators who told them that they had within their own borders all the requirements of a self-sufficient industrial polity, and that 'entirely from a commercial standpoint,...the preservation to Canada of the raw materials which now exist there is one of the simplest principles about which children could not dispute, much less grown men.'[20] Instead of free trade, home manufacturing was to be encouraged by controlling natural resources.

The result was the so-called 'manufacturing condition' of development, by which Ontario required that resources taken on Crown land be processed in Canada. This policy had been started in British Columbia in 1891, and began in Ontario in 1898 with an amendment to the provincial Crown Timber Act that prevented the export of timber cut on Crown land. Such a provision was the provincial equivalent of the protective tariff: 'Debarred from the opportunity of cutting logs for export, it is an absolute certainty that the American lumberman, in default of other sources of supply, will transfer his sawmill enterprises to Canadian soil.'[21] The principle of retaining Crown resources at home was extended to spruce pulpwood in 1900, and then to nickel mining. The latter produced a confrontation with the federal government; and facing royal disallowance, Ontario withheld proclamation of the legislation to prohibit export out of the province. But users of the province's natural resources were clearly being pressured to manufacture within Ontario. At the same time that Ontario sought to assist not only resource extraction but industrial development by protectionism, it also sought to encourage development through virtually free access to the province's natural resources, combined with strong technical assistance where needed; mining schools and forestry courses were encouraged. Many of the most energetic speculators were Americans.

The provincial involvement in resource development inevitably extended into hydroelectric power. Ontario had initially pursued the standard utility model for hydroelectricity, which meant parcelling out charters to syndicates of industrialists, many of whom had been impressed with the Canadian development of hydroelectric power in Latin America. Unfortunately the new companies dealt with the Canadian people as though they were Brazilians or Cubans, and soon a public-power movement began to emerge, part of a larger reform spirit of the time. Despite some considerable opposition from the capitalists, especially those who owned the power companies, a spirit of trust-busting invaded the hydro question. As the Toronto *Daily Star* observed as early as 1900:

> [T]he twentieth century will be kept busy wrestling with millionaires and billionaires to get back and restore to the people that which the nineteenth century gave away and thanked the plutocrats for accepting. . . . The nineteenth century shirked its duty, humbugged and defrauded the common people, played into the hands of the rich, and left the twentieth century with a host of perplexities.[22]

The manufacturing community saw cheap regulated power as essential to its growth and development, and the result was the establishment of the Ontario Hydro-Electric Commission in 1906, under the chairmanship of Sir Adam Beck (1857-1925). In Quebec the provincial government seemed less able to develop any resource policy, selling off most of its water rights before 1907, when it adopted a long-term leasing system. In 1910 the administration of Sir Jean-Lomer Gouin (1861-1929) joined Ontario in embargoing the export of raw pulpwood from Crown lands, but the ban was never extended to minerals before the Great War.

Along with public monopoly (at least in Ontario) came a more general public regulation of utilities, which by the turn of the century included telephone companies, water companies, electric light and power companies. The tramlines were the most profitable utilities—in Latin America as well as in Canada—and supported other ventures. Like industrial corporations, utility companies had a great urge for consolidation, both horizontal and vertical. A municipal entrepreneur like William Mackenzie could use the Winnipeg Electric Street Railway to gain a monopoly of gas, electricity, and public transportation in that city, and then amalgamate with similar companies in Halifax and Vancouver. The Winnipeg operation returned more than ten per cent on its investment for years. Even where there was competition, it was seldom for the same customers. Private utilities not only sought profits, but tended to drag their heels on the costly expansions of service so sought after by real-estate developers. The result could be competition—or regulation. Businessmen learned to deal with regulatory commissions, but they would have preferred not to have to do so. 'The ideal state of affairs, if you can secure it', wrote one tramline manager, 'is no Commission at all and freedom to run our business as we like.'[23] For the most part, commissions of regulation were not intended to break up cosy private monopolies, but simply to prevent them from becoming unbearable for the general public.

⤳ The Canadian Businessman

The mentality of the Canadian businessman, always agile in its unending quest for profit, was particularly flexible in this era. But there were some general guidelines. One was the insistence on government involvement in large schemes of public development, such as railroads. Another was a willingness to accept government power to grant monopolies of public service through charters, or access to Crown lands through advantageous leases. A third was to minimize competition wherever possible, even if public regulation was the price to be paid for the reduction. Small businessmen who could not combine institutionally to restrain trade—such as the small retailers—fought hard for early closings and price-fixing. Rhetoric about competition did not so much extol the virtue of the free-enterprise system as complain about unfair competition. The business community insisted that what it wanted was a 'living profit', a reasonable return on investment of time and capital. Sensing the development of the professions as a self-defining guild, Canadian businessmen wanted an equivalency for themselves.

The Canadian nationalism of businessmen was a fairly variable commodity. Most supported tariff protectionism ('the National Policy') and resource regulation ('the manufacturing condition') less in an attempt to keep Americans out of Canadian business than to bring the Yanks, their energy, and their capital into the country. At the highest levels of financial wheeling and dealing, Americans and Canadians could work together quite amicably. But it was also commonly accepted that Canadian businessmen and investors were not very adventurous, preferring familiar fields.

'In grain and real estate people will invest their money whether they gain or lose,' reported the *Monetary Times* in 1892, 'and they will continue to do so in a most persistent manner; while even one loss in mining operations seems to discourage them for a lifetime, so they will not touch the thing again.'[24] That same journal argued a few years later:

> The best sections both of agricultural and mineral-bearing lands in Canada are falling into the hands of our enterprising neighbours, while we ourselves are waiting Micawber-like to see how things will turn out. By the time we know the Americans will know, and Canadians will be listening open-mouthed to the tales of wondrous wealth in foreign lands.[25]

While Canadian business often envied the Americans, it sought neither to emulate nor to exclude them.

The backgrounds of businessmen in this era are interesting, paralleling the origins of those who supported Confederation in the 1860s. Most were immigrants or sons of immigrants, with Scots farmers over-represented in both categories. Few leading businessmen had begun at the bottom, although there were exceptions, such as Alexander Gibson (1819-1913) of New Brunswick, who began as a humble axeman in the lumber industry and ended at the head of a major industrial empire. French Canadians were seriously under-represented among larger-scale businessmen and industrialists, even within their own province, although again there were exceptions, such as the stockholder and politician Sir Joseph-David Forget (1861-1919), who became actively involved in the Montreal Street Railway Company, and in local power and navigation companies. Though there were some French-Canadian entrepreneurs—such as J.-E.-A. Dubuc (1871-1942), who pioneered in pulp and paper, Joseph Versailles, a cement baron; and Joseph Simard (1888-1963), a shipbuilder and prominent businessman of Sorel—most French-Canadian businesses remained small in scale, family-oriented, and confined chiefly to the province of Quebec. They were regionally, but not nationally, well integrated.[26]

Labour

On one subject Canadian businessmen large and small could agree. The organization of labour was regarded as an illegitimate combination designed to erode the right of the individual to run his business as he saw fit. While doubtless early labour organization was mainly successful in the more skilled trades, it was particularly hard to organize in the resource industries. The

Workers at looms, *c.* 1908. City of Toronto Archives, James Collection, 137.

growth of secondary manufacturing and a service sector created a working class (or proletariat) that clearly saw its interests as different from those of the 'bosses'. Organizing on the factory floor was not an easy matter, however, since one of the effects of industrialization was to reduce craft identification, and another was to employ semi-skilled workers, often women, on a less-than-permanent basis. But drives for more efficient utilization of labour combined with mechanization to produce considerable worker alienation. One showcase factory, the Lumen Bearing Company of Toronto, could boast of a 'staff boss', whose job it was to save time:

> He is on the floor all the time; he is corrective to slovenly practices. The stop watch is his gauge. By careful and accurate observations a basis is arrived at for piece work prices....In the Lumen Bearing Co.'s foundry a certain class of castings was formerly made at the rate of twenty-eight a day. That was in the day work era. Today the average production per man of the same casting is sixty-five. The history of the change in output from twenty-eight to sixty-five daily is the story in concentrated form of efficiency management.[27]

Such a history was also a built-in recipe for eventual industrial conflict.

Many of the late nineteenth-century labour organizations were foreign

A clothing manufacturer's shop in the City of Quebec, *c.* 1905. Archives Nationales du Québec, N 79-12, 43.
Both this photograph and the one on the left reveal the hierarchy in these mechanical jobs: a preponderance of women to carry them out—supervised by men.

imports, chiefly from the United States, although many Canadian labour leaders had British experience. The railroad brotherhoods moved into Canada with the expansion of the railroads in the 1870s and 1880s, and were joined in 1881 by the Noble Order of the Knights of Labor, a fraternal/industrial-type union that attempted, not very successfully, to combine unskilled and semi-skilled workers under one umbrella. The American Federation of Labor (AFL), led for many years by the cigar-maker Samuel Gompers, concentrated strictly on craft organization in certain industries. In the early years of the twentieth century more radical industrial-type unions than the Knights of Labor emerged, particularly the Industrial Workers of the World (the IWW or 'Wobblies'), which concentrated on resource-workers in western Canada. In Quebec, many unaffiliated Catholic unions emerged in the early 1900s. For Canada as a whole, the Canadian Labor Congress was established in 1883 as a holding body for local trade councils, and in 1892 became the Trades and Labor Congress of Canada—affiliated with the AFL. In 1902 the TLC expelled unions connected to the Knights of Labor, or that had an AFL affiliation. Seventeen of the twenty-three unions involved were from Quebec, and they became the backbone of the National Trades and Labour Congress of Canada (NTLC), founded in 1903. Not until the 1940s was an indigenous Canadian industrial union formed.

While there was no single factor that created labour unrest and confrontation with employers across Canada, this period saw unionism still trying to gain a permanent foothold, and most labour conflict revolved around the right to organize and the recognition of unions. The strike and lockout were the most common weapons of labour and management respectively, and despite the work of labour 'arbitrators' and of conciliators like William Lyon Mackenzie King (1874-1950)—who began his public career in 1900 as Canada's first deputy labour minister—there were few alternatives to open industrial warfare. The leading provinces for labour unrest were British Columbia and Quebec, although strikes became common everywhere after 1900. Except in the Far West, the majority of the workers involved in labour confrontations were skilled rather than unskilled, but much depended on local conditions. For example, in Ontario—which in its ten largest cities alone witnessed 421 strikes and lockouts, involving 60,000 workers, between 1901 and 1914—fewer than ten per cent of strikers came from the ranks of the unskilled or semi-skilled. But Ontario was highly industrialized. In the Maritimes, 324 strikes occurred between 1901 and 1914. Unskilled workers were involved in 37 per cent of these strikes, skilled in 28 per cent, and miners in another 18.5 per cent.[28]

Socialists were to be found everywhere in Canada after 1900, and both their existence and their political successes in local and municipal elections are still among Canada's best-kept secrets. The most militant socialists were in British Columbia, where socialism represented both a political and a labour movement, the two parts often conflicting with one another. On the other hand, the Socialist Party of Canada was organized in 1904 in BC as the result of a merger of Marxists and the Canadian Socialist League. BC labour unrest was particularly strong among miners, for whom the common categories of skilled and unskilled held little meaning. In this kind of environment, syndicalists and radicals (such as the Wobblies, or the 'Impossibilists', who insisted that the reform of capitalism could not happen) did very well.

There were all too many occasions when the civil authorities (in the person of policemen and even militiamen) intervened in labour conflicts—usually in the name of public order and inherently on the side of management—but it must be emphasized that the Canadian state had proved relatively receptive to the rights of labour to organize. Whereas in the United States public policy was almost universally hostile to labour organization, in Canada laws were put on the books fairly early—beginning in the 1880s—that legalized union activity. So it is not surprising that in Canada the incidence of strikes and lockouts actually increased in comparison with the United States. By 1914 approximately 155,000 Canadians belonged to organized labour unions, many of them affiliated with American 'internationals'. Labour unrest was endemic in Canada before and even during the First World War.

Technology

The period between 1880 and 1919 was a great age of science and technology throughout the Western world. Most fields of scientific endeavour transformed out of all recognition the basic theoretical assumptions that had dominated humankind for generations, and the number of inventions that altered in practical ways how people lived and worked was astounding. In pure science Canada offered no world leaders. While science was taught at most Canadian universities, it was done at a general level with virtually no laboratory experimentation, and the number of programs beyond the elementary level—except in engineering and medicine—was relatively small. Quebec tended to lag behind the low levels in the other provinces. Several world-class scientists, such as Ernest Rutherford (1871-1937) in physics and Otto Hahn (1879-1968) in physics and chemistry, passed through Canada on their way to international recognition. But no amount of special pleading could place Canadian science of the period on a footing equal to the nation's economic world standing. In science and technology, Canada tended to borrow heavily from Great Britain and the United States.

In some areas of technical application of science, however, Canada played an important role. The Geological Survey of Canada was founded in Montreal in 1842 and limited to the Province of Canada; it did not grow until after its move to Ottawa in 1881 as part of the Department of the Interior. Parliament was willing to fund the GSC because of its obvious utility in surveying the vast land area of the nation, and while some GSC geologists became well-known figures for their explorations, the bulk of the Survey's

Charles E. Saunders.
National Archives of
Canada, C-9071.

work was slow, time-consuming, and extremely technical. Similarly, research
in agriculture had recognized value, and following the establishment of the
Dominion Experimental Farms system by Ottawa in 1886, director William
Saunders (1836-1914) set up the Central Experimental Farm at Ottawa and
four other similar farms across the nation, albeit in imitation of American
practice. The great achievement of Canadian agricultural research in this
period was the creation of Marquis wheat in 1907 by Charles Edward
Saunders (1867-1937), the son of William. Maturing early and giving excellent yields, Marquis wheat took the West by storm. Less successful were
attempts at the experimental stations to discover ways of farming with low
moisture in the drybelt areas of the West. The scientists may even have misled
a generation of settlers into thinking that new techniques could substitute for
adequate rain and snow, thus encouraging the cultivation of the dry belt.

Despite the growing sophistication of pure science and technology, many
of the technical advances of the period were made by laymen, or at least by
individuals who were neither employed as researchers nor given access to
fancy publicly financed laboratories and equipment in the course of their
discoveries. Notable among the few men who did enjoy careers as profes-

sional inventors were the American Thomas Alva Edison and the Scottish-born Alexander Graham Bell (1847-1922), who worked with the deaf in Brantford, Ontario, producing in the early 1870s a long series of inventions to aid the hearing-impaired. The culmination of his work, the telephone, came in the mid-1870s while he was employed in Boston, Massachusetts. The invention made Bell rich, and he moved to Washington, DC, to supervise his patents, spending the remainder of his life in the laboratory and financing the research of others. He also made important breakthroughs with the phonograph. Although he summered at his home Brinn Bhreagh ('Beautiful Mountain') in Cape Breton after 1890, and occasionally carried out experiments at Baddeck (including the flight of an early aircraft in 1907 and various sheepbreeding activities), Bell was essentially part of the American research world. Less well known was the Ontario-born Thomas Ahearn (1855-1938), head of a firm of electrical engineers and contractors from 1882, who invented a number of electrical devices, including an electric snow-sweeper to clear tram-tracks (1891) and an electric stove, used to cook a meal at the Windsor Hotel in Ottawa in 1892 as part of his display at the Ottawa Exhibition of that year. He later introduced the electric automobile into Ottawa in 1899. There were many Bells who were attracted to the United States by the size of its markets, and many Ahearns who stayed in Canada and died in decent obscurity.

✐ The Great War

The First World War both accelerated and distorted virtually every economic development that Canada had experienced during the previous forty years. While there is always some tendency to regard wartime as aberrant and unusual, the way in which the Great War worked upon the Canadian economy suggests that, like its successor from 1939 to 1945, its powerful force not only created new conditions but transformed and emphasized old ones. The great stories of the First World War have always concerned the appalling Canadian casualty rates, the maturation of Canadian independence and identity, and the Conscription Crisis of 1917. But in Canada itself, the war brought about economic development that was positive in the short run and negative in the long run because of the sudden quickening of earlier trends.

The sequence of events that began with the assassination of Archduke Ferdinand at Sarajevo in August 1914, and ended with much of the Western world at war, took place against a backdrop of an international slump that had followed more than a decade of overheated boom. Nineteen fourteen was not a good year for Canada. The western wheat economy had died, unemployment rates in central Canada reached twenty-five per cent before seasonal adjustment, and the per-capita national income had shrunk by a full ten per cent. Thousands of the young Canadians who queued to volunteer for the Canadian army were motivated by the absence of employment alternatives as well as by sentiments of loyalty to Britain and the Empire.

The Gains of War

Canadian industrialists responded to the war with three successive strategies. First, they tried to move into markets the Germans had abandoned, chiefly in the United States, without very much success. Then they tried a 'Buy Canadian' campaign. For the very first time in Canadian history they even encouraged the government to create an Advisory Committee on Industrial and Scientific Research to find some new technology to exploit. But real success came only when the Canadian government managed to convince the Imperial War Cabinet that it had the iron and steel capacity to churn out artillery shells to supply the entire Allied force. Initially the government allowed Canadian businessmen to contract directly with the British government for munitions, and by March 1915 over 200 firms, mainly in central Canada, had converted to munitions manufacture. Later in 1915 the government set up the Imperial Munitions Board, chaired by businessman Joseph Flavelle (1858-1939), and Canadian munitions production rose dramatically, raising the export of iron and steel products from $68.5 million in 1915 to $441.1 million two years later.

In the latter years of the war nearly forty per cent of Canadian manufacturing found export markets, and Canadian industry employed 200,000 people in munitions production. In 1917 the Munitions Board alone had an annual budget three times that of the federal government of 1914. At one point 675 factories were operating full time producing war orders. By 1917 Canadian industry had geared up for more than munitions, and started turning out ships, airplanes, and motor vehicles in record numbers. Throughout the war the Canadian soldier was equipped with arms and kits manufactured in Canada, and fed by Canadian suppliers. Some firms profiteered, but most merely made huge gross profits on small margins and substantial volume.

Only central Canada and industrial Nova Scotia directly benefited from this bonanza, although the sinews of war obviously kept the resource industries of the entire country—particularly the metals sector—booming as well. However, most of the raw materials of the munitions industry, especially iron and coal, were imported from the United States and Newfoundland. Iron-ore imports from the United States in 1918 were 1,392,000 short tons and from Newfoundland 754,000 short tons; only 93,100 tons of domestic iron ore were processed. In coal, 861,000 tons were imported, and 561,000 produced domestically, mainly for use in Nova Scotia plants. Wartime demand for metals, of course, was highly artificial. Nickel production, which reached a height of 46,300 short tons in 1918, had dropped back to 8,800 short tons by 1922, and the post-war collapse in other metals was equally dramatic.

No sector of the Canadian economy was more affected by the Great War than agriculture, particularly western wheat production. From 1914 to 1919, in Canada as a whole, agricultural acreage cultivated and wheat exports doubled; acreage under seed increased in the three prairie provinces from 9.3

million acres in 1914 to 16.1 million acres in 1918. Wheat and oats covered over ninety per cent of the fields. 'Improved' land as a proportion of total land in these provinces increased from forty per cent in 1911 to over fifty per cent in 1921. Wheat prices trebled, and the wartime boom helped the rural population of the Prairie West to increase from 858,000 to 1,250,000, thus keeping pace with growth rates in Canada's cities. The number of prairie farms rose during this decade by an astounding twenty-eight per cent.

The Economic Costs of War

Agriculture   Canadian farmers were often regarded by other elements of the population as particularly favoured by the war. Their young men could gain exemption from military service and, as Stephen Leacock put it, the farmer's wartime profits could sustain the consumption of 'pianos, victrolas, trotting buggies, books, moving pictures, pleasure cars and so on'.[29] But while farmers could and did benefit from high international grain prices, the war was not without its economic costs. Although farmers' sons could gain exemption from conscription when it was introduced in 1917, by that time there were few young men left on western farms, for the region had outdone the remainder of Canada in rates of volunteer enlistment in the first years of the war. Moreover, the cost of increasing production was high. More land often had to be acquired, and land prices rose substantially in the process. The CPR, for example, still a major source, in 1917 sold land for $21.63 per acre that it had charged $13.55 per acre for only two years earlier. Labour costs increased commensurately, and the need for both land and labour forced farmers to buy new and ever-more-expensive agricultural equipment. Most farmers did not move to gasoline-powered tractors, however, partly out of conservatism and partly because of the unavailability of satisfactory models. Instead, the number of farm horses doubled from 1911 to 1921. (But farmers did buy automobiles in large numbers.) The cost of meeting external and internal demands was high, and many farmers—particularly the smaller ones—did so with borrowed money. Farm credit was easily available during the war, although at high rates of interest, and the rate of farm debt increased in proportion to everything else.

If debt levels were one potentially negative consequence of wartime expansion, the land itself—or, more precisely, the way the land was used—produced another. Farmers were encouraged, both by the pressures for increased production emanating from the Canadian government and by high prices, to move cultivation onto marginal land and to abandon most of the tested techniques of soil and moisture conservation that had hitherto been practised. Farms got larger—the average farm size on the Prairies increased from 289.4 acres in 1911 to 335.4 acres in 1921—and, given labour shor-tages, were often hastily cultivated. One farm journal complained: 'We have developed weeds to the extent that they are a very important factor,' and 'We have cultivated our land in such a manner that soil drifting has become a very serious problem.'[30] For a variety of reasons, therefore, western farmers would be in serious trouble when the price of grain inevitably fell on international markets, and when the cycles of climate produced equally inevitable short-falls of moisture, particularly in the drybelt regions.

Labour While farmers were encouraged to mortgage the future during the war, labour was required to defer expectations during the emergency. Although organized labour made some gains in the early years of fighting, it remained convinced that the government was permitting wartime profiteer-ing to benefit the industrialists at the expense of the workers. Constant inflation eroded the purchasing power of labour incomes—the cost of living in 1919 was sixty-four per cent higher than in 1913, and annual inflation rates reached double figures by 1916—while wages did not keep pace with inflation, particularly after the government began to control labour's bargain-ing effectiveness. Compulsory arbitration was introduced into all war indus-tries in 1916, and in the crisis year of 1917 the government announced its intention of outlawing strikes and lockouts. The situation in 1917 was becoming as desperate on the home front as in the trenches of Europe. That year saw at least 148 work stoppages and over a million working days lost through labour unrest. While eastern workers called for reform, western radicals wanted general strikes and even revolution. The president of the British Columbia Federation of Labour insisted, for example, that 'if our masters force us to fight, let us fight for our own liberty and cast from our limbs the chains of bondage.'[31] When the war finally ended, it did so in an atmosphere of rising union membership and labour discontent. That discon-tent would culminate with violence on the streets of Winnipeg in 1919.

The Aftermath of War: The Winnipeg General Strike

Many factors contributed to that famous 'Confrontation at Winnipeg', the Winnipeg General Strike of 1919. The Bolshevik revolution in Russia pro-vided radical labour leaders—some of whom came from the same eastern-European cauldron where Karl Marx was only one of a number of revolu-tionary theorists, and a relatively benign one at that—with an illustration of what could be done against a repressive capitalist system. It also provided Canada's government and its businessmen with an illustration of what might happen if popular unrest were permitted to get out of hand. Most of the conditions and issues that initially produced labour unrest in Winnipeg in the spring of 1919 were traditional ones exacerbated by the war: recognition of union rights to organize, higher wages, better working conditions. A walk-out by workers in the city's metal trades and building industries was quickly joined by other malcontents in a general sympathy strike, and on 15 May the strikers voted to close down the city's services. To some understandably worried businessmen, placards on wagons allowing essential deliveries by permission of the strikers became a symbol of the breakdown of public

The Winnipeg General Strike, 21 June 1919. Manitoba Archives, N2771, Foote Collection, 1705.

A demonstration of protest against the arrest and trial of the leaders of the Winnipeg General Strike. National Archives of Canada, C-37329 (courtesy Mary Jordan, Winnipeg).

authority. Workers in other cities, such as Toronto and Vancouver, responded with declarations of support, and Canadian authorities were easily persuaded that the Revolution Was Nigh. As usual, the Canadian government's response to anything that smacked of popular uprising was to repress it as quickly as possible.

A delegation of Canadian Cabinet ministers, headed by Arthur Meighen (1874–1960, acting minister of justice and soon, briefly, to be Canada's prime minister), recommended the introduction of militia and Mounted Police to maintain order, since the Winnipeg police force refused to promise that it would not join the strikers. Postal workers were ordered back to work, and in early June the Canadian Naturalization Act was amended to allow for the instant deportation of any foreign-born radicals who advocated revolution or who belonged to 'any organization entertaining or teaching disbelief in or opposition to organized government.'*[32] The bulk of the city's police force of 200 men was dismissed on 9 June, to be replaced by local militia units, the Royal North West Mounted Police, and 1,800 special constables recruited and paid by the Citizen's Committee of 1,000, representing the city's business and professional élite. A few of these constables were drawn from the ranks of demobilized servicemen who accepted the official assessment that the best way to end the strike was to 'clean the aliens out of this community and ship them back to their happy homes in Europe which vomited them forth a decade ago.'[33] But by and large the ex-servicemen refused to join the forces of law and order. Open violence between special police and constables erupted on 10 June. A few days later ten strike leaders (six of British background and four 'foreigners') were summarily arrested, although the Anglo-Canadian contingent was released a few days later. On 21 June ('Black Saturday') a public demonstration of strikers and returned soldiers, marching towards the Winnipeg City Hall, was met by Mounties on horseback. The result was a violent mêlée that injured many, killed two strikers, and resulted in a number of arrests of 'foreign rioters'. The militia mopped up the troublemakers, and two days later the Strike Committee offered to end the strike if a Royal Commission investigated it and its underlying causes.

The aftermath of the Winnipeg General strike was anti-climactic and is often overlooked—but it says much about industrial Canada in 1919. The Royal Commission found that much of the labour unrest in Winnipeg in 1919 was justified, and that the strikers' principal goal was to effect the introduction of collective bargaining, an ambition the tribunal supported. Separate deportation hearings, held in July 1919 against some of the 'foreign' strikers under arrest, also demonstrated that these men were concerned more with local issues than with radical revolution. Three of the four leaders

---

*A generation later Canadians would shake their heads in disbelief at the upsurge of Communist 'witch-hunting' in the United States, obviously ignorant of their own history.

arrested in mid-June were eventually released after public hearings. On the other hand, most of the 'foreigners' arrested on 21 June were summarily sent to an Ontario internment camp and ultimately deported in secret. The police magistrate who interned these men explained to Arthur Meighen:

> . . .as Police Magistrate I have seen to what a large extent Bolsheviki ideas are held by the Ruthenian, Russian and Polish people, whom we have in our midst. . . .it is absolutely necessary that an example should be made. . . .If the Government persists in the course that it is now adopting [presumably of confrontation and deportation] the foreign element here will soon be as gentle and easily controlled as a lot of sheep.[34]

Thus a strike that began as a local response to local industrial conditions, exacerbated by the Great War, ended as a concerted campaign that reached far outside Winnipeg's Anglo-Canadian community. The use of the civil arm to suppress radicalism, long a part of the Canadian tradition, was given a new meaning in post-war Winnipeg. Perhaps most significantly, the fragility underlying the nation's spectacular industrial growth was exposed after the Armistice of 1918. Canadian industry would not really recover until the country became involved in another world conflagration in 1939.

chapter three

Urban Canada, 1885-1919

In August 1919 W.D. Lighthall (1857-1954) of Montreal, honorary secretary of the Canadian Union of Municipalities (since its founding, partly at his instigation, in 1901), delivered a valedictory address to his colleagues. A Montreal lawyer, he had served as reforming mayor of Westmount from 1900 to 1903 and was a fierce opponent of corporate monopolies, especially by utilities and railroads. As is usually the case on such occasions, his tone was both congratulatory and exhortatory, pointing out that much had been done in terms of urban reform, while much remained still to do. He particularly emphasized the battle against 'the triumph of corrupt money', noting that if unchecked it would 'with logical certainty lead to what is now called Bolshevism, unless the forces of right and order could meanwhile find a remedy.'[1] He went on to propose a series of nine principles for Canadian municipalities, which expressed 'forms of our original British constitutional birthright of personal liberty and right.' As Lighthall stated them, the essential principles were:

1. The Canadian people shall not be ruled by any irresponsible monopoly.
2. They shall not submit to methods of fraud or corruption.
3. There shall be no perpetual franchise.
4. Our heritage of natural resources affecting municipalities must not be sold, but leased, if not publicly operated.
5. One generation cannot legislate away the rights of another.
6. Municipalities must control their streets.
7. Each Canadian shall have a fair deal from all who are granted corporate or other public privileges.
8. Some court or council must always exist free and equipped to enforce the fair deal.
9. The life of the poorest citizen must be made worth living, through his share of the best civic conditions and services.[2]

Such 'principles' were also in effect a statement of priorities, and suggested the battles that were being and had been fought in the context of urban development and urban reform. For between 1880 and 1914 the growth of Canadian cities was a major trend, largely unanticipated and initially not planned.

In 1881 Canada had a population of 4,325,000, 3,349,000 of whom lived outside urban centres. Forty years later, of the nation's 8,788,000 inhabitants, only 4,811,000 resided in non-urban areas, and 1,659,000 lived in cities with populations of over 100,000. Put another way, while the non-urban population had increased substantially (from 3,349,000 to 4,811,000), the number of city-dwellers had burgeoned from 974,000 to 3,977,000. Not only had Canada's cities grown significantly, but so had the complexities of their problems. The percentage of residents below the poverty line may not have increased substantially, but the total numbers that percentage represented had doubled or tripled since the middle of the nineteenth century. Canada's largest cities began to develop middle-class suburbs, and place of residence increasingly became associated with income and ethnic origin. Cultural and physical amenities grew in tandem with movements to reform the appalling disparities between rich and poor that were observable almost everywhere.

At the same time, the process of Canadian urbanization indicated more than simply the development of some very large metropolitan centres. If 1,659,000 Canadians lived in cities over 100,000 in 1921, another 2.2 million lived in small centres, with 1,058,000 in towns of 5,000 to 29,999 people and 765,000 in towns of 1,000 to 4,999. Although the typical small town tended in some ways to merge into the rural countryside, for which it served as a shopping and service centre, many of these towns, especially in rapidly growing western Canada, had aspirations to larger status. Perhaps equally to the point, many served as centres for rural folk, often having stores and services that reached beyond their local requirements. The market-town, therefore, developed many urban characteristics that made the life-style of its inhabitants substantially different from that of people living in rural areas.

The Cities

As in most other aspects of Canadian development in this period, urban growth was not equally distributed across the regions. Maritime cities grew fairly sluggishly, and none could establish any dominance over the region. Indeed, Halifax lost ground as its financial institutions were siphoned off to central Canada. In Quebec, Montreal continued its path to the status of the Dominion's premier city, with Quebec City and other towns lagging far behind. In Ontario, Toronto was plainly the 'Queen City', although a number of smaller cities (such as Hamilton, London, and Kingston) were vibrant; and Ottawa inhabited a world of its own as the nation's capital, as it always would. The most spectacular urban growth-rates were in the Canadian West, which in this era spawned two major cities, Winnipeg and Vancouver, and two contenders for such a rank in Edmonton and Calgary. Indeed, while western settlement is usually associated with farms and agriculture, urban development in the West was strong from the outset, with land speculation driving local pretensions, and many communities aspiring to become major entrepôts.

The Maritimes

Most of the growth in Maritime cities came in the first decades after Confederation, during the period of rural depopulation and rapid industrialization to take advantage of the National Policy. They stabilized, perhaps even stagnated, only when the process of de-industrialization and dominance by central Canada worked its way into the region in the early 1900s. Saint John continued to be dominant in New Brunswick even though, prior to this period, it was hit by various calamities: the disastrous fire of 1877 that destroyed much of the city; a drop in the demand for wooden ships; the end of a protected British market for Maritime timber; and the effect of the Intercolonial Railway, which brought Saint John's trade goods into competition with goods from central Canada. Halifax served Nova Scotia. In the late Victorian period Halifax was dominated by the Citadel—the massive fortifications built between 1828 and 1856 and manned by British troops until 1900. The notorious Barrack Street ran just under it, one wag in 1883 commenting that 'it formed the lowest street of the city instead of the best, as it is the highest.'[3] The city contained more than forty per cent Irish and three per cent blacks, who together made up the bulk of the poor and casual labour force. Halifax managed to escape major fires in the nineteenth century—unlike Saint John, St John's, Newfoundland, and other cities mainly built of wood—only to be devastated by the Halifax explosion in 1917. Charlottetown—still little more than a small town in the last quarter of the century—was by far the largest community on Prince Edward Island. No Maritime city got large enough to escape its central waterfront core, and in the larger centres the early years of the twentieth century saw much loss of employment, especially in the skilled artisan trades. Much of the Maritime urban growth was in the smaller industrial centres. Around the turn of the century, Moncton in New Brunswick and Yarmouth, New Glasgow, Amherst, and Truro in Nova Scotia added factories and briefly flourished.

Perhaps no town developed more rapidly or extensively than Amherst, located not far from the New Brunswick border on the main line of the Intercolonial Railroad. The visitor to Amherst can still see, in sections of the town, both the baronial stone mansions of the local business élite and the row cottages of the workers, located in different neighbourhoods on different streets, but not separated geographically very much from one another. The distance from cottage to mansion was psychological as much as physical. By the early 1900s Amherst employed over 4,000 people in a variety of indus-

ome of the devastation caused by the Halifax explosion. At 8:45 a.m. on 6 December 1917 the British lief vessel *Imo* collided with the French munitions carrier *Mont Blanc* in Halifax harbour; twenty-one ainutes later the *Mont Blanc* blew up, producing the world's greatest man-made explosion before liroshima. It destroyed much of Halifax's North End and left no part of the city undamaged. City of oronto Archives, James Collection, 2450.

tries, and was one of the ten largest manufacturing centres in Canada. The leading local industries were in the metal trades. The year 1910 was the high-point of Amherst's industrial and urban development, however, and as local industrialists were replaced by central-Canadian decision-makers, Amherst's industrial capacity was gradually reduced by plant consolidations that retained central-Canadian over Maritime operations. Many Maritime towns were increasingly dominated by single industries, and were thus particularly susceptible to the economic cycle. The First World War brought a final glow of prosperity to Nova Scotia's coal and iron towns, but it was an artificial flame.

Montreal

Montreal had always been the commercial and financial capital of the St Lawrence region, and with increasing industrialization it continued to flourish. By the end of the nineteenth century it had a population of 328,000, which had nearly doubled to 618,000 by the end of the First World War. Ethnically the city remained divided between French Canadians (about sixty per cent of the population) and Anglo Canadians (about half of them Irish), although an increasing number of immigrants from eastern Europe made the

Dominion Square, Montreal, in the early 1900s. The centre of the Anglo-Protestant district, it was developed in the 1870s after the city appropriated a large area that had been a cemetery. The buildings surrounding the park, with its statue to Sir John A. Macdonald, were designed in an array of architectural styles— High Victorian Gothic, Romanesque Revival, and Second Empire. On the left are St George's Anglican Church and (to the north) the original Windsor Hotel at Dorchester and Peel Streets. To the right of the Macdonald statue is the YMCA (later replaced by the Sun Life Building). This view is from the tower of Windsor Station. Municipal Archives of Montreal.

city the centre of Jewish culture in Canada. Economically and socially Montreal was divided into working-class districts below Mount Royal and prosperous suburbs that climbed the hill. The city's wealth was exemplified by the many mansions of its business élite: the houses of Lord Strathcona and Harrison Stephen on Dorchester Avenue; the James Ross house on Redpath; the Lunn house at Park Avenue and Sherbrooke; the Sir William Van Horne house on Sherbrooke; and the Henry Lyman house at the top of McTavish Street. As in all cities in Canada (and North America, perhaps even throughout the world), there was a direct correlation between social status and physical elevation. Most of the working classes lived in overcrowded tenements with substandard services and amenities: Montreal had terrible health conditions. The city's death-rate was very high by international standards throughout the period; around the turn of the century an infant's chance of surviving its first year was better in Calcutta or Shanghai than in Montreal.

Just below the hill was Sherbrooke Street—'Plutoria Avenue' as satirized by Stephen Leacock in his *Arcadian Adventures with the Idle Rich* (1914). Here lived steely-eyed capitalists and thoughtful university professors, almost all of them English-speaking and of British origin. 'Just below Plutoria Avenue,' which was 'the very pleasantest place imaginable,' wrote Leacock,

> ...and parallel with it, the trees die out and the brick and stone of the city begins in earnest. Even from the avenue you see the tops of the sky-scraping buildings in the big commercial streets, and can hear or almost hear the roar of

the elevated railway, earning dividends. And beyond that again the city sinks lower, and is choked and crowded with the tangled streets and little houses of the slums.

In fact, if you were to mount to the roof of the Mausoleum Club itself on Plutoria Avenue you could almost see the slums from there. But why should you? And on the other hand, if you never went up on the roof, but only dined inside among the palm-trees, you would never know that the slums existed—which is much better.[4]

Montreal was becoming not only a large city—it annexed 22 suburbs between 1883 and 1918—but a great city with great economic and social problems to match its status. When a syndicate, backed by the powerful Bank of Montreal, financed the building of the CPR, Montreal became the centre of the nation's railroad network, and in the early years of the twentieth century it housed the largest stock exchange in Canada.

Toronto

Toronto did not dominate Ontario to the extent that Montreal dominated Quebec (and the Maritimes, and to some extent Ontario), but it expanded rapidly once it became the hub and commercial centre of the region. As well as sending small railroads fanning out into the province, Toronto was the

oronto in 1903, looking north from the top of the Temple Building at Bay and Richmond (its domed rret and flagpole are seen in the foreground)—one-third of a 360⁰ panorama taken with a moving amera lens by W.T. Freeland. The four-year-old City Hall is in the centre, with (to the east) the T. Eaton ompany department store on Queen Street and Simpson's on the south side of Queen at Yonge. The ree towers are those of St Michael's Cathedral (Roman Catholic), Metropolitan Methodist Church, nd Confederation Life. Knox Presbyterian Church, across from Eaton's, would soon be demolished and s property acquired by Simpson's. National Archives of Canada, PA-30911.

terminus of the Grand Trunk Railway, and the CPR brought its tracks into the city and connected it with Buffalo, and thus Detroit and New York. Commerce was ruled by such wholesalers as John Macdonald (1824-90), William McMaster (1811-97), and his successor A.R. McMaster (his nephew); by the retailers Timothy Eaton (1834-1907) and Robert Simpson (1834-97); by many manufacturing enterprises, such as the factory for agricultural implements, the Massey Manufacturing Company (later Massey Harris), president, Hart Massey (1823-96); and the distillers and exporters Gooderham and Worts, president, George Gooderham (1820-1905). As a financial centre Toronto was second in Canada to Montreal—which had the powerful Bank of Montreal, banker to the government and the CPR, and the Royal Bank, as well as the leading stock exchange—but it was a strong rival as a centre of banking in the country. Its business district seemed to be dominated by splendid bank buildings, located in close proximity, that were consciously designed to emanate wealth and power, solidity and prestige: the Toronto Branch of the Bank of Montreal; the Bank of Commerce, founded in 1867 by William McMaster and second in assets only to the Bank of Montreal; the Bank of Toronto, whose president was George Gooderham; the Ontario Bank; the Dominion Bank; the Imperial Bank, which moved into the West in the 1880s; and the Toronto Main Branch of the Bank of Nova Scotia. Their shareholders were drawn from Toronto's élite, who lived in a style befitting merchant princes, building mansions such as A.R. McMaster's great house on Jarvis Street, which was later purchased and altered by Hart Massey (it is now a restaurant); the Timothy Eaton house (demolished) on Lowther Avenue; the George Gooderham house (now the York Club) on St George at Bloor Street West; and John Macdonald's 'Oaklands' (now part of De La Salle College) at the top of Avenue Road hill.

Like Montreal and most North American cities in the late nineteenth century, Toronto grew geographically chiefly by annexing communities adjacent to the urban centre, which in 1882 had stood at a mere 7900 acres. Thirteen communities were gobbled up between 1883 and 1893, and another eighteen between 1903 and 1912, with a resulting land area in excess of 20,000 acres. The city sloped gently upwards from Lake Ontario, and the wealthier northern suburbs, such as Rosedale, were on higher ground than the tenements of the poor. Toronto continued to be a British city. In 1901 the population comprised 94,021 of English origin and 96,070 of Scottish and Irish origin, out of a total of 208,040. A few thousand French Canadians and some Germans were the only substantial non-British element, although before the First World War many eastern Europeans entered the city. By 1921 the population was 521,000.

The West

The fastest-growing cities in Canada, however, were in the West. Indeed, urban growth there was generally substantial, especially after 1900. In the

Prairie Provinces between 1900 and 1916 the urban population grew from 103,000 to 606,000, and city-dwellers, who represented twenty-five per cent of the region's population in 1901, increased to thirty-five per cent ten years later. In British Columbia by 1921 Vancouver (117,217) and Victoria (38,727) contained twenty-five per cent of the population of that Pacific province.

Winnipeg

Winnipeg's tiny population of 241 in 1871 expanded in fifty years to 179,087. Unlike Montreal or Toronto, Winnipeg did not grow by annexing adjacent territory, but by immigration. Although commonly perceived as being predominantly ethnic, Winnipeg began as a British city, with 83.6 per cent of its population of British origin in 1881. It ended its period of growth with 67.1 per cent British in 1921. Though the percentage of British gradually declined between 1881 and 1911, it actually increased during the decade of the First World War. The eastern-European population of the city never exceeded twenty per cent of the total, while the French-Canadian percentage had stabilized by 1901 at just over two per cent. Not blessed with an excess of higher elevations, Winnipeg utilized its complex river and railroad systems to create socio/economic/ethnic divisions, and by the First World War it was perhaps the most thoroughly segregated city in Canada. The immigrant poor, mainly from eastern Europe, were largely confined to the north-central section of the city (the notorious 'North End'), while the business and professional community increasingly moved south of the Assiniboine River and west of the Red into the southwest quadrant of the metropolitan area— actually outside the city limits. The immigrant community was fairly effec- tively sealed off from social assimilation, a result that accorded with the generally unsympathetic attitude of the dominant British élite towards the eastern-European newcomers.

Winnipeg's municipal government was dominated by promoters and real- estate developers, who saw the administration of the city chiefly in terms of growth and expansion. This dominance applied to most Canadian cities but was more open and obvious in the West. The western urban business élite tended to be incorrigible 'boosters', but developers had a particular axe to grind, for outlying land could not be properly improved without an exten- sion of services. The Winnipeg city government— especially during the boom years between 1900 and 1913—amounted to little more than a contest among rival groups of promoters for the expansion of local improvements. Even its great public park, Assiniboine Park—established in 1904, although projected much earlier, and designed by the firm of the distinguished Ameri- can landscape-designer Frederick Law Olmstead (who had created Central Park in New York)—was little more than a thinly disguised effort by speculators to run tramlines into what was then a remote suburban district.

The intersection of Portage and Main had by 1885 become the centre of Winnipeg's commercial and financial district, and one of Canada's best-known (and famously windy) street corners. The surrounding blocks were dominated by buildings of the Grain Trade—such as the Grain Exchange Building (1882, rebuilt 1906); several classical bank buildings; and the extraordinary City Hall (1886, demolished 1962), described by one architectural historian as 'a grandly garish variant of the Second Empire...embellished with local imagination and pride.'[5] Of more enduring impressiveness was the Legislative Building (1912–20), built in the grand classical manner, with a high central dome and a circular rotunda below, and climaxing an impressive boulevard vista. Most provinces had already built, or were building, similar legislative monuments.

Winnipeg overcame its climatic disadvantages as the world's coldest city and countered its lack of natural scenery with a tree-planting program along its streets and boulevards, boasting in 1905 12,072 trees already planted. The summer profusion of trees and green grass astounded visitors to the 'bare Prairies'. Labelled by its civic boosters 'the Gateway City' and 'The Chicago of the North', Winnipeg made these claims because of its role as a transportation centre, with its railroads leading in all directions, permitting the city to become both a nexus for the financial aspects of grain marketing and the wholesale supplier for the entire prairie agricultural hinterland.

Vancouver

The railroad was the key to Vancouver's development. The CPR, after a flirtation with Port Moody, had decided to terminate its transcontinental line at the banks of False Creek. The city's rapid population growth—from a mere handful of people in 1881 to 117,217 by 1921—was fuelled chiefly by immigration. Even more than in Winnipeg, the bulk of Vancouver's new arrivals were of British origin, coming after the turn of the century. In 1911 one of every three Vancouverites had been born in the 'old country'. Vancouver was, if anything, even harder on non-British immigration than was Winnipeg, partly because many of the newcomers came from Asia rather than eastern Europe. The city saw a series of anti-oriental riots, and in May–July 1914 largely approved when a shipload of East Indian Sikhs aboard the *Komagata Maru* was determinedly refused entry to Canada by intrepid members of the Canadian Immigration Service. To some extent Vancouver's success came at the expense of Victoria, reflecting a shift in the emphasis of British Columbia's economy from Vancouver Island to the mainland of the province. While coal and salmon declined as major economic sectors of the BC economy, timber grew in importance, with the quantity of lumber cut in the province more than tripling between 1901 and 1910. Most of this lumber was shipped to the booming Prairie Provinces via Vancouver.

Other Western Cities

Calgary and Edmonton in Alberta, and Regina and Saskatoon in Saskatchewan, had their beginnings well before their respective provinces were formed in 1905. Fort Calgary was established by the North West Mounted Police in 1875 at the confluence of the Bow and Elbow Rivers. In 1884 the CPR laid out the site of Calgary, west of the Bow and south of the Elbow, and it was incorporated as a city in 1893, becoming the chief transportation centre in Alberta and, until the harsh winter of 1906-7, thriving as a centre for the meat-packing industry. Calgary also benefited from cash-crop farming after the turn of the century; and the first oil-strike in 1914 at Turner Valley, a few miles southwest of the city, presaged another source of revenue that would develop in the next decade. Between 1891 and 1921 the population rose from 3,876 to 63,305. Fort Edmonton was a centre for the western fur trade, but permanent settlement outside the fort did not begin until the 1870s. Edmonton, on the North Saskatchewan River—having access to the farmlands of central Alberta and to the northern hinterland—was incorporated as a town in 1892, as a city in 1904, and was made the capital of the new province in the same year that it acquired a transcontinental rail connection by being on the route of the Canadian Northern Railway. Its population grew slowly—it was only 50,000 during the First World War.

Like Calgary, Regina was located and laid out by the CPR. It was founded in 1882 and made the capital of the Northwest Territories in 1883 (and was therefore the locus of Louis Riel's trial in 1885). Its growth, which did not really begin until it was named the provincial capital in 1905, was determined by its location in the heart of the wheat-growing plains and its role as a distribution and service centre for southern Saskatchewan. The northern prairies and northern Saskatchewan were served by Saskatoon on the South Saskatchewan River, some 120 miles northwest of Regina. Three villages combined in 1906 and were incorporated as the city of Saskatoon, which—as a hub of western railways—became a major distribution centre. Edmonton and Saskatoon were made the seats of provincial universities in 1906 and 1907 respectively.

✦ Factors of Urban Growth

While it is obviously difficult to generalize about urban growth, given the variety of economic conditions and stages of economic development prevailing across a country as vast and as regionalized as Canada, there were some factors and patterns that cut across geographical differences.

Transportation

The first and most important factor was transportation, which in these years meant railroads. No urban centre could expect to prosper if it was not on a main line. This reality was clearly recognized, and during the several outbursts of railroad expansion—particularly between 1906 and 1915, when more than 14,000 new miles of railroad track were added to the Canadian transportation network, mainly in western Canada—efforts by aspiring communities to become main-line (or even branch-line) depots or junction points were prodigious. Conversely, rumours of new railroad construction were sufficient to create a village where none had previously existed. The extremes to which communities would go to publicize themselves and to attract railroads were occasionally ludicrous and usually expensive. When funds were in short supply, the boosters tried publicity—sometimes in the form of catchy slogans ('New York may be Big, but this is Biggar'; 'You'll Hear from Champion')—through local newspapers created for the purpose. Agricultural fairs, and the support of town bands and sports teams, also publicized communities. A brass marching band was regarded as one of the best advertisements a town could have.

But nothing succeeded like money. 'Bonusing'—financial inducements to railroads and business entrepreneurs alike—was a way of life in this period. The little community of Minnedosa, Manitoba, well north of the CPR main line, contributed in 1883 $30,000 for a railway bonus to the Manitoba and North-Western Railway, and the county added another $100,000 in inducements. Once it acquired its railroad, Minnedosa rejoiced. 'In no distant day,' exulted one resident, 'the little town in the valley will seem more like an eastern town of Ontario than the newly discovered, just put together town on the Little Saskatchewan.' Minnedosa proudly insisted, in descriptive pamphlets, that it was 'the most important grain and stock centre on the Manitoba and North Western Railway.'[6] The town did not continue to grow, however, partly because it had nearly bankrupted itself bonusing the railroad, and partly because neighbouring Neepawa was able to connect with both the Canadian Northern and the Manitoba and North-Western. Nonetheless, Minnedosa's population growth to 1,100 by 1911 was fairly substantial. For every Minnedosa there were dozens of villages across Canada that never passed beyond the stage of wishing for greatness, when some optimistic land-speculator would build a general store in the middle of nowhere. Main-line was better than branch location, main-line junction was better than simple main-line, and rail-head was perhaps the best of all. But in the early twentieth century, as the automobile gradually became more common, roads replaced railroads as the subject of intense lobbying. Towns bypassed by provincial highways often built connector roads to the main road at their own expense.

Land Speculation

If urban growth—ranging from great cities to the Neepawas and Amhersts of the nation—was based upon railroad and highway transportation networks, it was also carried out in a context of fairly blatant and open land speculation. The attempted creation of every new city in western Canada, whether successful or unsuccessful, began with a land boom, and the first stage of development usually ended with a collapse in land prices that required several years of recovery. The collapsed land-boom in Winnipeg in the early 1880s was only the most notorious of hundreds of similar economic disasters. Many small businessmen in the West made a decent living selling out in one community, just before the bust, and moving to a new townsite further down the rail-line. The false fronts on western small-town stores were symbolic of the transitory nature of local commitment. But speculation in land was hardly confined to businessmen. Almost all segments of the local community joined in real-estate speculation whenever they could. Indeed, the attempt to turn a profit by investing in undeveloped land must surely be one of the most enduring features of Canadian business. Speculation was different from development, the former involving the holding of land for future profit, the latter the translation of land—often acquired at bargain prices—into immediate profit as sites for houses or factories.

Suburbanization

In the larger metropolitan centres land speculation and development were inseparable from the process of suburbanization. Although we often associate the suburb with the twentieth century, in Canada it was really a creation of the later nineteenth century and was associated with urban expansion away from the commercial core of most cities. The growth of suburbs (often with longer commuting times to place of work) required substantial alterations in systems of public transportation, and the electric tramlines of the end of the century served to open up new territories to residential populations. There were basically three distinctive motives for suburban expansion, and several different types of suburbs grew up in response to them.

The Social Motive

This factor involved the prospering business and professional classes, who moved into new suburbs to escape the noise, odours, and bustle of the central city. For example, horse droppings on city streets were a major sanitary problem. Some suburbanites, of course, were also attempting to put physical distance between themselves and the growing slums of the industrializing city. They were attracted by the possibility of large lawns and landscaped gardens, by the opportunity to build proper carriage houses for horses and equipment—and later to construct garages to house large automobiles. The houses built for the suburban élites, before the turn of the century and after, tended to be substantial and impressive, both inside and out, with large lots and large square footages. The architectural style most closely associated with them grew out of the English Art and Crafts movement and was dedicated to expressing traditional domestic building forms and craft practices in a modern manner. It became known as the English Domestic Revival, of which three noted practitioners were Eden Smith (Toronto), Percy Nobbs (Montreal), and Samuel Maclure (Victoria). There was much regional variation. Thus in Vancouver, both California bungalows and English Tudor Revival were very common.

Internally suburban middle-class houses featured large formal rooms on the first floor, plus a servant's bedroom somewhere, and smaller rooms with lower ceilings in the upper storeys. The employment of household servants—particularly 'live-ins'—continued to distinguish the wealthy from the ordinary householder. Not until after the First World War did fireplaces become mostly ornamental as central heating became more and more common—usually some form of hot-water, hot-air, or steam heat, which reached only to the first floor on the principle that hot air rises. The author's house in Winnipeg, built in 1906 for a marble dealer, has one of the city's first forced hot-air systems. As soon as it was available in the 1880s, such houses had electrical service, supplied by privately owned facilities. Electricity was used at first chiefly for lighting—electrical appliances did not become widely available until after the First World War. But the large appliances, like washing machines, were luxuries even in the twenties and thirties. Nevertheless, electrical service, along with indoor plumbing and servants, helped distinguish the wealthier city and suburban dwellers from the remainder of society, at least until the opening years of the Great War; and they separated urban from rural Canada until after the Second World War. Every town aspiring to urban standards introduced a water system and a sewer system, as well as an electricity plant of some kind. Larger centres often also had gas service of some sort. By the early 1900s these amenities had reached as far north as Dawson City in the Yukon Territory. Although most cooking was done on gas, wood, or coal stoves, even in wealthier districts, the electric range was making some inroads by 1914.

The Cost of Land

A second motivation for suburban growth was the cost of land and rising taxes in the central city, which drove certain businesses—mostly those that required considerable amounts of land, particularly large industrial operations—out of the urban core. The result was the development of a number of industrial suburbs, such as Maisonneuve in Montreal, that flourished outside the city but within its orbit. Especially after 1910, lower land costs and lower taxes also attracted better-paid members of the working classes into working-class residential suburbs, which usually consisted of rows of virtually identical small cottages. As anyone familiar with such districts can attest, the sameness of houses we associate with the large suburban subdivisions of the post–Second World War era actually had its counterpart in many earlier suburbs constructed before the First World War. In these districts, lots were smaller than in middle-class subdivisions, but the focus was often on single-family dwellings, with some space for gardens front and back. The presence of a front lawn, however tiny, distinguished suburban housing of this period from earlier urban housing that tended to front directly on the street (and now contained poor working-class tenants).

Proximity to Work

The third factor that drew urbanites to newer suburbs was proximity to work. The upper and middle classes could afford to commute fair distances on newly constructed tramlines; few rode horseback or drove carriages to work—although as the automobile grew in popularity (the Ford Motor Company of Canada was founded in 1904), it became increasingly common to drive one into the central city. The automobile required nothing but parking space, and seemed easier to accommodate downtown than the horse, so long as only a few cars replaced a few horses. For the working classes, who already toiled for between 55 and 60 hours over a six-day week, long-distance commuting was considerably less popular. As industrial development moved outside the downtown urban core, which tended to become financial and commercial in its emphasis, workers were forced to follow their jobs into often inadequate new housing. Slums were soon created by absentee land-lords who discovered that their houses were more profitable rented out to people who wanted to be relatively close to their work.

The Towns

Suburban service towns were, almost by definition, not completely indepen-dent of the larger metropolitan centres, although the modern concept of the metropolitan area had not yet been developed. As noted earlier, both Toronto and Montreal grew in part by incorporating outlying communities, and—given the tendency on the part of industry and workers alike to keep moving beyond municipal taxation boundaries—this process was a continual one. The genuine Canadian 'small town' tended to fit one of two models: a community servicing the surrounding agricultural region; or a single-resource community, often located in remote portions of the various pro-vinces, that had usually formed around a mine or mining/smelter operation. Many resource towns, though not all, were company towns.

The Service Town

The typical service town consisted of banks, a post office, stores, a hotel or two, churches, schools (including the only secondary school for the sur-rounding area), the offices of professional men (such as doctors, dentists, and lawyers), a funeral parlour, and the inevitable railroad depot. In older estab-lished towns of eastern Canada, religious, ethnic, or political divisions—the first two often producing the third—resulted in parallel establishments for different clienteles. Occasionally the larger town might have a small hospital or a library, although these amenities seldom made their way into the smaller communities before the First World War. Few towns of any substance were without at least one newspaper, usually a weekly, and few did not have a

Chamber of Commerce or Board of Trade, which spent its time attempting to boost the town into greater prominence and prosperity. By 1910 even the smallest community was at least giving serious thought to an electrical plant and a public water system, although the costs of such facilities would increase the mill rate substantially. Most towns had some sports facilities, usually a baseball field and occasionally, after 1890, an unheated building that served as a combination hockey and curling rink.

But such a catalogue does not convey the essential importance of the town as a centre of social and recreational life for the surrounding district. Before the advent of the radio and telephone, the social life of small-town Canada was especially bustling, even impressive. Organizations of all kinds proliferated and flourished. Most towns had a variety of fraternal lodges (Masons, Elks, Moose), church- and school-related organizations, and an endless round of meetings, dances, and 'occasions', the last ranging from concerts, to plays, to sermons by visiting evangelical preachers, to lectures on such diverse subjects as temperance or exotic places. Lectures were often accompanied by lantern slides, and were replaced after 1910 by motion pictures. By the end of First World War, most towns had at least one 'movie house', or at least a hall where motion pictures could be shown on a regular basis. Towns were hardly isolated from the larger urban centres, and city newspapers and journals sold briskly in the local stores. Although some towns had bars in the hotels, or in the halls of fraternal organizations, many had exercised the local option permitted by provincial liquor legislation and 'gone dry'.

The Resource Town

Unlike the agricultural service town, the resource town was isolated. Places such as Glace Bay (Nova Scotia), Black's Harbour (New Brunswick), Murdochville (Quebec), and Snow Lake (Manitoba) were surrounded by wilderness and inhabited almost exclusively by single males and a handful of women. Many towns had a single industry, often creations of particular companies. Only in Nova Scotia, particularly in Cape Breton, and in Quebec, did resource towns develop with relatively normal family life and institutions, and even here those institutions tended to be dominated by the 'company', which provided credit at the local store and preaching on Sundays. Eastern resource towns were created chiefly by drawing in population from the surrounding region, and were more stable in social structure, although not necessarily in terms of labour attitudes. In most regions, particularly on the mining frontiers of northern Canada, retail establishments were limited in number, and churches and schools were rare. The centre of any western or northern resource town was its drinking establishment(s): there were precious few other sources of entertainment than booze and gambling. Workers often lived in huts or barracks, working long hours for relatively short periods, perhaps six to ten weeks.

Many of the workers in resource towns were recent immigrants, some of them 'sojourners' intending to return to their country of origin when they had accumulated enough capital. Such communities were both violent and restive. Their population was almost totally alienated from their work, ready to follow the leadership of radical labour organizers, who often provided the only cohesion within the district. Mine-owners seldom resided in towns like Sudbury, Flin Flon, Cobalt, and Timmins in Ontario, or in the Cape Breton coal-mining communities: they were represented by local managers who were rarely generous to their workers. A few planned or 'model' towns— such as Brûlé and Nordegg in Alberta—were created before or during the First World War, particularly in the coal districts of Alberta. Resource towns were susceptible to the boom-and-bust cycle of resource industries, and the virtually overnight shutdown of mines and smelters could put an entire labour force out of work—as happened in Dominion, on Cape Breton Island, when the Dosco steel plant closed, and in Cadomin, Alberta, when a coal mine shut down. Under the circumstances, labour-management relations in these communities were seldom satisfactory, and a good many bitter strikes and lockouts were waged.

Urban Social Problems

While urban Canada was far more than the relatively few large cities with which it is frequently associated, it was naturally the cities—the largest concentrations of population—that exposed most clearly the social problems of the later Victorian and Edwardian eras. Of these, the most important was poverty—as it always has been. As there were now far more Canadians living in the cities, there were inevitably far more urban poor. People below the 'poverty line' tended to live in the worst housing conditions, to suffer from the most serious health problems, and to provide a challenge to all urban institutions, including the educational system. Income data is very sketchy before 1921, but existing evidence suggests that perhaps up to half the Canadian urban working-class lived below, or around, the poverty line. In 1912, for example, a child-welfare committee in Montreal asserted that the typical unskilled labourer earned $1.75 per day or $550 per year, adding:

> To get this much. . .a man must have continuous work (six days a week, fifty-two weeks a year) with no sickness, no changes in jobs, and he must not waste his money on drink or dissipation. Granted all this he can give a family of five a mere existence. . . .No allowance is here made for sickness, recreation, church, house furnishings, lectures and savings.[7]

Such a family would have to 'live in unsanitary quarters, sometimes below street level', and would not have sufficient nourishment even if meals were prepared according to strict domestic-science methods.

A weekly shopping-list for one Toronto working-girl— intended to feed her, her mother, and two sisters—consisted of the following:[8]

Bread at 14¢ a loaf	85¢
Oatmeal	25¢
Milk at 6¢ a quart	42¢
Sugar	10¢
Butter	20¢
Lard	12¢
Meat	25¢
Potatoes	15¢
Currants	06¢
Coal oil	10¢
Soap and salt	10¢
	$2.60

The resulting meals—heavy in starch, and weak in fresh vegetables—were hardly likely to provide proper nourishment. Little wonder that most working-class families were glad to supplement the father's income with the small earnings of wife and children in menial occupations. And given the grinding conditions of their lives, it is not surprising that many sought release in alcohol, a tendency that aggrieved middle-class reformers enormously.

Housing

For those approaching the poverty line, unbalanced diets and even malnutrition were only the start of their problems. Their housing conditions involved overcrowding, poor sanitation, and a lack of open yards and spaces. No city in Canada provided adequate inexpensive housing for its working classes. There was concern and discussion about housing in Toronto, but no system for dealing with it. Government-subsidized housing was not a recognized concept, and in any case the city fathers were aware that the public would not stand for an increase in taxes that would provide sewers, electricity, and running water in the older parts of the city where there were still pumps at street corners. In Toronto, for example, the response was to build libraries, hospitals, parks, playgrounds, and to improve public transportation. Such amenities as sewers in the city core were not completed until the 1920s, when the public had become used to wartime taxation, and would accept a hike in taxes to pay for them. The entire Western world lacked inexpensive working-class housing, although public agencies had begun providing some in London by 1905. In Toronto a few philanthropists—such as the Gooderhams, Sir Joseph Flavelle (president of the William Davies Company, pork-packers, and vice-president of the Robert Simpson Company), and two of the Masseys— subsidized workers' houses near their factories in the 1880s.

Some attempts at creating working-class housing were made just before the Great War. In 1907 the Canadian Manufacturers' Association sponsored a

Riverdale Courts, Bain Avenue, Toronto. This complex of 204 apartments (including some on two floors with four bedrooms), designed by Eden Smith around three-sided courtyards facing both sides of Bain Avenue, is located in the neighbourhood of Riverdale, east of the Don River. Originally intended as low-cost subsidized housing, it is run today by tenants as a co-op. Photograph by William Dendy.

schedule to produce small houses that could be sold profitably but at reasonable prices. There was a recession that year, but in May 1912 the Association—together with the Toronto Board of Trade, the Toronto City Council, the Guild of Civic Art, and the local Council of Women—conceived the Toronto Housing Company to provide proper low-cost accommodation. The Ontario Housing Act was passed in 1913, which gave Ontario municipalities the power to guarantee bonds for a Housing Company of up to 85 per cent of its working capital, as long as the remaining 15 per cent was invested by the public. Out of this initiative there grew, in 1914, two Toronto developments of Cottage Style flats—apartments with their own front doors to the street—in Spruce Court, at Spruce and Sumach Streets north of Cabbagetown, and Riverdale Courts on both sides of Bain Avenue, east of the Don River. Very well designed, both are still in use. Originally the rents were $14.50 to $16 a month, including heat and utilities. This amount could not be afforded by the very poor, but it was within the reach of upper working-class families, who paid it gladly.

Driven by demand, rents in the tenement areas of the central city went inexorably upward, yet only the most thrifty and skilled of workers could afford to buy a house, even in a distant suburb. Home ownership was difficult, even for middle-class people, because of the nature of mortgages,

These workers' cottages in St John's Ward on the south side of Albert Street, Toronto, were built as rental houses in the 1830s. At the time this photograph was taken—February 1912—they represented Toronto's lowest level of housing, and the City Hall in the background seems to point to their imminent demolition. This is one of a series of photographs intended to document slum conditions in Toronto. Commissioned by the city's Medical Officer of Health, they were taken between 1912 and 1920 for the Department of Public Works by the city photographer, Arthur S. Goss. City of Toronto Archives, DPW 32-53.

which were hard to obtain and had to be paid off in very short periods of no more than three to four years. Single-family dwellings in Toronto in St John's Ward (more or less where the present City Hall stands) were turned into multiple-family tenements in the 1870s. 'The intensive use of land', reported one Toronto observer in 1914, 'has lent itself to the creation of slums, and the scarcity of small houses has resulted in a doubling up of families in houses, so that two, three, and in some cases even five families are housed in a building constructed for one family only and with but one set of sanitary conveniences.'[9] Intensive land use and overcrowding did not necessarily produce slums, as the Annex in Toronto demonstrated. But demand led to overcrowding in all cities, even in a young city like Winnipeg, where one health inspector reported:

> A house of ten rooms was found occupied by five families, also roomers—20 adults and two children. Three of the families had only one room each. There were eight gas stoves, and none of these had hoods or pipes for carrying off the products of combustion and the odors of cooking. Two girl boarders occupied a portion of the cellar. . . . There was one water closet, one sink, a bath, and a wash basin. Two faucets had been fitted on the water-service pipe, and buckets placed under same in lieu of sinks.[10]

A slum interior in October 1913, with a nursing mother (whose husband is presumably at work, or ooking for work), her many children, and their grandmother all living in a small space. City of Toronto Archives, DPW 32-243.

Sanitation was one measure of the problem. In 1884 the Toronto Board of Health inspected 5,181 Toronto houses, finding '201 foul wells, 278 foul cisterns, 814 full privies, 570 foul privies, 739 cases of slops being thrown into privies, 668 cases of slops in the streets, 1207 cases of no drainage whatsoever and 503 cases of bad drainage.' A mere 873 of the 5,171 houses had water closets, although the Board recommended earth closets because the sewer system was useless. It subsequently reported that in one block 67 by 200 yards in extent, fourteen to eighteen tons of 'solid excreta' were dumped annually.[11] As late as 1905, Winnipeg had 6,153 box-closets and 186 earth-pits still in use.

Malnutrition and evil housing conditions combined to produce high overall death rates and high infant-mortality rates in Canada's largest cities. Montreal's death rate peaked at 24.81 per thousand in 1895, and declined very slowly. Equally significantly, there were wide differentials between the poorer and better-off districts, ranging from 35.51 deaths per thousand in 1895, in one working-class ward in Montreal, to less than 13 per thousand 'above the hill'. In Winnipeg a death rate that had fallen to 11.4 per thousand in 1896—just before the new surge of immigration into the North End from central and eastern Europe—climbed as high as 23.2 per thousand in 1906. Statistics for infant mortality were even more appalling. In Montreal, between 1899 and 1901, 26.76 per cent of newborn children died before they were one year old. In Winnipeg in 1912 the figure was just under twenty per cent, with 1,006 deaths for 5,041 live births. Such statistics could be traced to impure water, impure milk, and failure to take advantage of known vaccinations against smallpox and diphtheria, in addition to generally debilitating conditions.

Education

Education was yet another measure of the effects of poverty on Canada's cities. In working-class districts it was extremely difficult to keep children in school beyond the lowest elementary grades. In Montreal in 1905, for example, the Montreal Catholic School Commission reported that it had 3,442 students in grade one and 426 students (with an average age of thirteen) in grade five. Ten years later, Montreal Catholic Schools had 25,792 students in grade one and 2,848 in grade five, while Montreal's Protestant schools (almost all 'above the hill') had 1,187 in kindergartens (which were not in service in Catholic schools), 4,197 in grade one, and 2,761 in grade five. Less than twenty-five per cent of the total enrolment in Montreal's schools was beyond the elementary level in 1917—a figure inflated by the Protestant Anglos above the hill—while that figure was 33 per cent in Toronto and 37 per cent in Ottawa, but only 5 per cent in Winnipeg. Pressures for compulsory education were, as we shall see, strenuously resisted by the poor in all Canadian cities.

Transiency

While urban Canada had poverty and unemployment problems, Vancouver by the early twentieth century revealed a unique pattern of both. The relatively mild climate encouraged the seasonably unemployed to sojourn in the city over the winter months, turning up on the unemployment rolls when their money ran out. More than most Canadian cities', Vancouver's unemployed consisted of transient, single, able-bodied men, often prepared to become violent when not granted sufficient relief assistance. When Vancouver's City Council announced in 1915 that it would no longer feed non-resident single men, the result was a series of public meetings, allegedly addressed by 'alien enemies' and resulting in some broken restaurant windows on Hastings Street. The problem of unemployed transients reappeared there in 1919, when the Canadian government permitted demobilized soldiers recruited across the country to take their discharge in British Columbia. 'Our streets are rapidly becoming filled with idle men whose patience is almost at the breaking point,' reported one observer.[12] 'Floating' transients would continue to be a problem over the ensuing years.

Urban Government and Politics

Governance

The extent of the growth of urban Canada between 1880 and 1919 was largely unanticipated, and cut against most of the dominant ideologies of the time, which were relatively traditional and rural. Towns were comprehensible, while huge cities were not. Because of the unplanned, unconsidered nature of urban expansion, the institutions of urban government were not well integrated into the overall Canadian political system. The Fathers of Confederation had thought of provincial governments as the equivalent of British municipal corporations and produced a constitution that left little room for city government, much less the government of cities (Montreal, Toronto, Winnipeg) that would have budgets and revenue as large as those of the provinces in which they were located. The result, especially after 1885, was continual friction between provincial legislatures—which tended to be dominated by rural politicians—and the cities, which were usually under-represented at the provincial level, partly because their populations were growing faster than seats could be redistributed. At the start of this period both towns and cities were governed by councils, those in the larger urban centres elected on a ward-by-ward basis. The basic source of revenue was a land or real property tax, and cities were slower than other levels of government in abandoning property qualifications for voting. Few places went so far as Winnipeg, which allowed property owners to vote in any voting district in which they paid taxes, thus over-representing the wealthier inhabitants. In many towns and cities tenants were commonly excluded from voting (Montreal tenants gained the right to vote only in the 1960s) and in those places that did allow everyone to vote, there were efforts to correct the many abuses that this democratic franchise created.[13]

As urban government tended to operate outside the structures of Confederation, so did urban politics. Provincial and federal politics represented separate levels of operation, and the use of the same party labels federally and provincially often led to confusion, since parties had relatively independent federal and provincial wings with quite distinct policies, though there was some connection and overlap in personnel and party administration. Municipal politics, however, was quite removed from the party system, and politicians seldom aspired to political office at the senior levels of government, although after 1880 they expected to make careers at the municipal level. Municipal politics had not only its own agendas but distinct party labels, which were gradually replaced in this period by various efforts at non-partisan city government, such as in Montreal in the mayoralty election of 1903, or through the victory of the City Improvement League (CIL) in 1910. The ward system—particularly in cities with democratic franchises, such as Toronto or Halifax or Saint John—was heavily criticized for its tendency to produce ward-heeling municipal politicians who curried favour with the electorate and whose 'corruption' in this regard led them into other political abuses. That certain people were drawn into urban politics out of economic self-interest became a major problem in most Canadian cities. Businessmen saw the 'success' of the city as essential for their operations, with the result that city councils tended to be dominated by local merchants and real-estate promoters.

Urban Reform

By the 1880s most of Canada's major cities had begun to produce a group of urban reformers who would gradually coalesce into a reform faction within the city. The arguments for municipal reform were fairly obvious, although the reformers often had difficulty in agreeing on priorities, such as where to put the emphasis in planning. The earliest reformers were the humanitarians. They often became involved with the city through charitable work among the poor, or as professionals concerned with social and educational services; many of the former turned into the latter. Their concerns were to make the city healthy, moral, and equitable in its treatment of its citizens—quite a different agenda from that of businessmen who converted to the 'corporationist' reform movement after the turn of the century. They were concerned with the city's services, chiefly its utilities, and saw public ownership as a way to increase revenue without increasing taxes, which at the same time would eliminate greedy capitalists and permit the extension of essential services to the less-prosperous members of the community. Both humanitarians and corporationists could agree on the need for urban planning, however, although they often disagreed on priorities.

Both reform wings, frustrated by the seemingly intractable difficulties of achieving change, given existing municipal government and politics, turned to reconstructing these aspects as a first step. Thus better government or 'good government' became the rallying cry for urban reformers of various persuasions.* Their platforms and activities say a good deal about the strengths and weaknesses of urban reform in this period. While the existing system had its weaknesses, the advocacy of reform tended to be concentrated in the hands of the business and professional élites. The victims of injustice were seen as objects to be helped rather than as people to be consulted or involved in the process of assistance. Indeed, for some reformers the victims themselves constituted the principal obstacle to be overcome on the way to improved conditions—a classic case of blaming the victim. Much of the reform was seen in structural and even in business terms: increasing

---

*Theodore Roosevelt in the United States called the progressive city reformers the 'goo-goos', and Stephen Leacock wrote a scathing chapter in *Arcadian Adventures* on 'The Great Fight for Clean Government'.

efficiency and planning, for example, or adding more regulatory agencies. As G. Frank Beer, a city planner, wrote in 1914: 'Slums produce inefficiency— inefficiency begets poverty and poverty of this character means disease and degradation.' He went on to add: '. . .as population centralizes, *the power of the individual to shape his environment lessens and the responsibility of the state increases.*'[14]

Urban reform in Canada was carried out against a background of similar activity in Europe (especially Britain) and in the United States. Canadian reformers were well aware of developments abroad, and often modelled their efforts and organizations on those they read about in books and magazines. Montreal businessman Herbert Brown Ames (1863-1954)—who produced a pioneering sociological study of Montreal called *The City Below the Hill* (1897)—had a number of British studies to serve as models, some dating back to mid-century. Ames attempted to describe working-class Montreal to those who lived 'on the hill', people he insisted knew more about Europe than about their own city. He pioneered in the use of maps to describe visually the statistics he had collected on the working-class districts. What seems most significant about the Ames book in this context was how limited and incomplete his research was. (It was not nearly up to the exhaustive standards set by Henry Mayhew's *London Labour and the London Poor* [1851], Charles Booth's *Life and Labour in London* [1893], or the various studies by Fabian reformers such as Beatrice and Sidney Webb, which included detailed case studies as well as statistical tables.) By and large, Canadian reform efforts (and the evils targeted for their zeal) lagged fifty years behind those in Britain, and were at least a generation behind those in the United States. To some extent this lag reflected the later development of urbanization in Canada, though this ought to have made it possible for Canadians to avoid some of the mistakes, particularly of rapid growth and unplanned development, made by their British and American counterparts. While Canadians got much of their initial urban-reform inspiration from abroad, they then proceeded to rein- vent the wheel.

Humanitarian Reform

Humanitarian urban reformers were usually the first on the ground in any city situation. Their focus tended to be on the human victims of disastrous urban conditions, and their tone tended to be moralistic. A short term as mayor of Toronto by William Holmes Howland (1844-93) is an early exam- ple of reform politics in that city. From an established and moneyed family— his father, Sir William Pearce Howland, was a Father of Confederation— Howland had a successful business career while still a young man, but he was predominantly an evangelical Christian and a supporter of the temperance movement. He was active in some philanthropic organizations, focusing his attention on St John's Ward, a poor and vice-ridden district in the centre of the city, and was one of the founders in 1884 of the Toronto Mission Union, a non-denominational organization devoted to aiding the poor by various forms of social assistance. In 1886 the reformers in the city— who wanted to rid it of the power of ward-heelers—and the prohibitionists backed him for mayor. With the additional help of the city's newly organized labour movement, and of women—spinsters and widows who owned property were entitled to vote for the first time in this municipal election—he was elected on the platform of reforming the social and moral life of the city. As mayor for two years, 1886-8, he became embroiled in a strike against the Massey Manufacturing Company and in a labour dispute with the Toronto Street Railway Company, in which he backed the workers; he also tried to end civic corruption, to close houses of prostitution and unlicensed liquor outlets, and reduced the number of liquor licenses. But he had his opponents, and there were many frustrations.[15]

Howland's passion for reform rather than his accomplishments provided a model for subsequent mayors and the electorate, and earned for the city the sobriquet 'Toronto the Good'. A decade later the city had not changed much when this phrase was used ironically in the title *Of Toronto the Good: The Queen City As It Is* (1898), an anecdotal study by C.S. Clark of what he saw as the various forms of evil and crime that existed in the city, with such chapter titles as 'The Social Evil' ('houses of ill-fame'), 'Street Walkers', 'The Poor of the City', 'Gambling Houses', 'Drunkenness', 'Crooks', 'Thieves', 'Swindlers'. He concluded his book by saying: 'If. . . I know that any reform has been accomplished through my efforts I shall feel that my work has not been in vain. It is customary in writing of a city to praise it. I have done no such thing. I have told you of the city as I have found it, and if it is not palatable, it is the city's fault and not mine.'[16]

The Social Gospel

In the 1890s a movement to combat the ills of the new industrial society, and to promote social reform, grew out of the churches—first the Methodist, and then all the Protestant churches—and lasted into the 1930s. It was called the Social Gospel and raised social change to a spiritual level in seeing God as its inspiration and the Kingdom of God on earth as an ideal. A wave of social-service activity followed—in city missions, such as the Fred Victor Mission in Toronto (1894), and in church settlement houses—that led in 1912 to the establishment of the Social Service Council of Canada. Perhaps the most famous humanitarian reformer was the social-gospel minister James Shaver Woodsworth (1874-1942), who as superintendent of All Peoples' Mission in Winnipeg from 1904 to 1913 became totally immersed in urban slum life and conditions and wrote extensively about them. In two well-known books, *Strangers Within Our Gates: or Coming Canadians* (1909) and *My Neighbor: A Study of City Conditions, a Plea for Social Service* (1911), Woodsworth analysed the problems of Canadian cities as he saw them.

In *Strangers* Woodsworth had concentrated on the 'motley crowd of immigrants' to Canada, seeing 'some of the problems of population with which we must deal' as being remedied by assimilating the newcomers

A Yonge Street mission in Toronto, 1915, where the Social Gospel was preached and food was distributed to out-of-work men. City of Toronto Archives, James Collection, 1964.

rapidly to avoid their ghettoization. He referred to a litany of problems: 'Ignorance of the language, high rents, low standards of living, incompetency, drunkenness and other evils.' In *My Neighbor* he saw urbanization as both a 'menace to our own civilization' in its vice, crime, and disease, and the 'hope of Democracy' in the new co-operative efforts to deal with the problems. While the earlier book clearly recognized that immigrants to Canada had special problems, it had a tendency to associate the difficulties they faced with the extent of their assimilability into the new Canadian environment. *My Neighbor* was considerably more general and more sympathetic to the new immigrants from eastern Europe. It mixed quotations and analyses of urban problems from the secular press with a call for a new Christianity in which a concern for social problems would be added to the emphasis on individual souls that Woodsworth saw as typical of the traditional churches. In his concluding chapter on social service, Woodsworth wrote:

> We can hardly be accused of under-estimating the value of social settlements, institutional churches, and city missions, but more and more we are convinced that such agencies will never meet the great social needs of the city. They serve a

A well-baby clinic at the Fred Victor Mission, Toronto, 22 July 1921. At the southeast corner of Queen and Jarvis, the mission was established by Hart Massey and named after his youngest son, who died of tuberculosis at twenty-two. City of Toronto Archives, DPW 32-632.

present need; they bring us face to face with our problem; they point out the line of advance. Then by all means let us multiply them and extend the scope of their work. But the needs will remain until the community at large is dominated by the social ideal. This is surely the mission of the Church, and yet the Church itself is hardly awake to the situation, much less fitted to meet it. Will the Church retain—perhaps we should rather say, regain—her social leadership?[17]

Reform and the Moral State Over the course of time many of the private agencies became conscripted as quasi-public ones under provincial legislation, serving as arms of the state in the intermediate period before the establishment of permanent government operations. Thus private child-welfare programs were often made officially responsible for abandoned, abused, and delinquent children while still carrying on private charity. The result was an increased tendency towards a professional approach, although still within the framework of the assumptions of individual morality. Women unable to care for their children because of male abandonment were 'good' clients; women unable to care for their children because they worked as prostitutes were 'bad' clients.

Indeed, every city had its periodic campaigns against the 'red light' districts, usually led by local Protestant clergymen. As one prominent Winnipeg minister wrote in 1910 in a pamphlet entitled 'The Problem of Vice in Winnipeg':

> ...a minority who choose to degrade the sacred powers of generation, and by the use of aphrodisiacs, and the cultivation of filthy imaginations, bring themselves into a pathological debasement, that seems to themselves a permanent institution of sexual vice, have no right, Divine or human, to maintain such an institution to the injury of the commonwealth.[18]

The trouble with such rhetoric—which associated the struggle of one or another campaign against social evil with a holy war to ensure the purity of 'future generations'—was that it failed to distinguish among evils, or to search for root causes beyond the fall from grace. Vice, crime, and poverty were common associations among the humanitarian reformers, although it was often not clear which of these evils they considered most important to attack first. Even those who appropriately focused on poverty attributed it to almost every other cause than a failure of the economic system to distribute wealth equitably. Moreover, the attack on poverty had a certain class specificity about it that involved one 'superior' class helping an 'inferior' one, thus suggesting class divisions and conflict.

The Professional Reformers   Another wing of humanitarian reform was often associated with various professional groups who became involved in urban problems through their work with private voluntary agencies and through their professional practices. Thus doctors were active in establishing a public-health system and in recommending ways of improving public-health care. The Quebec Board of Health, for example, was created by the Public Health Act of the province in 1886, and its medical members pressed for inoculations, regulation of the purity of milk, and water purification, among other reforms. Doctors in French Canada had long attributed much of the high infant mortality among French-Canadian infants to maternal practices of early weaning of children. While they were unable to control such practices by public regulation, they could concentrate on improving the milk supply for infants through grading and labelling and by making properly pasteurized milk available through milk depots (*Gouttes de Lait*). Doctors in Quebec and elsewhere also pressed for the establishment of public facilities to treat tuberculosis and for a general commitment to publicly financed health facilities to replace the largely private institutions of the past. One of the most common public-health recommendations from the medical profession—in Montreal, Halifax, Winnipeg, and Vancouver—was compulsory medical inspection of school children.

Not all children, however, were in schools. Members of the teaching profession were often in the front lines of urban reform, since adequate schooling was regarded as one of the best ways to prevent the children of the poor from following in their parents' footsteps, as well as the only way to assimilate the thousands of non-British and non-French foreigners who began flooding into the country after the mid-1890s. In this period educational reformers pushed not only for improved schooling but for the schools to assume a considerable amount of the burden of social services for the young, acting *in loco parentis* for the children of slum and ghetto dwellers. The greatest problem was school attendance, and this period saw the extension, on a province-by-province basis, of the principle of the availability of schools for all with compulsory school attendance to (usually) age 14. Such compulsory-attendance laws were in place everywhere in Canada by the First World War. Regular attendance would provide a more suitable environment for children than roaming the streets or working in factories, might enable them to learn skills that would lift them out of their poverty, and—in the case of the immigrant—was essential to assimilation into the values of Canadian society. In most parts of the country 'Canadian society' meant Anglo-Canadian society.

Reformers did not doubt their position. Thus in 1911 the editor of the *Manitoba Free Press*, J.W. Dafoe (1866-1944), saw 'the necessity of compulsory education as a self-evident truth, a law of right reason, an inescapable conclusion, a point of view that no intelligent citizen could oppose, a proposition that only the apathetic would fail to support.'[19] As another Winnipeg advocate of compulsory education put it:

> ...children are growing up without an education, save in wickedness. Every day they are becoming a serious menace to the country. The future, if this continues, is very alarming. There must be compulsory education. There must! The party, the parliament, the government which permits a venerable obstacle to stand in the way of this absolute necessity to the very safety of the Dominion, which permits love for office or power to delay the enactment or proper enforcement of proper legislation whereby every child shall be compelled to attend school had forefeited all right to the respect of the people, and whatever its merits, must be replaced by those who have vision and courage to discern and do what is imperative.[20]

When children went truant, or their parents insisted on education in some language other than English and kept them out of school, the 'lower orders' were seen as not appreciating the rules of the game.

While teachers and educational reformers plainly believed that compulsory education—and the use of the schools for reform purposes—was in the best interests of Canadian society, this advocacy was also in their best interests as well. Compulsory education opened many more teaching jobs, particularly at the higher-paid senior levels, and completed the professionalization of teaching. With compulsory education (and all the intellectual freight it carried) came the teacher as social expert, as a professional who knew as much, or more, about what was important for children than parents, particularly the parents of disadvantaged children. Compulsory education, medical examinations, school nurses, lunch programs, all were part of a new type of social engineering, conducted in the name of 'right reason', which would emerge to prominence after the First World War.

Corporate Reform

Although medical and educational reformers often bridged the gap between humanitarian and corporationist impulses, the latter were quite distinctive. The goal was structural alteration, and the model was usually sound business practice, including the elimination of wasteful graft and corruption through political reform, the creation of publicly operated (and profitable) utilities to cut down on unnecessary taxation, and the introduction of city and suburban planning to reduce the inefficiency of urban development. These movements all found allies within associated middle-class and professional groups. City planning, for example, was strongly supported by an expanding community of professional architects, who combined an urge to 'plan the city as a whole' with aesthetic considerations of coherence, visual variety, and civic grandeur.

The City Beautiful   The City Beautiful Movement—the idea that many of the city's ills could be overcome by a comprehensive program of social programs, new facilities, rational street and transportation planning, and overall beautification—gained attention at the Expositions of 1876 and 1893 in Philadelphia and Chicago respectively, and several Canadian cities were influenced by it. In Toronto it began with the formation of the 'Adornment League' at the 1895 convention of the Ontario Association of Architects. This organization turned into the Guild of Civic Art, which—in response to a major downtown fire in 1904—funded the next year a comprehensive plan involving the creation of park areas on landfill along the waterfront; a system of parks and driveways encircling the city; and a series of diagonal avenues connecting the core of the city with the suburbs. In 1909 the Civic Improvement Committee extended the plan, and the heart of it—a manifestation of the 'grandeur' aspect of the Movement—was Federal Avenue, a processional way leading north from Union Station to a monumental civic plaza that was designed by John M. Lyle (1872-1946) in 1911. The onset of the war prevented development of this plan, and the Depression intervened in its revival in 1929. Other projects rising out of the City Beautiful Movement were the Ottawa Improvement Commission (1899); a plan for Calgary (1914) by the English landscape architect and city planner Thomas H. Mawson that was never carried out; Mawson's designs for Wascana Park in front of the Legislative Buildings in Regina and the townsite of Banff; the beautification of Maisonneuve, a municipality on the eastern boundary of Montreal that was annexed to the city in 1918; and the entire design of a new west-coast city, Prince Rupert, incorporated in 1910.

Several cities in Canada (Calgary, Ottawa, and Toronto) and the United States (including Chicago, New York, and Washington) sponsored lavish books containing plans, drawings, and textual descriptions of projects for remodelled cities. An unusually fine example of bookmaking for the time— published in a limited edition 'under the auspices of the City Planning Commission'—is Thomas Mawson's *Calgary: A Preliminary Scheme for Controlling the Growth of the City* (1914), which contained many watercolour renderings of his grandiose proposals reproduced in colour.* Mawson stated his approach in an epigraph: 'City planning is not the attempt to pull down your city and rebuild it at ruinous expense. It is merely deciding what you would like to have done when the chance does come[;] little by little you may make the city plan conform to your ideals.' North Americans were in love with cities at this time, thinking of them as the culmination of civilization, and commissioning grand plans for urban centres and centre-pieces was the order of the day. There was, however, opposition to the grandeur approach in these undertakings. In 1911 an article in *The Canadian Municipal Journal* commented:

> Magnificent avenues, leading to grand buildings, are desirable. Lovely and artistic parks should be in every city. But the dwellings in which those live who cannot get away from their homes the whole year long, really decide whether any city is to be healthy, moral and progressive. The common people are in the great majority, their proper accommodation is the greatest problem.[21]

To some extent the Great War decided this debate over priorities. Neither side triumphed, and all money and energy were pumped into the European trenches. With the subsequent drain on manpower and, particularly in the West, the withdrawal of English-based companies and English capital, cities had to settle for more restricted developments, such as new railway stations, new city halls, hospitals—and, in provincial capitals, the imposing legislative buildings that had been completed before the war.

Reform of the Political Structure

Political alteration of municipal government was a goal on which most reformers of all persuasions could agree. At first 'progressive' individuals attempted to run for mayoralties or city councils on reform platforms, but they soon discovered that honest administration was more difficult to achieve than to advocate. In Montreal corruption at city hall served to unify reformers, who forced the appointment of a provincial investigating commission (the Cannon Commission) that exposed corruption, bribery, and extortion on a massive scale. The 1910 election swept 'the notorious 23' councillors

---

*It was produced in England and published by Batsford, the leading London publisher of books on art, architecture, and design.

◀ *The Civic Centre of Calgary as It May Appear Many Years Hence,* the frontispiece of Thomas Mawson's scheme for Calgary, which was inspired by the City Beautiful Movement. City of Calgary Archives, Town Planning Commission, File 6.

mentioned in the investigation out of office. But by 1914 the reform alder-men had disappeared, and the old guard was back in power. Many reformers combined 'throwing the rascals out' with structural changes to limit the damage they could do. Rationalization or elimination of the ward system—that traditional source of local graft and corruption—was a popular proposal. The typical committee system of council, which allowed those able to get elected continually to control critical sectors of decision-making through sheer seniority rather than capacity, was frequently criticized. Several cities, including Montreal after 1910, adopted the Toronto scheme of a Board of Control to administer the city as a sort of executive. The introduction of the American system of less directly democratic commission government appealed to many reformers, including Frank Underhill (1889-1971), later a founder of the CCF party. According to the young Underhill, writing in the University of Toronto student magazine in 1911, existing 'municipal machinery' had two flaws: 'it lacks all systematic organization among its parts; and we cannot induce good men to step in and work it' because the general disorder 'makes constructive effort almost helpless.' Underhill insisted that a small commission could be elected by the people and would not be undemocratic, but his major complaint was about the 'all-round inefficiency of the system', and his principal solution was to have 'big men' (for which read the local captains of industry) 'offer themselves for election.'[22] Almost all reformers complained about the relatively low turnout at munici-pal elections and the failure of the system to attract as managers 'our most successful citizens'. As the mayor of Winnipeg observed in 1916, the people 'usually look with suspicion and resentment on any suggestions by their Council to reduce or vary the control which they, as electors, have; but are themselves negative and indifferent to any improvements or remedies for community benefits.'[23]

Public Ownership of Utilities

Perhaps the fiercest battles were fought over the question of the public ownership of municipal utilities. Here the corporationist leaders were members of the local business community. While at first glance it may seem surprising that some businessmen advocated public ownership, their position was quite logical. Utilities had been developed by outside capitalists and siphoned off profits from the local business community, which saw greater benefits from local public control of the physical plant of the city, including lower taxes and reinvestment of profits in expansion of services. The struggle for public utilities serves to remind us that, in Canada at least, public ownership was not necessarily associated with socialism. While the utility barons complained of the attack on private enterprise, the corporationists countered by arguing that utilities were intrinsic monopolies that should be operated in the public interest. Municipal ownership or control of transit lines, waterworks, electrical plants, and telephone systems—all these public utilities were present in some cities, although few cities enjoyed them all—reflected statist rather than socialist thinking.

The urban-reform movement grew out of the enormous changes in Canadian cities between 1885 and 1914, involving not only the increase of slums, ghettos, and poverty, but the creation of a vastly larger urban middle class. The reform movement was really an alliance of various sectors of the urban middle class, particularly businessmen, professionals, and women concerned with humanitarian reform. In essence, the middle classes attempted to improve urban conditions for all residents, but with particular emphasis on the disadvantaged. Much of the impulse behind the reformers consisted in fear of class warfare and moral degeneration, and they did *for* the poor rather than *with* them. The result was a vast increase in the public apparatus of the state, and the growth of public bureaucracy—which came increasingly to employ a substantial number of the middle class.

Culture

Among the city's many amenities was a rich and varied cultural life, made possible by large numbers of people and the collective wealth they represented. The larger the city, the greater the opportunity for resident professionals, but in Canada, cultural life in the period before 1919 continued to be dominated by an amateur tradition of considerable vitality. Only in hockey did professionals gain the upper hand. The city made possible the creation of cultural institutions, in the form of both organizations and buildings. The construction of museums, for example, was characteristic of the late Victorian and Edwardian periods. The Art Museum of Toronto was founded in 1900, the Royal Ontario Museum in 1912 (it opened in 1914). Equally characteristic of the age was the formation of artistic organizations such as the Canadian Art Club (1907), organized in Toronto—but intended to be national in emphasis, although its founders had not the faintest idea how to achieve this goal—to exhibit new Canadian painting, as well as the growth of formal art schools. The major development of Canadian urban culture in this era was not so much the emergence of first-rate artists as the creation of an institutional infrastructure that might eventually make possible the appearance of major figures on a regular basis. Of a large range of cultural activities that deserve discussion, four—museums, paintings, drama, and sport—must suffice to suggest the richness of the whole.

Museums

The museum movement in Canada had its origins in the first half of the nineteenth century, chiefly in the Maritime region, where it was associated with the Mechanics' Institutes and scientists like Abraham Gesner (1797-1864), who spearheaded in 1842 the opening of a museum that became the New Brunswick Museum in Saint John. Most such museums were built around 'cabinets' of various sorts of scientific specimens, often of local origin. Around mid-century the scientific museum was joined by the art museum, such as the Musée des Beaux-arts de Montréal (1847) and the Musée du Séminaire de Québec (1852, opened to the public in 1876).

A new museum era began after 1890, partly because of the emergence of merchant princes who could afford, like their American cousins, to collect expensive things. Some specialized in art, mainly European Old Masters. Others collected antiques, and others artifacts, such as rare coins and stamps. Because it had the most and the oldest merchant families in Canada, Montreal also had the best museums before 1914. In 1892, for example, the Montreal Museum of Fine Arts, a small institution of limited collections, received a major bequest in the form of a collection of art and money for further acquisitions from John W. Tempest. Other gifts and bequests soon followed, from the collections of the Learmonts (Dutch masterworks), Lord Strathcona, and Sir William Van Horne. In Toronto, Professor and Mrs Goldwin Smith in 1911 bequeathed their home, The Grange, to the Art Museum of Toronto (now the Art Gallery of Ontario). An art gallery in Winnipeg opened in 1912, with its exhibits chiefly borrowed from the National Gallery of Canada. That august institution, founded in 1880, was only in 1910 provided with a full-time director, Eric Brown (1877-1939), and in 1913 with adequate parliamentary support, including incorporation and funds for administration and suitable acquisitions. The early years of the Gallery greatly benefited from the patronage of Sir Edmund Walker, president of the Bank of Commerce and himself a collector, who became the second chairman of the Gallery's Council in 1910.[24] Walker was also a founding patron of the Art Museum of Toronto, which became the Art Gallery of Toronto in 1919, and the first chairman of the board of the Royal Ontario Museum.*

Painting

Of all the arts, painting was the most vibrant and productive in this period, with many artists producing large numbers of canvases, some of them key works in the history of Canadian painting. The beginning of the period coincided roughly with the end of a tradition of landscape painting that had become dominant partly in response to the developing sense of national identity and the topographical beauties of the new country that were just being discovered. Lucius O'Brien (1832-99) and John A. Fraser (1838-98)

---

*A sterling patron of the arts, Walker played a central role in still other cultural institutions, including the Champlain Society, the Mendelssohn Choir, and the University of Toronto. His magnificent house, Long Garth—which was built in 1882 to display his works of art, his library, and his furniture—was on the east side of St George Street in Toronto, north of Hoskin. It was demolished in 1969 to make room for a parking lot for the new Robarts Library in the University of Toronto.

were two of numerous painters who travelled west in 1880 at the invitation of the Canadian Pacific Railway to paint the Rockies. O'Brien's most famous painting, however, is *Sunrise on the Saguenay* (1880). It is a remarkable depiction of the sublime in nature, while in its poetic, moody treatment of the romantic scene it is also a Canadian example of a style, popular in the United States, that came to be called 'luminism'. This painting was hung in the inaugural exhibition of the Royal Academy, of which O'Brien was the first president, and deposited in the new National Gallery of Canada.

Homer Watson (1855-1936) of Doon, Canada West, though largely self-taught, had a genius for painting rural landscapes that caused Oscar Wilde, after seeing his work in Toronto, to call him 'The Canadian Constable' (Watson did not know Constable's work at the time). Among Watson's best-known paintings are *The Pioneer Mill* (1880), purchased by the Marquis of Lorne for Queen Victoria; *The Stone Road* (1881); *Before the Storm* (1887); and *The Flood Gate* (1900). His friend Horatio Walker (1858-1938)—born in Listowel, Canada West—lived winters in New York and summers on the Île d'Orléans and specialized, with great commercial success, in striking, somewhat sentimental, interpretations of Quebec farm life in the style of Jean-François Millet, such as *Oxen Drinking* (1899), *Ploughing—The First Gleam* (1900), and *Evening, Île d'Orléans* (1909).

By 1890 young Canadian painters sought to study in the academies of Paris, the centre of the art world at the time. There they learned to paint large, richly detailed, subtly coloured, naturalistic canvases featuring the human figure and sentimental sub-texts. William Brymner (1855-1925) of Montreal was the first Canadian to study in Paris. His best-known painting is *A Wreath of Flowers* (1884), an arrangement of four young girls in a patch of wildflowers on a hillside. Robert Harris (1849-1919) of Charlottetown painted *The Meeting of the School Trustees* (1885) and *Harmony* (1886), a portrait of a woman (his wife) playing the harmonium. Paul Peel (1860-92) of London, Canada West—who studied in Philadelphia with the famous American painter Thomas Eakins, before moving to Europe—was the first Canadian painter to portray nudes: *A Venetian Bather* (1889) and *After the Bath* (1890) are two of the paintings on which his fame rests. (Peel died in Paris at the age of thirty-one.) George Reid (1860-1947), who was born on a farm near Wingham, Canada West, also studied with Eakins before going to Paris, where he and his first wife (the painter Mary Heister) were welcomed by Peel. His famous genre paintings are *Forbidden Fruit* (1889), showing a boy lying in a field reading a forbidden book (the model was given *The Arabian Nights* to peruse); *Mortgaging the Homestead* (1890), inspired by an incident in his childhood; and *The Foreclosure of the Mortgage*, which won a medal at the Chicago World's Fair in 1893, the year it was painted.

Two important painters of the period do not fit into this pattern. James Wilson Morrice (1865-1924) of Montreal, who graduated from the University of Toronto and began to study law before moving to Paris in 1890 to

George Reid posing before his oil painting *The Foreclosure of the Mortgage*, 1893, which is now in the National Gallery of Canada. Photograph by Violet Keene, in the collection of the E.P. Taylor Reference Library, Art Gallery of Toronto, LN216.

paint, remained there and became part of the Parisian art scene, though he made annual trips home and travelled extensively.* Influenced by the American-born painter James McNeill Whistler, who had settled in London, and by the Fauves of Paris and his friend Henri Matisse, Morrice employed violent colours and rhythmical composition in his paintings of foreign scenes, and aesthetic rather than representational elements in his depiction of Canadian subjects—an approach that set him apart from his contemporaries in Canada. Ozias Leduc (1864-1955) of Sainte-Hilaire, Quebec, was a retiring painter and church decorator who was inspired to portray the perfection of God's creations. This spirit suffuses his glowing still-lifes—such as *Les Trois*

---

*Morrice inspired characters in both Arnold Bennett's *Buried Alive* (1908) and Somerset Maugham's *Of Human Bondage* (1915).

Pommes (1887) and *Pommes vertes* (1914-15)—and *L'Enfant au pain* (1892), his memorable study of a hatted boy, his lips on a mouth organ, seated before an empty bowl and a half-eaten slice of bread.*

Drama and Theatre

There were two requirements for the emergence of drama in Canada: theatres and actors. Theatres, such as Toronto's Royal Lyceum (1848), had been constructed from the early years of the nineteenth century. Theatrical buildings became a measure of the status of a city, and many aspiring towns had their 'Opera House'. As early as 1891 Vancouver had a 1200-seat Opera House, Toronto's Royal Alexandra Theatre (1906-7) seated 1,525, and Winnipeg's Walker Theatre (1907; recently renovated as a theatrical venue) seated 2,000 in splendid comfort. These buildings were well used, housing mainly touring companies and local amateurs. By the 1880s virtually every major actor and actress of the time had toured North America, often including the major Canadian cities. Sarah Bernhardt visited Montreal in 1880, to the cheers of French-Canadian students, and toured western Canada in 1906, performing *Camille* in the Winnipeg Auditorium Rink. Despite terrible acoustics, the audience was enchanted. In 1913 she again toured on the Orpheum Circuit. Not only famous performers but famous companies went on the circuit, including the Birmingham Repertory Theatre, the Abbey Theatre, and a company from Stratford-on-Avon. American musical theatre and vaudeville, under the auspices of Charles Frohman and the Schubert brothers, also toured, giving Canadians a chance to see such musicals as Victor Herbert's *Babes in Toyland* and such performers as Charles Chaplin, who toured with Fred Karnos's English slapstick pantomime group in 1911 and 1913, before he went into the movies. English and American performers touring the US viewed Canada as an American province, but liked the money and the appreciative audiences.

Indigenous theatre (both playwriting and performance) faced two obstacles. One was the hostility of many (especially in the churches) to such entertainment, an animosity that went back at least to the Puritan Revolution of the seventeenth century. Why theatrical performances were singled out by the moralists is not entirely clear, but actors and actresses were held in low esteem, associated with all kinds of 'depravity and debauchery' (which many certainly practised). Bishop Ignace Bourget (1799-1885) of Montreal frequently thundered against the theatre, and one of his fellow bishops prohibited parishioners from seeing Bernhardt on her 1880 tour. Not merely performers but the plays themselves were held to be immoral and indecent. George Bernard Shaw, of course, deliberately set out to shock his audiences in plays such as *Mrs Warren's Profession* (1893), which dealt with a brothel-

---

*The Group of Seven, which began to be formed in this period and worked well beyond it, is discussed on pages 141-2.

keeping madam as if she were merely an ordinary businesswoman and parent. The other problem was the competition from the theatre centres of London and New York. A Winnipeg drama critic complained in 1891: 'One is sick and tired of listening to amateur would-be's if they could.' This was at a time when Canadian audiences in most of the main cities had become familiar with some of the biggest names in British and American theatre, and some of the leading companies. Sir Henry Irving came to Canada six times from 1884 to 1904, accompanied by Ellen Terry (except in 1904); Lillie Langtry came twelve times between 1883 and 1916, going as far west as Winnipeg. Mrs Patrick Campbell came eight times from 1908 to 1916, as did Martin Harvey, beginning in 1903. Among the many American stars who toured Canada before the end of the century were Edwin Booth, Minnie Maddern Fiske, and Maude Adams. In spite of the virtual non-existence of indigenous professional theatre, however, some Canadian actors emerged who achieved fame in New York and carved out distinguished careers for themselves—in both the US and Canada. They included Clara Morris (c. 1848-1925); the comedienne May Irwin (1862-1938); Julia Arthur (1869-1950), who was Lady Windermere in the first American production of Wilde's play in 1893; and Margaret Anglin (1876-1958).[25]

Not surprisingly, it was in francophone Quebec—less well served by the American theatrical producers and promoters, although visited steadily by the French companies—that professional theatre first emerged in strength. There were ten different professional organizations at work in Montreal in the 1890s, headed by La Troupe du Théâtre Français. In 1899 alone these companies gave 618 performances of 109 plays.[26]

Interior of the New Academy of Music in Montreal, an illustration that appeared in the *Canadian Illustrated News* on 4 December 1875. Until the early 1890s—when it went into a decline, housing vaudeville and burlesque—the Academy was Montreal's finest auditorium. Thomas Fisher Rare Books Library, University of Toronto.

The development of the motion picture and its subsequent popularization not only converted many urban theatres into picture palaces, but helped lure new Canadian talent south to New York and then Hollywood. The fast-changing world of film production could hardly keep up with the public's insatiable appetite for this new genre of popular culture. One Canadian film producer and promoter, Ernest Shipman (1871-1931), with experience on both sides of the border, entered the field with his film *Back to God's Country* (1919), based on a story by James Oliver Curwood, and produced six other feature films. But this and other early attempts at film production in Canada were smothered by the growing Hollywood monster, with its studio system and theatre chains that would cover North America and put a stop to Canadian film production until the government intervened with grants decades later.

Sport

In sport, as in other cultural milieus, cities were essential to furnish large audiences and an institutional infrastructure. The period 1885-1914 was the heyday of amateur sport in Canada, but professionalism also flourished and began to challenge amateur dominance. Both amateur and professional benefited from the late-Victorian penchant for organization, as well as from the emphasis on the so-called 'manly virtues' that were seen to be encouraged by organized athletics.

This era saw the growth of many multi-sport organizations in Canadian cities. The Montreal Amateur Athletic Association (MAAA) was the nation's first multi-sport club (uniting at first lacrosse, cycling, and snowshoeing), but it was soon joined by others, including the Halifax Wanderers. In 1887 the Charlottetown *Patriot* editorialized about the need for an 'athletic association in this city' to benefit 'our young men'. The Charlottetown Athletic Association was founded in 1891, reorganized as the Charlottetown Amateur Athletic Association in 1897 to build 'a facility for track and field, baseball, rugby, cycling and other summer sports', and incorporated as the Abegweits-Crescents Athletic Club in 1899.[27] This incorporation, designed to cover the whole Island and not merely Charlottetown, was the high point in a decade of development that saw most competitive sports introduced to PEI. The Abegweit organization enabled Island teams to compete on terms of equality with others in the Maritimes, occasionally in Canada, and was particularly useful in track and field, where in 1912 the Abegweits swept the Maritimes championships before over 2,000 people. With the Great War amateur athletics ended on the Island—and elsewhere in Canada—to be resumed under different conditions after 1919.

The Rise of Professional Hockey   In 1885 the first hockey league in Canada was organized as the Montreal City League, playing 'McGill Rules'. When Toronto accepted these rules in 1888, intra-city rivalries were possible. In 1890 the Ontario Hockey Association was formed, with the assistance of

The McGill University Hockey Club in 1881. Founded in 1877, it was one of the earliest clubs in Canada and formulated the McGill Rules for hockey that soon became widely accepted. McGill University Archives photograph loaned to the National Archives of Canada, C-81739.

Arthur Stanley (son of Governor-General Lord Stanley, who in 1893 donated the Stanley Cup as a symbol of Dominion amateur hockey superiority). A Halifax league was formed in 1896, and the Winnipeg Hockey Club (which sponsored the Winnipeg Victorias) in 1899. By the mid-1890s there was a passion for hockey across the nation, Stanley had given the Cup, and artificial ice had been introduced for the first time in 1895. Before 1900 there was little trouble over professionalism in hockey, since the sport was played—like most sports—chiefly by college students, sons of farmers, and members of the urban élite. Under such circumstances, those playing for money were mainly those without 'independent means', i.e., members of the working class. Amateurism was redefined in 1902 by the Canadian Amateur Athletic Association:

> An amateur is a person who has not competed in any competition for a staked bet, monies private or public or gate receipts, or competed with or against a professional for a prize; who has never taught or assisted in the pursuit of any athletic exercise or sport as a means of livelihood; who has never directly or

indirectly, received any bonus or payment in lieu of loss of time while playing as a member of any club, or any money considerations whatever for any services as an athlete except his actual travelling and hotel expenses, or who has never entered into any competition under a name other than his own, or who has never been guilty of selling or pledging his prizes.[28]

This stringent definition, designed to separate the 'gentleman amateur' from the rest, was one of the major reasons that the concept failed in hockey. Most competitive hockey players had already broken the code, and felt they might as well get properly paid for their efforts. Play for the Stanley Cup and other big prizes had led many small-town promoters to import paid players to help beat the 'big city bastards'. Hiring professionals like Fred 'Cyclone' Taylor (1883-1979)—who played for Rat Portage (Kenora), Ottawa, and Renfrew in rapid succession and became North America's highest paid athlete in the process—was regarded as the only way for small towns to even things up with clubs that could draw from larger catchments.

The other factor that brought professionalism to the surface in hockey was, of course, the gate attraction that hockey had turned out to be, particularly in the larger cities. Canadian professional leagues began to form. By 1909 it was necessary to attempt to regulate the professionals, who were not only more skilful and better motivated, but were also accused of violent and disruptive play. That same year saw the creation of the National Hockey Association (originally Cobalt, Renfrew, Haileybury, and Montreal), which lured the best players by spending lots of money. In the long run, this process would defeat the small towns, which could not afford to compete. In the short run, the rules were changed. Teams were reduced from seven to six players to save on salaries, and an extra intermission was introduced to allow the players a breather. The Pacific Coast Hockey League was founded in 1911-12 by the Patrick brothers— Frank (1885-1960) and Lester (1883-1960)—who lured 'Cyclone' Taylor west for the princely sum of $22,200 for fourteen games. In 1911 the Patricks also built arenas in Victoria and Vancouver; the arena in Vancouver was the best in Canada, seating 10,000 and costing around $350,000. The NHA and the PCHL agreed to meet for a championship in 1913-14. In 1917 the NHA became the National Hockey League, its members now the larger Canadian cities of central Canada, and expansion into the US, where the 'big bucks' were to be found, began to be discussed.

More than one Canadian has seen in hockey a metaphor for the Canadian experience. If so, what took place between 1880 and 1914 was an experience of developing maturity of infrastructure combined with increasing integration into the world of big money. At the highest levels of success, the amateur gentleman had been replaced by the skilled professional, and the city once again had flexed its financial muscle. In this process of development, hockey had solidified its male ethos. The earlier, less-organized period had seen many girls' and women's teams playing hockey across Canada. But many of them had vanished by the Great War.

The Canadian city was not transformed by reform so much as it was gradually altered by new technology and by organizational trends that were partly the product of its increasing size and wealth. Such incrementalism could not eliminate either poverty or greed, in all their various urban dimensions. But the city was a vastly different place in 1919 than it had been in 1880, particularly for those able to enjoy its many newfound amenities. Not all Canadians were touched directly by either urban problems or the changes that occurred in the urban world, although increasing numbers of Canadians who still lived in the rural sectors and conformed to non-urban patterns, assumptions, and life-styles were attracted by the lure of the city. James S. Woodsworth wrote in 1911 that the move from country to city in Canada was the most important Canadian development of the period. Such a comment could only have come from an urban perspective, and was not entirely true. While urban Canada expanded rapidly in this period, rural Canada continued to grow as well, and in 1919 there were still marginally more rural than urban dwellers in the nation. Rural Canada was more than simply the vast hinterland from which the cities drew much of their new population. To these people and their society we now turn.

chapter four

Rural Canada, 1885-1919

Early in April 1899, budding writer Lucy Maud Montgomery (1874-1942) sat down at her desk to take stock of her life over the preceding winter. Like many ambitious young women of her day, Montgomery had studied to be a teacher, first at Prince of Wales College in Charlottetown and then at Dalhousie University in Halifax. She had spent several years as a schoolmarm in small communities on her native Prince Edward Island, but in 1898 had been called home to Cavendish, PEI, where she spent some years looking after her aged grandmother, who had brought her up—much as her fictional character Anne of Green Gables, an orphan, would care for her beloved foster-parent Marilla. Maud Montgomery found these years in Cavendish difficult ones:

> In a way, I have been having quite a nice time this winter. I say 'in a way' because in reality the gayety was all on the surface and away down underneath my new inner consciousness was coiled up, brooding like a snake in its den and every once in a while darting a pang into my soul's vitals.[1]

Although the superficial rounds of village life warred with her soul, Montgomery was a sufficiently objective and interested observer to recognize that rural life was, in its own way, busy. Whether such activity could be stimulating and satisfying was another matter, and for a twenty-five-year-old unmarried woman a large part of the problem revolved around the limited number of suitable males.

Montgomery's report on her 'uneventful' winter tells us a good deal about rural life in much of Canada. 'The Literary Society', she reported, 'has been in a flourishing condition this winter and I owe to it the few books that have delighted my soul.' Moreover, she added, 'I have been to several concerts and "socials" this winter. I had to recite at most of them and as a rule enjoyed them.' Such events were, as Montgomery indicated, participatory rather than spectator-oriented. Then there was the 'sewing circle' organized in aid of the new church building fund, which was time-consuming but had its amusing aspects 'in our pleasant afternoons of work and gossip—strictly harmless and clarified gossip, of course, patented for the use of church sewing societies!—and our evenings of fun when the boys came in and we play games of the same brand as the gossip.'

As Montgomery instinctively recognized, gossip was at the heart of rural entertainment:

> We are losing our minister. He has accepted a call to Tryon and Hampton, and is 'flitting' today. I do not think he will be much regretted. He was a fairly good preacher but no pastor[,] and his wife and family were certainly fearful and wonderful creatures—whole reams of description could not do them justice. What Cavendish will find to talk about when Mrs Robertson is gone I really do not know. Her sayings and doings quite usurped the place of the weather in current greetings. 'Have you heard Mrs Robertson's latest?' or '*What* will Mrs R. do next?' being standard questions.[2]

Montgomery would eventually escape from Cavendish when the death of her grandmother in 1911 was soon followed by her marriage to the clergyman Ewan Macdonald and her departure for Ontario. She had previously achieved a remarkable success with the publication of her first novel, *Anne of Green Gables* (1908). As its popularity immediately became apparent, her American publisher naturally pressed her for a sequel, and *Anne of Avonlea* was published the next year.

Montgomery's novels and short stories have since held a strong appeal for generations of young female Canadians (and others) as a beguiling romanticization of adolescence and rural life at the turn of the century. A modern adult will discover that Montgomery played strictly fair. The 'seamy side' of rural life is quite accurately presented, not only the gossip but the family obligations and responsibilities that so many found constricting. It was not accidental that Anne Shirley found that she had to choose between her own future and her love and affection for Marilla, or that the future involved leaving the Island to which Anne was so attached. The circumstances of Montgomery's characters—minus the romantic aspects—were a veritable catalogue of the strengths and weaknesses of life in rural Canada, from the Cuthberts' need for an orphan to work on their farm to the very real problems Anne faced in the community.

Western Farming

The Prince Edward Island *Anne of Green Gables*, however, was never considered to be a symbol for rural Canada at the turn of the century because it was so untypical. With its established, self-contained communities, lived in by people of mainly Scots and English descent and close-knit by generations of intermarriage and friendship, the Island seemed a somewhat exotic place far removed in every way from the principal developments of the period in western Canada. The settlement of the West was undoubtedly a major Canadian event of the years between 1885 and 1919, although it was representative only of itself and not of the nation as a whole. Manitoba grew in population from 25,228 in 1871 to 461,394 in 1911, and the Northwest Territories from a few thousand in 1881 to 876,375 in 1911 (492,432 in Saskatchewan and 373,943 in Alberta, both of which were granted provincial status in 1905).

The Canadian West was obviously different from PEI because it was a new society, composed of immigrants from Europe and from the East, and emphasis was on the creation of institutions rather than on their perpetuation. Moreover, the concentration on grain, particularly wheat—in its market aspects and in the singlemindedness with which it was grown—marked off western agriculture from that of the rest of the nation. Wheat culture not only made many farmers prosperous, but its rhythms freed them during the long winter months, and for long periods during the summer, from much of the drudgery of farming routine. Both the potential prosperity and the relative freedom from year-round daily work compensated to some extent for the climate and the isolation of individual homesteads. After the initial hard years of settlement, westerners were able to become sociable. Much of their life, as in eastern Canada, revolved around church and school.

A Ukrainian family harvesting wheat on the Prairies in 1918. Here the labour problem for harvesting was solved by employing the entire family, including the children. National Archives of Canada, PA-88504.

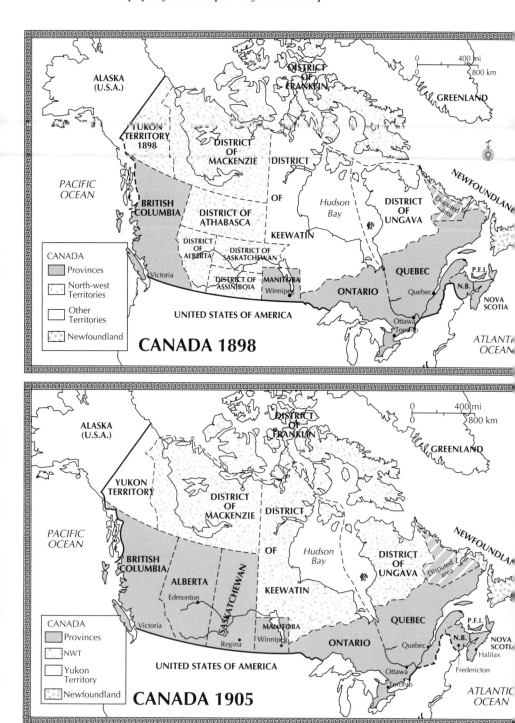

The Mythology of Pioneer Farming

The mythology of farming in western Canada, generated by immigration literature and encouraged by best-selling novelists such as 'Ralph Connor'— the Reverend Charles W. Gordon (1860-1937) of Winnipeg—was largely utopian, but nonetheless had a certain reality. It emphasized the opportunities that free land offered for beginning anew, with all that fresh starts entailed. The West was egalitarian and neighbourly, and offered an unparalleled chance to succeed from a standing start. As A.J. Cotton, a farmer of Swan River, wrote in 1903 to relatives in eastern Canada:

> Many a one have come to Manitoba with no capital and today are in easy circumstances. Farmers all over Manitoba say they are prospering and they look it, and if one prospers, can't another try, and where one meets with success, why can't another? This is true that Manitoba has advantages to offer the farmer that no other country has and there is no other country under the sun where farmers have and can do so well as in our Canadian North West. Prosperity reigns throughout and I like to see everyone come and take a share in it.[3]

Though a booster, Cotton was no simple utopian. He also warned:

> You cannot be promised ease or luxury. There will be a certain amount of hardship to endure, obstacles to contend with, and privations to overcome. Your first four years would be your greatest worry. After that you would be into shape to go ahead. Of course, the more capital you can put into it, the easier you can get through. Pioneering now is not what it used to be.[4]

Like other prosperous farmers, Cotton saw 'industry and good management' as the key to success. And like most successful people, he tended to view the hardships of earlier days through a golden haze, persuaded that though they had tested his physical and spiritual endurance, his triumph over them marked the end of a great quest, which Stephen Leacock once described as the Canadian equivalent of the search for the Holy Grail. Like most farmers as well, Cotton tended to say little about the contributions the women of his family had made to his success. Nevertheless, the celebration of western pioneers—whether they were wealthy Ontarians or impoverished Ukrainians—remains a central feature of Canadian mythology.

Utopianism

Alongside the myth of the pioneer was the association of nature with the 'Promise of Eden'. As W. C. Pollard later rhapsodized in his autobiographical *Life on the Frontier*:

> Did humanity ever set for itself a nobler task than that of pioneering in a new and virgin country, there the work of Nature can be seen on every side, and there avarice and selfishness are unknown, and all are engaged in Man's primitive occupations: tilling the soil, guarding the flocks and herds, fishing in the

waters, hunting in the wilderness and mining in the ground. There the brother-hood of man is amplified and common interests cement together social ties and friendships and there the works of the Creator are seen before man makes any contributions or contaminations.[5]

Utopianism was not simply rhetorical on the Prairies, for many communi-ties—such as Steinbach, Manitoba, or Thunder Hill, Saskatchewan—were founded by men and women who sought to create ideal new societies in the new environment. Many new communities were far from being solely products of British and Anglo-Canadian society. The Prairies appeared as a haven for dissenting Christian sects from central Europe and beyond. Some were founded by German-speaking Hutterites and Mennonites, and Rus-sian-speaking Doukhobors. About 7,400 Doukhobors—followers of Peter Verigin (1859-1924)—came to Saskatchewan in 1899 and registered for homesteads.* On the other hand, Cannington Manor, in southeastern Sas-katchewan, was the idealistic attempt of an Englishman, Captain Edward Michell Pierce, to found a self-contained farming community. He attracted about a dozen English families who emigrated in 1882 with their servants, racehorses, and grooms and turned out to be not interested in becoming serious farmers. A 26-room stone house, service buildings, a hotel, and an Anglican church were built, but by 1902 business and farm bankruptcies, along with Cannington's being bypassed by a new CPR line, contributed to its collapse. As this venture was grounded less in utopian socialism than in pastoral capitalism, its failure may also have had to do with the absence of a true collective ideology.

Pastoral Capitalism

Pastoral capitalism was certainly the dominant economic norm for western farmers before and during the First World War, and their early organizations and attempts at co-operation should be understood in this light. The basic unit of production throughout this period remained the family farm, usually producer-owned, although tenant farming increased over the years. The farmer operated his farm as an individual entrepreneur, and his efforts at co-operation focused on the movement and marketing of his grain, as well as on the acquisition of consumer goods essential to his success and the well-being of his family. Farmers tended to see eastern capitalists as their enemy, and attempted to construct alternative marketing mechanisms to those they felt were abusing them. Not surprisingly, the most successful element of agrarian co-operation in the West came with grain elevators, which stored grain along

---

*Verigin, who had been exiled to Siberia, did not join them until 1902. In 1905, when the Doukhobors refused to swear an oath of allegiance, their homestead rights were cancelled and Verigin led most of them to southern British Columbia, where a community of some 6,000 was founded.

railroad lines until it could be shipped to market. After 1910 a farmer-controlled co-operative elevator system grew rapidly, pledged to guaranteeing fair treatment for farmers through open competition with the private elevators dominated by the great railroads. But the co-operative in no way altered the free-enterprise system to which farmers were themselves committed.

The Position of Women

The family farm was operated on the principle of deferral of expectations and on considerable exploitation of those who would not in the end inherit a substantial share of the farm property. The system was particularly hard on women, who usually did not share in the ownership of the farm and whose labour was seldom remunerated (or indeed recognized as having monetary value, even by the Canadian Bureau of the Census, which persistently refused to include farm women as workers in its data). Western farmers were particularly hostile to 'anachronistic' legal concepts such as dower rights, which protected women's inheritances and were abolished in the Northwest Territories as early as 1886. Furthermore, the homesteading system was generally unsympathetic to the rights of women to set up in farming. Georgina Binnie-Clark (1871-1955), whose account of farming without a male partner in Saskatchewan, *Wheat and Women*, was published in 1914, was quite unusual if not unique. For many women in the West, as everywhere in Canada, the daily routine was much more continually demanding than that of men, since their responsibilities included not only the kitchen garden and the small livestock that had to be tended on a more regular basis than the grain fields, but care of the family itself. Life at harvest time was especially hectic, for a substantial farm required a large number of harvesters, whose feeding was the responsibility of the women. In spite of their labours, however, pioneer women complained most about the isolation of the farmstead when the farmhouse was as much as a mile or more from its nearest neighbour.

The Farm Labour Problem

The western farm had a contining labour problem, chiefly because at peak production times the farmer's family was seldom large enough to handle necessary tasks. The situation became particularly difficult during the autumn harvest, when in eastern Canada thousands of temporary workers were recruited as harvest migrants. But since few prairie farms had a full stock of boys old enough to do all the work necessary throughout the year, the 'hired hand' became a fixture in most operations. He was usually required to board with the family—a not-unpleasant experience, since a woman was in the kitchen cooking the meals. Many farm-hands were treated as members of the family, but such a position was often a mixed blessing. The typical farm-hand was a young man temporarily filling a job, either hoping to earn enough money to get a farm of his own or acquiring prairie farm experience as a sort of apprentice. Exploitation could work both ways. One farmer in 1907 complained:

> Last spring I hired a man for $210.00 for seven months. He is with me yet, but he feels just like as if he were in jail. He knows he could get $3.00 a day if he were free, and he reminds me of that fact quite often. He is the boss and I am the roust about. . . .He does just as he likes and knows I have to put up with it.[6]

There was a general perception among farmers that a close sense of community between farmer and hired hand had been lost after the turn of the century, with the relationship becoming increasingly an economic one.

The unequal treatment of women also contributed to the labour problem. The failure of many farmers to provide adequately for their daughters in their inheritance strategies, combined with the amount of work demanded, encouraged young women to depart for the city, where conditions could hardly be any more onerous. 'Servant girls', to help with the domestic responsibilities, had to be recruited, often from among recent immigrants stranded in the western cities. But they were usually in short supply and were not treated generously. While male hired hands usually worked specified hours, women employees—like the wives who supervised them—were expected to be available continuously.

After 1900 farmers turned increasingly to other sources of labour, including young immigrants from Britain brought out by charitable and philanthropic institutions to gain a fresh start. More than 50,000 of these 'home children' were imported into Canada before the First World War, most of them recruited in British slums. Many were encouraged to go by their parents; others were literally seized from parents and sent overseas 'for their own good'. The results were rather mixed, although the worst experiences were suffered by children—both male and female—sent into rural homes. While many farm families in effect adopted these newcomers—as Matthew and Marilla had done with Anne Shirley—others treated them only as a source of labour to be exploited.

Changing Patterns of Western Life

Except in the more isolated districts, after the turn of the twentieth century the western experience lost much of its quality of adventure and testing. Schools and churches had been built, the land had essentially filled up with settlers, and the prosperity created by the wheat boom of the early twentieth century made life considerably less harsh than it had been a generation earlier. Enough surplus was left after farm expenses had been met to provide some amenities for the farm-wife, particularly in the kitchen, although rural electrification and indoor running-water were slow to make their way everywhere in Canada before 1919. Nevertheless some farmers constructed their own electrical generators, and all obtained telephones as quickly as they could organize the stringing of the lines. Many of the more prosperous wheat farmers began to visit friends and relatives back east during the winter months, and some even began wintering in warmer climates in the United States. Almost everywhere across western Canada the pace of organized social activities in the nearest village or town increased. Farmers travelled long distances by horse and buggy—or in the winter by horse and sled—to participate in dances, church socials, and cultural affairs in their nearest community.

As in eastern Canada, the closest market-town or village became an integral part of the rural environment, and conditions in general became more akin to those of the East. The isolation of daily life was tempered by the growth of social institutions and social activity. 'A working day...was from about 4:30 a.m. to 11 o'clock at night,' reported one farmer, 'but this was only in seeding and harvesting time. In the winter we used to really have fun.'[7] Travelling long distances in the winter was fraught with constant danger on the Prairies, and newspapers continually reported casualties. But everyone took the risks, and journeys of up to twenty-five miles on horseback or by horse-drawn sleigh or sledge to see the local drama club or to attend a Women's Institute meeting were not uncommon. Social gatherings lasted well into the morning hours, since few attending from remote farmsteads had any intention of going home early. Given the distances involved,

A prosperous farmstead near Darlingford, Manitoba, established before the First World War. The large house and barn are screened by trees on the north and west and are open to the sun on the southeast. Photograph by Eberhard Otto.

little socializing was spontaneous. Events were planned and publicized well in advance, and even afternoon teas were organized.

The organized structure of rural life in western Canada was not unique; it was imported from other regions in Canada and the United States. In all parts of the nation, winter was the time when rural social life really came alive, partly because farming families had more time, partly because travelling conditions (despite snow and cold) were relatively easy. The dangers from region to region were not dissimilar and were met with equanimity. Thus Maud Montgomery, in late January 1897, travelled by sleigh to a distant village in Prince Edward Island for a concert and supper. When she and her friends left for home at about eleven in three sleighs: 'It was fine and calm all the way down to the ice but we had scarcely driven a mile on the latter when suddenly there came up a blinding snow-squall. In the twinkling of an eye we were enveloped in a white whirl so thick that we could not see from one bush to another.'[8] The vivid portrayal in Montgomery's journals of the importance of church and school to social life in Prince Edward Island before the turn of the century could well apply virtually everywhere in the settled parts of rural Canada.

The Rise of Specialized Farming

If the Prairie West, particularly after 1900, was quite similar to the rest of the country in its organized social activity, it remained quite distinctive in its monolithic concentration of grain cultivation. For most of western Canada, the only other significant commercial farm production had to do with horses—the raising of them and the growing of grain to feed them, which represented less a diversification than an essential feature of the production of grain itself. Cattle-ranching was not farming. But agricultural diversification had actually been occurring, though with uneven results, in other regions of Canada—such as southern Ontario. Much of the movement was to 'mixed farming', although most farmers realized that non-specialized farming was merely the solution to holdings too small or not fertile enough to grow a commercial crop. Specialization was the order of the day wherever possible.

One of the ironic effects of the shift into specialized farming, such as dairying, was that parts of farming previously consigned to women—and which often provided them with a small income independent of their husbands—were taken over by males. Almost every farm, and indeed many a non-urban household, kept a cow and some chickens; even a fishing family in Newfoundland or the Maritimes had its cow. So long as the animals were part of the subsistence economy they were the women's responsibility, and surplus production was frequently sold or bartered in the community to produce the well-known supplement called 'egg money'. But once this sideline became the major business of the farm, the woman was denied the opportunity to become autonomous. She still assisted with the cows, but not with the milking if this task became a large-scale operation.[9]

Not all regions of the nation or districts of a region were able to move easily to specialized farming. In the Maritime Provinces, for example, the agricultural sector peaked in size and importance in 1891, with strong concentrations on Prince Edward Island, in north-central Nova Scotia, and in southeastern New Brunswick. Then wheat production declined in importance, though dairying increased, and some farmers found new crops in which to specialize, particularly potatoes and fruit. But between 1891 and 1921 the Maritimes lost 22,000 farms and 630,000 hectares of farm acreage under cultivation. Farms continuing in operation had less than half the investment of central Canada in equipment and livestock, and large-scale commercial agriculture was on the decline almost everywhere except on Prince Edward Island.

Substantial changes in agriculture certainly occurred in central Canada. In Ontario farmers shifted from wheat to specialized high-quality consumer production, becoming increasingly dependent on off-farm processing, particularly of cheese and butter. By 1900 Ontario had 1,200 cheese factories that had captured over half the British market, so that the value of cheese exports from the province exceeded that of wheat. The production of meat—both beef and pork—for the dinner table at home and abroad also grew substantially. Similar shifts occurred in Quebec, although the relative poverty of many Quebec farmers, and the marginality of much of their land, inhibited the process. In Quebec, dairy products accounted for less than twenty per cent of agricultural production in 1900-10. In 1918 field crops still produced nearly seventy per cent of agricultural income, which rose from a gross value of $42 million in 1890 to a high of $266 million in 1920, when the bubble broke. Nevertheless, the acreage under cultivation in Ontario and Quebec constantly expanded. While the production of wheat constantly declined, the increase in livestock and of the hay and grain to feed them was steady. Districts around the larger cities profited most from the changes in farm production in both provinces, although the area of the St Lawrence lowlands around Montreal suffered a dramatic rural exodus. Some districts—like the Eastern Townships of Quebec, where French Canadians had virtually overwhelmed the English by the close of this period—were economically very stable. In many parts of Quebec subsistence agriculture remained resilient.

Specialty farming was very remunerative for those able to engage in it. Few Maritime farmers were able to respond to changing circumstances as well as those in the Annapolis Valley, where the development of an apple industry to serve the British market was encouraged in the 1880s by improved steamship service and reduced freight rates to Britain. By 1911-12 the Valley was producing a bumper crop of over one million barrels of apples, and had introduced co-operative marketing. An extensive program of tree-planting just before the First World War would not bear fruit until the 1930s, but farmers were actively experimenting with new techniques and new varieties. The strength of the British market also increased the region's commitment to the Empire, and successful candidates in the 1911 election campaigned in the Valley on the slogan 'No truck with the Yankees.'

During the same period another fruit growing district developed in the Niagara peninsula, and a third in British Columbia in the Okanagan Valley, which was opened by land speculation that attracted members of Britain's landed aristocracy and wealthier commercial classes. The Okanagan land-boom—encouraged in the 1890s by Governor-General Lord Aberdeen and his wife, who owned a large range of land in the northern part of the Valley—extended into southern mountain valleys of the British Columbia interior after the turn of the century. At the peak of the boom, land planted with maturing fruit-trees was selling at prices of up to $1000 per acre.

Apart from the relatively small number of fruit-farmers—who were of course restricted to a few regions with particularly favourable soil and climatic conditions—the aristocracy of Canadian farming outside the Prairies were the dairy farmers, whose success was inextricably connected with the growth of the Canadian city. Dairying had begun in earnest in central Canada in the 1860s, and its chief products were butter and cheese for export. By the 1890s a dairy community in most provinces was also involved in supplying milk (and collateral products, such as ice cream) to its nearest city. Successful dairy farming increasingly involved substantial capital investments—in herds, barns, and machinery—and it was quite labour-intensive. No branch of specialized agriculture was more demanding of time, for cows had to be milked twice a day regardless of other circumstances, and while competent dairy farmers could count on a decent return on their investment of capital and labour, they were more closely tied to their operation than any other farmers.

Successful dairy farming required capital and time; it also involved an expertise that was not known to many earlier settlers. Successful animal husbandry had not often been practised in pioneer Canada, and after the 1880s new breeds, such as the Holstein cow, required pure-breeding and constant improvement. Moreover, the farmer increasingly had to be a businessman, dealing not with a distant wheat-marketing system but with local industrialists who bought and processed his products and insisted on high quality at the lowest price. Given the specialized farmer's investment in equipment and labour, his need to achieve efficiency in production was as great as that of the factory owner. Those who did not keep careful books, and balance the appropriate elements, soon found themselves in trouble. Dairy farming was not without its problems. After 1910 New Zealand products began to compete in the lucrative United Kingdom market, and over-specialization was always a danger—as Quebec farmers realized when they suffered as a result of emphasizing the production of butter to the neglect of cheese. Another problem was the high cost per unit—again, a particular difficulty in Quebec.

The Introduction of New Technology

From 1885 to 1919 technological change was a powerful force in rural districts, as it was in urban Canada, but it had more importance in some aspects of farming than in others. In Ontario, Hart Massey—who had inherited from his father, Daniel Massey, the Newcastle Foundry and Machine Manufactory—acquired the patents for innovative American mowers and reapers, and introduced the Toronto Light Binder, all of which had a transforming effect on agricultural production in Canada. In 1870 he had incorporated the Massey Manufacturing Company, which moved to Toronto in 1879, and in 1891 merged with its chief rival, A. Harris Son and Co., to become Massey-Harris Company Limited, the leading farm-implement firm in the British Empire. The pace of the mechanization of agriculture, particularly the time-consuming and labour-intensive harvesting process, had increased. Mechanical hay mowers were introduced in the 1880s, enabling a man to cut ten acres of hay a day rather than a fraction of an acre. The reapers, mowers, drills, and threshing mills of the 1880s were in the 1890s supplemented by a variety of other agricultural equipment—all horse-drawn—that would serve Canadian farming well into the tractor era.

New labour-saving technology enabled one man in 1900 to produce a bushel of wheat in less than one-hundredth of the time required in 1870. The centrifugal cream-separator, introduced at the turn of the century, revolutionized dairy farming. The gasoline-powered Wallis Tractor—introduced into Canada in 1927 by Massey-Harris—would ultimately complete the process. Technology saved time and labour, but as it was extremely capital-intensive, its introduction separated the well-established and profitable farmer—who was enabled to reach new heights of production—from his less-successful fellows. Another important aspect of new technology was the processing and shipment of foodstuffs, particularly the perfecting and popularizing of canning as a means of preservation. The use of refrigeration for shipping, and new processes for the production and preservation of dairy products, were equally influential, enabling the Canadian farmer to grow more and to concentrate on certain products with high consumer demand.* Probably no new technology made more difference to the quality of rural life, particularly for isolated farm women, than the telephone, which made it possible for farm dwellers to talk on a regular basis with their neighbours, even if they lived miles away. Social activities could be planned, advice

---

*Though the tractor theoretically replaced the horse, many farmers continued to grow oats to feed horses they still owned, but no longer used.

solicited, business transacted, and gossip—that heart of rural life—exchanged.

The Rural Patriarchy

In this period, Canadian rural society continued to be inherently patriarchal in its organization. Men owned the land and usually made the decisions—including the decision to uproot and resettle, often against the wishes of their wives. One daughter of a Saskatchewan pioneer described what happened when a man named Robert Jaques

> came to visit dad one day in January 1902. They were in the parlor talking and laughing together. . . . Suddenly the folding doors between the two rooms opened and dad stood in the doorway (I can see him yet) and loudly announced to my mother, 'We're leaving Collingwood [Ontario].' Taking a long breath he said, 'We're going homesteading in the Northwest Territories. . . .' My mother fainted.[10]

Such a scene could also have been played out in Quebec, where the destination would be a remote part of the province, either further into the Laurentian and Appalachian Highlands, or to the Hudson Bay side of the Canadian Shield. By 1910 the Lac Saint-Jean district was fully settled, and the Outaouais and Temiscamingue districts were rapidly filling, as was the Baie-des-Chaleurs coast of the Gaspé. The Abitibi region was opened in 1912, while the National Transcontinental Railway (the NTR) was being built (between 1906 and 1914) in northern Quebec and Ontario, chiefly in an effort to develop an empty wilderness. The NTR would become part of the Canadian National system. The colonization movements into these regions were led by the clergy, with the government providing little assistance but road construction. For the most part the land was marginal, and settlement was closely tied to a neighbouring resource industry—usually lumbering, but sometimes fishing or mining.

The rural patriarch—intensely self-righteous, but essentially a land-hungry, materialistic tyrant—became a common motif in Canadian fiction of the period, especially from the prairie region. Novels by Robert J. C. Stead (*The Bail Jumper*, 1914, *The Homesteaders*, 1916), Martha Ostenso (*Wild Geese*, written in 1921 and published in 1925), and Frederick Philip Grove (*Our Daily Bread*, 1928, and *Fruits of the Earth*, 1933) all featured an insensitive farmer controlling and subjugating his family—especially the women, who smoulder in unfulfilled rebellion. The rural patriarch, who had always existed, was now being criticized for his acceptance of the values of modern industrial society, particularly the 'cult of Mammon'. Patriarchy meant something quite different for sons, who would inherit the land, than for daughters, who would not; but the very family-oriented nature of the typical farm meant that its operation and ultimate disposition had to be intensely practical. In fairness to the acquisitive patriarch, his greed for more and more land usually had its roots in a desire to provide security for his sons—who were seemingly more dependent on their father's largesse than his daughters, who were expected to marry and acquire their own households.

By and large, those who succeeded in making the shift to specialized agriculture did so on land they had inherited, not on land they could afford to acquire on the open market, or pioneer in some remote district. The emergence of highly specialized agriculture, and the boom in western wheat, also increased the distinction between prosperous farmers and those who subsisted on varying degrees of the economic margin—though both categories wished to provide some patrimony for their sons.

In this period of declining stocks of decent arable land and rising prices, entry into agriculture was still possible: hence the rush to districts like the Swan River Valley in Manitoba, southern Alberta, the Peace River district of northern Alberta and British Columbia, and the continued movement into northern Ontario and Quebec. French Canadians—who were perhaps discouraged by the hostility to their culture on the Prairies, and encouraged by the Quebec government and the Church to perpetuate French Canada on the frontiers of Quebec—were virtually excluded from the 'Last Best West'. The most famous French-Canadian novel of this period, perhaps of all time, was *Maria Chapdelaine* (1916), written by a Frenchman, Louis Hémon (1880-1913). In the harsh and remote Lac Saint-Jean region of Quebec, Maria rejects a chance to marry a man who would take her to the United States—when the migration of Québécois to the northern States was becoming heavy—and instead sacrifices herself to another in order to safeguard her family and her community.

The inheritance process in Quebec was not much different from that in the remainder of Canada. Basically there were two strategies that could be adopted. One possibility was to send the older boys off to establish new farms, more viable in the earlier period when land was still available. In Quebec this strategy overturned the traditional right of primogeniture:

> In certain parishes, it is almost always the youngest who inherits the paternal estate. Canadians marry young and these marriages are productive. When the eldest boy reaches the age of settling down, his father and mother are still in possession of all their strength and do not even think of giving up work; they are thus satisfied with providing their son with the means of starting a farm in a parish not far from their own but settled later, where land is therefore cheaper. The same plan is adopted with regard to the second, third, and each following boy; by the time the last one is in a position to manage a rural estate, the father is approaching old age and feels the need to retire; if the youngest is intelligent, he becomes owner of the property, in return for a life annuity assured his parents by a contract signed before a notary.[11]

The disappearance of arable wasteland, however, tended to increase the dependence of the farm family on more traditional inheritance strategies. As one observer in Quebec described the alternative approach:

It is not customary to break up landed property as is done in France. The head of the family works hard at economizing and acquires a piece of land for each of his sons who is old enough to cultivate. If his resources do not allow him entirely to accomplish this task, to which he attaches an extreme importance, he bequeaths the patrimonial estate to his most intelligent son, delegating to him the responsibility of helping his brothers and sisters and, little by little, setting them up properly.... The patrimonial estate remains intact in the midst of the ups and downs undergone by the family, which becomes divided without the property itself being broken up; the successive emigrations which leave to populate neighbouring parishes radiate from this traditional center....[12]

This strategy would become a veritable recipe for rural depopulation when adjacent parishes no longer had available land.

✒✒✒✒ *Rural Mobility and Its Alternatives*

In the process of agricultural development, families that persevered were rewarded, and few newcomers were able to gain entry into the community of prosperous specialized farmers in the established agricultural regions of eastern Canada. Those farmers who, for one reason or another, did not move into the West, or who did not enjoy a family inheritance of decent arable land adjacent to a market (they were extremely numerous), had to adopt other strategies for survival. Indeed, some farmers, especially in French Canada, were driven off the farm for part of the year in search of additional income, or were forced to move into newly colonized districts.

The history of rural Canada in this period continued to be one of constant mobility and family fragmentation. Few farmers were as successful as A. J. Cotton in accumulating enough wealth and land to provide autonomous farms for his four sons—and even Cotton had found it necessary to move to a newly opened district in the Swan River Valley in order to do so. Those sons who would not inherit moved on, with the financial assistance of their parents, if possible (or without it, if necessary).

Urban Migration

A basic component of urban growth continued to be, as it always had been, surplus rural offspring, and an increase in population was arguably the most important surplus Canadian agriculturalists produced in this period. Some young people moved deliberately into cities and city factories, while others ended up there less intentionally. Many of the eastern migrants to the Prairies, for example, probably intended to settle on farms, but did not. As one commentator in 1915 pointed out:

The cities were bright: there were people, moving picture shows, taverns, music halls, churches, life and electric light.... The city seemed happier. There was work in the city at good wages; and the hours of such work were regular,—just so many hours per day. Evenings and Sundays were for pleasure and self-indulgence. And like seafaring men, farm hands acquire a faculty enabling them to shape well in many branches of labor: Therefore, they had little difficulty in doing well in our cities.[13]

Permanent residence in the city, however, was not the only possible goal of those forced off the farm by inheritance patterns or economic marginality. Two others were equally common.

Agro-fishing and Agro-forestry

One alternative to urban migration was the entrance of displaced farmers, often on a part-time basis, into the traditional resource industries of the nation, chiefly fishing and lumbering. This strategy was a time-honoured one, and the choice of industry depended both on location and on individual predilection. Along the coasts of the Maritime Provinces, for example, the emergence of new markets (particularly for shellfish, such as lobster, which could now be canned and sent long distances) encouraged many farmers to supplement their agricultural income with fishing during relatively constricted seasons. In the interior of New Brunswick and Quebec agro-forestry continued to flourish throughout this period, with males farming on marginal holdings during the summer and working in the woods during the winter. While neither agro-fishery nor agro-forestry patterns were productive of much real economic advance for those who engaged in them, their adherents were probably better off than fishermen on the Gaspé, or in places like Grand Manan Island, who worked on a full-time basis and had little access to the produce of a subsistence farm. Some small communities could be really creative about their alternative incomes. For example, on 1500-acre Tancook Island off the coast of Chester, Nova Scotia, the inhabitants—descendants of the Germans of Lunenburg—not only fished, but grew cabbages and made sauerkraut for the mainland market.

Agro-industry

Industrialization permitted another pattern to develop, perhaps most strikingly in the Maritimes, but possibly everywhere in rural Canada: agro-industry. The rise of factories in rural districts, often to process farm products or resource products such as fish, offered an opportunity for part-time employment for local residents. Like the products they processed, most of these factories were seasonal in their operation. The cheese and butter plants of central Canada were unusual in the length of their seasons, but even they were controlled by the lactation period of the animals. More typical were the fish-packing plants on both coasts, especially those involved in the new processing technology of canning. Geared to the 'run', whether of salmon or lobster, such plants would spring into operation for a few weeks each year, usually employing female workers recruited from the surrounding community and providing income supplements for their families. In 1902 in British

Columbia, for example, nearly one hundred plants packed over 1,200,000 cases of canned salmon. Fruit-packing warehouses in regions like the Annapolis Valley similarly employed seasonal local workers at harvest-time. In some areas men were able to work in nearby mines and mills, while their families kept alive some pretension of subsistence farming.

The Implications of Occupational Pluralism

Rural occupational pluralism—whether it meant combining agriculture with fishing, lumbering, or manufacturing—had several important implications and consequences. In the first place it was a survival strategy for the less-prosperous members of the rural community, who could be either unsuccessful practitioners of an otherwise flourishing local agriculture or typical residents of a region that was generally marginal and depressed. But it had both positive and negative consequences. On the plus side, occupational pluralism enabled families to remain together, and to find some external source of income to supplement limited agricultural production. It was an alternative to permanent removal to the city, and in many regions it became elevated into a way of life seen as preferable to full-time urban or industrial employments. Such a strategy, usually geared to the seasons, left room for hunting in the autumn and provided ways of escaping from the drudgery of regular work, particularly for the men. On the negative side, rural occupational pluralism was associated with slovenly agricultural practices and work attitudes. Since income was derived less from farms than from other work, the land did not have to be efficiently and expertly cultivated. Moreover, marginal lands could be kept in cultivation and the farm-owner did not have to make hard economic decisions. Finally, occupational pluralism contributed to the difficulties of labour organization in rural sectors of the economy, and few attempts at this were made in the period before 1919.

Rural Hierarchies and Their Institutions

Canadian rural society was not only patriarchal, but intensely hierarchical. Even the basic unit—the family farm—was organized in hierarchical layers, with the father at the top, the male children favoured over the female, and a considerable gulf between 'the family' and the help. On the larger scale the prevalence of land ownership, and the distances that frequently separated farms, fostered illusions of social equality among families. The extent to which an individual rural family was conscious of its socio-economic position depended on the extent of its involvement in the community, as well as on the tendency of status-conscious merchants and professionals to cluster in villages and small towns rather than in the countryside itself. Every village had its clergyman and teacher, however, and larger ones added doctors and a few other professionals as well. As for the farmers, they divided into the prosperous—most of the substantial farmhouses and barns that still

The first school in Edmonton, built in 1881. National Archives of Canada, C-3862.

dot the rural landscape, and once served as the visible signs of success, date from the period 1880-1919—and the not-prosperous. Persistence was another factor that helped stratify rural society, particularly outside the newly settled western region. Those families whose roots went back to the period of early settlement had claims to status and importance—whatever their material condition—that no newcomer could ever hope to enjoy.

The School

School districts were often the only sign of public organization in the vast regions of rural Canada that remained politically unorganized. A local school was jealously guarded and operated by those it served. The one-room rural schoolhouse, taught in by a series of young schoolmarms and older school-masters, was standard in these years. The school year was commonly geared to the agricultural season, and girls attended more regularly and longer than boys. Maud Montgomery's response to her first such school as a newly appointed teacher, in 1895 at Bideford, was probably typical:

> This morning Mr Millar drove me up to the school and I went in, feeling forty ways at once and rather frightened into the bargain. The school is rather big and bare and dirty. There were about twenty children there, from six to thirteen years, and I called them in, said a few words to them and took down their names, feeling as idiotic and out of place as I ever did in my life.[14]

A classroom in School District No. 3, Glenelg, Ontario, 1910. The teacher is J.L. MacDonald.
National Archives of Canada, C-15490.

Schoolmistresses were expected to take a certain cultural lead in the community, both in school and outside it. Their problems ranged from the difficulties of finding suitable lodging, to disciplining young men considerably bigger and often nearly as old as they were.

The one-room school dominated rural Quebec as well as rural anglophone Canada. The most common Quebec school in the 1913 census was one-roomed, built at a cost of $1,200, with a young female teacher, paid less than $200 annually, whose pupils ranged from ages 6 to 14.[15] In both French and English Canada, some external standards were maintained by the school inspector, appointed by the province, who visited the classroom once a year to assess the teacher's performance and the school's facilities. In Quebec the inspector was usually accompanied by the parish priest.

The Clergy

Along with the schoolmarm, the resident clergy set the cultural and moral tone for any rural district. In Quebec the clergyman was a Roman Catholic priest, the fabled *curé*, but in most other regions of Canada he was an Anglican priest or a Methodist or Presbyterian minister. As might be expected, denominational allegiances became less important the further west one moved. In the older parts of eastern and central Canada, denominational loyalty persisted through life. In newly settled areas of the West, however, residents were usually happy to attend whatever church had managed to organize and attract a minister. Whether Protestant or Catholic, rural Canadians took their religion seriously. Sermons served as topics for daily conversation, and the activities of various auxiliary groups connected with any church were well attended, particularly the picnics and socials they organized. Churchmen often took the lead in social and political matters, and church journals regularly supplied reading material for rural areas.

Rural Culture and Values

Rural Canada was by no means a wasteland of unlettered country bumpkins, despite frequent cases of isolation and educational limitations. A relatively efficient postal service provided contact with the wider world, and while current books may not have been widely read, they were available for those who wanted them, as Montgomery's *Journals* clearly demonstrate. Rural Canadians voraciously devoured newspapers and magazines that often required far more of readers than do their modern counterparts. Many farm families received at least one daily newspaper (seldom on the day it was published), but most relied heavily for their edification on farm journals such as the *Grain Growers' Guide* (1908-28), and more general magazines like the *Christian Guardian*, the voice of the Methodist Church that was begun in 1829 by Egerton Ryerson and continued under this name until 1925 (it was the forerunner of the present *United Church Observer*). Formal statistics of circulation figures for such periodicals do not indicate their influence; a better measure is perhaps the wide range of letters to the editor that most included in every issue. Rural Canada had its own ideologies, and they were both shaped by and reflected in the literature of the time.

Canadian Pastoralism

Despite the rapid growth of Canadian cities, a vast majority of Canadians continued to hold rural values and to think of the nation in essentially pastoral terms. Those who read Canadian literature or looked at Canadian art were exposed to little but Canadian Nature, and foreigners could be forgiven for thinking that Canada was essentially an undeveloped country and Canadians a rural people. In the 1880s and 1890s Archibald Lampman (1861-99) and Charles G.D. Roberts (1860-1943) liberated Canadian poetry from unfelt Romantic simulations of the English experience by interpreting Canadian nature as they saw it—romantically in their cadences, but exactly in their imagery, as in Lampman's 'Late November':

> The hills and leafless forest slowly yield
> To the thick-driving snow, a little while
> And night shall darken down; in shouting file
> The woodmen's carts go by me homeward-wheeled,
> Past the thin fading stubbles, half-concealed,
> Now golden-gray, sowed softly through with snow,

Archibald Lampman in May 1895. National Archives of Canada, PA-25827.

Where the last ploughman follows still his row,
Turning black furrows through the whitening field.

Far off the village lamps begin to gleam,
Fast drives the snow, and no man comes this way;
The hills grow wintery white, and bleak winds moan
About the naked uplands. I alone
Am neither sad, nor shelterless, nor gray,
Wrapped round with thought, content to watch and dream.

(November 1887)[16]

French-Canadian romanticism could be very similar. Louis-Honoré Fréchette (1839-1908), sometimes called Quebec's 'national bard', included in his *La Légende d'un peuple* (1887) this ode to America (translated):

When, your brow covered with giant trees,
Virgin, on the banks of the ocean, you cast off
Your veil of folds bathed in flashes of light,
When, draped in billows of waving woody vines,
Your great shadowy forests, filled with singing birds,
Impregnated the greens with their pungent smells. . . .[17]

Enraptured by nature's beauty, the poets tended to concentrate on its more benign aspects.

The violence in nature was best captured in prose, by Ernest Thompson Seton (1860-1946) and Charles G.D. Roberts. Both writers originated a new

Charles G.D. Roberts, *c.* 1884.
National Archives of Canada,
C-6718.

kind of animal story that grew out of close observations of animal behaviour and, in Seton's case, the knowledge of an observant naturalist. Seton, who was born in England and brought up in Ontario, moved to Manitoba in 1882. He was a self-taught naturalist and artist whose first book was *The Birds of Manitoba* (1891). When he moved to Paris for formal study, his painting entitled 'The Sleeping Wolf' won a prize at the Paris Salon in 1891, but one called 'Triumph of the Wolves', in which animals are seen devouring a man, caused such a furor that he returned to Canada. Thompson's first collection of animal stories, *Wild Animals I Have Known* (1898), was followed by many others, increasingly tailored for children, in which the violence of animal activity is seen through human eyes.

> All that day, with growing racking pains, poor Redruff hung and beat his great strong wings in helpless struggles to be free. All day, all night, with growing torture, until he only longed for death. But no one came. The morning broke, the day wore on, and still he hung there, slowly dying, his strength a curse. The second night crawled slowly down, and when, in the dawdling hours of darkness, a great Horned Owl, drawn by the feeble flutter of a dying wing, cut short the pain, the deed was wholly kind. ('Redruff, The Story of the Don Valley Partridge')[18]

Roberts, author of nineteen collections of animal stories among many other books, was a lesser naturalist but a greater writer. He was fond of portraying the role of 'Fate' in the animal world, where unexpected elemental forces clash, and his later stories often involved epic battles between courageous beasts, usually to the death. The animal world described by Roberts, like that of Seton, was one of amorality and the struggle for survival:

> When, at last, the salmon came blindly into the eddy and turned upon his side, the bear was but a few feet distant. She crept forward like a cat, crouched,—and a great black paw shot around with a clutching sweep. Gasping and quivering, the salmon was thrown upon the rocks. Then white teeth, savage but merciful, bit through the back of his neck; and unstruggling he was carried to a thicket above the Falls. ('The Last Barrier')[19]

Both Seton and Roberts portrayed nature as dominant over humans.

Other writers described the conflict differently, depicting people triumphing over nature. This theme was especially common with Prairie writers, who were so conscious of the difficulties of pioneering—of taming the land and surviving the harsh climate of the West. For example, several novels by Robert J.C. Stead (1880-1959)—notably *The Homesteaders* (1916), which was reprinted five times by 1922—are replete with graphic descriptions of hostile nature. Quebec novelist Antoine Gérin-Lajoie (1824-82) had earlier worked similar territory in his two-volume novel *Jean Rivard*—subtitled *Le Défricheur* (1874) and *L'Économiste* (1876). One of the most popular French-Canadian novels of the nineteenth century (reprinted seven times before the close of the century), it was written in an attempt to stop, or slow down, the mass immigration of French Canadians to the industrial towns of New England, and to encourage settlement in the uninhabited regions of Quebec.

Ralph Connor—who, before and after the turn of the century, was one of the most popular novelists in the world, selling more than five million copies in America alone before his death in 1937—was a Presbyterian minister in Winnipeg who wrote his books chiefly in the summer at a cottage on the Lake of the Woods. In such novels as *Black Rock:A Tale of the Selkirks* (1898), *The Sky Pilot:A Tale of the Foothills* (1899), *The Man from Glengarry:A Tale of the Ottawa* (1901), and *The Foreigner:A Tale of Saskatchewan* (1909) he wrote about larger-than-life heroes in contest with sin and anarchy. By sheer force of character, Christian conviction, goodness, and often physical strength, they triumph over unregenerate men, a rough, uncaring community, and the environment—transforming them in the process. Ralph Connor's heroes, some of them Presbyterian ministers like himself, represented not only 'muscular Christianity', but the forces of civilization and progress.

Connor's theme struck a chord with Canadians who sought to identify progress with growth—an increase in population, the expansion of cities—and the taming of nature, in what Sir Wilfrid Laurier had proclaimed would be 'Canada's Century'.* The Reverend F. A. Wightman (1860-1939)

---

*During the general elections of 1904, which the Liberals won, Laurier prophesied: 'The twentieth century shall be the century of Canada and of Canadian development!'

Ralph Connor in 1910.

of New Brunswick pointed out, in a paean of praise for Canada published in 1905, that the entire population of the vast expanses of Canada was less than that contained within the environs of the City of London. He contemplated with equanimity a growth of population to 65 or 70 million by the end of the century, and the creation of many new cities 'in the heart of the country.' Sydney, Nova Scotia, might well contain one million inhabitants by the year 2000! Other great cities would spring up on the east coast of James Bay, at Churchill, on Great Slave Lake![20]

Romanticizing Rural Life

Not everyone was quite so certain. Contrary responses took several forms. One was a romanticization of the farmer. Sir Andrew Macphail (1864-1938), a native of Prince Edward Island who had a medical degree, taught the history of medicine at McGill University and was also a writer. Among his books was *The Master's Wife* (1939)—a family reminiscence, published posthumously, that has become a classic of Canadian social history. In 1912 Macphail had written:

> The man who farms only for the money there is in it is a fool, because one who can make money out of farming can make a great deal more out of something else. But for the man who would live a quiet, interesting, reasonable and useful life there is no other occupation which affords so favorable an opportunity. It demands the exercise of every faculty. Every moment of the day is full of

surprise, and every effort has its immediate reward either in success or failure. For the finest minds it affords an outlet for activity; for the poorest it affords a living without the sordid accompaniment of poverty.[21]

Macphail later confessed in *The Master's Wife* that as boys on the farm he and his brothers 'worked thinking only of escape.' But his colleague at McGill, Stephen Leacock, thought Macphail possessed 'a deep-seated feeling that the real virtue of a nation is bred in the country, that the city is an unnatural product.'[22] The novels of L.M. Montgomery frequently present the same dilemma: Prince Edward Island is the most beautiful place in the world, but the action is somewhere else—usually in the cities of central Canada or New England.

Antoine Gérin-Lajoie's Jean Rivard conducted a lengthy correspondence with a former schoolmate still bound to the city, extolling the virtues of his rural existence. The painter Horatio Walker, working on the Île d'Orléans, described his own preoccupations in this way:

> The pastoral life of the people of our countryside, the noble work of the Habitant, the magnificent panoramas which surround him, the different aspects of our seasons, the calm of our mornings and the serenity of our evenings, the movement of ebb and flow of our tides which I have observed on the shores of my island which truly is the sacred temple of the muses and a gift of the gods to men: such are the preferred subjects of my paintings. I have passed the greatest part of my life in trying to paint the poetry, the easy joys, the hard daily work of rural life, the sylvan beauty in which is spent the peaceable life of the habitant, the gesture of the wood cutter and the ploughman, the bright colours of sunrise and sunset, the song of the clock, the daily tasks of the farmyard, all the activity which goes on from morning to evening, in the neighbourhood of the barn.[23]

Such idealizations, expressed also in paintings like Walker's *Evening, Île d'Orléans*, were typical of the romantic view of Canadian rural life.

Folklore

Another form of romanticization of rural life was to be found in its folklore and folk songs. Folklore societies flourished briefly in Montreal and Toronto, but most of the work of collecting was done by people operating on their own or through Canadian museums. Although Ernest Gagnon (1834-1915) had produced the first significant Canadian folklore collection in 1865, *Chansons populaires du Canada* (which went through six editions by 1913), only in the 1890s did the movement to preserve the rural heritage of the nation gain strength. *The Family Herald and Weekly Star* (Montreal) began publishing folk songs in a weekly column beginning in 1895; W.P. Greenough's *Canadian Folk-Life and Folk-Lore* was published in 1897; William John Wintemberg began publishing material on the German dialect of Waterloo County in 1899; and around 1908 W. Roy Mackenzie (1883-1957)—a native Nova Scotian teaching at Washington University in St Louis—started

Horatio Walker, *Evening, Île d'Orléans*, 1909. Oil on canvas. Art Gallery of Ontario.

using his summer cottage in Nova Scotia as a base to search for traditional singers and songs. This effort was described in his book *In Quest of the Ballad* (1919):

> My constant purpose has been to portray, as faithfully as in me lies, the popular ballads which it has been my high privilege to encounter in their natural state and the reserved but simple and profoundly human old men and women who are still maintaining them in that state.[24]

Marius Barbeau (1883-1969), the first great Canadian collector of folk traditions, was appointed in 1911 an anthropologist in the Museum Branch of the Geological Survey of Canada (now the National Museum of Canada), where he remained until his retirement in 1949—and as a consultant into the 1960s. Some thousand Barbeau publications, and thousands of texts and songs he recorded (now preserved in archives), document not only the traditional folk traditions of rural Quebec, but also the myths of the

Tsimshian Indians of British Columbia. The folkways and songs Barbeau and others collected were part of the traditional rural experience of Canada; almost nothing was of urban origin. Dialects, riddles, tall tales, children's rhymes—all of which told more of the everyday life of the people than most other evidence—were often gathered up for fear these traditions would be lost in the rapidly changing society of the period.

Native People and Farming

The dominance in Canada of the rural/agricultural myth is well illustrated by the various efforts, particularly in the period 1867-1914, to turn native peoples into 'peaceable agricultural labourers'.[25] For those Canadians—whether government bureaucrats or private reformers—who concerned themselves with the natives, converting them from wandering hunters to settled agrarians appeared to be a simple panacea for the ills of Indian society. Towards the end of the nineteenth century Hayter Reed, the deputy superintendent-general of Indian Affairs, expressed his view of native people:

> Corn precedes all civilization; with it is connected rest, peace and domestic happiness, of which the wandering savage knows nothing. In order to rear it nations must take possession of certain lands; and when their existence is thus firmly established, improvements in manner and customs speedily follow. They are no longer inclined for bloody wars, but fight only to defend the fields from which they derive their support. The cultivation of corn, while it furnishes man with a supply of food for the greater part of the year, imposes upon him certain labours and restraints, which have a most beneficial influence upon his character and habits.[26]

While his remarks focused on Indians, the underlying assumptions of his address extended beyond Canada's native population.

Although agrarian ideology assumed particular importance for Indian policy, since it both justified dispossessing the natives of their hunting-grounds and provided a solution when they gave up territory, it also served as the basis for much of Canadian life, particularly in the Prairie West. Before the Great War most Canadians regarded agriculture as 'the mainspring of national greatness', and farming as a way of life that uplifted one 'morally and emotionally'.[27] Scientists—and those who had pretensions to science, such as the anthropologists—saw agriculture as a crucial and unavoidable step on the ladder of progress to civilization for any primitive people, be they ancient Celts or Canadian Indians. As a result, other ways of using the land, such as mining or lumbering, were regarded as inferior—and the people engaged in such enterprises as somehow tainted. The fact that neither mining nor timbering encouraged a settled family life added to their disrepute.

Indians could be displaced by treaties, removed to reserves, and encouraged to farm. But encouragement was not synonymous with useful practical assistance. Native Canadians needed a good deal of help to shift from a nomadic hunting/gathering existence to a settled agricultural one, and they did not consistently receive it. Government aid was sporadic, cheese-paring, and patronizing.

The natives of the Treaty Four territory in what would become southern Saskatchewan had began the conversion to farming with some enthusiasm, which waned as quickly as the government subsidies. When they resisted in the early 1880s, they were quickly suppressed militarily. The native response became merged with the second Riel uprising: the Treaty Four Indians were among those defeated at Batoche—and this, according to one observer, 'knocked the bottom out of every Indian on the Reserve,' leaving them 'completely subdued and quite tractable ever after.'[28] After 1885 coercion replaced subsidization as the major weapon of the federal government to impose agriculturalism on the reserves. Not surprisingly, the policy failed.

Conservation

Agonizing over the question of whether to choose progress (usually in an urban garb), or nature, was not the only possible response to the implications of 'Canada's Century'. Another was to mount crusades to preserve Canada's natural environment in the face of encroaching civilization. One leader here was Dominion entomologist Charles Gordon Hewitt (1885-1920), who was the Canadian representative on the International Commission for the Protection of Nature, and led the fight for the conservation of Canadian wild life. Hewitt recognized that 'the opening up of enormous areas of land by agricultural development, the penetration of virgin forest by railroads, lumbermen, and prospectors, and the reclamation of the wilderness have led to widespread destruction of the haunts of our wild life, with a consequent destruction of the greater portion of it.'[29] He supported the establishment of game reserves by the federal and provincial governments, and sought legislation to curb indiscriminate hunting, one of the principal reform interests of Canadian conservationists.

Summer Vacationing in the Wilderness

Most Canadians caught in the progress/nature dichotomy resolved their ambivalences with half-measures. Thus, alongside the growth of Canadian cities came the growth of summer cottages and resort hotels, located at lakeside or seaside, and frequently served directly by rail. The phenomenon pushed its way even into wilderness areas—such as Temiskaming in Ontario. Sir Andrew Macphail summered at the family farm on Prince Edward Island, Ralph Connor had his lakeside cottage on the Lake of the Woods, and even Stephen Leacock—who had a less romantic view of rural Canada than most Canadians—spent as much time as he could at his summer home at 'Old Brewery Bay' on Lake Couchiching near Orillia, Ontario. Weekend train services poured middle-class urban Canadians by the thousands into the Laurentians of Quebec, in Ontario into the Muskoka district and the regions of Algonquin Park and Haliburton, and from Winnipeg into the Lake of the Woods district just across the Manitoba border in Ontario. The rich travelled regularly abroad, but for most middle-class Canadians a few weeks away from the city became the newly ritualized holiday. A tourist industry began to develop along the shorelines of lakes and oceans alike.

Wilderness Travel

Other Canadians became fascinated with the recreational possibilities of wilderness travel, and the waterways of Ontario and Quebec became crowded with weekend canoeists. After 1905, when a railroad opened the Temagami forest 300 miles from Toronto, canoeists were able to enter the James Bay watershed on longer voyages. The best early canoeing manual was by James Edmund Jones, entitled *Camping and Canoeing* (Toronto, 1903), which offered advice that did not pamper the prospective canoe camper ('the men of the North are stalwart'), and was strongly moralistic ('the man who desires stimulants while he is living a pure and natural life in the open air ought to be ashamed of himself'; 'it is illegal as well as immoral to treat or debauch an Indian').[30] The menus included root-beer tablets, as well as 'evaporated' potatoes and apples. Canoeists could return to their routine refreshed by the 'brief bright experiences of a very pleasant trip.' The rewards included

> a manlier heart and tougher muscles, the glory of the sunset and the freshness of the dawn, the moonlit stillness of the Lake and the sweep of the river as it flushed and gurgled among the stones. A brief return to the evidences of nature; a brief renunciation of the artificiality of business and social life; a brief enjoyment of skies and lakes and rocks and pine trees at their freshest and best. Then, with firmer grip and steadier purpose, back to the work or the waiting, back to the rush and bustle of the city.[31]

A junior version of this outdoor activity was promoted by Ernest Thompson Seton, who had founded an organization called Woodcraft Indians in 1902; in 1910 he participated in establishing the Boy Scouts of America. Seton's classic *Two Little Savages; Being the Adventures of Two Boys Who Lived as Indians and What They Learned* (1906) drew on his own boyhood experiences near Lindsay, Ontario. It also provided a new context in which to view native people. British author Hesketh Prichard offered another version in a series of detective stories in which the sleuth was 'Indian Joe', a man for whom every blade of grass and moss-covered tree in the wilderness provided possible clues to events occurring there.[32] James Fenimore Cooper had introduced the Indian scout as a fictional hero earlier in the nineteenth century, but Prichard combined Conan Doyle's Sherlock Holmes with Cooper's last Mohican. Indian Joe was not only a very clever chap, but one for whom the wilderness held no mystery. Grey Owl and the Hollywood Indian could not be far behind.

The Group of Seven

Some of the best publicists for the canoe and the wilderness of the Canadian Shield were painters, beginning with J.E.H. MacDonald (1873-1932) and Lawren Harris (1885-1970), who attracted other like-minded painters to them and eventually formed the 'Group of Seven'. One of their haunts was Algonquin Park, Canada's first official wilderness area, created by the Ontario government in 1893. While such parks were partly intended as game preserves, their recreational possibilities were appreciated very early, especially if they were located within striking distance of a large city. Certainly Algonquin Park fitted that description. Although the Group of Seven was not officially formed until 1920, its members—mainly English-born Torontonians making a living as commercial artists—had begun travelling north to Georgian Bay and into the Algonquin wilderness to refresh themselves and to paint as early as 1911. In 1912 fellow artist Tom Thomson (1877-1917), a farm boy who had migrated from Owen Sound to Chatham to Seattle to

Arthur Lismer and Tom Thomson fishing, Canoe Lake, Algonquin Park, 1914. Photograph by Bud Callighen. McMichael Canadian Art Collection Archives.

Toronto, also became a wilderness enthusiast. Thomson never totally gave up Toronto—he spent his last two winters in a shack next to Lawren Harris's Studio Building in Rosedale ravine, where he escaped from 'all that otherwise made Toronto'—but he became identified with Algonquin Park. His drowning in Canoe Lake there in 1917 came to symbolize his devotion to the north. Thomson, and his friends who later formed the Group, began painting the Canadian wilderness in the midst of the new recreational movements, and their work gradually became accepted as the first 'truly Canadian' art. They captured the iconographic essence of the Canada most beloved by those who lived in its cities—a bleak and sombre, unpopulated landscape of jack pines, rock outcroppings, and storm-driven lakes.

While urban Canada revelled in its neighbouring wilderness, rural Canadians remained somewhat more ambivalent about the joys of living without electric lights and indoor plumbing. By 1900, rural areas of Ontario, Quebec, and the Maritime Provinces were all experiencing the problems of urban migration and depopulation. As the *Farmer's Advocate* put it in 1911, the most important issues of the day were not 'those touching important practical problems of soil culture and stock husbandry, but the ones aroused by disputatious views on matters of social and business relationships...the perennial debates as to "Why the Boys Leave the Farm"....'[33] One newspaper compared the population rupture to consumption:

> At first there is a slight cough, a little weakness, but no serious symptoms to cause alarm. Then the cough gets worse. Spasmodic attempts are made to check the disease, but neither the patient nor his friends are seriously alarmed. But if the disease is not resolutely taken in hand at this stage, it is almost certain to result in suffering later and perhaps death.[34]

In the years before 1914, farmers in Ontario joined their fellows elsewhere in the country in calling for political reform to prevent urban concentrations of wealth and power from destroying their way of life. Some of the agrarian community's demands for reform would be met during the course of the First World War. But by the beginning of that conflict Canada's farmers— particularly in the English-speaking parts of the country—already had their agrarian crusade well under way. An urban-rural confrontation had long been building in Canadian politics, and its place in the political history of Canada will be discussed in Chapter six.

chapter five

Imperialism, Racism, and Reform, 1885-1919

In 1906 the young French scholar André Siegfried (1875-1959) published a classic work that appeared the following year in translation as *The Race Question in Canada*. A cogent and illuminating study of the nation—the result of three visits, the most recent one during the election of 1904—it presented a revealing portrait of the two 'races' and of political life in Canada, combining French lucidity and wit with anti-clerical sympathies that only an outsider (in this case a French Protestant) could have expressed. Accustomed as Siegfried was to the complex politics of the Third Republic in France, with its plethora of political parties organized in terms of issues and doctrines, he found Canadian national politics quite difficult to characterize. Political parties, apparently without ideologies, seemed little more than machines 'for winning elections':

> In the absence of ideas or doctrines to divide the voters, there remain only questions of material interest, collective or individual. Against their pressure the candidate cannot maintain his integrity, for he knows that his opponent will not show the same self-restraint. The result is that the same promises are made on both sides, following an absolutely identical conception of the meaning of power. Posed in this way, the issue of an election manifestly changes. Whoever may be the winner, everyone knows that the country will be administered in the same way, or almost the same.[1]

Only occasionally, said Siegfried, when 'some great wave of opinion sweeps over the whole country', did Canadian politics escape from its 'sordid preoccupations of patronage or connection.' Canadian politicians did their best to avoid such major confrontations. A few paragraphs later he added: '. . . the parties borrow one another's politics periodically, displaying a coolness in this process that would disconcert us Europeans.'

Siegfried's characterization did a considerable injustice to the Canadian political scene by implying an absence of ideological issues and debates. Those debates may not have been reflected in the platforms of the national parties, but they nevertheless continually engaged Canadians of the period. Indeed, some of the most serious and profound issues ever confronting Canadians and their political culture were faced and discussed during these years. The chief issue was the so-called 'Canadian Question', which bore in various ways upon the very future of the young nation, and often appeared to be a debate between those who sought to keep Canada within the British Empire and those who wanted it to assume sovereignty. But into this discussion merged several related matters, including the 'race question'—which involved more than merely the future of French Canada within an evolving Anglo-American country—and the 'reform question', which had to do with instituting change through public policy, particularly legislative enactments. Debate and disagreement over imperialism, Anglo-French antagonisms, and reform—the three strands were loosely if inextricably linked—kept political Canada bubbling with scarcely suppressed excitement from the late 1880s to the beginning of the Great War.

The Nature of Canadian Party Politics

The sheer magnitude of debate helps to explain why Canadian political leaders so assiduously sought consensus, as the Canadian educator James Cappon (1854-1939) suggested in 1904 when he speculated on what would replace the party system. Would not the result, he asked, be

> ...the unchecked conflict of class interests, provincial interests, religious interests, the free play of jealousy and prejudice? At present all these antagonisms are to a great extent modified and controlled by the party system of government and a certain amount of moderation and mutual understanding. What other system could do that work at present? It is a useful training for nations composed of heterogeneous elements; it has really created our national unity, and it produces probably the best and clearest expression of national opinion and will at which we could arrive. And it remains to be seen whether Canada is capable of making it a good deal better than it is at present.[2]

Although the Fathers of Confederation had not written political parties into the Canadian constitution, by the mid-1880s a two-party system had evolved at both the federal and provincial levels (at least east of Manitoba) that would survive virtually unchanged until the First World War. Indeed, this period was in many respects the Golden Age of Canadian politics, an era in which party affiliations were taken seriously, and being a 'Liberal' or a 'Conservative' was a lifetime commitment passed on from father to son. The seeming vitality of the two-party system disguised, to some degree, the extent of underlying tensions within the expanding Canadian federation, but until

1914 the traditional parties seemed flexible enough to contain various currents of conflict and reform.

Both national parties developed consensual styles capable of holding a vast array of differing ideologies, as well as various sectional and interest groups. Reformers and Tories, regionalists and nationalists, could co-exist. Individuals from all regions and all walks of life could be found within each of the parties. The key to the successful functioning of the national parties—and the allegiances of their adherents—was in large part to be found in the power of patronage. The reform of government service along the lines of a merit system was slow to develop in Canada, partly because the process of industrialization lagged behind that in Great Britain and the United States and partly because those who supported the parties continued to prefer to see them as a source of employment. Both national parties were firmly committed, when in office, to distributing honours and jobs to their leading supporters, employing careful systems of apportionment to adherents whose qualifications were judged solely in terms of political service and loyalty. A 1907-8 Royal Commission studied the public service outside Ottawa, concluding:

> As a rule, in the outside service...politics enter into every appointment and politicians on the spot interest themselves not only in the appointments but in the subsequent promotion of the officers. . . .In the outside service the politics of the party is of greater importance in making appointments and promotions than the public interests of the Dominion.[3]

The patronage system worked similarly for both parties, with Members of Parliament making the actual decisions based on recommendations from local party organizations. Even those who did not seek the fruits of patronage in the form of appointments expected assistance from their MPs, invoking party loyalty in their requests. Only on the very eve of the First World War were serious questions raised about the efficacy of such a system.

The patronage system chiefly rewarded those members of the Canadian professional and business élites (mainly from the so-called 'middle class') who ran the two political parties. It tended to diminish ideological and regional differences, offering French Canadians their own opportunities for advancement. Patronage thus encouraged a stable party system in which matters of principle were less important than division of the spoils of victory, and many of the festering problems of the nation were capable of being ignored. At the same time it would be a mistake to regard patronage as totally negative, since it had at least the merit of opening office to a larger array of people than in the early years of reform, when the civil service tended to be very élitist.

The pervasiveness of party patronage, handled identically for English and French Canadians regardless of their other differences, was not the only feature of Canadian politics in this period. Another was the complex relationship between the federal and provincial governments, and indeed between

Oliver Mowat. National
Archives of Canada, C-8361.

the federal and provincial wings of the two major Canadian parties. Sir John
A. Macdonald's centralizing vision of the nation had met with opposition
from the provinces, expressed initially by Sir Oliver Mowat (1820-1903), the
Liberal premier of Ontario from 1872 to 1896, who was determined that the
provinces remain important political units. His province was too rich and
powerful to be bullied into submission to federal domination, and Mowat
sought provincial control over economic development. He successfully confronted the federal government in 1882 over the question of provincial
boundaries particularly, persuading the Judicial Committee of the British
Privy Council (the court of last resort for federal-provincial disagreements)
to reject a federal proposal to turn the territory west of the Lakehead over to
Manitoba. Responding to his success in asserting provincial rights over a
wide range of responsibilities and extending provincial boundaries, he said to
one audience in Niagara Falls:

> I rejoice to know that the one great cause, the principal cause of your enthusi-
> asm, is that you love Ontario as I love it. The display that you have made this
> night shows that you are for Ontario, and that you are for those who maintain
> Ontario's cause.[4]

Other provinces were forced to contend with the federal government for
'better terms', which W.S. Fielding's Liberal government in Nova Scotia
insisted upon in 1886 and 1887, but Ontario consistently held out for a

constitutional arrangement in which the provinces held a veto. In so doing, Mowat helped elaborate a 'compact' view of Confederation—in which each province was an equal partner in the constitutional agreement—that would ultimately become quite influential.

Provincial parties of the opposite persuasion to the party in power in Ottawa were often in a stronger position to confront the federal government because they were not tied to it, or associated with it. Canadians were not slow to appreciate the point, thus establishing two of the verities of Canadian politics: first, complain about Ottawa; second, vote into office the provincial party that has promised to confront the federal government. A succession of Ontario Conservative leaders complained that the patronage of the federal government insufficiently benefited their party to compensate for its identification with Ottawa. On the question of provincial rights, which Mowat had made a crucial and continuing issue, the Ontario Tories were disadvantaged. Mowat's Liberals took over the ground, leaving his provincial opponents the dubious choice of supporting the federal government or splitting the party. Moreover, the increasing hostility within Ontario to French Canada, best exemplified by the reaction to the Riel uprising of 1885, could not be harnessed by the provincial Tories while Macdonald's government relied on Quebec support. Only with the success of Laurier's Liberals in 1896 were the Ontario Tories freed from the incubus of a federal Conservative party, and they moved quickly to disassociate themselves from the national politicians, ultimately winning power in the province in 1905 that they would seldom relinquish over the next eighty years.

One of the great ironies of Canadian Confederation was that French Canada, while it had been successfully isolated in Quebec, remained the region upon which national political success had to be built. A national party had to win in Quebec while also picking up sufficient strength in the other provinces to put together a majority. Until the death of Macdonald in 1891, the Conservative Party had successfully appealed to French Canadians with a judicious combination of political patronage and continuing national leadership. But even before Macdonald's death, the signs of a political shift within Quebec had become evident, notably in 1885 when Louis Riel was tried for treason and sentenced to death, despite fierce opposition from French Canadians. The shift finally settled in 1896 when Wilfrid Laurier (1841-1919) became the national 'chief/*chef*'. Laurier carefully put together a coalition of provincial Liberal parties, and his notions of consensus were considerably less blunt than those of Macdonald. His agonizing over the Manitoba Schools Question of the earlier 1890s, when his distaste for a unilingual language policy for Manitoba schools came into conflict with his support of the rights of provinces to run affairs within their general mandate, was a pure reflection of the Laurier mind, which favoured conciliation. 'My object', he wrote in 1904, 'is to consolidate Confederation, and to bring our people, long estranged from each other, gradually to become a nation. This is the supreme

Sir Wilfrid Laurier campaigning on 26 October 1908. National Archives of Canada, C-932.

issue. Everything else is subordinate to that idea.'[5] Laurier saw national unity and national harmony as identical, and, not surprisingly, viewed a biracial state as essential to the quest. He was able to survive politically, on the strength of a great period of national prosperity, until 1911, when the Liberal program of establishing a Canadian navy and limited free trade with United States brought defeat. The Liberals became a minority in Quebec and, in Laurier's words, 'Ontario went solid against us.'

Laurier's Liberals were succeeded in 1911 by the Conservatives of Robert Borden (1854–1937), who managed to split the Quebec vote by traditional means (including bribery) while almost sweeping Ontario, thanks in large measure to the support of the Ontario provincial party. Borden's victory was a triumph for the imperialistic view of Canada and the advocates (mainly the Anglo-Canadian middle classes, both urban and rural) of certain public reforms that Borden had set out in his 'Halifax Platform' of 1907. He had called for civil-service reform, public ownership of telephones and telegraphs, a reformed senate, and free mail delivery in rural areas. Laurier had enacted some of Borden's planks, including civil-service reform, in 1908, but the Nova Scotia-born prime minister was able to achieve some of his imperial vision only with the beginning of the war, when he attended the 1917 Imperial War Conference and argued successfully that Canada and other dominions deserved recognition 'as autonomous nations of an Imperial Commonwealth'.

The Conscription Crisis of 1917 completed the process, begun in 1911 with the defeat of Laurier, of the political isolation of French Canada, while not satisfying either the Maritimes or the West. Borden represented the 'progressive' forces of Anglo-Canadian society and reform that had been marshalling strength since the mid-1880s. In this sense Laurier's conciliatory policies had been a check on a principal underlying current of Canadian public affairs in the thirty years before the war, particularly outside French Canada.

Canadian Imperialism and Its Opponents

Years of internal and external crises following Confederation had been trying for the young nation. Against a constant backdrop of struggle between the federal government and the provinces over control of economic development occurred a series of well-publicized confrontations that suggested an equally critical cultural dimension: the New Brunswick Schools Question of the 1870s, the Riel Rebellion of 1885, the rise of the Equal Rights Association in Ontario (organized in 1889 in response to Quebec's Jesuit Estates Act* and profoundly anti-Catholic), and the notorious Manitoba Schools Question of the 1890s. The presence of an increasingly powerful southern neighbour meant a continuing fear of 'Manifest Destiny'—the urge to continental expansion of the United States, which had fought Spain in 1898 in the Caribbean and elsewhere and would make menacing noises about the Alaska boundary. The flood of a new generation of immigrants into Canada, particularly into the developing western region, brought a new infusion of 'British' sentiment to the nation, along with a new 'alien' population, neither French nor British in origin, that settled mainly in the mid-West.**

As Britishness sought ways of expressing itself in Canada, Great Britain

---

*Disagreement over the settlement of the considerable property and seigneuries that had once been owned by the Jesuits in Quebec was resolved—with the help of Pope Leo XIII, who acted as arbiter—in July 1888 when the Jesuits' Estates Act was passed by the legislative assembly of Quebec, providing payments to the Jesuits and several educational institutions. Papal involvement angered the Orange Order in Ontario.

**The notion of a 'British' ethnicity was very Canadian. Despite political unity, those in the British Isles clung tenaciously to their traditional national cultures—Scots, Irish, English, and Welsh.

itself began to shed its commitment to 'Little England' sentiments and to the colonies, and to the international free trade that had so distressed some British North Americans in the 1840s. Anti-colonial attitudes in Britain gradually disappeared, however, as the world's shopkeeper discovered that it was impossible to guarantee raw materials and markets solely in economic terms. Simultaneously British overseas adventurers found that substantial windfall profits were to be made by exploiting the economies of underdeveloped sectors of the world, especially in Africa. Canada first faced the implications of the resurgence of Britain's imperial pretensions in 1884, when it was asked to contribute to an expedition to relieve General Charles Gordon, besieged by thousands of Muslim religious fanatics at Khartoum in the Egyptian Sudan. Macdonald's immediate response was to wonder 'Why should we waste money and men in this wretched business?', adding that 'our men and money would be sacrificed to get Gladstone & Co. out of the hole they have plunged themselves into by their own imbecility.'[6] But Macdonald ultimately found it politic to allow Canadian civilian 'volunteers' to assist the British Army: a contingent of 367 men, mostly French-Canadian raftsmen but also including a few Caughnawaga Indians, participated in the relief expedition. Great Britain would increasingly expect her major 'settlement colonies'—Canada, the Australian states, and New Zealand—to assist her militarily; and just before the turn of the century Joseph Chamberlain at the Colonial Office began to advocate that these colonies be joined together in some pan-Britannic political and economic union, the so-called 'Imperial Federation'.

Against this background of continuing internal dissension (among political parties, regions, and 'races'), and growing imperial pressure, a number of Canadians by the 1890s had begun to make reputations by speaking and writing about the problems that faced Canada in both imperialist and anti-imperialist terms—although within each camp there were several sub-groups. Neither those supporting imperialism nor those opposing it could ever be neatly fitted into monolithic straitjackets. They were essentially publicists, pamphleteers, and editorialists, more eager to persuade with rhetoric than to convince with impeccable logic. That the debate over the 'Canadian Question' was carried on with more heat than light ought to surprise no Canadian who has lived through the recent discussions over free trade. But the absence of careful argumentation did not mean that the questions discussed were not taken seriously.

The Imperialists

The predominant imperialist view was essentially an Anglo-Canadian perspective, promulgated by men from central Canada and the Maritime Provinces. The leading spokesmen for the cause were George Denison (1839-1925), George Parkin (1846-1922), George Monro Grant (1835-1902), Charles G.D. Roberts, and Stephen Leacock. Their position was on one level conservative, attempting to preserve the status quo arising out of the strong Loyalist traditions still prevalent in eastern Canada. Their sense of imperial destiny was not necessarily anti-nationalistic, for they saw no inconsistency between the promotion of a sense of Canadian unity and a larger British empire. 'I am an Imperialist', argued Stephen Leacock in 1907, 'because I will not be a Colonial. This Colonial status is a worn-out, by-gone thing.'[7] What Leacock wanted, he said, was 'something other than mere colonial stagnation, something sounder than independence, nobler than annexation, greater in purpose than a Little Canada.' Such a pan-Britannic nationalism was quite common to all the major 'white-settlement' colonies of the British Empire. It expressed itself concretely in the form of demands for Imperial Federation, which one advocate defined 'as a union between the Mother Country and Canada that would give Canada not only the present full management of its own affairs, but a fair share of the management and responsibilities of common affairs.'[8]

While the imperial sentiments of those Anglo-Canadians born in the first half of the nineteenth century had their roots in historical experience, much of the rhetoric of younger advocates in the second half of the century had an intellectual basis in the revival of the philosophy of Idealism. The prevailing ethos of industrialization and free trade had been utilitarianism ('the greatest good for the greatest number'), which combined with evolutionary Darwinism into a world-view where only the fittest who fought the hardest survived. The resulting Social Darwinism—associated with the writings of Herbert Spencer in Britain and William Graham Sumner in the United States—was a philosophy of rampant individualism that exempted the state or community from any need to interfere in the natural processes of life. Reacting against this creed, many thoughtful individuals throughout industrializing society quickly extended the abstract conceptualizations of Idealism into a practical philosophy that centred on duty and responsibility and emphasized the community's needs rather than those of individuals. The Idealists also rejected the materialism and secularism of individualism, while enlarging their vision of community to include larger political entities, such as the British Empire.

The prevailing philosophy of Canadian and British universities in the last quarter of the nineteenth century, Idealism was the perfect philosophical underpinning for a generation of paternalistic imperialists. It exalted British civilization and political progress into the perfect Idealist state, fully worthy of its Empire, and insisted that every member of that Empire had a duty to promote its principles. 'The Empire to which we belong', wrote Principal George Monro Grant of Queen's University in 1890,

> is admittedly the greatest the world has ever seen. In it, the rights of all men are sacred and the rights of great men are also sacred. It is world-wide and therefore offers most opportunities for all kinds of noblest service to humanity, through the serving of fellow-citizens in every quarter of the globe. . . . Of the few great

nations of the future the English-speaking people is destined, if we are only true to ourselves, to be the greatest, simply because it represents most fully the highest political and spiritual life that humanity has yet realized.[9]

How could one be satisfied with less?

The Anti-Imperialists

Unfortunately for the imperialists, a good many Canadians were not impressed by their arguments. Of several anti-imperialist strands abroad in Canada around the end of the nineteenth century, one was pro-American and was notably advocated by the political journalist Goldwin Smith (1823-1910), who had settled in Canada in 1871 after a successful career as Regius professor of history at Oxford.* Smith was an anti-statist liberal with utilitarian leanings, a proponent of free trade, and unsympathetic to notions of a far-reaching British Empire. He was a great admirer of the United States, however, and after an early flirtation with Canada First he became persuaded that Canada's future lay within a continental union with the United States. His most famous formulation of this argument was presented in *Canada and the Canadian Question* (1891). Smith was a firm believer in the 'invisible hand' of the market and an opponent not only of economic regulation but of any transcendence of natural processes. He insisted that the geography of North America worked against Canadian nationalism, and that the *continent* was Canada's national market, concluding his study by advocating 'Commercial Union' with the United States. He had earlier identified four forces that would ultimately lead to the severance of the political connection with Britain: 'distance, divergence of interest, divergence of political character and the attraction of the great mass of English speaking people which adjoins us on this continent.'[10] He saw little in common between Canada and most of the rest of the British Empire, which included 'an Asiatic dominion extending over two hundred and fifty millions of Hindoos, [or] a group of West Indian Islands full of emancipated negro slaves.'[11]

Smith has always been labelled an 'anti-imperialist', but a persuasive case could be made for his being merely an anti-British imperialist who preferred Canadian absorption into the United States to a merger with the mother country. Certainly his arguments were pragmatic rather than abstract, and quite different from those of the mainstream of Canadians, who criticized imperialism from the perspective of the need for the development of eventual Canadian independence and sovereignty. Many Canadians found American annexationism a frightening prospect, but no group was more unsympathetic than the Quebec clergy, as André Siegfried noticed:

The policy of annexation has no more resolute opponents than the clergy of

---

*In 1875 Smith married Harriette, the widow of William Henry Boulton (son of D'Arcy Boulton Jr), and took up residence in The Grange, Toronto.

Quebec, for they realize that on the day the province should be swept into the American vortex there would be an end to its old isolation, and it would be overwhelmed by the torrent of new ideas. It would mean the end of Catholic supremacy in this corner of the world, perhaps the deathblow to the French race in Canada.[12]

Many Anglo-Canadian advocates of full Canadian sovereignty were lawyers like John S. Ewart (1849-1933), who was born in Upper Canada and was largely self-educated before his admission to Osgoode Hall Law School in the late 1870s. He moved to Manitoba in 1881, abandoning the Presbyterian church of his family and becoming an Anglican, attracted by that church's tolerance and lack of doctrinal rigour. Ewart rejected moral absolutes, displaying little sympathy with abstract arguments of any description. He had made a public reputation as the leading lawyer for Manitoba's Catholic minority in its constitutional appeals connected with the Manitoba Schools Question. His arguments for independence tended to be legalistic and constitutional. He found colonial status degrading, for 'Colony implies inferiority—inferiority in culture, inferiority in wealth, inferiority in government, inferiority in foreign relations, inferiority and subordination.'[13] He did not advocate the breaking of the imperial connection with the Crown, but envisioned an evolutionary progression by which the government in Ottawa would have the same standing as that at Westminster. Canada had no responsibility for shouldering any of the burdens of Empire. It had ceased to be a subordinate state, and all that remained was 'the semblance and appearance of subordination.'[14] Insofar as Canadians had a duty, it was to reject the final tie and become truly independent. Like most other nationalists, Ewart was concerned that British sentiments stood in the way of the creation of a genuine home-grown Canadian national consciousness:

Our unofficial orators have held up to us, not Canadianism, but Imperialism, and their failure to achieve success is similar to that of those who endeavour to love God and yet remain out of sympathy with their fellow-men. How can Canadians love the British Empire which they have not seen when they do not love their own country which they have seen?[15]

Such arguments were as close as Ewart would come to a transcendent vision.

A different perspective was enunciated by the chief French-Canadian opponent of imperialism, Henri Bourassa (1868-1952), who belonged to a leading Quebec family (his grandfather was Louis-Joseph Papineau). First becoming prominent in 1899 when he resigned his seat in parliament over the Laurier government's decision to permit Canadian volunteers to assist Britain in South Africa without parliamentary approval, Bourassa was re-elected unopposed and pursued unsuccessfully his insistence on the right of the Canadian Parliament to declare war. He helped defeat Laurier in 1911 over the prime minister's willingness to build a Canadian navy that could be turned over to Britain in time of emergency. Unlike Ewart, who seldom

Henri Bourassa in 1917.
National Archives of
Canada, C-9092.

argued in English-French terms, Bourassa stood for a fully articulated bicultural Canadian nationalism. Indeed, he wrote:

> The only possible basis for the solution of our national problems is one of mutual respect for our racial characters and exclusive devotion to our common land. . . . We are not asking our neighbours of English extraction to help us develop a political reconciliation with France, and they have no right to use their strength of numbers to break the rules of the alliance, forcing us to shoulder new obligations towards England, even if these were completely voluntary and spontaneous.[16]

Although he admitted that 'My *own* people. . . are the French Canadians,' Bourassa maintained that he respected English-speaking Canadians and did not see them as foreigners:

> My native land is all of Canada, a federation of separate races and autonomous provinces. The nation I wish to see grow up is the Canadian nation, made up of French Canadians and English Canadians.[17]

As an opponent of Quebec separatism Bourassa saw his vision of Canada as the only viable alternative to national disintegration and chaos. In his ultimate insistence on full Canadian sovereignty he was in agreement with Anglo-Canadian nationalists like Ewart, but he reached that point only in 1917—however much full sovereignty was implicit in his arguments. In his philosophical position and his concerns with race, community, and political power, Bourassa had much more in common with the Imperialists than he would have liked to admit. Bourassa was essentially an Imperialist turned upside down.

The Bourassa version of nationalism, while obviously inspired by a French-Canadian perception of Canada, was hardly the only one current within Quebec in this period. There was also a more traditional nationalism that had its origins in earlier times but had been considerably sharpened by Quebec's experiences since 1867. Its clearest statement came in the newspaper *La Vérité* in 1904:

> Our own brand of nationalism is French-Canadian nationalism. We have been working for the last twenty-three years toward the development of a French-Canadian national feeling: what we want to see flourish is French-Canadian patriotism; our people are the French-Canadian people; we will not say that our homeland is limited to the Province of Quebec, but it is French Canada; the nation we wish to see founded at the time appointed by Providence is the French-Canadian nation.[18]

That nationalism was simultaneously defensive and aggressive: French Canada had a mission to uphold the Roman Catholic faith and the rights of French Canadians, not only within Confederation but everywhere in North America. In its own way, such a nationalist vision had imperialist overtones, for it saw Quebec as a 'mother country' for francophones across the continent.

✐ Imperial Defence

The most common public confrontations over the role of Canada in the Empire occurred in the context of imperial defence. As colonial secretary, Joseph Chamberlain used the occasion of Queen Victoria's Jubilee celebration in June 1897 to assemble the leaders of the various 'colonies' of the Empire. He saw to it that Laurier was knighted, and pressed 'for some adequate and regular system of contributions to sea-power' and exchange of troops. Those colonies for the most part were unenthusiastic about any of Chamberlain's concrete proposals, concluding that political relations were 'generally satisfactory under the existing condition of things.'[19] The question of Canadian assistance to Britain rose again in July 1899, when the mother country requested Canadian troops for the forthcoming war in South Africa against the Boers. Laurier temporized, but the issue would not go away, particularly when shooting began on 11 October 1899. The popular press in English Canada responded with enthusiasm to the idea of an official Canadian contingent. The press in French Canada, however, opposed Canadian involvement in Britain's overseas adventures, *La Presse* stating: 'We French Canadians belong to one country, Canada; Canada is for us the whole world; but the English Canadians have two countries, one here and one across the sea.'[20]

The government compromised by sending a force of 1,000 volunteers, insisting that it was not setting a precedent.* When Bourassa asked, in the Liberal caucus, whether Quebec's opinion had been taken into account in the decision, Laurier answered: 'My dear Henri, the Province of Quebec has no opinions, it only has sentiments.'[21] Laurier rode out the storm of objection, but the whole business did not incline him towards supporting imperial entanglements, much less imperial federation. He continued to attend imperial conferences called by the British. But at those meetings he firmly resisted any moves to regularize imperial authority, conscious of the gathering strength of anti-imperialism in Quebec, which had even produced mutterings about the organization of a new nationalist party within the province.

The defence issue emerged again in 1909, this time over naval policy. Britain had been pressing her colonies, since the mid-1890s, for naval contributions that would be integrated into the Royal Navy. At a naval conference in 1909, Canada finally agreed to produce a unit of five cruisers and six destroyers, having been assured that the Admiralty would not insist on a unified command (except, of course, in time of war). Thus the Laurier government introduced a Naval Service Bill in January 1910, with predictable results. Many in English Canada—led by Conservative spokesmen, joined by the country's leading Tory provincial premiers—sneered at this 'tin-pot navy', insisting that the legislation did not go far enough towards assisting the British. In Quebec it only touched off another round of threats of new party reconstructions, with the nationalists and the Conservatives joining forces to fight for repeal of the Naval Service Act.

In the context of imperialism, however, defence was a secondary issue, particularly in English-speaking Canada. In the finest Canadian novel of the period, *The Imperialist* (1904) by Sara Jeannette Duncan (1861-1922), the question of imperialism was intricately interwoven with the social values of late-Victorian Canada. For Duncan's protagonist, young politician Lorne Murchison, Canada's continuation as a British nation was morally rather than strategically important:

---

*The thousand untrained infantrymen, who sailed from Quebec on 30 October, were followed by 6,000 more volunteers in Canada's second contingent, and later another thousand men—all equipped, transported, and partially paid by the Canadian government. Another contingent, Strathcona's Horse, was supported entirely by Lord Strathcona (Donald Smith), Canada's high commissioner to Britain. The Canadians took part in twenty-nine engagements before the war ended on 11 May 1902.

**Troops leaving Winnipeg for the South African War. In the upper left is the old City Hall
on Main Street. National Archives of Canada, C-12272.**

We're all right out here, but we're young and thin and weedy. They did not
grow so fast in England, to begin with, and now they're rich with character and
strong with conduct and hoary with ideals. I've been reading up the history of
our political relations with England. It's astonishing what we've stuck to her
through, but you can't help seeing why— it's for the moral advantage. Way
down at the bottom, that's what it is. We have the sense to want all we can get of
that sort of thing. They've developed the finest human product there is, the
cleanest, the most disinterested, and we want to keep up the relationship—it's
important.[22]

For Murchison, Britain needed help because 'industrial energy' was desert-
ing her, and Canada could provide reciprocal benefits.

Racial Sentiments

The 'Canadian Question' could not be debated in isolation from racialism
and reform impulses of the moral-reconstructionist variety, in either English
or French Canada. The Anglo nationalist-imperialists had no doubt about

the superiority of the Anglo-Saxon race, and most of them waxed eloquent on the subject. George Parkin claimed that one of the Anglo-Saxons' great assets lay in their 'special capacity for political organization' and stability. Never before had 'any branch of the human family been so free to apply itself to the higher problems of civilization.'[23]

The historical development of Great Britain, the United States, and Canada demonstrated to the imperialists the special genius of the race. But Canada had advantages over both the United States and Britain. As Social Darwinists, many imperialists believed that climate was an important factor in the process of natural selection, and that Canada's 'strenuous climate' would ensure that only immigrants 'belonging to the sturdy races of the North' would come to Canada. Although such immigrants would increase Canada's population slowly, 'quality would be balanced against quantity.'[24] The United States, on the other hand, was attracting less-desirable immigrants from 'the vagrant population of Italy and other countries of Southern Europe' — it was understood that the Canadian climate was inhospitable to those who would not work and provide shelter for themselves. In parts of the United States it was possible for people to sleep outside and so have an easier life; furthermore, there were a large number of blacks who were regarded as even further down the scale of evolution than southern Europeans. The population of the United States, like that of Britain, was further debilitated in this view by industrialization and urbanization. Goldwin Smith shared in the prevailing assumptions of Social Darwinism, arguing that his concept of continentalism would ensure the continuance of the Anglo-Saxons in North America. For him, the democratic American system was 'hard pressed by the foreign element untrained to self government.'[25] But after 1896 those same 'foreign elements' began entering Canada in large numbers from Italy and eastern Europe — an incursion that worried the imperialists greatly.

The condescending attitude of English Canadians towards French Canadians, their fellow citizens, was more serious, however, and held the seeds of generations of suppressed mutual antagonism. It was described by André Siegfried:

> The English Canadians consider themselves the sole masters of Canada; they were not its first occupants admittedly, but it is theirs, they maintain, by right of conquest. They experience, therefore, a feeling of indignation at the sight of the defeated race persisting in their development instead of fusing or being submerged. And to the classic cry of the mother country — 'No Popery!' — they add another of their own — 'No French Domination!' English Protestants and French Catholics thus find themselves face to face every day in the political arena; and the English obstinately make it a point of honour not to let themselves be surpassed by adversaries whom they judge backward and inferior.
>
> An attitude frequently adopted in Anglo-Canadian circles is that of ignoring deliberately the very presence of the French. From their whole bearing and conversation, you might suppose that the French element in Canada was quite

insignificant. You might spend many weeks among the English of Montreal without anyone letting you realize that the city is two-thirds French. Many travellers never suspect this.[26]

Nevertheless, many Anglo imperialists were willing to accept French Canada. Quebec, after all, had northern origins, and it had grown and developed politically under British influence. According to George Monro Grant, French Canadians were politically 'British and their hearts are all for Canada.' But the imperialists, and some of their English-speaking opponents, were disturbed by the Roman Catholic peasant mentality they saw in French Canada. French Canadians, wrote Goldwin Smith dismissively, were 'tractable, amenable and while they are neither cultivated nor aspiring, their life is above that of the troglodyte of *La Terre*.'* [27] According to George Parkin: 'One has no hesitation in discussing frankly this question of race inertia in Quebec. The most clear-sighted men of the province admit and deplore it.'[28] The French-Canadian people were 'simple and docile', and needed to be saved from their 'narrow, bigoted, and isolated ways'. The poet Wilfred Campbell (1858-1918) saw French Canada as 'useless, despotic, intolerant, and ultra-conservative in her body politic and her social ideas.'[29]

Such judgements—which today would be labelled racist, a concept and term that was unknown at the time—were not confined to English-speaking intellectuals, as the newspaper debate over Louis Riel in 1885 had well illustrated. 'The masses of the French-Canadian people are simple and ignorant,' blithely declared the *Toronto Weekly News* in May 1885. On a higher plane, the Toronto *Mail* editorialized in July of that year:

> In Quebec there is a caricature Ontario, and in Ontario a caricature Quebec, both invented by politicians; and until those wretched figments are replaced by more truthful and intelligent conceptions, we cannot hope to become an united Canada.

The *Mail* went on to say that the problem was not simply a tendency on the part of English Canada, particularly Ontario, to disparage the ordinary French Canadian. The great newspaper war over Riel demonstrated the extent to which French Canadians were prepared to respond in kind, and with an equal amount of intellectual justification, based on history and the notion of French-Canadian distinctiveness.

Much of the French-Canadian definition of 'the French race in North America' derived from the clergy, who, since 1840, had preached to their flocks about the providential mission of French Canada. According to one well-known oration by Mgr L.-A. Paquet (1859-1942), on the simultaneous

---

*'*La Terre*' refers to the idealization in French-Canadian novels of the time—the *romans de la terre*—of the rural way of life and the illiterate *habitants*.

occasion in 1902 of the fiftieth anniversary celebration of Laval University and the sixtieth of the Saint-Jean Baptiste Society in Quebec:

> We are not only a civilized race, we are the pioneers of civilization; we are not only a religious people, we are the messengers of the religious idea; we are not only submissive sons of the Church, we are, we ought to be, numbered among its zealots, its defenders, and its apostles. Our mission is less to manipulate capital than to change ideas; it consists less in lighting the fires of factories than to maintain and to make shine afar the luminous fire of religion and thought.[30]

Earlier expositions of such Messianism had often used the term 'people' instead of 'race', but after the turn of the century French-Canadian writers commonly used the latter word, not always in an anthropological sense. Henri Bourassa, for example, in a published speech of 1912 entitled *La Langue française et l'avenir du notre race* (The French Language and the Future of Our Race, 1913), referred to the 'Irish race, which has continued to exist and preserve its ethnic character, although it lost its language a long time ago.' He went on to discuss the 'Scottish people' who, 'by losing their language and being intellectually assimilated into the Anglo-Saxon race,... have furnished England and the British Empire with a moral and intellectual factor of undeniable value.' Bourassa concluded:

> When a race ceases to express its thought and feelings in its own language, the language that has grown with it and has been formed along with its ethnic temperament, it is lost as a race. The preservation of language is absolutely necessary for the preservation of a race, its spirit, character, and temperament.[31]

The French-Canadian definition of 'race' was chiefly home-grown out of historical experience. Not until the very eve of the First World War were French-Canadian intellectuals, such as the Abbé Lionel Groulx (1878-1967), exposed to elements of European racial theories, particularly those of the Comte de Gobineau. At the same time, in its anti-Semitism French Canada demonstrated that it was equally capable of intolerance. In 1906 Henri Bourassa argued in the House of Commons that the Jews '...are the least remunerative class that we can get—that class which sucks the most from other people and gives back the least'—adding that 'they are the most undesirable class that can be brought into the country' and 'vampires on the community.'[32](Bourassa was opposing exemptions for Jews from the Sabbath Day legislation that was currently before the House.) French-Canadian suspicions of Protestant Canada were also deep-seated: in Siegfried's words, 'their mutual animosity is too distinctive for any complete understanding to be possible between them.'[33]

The 'race question in Canada' was not really about race at all, as many contemporaries well recognized. 'It is unfortunate that this matter has to be referred to in terms of race,' wrote Robert Macdougall in 1913, 'inasmuch as it is not racial in essential character. There is absolutely no racial barrier to preventing our French and English-speaking peoples commingling.'[34] As Macdougall implied, 'commingling' involved other peoples besides the two founding ones. Many saw the new immigrants, whether Chinese or Polish, as a genuine racial threat. Almost no Canadian of the time had any vision of encompassing these new 'races' other than by assimilation, at best, to the dominant values of the two founding peoples. Even J. S. Woodsworth had argued in *My Neighbor* for no more than a policy of assimilation.

Throughout Europe and the United States, racial arguments and analyses of various kinds were being espoused—and filtered into Canada—as part of what was regarded as 'science' at the time. For example, the concept of natural selection, introduced in Charles Darwin's *On the Origin of Species by Means of Natural Selection* (1859), was taken as the basis for various social theories, although it had been intended only as a biological construct. Social Darwinists offered not a philosophic but a scientific 'truth': the strong must control society in order to eliminate the 'bad' elements of heredity. By the turn of the century this movement had developed what became known as the 'science of eugenics': inheritance was the key to evolution, and races had been formed by natural selection on a very unequal basis. Led by the British scientist Francis Galton (a cousin of Darwin), the eugenicists opposed another group—the environmentalists (who traced their ancestry back to the French scientist Jean-Baptiste Lamarck)—who were equally convinced of the importance of heredity.[35] The principal issue, still with us in a different guise, was whether heredity (nature) or environment (nurture) was the key to human characteristics. The Lamarckians believed in the inheritance of acquired characteristics, which meant that if one ameliorated the environment of the less-privileged members of society through reform, one could improve the characteristics of the younger generation. The eugenicists, on the other hand, insisted that social reform would merely perpetuate the weak and 'degenerate'. Ethel Hurlbatt, a Montreal suffragist, asked in 1907:

> Can we, by education, by legislation, by social effort change the environmental conditions and raise the race to a markedly higher standard of physique and mentality? Or is social reform really incapable of effecting any substantial change, nay by lessening the selection death rate, may it not contribute to the very evils it was intended to lessen?[36]

Both eugenicists and environmentalists, however, accepted the need for improvement in the race, and were continually concerned about its potential degeneracy. 'Race regeneration' was thus one of the central themes of the reform movement, especially in English-speaking Canada. Connected with this was the demand for social purity, sometimes through restrictions on the consumption of alcoholic beverages, but also through concerted campaigns against prostitution, venereal disease, and sexual exploitation of various kinds.

The desire for racial regeneration and the restoration of social purity was one of the major links between racial attitudes in Canada and the various movements of reform that were so prevalent in this period. In British Columbia, for example, one opponent of Chinese immigration stated in 1908:

> ...the fact remains that British Columbians object to a vast alien Colony, exclusive, inscrutable, unassimilative, with fewer wants and a lower standard of living than themselves, maintaining intact their peculiar customs and characteristics, ideals of home and family life, with neither the wish nor the capacity to amalgamate, which gradually by the mere pressure of numbers may undermine the very foundations of *their province*. They have to safeguard the future and the distinctiveness of their race and civilization.[37]

In its own way the campaign for Oriental and Asiatic exclusion came out of the same stock of assumptions about heredity and environment that informed many reform movements of the period. Social and moral aspects were frequently emphasized, and the belief was commonly held that these newcomers would not assimilate; but if they did, the result would be 'a lowered standard of civilization'.[38]

The Suffrage Movement

Mainstream Canadian reform movements were spearheaded by Anglo-Canadian members of the middle and professional classes who shared the common assumptions of the age about regeneration and social purity. Women, because of their general nurturing role in society, played a critical part in almost all aspects of reform. Those from middle-class Protestant backgrounds were at the forefront in Canada, particularly in the areas of temperance/prohibition, public health, education, and women's suffrage. Because they were acting out of their traditional functions as nurturers and civilizers rather than protesting against those functions, Canadian women were not seriously concerned to restructure gender roles in society. Instead they tended to concentrate on what modern scholarship has come to call 'maternal feminism' or 'social feminism', supporting movements that emphasized either the need for regeneration or the traditional Protestant middle-class virtues of chastity and sobriety. Even potentially radical change was often justified in maternal terms. In both cities and rural areas existing women's organizations were harnessed to the cause of reform, although frequently to different aspects.

The political powerlessness of women was addressed by trying to obtain for them the right to vote. The suffrage movement was chiefly an urban one, dominated by well-educated middle-class women who wanted to obtain some political power in order to bring about other legislative changes that would help control the 'evils' of a degenerating and decadent society, such as the liquor trade and the 'white-slave trade', or to correct injustices against women, such as unequal wages, bad working conditions, and legal discrimination.* The suffragist élite—almost exclusively Canadian- or British-born—belonged to the main-line Protestant churches; less than 5% of the suffragist leaders were Roman Catholics, although nearly 40% of the anglophone population of the country were Catholic. Significantly, well over half (60%) of the female leaders were gainfully employed, chiefly in middle-class occupations, although only about 15% of Canadian women in the early twentieth century had jobs. The single largest concentration of employed women was in journalism and writing. While 42% of them were single, most of the rest were married to middle-class and professional husbands. Well over half this female élite had some form of higher education.[39]

An early proponent of women's rights and political activism was Emily Stowe (1831-1903), the first Canadian woman doctor and the founder, in 1876, of Canada's first suffrage organization. Gradually, around the turn of the century, the goals of the suffrage movement shifted, as did the composition of its leadership. As more women entered professional life, the predominantly male society around them adjusted—at least superficially—to their presence, and discrimination became less blatant. But many women—perceiving how deeply rooted male domination was, and how difficult it would be to eradicate it—chose to get on with their work instead of pursuing the right to vote. They became skeptical about suffrage, and as a result the movement was taken over by women from the upper and middle class who were not gainfully employed, and for whom social service—'volunteer work', it was called—was extremely important. The key organization became the National Council of Women of Canada, founded in 1893. For many women, social reform came to take precedence over the vote itself; indeed, achieving the vote for women was increasingly justified in terms of its impact on recalcitrant governments, rather than on the grounds of the personal changes it would bring in its wake. According to one women's journal in 1909: 'The hour is now come to call the women of Canada to redress the political, electoral and social evils from which the country suffers.'[40]

As the suffrage movement changed its emphasis, it lost contact with working-class women. Suspicious of the class bias of both suffrage and reform movements, many working-class women refused to support them. As for farm women, their organizations could agree with the urban suffragists over the importance of correcting injustice and increasing moral purity via the vote, for women voters would 'throw the rascals out' and insist on having politicians with new policies. But they were unable to persuade their urban counterparts of the urgency of the particular concerns of the farm sector.

---

*Not all supporters of women's suffrage were women: about one-quarter of the leaders of the movement in this period were men.

Adelaide Hoodless and her children, Hamilton, Ontario, 1887. National Archives of Canada, PA-128887.

Many of the most active organizations among farm women were 'special-interest' branches of larger, male-dominated farmer groups, such as the United Farmers of Alberta and the Saskatchewan Grain Growers, or creations of provincial governments designed to deal with the particular problems of rural farm women, like the Women's Institutes, a movement that spread round the world. The first Institute was founded in 1897 by Adelaide Hoodless (1857-1910) at Stoney Creek, Ontario.* (In Henry James Morgan's biographical compilation *The Canadian Men and Women of the Time*, 2nd

---

*Hoodless (née Hunter)—whose infant son's death in 1889 from drinking impure milk impelled her to work for women's causes—also helped found the National Council of Women, the Victorian Order of Nurses, and the national YWCA.

ed. 1912, she is listed under the name of her husband John, who was a furniture manufacturer in Hamilton.) Women's Institutes were intended to promote appreciation of rural living and also to encourage better education of all women for motherhood and homemaking. By 1913 there were Institutes in every province; and in 1919 the Federated Women's Institutes of Canada was formed, with the motto 'For Home and Country', reflecting their aims to promote rural values and study national and international issues, and to achieve common national goals. More radical women felt the Women's Institutes had been encouraged by provincial governments eager to defuse potential feminism, particularly in rural districts. Once urban suffragists became involved in such organizations, they were regarded with suspicion by many farm women: urban and rural women saw the world quite differently. Both wanted the vote, but the reforms they sought were quite different. For example, farm women wanted something done about rural depopulation, while urban suffragists sought to improve working and living conditions in the nation's cities.[41]

While many women's farm organizations concentrated on agrarian issues, one reform organization, the Women's Christian Temperance Union (WCTU), had rural and urban memberships that were equally strong. Founded in 1874 in Owen Sound, Ontario, the WCTU by 1900 claimed 10,000 members, and had an influence that ranged far beyond that number. Despite the inclusion of 'temperance' in its name, the WCTU was committed to *prohibition*, and soon came to see the elimination of alcoholic beverages as a panacea for many of the ills currently besetting Canadian society, which included crime, the abuse of women and children, political corruption, and general immorality. A speech made in 1898 by Jessie C. Smith, called 'Social Purity', expressed the spirit of the WCTU:

> *What strength, what purity, what self-control,*
> *What love, what wisdom should belong to her*
> *Who helps God fashion an immortal soul.*

That is the burden that rests on Christian Mothers, helping God fashion immortal souls, and our W.C.T.U. true to God, and Home, and Native land, sets itself to help Mothers, and Fathers too, in laying, as the hearthstone of every home, the foundation of Social Purity in Canada, let us, then, like charity, begin at home.[42]

The WCTU was only one of several members of the Dominion Alliance for the Total Suppression of the Liquor Traffic. Like most Canadian reform movements, prohibition required state intervention in order to be effective. The WCTU was unusual, however, in its ability to generate credible political candidates, who campaigned outside the two major parties (which generally tried to ignore the question) on a prohibition platform and appeared regularly in most provinces. Inevitably the political goals of prohibition drew its supporters into women's suffrage. As the president of the WCTU explained in 1914:

During all the time since ever liquor was introduced women have ever and always been its chief sufferers. Its sword has pierced her very soul; she has again and again seen the lord of her life, her husband, transformed into a veritable beast through its malignant spell; and if there be one thing harder than this I think it must be for a mother to see the idols of her soul, her own children, dragged down to the nethermost depths because of it. Is it any wonder, then, that the W.C.T.U. ardently desires the enfranchisement of women: Why? Not from such low aims as to add a little paltry power to their positions; ah, not so, but because we realize that the ballot in the hands of the women must mean eventually the outlawry of the liquor traffic.[43]

On one level this appears to be yet another illustration of maternal feminism, but arguments of this kind had an important impact in their day.[44]

As a movement, prohibitionism contained some of the best and worst features of reform. Strongly based in the Protestant churches, it had only limited support in Catholic districts and in Quebec, and none among the urban working classes, who regarded it with suspicion on several grounds. Many urban workers were recent immigrants of Catholic background, and felt personally attacked by the prohibitionists, who often attributed their political failures to an unholy alliance between the 'liquor interests' and the 'Catholic vote'. Other workers regarded prohibition as a class issue, an attempt by the middle classes to eliminate one of the few pleasures they enjoyed in a hard and otherwise impoverished life. Anti-liquor organizations, such as the WCTU, were frequently over-zealous in their desire to suppress related 'vices'—such as public dancing, gambling, theatre attendance, and the reading of 'trashy novels'—that were acceptable to most Canadians at the time. Even when their campaigns were directed against social evils that most of society shared in condemning—such as prostitution and brothel-keeping—the moral fervour and singlemindedness of the prohibitionists turned much public opinion against them. In 1898 the WCTU was extremely critical of the approval by one of its international officers of the British Contagious Diseases Act, instituted to license brothels. And attempts to secure curfew laws for minors in several provinces, while well intentioned, were not universally popular. Much prohibitionist sentiment tended to be morally old-fashioned, even puritanical. Organizations like the WCTU were especially traditional in their attitudes towards women, exalting their role as moral guardians of society. In addition, many prohibitionists were unabashed eugenicists, despite a fundamental contradiction: if 'evil habits' were inherited, the effort to legislate them out of existence would seem pointless. For a great many Christian anti-liquor campaigners, supporting prohibition served as an outlet for energies that in earlier days might have found expression in religious revivalism.

In Quebec, although the conditions for a social-reform movement certainly existed—and Quebeckers (including many French-Canadian males) were active on a variety of fronts connected with the consequences of

The front page of the women's section of *The Toronto Sunday World*, 14 March 1915.

urbanization and industrialization—French-Canadian women were significantly under-represented in most national reform movements, and had great difficulty in creating viable organizations. The bicultural Montreal Local Council of Women (WCLU) was founded in 1893, and in 1907 the Fédération Nationale Saint-Jean-Baptiste (FNSJB) was created by Marie Gérin-Lajoie, whose call for action sounded little different from that of her anglophone sisters:

> Ladies, do you realize how important it is for you to vote in the municipal elections. . . . You will complain that your son dissipates his health and fortune in the neighbourhood bar, you will be overcome with sorrow at the sight of your daughter whose virtue is gradually being eroded by immoral theatre, you will condemn the death of a child, contaminated by the filth in the streets and still you do not attempt to remedy these evils.[45]

The status of women in Quebec, particularly for French Canadians, was much limited by the anti-feminist ideology of the traditional society, promulgated in large measure by the Roman Catholic Church. Nuns were allowed an active role outside the home, but most women were encouraged to remain there as mothers and homemakers. Though the FNSJB distinguished between 'good' feminism, which did not challenge traditional roles, and 'bad' feminism, which searched for alternatives to them, the organization became actively involved in various social-reform movements, including the campaign against liquor. It sought not prohibition, however, but a reduction in the number of outlets in Montreal, and was able to co-operate with the WCTU in an Anti-Alcoholic League that ran candidates in municipal elections. The WCLU fought, not always successfully, to prevent the Quebec government from revoking some limited voting privileges enjoyed by women in the province. It did manage, in 1902, to prevent the City of Montreal from withdrawing the vote from women who paid property taxes. In general, however, women in French Canada faced an insurmountable hurdle in the male-dominated attitudes of society and Church.

By 1914 the Canadian social-reform movement had many achievements to its credit, including a total overhaul of urban school systems and the introduction of new notions of child care (both public, and at the level of the individual family). Perhaps nowhere had social reform been more successful than in the areas of education and child care, although some inroads had been made in most areas of urban life and society. Since reform was middle-class and professional in orientation, it was most successful in those arenas where professionals held sway, such as the schools, and where its objectives were limited. In those arenas where successful reform demanded state intervention—such as housing or poverty—the record was considerably more mixed. The reformers were convinced that most opposition to their endeavours was caused by conspiracies between corrupt politicians and equally corrupt businessmen. But as reform shifted in the early years of the century—from the search for remedies for specific abuses and evils towards generalized efforts at moral regeneration—the opposition to reform became much more widespread and complex, while the chance of real accomplishment diminished.

In 1906, for example, the House of Commons passed a bill prohibiting most commercial work and even unpaid labour on Sunday, as well as most forms of commercial recreation. The bill was the result of both pressures from Protestant churches (through the interdenominational Lord's Day Alliance, founded in 1895) and support from the Church in Quebec, combined with considerable sympathy from the ranks of organized labour. It was heavily criticized in the House as class legislation, since it prevented most Sunday recreation for which daily admission fees were charged, while allowing golfing at private clubs where membership fees were levied on a different basis. It was also attacked by some French-Canadian members of the House as an attempt to impose the values of Ontario Protestantism upon all Canadians. The chief legacy of the bill was the principle of the total Sunday closure of commercial activity, which remained in force throughout much of Canada until the 1960s. But it was relatively ineffectual in its efforts to close down industrial production on Sunday.

Prohibition met with similar criticisms on the grounds of class and religious interests. Despite Laurier's national plebiscite in 1898, which its supporters narrowly won, the Prime Minister refused to implement national legislation for prohibition because only twenty per cent of the total electorate had supported the principle. The prohibitionists turned to the provinces, where they succeeded in passing legislation in Prince Edward Island in 1900 and in Nova Scotia in 1910. Local option was even more effective, since it permitted local jurisdictions, where prohibitionist sentiment was strong, to have their way without requiring hard-to-obtain provincial majorities that would have needed the support of hostile urban dwellers and French Canadians. Equally local were most of the victories for women's political rights, many of which consisted in preventing the removal of existing rights in jurisdictions where votes were granted to women who paid taxes or held property.

The First World War

Whether or not the reform spirit had peaked by 1914—and a case can be made on either side—the entrance of Canada into the First World War, which marked a triumph of sorts for Canadian imperialism, also completely rejuvenated Canadian reformers. At the same time that the war was inflicting extremely heavy Canadian casualties—60,661 were killed in action and 172,000 were wounded out of some 620,000 Canadians who served, in a population of 8 million—both the patriotic fervour of the war and the eventual political isolation of French Canada, sealed by the Conscription Crisis of 1917, made possible sweeping national reform on a number of fronts. Reform had always required an active policy of state intervention, and wartime conditions encouraged the intrusion of the Canadian government in almost all areas of life and work.

It hardly needs to be said that Canada entered the war with no conception of its ultimate length, intensity, or essentially futile savagery. The initial enthusiasm of English-speaking Canadians was predicated on a short and swift defeat of the Germans and their allies. By 1917 support for the war effort had come to be based on the sheer extent of the sacrifices that had already been made, given the fact that the war on the European front had been fought for years without victory. Canada's military contribution was substantial. Serving as the shock troops of the Empire, Canadians rapidly achieved a reputation for bravery and fierceness. They were continually thrown into the most difficult situations and performed well. The list of battles at which they fought heroically was a long one, beginning at Ypres in 1915 and continuing through to the Belgian town of Mons, where fighting ended for the Canadians at 11 a.m. on 11 November 1918.

The Canadian government had not only totally mobilized for victory—Arthur Meighen (1874-1960), as Secretary of State, once declared in the Commons that he would bankrupt the country, if necessary, in support of the war effort—but had increasingly, and ultimately successfully, fought for a say in imperial war policy and for the maintenance of separate Canadian units and command structures. To some extent Canada's arguments for autonomy, and the need to prove their legitimacy by providing manpower, dragged the government ever deeper into the quagmire. By the time of the Canadian triumph at Vimy in April 1917, Canada could no longer recruit new troops to replace the mounting casualties and was finding it difficult to meet the military responsibilities it had agreed to shoulder. Conscription was seen as the only solution.

Conscription ran against the entire grain of French-Canadian attitudes towards the war—and the British Empire. In the words of Henri Bourassa: 'I find that Canada, a nation of America, has another mission to accomplish than to bind herself to the fate of European nations and of despoiling empires . . . .'[46] From the standpoint of Anglo Canadians, French Canadians had not borne their fair share of the burden of the war effort. Of over 424,000 Canadian volunteers, it was argued in April 1917, less than five per cent came from French Canada, which had twenty-eight per cent of the total Canadian population. On the other hand, French Canadians had for years felt increasingly beleaguered by English Canada. They had fastened on the plight of francophones in Ontario as a symbol of their situation. To Regulation 17 of 1915, which seemed to impose unilingualism on Ontario's elementary-school system, French Canada responded with anguish, and the subsequent debate split along ethnic lines. For English Canada the war was an imperial crisis, and Canada's contribution was considered to be deficient; while for French Canadians the language restrictions of Ontario were central

Canadian battalion going 'over the top', October 1916. National Archives of Canada, PA-648.

Canadians washing their feet in a flooded shell hole, June 1917. National Archives of Canada, PA-1456.

to their resistance to supporting it. Ignoring the opposition by French Canadians, the Borden government imposed the Military Service Act, which became law in August 1917 and led to conscription. Virtually all French-Canadian members of Parliament opposed it. But in its wake, and with a federal election upcoming, the government took advantage of the isolation of Quebec over the issue and created a Union Government out of ruling Conservatives and those Anglo members of the Liberal party who had broken with Laurier over his opposition to conscription.

French Canada was not alone in becoming isolated by the war. Members of Canada's other ethnic minorities, many of them originating in parts of Germany and the Austro-Hungarian Empire, found themselves under severe attack. In 1914 the Canadian government attempted to distinguish between the 'German people' and the 'German government', but the distinction soon collapsed under a spate of hate propaganda against the enemy. Canadian Germans ceased to be 'privileged' ethnics and became associated with the despised 'aliens', and many towns changed their German names to more acceptable ones, with Berlin, Ontario, becoming Kitchener, and Dusseldorf, Alberta, becoming Freedom. The fairly recent arrivals of Ukrainians from the Austro-Hungarian Empire comprised a much larger segment of so-called 'enemy aliens', to whom objections increased as the war continued. In the end, over 8,000 'aliens' were interned by the Canadian government by Order-in-Council, and the foreign-language press was greatly restricted. Pacifist members of German and Russian sectarian groups, such as Mennonites and Doukhobors, also met with much public hostility. In the Wartime Elections Act of 1917, Canadians of enemy origin were ruthlessly disenfranchised with little objection from the English-speaking Canadian community, who were of course in the majority.

The Wartime Elections Act of September 1917 and the Union Government that took office the next month under Sir Robert Borden completed the process of turning the wartime Canadian government into one enthusiastically supported only by English Canadians on a bipartisan basis. The very bipartisan nature of the government completed one of the most important political planks of the pre-war period, and it was now able to implement other reforms favoured by its Anglo-Canadian supporters. In the early years of the war several provinces had granted women the vote; and Borden's government, with the Elections Act, quite cynically granted the federal franchise to women with close relatives in the war, in the accurate expectation that they would support both the government and its conscriptionist policies. But during the war women had been arguing for general suffrage on several grounds, of which the most powerful were that they needed to vote so as to bring the war to an end, and to have a voice in post-war reconstruction. Finally—and ironically, given the pre-war pacifism of the women's movement—women were granted the vote federally in 1918, in order to increase support for the war effort. And, as one war widow put it: '*We won't let it go back. We've paid too much to let it go back.*'[47]

The other great reform demand of pre-war Canada, prohibition, also triumphed because of the needs of the war. It was seen as necessary not only to keep the soldiers pure and to ensure that the country to which they returned would be a better place, but also for the war effort, to prevent waste and inefficiency. Previous arguments about infringing personal liberty lost their cogency during wartime. As the popular writer and activist for women's rights, Nellie McClung (1833-1951), put it: 'We have before us a perfect example of a man who is exercising personal liberty to the full...a man by the name of William Hohenzollern.'[48] With many of the earlier opponents of prohibition effectively silenced, the provinces began introducing it, and many supporters of the Union Government expected to see it implemented after the election of 1917. They were correct, and the federal government introduced national prohibition by Order-in-Council on 1 April 1918.

The Great War thus had a profound impact on Canada in almost all aspects of life. Its rhetoric, however, was of present sacrifice for future benefits. This war to end all wars would make the world safe for democracy, and would be followed by an era of full social justice. That Canada's contribution had been made with little regard for civil liberties or for the legitimate opinions of minorities at home was an irony that eluded most contemporaries. For Canada, the war's conclusion amounted to a triumph of Protestant Anglo-Canada; little thought was given to the tomorrows that would follow the coming of peace. A country that had drawn heavily on its resources to contribute to the ultimate victory was hardly prepared to deal with the negative legacies of its Herculean efforts.

chapter six

Economy, Polity, and the

'Unsolved Riddle of Social Justice', 1919-1945

Once the war had ended and peace was welcomed everywhere, most Canadians did their best to put the conflict behind them and, in the phrase popularized south of the border, tried to 'return to normalcy'. Such a collective enterprise would not be easy to accomplish. Perhaps symptomatically, certainly symbolically, during demobilization Canada experienced one of the most devastating epidemics of modern times, the Spanish Flu outbreak of 1918-19. The situation was so desperate in November 1918 that the government actually attempted, without success, to postpone public celebrations of the Armistice for fear of spreading infection. Canada's deaths from the flu ran ultimately to 50,000, only some ten thousand fewer than the number of Canadians who had died in battle. Fatalities had shifted from the front to the homefront.

Many thoughtful Canadians understood the potential difficulties, but few expressed them as articulately as Stephen Leacock, who wrote a series of articles for the *New York Times* in the autumn of 1919 that he published a year later in *The Unsolved Riddle of Social Justice*. Disengaging himself from his well-established role as a humorist and writing as an economist, the head of the Department of Economics and Political Science at McGill University, he stated:

> These are troubled times. As the echoes of the war die away the sound of a new conflict rises on our ears. All the world is filled with industrial unrest. Strike follows upon strike. A world that has known five years of fighting has lost its taste for the honest drudgery of work. Cincinnatus will not back to his plow, or, at the best, stands sullenly between his plow-handles arguing for a higher wage.[1]

Stephen Leacock in 1914. McCord Museum of Canadian History, Montreal, Notman Photographic Archives.

Neither a social revolutionary nor an arch-reactionary, Leacock attempted desperately to make sense of the future, both for himself and for his readers. Technology, industrialization, and war had profoundly altered the modern world, and there was no turning back.

> With all our wealth, we are still poor. After a century and a half of labour-saving machinery, we work about as hard as ever. With power over nature multiplied a hundred fold, nature still conquers us. And more than this. There are many senses in which the machine age seems to leave the great bulk of civilized humanity, the working part of it, worse off instead of better.[2]

Despite the immense destruction of war, in which 'some seven million lives were sacrificed; eight million tons of shipping were sunk beneath the sea; some fifty million adult males were drawn from productive labour to the lines of battle', the 'productive machine' never ceased to function. Industrial society did not normally employ its full potential. Leacock could only hope that the destructive energy of war could be harnessed for peacetime reform

and be directed at ensuring for every child 'adequate food, clothing, education and an opportunity in life.' Writing for an international audience,
Leacock left out most references to Canada in his discussion, although
towards the end of his extended essay he raised the wartime concept of
'conscription'—a term to which Canadians were particularly sensitive—
emphasizing that it was seen as part of a democratic obligation. 'But', he
added, 'conscription has its other side. The obligation to die must carry with
it the right to live.' Unemployment should become a 'social crime', said
Leacock, for states that could wage total war should be capable of eliminating
such a scourge. His version of economics could not sustain such a position,
but Leacock had at least addressed it.

The development of Canada over the next two decades demonstrated that
in peacetime Canadians had trouble coming to terms with the paradox
Leacock had suggested. What he did not emphasize overmuch in his discussion was the need for a unified body politic to implement the new society he
envisaged. While Leacock understood the importance in wartime of creating
a public consensus, and was correct in his assertion that the war had demonstrated the immense power of the state, for both destruction and construction, he failed to observe the extent to which war—at least in Canada—had
mortgaged the future.

Regional Protest in the 1920s

The war had set off, or perpetuated, a number of economic trends in Canada
that would trouble the nation in its post-war readjustment. The decade of the
1920s is usually associated with prosperity, but in truth the years immediately
after the armistice were difficult ones economically. Inflation was not brought
under control until 1921-3. The boom of the twenties did not begin in
earnest until 1924, and it was not shared equally by all sections of the country
or by all sectors of the economy. After an initial round of strikes in 1919 and
1920, responding to inflation and the deferral of expectations from the war,
industrial unrest remained high through 1925, when it collapsed in the face
of the boom and the introduction of the open shop. By 1921, labour
candidates sat in seven of nine provincial legislatures, and in the election of
that year over thirty federal constituencies had labour candidates of some
description, although only four were actually elected. Labour unrest continued to be most prevalent at the geographical extremes of the country, with a
number of notable strikes in Cape Breton in the East, and in Alberta and
British Columbia in the West—particularly in the coal fields: 22,000 coal
miners were on strike in August 1922,[3] and a number of unions were broken
in some of the bitterest labour violence that Canada had ever seen.

Most of the social and economic unrest of the 1920s found expression in
movements of regional protest. The collapse of the international wheat
market in 1921, and the beginning of serious drought conditions in parts of

western Canada, meant that the prairie farmer would never fully share in the prosperity of the twenties. In Maritime Canada the dissatisfaction before war's end over the inability of the wartime government to encourage the growth of the economy there only increased after the war. Both regions responded with movements of political protest directed against central Canada. The unhappiness of Quebec was not so directly related to economic factors, but it elaborated its own form of protest. Only in Ontario, which by 1921 had the sole self-sustaining economy in the country, was regional protest muted. Buoyed by a major resource boom in pulp and paper, mining, and hydroelectricity, Ontario's economy recovered more quickly from postwar problems. The early Canadian demand for automobiles had been responded to by the Ford Motor Company of Canada in Windsor, formed in 1904 soon after Henry Ford began production in Detroit, and by countless Canadian manufacturers, including the McLaughlin Motor Company (1907) in Oshawa, which produced the McLaughlin-Buick and later the McLaughlin-Chevrolet. The business sold out to General Motors in 1918 and became General Motors of Canada, with R.S. McLaughlin (1871-1972) as president. By the twenties no independent Canadian company survived, and the growing market for cars was controlled by American branch plants—Ford, Chrysler, and General Motors—encouraged by a preferential tariff on the entry of parts from Detroit into Canada and the entry of finished cars into all British countries.

Ontario farmers had been upset about conscription and rural depopulation, and voted their concerns in the 1918 provincial election and the 1921 federal one. But the Ontario farm economy, more mixed and less dependent on grain monoculture than its prairie counterparts, recovered more quickly. Ontario prospered, as it usually has, and wondered why the remainder of the country complained.

The Progressive Party

Certainly nobody felt harder done by after the Great War than the farmer. The movement of farm protest reached its height in the 1921 election, before the wheat market collapse and the spread of drought conditions had really begun to bite. In 1919, when agrarian discontent was most serious, Thomas A. Crerar (1876-1975) resigned as Liberal minister of agriculture and, with the backing of prairie and Ontario farmers on the Canadian Council of Agriculture, and dissident Liberals who (like Crerar) rebelled against the government's tariff policies, became leader of the new Progressive Party in 1920. In the 1921 election it won 64 seats and—alongside 50 Conservatives and 117 Liberals in the House—achieved a position of power in Parliament, breaking the established two-party tradition. Though they might have become the official opposition, the Progressives were split by the differing philosophies of former Liberals, who simply wanted free trade, and the farmers' representatives who wanted a more radical party. In the elections of

1925, 1926, and 1930 they were gradually reduced to a small 'Ginger Group' that eventually merged with the Co-operative Commonwealth Federation (CCF) in 1932. The Progressive Party's failures in Ottawa, however, were not matched at the provincial level in Alberta and Manitoba, where Farmer parties controlled the governments, or in Saskatchewan, where farmers dominated the ruling Liberal Party. Nevertheless, the decline of Progressivism as a phenomenon of national importance coincided with the farmer's own during the twenties. Its rise had really been associated with cumulated grievances deferred or exacerbated by the Great War, rather than with the deep-seated problems produced by international conditions and the overproduction of the war years.[4]

Western farmers, whose problems were the most serious, had long been persuaded that a national policy that included protective tariffs was not in their best interests. That both Liberals and Conservatives had accepted protectionism while in office served to convince the farmer that there was no major difference between the two parties on the tariff question, and encouraged him to think in terms of a third party, particularly in the years immediately preceding the war, when tariffs had been substantially increased. The western farmer had earlier been alienated by the failure of Laurier's Liberals to take advantage of American offers of reciprocity in 1911. In the United States, similar discontents were expressed in the 'populist' movement, which provided a rhetorical vocabulary for Canadian farmers, while American immigration to western Canada supplied a number of leaders who called for a new political organization that was free from the influence of the 'eastern capitalists' and committed to truly democratic principles.

Despite farmers' relative prosperity during the Great War, they remained convinced that they were at the mercy of central-Canadian profiteers. Inflation, after all, affected farmers as much as anyone else. The farm country of English-speaking Canada had supported conscription, but with the understanding that farm labour would be exempt from its pressures. When Ottawa revoked this exemption in the spring of 1918, farmers, particularly in Ontario, became most resentful. The isolation of French-Canadian Liberals and the achievement of the Union Government in 1917, however, momentarily dampened prairie discontent, while opening the door to change in the two-party system. Farmers had high expectations for the coalition government, but only some of these were realized—such as the nationalization of the railways. In economic policy, two issues were important. One was wheat marketing, which during the war years had been done under the auspices of a national Wheat Board; the government abandoned the program in 1919, starting with the 1920 crop. The other was the tariff. Here the government temporized in 1919, and Crerar resigned as minister of agriculture over the issue, being joined in his vote against the budget by other western supporters of the 'bipartisan' Union government. In the two years immediately after the war, farmer discontent was not confined to the Prairie West. The United

Settlers from Colorado arriving by special train at Bassano, Alberta, March 1914. Glenbow-Alberta Institute, Calgary.

Farmers of Ontario formed a minority government in that province in October 1919, and farmers elected a half-dozen MLAs each in Nova Scotia and New Brunswick in provincial elections of 1920. Nonetheless, it was chiefly from the West that the new national party emerged in 1921, finishing the process of wiping out the traditional two-party system.

Whether the new Progressive Party could make anything of its success in the 1921 federal election was another matter. It won 64 seats in six provinces (37 on the Prairies, 24 in Ontario, one in New Brunswick, and two in British Columbia) and held the balance of power in the new federal Parliament. But eastern and western farmers did not see eye to eye on many issues, such as railroad rates and regulation, and—like other national third parties throughout the century—the Progressive Party failed to make any inroads in French Canada, collecting under four per cent of the popular vote in Quebec. Progressivism was very much Anglo-Canadian, perhaps even more than it was regional and occupational. The new party was also badly divided between two philosophies, one of which (exemplified by Crerar of Manitoba) sought to reform the existing Liberal party along low-tariff lines, while the other—best articulated by Alberta's Henry Wise Wood (1860-1941)—wanted to reject the existing party system and adopt an essentially occupational ideology centring on farmers' grievances. The only action that both

The 'dust bowl'—the Prairies in the 1930s. Agriculture Canada, Research Branch, Research Station, Lethbridge.

wings could agree on was refusal to become the official opposition in the Commons, although the party had won more seats than the Conservatives of Arthur Meighen. More divisive was the idea of coalition with the Liberals. When this possibility was ultimately rejected, the party was hopelessly trapped. Refusing to behave as a distinct party of opposition, and unable to achieve coalition with a minority government, it was condemned to being blamed by both traditional parties for the failure of the Fourteenth Parliament.

While a collection of inexperienced farmer-MPs—many of them committed to impossible political principles—attempted in Ottawa to deal with the political pirouettes of the new Liberal Prime Minister, Mackenzie King, economic conditions in western Canada continued to worsen. Two disasters struck almost simultaneously. First, in 1921 the bottom fell out of wheat prices, which dropped from over $2.00 per bushel to less than $1.00 for the 1922 crop. Second, drought conditions, which had begun in the later years of the war, refused to go away. The situation in the dry-belt region of southern Alberta and western Saskatchewan became desperate. Average rainfalls of under ten inches were accompanied by above-average temperatures, and no matter how farmers in the region operated, crop failure was virtually guaranteed. The result was a widespread inability to meet mortgage payments and foreclosure. Provincial governments struggled desperately to prevent farmers from losing their property and mortgage companies from losing their investments. In the end, neither effort succeeded, and much of the land in the dry-belt region reverted to the state for unpaid taxes. Credit facilities in the region virtually dried up, and one farm journalist reported in 1925 that 'it is today impossible to negotiate a desirable farm loan in the west.'[5] The spillover effect on towns and villages in the western farm country was substantial, and many prosperous places began to take on the appearance of ghost towns. The virtual collapse of the federal Progressive Party in the 1926 election was accompanied by the failure of the western farm economy. Many farmers were simply too disheartened to continue to fight, and some turned to less confrontational tactics, such as the co-operative movement.

The Maritime Rights Movement

A similar fate befell the Progressive Party's eastern protest equivalent, the Maritime Rights Movement. At the end of the Great War, which was followed by a slump, the three Maritime Provinces were faced with a veritable disaster, as they had been relying heavily on resource production that no longer had markets. Immediately after the war the region had toyed with a series of provincial farmer-labour coalitions that had achieved some brief success but not power, though they shared a sense of grievance, particularly in their deteriorating economic positions under runaway inflation. But the general international economic collapse of 1921 greatly weakened the unions, and led many Maritimers to believe that proper representation in Ottawa, especially in the ranks of the governing party, was more important than new political parties. Understandably, the farmer-labour parties found great difficulty in making common cause with western farmer organizations, particularly the Progressive Party; and the westerners, seeking free trade, failed to understand Maritime desires for increased protectionism. The government in Ottawa exploited these incompatibilities between the eastern and western peripheries of Canada.[6]

The Maritime region was acutely conscious of its increasing disadvantages within Confederation. Part of the problem was its lack of political clout. As the region's population base stagnated, and even declined in proportional terms, central and western Canada continued to grow. Early in 1920 the legislatures of the three Maritime Provinces agreed that only joint action—particularly on the contentious freight-rate issue—would serve the needs of the region. When the Canadian government sought to make the Intercolonial Railway begin to pay its own way, Maritimers protested that they could 'no longer successfully compete in the markets of Central and Western Canada which they are obliged to do to market their surplus production.'[7] By the end of 1921, farmer-labour support had drifted into the camp of the Maritime Rights Movement, which combined a drive for equitable freight rates with a variety of particular provincial demands, producing widespread public agitation. Unfortunately, farmer-labour allies were never able to agree on a tariff policy. In the 1921 election King's Liberals did extremely well in the region, chiefly because they alone sought to mobilize regional sentiment. But once elected, the Maritime Liberals found themselves with insufficient strength to influence party policy, continually seeing their demands sacrificed to the Prime Minister's need to appease the Progressives.

Eschewing the third-party route of the western farmer, the Maritime Rights leaders decided in 1923 to appeal to the remainder of the country over the head of Mackenzie King. Efforts were made to persuade Canadians through advertising and public relations that the Maritimes represented more than economic backwardness and old-fashioned political corruption. While that program would eventually have some success, it was far from enough. Martimers would have to abandon the Liberal Party and begin voting Conservative. This they did, starting with by-elections in Halifax, and in Kent, New Brunswick, late in 1923. Instead of attracting attention to the region's grievances, however, this voting pattern merely angered the Prime Minister, who continued to tailor government policy to meet the demands of the moderate Progressives and to refuse to deal with Maritime needs. By the 1925 federal election, when the shift to the Tories was virtually complete (23 of 29 seats), the King government offered nothing more than an investigation of Maritime grievances by a royal commission; then it proceeded to buy off the region as cheaply as possible through concessions on freight rates, subsidies, and port development. In the end, working through the two-party system achieved even less for the Maritimes than creating a third-party movement did for western Canada. Perhaps the inability of protest in the Maritimes and the West to find common ground made a significant point about the conflicting demands of the two regions, particularly on freight rates and tariffs. For the most part, however, neither side could see beyond regional interests. And regional political protest—which was kept divided— was unable to achieve anything much of substance.

Quebec 'Nationalism' in the Twenties

While the West and the Maritimes protested, relatively unsuccessfully, on the national level, Quebec turned increasingly inward in pursuit of a narrow nationalism (or provincialism) that was a reaction against its sense of isolation from the rest of Canada that had developed during the war. The chief outlet for the new nationalism was the journal *L'Action française,* founded in 1917 on the eve of the conscription crisis by the Ligue des droits de Français. This movement started out to save the French language, but gradually shifted to a broader-based agitation.[8]

The inspiration for both movement and journal was the Abbé Lionel Groulx (1878-1967). Born at Vaudreuil, Quebec, of rural parents, Groulx had begun his education in village schools and then was sent on to the seminary in Ste-Thérèse. He punctuated a career as a young schoolteacher and an ordained priest with three years (1906-9) of graduate study in France, where he imbibed most of the latest intellectual ideas of the time. A self-taught historian, Groulx was appointed in 1915 to the first chair of Canadian history at the Université de Montréal. His 'nationalism' was heavily tinged with racism, both in its attitude towards French Canada itself, and in its sweeping hostility to alien influences: '. . . it is this rigorously characterized French type,' Groulx insisted, 'dependent upon history and geography, having ethnical and psychological hereditary traits, which we wish to continue, on which we base the hope of our future; because a people, like all growing things, can develop only what is in itself, only the forces whose living germ it contains.'[9] To nurture this 'living germ', Groulx undertook to refashion the history of French Canada. The subordination of Quebec by a 'beneficial' British presence must no longer be accepted; the Conquest must be seen as a disaster and the history of French Canada as a constant struggle to survive in the face of oppression. Groulx's novel *L'Appel de la race* (1922)—which was published anonymously and was notorious in its day for its racist arguments—is about Jules de Lantagnac, a French-Canadian lawyer in Ottawa, who had been educated at McGill, and his wife Maud Fletcher, an Anglican who had converted to Catholicism to marry him and is a stereotype of the rigid Anglo-Saxon 'dominated by ethnic pride'. The novel reflects the tensions over Ontario's Regulation 17 (1912; revised 1913), which limited French instruction to one hour a day even for francophone students, and Lantagnac's response to this measure leads to the break-up of the marriage and the family of four children, two of whom go to each parent. This novel, and Groulx's other writings, were responsible for some of the excesses of French-Canadian historiography in the interwar period, including the cult of Dollard des Ormeaux (1635-60) as a nationalist symbol.*

Like many French Canadians—indeed, like many other Canadians—Groulx worried about the survival of traditional elements in the face of an increasingly alien and materialistic environment located 'in the middle of an immense Anglo-Saxon ocean.'[10] In the 1920s—when he shared in the sense of a post-war crisis—he continually denied that his arguments advocated separatism; but they nonetheless pointed in that direction. Groulx led the way in calling for a commitment to building the Quebec economy, using French-Canadian capital and skills to prepare for a future in which Confederation was broken up. He may only have wanted to be prepared for a political collapse resulting from other regional pressures, but he did wonder whether the British Empire was 'an organization of peoples which has become artificial, an outworn political formula, unable to sustain the shock of approaching realities.'[11] During the later 1920s Groulx's monthly journal

---

*In late April 1660 Dollard and sixteen other Frenchmen, and some Hurons and Algonquins, set out from Montreal to ambush Iroquois hunters coming down the Ottawa River, but at the foot of the Long Sault rapids they were discovered by some 300 Iroquois. They were besieged for a week before all the Frenchmen lost their lives. The cult portrayed Dollard as a national saviour.

L'Action française lost the support of many French Canadians as prosperity, and the return to federal power of Quebec, bled off much of the radical discontent in the province. Instead of commanding large crowds at public gatherings, Groulx was reduced to lecturing to relatively small classes at the Université de Montréal, as merely another university professor.*

∾∾∾∾ An Artificial Boom and a Depression

The wave of economic prosperity of the later 1920s was in large measure an artificial boom based on speculative activities in real estate, in the stock market, and in commodity futures. It was also encouraged by a substantial growth in new housing construction, mainly in the suburban areas of larger cities, and by a great wave of consumer spending on automobiles and various electrical appliances for the home, including radios, vacuum cleaners, washing machines, and phonographs. Not only houses and the goods to go in them but also automobiles were now for the first time in Canada financed on credit and promoted seriously by a newly expanded advertising industry. If the banks were reluctant to lend money on the security of an automobile, the automobile manufacturers were not. They therefore created their own finance companies to add to their profits. Just as the nation had mortgaged its collective future in the Great War, its citizens now mortgaged their individual futures by 'selling short' in the market and by borrowing substantial sums of money to buy consumer goods. Between 1926 and 1929 one company of Canadian stockbrokers—Solloway, Mills and Company Ltd, specializing in penny stocks to open the Canadian resource economy—expanded from one small office in Toronto to forty offices across the country, with more than 1,500 employees.[12] The newly minted millionaire became one of the folk-heroes of Canadian society. British Columbia alone could boast 83 millionaires, not one of whom, we are told, gave anything to a university or sponsored a major civic enterprise.[13] Some of the newly rich had made their money in the shadowy business of producing alcoholic beverages in Canada and distributing them south of the border, where efforts were much more serious to legislate prohibition than in Canada. Most important, Canadian law did not prevent the manufacture of booze for export; what was illegal was getting it into the United States. But fortunes were to be made here, as in many other industries. The Bronfman family of Montreal, the owners of Seagrams, has permitted its illicit activities in the prohibition period to be discussed only in tones of reverence.[14] Gambling became big business, particularly on sporting activities from boxing to soccer to horse racing.

---

*On the other side of the city, Stephen Leacock 'saved the empire three times a week' in his introductory political economy classes and was regarded by many McGill students as an increasingly old-fashioned 'fuddy duddy'.

But the good times could not last. Most Canadians, like their American cousins, have always associated the coming of the Great Depression with the stock-market crash of October 1929, when Wall Street led the way for a record collapse of stock prices that encompassed every North American exchange, including those in Canada.[15] The stock market was badly regulated, with a number of dubious practices. The best-publicized was the process of buying 'on margin', in effect on credit, in the expectation of further increases in prices of already over-valued stocks. Many speculators, including this author's grandfather, lost their shirts—and their paper fortunes—in the overnight collapse that reached panic proportions. Orders to sell could not be executed swiftly enough. But businessmen at the time did not regard the violent market readjustment of 'Black Tuesday', 29 October 1929, as necessarily related to the overall economy. Some had won and some had lost in the 'speculative orgy' that had now sorted itself out: the economy was fundamentally sound. Perhaps. But just as the boom of 1925-9 had been based on an upsurge of consumer and business confidence, the economic collapse was partly brought about by a lack of confidence.

The Depression that followed Black Tuesday was hardly a distinctive Canadian or even North American phenomenon. It was one of those periodic international economic turns, or cycles, that can be properly analysed only in terms of world-wide conditions. Though Canadian behaviour was not responsible for the downturn, Canadians certainly felt its effects because the Canadian economy was so closely tied to international resource and raw-material demands. In difficult economic times resources are the first commodities to be affected and the last to recover. The world-wide fall in prices—which had not readjusted from the inflation of wartime and the post-war period—seemed impervious to conventional national economic policies, and in their wake came decreased orders for the commodities in which Canada specialized. An international failure to buy left Canada and other major resource producers—such as Argentina and Australia—with a serious problem. Trade deficits mounted, and nations that owed Canada money were unable to pay. The dollar fell, and in 1931 so did a number of major Canadian financial institutions, brokerage agencies, and insurance companies. The country would not fully recover until after another war erupted, in 1939.

For most Canadians the depression of the 1930s was always the Great Depression. People lived in its shadow, and those who had experienced it had their own lives shaped by its message for decades to come. What the Depression meant, first and foremost, was unemployment. Official statistics are totally meaningless as a measure of unemployment's extent, much less its significance. According to the publication *Historical Statistics of Canada* (1983), reflecting contemporary government data, unemployment in Canada rose from 116,000 in 1929 to 741,000 in 1932 to 826,000 in 1933, ultimately declining to 411,000 in 1937 and increasing to 529,000 in 1939. It is virtually impossible to interpret these figures as a percentage of the total number of employable persons, not least because no farmers, or fishermen, or their families were counted among the ranks of the unemployed during the decade. Non-agricultural unemployment was something over 27 per cent in 1933, in the depths of the Depression; and when underemployment and the lack of work for women seeking to re-enter the workforce is added, it was probably closer to 50 per cent. Regarded as self-employed businessmen by the Canadian government, farmers or fishermen (and their families) merely lost money (and sometimes their 'businesses') during the Depression. At the same time, a farmer whose expenses exceeded his income was probably in better shape than an urban resident who had no job and whose expenses similarly exceeded his intake. Farmers at least had some land on which foodstuffs could be grown. In the 1930s many members of farm families who had gone off to the cities returned to the family farm, and the decade was the first since the 1880s—and the last—in which the rural population grew at about the same rate as the urban one.

Although the fall in prices meant that things were cheaper for the other 50 per cent of Canadians who continued to work throughout the Depression, wages also fell, and almost all of them held their breath each time payday rolled around. Yet for the half of the population who had steady incomes, life was reasonably good. Houses could be purchased for a song, and rented or leased at advantageous terms everywhere in Canada. In Montreal a private chef could be hired for $40 per month (plus room and board) at the height of the Depression, and laundresses who washed and ironed by hand in their own homes earned $2.00 a day.[16] While university professors took substantial pay-cuts, they did so from a typical pre-Depression salary of $3,000 per year, and were still able to afford a servant. In the industrial and resource sectors, the Depression was met by layoffs, plant and mine closures, and general retrenchment. Canadian business corporations actually suffered losses (or negative profits) only in 1932, chiefly because they had not responded quickly enough to the slump by laying off employees and limiting operations; in 1933—the lowest point on the economic curve—they ended up collectively in the black. Retrenchment was relatively simple: excess workers were fired or laid off. Large corporations, such as those in the Ontario automobile industry, rebounded so well that by 1937 they were above 1929 production figures. Small businessmen were obviously not in the same favourable position as the larger corporations, however, and many experienced bankruptcy.[17] The gradual recovery in the economy after 1935—with another slight slump in 1939—alleviated some of the distress experienced in the first half of the decade.

Farmers in the thirties were in serious trouble and remained so. The slump in international grain prices, which had begun long before the Depression, did fundamental harm to the agricultural economy, while continued drought and related dustbowl conditions made it difficult for many farm families to harvest a crop. Omnipresent dust became the desolate symbol for the Depression on the Prairies. At the same time, because farm problems had predated the current crisis and because farmers had long had their own organizations and political movements, provincial governments tended to respond sympathetically to their plight, although perhaps not as rapidly as they would have wished.

The real victims of the Depression were the urban unemployed, who found that their relief became the great political football of the thirties. Traditionally Canadian municipalities and private charities had looked after the poor and the jobless, but now the challenge was more than any city could handle, at least without the full co-operation and assistance of senior levels of government. Mackenzie King's notorious remark about not giving a five-cent piece to help a Tory provincial government relieve unemployment—which some thought cost him the election in 1930—suggested the partisan tensions that existed between the two levels of government. King's successor, R.B. Bennett (1870-1947), was apparently a kindly gentleman who often assisted, out of his own pocket, people who wrote begging letters to him as Prime Minister.[18] But he was also more concerned to end unemployment by manipulating tariffs than to relieve it by spending money on the unemployed, whatever his campaign promises. He had long opposed 'the dole system', resolutely balancing the federal budget and passing the buck to the provincial governments. They in turn passed it over to the municipalities, which had to balance declining revenue from property taxes against increasing expenditures on the unemployed and welfare. By 1933, for example, tax arrearages in Burnaby, BC, stood at 72 per cent of taxes levied, while arrearages for neighbouring municipalities stood at 64 per cent for North Vancouver City, 60 per cent for West Vancouver, and 144 per cent for North Vancouver District.[19] Tax sales proved increasingly impossible for want of buyers. Most municipalities distinguished unemployment rolls from relief rolls, regarding the latter as more permanent (and managing them more stringently). As one Member of Parliament vainly pointed out in 1930: 'Unemployment is created by conditions over which the municipality has no control whatever. [It is] merely the victim of circumstances.'[20] If municipalities were victims, so too were the recipients of their assistance. As James Gray (b.1906) recounts in his autobiographical account of life in Winnipeg during the Depression, municipal assistance to those in need was given grudgingly, almost always in the form of credit vouchers to be redeemed at local stores rather than as cash that might be spent on frivolities or worse. The relief lines were not called 'the dole' for nothing. Gray recalled that the radio was the last material possession held onto by many families, since it represented their principal enjoyment and contact with the outside world.[21] For the single unemployed male, most cities had nothing to offer them but advice to go somewhere else—perhaps to one of the work-camps organized in the frontier districts of the West.

(*Right*) Jobless men lining up for a free meal at a 'soup kitchen' in 1934. City of Toronto Archives, 1683.

(*Below*) Workers on Relief Project No. 27 inside their hut at Ottawa, March 1933. National Archives of Canada, PA-35133.

The relationship between the provinces and the federal government was certainly not a harmonious one during the Depression, although the constitutional wrangling over placing responsibility for assistance was unedifying and irrelevant to those Canadians looking for help. Throughout most of its term of office Bennett's government imposed tight controls on expenditures for the unemployed, arguing 'constitutional limitations'. Not until an election loomed did Bennett listen to those voices within his own party who pressed for a more active role. What he apparently found persuasive was the popular success that Franklin Delano Roosevelt had achieved in the United States with more dynamic policies; the rejection by the electorate of Herbert Hoover, another honest, upright conservative, was equally instructive. Influenced by his brother-in-law William D. Herridge (1888-1961), Canadian minister to Washington, Bennett converted to his own version of a 'New Deal'. He announced his new policy in a live radio address to the nation early in January 1935, saying: 'I am for reform. I nail the flag of progress to the mast. I summon the power of the state to its support.' He spoke of programs that echoed the sentiments of Stephen Leacock in 1919— legislation regulating working conditions, insuring against unemployment, extending credit to the farmer. Like Leacock, Bennett in 1935 had apparently come to appreciate that only an active state intervening on behalf of the working people could save the system of capitalism and the profit system that was its base. Unfortunately for Bennett, however, his radio proclamations ran well ahead of the practical legislative program he and his cabinet had ready for Parliament, and Canadian voters rejected the Prime Minister and his party in favour of Mackenzie King's Liberals, who had offered few rhetorical promises but had the solid backing of Quebec.[22]

Nevertheless, Bennett's 'conversion' to New Dealism symbolized more than political desperation. It also represented a growing realization by large parts of the Canadian business and professional communities that stabilizing the economy of the nation was necessary to prevent a more serious upheaval from taking place.[23] Broad sectors of the business community had responded to the Depression by seeking to reduce competition—always the aim of most businessmen within their own industries—through using government regulation of the market. Thus many Canadian businesses had been persuaded by the price-fixing schemes introduced in the United States under Roosevelt's National Recovery Administration (NRA), and advocated a similar agency in Canada. One speaker before the Canadian Pulp and Paper Association in 1934 argued:

> Our government might do well to consider some such scheme for the stabilization of Canadian industry, which could be brought about by the vesting in industry of certain powers and authority which would enable it through trade associations to control itself in all its main phases, working hours, wages, manufacturing and marketing.[24]

Most mainstream reform policies advocated during the Depression had considerable support among the business community, which saw these proposals as stabilizing alternatives to the economic and social chaos of the period. Some businessmen continued to oppose government interventionism, but many leading businessmen and financiers were statists—providing they could control the reforms and assuming that the expenditures made benefited their industries. As economist A. F. Grauer explained in 1939:

> Since the Great War, the Great Depression has been the chief stimulus to labour legislation and social insurance. The note sounded has not been so much the ideal of social justice as political and economic financial expediency. For instance, the shorter working week was favoured in unexpected quarters not because it would give the workers more leisure and possibilities for a fuller life but because it would spread work; and the current singling out of unemployment insurance for governmental attention in many countries is dictated by the appalling costs of direct relief and the hope that unemployment insurance benefits will give some protection to public treasuries in future depressions and will, by sustaining purchasing power, tend to mitigate these depressions.[25]

While he was prime minister, Bennett himself had advised: 'A good deal of pruning is sometimes necessary to save a tree and it would be well for us in Canada to remember that there is considerable pruning to be done if we are to preserve the fabric of the capitalist system.'[26]

Protest Movements of the Thirties

The system had to be preserved from an increasing series of attacks on it. While all were in some senses 'radical', not all came from the traditional left, associated with organized labour, socialism, and Communism. Few were truly national in either their outlook or their organization, being chiefly confined to particular provinces. These regional reactions said a good deal about the extent to which the federal level of government was considered responsive to public concerns. During the Depression, Canadians thought regionally or provincially rather than nationally. The federal government lost a lot of credibility in the 'Dirty Thirties', and the cause of Canadian nationalism was significantly retarded.

Social Credit in Alberta

One radical movement—not of the left—was the successful Social Credit Party in Alberta, where farmers in the dry-belt region of the Prairies had suffered most severely from drought and depression. Alberta farmers had been heavily hit by mortgage foreclosures throughout the 1920s, and the provincial government run by the United Farmers of Alberta had tried many expedients to control the damage wrought by the credit institutions of the province. Albertans were thus inherently hostile to banks and mortgage companies, and quite responsive to the ideas of a Calgary radio preacher, William G. Aberhart (1878-1943), who since 1924 had used his Sunday broadcasts for the Prophetic Bible Institute over CFCN (the most powerful radio station in Canada at the time) to build up a substantial personal following attracted to Protestant fundamentalism. In 1932 Aberhart added a secular dimension to his broadcasts following his conversion to the economic ideas of a Scottish engineer named C.H. Douglas.[27]

The most dynamic part of Douglas's philosophy was its monetary theory, which held that capitalism intrinsically maintained a permanent deficiency of purchasing power among the masses. The credit system, in the hands of bankers, was not concerned to utilize the productive system to its fullest extent. Douglas advocated distributing money, in the form of 'social credit', to make it possible for people to buy the goods and services produced. Here was Leacock's riddle of social justice, the existence of 'Poverty in the Midst of Plenty', which became one of Aberhart's major slogans. Aberhart never thoroughly understood Major Douglas's economic theories, and he assured his Alberta audience that they need not understand them either. But from them he derived a practical platform that emphasized the need for the state to make up the difference between the purchasing power of consumers and the total costs of production by issuing 'social credit' as a national dividend to all citizens as part of their cultural heritage. This social dividend was eventually set by Aberhart at $25.00 per month.

With the assistance of Ernest Manning (b. 1908), Aberhart organized the Social Credit Party early in 1935, and its leadership came from those previously politically inactive. The new party swept to success at the polls, despite criticisms of its program from the traditional parties, taking 56 out of 63 seats and winning 54 per cent of the popular vote.* It would maintain public support and credibility over the next few years in the face of vehement opposition to its legislative program—particularly mortgage, debt, and banking legislation—from the dominion government and the federal courts, which ultimately disallowed thirteen Alberta acts. The Social Credit government in Alberta would thereafter move to more traditional (and conservative) fiscal practices, blaming Ottawa and eastern big business for its failure to enact its program. The federal activity against Aberhart's legislation stood in marked contrast to the Mackenzie King government's generally cautious attitude in dominion-provincial relations. But the preacher's popular success simply demonstrated that attacks on the existing capitalist system could come from those who wished to return it to some sort of pristine purity as well as from those who wished to eliminate it.[28]

Maurice Duplessis and the Union Nationale in Quebec

Among regional or provincial political responses to the Depression, Quebec presents an interesting problem. The political movement that emerged there was constructed out of distinctly French-Canadian elements, but its overall

---

*Under Aberhart, and following his death in 1943 under Manning, Social Credit won nine successive elections in Alberta and governed the province until 1971.

patterns of response were not appreciably different from those in Alberta, or even Ontario. Not only did a popular political leader emerge—with all the trappings of a demagogue—but there was a good deal of searching for convenient scapegoats and offering of simplistic solutions within a highly paternalistic framework.

The new leader was Maurice Duplessis (1890–1959), son of a small-town lawyer in Trois-Rivières. The Duplessis family were active Conservatives, and the young man from the outset had only one ambition: to be Premier of Quebec.[29] He trained as a lawyer, and all his energies were spent on politics and politicking. In 1933 he became leader of the province's minority Conservative Party without having committed himself to any particular position on Quebec's growing economic and social crisis. Duplessis knew that the Quebec Conservatives were too fragmented to win an election, and he sought new directions and allies. He found them in two burgeoning Quebec movements of the early 1930s: the Catholic social action of the École sociale populaire and the Liberal radicalism of the Action libérale nationale (ALN).

Catholic social action proposed an alternative to socialism that attempted to reconcile the need for reform with the teachings of the Church. It was critical of 'capitalism' and supportive of government intervention to redistribute wealth, protect farmers and workers, and regulate large corporations in the interests of all. Capitalism, argued Father Louis Chagnon, needed to 'be subject to the Christian law of justice and charity, socially managed, and directed by government action and the organization of professionals.'[30] From the ALN Duplessis took a program of economic nationalism. Quebec's problem was that it was owned by 'foreigners', so that the inferior status of French Canadians was not so much a class matter as it was one of colonial oppression. Most Quebec nationalists could agree on the need to preserve traditional rural virtues and '*l'achat chez nous*'* in order to support small-scale French Canadian industry, but the ALN merged Quebec nationalism with the new Catholic reform. It wanted agrarian reform, new labour legislation, the promotion of small industry and commerce; but it also sought 'to destroy, by all possible means, the hold that the great financial establishments, the electricity trust and the paper industry have on the province and the municipalities.'[31] It sought banking regulation and a government not clandestinely linked through shareholding and directorates to the capitalist system.

Duplessis negotiated with the ALN (which won 26 seats in the 1935 Quebec election) an agreement to form a new party, the Union Nationale. It would be composed of both the ALN and the Conservatives, and would campaign on the ALN's reform platform. The new coalition party swept to an easy victory in the 1936 election, winning 76 seats and 58 per cent of the

---

*This slogan of small businessmen (translated as 'buy from our own') had an anti-Semitic sub-text that lost its currency in the late 1930s when fascism became so threatening.

Maurice Duplessis attending a bridge opening at Ste Thérèse, Quebec, 18 August 1946, with the Most Reverend Joseph Charbonneau, Archbishop of Montreal. Three years later, in May 1949, the two men came into conflict over the Asbestos Strike. National Archives of Canada / *The Gazette*, Montreal, C-53641.

popular vote. Duplessis, now premier (or 'prime minister') of Quebec, quickly purged his government of ALN people and quietly abandoned the reform program that had brought him to power. What remained were the shards of the old platform: a concern for provincial autonomy in federal-provincial affairs, anti-Communism (expressed in Duplessis's infamous 'Padlock Act' of 1937 that closed any place where it was suspected that communism was being propagated), and paternalistic grants and handouts for the disadvantaged, carefully calculated to achieve maximum electoral effect. Duplessis did not approve of the closed shop, and his labour legislation essentially imposed settlements from above if they could not be achieved through collective bargaining. Like Social Credit in Alberta, the Union Nationale in office was quite different from what its campaign promises had suggested it would be. But, as in Alberta, once in power the party was extremely difficult to dislodge.

The Antigonish Movement in Nova Scotia

In the eastern-shore and Cape Breton regions of Nova Scotia another movement arose that reacted to the Depression in a non-revolutionary way.[32] These regions were composed mainly of farmer-fishermen, small producers who controlled production but not marketing and distribution. The population was largely made up of the descendants of Catholic Scottish Highlanders. The Antigonish Movement was begun by two extraordinary Roman Catholic priests at St Francis Xavier University in Antigonish: Father James J. ('Jimmy') Tompkins (1870-1953) and Father Moses Coady (1882-1959). Cape Breton's depression had started long before 1929, and its population was as ripe as Alberta's for some sort of social catharsis. Tompkins and Coady provided it, with the latter supplying a theoretical formulation in a book entitled *Masters of Their Own Destiny* (1939). The industrial revolution, Coady maintained, had taken economic power away from ordinary people, and capitalism had failed. The capitalists were not to blame; the system had a weak foundation, however, and needed reconstruction. The solution was for small producers to regain power over their own production and consumption through economic co-operation. The need was for co-operative banks, stores, and marketing agencies, and the Antigonish Movement built gladly on earlier examples provided by farmers. It established its first credit union in 1932 and attempted to help a region to survive.

The ideology of Antigonish, like western populism, was a curious mixture of radical rhetoric and conservative attitudes, well suited to a population of individualistic small producers. Thus it criticized the 'bourgeoisie' as economic parasites, but insisted that it did not advocate class warfare. It was not socialistic and opposed labour unions, deriving much of its strength from humanistic principles of the Catholic Church that were not always shared by the Church's hierarchy at the time. But Coady insisted that the workers owned whatever they produced, and that any outside attempt to claim ownership was exploitation.[33] In its own way the Antigonish Movement— which swept across the Maritimes in the thirties—was wrestling with the unsolved riddle. Like Social Credit, it demonstrated the need and desire of the victims of economic depression in Canada for some kind of transforming solution to their problems. In its consciousness-raising transcendence of the existing capitalist system, the movement may have prepared the way for more radical measures among a very traditionalistic population. But Antigonish did not advocate political activism, much less support parties to the left, such as the CCF.

The CCF

To the problems created by the Great Depression, the most important alternative political response based in the socialist tradition came from the Co-operative Commonwealth Federation (CCF). It was founded in Calgary in 1932 as a coalition of farmers' organizations, labour unions such as the Canadian Brotherhood of Railway Employees, and labour-socialist parties in the four western provinces. Its platform, however, was provided by another socialist group that formed earlier and grew out of the concerns of thinkers like F.H. Underhill, professor of history at the University of Toronto, that

F.R. Scott, *c.* 1941. Photograph by John Steele, Toronto.

Eugene Forsey in the late 1930s. Courtesy Margaret Forsey.

mass unemployment and hardship presaged an economic breakdown. He received the support of many colleagues—including F.R. Scott (1889-1985) and Eugene Forsey (1904-91), who taught at McGill, David Lewis (1909-81), a law student there, and J. King Gordon (1900-90), professor of Christian Ethics at the United Theological College in Montreal—and in 1931 they formed the League for Social Reconstruction (LSR), with J.S. Woodsworth as honorary president and Frank Scott as president. The declaration of principles that was approved at the first convention in Toronto in January 1932 deplored the fact that 'In the advanced industrial countries [the present capitalist system] has led to the concentration of wealth in the hands of a small irresponsible minority of bankers and industrialists whose economic power constantly threatens to nullify our political democracy.' It stated that the League would work 'for the establishment in Canada of a social order in which the basic principles regulating production, distribution and service will be the common good rather than private profit'—by substituting 'a planned and socialized economy for the existing chaotic individualism'.[34]

The LSR was heavily influenced by British socialism, particularly the wing that was led before the First World War by Sidney and Beatrice Webb and Bernard Shaw, the leading exponents of Fabianism. The Fabian Society (it took its name from Quintus Fabius Maximus, nicknamed 'the Delayer') was founded in England in 1884. Fabians believed in the gradual conversion of society to socialism through what Shaw called 'permeations' of the body politic by indirect influence. They were proudly non-Marxist and non-revolutionary, although vehemently committed to a welfare state and the takeover by the state of key industries.* These general goals were shared by the LSR, which considered itself to be an educational organization.

The inevitable connection between the LSR and the CCF was made through individual LSR members who became active CCFers. Before the first annual CCF convention took place in Regina in 1933, Underhill was asked to prepare a statement of principles and a program for the new party. He did so, in collaboration with some of his LSR colleagues—using the LSR manifesto as a model— and the famous Regina Manifesto was the result. It promised a heady brew of political reform and action once the CCF came to power. All industry 'essential to social planning' would be nationalized, the former owners suitably compensated. A series of universal welfare measures—hospitalization, health care, unemployment insurance, pensions— would be introduced after amendments had been made to the British North America Act. The 'Co-operative Commonwealth' it defined as 'the full system of socialized planning'.[35] The Regina Manifesto, in its emphasis on the need to place social planning in the hands of 'public servants acting in the public interest and responsible to the people as a whole', harked back to the days of the Progressives. (Indeed, the latter's 'Ginger Group' were among its founders.) In choosing the party's leader the Regina meeting compromised between its academic and popular membership—who were not entirely sympathetic—by appointing the former Methodist minister James Shaver Woodsworth. Pacifist, idealist, and moralist, Woodsworth had since 1921 (two years after the Winnipeg General Strike, in which he participated) led a small cadre of labour-supported MPs in Ottawa.[36]

The new party attracted over 300,000 votes in the 1933 British Columbia provincial elections, more than 30 per cent of the popular vote. The *Vancouver Sun* described its platform in Sir John A. Macdonald's phrase, 'Something to get in on—not to stand on.'[37] But while this support brought it seven provincial seats and made it the official party of Opposition, Liberal Duff Pattullo (1873-1956) took thirty-four seats and formed the government. On the national level, in the 1935 election the party obtained 8.9 per cent of the popular vote, which translated into seven CCF seats—including one held by T.C. Douglas (1904-1989) of Saskatchewan. Woodsworth himself led the new MPs into the House, convinced that the CCF was 'a distinctly Canadian type of socialism'. While the party had high hopes of future success after its

---

*The Fabian Society assisted in the formation of the Labour Party, which elected 29 members to the British Parliament in 1906. In 1922 it became the official opposition and in 1924 it formed its first ministry.

J.S. Woodsworth speaking at a meeting of unemployed. One placard behind him reads: 'Work and Wages NOT Relief'. National Archives of Canada, C-55451.

early showings both provincially and federally, during the thirties it would flourish only in a few provinces (especially BC and Saskatchewan) and would not attract broad-based national support.[38] Quebec refused to support anything that smacked of secularistic socialism, but that response was to be expected. More significantly, Alberta's discontent with the system was swept up by Social Credit at the provincial level, and Cape Breton's potential support was eased away by the Antigonish Movement.

The Communist Party of Canada

The nation's politicians and businessmen grimly viewed the CCF as a movement on the radical left, completely failing to appreciate that the new party provided a far more restrained left-wing alternative to the only genuinely radical party in existence in the early years of the Depression: the Communist Party of Canada, which became a legal party in 1924. At the outset of the Great Depression, only the Communist Party had offered an organized outlet for Canadian popular discontent, creating in 1930 a National Unemployed Workers' Association that by the next year had attracted 22,000 memberships across the nation. The Communists, however, operated under several serious disadvantages. One was the charge that they were 'un-Canadian' members of an international conspiracy, and it was true that most

On-to-Ottawa trekkers, 1935. City of Toronto Archives, James Collection, 2181.

of the party's leaders were strongly influenced by the Communist International. But it was equally true that the party was badly divided into any number of factions with varying attitudes towards Moscow. Yet another disadvantage was the willingness of the Canadian government to repress the party in any way possible, using Section 98 of the Criminal Code, introduced in 1919 at the time of the first 'red scare' to outlaw the advocacy of revolutionary agitation. Thus eight Communist leaders were arrested in August 1931; they were easily convicted and sentenced, but were gradually released from prison after continual demonstrations on their behalf.[39]

Nevertheless, the party had lost its momentum at the grass-roots level during the battles of its leaders with the government and the courts, and never recaptured it, becoming instead increasingly affected by rapidly changing instructions from the Comintern and by events in Europe. The Communists were credited in 1935 with organizing, through the Workers' Unity League, a mass march on Ottawa known as the 'On-to-Ottawa' trek. The trekkers came out of the unemployment relief camps in BC, where single unemployed young men found their only refuge. Conditions in the camps were often degrading, and not even the Communists themselves claimed that the outbreak of trouble was anything but spontaneous. The trek began in Vancouver, and was halted by the RCMP at Regina. A delegation of eight trekkers was allowed to take grievances forward to Ottawa, but the talks broke down and they returned to Regina, where the Mounties moved in, waving 'baseball bat batons', and a riot ensued, involving 500 Mounties and local police and hundreds of trekkers. Downtown Regina was reduced to a shambles and 120 protesters were arrested. Most of the remainder accepted offers of passage back home. In 1937 many Canadian Communists were attracted into the European struggle between the Communist-supported Republican government and Franco's fascists in Spain, joining the Macken-zie-Papineau Battalion that was mustered into the XVth International Brigade.

Popular Violence

While the thirties were punctuated continually by outbreaks of public discontent that often turned to violence, two points must be made about that violence. The first is that with most of the spontaneous demonstrations—even the march on Ottawa—the bulk of the damage to person and property resulted from the efforts of the authorities to break up what were regarded as ugly crowds. When men from the relief camps gathered in Vancouver in April 1935, they were orderly for days before starting a demonstration and breaking some showcases in the Hudson's Bay Company store. They then marched to city hall, where Mayor Gerry McGeer (1888-1947)—convinced the city was 'being victimized by an organized attempt to capitalize, for revolutionary purposes, the conditions of depression which now exist'—read them the Riot Act, touching off street battles between police and protesters.[40] The second point is that much of the violence of the period resulted, as might be expected, from confrontations between organized labour and the authorities. These gained in intensity and frequency after 1937, when economic conditions had improved and workers attempted to organize industrial unions to represent those in large factories. One particularly nasty series of incidents occurred in April 1937, when more than 4,000 workers in the large General Motors plant in Oshawa, Ontario, struck for an 8-hour day, better wages and working conditions, and recognition of the new union of United Automobile Workers (UAW), an affiliate of the recently formed Congress of Industrial Organizations (CIO), which was organizing throughout the US. Premier Mitchell Hepburn (1896-1953), who sided with General Motors in its refusal to negotiate with the CIO, clashed with the prime minister over King's refusal to send RCMP reinforcements for the local police (the premier organized volunteers, Hepburn's Hussars). General Motors eventually agreed to most UAW demands, while not recognizing the CIO (though the settlement was widely seen as a CIO victory). Hepburn's tenuous relation-ship with the Prime Minister broke down, and he resigned as premier of Ontario in 1942.

The Second World War and Economic Recovery

The obvious tensions between Ottawa and the provinces during the 1930s, as well as the failure to resolve the constitutional constraints of the British North America Act during a time of economic emergency, led the federal government to appoint a Royal Commission on Dominion-Provincial Relations in 1937, chaired first by Newton Rowell (1867-1941) of Ontario and then by his successor Joseph Sirois (1881-1941) of Quebec. Taking two-and-a-half years to deliberate, the Commission did not report until May 1940, when the nation was once again at war. Its research had been extensive, and its conclusions were relatively clear-cut. The Rowell-Sirois report stated that, despite the division of responsibilities in the British North America Act, regional or provincial governments could not maintain expensive functions such as providing for the unemployed. It recommended that the federal government take over certain taxation powers (including taxes on personal incomes) from the provinces, relieving them of their debt burdens by providing adjustment grants. Seeing the reform of dominion-provincial relations almost entirely in fiscal terms, the Commission proposed a quite profound, and more equitable, restructuring of public finances that would not be implemented until after the war.

Embarkation of the 1st Division Canadian Active Service Force (CASF), Halifax, December 1939.

The entry of Canada into the Second World War on 10 September 1939 began the completion of a process of economic recovery that had started in 1935. The country was not prepared militarily; but, as in the First World War, it mobilized resources remarkably swiftly when war was the objective. The British Commonwealth Air Training Plan (BCATP) had been quickly accepted by Canada as its principal war commitment, and the details of the scheme were agreed to by Britain and Canada on 17 December 1939. Within months the BCATP's first graduates emerged from Camp Borden, Ontario, and it eventually graduated 131,533 Commonwealth airmen, 72,835 of whom were Canadian, at a cost of $1.6 billion. A country of less than 12 million people would eventually put over one million men and women into uniform and, using the War Measures Act, succeed in mobilizing its economic resources in a way that had seemed impossible during the Depression. The economy was totally managed and regulated, so that by 1943 unemployment was well under two per cent, a figure regarded in most quarters as representing 'full employment'. Federal spending rose from 3.4 per cent of the Gross National Product (GNP) in 1939 to 37.6 per cent of GNP by 1944—a full $4.4 billion in that year. Industrial growth was better distributed across the regions than in 1914-18, inflation was controlled, and consumption was regulated. Canada's total GNP rose from $5.6 billion in 1939 to $11.9 billion in 1945, and Canada became one of the world's major industrial nations, producing 850,000 motorized vehicles and over 16,000 military aircraft. Of Canada's war production, only about one-third supplied the Canadian forces, with over half going to other countries of the Empire.[41] The government not only spent more money, but it also collected much more in taxes and borrowed heavily, chiefly from its own citizens in the form of war bonds. While Canada's achievement was on one level a great economic success story, it strongly suggested that the problems addressed by Stephen Leacock in 1919 had not yet been resolved. Canada appeared far more capable of efficient utilization of its productive capacity to fight external enemies than to battle the domestic ones of poverty and unemployment.

The man most closely identified with Canada's wartime production was Clarence Decatur Howe (1886-1960), a ninth-generation New Englander who had moved to Canada in 1908, at the age of 22, to teach engineering at Dalhousie University in Halifax. He left the university in 1913 to design elevators for the Canadian Board of Grain Commissioners, and in 1916 formed his own successful engineering firm. In 1935 he entered federal politics and was elected to a Liberal seat for Port Arthur (Thunder Bay), Ontario. He was soon appointed minister of transport in Mackenzie King's cabinet. In November 1939 Howe took over the task of mobilizing defence production, and he became minister of the Department of Munitions and Supply (DMS) in April 1940. Chiefly at Howe's instigation, DMS moved quickly into government manufacturing, in preference to private enterprise, developing a new entity, the Crown corporation, to do the job. Before the

The Consolidated 'Catalina' flying boat—the Canso amphibian—in production at Canadian Vickers, Montreal.

The 9th Canadian Infantry Brigade landing at Bernières-sur-Mer, France, on D-Day, 6 June 1944. National Archives of Canada, PA-137013.

was over 28 Crown companies had been created by Howe under DMS. He also insisted that Canada could produce any wartime commodity the nation needed, and encouraged private enterprise to bid on defence contracts. Howe managed to get away with autocratic and peremptory behaviour under the exigencies of wartime, and his most notorious quips—'What's a million?' and 'Who would stop us?'—entered political lore. But his vision of post-war prosperity for Canada was real enough when, as Minister of Trade and Commerce after the war, he converted Canada's economy to a free-enterprise system.[42]

As in the Great War, Canadians fought well whenever called upon; and, as in the previous conflict, they were often employed as shock troops. In the disastrous landing of the 2nd Canadian Division at Dieppe in August 1942, of the 5,000 Canadians who embarked, nearly 2,700 were killed or captured. The Dieppe raid became a classic example of military bungling because the Canadian troops were sent into combat under circumstances that almost guaranteed disaster. On the other hand, the eagerness of Canada's armed forces in Britain to get into the thick of things contributed to the failure of its leading officers to protest effectively the British planning for Dieppe.

The First Canadian Army, formed in 1942 under the command of General A.G.L. McNaughton (1887-1966), was composed of five divisions that were eventually split up between Italy and Northwest Europe. (Canadian casualties in Italy were heavy, with 18,500 soldiers dead, missing, or wounded.) McNaughton,* and his successor General H.D.G. Crerar (1888-1965), maintained close consultation with Ottawa in deploying these troops, except in matters of grand strategy. On the other hand, the Royal Canadian Air Force (RCAF) and Royal Canadian Navy (RCN) were pretty well integrated into their British counterparts. Most RCAF personnel joined RAF units, though Canada eventually sent 43 squadrons overseas. The RCN, which grew to 365 ships, spent the war mainly protecting convoys on the North Atlantic route, achieving such expertise in this duty that by May 1943 a Canadian, Admiral L.W. Murray (1896-1971), was given command of the Canadian Northwest Atlantic theatre. For the most part, however, the Canadian military machine was led by inexperienced officers—which was understandable, considering that Canada's pre-war military complement was very weak—and this was the major criticism levelled by its allies.

Canadian assistance to American and British efforts in the Pacific and Southeast Asia was largely token, occurring for the most part in the last few months of the war against Japan. In October 1941, however, two Canadian battalions set sail for Hong Kong to reinforce the British garrison there. Japan attacked Hong Kong on 7 December (the same day it attacked Pearl Harbor). Hong Kong fell on Christmas Day with 290 Canadians killed and almost

---

*McNaughton was appointed Minister of National Defence in November 1944.

double that number dying in the Japanese camps. (The 1,421 who returned home were forced to fight for 23 years to win proper veteran's benefits from the Canadian government.) Despite Canada's declaration of war against Japan in the wake of this disaster, its commitment until the end of the war was almost entirely in the Atlantic/European theatre in support of the British.

As in the Great War, casualties were heavy: 42,642 Canadians lost their lives. Since most of these losses occurred in the later years of fighting, when it had become clear that the Allies were winning, the total casualties were perhaps a little easier to accept than in the First World War, when they had a less discernible explanation.

The War and Domestic Politics

In six years Canada had gone from mass unemployment and general hardship to relative prosperity and a booming economy. And with the third largest navy, the fourth largest air force, and an army of five divisions, it had also become something of a power in the world—a transformation that, sadly, it had taken a global conflict to achieve.

The internal politics of the war revolved around two major questions: conscription and French Canada, and the twin issues of social policy and post-war reconstruction. As in the Great War, the extent of support for the war effort was not evenly balanced among Anglo and French Canadians. The differences were clearly revealed in a national plebiscite held on the question of conscription in the spring of 1942. While the nation voted 2,945,514 to 1,643,006 to release the government from an earlier pledge not to conscript for overseas service, Quebec voted strongly against this option. Public-opinion polling (a new wrinkle imported from the United States) indicated that most French Canadians were willing to fight to defend the country at home, but not to serve overseas. However, there were 50,000 French-Canadian volunteers in the army, over half of whom served in anglophone units. The issue emerged again in 1944, when the military insisted (as in 1917) that it was necessary to ship overseas conscripts who had been drafted with the promise that they would not be required to serve abroad. Prime Minister King accepted the resignation of his minister of defence, J.L. Ralston (1881-1948), over the question as a symbol of his concern, and then allowed conscription to go ahead when the new minister, General McNaughton, was unable to find enough volunteers.

Conscription, and the whole question of Quebec, probably seemed less urgent politically to the government of Mackenzie King than the increasing threat from the left posed by the CCF. By 1941, two years into the war, the mood of much of English Canada was quite different than it had been at a similar point in the previous war. Many Canadians had apparently come to realize that during the interwar period neither constitutional nor technical reasons had stood in the way of a more concerted assault on the 'unsolved riddle of social justice'. The problem was the essential unwillingness of

The War Committee of Mackenzie King's cabinet. Seated l. to r.: C.G. ('Chubby') Power, T.A. Crerar, King, J.L. Ralston, J.L. Ilsely. Standing l. to r.: A.L. Macdonald, J.E. Michaud, C.D. Howe, Louis St Laurent.

governments to act, since they were now demonstrating in the wartime emergency how well they could mobilize the country if they so desired. The shift began first, perhaps, in British Columbia, where the Liberal government of Duff Pattullo was devastated in a late-1941 election. British Columbia remained out of the hands of the CCF only by the expedient of a coalition of the two traditional parties. But overall public support for the CCF grew significantly in 1942. While weak in Quebec and the Maritimes, it was very strong from Ontario westward. In early 1942 Arthur Meighen attempted to return to Parliament after having been chosen leader of the Conservative party for the second time. He ran as a strong conscriptionist in a by-election in York South and was badly beaten by an obscure schoolteacher named Joseph Noseworthy, who ran on a platform of winning both the war and the subsequent peace. Between the federal election of 1940, when the CCF had received 8 per cent of the popular vote, and September 1943, when it had attained the support of 29 per cent of the electorate in the polls, Canadian public opinion had significantly shifted. Even the Conservative Party sensed the new wind and replaced Meighen as leader with John Bracken (1883-1969), the long-time premier of Manitoba, who insisted that the party rename itself 'Progressive Conservative' and adopt a platform of social reform.

In a 1944 election in Saskatchewan, a long-serving Liberal government was wiped out and replaced by a CCF one led by Tommy Douglas, giving the CCF its first ministry, albeit a provincial one. The election debate in Saskatchewan had been chiefly about social services and federal policy that discriminated against the ordinary Canadian. Saskatchewan was enough to change Mackenzie King's thinking. He had previously held out against reformers within his own party who had long advocated the wholesale introduction of social-welfare measures. But the Prime Minister now understood the political urgency of such a policy. Most political pundits agreed that the CCF was for the first time successfully polarizing Canadian politics, and could see that it was drawing much of its support from Liberal rank-and-filers. It would have to be politically outflanked.

In theory King had supported social welfare since the First World War. Beginning in 1939 his government had accepted the necessity for deficit spending to promote recovery from Depression conditions, thus adopting the new orthodoxy put forward by John Maynard Keynes in his *General Theory of Employment, Interest and Money* (1936). King's minister of finance, Charles Dunning (1885-1958), in his defence of the new policy in the Commons, made clear that the government did not regard public spending as a 'substitute for private enterprise'; but he also emphasized that if business would not spend, then government must as a matter 'of sheer social necessity'. In 1940 the government introduced unemployment insurance, and King's reconstruction program included family allowances and proposals for health insurance. But the time had not been ripe to introduce such measures. Now, in 1944, it was. King declared in the House of Commons in July 'a wholly new conception of industry as being in the nature of social service for the benefit of all, not as something existing only for the benefit of a favoured few.' The introduction of social reform was necessary not only to steal ground from the CCF, but also to prevent possible public disorder at the conclusion of the war. The two matters were of course related, for the CCF had been gaining ground on the strength of its willingness to press ahead with 'post-war reconstruction'.[43]

Once the decision had been made at cabinet level to implement social reform, there was little problem in producing the necessary legislation. The Great Depression had already created the required climate of public opinion—one favourable to the concept of 'social security' advocated by men like Stephen Leacock in 1919—and remembering the social unrest that followed the First World War, the Canadian government was concerned about post-war planning almost from the outset of the conflict. Part of the result was the well-known 'Report on Social Security for Canada', tabled in the House of Commons Special Committee on Social Security by economist Leonard Marsh (1906-82) in 1943.[44] His report—which exemplified the

T.C. (Tommy) Douglas at the founding convention of the New Democratic Party in July 1961, when he became its first leader. National Archives of Canada, C-36219.

increasing employment of Canadian academics during and after the war in preparing policy documents for government use—went further than the King government would go in 1944 and 1945, calling for a scheme of national health insurance as well as the more acceptable unemployment insurance, old-age pensions and retirement insurance, and children's allowances. But King and the Liberals had introduced enough social-security benefits to regain power in 1945 and to save Canada from a turn to socialism, such as Britain experienced in that same year.

The 'unsolved riddle of social justice' was finally being attacked seriously by Ottawa, although whether the King government was prepared to go far enough fast enough was another matter. That the Liberals saw reform within capitalism as an alternative to socialism was perfectly plain, however, and the results of the 1945 election suggested that most Canadians agreed.

chapter seven

Canadian Society and Culture, 1919-1945

In the warm spring days of late May 1934 the family of Oliva and Elzire Dionne achieved headlines around the world. The Dionnes were a French-Canadian Roman Catholic farming couple living in northern Ontario between Callander and Corbeil, just east of Lake Nipissing. Like many family farms during the Depression, theirs lacked plumbing and electricity, though the Dionnes were not as poor as their neighbours—they owned 195 acres, a car, and had five children. Now, in one stroke, the Dionne children were doubled in number when Elzire gave birth to identical quintuplets—the third set recorded before hormonal tampering, and the first to live beyond a few days. Curiously, the acclaimed person in this miracle was not Elzire Dionne, who had borne the children, but Dr Allan Dafoe (1883-1943), the middle-aged small-town physician who delivered them safely and kept them alive during their first precarious days. For a generation of Canadians, Dafoe became a mythic figure through his portrayal on radio and in Hollywood films by Jean Hersholt. The Dionne parents, for their part, became semi-villains, who appeared to stand in the way of a better life for their children.[1]

Complex questions of benevolence, public responsibility, professional expertise, and private poverty soon swirled around the photogenic quints. The Province of Ontario swiftly removed the children from the control of the impoverished and somewhat stunned Dionnes, who were helpless before the importunities of the media and of crass commercialism. Ontario managed the quints as a major provincial asset and tourist attraction, putting nearly a

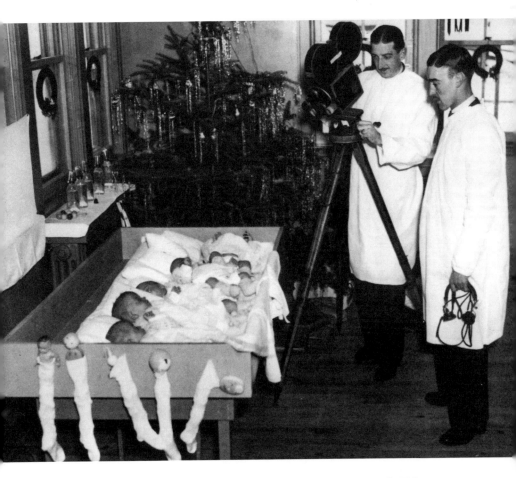

The Dionne quintuplets at the time of their first Christmas, 1934. Photo–Canada Wide.

million dollars aside in a trust fund built on strategically authorized commercial endorsements, and moving them away from their family into a specially equipped hospital under the care of Dr Dafoe. By early 1935 the quints were declared wards of the Crown, though a horde of specialists would contend for years over control of their upbringing. Almost ignored in the sorry drama were the interests and concerns of the Dionnes themselves.

In a period when the birth rate was in a slump, the birth of five children at one time was a truly newsworthy event, providing the media and public alike with a long-lasting topic of universal interest. And it gratefully superseded another child-related news sensation of two years before: the kidnapping and murder of the son of the American aviator Charles Lindbergh. When being poor was so commonplace, it was somehow reassuring to know that the state occasionally interposed itself between poverty and its innocent victims.

Yvonne, Émilie, Cécile, Annette, and Marie would soon join the ranks of Depression moppets, the most famous of whom was Shirley Temple. As a compelling mixture of 1930s hoopla and poverty, nicely seasoned with professional management, the Dionne story was hard to beat. It demonstrated the extent to which the entertainment media had taken over, in Canada as elsewhere.

Demographic Trends

For more than half a century before 1919, Canada had been involved in the gradual transition from developing frontier nation to modern industrial nation. All Canadians were aware of the most apparent changes: the rapid growth of cities, the eventual decline of rural population, the appearance of factories. What they did not so clearly appreciate were the major demographic changes in Canadian society that operated beneath the surface, and that reflected the shift in buried but extremely profound ways. The failure of the federal government, until 1921, to begin accurate national record-keeping assisted in disguising the profundity of the transition, while the enormous burst of immigration between 1896 and 1913 also helped to prevent the new demographic realities from becoming too apparent. Even before the war, some commentators had begun to emphasize one of the major themes associated with the new society: the collapse of the family as the fundamental unit. To some extent the perceived change in the family unit was more a moral than a statistical point, and it was of course associated with significant alterations in the legal and practical status of women. The Great War contributed variations on that theme, and the ensuing decades added their own particularities.

But the demographic patterns that characterized Canada between the wars were not, in overall shape, very much different from those that affected all industrialized and 'advanced' countries of the world. First, mortality rates declined, then fertility rates. The extent to which the fall in the birth rate reflected a new attitude on the part of women is not entirely clear, but the two were plainly related in some way. Certainly increases in divorce were associated with changes in the legal status of women. But there was a wild card in the Canadian demographic situation (which had existed in the past, and would be even more evident in the future): immigration.

The Death Rate

For some time before 1921, particularly in the critical area of infant mortality, the death rate had been steadily declining. But among infants it took another major drop (after the nineteenth century) in the course of the 1930s, and the overall death rate drifted perceptibly downward throughout this period, with the standardized death rate (after controlling for age structure of the population) dropping from 12.9 per thousand in 1921 to 9.9 per thousand in 1946, and the median age at death rising from 41.3 for males and 43.5 for females in 1921, to 63.1 for males and 65.3 for females by 1946. Canadian society had begun to produce substantial numbers of older people beyond the age of working, so that the rise in concern for old-age pensions in this period was hardly accidental. The difference in life expectancy between males and females of this era would only widen in subsequent years. The decreasing death rate (for both adults and infants) was associated with a variety of factors, including an improved standard of living—making possible declines in fetal mortality as well as in infant deaths—and better medical treatment. Better sanitation and an increased medical ability to control contagious disease were also significant factors. In 1921-6 pulmonary and communicable diseases were among the top causes of death in Canada. Over 270 out of every 1,000 deaths were due to these diseases, but after the Second World War such fatalities dropped to just over 60 of every 1,000 Canadian deaths. Cardiovascular problems, renal disease, and cancer had become much more important killers. Nevertheless, Canadians in these years were living longer—despite the Depression and the war—and this fact pressed in different ways on society's needs and capacities to deal with its population.

The Birth Rate

Related to changes in mortality were profound alterations in fertility patterns. Increased urbanization made large families less desirable. And by receiving into the work-force married women, who found it difficult to work and care for small children, industrialization played its part. Declines in infant mortality, particularly during the thirties, meant that couples were producing fewer babies—not more to ensure living children. And many women realized that there were alternatives to the traditional child-bearing function: more women over thirty began to limit their number of births, practising some form of contraception. Birth rates, which began to fall in Canada before 1919, continued their fall in the twenties and thirties, recovering only in 1941 from an extremely low point in the mid-1930s, to increase sharply after 1945. Ironically enough, while the medical and health improvements of modern industrial society maximized the span of child-bearing years for most women, many chose to have small families or no children at all. Thus Canadians exulted in the birth of quintuplets—but managed to find ways not to honour their mother, who had somehow broken an unwritten rule. The age of marriage for both males and females dropped after 1921, but this did not greatly increase fertility rates. The number of marriages dropped between 1929 and 1932 from 77,000 to 62,000 annually, but gradually recovered throughout the rest of the decade.

One important differential was between Quebec and the remainder of Canada, for the birth rate in French Canada remained significantly higher (although sharing in a general decline) throughout this period. Another difference was between urban and rural, with substantially greater birth rates in the latter. A third differential occurred between Catholic and Protestant, although certain subgroups within the Protestant ranks (Mennonites, Mormons) had higher rates than the overall Catholic population. Finally, as we shall see, birth rates remained substantially higher among native peoples than within the general population.

Divorce Rates

If mortality rates and fertility rates fell persistently in Canada over many years, merely continuing well-developed trends in the period before 1945, substantial increases in divorce rates were a relatively new characteristic of this period. Before the First World War the total number of divorces in Canada in any given year was remarkably small. There were divorce laws in existence, in some provinces predating Confederation and in others extended by judicial decision to provincial courts. But the grounds for divorce were extremely limited and quite inequitable. Thus before 1925 males could dissolve a valid marriage on grounds of adultery alone, or obtain annulment because of impotency, while in most provinces women had to establish adultery plus some other abuse (such as incest, bigamy, rape, sodomy, desertion, or cruelty). After 1900 an increasing number of marriages were ended by the courts through judicial separation, but this strategy did not allow parties to remarry. The divorce laws were not reformed at all until 1925, and then only partially, because of strong opposition in Parliament from the Quebec members and from others concerned to uphold the sanctity of the family.

Even before reform, the social upheavals of the Great War had increased the incidence of divorce. Immediately after the war many suits were brought by wives who were able to demonstrate that their husbands—usually while serving abroad in the Canadian forces—had added one or more other causes to the standard one of adultery. For their part, husbands sued for divorce because wives had made other arrangements and liaisons during their absence. The year 1918 saw only 114 divorces in all of Canada, a rate of 1.4 per 100,000 people; but the number increased greatly in 1919 and 1920 and slowly but inexorably continued to grow thereafter. In 1925 a revision of the divorce laws made it possible for a wife to obtain a divorce on grounds of adultery alone, although the proof of such action was quite stringent. Not in 1925—nor in 1930 or 1938, when divorce was again debated in Parliament—were other causes such as insanity, desertion, or extreme physical cruelty found acceptable without adultery. Ontario courts obtained divorce jurisdiction in 1930. After that year, in cases of desertion a wife could bring suit for adultery in the province of the husband's last residence; but if he hadn't deserted her, she could sue only in the province of the husband's present domicile, regardless of her own residence. By 1929 the divorce rate had reached 8.2 per 100,000, rising to 18.4 per 100,000 in 1939 and to 65.3 per 100,000 by 1947. There were strong regional differentials, caused partly by the fact that divorce for Quebec residents was possible only upon application to the Parliament of Canada. Throughout the period, and especially during the Great Depression, most marital dissolutions never reached a court and resulted from desertion of the wife by the husband. Nevertheless, the Second World War brought another substantial increase in the number of divorce cases heard before the courts.[2]

Exceptions to the Rules: The Native Peoples

Not all Canadians exemplified the overall demographic trends, and no group deviated from them quite so extensively as the native peoples. While Ottawa could evade direct responsibility for the plight of the unemployed by insisting that social welfare was not a federal responsibility, Canada's treaty Indians and Inuit were wards of the federal government. Many groups had signed treaties with the government by which they surrendered title (or at least control) of their lands in return for guaranteed assistance and protection. The final treaty was signed in 1923 in northern Ontario. The federal Indian Act (which first came into force in 1876 and was frequently revised) specified who was and who was not a status (or 'legal' or 'registered') Indian eligible for government support. Only about half the native population came under the Act, and hence under the supervision of the Department of Indian Affairs; the Métis, among others, were excluded. The Inuit (and to some extent Indians) living in the Territories came under the separate jurisdiction of the Department of the Interior's Northwest Territories and Yukon Branch. The treaties and the Indian Act combined to turn at least the status Indians into an isolated rural people, far removed from the centres of population on remote reserves of land considered marginal. Many Métis and non-status Indians lived in urban areas, but the very structure of the Indian Acts insisted, almost dictated, that status Indians live in bands on reserves, chiefly located in the North.

Until 1960 it was impossible to obtain sufficiently precise statistics about Indians and Inuit to talk about their demographic characteristics. The Bureau of the Census did not isolate such data, and neither Indian Affairs nor Interior collected it. This vagueness in itself tells us much about the government's attitude towards native peoples between the wars. Not until the 1940s (and later) did the governments of Canada respond to pressure, mainly from native peoples themselves, for more than token involvement with their affairs.[3] Between the wars, apart from the handouts guaranteed by treaty and by legislation, government concerned itself with native peoples chiefly by encouraging the establishment of boarding schools off the reservations. The number of native children enrolled in such schools was the chief statistic proudly publicized by Indian Affairs, as a perusal of *Canada Yearbooks* for the period quickly illustrates. Public-health care in the isolated northern regions inhabited by native peoples was virtually non-existent, particularly during the Depression, when budgetary cutbacks affected all government departments.

Given these factors, it was hardly surprising that population trends within the native population would deviate substantially from national norms. Indian birth rates, for example, were considerably above the national average. Under-recording of births at the time masked the difference to some extent, but recent scholarship has calculated the Indian crude birth rate of the interwar period to be something over 40 per thousand, while Canadian rates were closer to 20 per thousand.[4] Unlike overall Canadian rates, which were those of industrialized and urbanized modernity, Indian and Inuit fertility was that of a developing nation. High by modern standards, it was capable of going much higher still at the first sign of improved living standards. The birth rate for native peoples would jump to near 60 per 1,000 by the 1950s.

The other side of fertility was mortality. Death rates among native people were astoundingly high, nearly four times that of the overall Canadian population in this period. In 1929, for example, with a Canadian death rate of just over 10 per thousand, the figure for status Indians was 39.7 per thousand. Infant mortality ran at more than twice the national average, with 200 deaths per 1000 births among native peoples in 1940, while in all of Canada infant deaths ran well under 100 per 1000.[5] In addition, a large number of native mothers died in childbirth, with one study showing 21.8 per cent of all female deaths in this period attributable to this cause.[6] Before 1940 less than two per cent of Indian births in the James Bay region of Quebec were in hospital, with more than half the babies delivered at home and over 40 per cent in the bush.[7] In addition, Indians suffered two to three times more accidental deaths (more common among males) than Canada's non-native population, and a very high suicide rate. Accidents were second only to 'combined diseases' as the major cause of death among Indians.

Before 1940 most Indians and Inuit died of communicable rather than chronic diseases, with tuberculosis the big killer. In British Columbia in 1938, for example, Indian deaths from TB were 8.1 per 1000, while for the remainder of the population in the same area such deaths ran at 0.45 per 1000.[8] Nutritional surveys in the 1940s indicated that Indians in northern Manitoba and James Bay were deficient in both caloric intake and vitamin nutrients, which contributed to a susceptibility to many communicable diseases.[9] However, native peoples on the whole were relatively free of several modern health problems. Their teeth showed little evidence of decay because they did not eat much sugar, and heart disease and cancer were not prevalent among these northern populations—partly because their life expectancy was so much shorter. In the context of demographic characteristics, Indians and Inuit plainly lived in a different Canada from the majority of the population.

Most Canadians' impressions of Indian life had their source in Hollywood movies or the writings of a few popular romanticizers. Chief among these writers was Archie Belaney (1888-1938), the Englishman who had been adopted by the Ojibwa and assumed the name Grey Owl, producing bestsel-

Grey Owl with Anahareo, his
companion from 1926 to 1934, at
Squatteck, Quebec, 2 November
1929. National Archives of Canada,
C-28198.

ling books about life in the bush—*The Men of the Last Frontier* (1929),
Pilgrims of the Wild (1935), and *Tales of an Empty Cabin* (1936)—that stressed
Indian communion with nature. 'For we are Indian, and have perhaps some
queer ideas,' Grey Owl wrote in *Pilgrims*, 'yet who among you having a faith
of any kind, will deny us our strange fancies and tell us we are wrong, or say
us no.'[10] The message of his writings was not so much wrong about the native
relationship with nature—he was an exceptional naturalist and environmen-
talist—as one-sided in its approach. The vital statistics told a different story
about Indian life.

Other Demographic Factors

Immigration between 1931 and 1945 fell to the lowest point it would ever
reach in the post-Confederation era. Some attempt was made immediately
after the Great War to find land for demobilized imperial soldiers through the
Empire Settlement Act of 1922, which brought 120,000 British immigrants
into the country, and 185,000 Central Europeans were brought by the
railroad companies in the mid-1920s. But public opinion reflected in government policy was not favourable to immigration in these years. Many Canadians felt that as most agricultural land was now settled, new arrivals would
compete for jobs and alter the ethnic composition of the population. Immigration dropped to an average of just over 124,000 per year during the 1920s,

and then to around 20,000 per year during the thirties. The government discouraged all immigration during the Great Depression except that of farmers with substantial capital, and during the years 1930-3 it even deported over 23,000 residents who were charged with 'undesirability', some of them for political reasons and others because they were held to be 'public charges'. There were also Canadians who decided that a future outside Canada— especially in the United States—held more promise; and Canada actually had a net loss of population from migration during the decade 1931-41. Canada operated its immigration policy on a 'preferred nation' basis, discouraging new arrivals from outside the ranks of the 'founding peoples' and demonstrating hostile indifference to immigrants from non-European nations.

The result of this period of minimal immigration was to encourage assimilation of the non-founding peoples who had arrived between 1896 and 1913 into the two major linguistic/cultural groups that made up the nation, although most such findings would show up only in the 1951 census—and beyond. The number of Canadians speaking languages other than English or French dropped off precipitously, and many surnames were adjusted to new cultural conditions.* Moreover, since immigration had long supplied a new population that was gender-skewed (predominantly male), the fall in immigration allowed a more evenly balanced male/female ratio to emerge in most provinces. During this period of linguistic and cultural consolidation, the numbers of francophones outside Quebec declined everywhere except in New Brunswick. And far more francophones than anglophones were bilingual.

Although the trends recorded by the 1941 census were not major ones, this census was the first to show that more Canadians lived in urban rather than rural places: there had been a substantial increase in urban population during the 1920s. The 1941 census was also the last one in which a pattern of continual growth in total rural numbers was maintained. The 1951 census would document fewer rural dwellers than in 1941, and the decline was even more significant for the farm population of Canada, which having fallen slightly between 1931 and 1941, would drop substantially and constantly thereafter.

The Child-Care Experts

Like the middle classes whose aspirations they attempt to satisfy, experts have always been rising—and advising. Each generation sees its intellectual and technological breakthroughs translated into new categories of professionals with new skills and pretensions. What is important is not that experts

---

*One of the most graphic presentations of the thrust for assimilation of these years is contained in John Marlyn's novel *Under the Ribs of Death* (1957).

rise, but the particular body of experts that becomes fashionable, heeded, and admired in a given historical period. Between the wars in Canada, the most respected experts were those who worked in child care or performed other services relating to children: doctors, schoolteachers, guidance counsellors. Such people had been developing their territory since the 1870s, but only after the Great War did they really come into their own. Canada's most famous medical figure in this era was Dr Frederick Banting (1891-1941), the instigator and member of a research team, which included Charles Best (1899-1978), at the University of Toronto that in the winter of 1921-2 discovered insulin as a treatment for diabetes mellitus, a disease that tragically affected young people as well as adults. Dr Alan Brown (1887-1960), a renowned pediatrician who was chief physician of the Toronto Hospital for Sick Children, halved the infant mortality rate there. He was a co-developer of Pablum, the first pre-cooked vitamin-enriched cereal, which was marketed internationally in 1930 (with proceeds going to the hospital's Pediatric Research Foundation). In 1925 Dr William E. Blatz (1895-1964) founded the Institute of Child Study, at the University of Toronto, to explore children's psychological development. The birth of the quintuplets, and their well-publicized supervision by Dr Dafoe, increased interest in child care.

Charles H. Best and Sir Frederick Banting on the roof of the Medical Building, University of Toronto, with one of the dogs in which they arrested diabetes by using insulin. University of Toronto Archives.

There were complex reasons for the emphasis on children, and for the unquestioned respect, bordering on reverence, for those who dealt with them. One was the fact that medical science was making a number of well-publicized breakthroughs that were cutting deeply into infant mortality and childhood diseases. Reduced birth rates meant that children deserved greater attention. Another input was the much-discussed breakdown of the traditional family under the pressures of industrialization, new moralities, and during the thirties economic hardship. Those professionals who addressed the problems caused by family disintegration were performing socially useful work. A third factor was the heavy toll taken on the generation of young men who had died in the trenches of the Great War. All Canadians hoped that the next generation would have a better chance at life than the Class of 1914-18, and viewed those attempting to improve those odds, particularly under the trying conditions of the Depression, as peacetime heroes and heroines. The mentality of the Great War itself, with its concern for selfless commitment to the state, also played a role here. In 1917 a British Columbia meeting of health officials had been told: 'The child is the asset of the State, and all conditions should be arranged as far as possible to get the best results from that child. . . . We do not want inferior products turned out that may or may not answer the purpose, but as perfect a thing as can be produced; something to be proud of; something with stability and quality, that can be used for the purpose of development and advancement and for protection, if need be, of the State to which it belongs.'[11]

While most Canadians were probably unaware of the concentration on the 'appropriate' upbringing of youth by the Soviets, the Italian Fascists, and the German Nazis—and would have denied any connection between these authoritarian tendencies and those in Canada—the interwar years saw almost everywhere in the world an enormous public and private investment in the welfare of the young. Canadian society did not quite indulge its young—that breakthrough would come only after the Second World War—but it was heading in that direction. The experts had already identified a new stage in growing up: the adolescent, who inhabited the years between puberty and full adulthood. The Depression prevented these adolescents from coming into full flower, except in relatively prosperous families that could afford to encourage them to stay in school beyond the leaving age of 16 and send them to university. During the thirties, less than half of Canada's 16-year olds were still in school, but as soon as times improved young people clearly would be required to obtain more education.

Much of the ideological baggage of the emerging experts came from the newly respectable social sciences, particularly psychology. Attempts at formulating a science of the mind went back a long way, as far as Plato and the ancient Greeks, through the Renaissance into the seventeenth-century psychology of the senses developed by John Locke, and on to a host of nineteenth-century schemes such as mesmerism, spiritualism, and phrenology.

Sigmund Freud had added another whole dimension to the enterprise with his discovery of the unconscious level of the mind beneath the superficial one; more controversially, Freud insisted that the basic drive of the unconscious was sexual. The Russian scientist Ivan Pavlov introduced the notion of conditioned learning through repetition of stimuli. The American philosopher John Dewey combined the long-standing concerns of education for the inculcation of moral virtues with the new psychology of personality development. He insisted that educators needed to be concerned with the 'whole child' rather than with simple academic subjects taught through memorization and intimidation.

Examples of all these influences could be found everywhere in child-rearing advice and educational practice between the wars. Infant sexuality was seen as a normal part of the developmental process, not to be 'repressed'. Children could be toilet-trained at a very early age by not very subtle adaptations of the experiments of Professor Pavlov with his dogs. In schools the 'progressive' ideas of John Dewey were advocated against traditionalist educators and administrators by a generation of reformist teachers who complained about the mechanized quality of the older process. The problem was that in the hands of the unimaginative, progressivism could be equally mechanical, and even more insidious. The Alberta Department of Education's 'Programme of Studies for the Elementary School', for example, stated in 1942: '...the proper adjustment of the personality of the school child is another of our educational objectives. The school has a two-fold function— it holds before him the attitudes, standards, principles which have society's approval, and provides a supervised social situation in which these behavior tendencies can be realized and undesirable patterns inhibited.'[12] The seeds of post-war 'conformity' were being well planted.

✐ New Technologies

The Automobile

Despite the nation's uneven economic record between 1919 and 1945, Canadians in these years experienced an increase in the rate and nature of technological change. The use of new technology was most evident in the mass adoption of the internal combustion engine in the form of the automobile and the tractor. Before 1910 automobile ownership had been almost entirely an urban phenomenon, but by 1920 it had become more general. In 1904 there were fewer than a thousand motor vehicles in Canada; in 1918 there were half a million. From 1918 to 1923 Canadian manufacturers, allied to US companies, were the second-largest car producers in the world and made Canada a major exporter. By 1930 only the United States had more cars per capita than Canada. One significant feature of the automobile was that it was individually owned and operated as an extension of a private

A Toronto traffic jam in 1924. The motorists are out for a Sunday drive on the newly built Lakeshore Boulevard. City of Toronto Archives, James Collection, 2530.

household, representing private rather than public transportation. No other single product operated so insidiously against communalism as the automobile. It also had tremendous spin-off consequences, not merely in the industrialization required to manufacture it but in its secondary impact on both the Canadian economy and Canadian society. For example, the automobile required roads, and provincial governments that had neglected road-building obligations during the railroad era were forced to reassume them. Road mileage in Canada grew from 385,000 miles in 1922 to 565,000 miles in 1942, with much of the construction undertaken in difficult physical and economic conditions. Motorists wanted not only roads but surfaced ones, and the thirteen per cent of roads surfaced in 1922 gradually increased over the ensuing decades, although nearly two-thirds of Canadian roads in 1945 were still of earth construction, and gravel was regarded as an improvement. Only Australia had a greater road network per capita than Canada. Gradually the extent of the road network cut into the railroads' passenger business, and into their freight business as well. Automobiles ran on petroleum products; and not only did they encourage petroleum production (chiefly in Alberta), they also created the gasoline station and the garage as new service industries. In addition, people travelling by automobile needed to eat, drink, and even sleep. The result was the growth of restaurants and rural hotels, even primitive motels, to serve a newly mobile population.

Door-to-door mobility—rather than the station-to-station kind that had characterized the railroad/streetcar era—was one of the principal effects of the automobile revolution. The car made possible a new round of suburban expansion and greatly reduced the isolation of rural farm families, who were now able to pile into their Model-T or Model-A Ford to visit friends or to get to the nearest city. While the automobile provided an important source of tax revenue for both federal and provincial governments—with Ottawa imposing a 1% sales tax on automobiles in 1922 and an excise tax in 1922, often stepped from 5% to 10%, depending on the price of the vehicle; and the provinces collecting about 20% of their total budgets from gasoline taxes and various fees—neither level of government made any serious effort to impose rules on the use of motor vehicles, aside from some fairly minimal regulations and the issuing of drivers' licences. The pre-war attempt of Prince Edward Island to prevent the introduction of passenger motor vehicles into its jurisdiction—through legislation voted by the provincial legislature in 1908 and partially revoked in 1913—was significant mainly for its uniqueness. The car quickly became the symbol of North American independence and individualism, as well as serving as a combination status and sex symbol.

Most technological innovation and change in Canada progressed relatively unregulated by government in this period. No technology had more implications for provincial governments than the automobile, for road construction was a provincial responsibility under the British North America Act. Most jurisdictions, however, shied away from the implications of the automobile even in matters such as roads and bridges, and refused adamantly to touch the machinery itself. Despite its importance, the automobile—made of up to 20,000 parts—was produced entirely according to manufacturers' standards and consumer desires. The vast world of electrical appliances similarly had no national controls imposed upon it beyond minimal levels of standardization regulated by the manufacturing industry itself. Consumer protection was not a recognized public principle, and the buyer had to beware. In this world of private enterprise radio was unusual: the broadcasting of programs was regulated, though not the receiver.

Radio

The transmission and reception of sound via radio waves had been developed as a technology before the First World War, initially as an aid to ships at sea. The war saw improvements, and radio began to take off after the armistice. The production of radio sets led the federal Department of Marine and Fisheries to attempt to license their use, chiefly because most early radios were both receivers and transmitters. But supplying radio owners with a signal to listen to was an obvious way to go, and in 1919 the Canadian

This photograph, though staged, conveys the avid interest in radio in 1935. For those who could afford one, the receiver was a large piece of livingroom furniture, like the walnut-veneer cabinet of this Canadian General Electronic radio. Canadian Motion Picture Bureau/National Archives of Canada, C-80917.

Marconi Company had a transmission station in operation in Montreal. By 1929 eighty-five broadcasting stations were operating in Canada under various ownerships. The Canadian government regulated wave-lengths to prevent interference, but did not initially attempt to control broadcasting itself. It eventually became involved in the broadcasting question chiefly because Canadians spent much of their time listening to more powerful American stations, which by the late 1920s were organized into networks with national programming originating from the entertainment capitals of New York and Los Angeles. Private radio broadcasting in Canada was not all bad, but it was most uneven and not well financed.[13]

A royal commission on broadcasting—the Aird Commission, appointed in 1928 and reporting in 1929—recommended the nationalization of radio to foster national unity and to be financed by listener licences, parliamentary grants, and indirect sponsorship. Its advice was not immediately taken. Private broadcasters campaigned against the Aird Report until the Canadian Radio League, a citizens' lobbying group organized by Graham Spry (1900-83) and Alan Plaunt (1904-41), persuaded the government of R.B. Bennett to introduce the Broadcasting Act of 1932, which led to the formation of the Canadian Radio Broadcasting Commission to establish a national network and to supervise private stations. In 1936 this Commission became the Canadian Broadcasting Corporation, with extensive English and French networks.[14] The CBC had to contend with nearly insuperable obstacles, ranging from limited financial resources to competition from American programming featuring far more popular entertainment emanating from New York and, more and more, from Hollywood. Only its hockey broadcasts and current-events programming—such as the 1936 abdication speech of Edward VIII, and wartime news broadcasts—drew truly impressive audiences. But beginning in 1943 the English network managed to air literally thousands of radio dramas—including those in the famous Sunday night 'Stage' series produced by Andrew Allan (1907-74) from 1944 to 1956—written and acted by Canadian talent, and even earlier it had begun to broadcast innumerable concerts of live music both classical and popular, commissioning a good many works from Canadian composers. In the realm of the national encouragement of Canadian culture, the CBC was not only pre-eminent in this period, it often seemed to stand virtually alone.[15]

✐ Canadian Nationalism

The creation of the CBC was the major domestic institutional response, albeit a tardy one, to a resurgence of Canadian nationalism during the 1920s, particularly in English-speaking Canada. The Great War may have been fought for the Empire, but its course and outcome were to make Canadians more conscious of their country's distinctiveness, particularly where Great Britain was concerned. In the 1920s Canadian nationalism had a dual purpose: both to reflect a new international status and to control both the receding British and the rising American tides of culture.

The painter Arthur Lismer wrote: 'After 1919, most creative people, whether in painting, writing or music, began to have a guilty feeling that Canada was as yet unwritten, unpainted, unsung. . . . In 1920 there was a job to be done.'[16] That job was not only to write books and paint pictures that captured the true Canadian spirit, but to organize national cultural organizations that would mobilize a new sense of national consciousness. The postwar period saw the establishment of several Canadian magazines and journals to serve as vehicles for Canadian ideas. These included the *Canadian Bookman*, founded in 1919, and the *Canadian Forum*, the *Canadian Historical Review*, and the *Dalhousie Review*, which were all founded in 1920. The readers of these journals tended to come from a relatively tiny élite of academics, artists, and journalists. Only the Association of Canadian Clubs, reorganized in 1925 and 1926, had any claim to popular support, with 40,000 members in 115 local clubs by 1930. The Canadian Authors' Association (1921)—whose 800 members included many hopeful writers who were not professionally employed as such—backed campaigns promoting Canadian writers, proclaiming on one poster: '700/Canadian Authors/ in our Wonderful Canada/ Have you read their books?'[17] The Association also sponsored summer schools on Canadian literature and attempted to get literary prizes established, although it was not until the mid-thirties that it succeeded in persuading the Governor-General, Lord Tweedsmuir—the famous Scottish novelist John Buchan (1875-1940)—to establish the prestigious Governor-General's Awards, which the CAA launched in 1937.

By the 1920s it was indisputably clear that Canadian cultural nationalism, especially in English-speaking Canada, would have to confront American popular culture, which was expanding its influence at a rapid rate. While Canada had long imported much of its culture from abroad, it had usually achieved some kind of balance between the United States and Great Britain. That balance was now broken in a number of areas, including periodical publications. By 1929 Canadians spent $100 on American magazines for every dollar on British ones, and imported eight magazines from the United States for every one printed at home. The four leading Canadian magazines—*Maclean's, Chatelaine, Mayfair, The Family Herald and Weekly Star*—had circulations within Canada that were less than half those of their popular American counterparts, although in 1929 *Maclean's* had the largest circulation of any magazine in Canada at 160,000 copies per monthly issue.[18] Canadian periodical publishers attempted desperately to stem the tide, but with little success. Efforts to maintain low postal rates on second-class mail failed in 1922. A year later the House of Commons agreed unanimously that 'it is desirable that measures should be adopted to encourage the publication of Canadian magazines and periodicals', but the politicians could not agree on how to implement such a generality.

Later in the decade the publishers, through the Magazine Publishers' Association of Canada (MPAC), pressed for a protective tariff against American imports in order 'to build up a strong Canadian literature, a matter of first importance to Canadian unity, the preservation of Canadian tradition and ideals, and the development of a national consciousness.' The MPAC was opposed initially by the newsdealers of Canada, and later by book publishers. *The Grain Growers' Guide* insisted that lower tariffs on raw materials were a more effective way to encourage Canadian publishing. One statement of opposition to protectionism read:

> It is utterly impossible to conceive that an English speaking population or a French speaking population of five million or less could maintain any large number or any wide range of high grade magazines. For that reason it would be nothing short of national tragedy for the Canadian people to cut themselves off from the privileges which they now enjoy in the way of periodical literature without any possibility of it being replaced by home productions. It would be nothing more or less than a heavy tax or a prohibition upon the dissemination of knowledge.[19]

To some extent the struggle was between those in central Canada who were still residually British-Canadian (and anti-American) and those in western Canada who found far less to fear from American influence than their eastern counterparts.

In the end, the only action on the tariff issue taken by the King government was the reduction of duties on some types of paper in 1928. When Bennett's Conservative government, which took office in 1930, did bring higher tariff protection into the publishing industry, it was probably less for cultural than for fiscal reasons. The results, perhaps not surprisingly, were substantial increases in Canadian periodical circulation during the early 1930s and corresponding decreases in American, combined with an increase in American branch-plant publishing. Canadian policy was protectionist during the Depression, but that position was justified by economic necessity rather than by nationalism. During the thirties Canadians were concerned about more urgent matters than national identity.

Popular Culture

Between the wars Canada's love affair with American popular culture blossomed. During the 1920s radio, motion pictures, and the great expansion of professional sports all represented Yankee incursions into the Canadian consciousness. In sport the loudest critics of creeping Americanization usually operated from some sort of pro-British perspective. The cult of amateurism in sport had long been associated with the English 'gentleman', and terms like 'commercialism' and 'professionalism' had become pejorative codewords for Americanism. The foes of American popular culture did not concede without a fight, but they could not find a ground on which to stand.

In the world of film, Hollywood's success was also in a curious way Canada's, since there was no shortage of Canadian talent in the formative years of Tinseltown. What happened, of course, was north-south integration and the disappearance of Canadian talent into the great American marketplace. Mack Sennett, Sidney Olcott, Louis B. Mayer, Jack Warner, Walter Huston, Mary Pickford, Norma Shearer, and Marie Dressler were all Canadian-born. Pickford, Warner, and Mayer founded three of the major Hollywood studios between 1919 and 1924. In this period Canada had only the shards of a Canadian film industry, comprising mainly the seven films produced by Ernest Shipman, of which *Back to God's Country* (1919) is a Canadian silent-film classic. Otherwise film-making in Canada was confined chiefly to newsreels and documentaries that were appended to American features. By 1922 American studios were including Canadian receipts as part of domestic revenue, and in 1923 the leading Canadian cinema chain, Allen Theatres, was taken over by Famous Players' Canadian Corporation, a subsidiary of Mary Pickford's former studio. Thus at the height of the silent-film era Hollywood succeeded in gaining a stranglehold on the distribution of film in Canada.

Other nations around the world took some sort of defensive action against the Hollywood juggernaut, either placing quotas on imported films or providing tax incentives to native productions. Canada did neither, contributing to a ceaseless outflow of talent nurtured at home and seeking the brighter lights and better opportunities that existed elsewhere. In 1922 Raymond Massey (1896-1983)—son of one of Canada's richest business families, brother of a future governor-general—made his acting debut at the University of Toronto's Hart House Theatre (named for his grandfather). Soon after he went to England, where he began a long and distinguished career, becoming in the next decade a star in British films and the London theatre, and on Broadway. Canadians enjoyed the irony of his achieving international acclaim playing the greatest American President in *Abe Lincoln in Illinois* (1938) on the New York stage and in the Hollywood movie (1939). In fact, this was a double irony, for Massey's film portrayal of Lincoln had been preceded by that of another Canadian, Walter Huston (1884-1950), in 1930. So closely were Americans and Canadians identified.

During the Great Depression, when the Dream Factory provided blessed release from the cares and woes of everyday life for millions of Canadians, that dream was very clearly American, even when the content was supposed to be Canadian. Hollywood made hundreds of films with Canadian settings—particularly the North and West, and especially about the Mounties—which allowed for the introduction of some favourite stereotypes: the Mountie who always gets his man, fearsome Indians (usually Blackfoot), and the wicked male halfbreed (always half French Canadian, always with a moustache, and usually wearing a toque). *Rose Marie* (1936)—in which Nelson Eddy plays a singing Mountie—is probably the best-remembered of these films. Cecil B. DeMille's epic *North West Mounted Police* (1940) was about the Riel Rebellion of 1885 and the massacre at Duck Lake. (A memorable still from the film shows Paulette Goddard, playing a Métis, with a knife clenched between her teeth.) The battle is fought in 'absolutely authentic' costumes against the geographically impossible backdrop, for Saskatchewan, of the Rocky Mountains; and Hollywood, which could never quite decide how Mounties' uniforms really looked, gave many of them fur hats, as though they were worn all year round. But Canadians of the time were uncritical of such inaccuracies, enjoying the film for itself—as they enjoyed portrayals of the American semi-fantasy world of gangsters and gun molls, along with Shirley Temple (who starred in her own Mountie film, *Susannah of the Mounties*) and other tots who cavorted through Hollywood films of the thirties.[20]

Canadians played a much more influential role in hockey. The National Hockey Association (NHA) was formed in 1909 in eastern Canada, and on the west coast, where hockey had been slower to take hold, Frank and Lester Patrick, in 1911-12, formed the Pacific Coast Hockey League, which defeated an NHA team for the Stanley Cup in 1915. In 1917 the National Hockey League (NHL) was formed out of the NHA. The Pacific Coast Hockey League folded in 1925, and that year the NHL granted a franchise lease to the Boston Bruins and became the top professional hockey league in

North America. The New York Rangers and the Pittsburgh Pirates followed, and Chicago and Detroit were awarded NHL franchises in 1927, bringing to nine the number of Canadian and American clubs playing in the NHL. The Toronto Maple Leafs (and indirectly the NHL) acquired a kind of physical presence when Maple Leaf Gardens was built as their home. At the opening on 12 November 1931 Foster Hewitt (1902-85) broadcast his first 'Hockey Night in Canada', describing the game from a gondola overlooking the rink. For three decades thereafter his high-pitched voice—and his excited refrain, 'He Shoots! He Scores!'—was the voice of hockey.

At the height of the Depression people needed entertainment, and professional sport and movies both benefited. At the Gardens on 3 and 4 April 1933 the Maple Leafs and the Boston Bruins played the longest game in the history of hockey. It lasted for nearly seven hours before the tie was broken, was witnessed by 14,500 exhausted fans, and all of it was described on air by Foster Hewitt. In the same year over 3,000 people attended the Dominion Day horse races in Summerside, PEI. Canadian football—which in the 1930s was becoming Americanized with the introduction of the forward pass and many American players—still created excitement over the annual Grey Cup games. 'Depression, unemployment, its railway problem, the wheat problem,

Maple Leaf Gardens, Toronto, in 1932, the year after it opened. Metropolitan Toronto Library Board, T 10161.

all the host of troubles sent to Winnipeggers were just as much nonsense to the citizens Saturday night as they set about the serious business of celebrating the glorious victory of their championship rugby team,' wrote the *Winnipeg Free Press* on 9 December 1935, when the Winnipeg club brought the Grey Cup to the West for the first time. While baseball never stopped being played in city parks, the Depression hit the professional game. The Montreal Royals and Toronto Maple Leafs both experienced financial difficulties—in Toronto because the admission prices to Maple Leaf Stadium, of 50¢ and $1.25, were considered too high. And by 1939 the NHL had suffered the loss of all but two of its Canadian teams: the Maple Leafs and the Montreal Canadiens. The centre of power shifted to the United States, and many Canadian players followed.[21]

High Culture

Although films, radio, and sport provided the most popular forms of escape from the stresses of the time, books also played their part. During the Depression many Canadians used their enforced leisure to read more; library memberships and circulations increased substantially. Between 1920 and 1940 over 750 Canadian novels were published, most of them escapist fiction in the form of historical romances; crime, mystery, and adventure novels; and regional idylls.* Two novels won major American literary prizes: *Wild Geese* (1925) by Martha Ostenso (1900-63), who was really a Norwegian-American but lived most of the first twenty years of her life in Manitoba, where her novel was set; and *Jalna* (1927), by the Ontario novelist Mazo de la Roche (1879-1961), which had sold close to 100,000 copies a few months after publication and gave rise to many sequels. Morley Callaghan (1903-90) also gained a North American reputation when his first two books were published in New York by Scribner's.

In addition to many forgettable works, a small number of strong, confident, realistic novels were published in this period that formed the foundation of modern Canadian fiction. A notable example is the Great War novel *Generals Die in Bed* (1930) by Charles Yale Harrison (1898-1954), which compares favourably with Hemingway's *A Farewell to Arms* and Remarque's *All Quiet on the Western Front*. (In 1928, the year before these novels were published, portions of *Generals Die in Bed* appeared in English and German magazines.) The short, direct sentences of the first-person

---

*An unrepresentative footnote to the period is provided by the surprising career of Canada's bestselling fiction writer, 'Frederick W. Dixon' (Leslie McFarlane, 1902-77), who, beginning in 1927, wrote for the Stratemayer Syndicate of New Jersey 89 books in the voluminous *Hardy Boys* series, the sales of which in 1982 had reached some 50 million copies.

narrative of *Generals Die in Bed* evoke unforgettably the horrors of life at the Front. *Generals Die in Bed* is in a class by itself, both in its setting and in its stylistic assurance. Other novelists introduced into Canadian fiction prairie realism or the psychological tensions of industrialized urban society. Manitoba was the setting not only for Ostenso's *Wild Geese* but also for *The Viking Heart* (1923) by Laura Goodman Salverson (1890-1970), about the Icelandic immigrants at Gimli and three generations that succeeded them; and for *Grain* (1926) by Robert Stead (1880-1959), who followed his popular romantic novels about pioneering on the Prairies with this classic of prairie realism. Another classic is *As For Me and My House* (1941) by Sinclair Ross (b. 1908). Narrated in diary form, it is Mrs Bentley's portrayal of her frustrated clergyman husband, of the couple's responses to the isolation and barren environment of the small Saskatchewan town they live in, and of the effects on them of drought, dust, and bad economic times at the end of the Depression. The novel was barely noticed when it was published and was not recognized as a distinguished work until the 1950s.

Of the major novelists of the interwar period, Felix Paul Greve/Frederick Philip Grove (1879-1948) was the most fascinating because he invented a persona for himself in two autobiographies, claiming to have been born to English parents in Sweden, when he was really born to German parents in Germany, and omitting to mention his imprisonment for fraud in 1903-4. After working for five years as a translator into German of famous English works, and having had two German novels published, he left Europe for North America in 1909 and worked as a labourer in the US and Canada, settling finally in Manitoba as a schoolteacher under the name of Grove. *Settlers of the Marsh* (1925) was the first of his four prairie novels, all of them reflecting the naturalism of Émile Zola and other European novelists of the late nineteenth century in featuring rather bleak character studies, psychological realism, emotional confrontations, and accurately observed social detail. They are burdened, however, by the ponderous style and awkward diction of a writer for whom English was a second language.

In these beginnings of a realistic, unsentimental tradition in Canadian fiction, other writers were attracted for subject matter to urban or industrialized Canada. Morley Callaghan's first novel, *Strange Fugitive* (1928), and his first collection of stories, *A Native Argosy* (1929), were followed by three of his most important novels: *Such Is My Beloved* (1934), *They Shall Inherit the Earth* (1935), and *More Joy in Heaven* (1937), which deal with various forms of morally weak or criminal behaviour, and the question of redemption, in an unnamed city that suggests Toronto. *The Magpie* (1923) by Douglas Leader Durkin (1884-1968) treats opposing views of labour and social justice around the time of the Winnipeg General Strike of 1919; and *Waste Heritage* (1939) by Irene Baird (1901-81), about labour unrest and chronic unemployment in Vancouver during the Depression, powerfully evokes the tensions between

Gabrielle Roy in the 1950s. National
Archives of Canada, C-18347

those who were for and against radical reform. Grove's *The Master of the Mill* (1944) is a complex look at the effects of industrialism on three generations of the owners of a flour mill that began small and grew into a mechanized colossus, symbolizing for Grove a threat to humanity.

After achieving success and a wide readership with his first novel, *Barometer Rising* (1941), a semi-autobiographical account of the Halifax explosion of 1917, Hugh MacLennan (1907-90) received even more acclaim for *Two Solitudes* (1945), whose title (from Rilke) injected into Canadian discourse what is now a cliché for the profound alienation of French and English Canadians in Quebec. Covering two periods, 1917-1921 and the 1930s, the novel is dated in its simplistic suggestion that mutual understanding was bringing about a transformation in the relationship of French and English. Nevertheless, it was a singular attempt to portray the tensions and differences that existed in Quebec's recent past. A more realistic Quebec novel of the time was *Bonheur d'Occasion* (1945)—set in Saint-Henri, the slum district of Montreal—by Gabrielle Roy (1900-83). With its English translation, *The Tin Flute* (1947), Roy was recognized internationally as a new writer of distinction. Depicting the pathetic yearning of Florentine Lacasse to escape from her squalid environment, the novel also portrays the gradual disintegration of the Lacasse family, torn by poverty and war, and throws a harsh light on an aspect of urban Quebec that was outside Hugh MacLennan's experience. *The Tin Flute* was the first modern novel by a French Canadian to have a wide readership in English Canada, where Roy's books remain popular to this day. *Bonheur d'Occasion* won for the author—a Franco-Manitoban then living in Montreal—the Prix Fémina, making her the first Canadian writer to be awarded this major French literary prize.

Canadian poetry between the wars found itself caught between the last gasp of Victorian romanticism and new experimental forms that sought to downplay metrical and other conventions, to use modern language, and to expand subject matter. As A.J.M. Smith (1902-80), one of the best of the new poets, put it in the *McGill Fortnightly Review* (1925-7), the task was 'to bring the subject-matter of poetry out of the library and the afternoon-tea salon into the open air', dealing in the language of present-day speech with subjects of living interest.'[22]

The major poet of the period was E.J. ('Ned') Pratt (1882-1964), a Newfoundlander who was educated at Victoria College, University of Toronto; was ordained a Methodist minister; and taught English at Victoria until his retirement in 1953. With *Newfoundland Verse* (1923) he began a long and productive career as a poet, drawing often on his Newfoundland heritage of the sea and becoming famous for his narrative poems, which in this period included *The Titanic* (1935) and *Brébeuf and His Brethren* (1940). Employing assiduous research and witty diction in a conservative poetic form—having, in the words of Northrop Frye, 'the power to make something poetic of what everybody had just decided could no longer be poetic material'—he became a kind of epic bard, transforming the events he wrote about into myths.

More responsive to the new trends in poetry and to social conditions of the time were Dorothy Livesay, F.R. Scott, and A.M. Klein. Livesay (b. 1909) was an active member of the Communist Party in the thirties and her poems in *Day and Night* (1944) concern workers in wartime industry ('One step forward / Two steps back / Shove the lever, / Push it back'—'Day and Night'). Scott—a law teacher at McGill and a political activist who was one of the founders of the CCF—believed in the power of poetry to change society. His first collection, *Overture* (1945), contains poems written from the twenties to the forties. Beginning with 'Dedication' ('Till power is brought to pooling / And outcasts share in ruling / There will not be an ending / Nor any peace for spending'), it includes nature poems ('North Stream', 'Old Song', 'March Field') as well as satires both political ('Ode to the Politician', 'Social Notes') and literary ('The Canadian Authors Meet'). Klein (1909-72), another Montreal poet who was trained in law, was especially a barometer of the time, as his Jewish roots led him from social observation in the mode of T.S. Eliot to deeply felt statements about anti-Semitism in the world around him that culminated in *The Hitleriad* (1944).

In the realm of the visual arts, the twenties were dominated by the popular successes of the Group of Seven. When officially formed in 1920, it was made up of Franklin Carmichael (1890-1945), Lawren Harris, A. Y. Jackson (1882-1974), Frank Johnston (1888-1949), Arthur Lismer (1885-1969),

Arthur Lismer, *Emily Carr and the Group of Seven,* **c.1927. Charcoal. Lismer depicts in this cartoon the imaginary meeting of Emily Carr and some members of the Group—himself, Frank Carmichael, A.J. Casson (a later member), J.E.H. MacDonald, A.Y. Jackson, Lawren Harris—along with fellow artist Bertram Brooker. Private collection. Photograph courtesy McMichael Collection of Canadian Art.**

J.E.H. MacDonald and F.H. Varley (1881-1969). They consciously sought to create a Canadian mythology, and according to their first exhibition catalogue of 1920 their vision was simple: 'An Art must grow and flower in the land before the country will be a real home for its people.'[23] Toronto and Montreal (along with Ottawa, because of the National Gallery) controlled the world of art in Canada, and more than one regional artist railed unsuccessfully against the tyranny of metropolitanism.

A few regional figures made it to national prominence, particularly British Columbia's Emily Carr (1871-1945). Born and brought up in Victoria, Carr had studied art in San Francisco, England, and Paris, picking up from the last a post-Impressionist style that she applied back in British Columbia to paintings of Indian sites and artifacts. By combining French post-Impressionism with Indian forms and bold colours, Carr gradually created a distinctive and powerful art. But she was known only locally until 1927 when, at the age of 57, she travelled east for an 'Exhibition of Canadian West Coast Art' at the National Gallery, in which her work was represented. Enthusiastically encouraged, and then influenced, by Lawren Harris and other members of the Group of Seven, Carr went on to produce some of her most famous paintings, many of them depicting sculptural forests and pulsating skies inspired by the British Columbia interior. Emily Carr also made her mark on

Canadian literature with the first of three books published in her lifetime, *Klee Wyck* (1941), a collection of stories based on her visits to Indian villages that won a Governor General's Award. She had triumphed not only over the disadvantages of Canadian geography, but over the limitations faced by any woman who aspired to more than genteel 'dabbling' in art, especially in a town like Victoria.

If the Group of Seven assisted Carr and a few other artists, their success as national symbol-makers prevented other painting styles from making much headway with the Canadian public. In retrospect it is surprising that during the Depression, when most painters had to live at subsistence level, so many works we now value highly were produced, not only by Carr but by other English-Canadian artists, such as Bertram Brooker (1888-1955), Paraskeva Clark (1898-1986), LeMoine FitzGerald (1891-1952), Prudence Heward (1896-1947), Edwin Holgate (1892-1977), Jack Humphrey (1901-67), John Lyman (1886-1967), David Milne (1882-1953), Walter J. Phillips (1884-1963), Goodridge Roberts (1904-74), Carl Schaefer (b. 1903), and Philip Surrey (1910-90).

Canadian painters in this period, along with writers, were also sensitive to the international trends and the immediate environment. At the age of nineteen Alfred Pellan (b. 1906), of Quebec City, received a bursary that enabled him to study in Paris. He went there in 1926 and achieved a name for himself before he returned to seek a job at his old school, the École des Beaux Arts in Quebec. After expressing his interest in the styles of Picasso and Matisse, Pellan was informed that 'with such ideas I could never be accepted.' He returned to Paris, coming home only when Hitler's armies overran France. At a Montreal exhibition in June 1940 of his Cubist-influenced work and abstractions, he was praised as a 'European painter. . .born in Quebec'.[24] In the meantime another Quebec painter, Paul-Émile Borduas (1905-60), had become interested in Surrealism, relying on his unconscious to produce a series of 'automatic' abstract paintings that were exhibited in April 1942 to great acclaim in the French-Canadian press. Before he died in 1960 Borduas had achieved an international reputation. Three English-Canadian painters attracted to abstractionism were Lawren Harris and Bertram Brooker of Toronto and Marian Scott (b. 1906) of Montreal; but most painters of the thirties worked in more realistic modern styles.

Two paintings sum up the mood of the time. Scottish-born Charles Comfort (b. 1900), who had worked as a commercial artist in Winnipeg and then Toronto, painted a fellow artist, Carl Schaefer, as a generic *Young Canadian* (1932). Against a rural background of barn and menacing sky (on the Schaefer farm in southwestern Ontario), the young man—his paint-box before him and a brush in one hand—is ready to take up work. The bleak expression on his face could be seen to portray both the depressed artist having to pursue his vocation in an unreceptive period, or the worker willing to start a job if only one were to be had. A few years later a pupil of Schaefer, the Polish-Canadian Nathan Petroff (who soon moved to New York), pro-

Charles Comfort, *Young Canadian*, 1932.
Watercolour. Hart House, University of
Toronto.

Nathan Petroff, *Modern Times*, 1937.
Watercolour. National Gallery of
Canada, 4314.

duced a watercolour entitled *Modern Times* (1937), showing a young woman despondently leaning over the want-ads searching for a job. Under the classified section is part of the paper's headline: 'SHELL MADRID'. Unemployment and an international crisis were here inextricably linked.

➤➤ *Protestant Church Union and Prohibition*

In the field of religious organization a large number of Canadians pursued a course that was quite different from anything occurring to the south. Whereas the United States had a long history of sectarianism and schismatic tendencies within Protestantism, the development of Protestantism in Canada had tended towards unification and centralization rather than division. Everywhere in the Protestant world there had long been talk of unification. But only in Canada after the Great War was substantive union achieved when, in 1925, the Methodist, Presbyterian, and Congregational churches— the first two among Canada's largest denominations—merged as the United Church of Canada. As three of the most 'liberal' denominations in Canada, home of much of the 'social gospel' commitment to Christian reform of secular society, they hoped to strengthen the social gospel and liberal religion through unification, which was first discussed in the early 1920s against a background of declining reform fervour.

The failure of the Prohibition experiment symbolized the decline of reform. The death-knell of Prohibition sounded when various provinces voted 'wet' between 1920 and 1924, and when the Liquor Control Act replaced the Ontario Temperance Act in 1927. But there was considerable evidence that the elimination of spirituous beverages had made a difference in society—the jails were largely emptied in most places, since alcohol-related offences were by far the most common. The Ontario Alliance for the Total Suppression of the Liquor Trade claimed in 1922 that the number of convictions for offences associated with drink had declined from 17,413 in 1914 to 5,413 in 1921, and drunkenness cases decreased in the province's major cities from 16,590 in 1915 to 6,766 in 1921. Opposition to Prohibition after the war had found a new argument to add to the old one that private conduct was being publicly regulated: attempts to enforce Prohibition encouraged flaunting the law, and even organized crime and vice. Too many people were prepared to ignore the law and drink illegally, said Prohibition's opponents, who found new, more acceptable slogans of their own in 'Moderation' and 'Government Regulation'. The possibility of obtaining provincial revenue for tax-starved coffers led several provinces to introduce government control of the sale of alcohol, and by the mid-1920s Prohibition was fighting a losing battle. Conservative Protestantism was feeling more than a bit beleaguered by 1925.[25]

Not everyone within the three denominations that became the United Church was prepared to water down statements of doctrinal belief in the interests of ecumenicalism, or to stand by while the churches united.[26] Opposition to union was particularly strong among the Presbyterians, many of whom insisted that the unionists were leaving the traditions of Presbyterianism and ought not to drag the entire church with them. The battle was hard fought because church property and assets were involved. In the end, congregations could stay out of union by so voting, and 784 Presbyterian and 8 Congregational churches so declared, while 4,797 Methodist, 3,728 Presbyterian, and 166 Congregational churches joined in the United Church of Canada. The new church was the most sizeable Protestant communion in Canada, a national denomination generally committed to liberal theology and the social gospel.[27] Not all Protestant Canadians approved of its principles, however, and the union was particularly worrisome to conservative adherents of traditional doctrine, especially those who still believed in a literal interpretation of scriptures, which most ministers of the United Church had long since abandoned. The fear of liberal theology worked its way into Canadian society in a curious variety of ways. One was in the popular support given in the later 1920s to the Ku Klux Klan.

Racism

If Canada exported film people and hockey players to the United States in the 1920s, it imported a good many items in return. One of the least desirable was the Ku Klux Klan, which had experienced a revival in the United States after the First World War. The original Klan had been founded in the American South after the Civil War to prevent blacks, through intimidation, from voting and assuming full rights as citizens in the post-war reconstruction period. In the United States the revived Klan was devoted to spreading anti-black and anti-Catholic hate propaganda under the guise of a fraternal organization. In its secret rituals, fundamentalist Protestantism, and social operations, the Klan appeared to some Canadians little different from a host of other secret societies. Like many American organizations, the Klan in Canada assumed a Canadian face, posing as the defender of British nationality against the alien hordes and 'incorporating' as the 'Ku Klux Klan of the British Empire'. Many of its most outspoken supporters were conservative Protestant ministers. Although the Klan had some success everywhere in Canada, it made particular headway in the late twenties in Saskatchewan, where by 1929 there were over 125 local chapters. Emphasizing conservative Protestantism and hostility to Catholics, the Klan in Saskatchewan was supported by a number of ministers who objected to the increasingly liberal leanings of the mainline Protestant churches. It found some unofficial political backing in its implicit critique of the policies of the Liberal government of the province, and was supported by a number of powerful Conservatives and Progressives. Distancing itself from its American origins, the Klan in Canada trumpeted its Canadian nationalism—despite its organization by Americans—and its inherent respectability. It did, after all, sponsor a number of baseball teams in the province. Its rapid growth produced considerable public debate in Saskatchewan, critics pointing to its past American record as a racist organization and its defenders insisting that it was an acceptable instrument for the legitimate interests of the population of the province. Apparently few of its members associated it with American-style cross burning and midnight lynch mobs, although the former was not an uncommon part of Klan ritual in its Canadian heyday.[28]

Whatever the Canadian KKK was or was not, its appeal was plainly to a beleaguered conservative Protestant population in Saskatchewan, heirs to the old spirit of WASPishness so prevalent in large sections of rural Canada. Like the Orange Order, it was unabashedly racist and exclusionist in its rhetoric, appealing to popular fears of various sorts.

A similar rhetoric infused the anti-Oriental movement in British Columbia that flourished during the interwar period.[29] As the province through which immigration from Asia was bound to come, British Columbia felt itself particularly threatened. Much of the criticism of the Oriental 'menace' was economic in nature, although underlying this objection was a general concern for the racial integrity of the province as a 'white' civilization. Exclusion of Asian immigrants continued to be a major goal, and attempts were made to limit both the amount of land held by Orientals, particularly in the agricultural sector, and competition in retail trade, especially from small stores run by Chinese grocers and their families. The general argument was that the newcomers would not assimilate, although there was considerable evidence that the Japanese were acculturating rapidly. Moving onto small holdings in the Fraser Valley and into salmon fishing along the coasts, the Japanese were regarded as a potential military threat to the province should their homeland—which had been militarily aggressive in the Pacific since the Russo-Japanese War earlier in the century—attempt to expand into Canada. Despite claims that the Oriental population of British Columbia was growing, its percentage of the total population actually declined marginally during this period. And if the Orientals were highly visible in some areas and some industries, that fact was partly explained by their exclusion—in law and in practice—from so much of the life of the province. The increasing territorial expansionism of Imperial Japan in the 1930s only increased the concern of British Columbia about its Japanese residents. Ironically, British Columbians were captives of their own sense of racial and cultural superiority. Few of them would have chosen to immigrate to Japan (or anywhere else) and become loyal citizens of the Japanese empire, yet they were quite unable to understand that the Japanese might behave differently than they.

British Columbia's sensitivity to the possibility of Japanese expansion was the exception. Canadians as a whole in the 1930s were slow to appreciate that the peace of the world was being menaced by the actions of Germany, Italy, and Japan. Indeed, Canada spoke sympathetically at the League of Nations in

The executive of the Canadian Jewish Congress at the King Edward Hotel, Toronto, 27 January 1934.
Revived seven months before, partly as a means of furthering plans for the relief of German Jews and to
form a permanent Dominion Relief Committee for this purpose, the Congress included in its platform
the following resolutions: 'To safeguard the civil, political, economic and religious rights of Jews' and
'To combat manifestations of anti-semitism in Canada by means of an intensive campaign of
enlightenment and education among non-Jews, as well as through legislative channels.' Courtesy the
Canadian Jewish Congress.

1932 in support of Japanese claims to Manchuria, and most Canadians
regarded German actions in Europe as legitimate attempts to recover German interests. At the Berlin Olympics in 1936 the Canadians were the only
Commonwealth team to give Hitler a Nazi salute at the opening ceremonies
(which represented a refusal to protest German policy, including the persecution of non-Ayrans). While it would be simple enough to blame the nation's
failure to open its doors to Jewish refugees in the 1930s on the anti-Semitism
of Mackenzie King and the mandarins in Ottawa who advised him, there was
little public demand for a more liberal policy. In the event, the episode was
one of the most disgraceful in the country's history: between 1933 and 1939
Canada accepted only 4,000 of the 800,000 Jews who had escaped from
Nazi-controlled territory.

Canadian fascists were not very important numerically, and were almost
completely ignored in Canada until 1938, when the RCMP added Nazis to
Communists and Japanese as 'foreign' elements to monitor, and in some cases
harass. But the very presence in Canada of fascists underlined the significance
of the rise of right-wing totalitarianism in the international arena.

✔✖ Women

Canadian women emerged from the Great War with the vote in hand and great optimism for the future 'New Day'. As some feminist critics had argued before the war, however, the achievement of woman's suffrage was no panacea for the second-class position of women in Canadian society. Women between the wars did not run very often for public office, did not constitute any recognizable voting block to which politicians needed to pay attention, and for the most part continued in their traditional stereotyped roles. Although the 'flapper'—with her bobbed hair, short skirts, and spirit of independent adventure—was the symbolic 'New Woman' of the twenties, she was hardly typical. Most Canadian women did not smoke or sip cocktails or dance the Black Bottom. The 'gay young things' were relatively few, and only in the larger cities. About all that many Canadian women had in common with the flapper was the fact that, like her, they worked outside the home. More women worked in 1931 than in 1921, making up 16.96 per cent of the Canadian labour force in 1921. A few reached the top of their chosen occupations—even though most employers practised discrimination against women's entrance into positions of authority—but most were stuck in relatively dead-end jobs. Women were still expected to find their chief fulfilment as wives and mothers. They used the new labour-saving appliances in their homes—only to find that they still worked just as hard as ever.

As Petroff's *Modern Times* suggests, the Depression was particularly difficult for Canadian women. The initial response to the economic crisis in many families was a transfer of breadwinning responsibility from the males to the females, who worked for lower wages in service sectors of the economy. But gradually public opinion turned against women, particularly married women, who held jobs that could be done by men—though in several traditionally female industries, such as garment-making, men, in desperation, worked for even lower wages than the women. Most relief programs were geared to men, partly because it was not anticipated that women would threaten the social order. Many women were deserted by their husbands; and even where families remained together, it was the wife who did most of the patching and scraping to keep it functioning. The reminiscences of women in Barry Broadfoot's oral history, *Ten Lost Years: 1929-1939* (1973), are easily the most poignant in the book.[30]

✔✖ War and Public Attitudes

Canada's attitude towards its women, as towards so much else, changed rapidly after the beginning of the Second World War. Women were expected from the outset to manage the home front, keeping track of rationing coupons and planting victory gardens to supply extra food. After 1942, when military and industrial needs had exhausted the pool of unemployed Canadians, women were also expected to enter wartime industries on an emergency basis. By June 1943, 255,000 women were employed in war industry, and a year later over 40,000 were engaged in munitions manufacture in Quebec and Ontario. It was claimed that they were much better at tedious jobs than men because they were accustomed to the boredom of housekeeping. By 1945, over 43,000 women were serving in Canada's armed forces, 21,000 of them in the Women's Army Corps. But a 1944 Gallup poll indicated that most Canadians, including 68 per cent of the women polled, believed that men should be given preference for employment in the post-war reconstruction. A report on the question of the future of women active in Canadian war industry—reluctantly commissioned by the government in 1943—was ignored almost completely, and governments moved with unseemly haste at war's end to dismantle the machinery, including daycare centres, that had been created to encourage women to work in critical industries.[31]

While the active participation of women in the Canadian war effort was welcomed with open arms, other elements of Canadian society did not fare so well, even in the short run. As in the Great War, dissent was met with persecution. The Canadian government proved almost totally insensitive to the beliefs of pacifists, including those of religious groups, such as the Mennonites, that had long been 'guaranteed' understanding of their doctrinal opposition to war. J.S. Woodsworth was forced to step down as leader of the CCF—not by the government but by the war's supporters within his own party—because he opposed the war as a matter of conscience. The War Measures Act was used to intern thousands of Canadians without trial, including many young German emigrants, who stayed in Canada and later made highly successful careers. While some of those detained were enemy sympathizers, others—such as Camillien Houde (1889-1958), the mayor of Montreal—were merely outspoken critics of government policy, in Houde's case of registration for national service.[32] But the major abuse of the power of the state in the Second World War was the treatment of the Japanese.

Decades of paranoid hostility in British Columbia to the 23,000 Japanese resident in the province virtually exploded in the weeks after the Japanese attack on the American naval base at Pearl Harbor on 7 December 1941. Many British Columbians were convinced that among the loyal Japanese— and the majority of those in British Columbia had been born in Canada— were potential spies and fifth columnists waiting to surface. RCMP investigations at the time were unable to uncover more than a handful of people who were even suspicious, and the passage of time has not identified a single Japanese spy in Canada. Nevertheless, the press and the politicians in BC called for action, mainly in the form of internment of all Japanese so as not to miss the few possibly dangerous ones. And although the King government did not for a moment believe that Japanese Canadians represented any military danger, it yielded to provincial pressure and used the excuse of the need to protect the Japanese from the white majority to evacuate most of them from the West Coast. Most were sent to internment camps in the

Japanese Canadians in Vancouver begin their journey into the interior for three years of internment. National Archives of Canada, C-46350.

British Columbia interior, although some were scattered across the country. Their land was seized and their property was sold at auction. A few young Japanese men were permitted to serve in special units in the Canadian army in the later stages of the war, but on grounds of 'national emergency' the government refused to acknowledge any injustice in the treatment meted out to Japanese Canadians as a group.[33]

Although wartime propaganda by the state was as old as war itself, the Second World War gave rise to a new sophistication in the process. The effective propaganda of the Great War was crude by comparison with the operations of Canada's Bureau of Public Information and the Wartime Information Board. The dissemination of propaganda now became the 'management of information', and was placed chiefly in the hands of academic social scientists, who used the findings of sociology, psychology, and political science to achieve the desired results. Though this employment of experts characterized the entire government propaganda effort during the war, the academics did not achieve their influence without a struggle. Politicians were initially reluctant to allow public opinion to be insidiously moulded by outside experts, preferring instead to listen to journalists who wanted merely to choose the appropriate news to report. The general manager of the Canadian Press Association argued in 1939 that 'the most efficient propaganda lies in the selection of news', and Prime Minister King apparently felt that the right information would, as his personal secretary later reported, 'ooze out by osmosis untouched by human hands'. The government soon overcame its scruples, however, although journalists and academics continued to contend with one another throughout the war.

The management of information gradually replaced blatant journalistic sloganeering as the essence of the wartime approach. Citizens needed to be educated in order to maintain 'faith and hope' and to eliminate 'potential elements of disunity'. In 1939 Scottish-born John Grierson (1898-1972) was appointed the first Government Film Commissioner of the National Film Board of Canada, which he headed, and where he introduced his philosophy of the documentary film, supported by the state. He regarded himself as an expert in 'mind-bending'—this was effectively revealed in the NFB's *Canada Carries On* and *World in Action* series, narrated by Lorne Greene (1915-87) to an original orchestral accompaniment. Grierson recognized that the war was an opportunity for social planning, for the integration of 'the loyalties and forces of the community in the name of positive and highly constructive ideas', and saw 'information services—propaganda if you like' as an inevitable consequence of government action. He managed to persuade the Prime Minister, at least some of the time, of the political advantages of scientific information management. Even after his resignation in 1945, the NFB remained committed to his principles, and began to employ public-opinion polling as a means of discovering what information the public needed.[34] Although throughout the war those involved in the NFB wrestled with the problem of reconciling the manipulation of public opinion with democratic principles, opinion was nonetheless continually manipulated. And the principle of consulting the polls to establish the direction of policy became well entrenched.

Despite tragedies, injustices, and some deprivations, the Second World War was on balance a unifying and positive experience for most Canadians. Full employment, after a decade of Depression, helped. So too did the fact that the enemy had behaved, and continued to behave, with considerable brutality over many years. Wartime propaganda was a good deal less blatantly self-serving (although no less manipulative) than had been the case in the First World War, in large measure because the Nazis, the Italian Fascists, and the Japanese were all felt to have condemned themselves by their actions. Rationing probably produced a more balanced diet for many Canadians, since much of what was rationed (such as sugar) was not necessary to dietary balance anyway. Canadians ate less meat and butter, consumed more fresh vegetables (grown in thousands of Victory Gardens), and became healthier in the process. Limited leisure time and the absence of consumer goods in the stores, especially durable big-ticket items such as automobiles and household appliances, forced many Canadians to save, often by purchasing War Bonds. There were some harmless, unexpected side-effects, as when the openness of Montreal night-life during the war, created by people with money to spend who sought release from the pressures of the day, encouraged the growth of a jazz movement in the city. The principal figure in that development was the pianist Oscar Peterson (b. 1925). By war's end, however, a fifteen-year deferral of expectations had produced a powerful desire for normal conditions and the opportunity to enjoy material comforts. It would lead Canada into a new era of affluent consumerism.

chapter eight

Canada and the World, 1919-1973

~~~~~~

As a result of both its geographical position and its colonial situation, Canada before 1914 had been able to enjoy relative isolation from the turmoil of international politics, concentrating on its own domestic development. Like Americans, most Canadians were relatively inward-looking, even isolation-ist, in their attitudes to the wider world. Most French Canadians saw themselves as an automonous people without close European or international connections; and although Canadians of British origin could identify with the mother country, the vast majority of citizens felt no particular tie to the British Empire. Beyond the ongoing relationship with the United States and continuing interest in the British Isles or France, there seemed little need for Canadians to have an opinion on either the domestic developments in other nations or international affairs. Whitehall looked after most such matters, and the government in Ottawa, however awkwardly in constitutional terms, had input into international issues when specifically Canadian interests were at stake.

While many Canadians felt no need to be citizens of the world before 1914, most had considerable access to international news. The larger daily newspapers covered foreign affairs far more assiduously than their modern equivalents, and religious magazines and even farm weeklies often contained overseas news. Canadians were not likely to read about their own govern-ment's foreign activities in such sources, for Canada's corps of diplomats was very small. Canadian prime ministers attended periodic Imperial Confer-ences in London, Canada had had informal representatives in London (a High Commissioner) and in Paris (a Commissioner General) since the 1880s, and an International Joint Commission had been created in 1911 to deal with Canadian-American problems on the Great Lakes. A small Department of External Affairs, instituted in 1909, supervised and co-ordinated Canada's sporadic formal relations with the world.

After the Great War, Canada's international position changed rapidly, and it is at least arguable that the nation possessed its greatest degree of real autonomy in the interwar period, as it gradually broke its imperial ties, became an independent dominion in the newly organized 'Commonwealth' in 1931, and began seriously to construct its own foreign policy and diplomatic apparatus. Before 1939-40, American direct influence over Canadian foreign and defence policy was minimal, and the Canadian military as late as the 1920s still thought of the United States as a potential enemy against which Canada might need to be defended. External Affairs, like other departments of the federal state, developed under the leadership of a new class of professional civil servants, an élite cadre of 'mandarins'.[1] The Second World War both completed the process of Canada's withdrawal from the British Empire and initiated the process of its integration into a less formal American empire. Canada's scope for genuinely autonomous international action declined markedly in the years after 1945, although most Canadians were reasonably content with the nation's situation and performance as they understood them. Nevertheless, the period 1919 to 1973 did see Canada pass in international affairs from one sort of colonial status to another.

Canada and the League of Nations

Even before the First World War, Canadian political leaders such as Prime Minister Robert Borden had indicated the potential reasons for a change of attitude. As Borden put the case in debate over the naval controversy in 1910:

> If Canada and the other Dominions of the empire are to take their part as nations in the defence of the empire as a whole, shall it be that we, contributing to that defence of the whole empire, shall have absolutely, as citizens of this country, no voice whatever in the councils of the empire touching the issues of peace or war throughout the empire? . . . I do not believe the people of Canada would for one moment submit to such a condition.[2]

Borden did not immediately pursue to its logical conclusion the position he had so clearly enunciated, but the Great War brought the point home to both Canadian politicians and the people in graphic fashion. Canada found itself involved in a war not of its own making, and its enthusiastic support of the imperial war effort only increased the frustrations of its leaders over the lack of direct participation in imperial war councils. Borden took the lead in pressing for change, arguing privately in 1916 that 'it can hardly be expected that we shall put 400,000 or 500,000 men in the field and willingly accept the position of having no more voice and receiving no more consideration than if we were toy automata.'[3] Eventually the new British War Cabinet of December 1916, headed by Lloyd George, took the unprecedented step of inviting Dominion ministers to sit in imperial council. This 'Imperial War Cabinet' of 1917 may have been largely cosmetic in terms of the direction of the war, at least until 1918, and certainly provoked constitutional concerns among the purists. But it did put on record the need for a 'full recognition of the Dominions as autonomous nations of an Imperial Commonwealth' and discussed the broad outlines of the eventual peace settlement.[4] The dominions insisted on full representation as participants in the Paris Peace Conference of 1919, although in the end they had to settle for being no more than members of the delegation from the British Empire.

Borden himself led the Canadian delegation to Paris. For Canada, the particularities of the peace settlement were less important than its status in the League of Nations, which was constructed at the conference. Canada had some major differences of opinion with its powerful allies over the responsibilities of the League, especially regarding the question of universal guarantees to all members against aggression, which it opposed as providing a blank cheque that might well involve nations 'in all the horrors of wars in which they have no interest.'[5] What Canada really wanted was not only to be a member of the League, but to be a full member apart from the British Empire, as a symbol of full Canadian sovereignty. Borden insisted that the British, French, and Americans agree in a separate memorandum that Canada was eligible to sit on the League Council, and forced the negotiators of the treaty to change its language so that Canada could be a separate member of collateral League bodies like the International Labour Organization.

Once Canada was admitted to the League of Nations as a full member it became a regular if uninfluential participant, frequently lecturing Europe on its past and present failures. One Canadian delegate to the League Assembly in 1924, for example, observed that 'Not only have we had a hundred years of peace on our borders, but we think in terms of peace, while Europe, an armed camp, thinks in terms of war.'[6] Taking a position from such a high moral ground became a durable characteristic of Canada's external relations, although it did not always make the nation popular at the conference table. If Canada assumed no major role at the League, part of the reason was that the major problem of its external relations in the 1920s was assumed in Ottawa to be the continuing process of redefining the nation's role in the British Empire. Under the umbrella of the Empire, Ottawa was prepared in the first years after the war to participate in international conferences, such as the one held at Washington in 1921 over Far Eastern questions. But this was the last time this approach was deemed acceptable. Pressure for a new imperial arrangement built up rapidly after 1921.

Canada's ambivalent attitude towards the League of Nations in 1919 not only foreshadowed its ambiguous involvement in that organization over the next twenty years, but also illustrates the essential dichotomy and tension of

Canadian external policy over that period, and beyond it. On the one hand, Canada sought to give priority to full sovereignty and accompanying international status as an independent nation. On the other, rights imply responsibilities, and Canada was never convinced that its best interests were served by full involvement in the international world of crisis politics, or in the maintenance of the military machine that such participation implied. Its isolationist instincts and its ambitions for both sovereignty and full international status were continually at odds. Interwar external management concentrated on achieving full international sovereignty in several ways. First, the nation needed to develop an infrastructure for implementing Canada's role in the world independent of the Empire. Second, it would be necessary to complete the process of redefining the British Empire to fit Canada's needs. Finally, there would have to be a foreign policy or policies, as well as a military establishment, capable of providing some response to the increasingly frequent crises of the 1930s.

External Affairs and the Mandarins

No aspect of modern government is ever truly democratic, but the conduct of foreign relations almost by definition has to be more insulated from the vagaries of public opinion than domestic policy. Canadian external affairs were generally constrained by two public factors always recognized by those who managed them. Canada had no tradition of militarism, which meant that the military means available to the nation would always, at least in peacetime, be limited. Canadians, moreover, were a complex mixture of peoples with conflicting foreign allegiances and a tendency to look inward rather than outward.

Between 1912 and 1946 the Secretary of State for External Affairs was also by law the Prime Minister of the country, which meant that the Prime Minister at least in theory had the capacity to dominate foreign policy. Gradually, however, the Department of External Affairs collected a small cadre of highly capable officers who thought very much alike, and constituted an élite body of prime-ministerial advisers. Other departments acquired similar groups in the interwar period, but External's was both the biggest and, in many ways, the most significant.

The architect of the new Ottawa civil service so well exemplified at External Affairs was O.D. Skelton (1878-1941), who served as Undersecretary of State at External from 1925 to 1940. Skelton came from Ontario small-town, middle-class, Protestant stock, and went to Queen's University with the aid of a scholarship. He was a Canadian nationalist, described in 1923 as a 'narrow-minded extreme autonomist, whose time has been spent in hack writing and who is nervously jealous of what he suspects as English "superiority." '[7] He had received a doctorate in political science at the

O.D. Skelton and Lester
Pearson on board the
Barengaria in the 1930s.
National Archives of Canada,
PA-117595.

University of Chicago.* He returned to Queen's as John A. Macdonald
Professor of Political Science and Economics, becoming Dean of Arts in the
years before his appointment to Ottawa in 1924, initially on a temporary
basis. Skelton's tenure in Ottawa coincided with the elaboration of civil
service reform earlier agreed upon in principle, such as the introduction of
competitive exams for appropriately prepared candidates in place of purely
political appointments. Such reform was, of course, hardly democratic.
Qualifications for External Affairs included a university degree and special
training in political economy and international law, as well as skill in a foreign
language (often overlooked in the event). University education in Canada in
the interwar period was still extremely élitist in nature.

Canada recruited young men of talent such as Lester Pearson (1897-1972),
Norman Robertson (1904-68), Hugh Keenleyside (1898-1992), and Charles
Ritchie (b. 1906). These men exemplified 'all-round ability, capable of performing in widely different assignments at short notice', as Skelton once put
it.[8] But the nation took them from a fairly narrow spectrum of Canadian
society: 'affable' males, typically of WASP middle-class origins (though they
included one Jew and several Roman Catholics), with a strong sense of public

---

*In those days Canadians went abroad for graduate work; it is interesting that
Skelton chose the United States rather than Great Britain to pursue his education.

duty, who were educated at Queen's, Toronto, McGill, Manitoba, Dalhousie, or UBC with postgraduate studies at Oxford (four were Rhodes Scholars), Cambridge, or the London School of Economics. In Ottawa, on salaries of a few thousand dollars a year, they enjoyed a relatively comfortable, unostentatious lifestyle, which included a maid, and worked together in one building in the East Block. They ate lunch together, and their wives socialized with one another. 'The web of interconnections', as J.L. Granatstein has pointed out, 'was intense, embracing family, class, school, associations, and work.'[9] Such men did not always agree with each other, and conflict could be heated, but their arguments occurred within a relatively narrow range bounded by their background and experiences.

In many respects these early mandarins resembled another cadre in Canadian society of the time: the university professoriate from which many were recruited and that was regarded as the most suitable alternative employment to the civil service. The chief difference, of course, was that university professors were not in positions of public power and authority. The chief civil servants did not exercise unrestricted power, for they were all responsible to ministers and ultimately to Parliament, which provided a considerable check, particularly on adventuresome innovation. But as the men who provided the continuity in Ottawa, managed the departments, and drafted the policy statements, the mandarins were far more significant in the daily operation of government than popularly elected ministers who seldom remained very long in any portfolio. Whatever their positive influence on policy, their negative potential was enormous; few initiatives could succeed without their full support. Such were the people who operated Canada's external affairs, as well as its domestic policy, in the interwar years—and beyond, although domestic affairs were more amenable to older pressures, such as political patronage. Under Skelton's tutelage External Affairs also expanded abroad. A Canadian Minister to Washington was appointed in 1926, and similar legations were opened in Paris and Tokyo in 1928. The result was that Ottawa received some foreign diplomats in return, including a British High Commissioner, becoming a less parochial city in the process.

✑ Towards the Commonwealth

In 1921 the Liberal Party, under William Lyon Mackenzie King, came to power, and while foreign affairs were not an explicit issue in the election that brought the Liberals to Ottawa, King was no supporter of the Tory (or Union) view of the British Empire. He had had no military experience in the Great War, and had not been closely associated with its prosecution. He worked closely with Skelton to mould External Affairs into a more autonomous agency, but even before he began this process he had been forced to respond to his first challenge, the Chanak Affair of 1922. The British government had decided on interventionist policies in the Dardanelles, and automatically expected its dominions to support it. King refused 'to play the imperial game', and saw the issue as one of 'Canada vs. Imperialism, the people vs. the jingoes.'[10] He and his cabinet (which was not united on the question) insisted that Canada would not participate without Canadian parliamentary approval. King had already informed the British that a possible treaty with the Americans about naval armaments on the Great Lakes would be signed only by Canada. At his first Imperial Conference in 1923, he continued (with O. D. Skelton's support) to insist on Canadian autonomy. He found an unexpected ally in the British government itself, which had no desire to have its own hands tied by its dominions and so abandoned its insistence on dominion co-operation. King was prepared to live with the result: the British could have their own policies without consultation, and Canada would remain aloof from them. At another Imperial Conference in 1926 the British themselves suggested constitutional alterations. In the Bal-

Mackenzie King in 1915, when he was out of office. In 1919 he succeeded Laurier as Liberal leader, and in 1921 he began nearly 22 years as Prime Minister.

four Report, a resolution moved by former Prime Minister Arthur Balfour and adopted, Great Britain and the self-governing dominions were defined as 'autonomous communities within the British Empire, equal in status . . .'. The implementation of this proposal became the task of the well-known Westminster Conference of 1930.

By the time of that conference, Mackenzie King had been defeated at the polls by R.B. Bennett's Conservatives. Bennett himself headed the Canadian delegation to London, which did not include Skelton. Despite the slight to Skelton and the continuance of older imperialist sentiments in segments of his party, Bennett was hardly in a position to initiate another major shift in Canadian policy. The Tories had not opposed new constitutional arrangements in a preliminary parliamentary debate before the election, and Bennett himself had little time to familiarize himself with the issues. Given the world economic collapse, he might have been pardoned for thinking he had more important matters on his plate than tidying up constitutional niceties. He did insist that the Canadian provinces must be consulted before amendment of the British North America Act, but otherwise accepted the Statute of Westminster agreed to by the conference, which made six dominions (Canada, Australia, New Zealand, South Africa, the Irish Free State, and Newfoundland) legislatively independent. That the Statute of Westminster was brought into existence under a Conservative government was in some respects useful, since it symbolized the reality that autonomy was a bipartisan policy. King George V assented to the Statute on 11 December 1931. Although amendment to the British North America Act remained in the hands of the British Parliament, Canada was for all intents and purposes independent, a member of a 'Commonwealth of Nations' that had no binding authority over anyone and was united mainly by allegiance to a single ceremonial monarch. As Bennett himself said at Halifax immediately after the Statute of Westminster became law, with its adoption 'the old political Empire disappears.'[11] But, he went on to add, he hoped that there would be laid instead 'the foundations of a new economic Empire.' Canada was not yet done with the British connection.

✦ The Thirties

From the perspective of foreign affairs, the decade of the 1930s divides fairly neatly into two periods, broken at 1935. While that year saw the defeat of Bennett's Conservatives and the return to Parliament of King's Liberals, the election was less the dividing-point than were larger international developments. Apart from the important constitutional revisions at Westminster, accepted by imperial statesmen almost absent-mindedly, the foreign relations of Canada from 1930 to 1935 were dominated almost exclusively by economic considerations—which equally concerned most of the industrialized world. Developments in Germany and Italy that otherwise might have received more attention were virtually ignored. Not until Mussolini's invasion of Ethiopia in 1935 did the world discover the threats posed by nations that had resolved their economic problems with military rearmament. After Ethiopia, as other nations gradually emerged from the Depression they found themselves in the midst of an escalating international crisis that ultimately resulted in another world war.

Bennett's Tories had swept into office in 1930 chiefly because no government, not even one led by King, could withstand the effects on the electorate of the economic crisis. Bennett's campaign promises had emphasized getting the nation back on its feet, chiefly through new tariff policies more favourable to Canada. Revisions of tariff arrangements are, of course, matters for negotiation between or among nations. Both Bennett and his colleagues at Westminster in 1930 were really more interested in economic than constitutional matters, and one of the outcomes of the Imperial Conference of that year was a commitment to a thoroughgoing re-examination of imperial economic policy, which was eventually undertaken at a conference that was convened in Ottawa in July 1932. At Westminster Bennett had declared Canada's general attitude towards the future conference when he announced a 'Canada first' protectionist policy to be combined with imperial preference:

> I offer to the Mother country, and to all other parts of Empire, a preference in the Canadian market in exchange for a like preference in theirs, based upon the addition of a ten percentum increase in prevailing general tariffs, or upon tariffs yet to be created. In the universal acceptance of this offer, and in like proposals and acceptances by all the other parts of Empire, we attain to the ideal of Empire preference.[12]

None of the major participants were much taken by Bennett's proposition—the British Secretary of State for the Dominions commented 'there never was such humbug as this proposal'—but nations in trouble could not afford to overlook any possibility, including imperial co-operation. When Bennett invited the Westminster conferees to reconvene in Ottawa within twelve months, the offer was accepted. Canada would obviously chair the new meeting and prepare its agenda. It provided an opportunity to be at the centre of affairs and in the public spotlight that no Prime Minister could afford to ignore. Unfortunately, Canada did not do its homework and did not show to advantage at the conference, although Bennett thought he had obtained major concessions. The meeting was not aided by the humid heat of an Ottawa summer in the days before air conditioning.

All participants were to exchange a schedule of items for tariff concessions. Bennett asked the Canadian Manufacturers' Association to prepare Canada's list of goods, 'of a class or kind not made in Canada.' The list of 9553 items did not arrive until after the conference had opened and was not likely to win friends, since Bennett was obviously prepared to make concessions only on goods Canada had no need to protect. Canada did not examine other

R.B. Bennett, Conservative
leader and Prime Minister
from 1930 to 1935.
National Archives of
Canada, C-687.

schedules in advance. Bennett himself prepared the agenda—without much
consultation abroad—and designed it to suit Canadian purposes, including
such matters as Russian trade and monetary policy that most participants
preferred to ignore. Australia joined Canada in a highly protectionist mood,
but none of those nations attending had any real experience in complex tariff
negotiations. Neither of these realities boded well for the achievement of
anything significant, and in this sense the conference met everybody's expectations.

The failure of the Ottawa Conference to undertake a serious discussion of
monetary policy—which Canada had proposed in a not very persuasive or
constructive way—was probably a tragedy. Instead, the negotiators concentrated on tariff reform, with little real success. Because so much was expected
of this Conference, some face-saving results were required. The delegates
agreed to the principle of gradual reduction of tariffs, protecting only
'plausible industries' (the Canadian position) on the basis 'of the relative cost
of economical and efficient production'. Some concessions were made, few
of them critical. Canada did gain British agreement to a duty on foreign
wheat, removable if dominion wheat rose above the world price. (This point
took Britain back to the nineteenth-century Corn Laws.) In the course of
the negotiations Bennett made himself even less popular with his foreign

counterparts by bargaining almost exclusively in terms of Canada's immediate advantage. He did achieve success of a sort by gaining a substantial increase in Canadian exports to the United Kingdom and a favourable balance of trade with the British by 1935. But from the standpoint of a 'new economic Empire', the Ottawa Conference was a complete bust.[13] The failure was not entirely Bennett's fault, since none of the nations involved were any less concerned than Canada with the immediate economic consequences of the negotiations. But a golden opportunity for constructive statesmanship in producing international co-operation on monetary and economic questions had been bypassed, even by those who still had hopes for the Empire.

In 1930 the United States and Canada had responded to worsening economic conditions with an exchange of high protective tariffs that set up the most severe trade barriers ever seen between the two nations. For Canadian nationalists such a situation was good news—although it would not continue. Gradually the two countries resumed normal co-operative relations. Both Canadian parties had supported a St Lawrence waterway in the 1930 election, and a treaty was finally signed in July 1932 for 'a deep waterway, not less than twenty-seven feet in depth, for navigation from the interior of the Continent of North America to the sea, with the development of the water-power incidental thereto.' The United States Senate rejected this treaty, which had been negotiated by the outgoing Hoover administration and was opposed by many interests in New York, the home state of the new American president, Franklin Delano Roosevelt. However, Roosevelt invited Bennett to Washington, a visit that produced a joint statement about agreeing 'to begin a search for means to increase the exchange of commodities between our two countries.'[14] By this time Bennett had come to see improved trade with the Americans as favourable to his chances of re-election, and the Canadian government pressed hard for a major agreement in 1935, without any success. Mackenzie King made American negotiations one of the first points on the government's agenda after his electoral success in 1935. In a conversation with the American minister in Ottawa, King had emphasized 'that there were two roads open to Canada', and that 'he wanted to choose 'the American road', adding: 'From every point of view it was important that our attachments should be strengthened and our relations brought closer in every way, politically as well as economically.'[15] Over the years King would certainly achieve this goal.

With the benefit of hindsight it is easy to see King's 1935 statements as prescient, and the ensuing hastily negotiated trade agreement with the Americans as a turning-point in Canadian history. On 15 November 1935, King signed a most-favoured-nation treaty with the United States. Neither country was to allow duties on anything to be higher than those allowed to the most favoured outsider, although Canadian preferential agreements with the British were excepted. Despite special American concessions on some items, the Yanks held fast on cod and table potatoes, and there was much muttering in Ottawa that the Americans had benefited more than the Canadians from the deal. But in his earlier comments to the American minister King was only reflecting the reality of the Canadian position in 1935 and the probable inclination of the Canadian people when the chips were down. The other road to which King had referred in his conversation with the American minister was not for a fully sovereign Canada to go it alone in an increasingly nasty world, but rather for it to seek some form of imperial economic and military arrangement with Britain.

The Depression had demonstrated the nation's dependence on foreign trade, and the Canadian military was in no position to defend Canada in an age of renewed aggression. Canadian governments in the 1920s had reduced the military establishment as far as possible. By 1922/3 the military (including the militia and reserves) cost Canadians a mere $1.46 per capita, which increased slightly by 1929 and then was sharply cut during the Depression. The regular force of 3,000 and the militia were maintained chiefly to provide domestic security, but nobody could accuse Canada of responding to the economic crisis by rearming.[16] A confidential memorandum prepared in 1935 by the Chief of the General Staff, Major-General A. G. L. McNaughton, made no bones about the serious state of the nation's military unpreparedness, even for defensive purposes. The country had no modern anti-aircraft guns, not a single operational aircraft, and just about enough artillery ammunition for '90 minutes fire at normal rates'.[17] In dealing with the Americans, King in 1935—in spite of Canadian military weakness— probably saw no further than the need for visible gestures to revive the economy and did not consider that Canada might shelter under the American military umbrella. But if the spirit world, which he regularly consulted in private seances, had been able to give him an accurate glimpse of the future, he would have behaved no differently.

The trade agreement with the Americans was a turning-point in another sense. It marked the shift in the 1930s from an economically driven external policy for Canada to one that had to deal with an escalating series of political and military crises in several parts of the world. Mussolini had already invaded Ethiopia, and a Canadian voice at the League of Nations was virtually silenced by the upcoming elections. In 1935, with the transition from one government to another, W.A. Riddell (1881-1963), the Canadian adviser at Geneva, was allowed to take the Canadian position closer to actual leadership for sanctions against Italy than the new government preferred, but his actions were publicly disavowed. The result was a mini-controversy in which many French Canadians supported Italy, the home of the Papacy. King himself led the 1936 Canadian delegation to the League, emphasizing 'mediation and conciliation' in place of collective security. Instinctively a mediator, King could not be blamed for failing to recognize the futility of such an approach with the dictators and militarists of the day. Like many Canadians, he resented being drawn into international conflicts, and hoped they would go away.

The years between 1936 and 1939 saw a greatly increased interest in international affairs in the Canadian press and the emergence of a genuine public debate over foreign policy. The Canadian Institute of International Affairs (CIIA), founded in 1920 by Sir Robert Borden and John Dafoe, was particularly active in pressing for more recognition of Canada's role in the world. The focus was mainly on Europe, although Japan had provided evidence of its own ambitions in its 1931 occupation of Manchuria, and continued to behave aggressively in the Far East. In 1936 Canada began a modest program of rearmament, less by increasing expenditures than by co-ordinating forward planning for the next five years. The first serious debate in Parliament in years over external policy came in 1937, when the pacifist J.S. Woodsworth moved a resolution of strict Canadian neutrality 'regardless of who the belligerents might be.' The government's response was that its hands should not be tied, and that 'with respect to participation and neutrality...parliament will decide what is to be done.'[18]

In the 15 May 1937 issue of *Maclean's Magazine*, the historian Frank Underhill insisted: 'Canada should emulate Ulysses and his companions, and sail past the European sirens, our ears stuffed with the tax-bills of the last war.' But such isolationism was rapidly overtaken by events. Although at the 1937 Imperial Conference connected with the coronation of George VI, Mackenzie King opposed any Canadian commitments, privately he admitted to British leaders that Canada would again support Britain in a war against European aggression.* In a meeting with Adolf Hitler early in the summer of 1937, however, King was mesmerized by the Nazi leader's personality and persuaded by his assertions that Germany wanted no war. Fully understanding the threat of war, Canada quietly supported the British policy of 'appeasement', of accepting an escalating series of aggressive moves by Germany—in the Rhineland, in Austria, in Czechoslovakia—as a legitimate quest for *lebensraum* and consolidation of German-speaking peoples. However, by 1938, when Neville Chamberlain's Munich agreement promised 'peace in our time', a vocal minority was arguing against appeasement as an immoral and futile policy.

While appeasement may have been pusillanimous, it was arguably necessary and unavoidable, particularly for nations that were as ill-prepared militarily as were the western democracies in the later 1930s. Less defensible was Canadian policy towards the victims of the Nazi program in Europe, particularly the Jews. Refugees from Nazi Germany had begun an exodus from that

---

*On this visit to London, the Prime Minister had the first discussions about the Royal Tour of George VI and Queen Elizabeth, which took place in May/June 1939 (with a brief visit to the United States) and greatly strengthened emotional ties to Britain on the eve of war.

country soon after Hitler's takeover of power. Some were radical political dissenters, like Arthur Koestler, but many left in response to the anti-Semitic policies of the new Nazi state. Canadian authorities displayed little interest in accommodating these refugees, and in 1938 actually began restricting Jewish immigration. Prime Minister King himself, in a cabinet discussion, rejected 'humanitarian grounds' in favour of political 'realities' as a basis for Canadian action, over the protests of the minister of immigration, T.A. Crerar. Those realities included a general Canadian suspicion of Jews, and what appeared to be a positive hostility to their admission to Canada in Quebec. *Le Devoir* asked: 'Why allow in Jewish refugees?...the Jewish shopkeeper on St. Lawrence Boulevard does nothing to increase our natural resources', and the St Jean Baptiste Society produced a petition to the House of Commons against 'all immigration and especially Jewish immigration', signed by 128,000 of its members.[19] With great reluctance Canada agreed to attend an American-backed international conference on the refugee problem in 1938. Even more pointedly, in 1938 a cabinet committee refused to hear a proposal from the Jewish community that Canada bring to the conference a plan to accept 5,000 Jewish refugees over the next four years, none to be placed in Quebec and their costs to be guaranteed and borne by Canadian Jews.

The most that can be said for the official Canadian attitude towards the Jewish refugees was that it was consistent with past national policy. Canada's immigration policy had never been strongly influenced by humanitarian considerations, and Canadian authorities had always been obsessed by the need for assimilable newcomers. As it turned out, the conference on the refugee problem held at Evian, France, did not force Canada to alter its policy. Instead, the delegates of the assembled nations mouthed platitudes and resolved unanimously that they were 'not willing to undertake any obliga-tions toward financing involuntary immigration.'[20] As the European situation worsened, Canada's Jews mounted a desperate series of public demonstra-tions to arouse support for a change of policy, and on 23 November 1938 a delegation of Jews met with Mackenzie King, and T.A. Crerar, to plead for the admission of 10,000 refugees at no expense to the government. They were rebuffed. On the other hand, mounting pressure on the government led to some internal discussion among the mandarins, one writing: 'We don't want to take too many Jews, but, in the present circumstances particularly, we don't want to say so.'[21] On 13 December 1938 the cabinet agreed to keep existing immigration regulations but to interpret them 'as liberally as possi-ble'. Since the existing system allowed into the country only farmers with capital, such a concession was not significant. Immigration officials were themselves convinced that few Jews really wanted to farm. They were equally persuaded that refugees would say anything to be admitted, and systemati-cally rejected highly skilled professionals and intellectuals (including doctors, scientists, and musicians) as 'inadmissible' applicants.

For a nation as limited in world-renowned scientific, intellectual, and cultural talent as Canada, the result was a cruel—if totally deserved—shortfall. Other countries, particularly the United States, benefited greatly from Nazi persecution in fields as diverse as physics, medicine, theatre, music, and education. Canada did not. Even in the crassest of non-humanitarian terms, Canadian policy was a disaster. But it was inexcusable in a moral sense—particularly on the part of a country that constantly lectured the rest of the world about its shortcomings.

Canadian External Relations in Wartime, 1939-1945

The greatest value of appeasement, apart from buying a bit of time for reinvigorating long-neglected military establishments, was that it delayed war until only the most ardent pacifist or isolationist could deny its necessity. By the summer of 1939 no informed observer could doubt that the next German aggression would be met firmly by the allied governments. When Hitler invaded Poland on 1 September 1939, the Prime Minister summoned Parliament to meet a week later, and on 10 September Canada joined Britain and France in declaring war against Germany. Only four MPs—three from Quebec and J.S. Woodsworth—spoke against the action. Having learned its lesson in the First World War, the Canadian government had no intention of trying immediately to ship thousands of volunteers (much less conscripts) overseas. Instead Canada's first response to war would be limited to overseas military action involving the air force, with a corresponding emphasis on economic support to its allies. From the outset, Canada understood the importance of close ties with the United States, which of course was to remain officially out of the international conflagration until December 1941. Despite American neutrality, Canada found the Roosevelt administration receptive to mutual defence undertakings. When France fell to the Germans in 1940 and Britain stood virtually alone against the Nazi war machine, Canada simultaneously supported the British—if somewhat gingerly—in Europe while coming inexorably under the American umbrella.

Virtually from the outset of the war it was obvious that Canada's connection with Britain would be reduced as a consequence of it. The British asked Canada to assist in financing essential supplies, for example, and this aid partly took the form of the 'repatriation of Canadian securities held in London', a process that would eventually lower British investment in Canada substantially by war's end. American neutrality encouraged the two governments to keep their distance from each other until 1940, although Congress extended the trade treaty with Canada. In late April 1940, Roosevelt and King met in Warm Springs, Georgia, and worried together about the possible collapse of the French and the British without actually agreeing to anything. Within little more than a month, even the United States came to realize that its European friends were in serious trouble. The Americans moved quickly to rearm themselves and achieve a state of military readiness, and they sought desperately to prop up the tottering British, left alone after Dunkirk, facing a German air blitz that everyone feared was a softening-up process before an invasion. Washington's recently formed friendship with its northern neighbour made it possible to use Canada to facilitate assistance to the British while still remaining officially neutral.

In August 1940 Franklin Roosevelt on his own initiative invited Macken-zie King to Ogdensburg, New York, where the two leaders—according to their joint statement to the press—'agreed that a Permanent Joint Board on Defence shall be set up at once by the two countries.' The Ogdensburg Agreement was the product of two converging factors. One was that the United States, which was officially neutral, needed Canada as a conduit for assistance to Britain. The other was that the US needed the assistance of Canada—which was legally able to gear up for wartime production—to rearm. Shortly after Ogdensburg, the Americans sent the British fifty des-troyers in return for long leases on military bases within the British Empire, including Newfoundland. Since that island had surrendered its dominion status in 1933 as an alternative to bankruptcy and was now technically a British colony, its government was not consulted about the British conces-sions. Canada attempted unsuccessfully to get the Newfoundland deal con-sidered separately, but had to settle for a discrete protocol recognizing its 'special concern' about the defence of Newfoundland. Newfoundland was of critical importance to the Allies throughout the war, since it served as a staging and refuelling base for aircraft incapable of flying the Atlantic non-stop. American military investment on the island helped turn around its economy.

The next step in the process of Canadian-American co-operation was the Hyde Park Declaration in April 1941, which consisted of a statement that 'each country should provide the other with defence articles which it is best able to produce, and above all, produce quickly, and that production pro-grammes should be coordinated to this end.' Britain's investment in Canada could not be converted into cash fast enough to keep up with her war purchases, which in turn required the importation of American materials in record amounts. The result of the production and sale to Britain of such items as ships and munitions was an even more unfavourable balance of trade with the United States and a Canadian initiative in 1948 for further economic integration. In the short run, Hyde Park meant that the Americans ordered military equipment made in Canada under the war-production program of the Ministry of Munitions and Supply, headed by C.D. Howe, who had created this program using American technology and money. He now devel-oped a new Crown company, War Supplies Limited, to deal with the Americans. Until American industry was fully geared for war, the Canadian production would prove quite useful.[22]

Even before formal American entrance into the war following Pearl Harbor, and certainly after it, the principal allied partnership was between

Some of the Canadian delegation at the San Francisco Conference, April–June 1945. In the first two rows, l. to r., are: Louis St Laurent, Mackenzie King, (behind) Hume Wrong, Norman Robertson, Charles Ritchie. National Archives of Canada, C-22720.

Franklin Roosevelt and Winston Churchill. Mackenzie King and his advisers seemed reasonably satisfied with the arrangement and prepared to bask in its reflected glory—at least most of the time. As in the Great War, Canada had great difficulty gaining information about many high-level decisions, much less obtaining access to the corridors of power. Ottawa never pushed for access to the high-level military-planning committee, the Combined Chiefs of Staff, which was strictly an Anglo-American operation; but it did try to gain representation on such middle-level co-ordinating bodies as the Munitions Assignment Board, the Combined Production and Resources Board, and the Combined Food Board. Canada had more leverage over the British than the Americans because of its substantial financial assistance to Great Britain, and finally won some representation on the less-important of these civilian boards.

When, in 1942, the British began the planning of post-war world rehabilitation policy, Canada insisted that as a principal contributor to such assistance it deserved to be fully represented on any formal organizations, such as the United Nations Relief and Rehabilitation Administration (UNRRA), formed in 1943. A Canadian position on such matters was developed at External in the spring of 1943. Called 'functionalism', it expressed a Canadian attitude to international organization that would continue until well into the 1960s. Canada insisted that authority in world affairs be neither concentrated solely in the hands of a few superpowers, nor equally distributed among all sovereign states. Instead, 'representation on international bodies should be determined on a functional basis so as to permit the participation of those countries which have the greatest stake in the particular subject under examination.'[23] In its insistence on some direct share in UNRRA, which it received, Canada developed one of its most typical post-war techniques of dealing with the superpowerful United States. This approach consisted of demanding a lot and compromising for much less. The UNRRA debate also served as a dress-rehearsal for the much more complex business of organizing the United Nations.

Canada's role in the creation of the United Nations was, in the minds of many Canadians, the nation's finest moment in international affairs. Out of Canadian self-interest came a concern for finding a middle ground between superpower domination of the new organization and its potential deterioration into a mere international debating body like the League. The Canadian delegation at the 1945 San Francisco Conference that drafted the United Nations Charter consisted of a veritable Who's Who of Canadian mandarins and diplomats. Besides King, in attendance were External's Escott Reid (b. 1905), Lester Pearson, Louis St Laurent (1882-1973), Hume Wrong (1894-1954), and Louis Rasminsky (b. 1908). The Canadians made some major contributions to the Charter's ultimate acceptance as an international document. Most important, they fully supported the notion that security issues were no more crucial than economic and social ones in establishing any new basis for world peace. Since Canada was one of the few nations in a position to make a positive financial contribution to global reconstruction, its opinion mattered. Canada was not enthusiastic about all the specialized agencies, however. It never much liked the United Nations Educational, Scientific, and Cultural Organization (UNESCO), for example. But it did support the World Health Organization (WHO). Canada also was a principal figure at Geneva in 1947 when twenty-three nations signed the General Agreement on Tariffs and Trade (GATT).

The Cold War

By the conclusion of the Second World War, Canada was probably too deeply enmeshed in its linkages with the United States ever to cast them aside. Great Britain was not likely to provide much of a counterweight, having only barely survived the war financially. As one British official had laconically explained earlier in the war, 'Boys, Britain's broke.'[24] Canadian economic policy during the war had attempted to avoid making choices, although Britain's insistence on its own fiscal interests was very annoying. As Hume Wrong put it to Vincent Massey, when he was High Commissioner in London during the war, 'the U.K. is very prolific with its requests on Canada and much less prolific with its appreciation of what we have done.'[25] Canada continued to try to help Britain recover something of its international economic position after the war, chiefly to avoid a total reliance on bilateral trade with the United States. But the American economy was very seductive, and Canadian involvement in the Cold War was probably inescapable.

The alliance between the Soviet Union and the Western democracies had never been a comfortable one. There were numerous signs in the latter years of the war that the Russians and the Americans were the emergent world superpowers, eager to carve up the world into respective spheres of influence. There were equally strong signs that the British and French were simply not strong enough any more to count for much, and were satisfied to be allowed to participate in some of the major decisions. Countries like Canada found themselves virtually excluded from the process of making peace with the defeated enemies, as well as from most of the significant diplomatic manoeuvering of the post-war years. As a result of the war Canada had substantially increased its overseas diplomatic contacts, with 25 posts abroad in 1944 and 36 by 1947, but hardly improved its international position. Towards the close of the war Canada tried to establish some diplomatic distance from the Americans in their continual arm-wrestling with the Russians. But the notorious 'Gouzenko Affair' made it difficult for Ottawa to remain sympathetic to the Russians, and probably crystallized Canadian public opinion at the same time.

Igor Gouzenko (1919-82) was an obscure cipher clerk in the Russian Embassy in Ottawa who brought to the RCMP in September 1945 material that demonstrated how the Russians had organized a spy ring in Canada during the war. A handful of Canadians had been recruited to provide classified information to the Russians from a number of government departments, including the National Film Board, which had little top-secret intelligence to disclose. From today's perspective the revelations, made public early in 1946, seem quite tame and unsurprising. It is understood that foreign nations 'spy' (or gather intelligence) through their overseas embassies, and inevitably a few local individuals can be found to provide them with classified data, for either ideological or financial reasons. But at the time Gouzenko's information and the subsequent arrests of Canadian citizens (including one Member of Parliament) were absolutely shocking. Canada did not exchange ambassadors with the Russians again until after 1953, and in 1946 Canadians proved in public-opinion polls far more willing than people in other nations to believe that Russia sought to dominate the world. The Gouzenko business would also send shock-waves across the Western world, for as other nations pursued loose ends from his files it became apparent that the Russians had not confined their activities to Canada. Knowledge that some American citizens were prepared to assist a foreign power, often for ideological reasons, contributed to the Communist 'witch hunts' in the United States in the late 1940s and early 1950s.

Part of the spin-off from Gouzenko was the growing awareness that the tight security connected with research on atomic energy carried out in Montreal had been breached. The Russians had received most of the results of 'Project Manhattan'—the atomic-bomb development project at Los Alamos, New Mexico—which may have assisted them in developing their own atomic bomb, tested in 1949. As a result of these revelations, the Americans became even more secretive and possessive about their atomic-energy research; and while the Canadian government complained about this policy, it otherwise accepted it because it 'had no plans for military use of atomic energy.'[26] But Soviet nuclear capability, which became a proven reality in 1949, meant that Canada was now geographically located between two great superpowers with atomic bombs capable of overwhelming destructive force. Neutrality was impossible, and so Canada was increasingly pushed into becoming a 'Cold Warrior'.

Economic considerations impelled Canada in the same inevitable direction as the military situation. Canada did its best to trade with the United Kingdom, selling wheat there in 1946 at bargain prices—in a four-year contract that considerably disadvantaged Canadian farmers. The home economy boomed, for—as C.D. Howe and others had predicted—years of consumer deprivation had produced a substantial pent-up demand that Canadian industry had trouble meeting. But the Canadian exchange position in a world dominated by the American dollar was weak, and in 1947 the nation was forced to put strict controls on imports. Howe even attempted to limit Hollywood's free access to the Canadian market in an effort to preserve precious dollars. When, early in 1948, the American Congress approved the Marshall Plan, by which the United States proposed to rebuild war-torn Europe with unrestricted gifts of money and goods, Canada was forced to do something. If European reconstruction was limited solely to American purchases and gifts, Canadian trade there would shrink to nothing. Canada had no desire to provide any of the financial assistance, arguing that it was already doing enough in helping out the British. What it wanted was market access into the American program, permission for Europe to use the American money to buy Canadian goods. The United States readily agreed, for the process further integrated the Canadian economy into the North American one dominated by itself.

The Canadian government, thanks to Mackenzie King's forebodings, rejected a scheme for a return to the complete economic integration of wartime initiated by the Americans and discussed by leading civil servants, including Lester Pearson, on both sides of the border.[27] One American official described these free-trade discussions as 'a unique opportunity of promoting the most efficient utilization of the resources of the North American continent and knitting the two countries together—an objective of United States foreign policy since the founding of the Republic.'[28] Canadian financial mandarins were equally enthusiastic, for by freeing itself from dependence on the 'uncertain markets of Europe', Canada would 'maintain, as far as could be maintained, the prosperity of this country.'[29] King did not think Canada was ready for peacetime 'reciprocity', and he was probably right. Nevertheless, after 1948 Canada and the United States were closer economic partners than ever before, because the bulk of Canadian trade was with the United States, which was increasingly investing in Canadian industry and natural resources.

At about the same time that the Finance people were discussing in Washington a free-trade agreement, the diplomats were meeting there to talk about North Atlantic security. Neither Canadian contingent was aware of the presence of the other, until the Prime Minister saw in North Atlantic security a way out of continental free trade. King observed that 'I felt trade proposals might be made to fit as it were into the larger Atlantic Pact.' He elaborated:

> ...if, for example, the Atlantic Security Pact were agreed upon and were brought before Parliament and be passed as it certainly would be, we might immediately follow thereafter with trade agreement as being something which still further helped to further the object of the Pact, namely, the removal of restrictions to trade within the area arranged by the Pact.[30]

Thus, by one of those cruel ironies that have always governed Canadian-American relations, Canada took the initiative in the creation of the North Atlantic Treaty Organization, which the Americans would dominate for decades. As Canada saw matters at the time, a security treaty would not only deflect reciprocity, but as a multilateral arrangement might provide an international counterbalance against American military domination of Cold War defence. According to Pearson's memorandum to the Prime Minister dated 1 June 1948, 'the joint planning of the defence of North America would fall into place as part of a larger whole and the difficulties arising in Canada from the fear of invasion of Canadian sovereignty by the United States would be diminished.'[31] Since King 'felt sure that the long objective of the Americans was to control this Continent...[and] to get Canada under their aegis', Pearson's argument was compelling.[32] With the British in earlier days and now with the Americans, Canadian policy was always to involve as many other nations as possible in international agreements, on the grounds that such multilateralism reduced the subordinate position that Canada would experience in a bilateral arrangement with an overpowerful partner.

In the case of North Atlantic security, the United States was not totally enthusiastic about the notion of a multilateral arrangement. Some opponents of NATO argued that the American Senate (which had to approve all foreign treaties) would never accept it, while others (led by George Kennan and Charles 'Chip' Bohlen) insisted that it was not only a step unprecedented in American history but one that drew Russian attention to the weakness of Atlantic defences, while foreclosing on an unforeseeable future. But Canadian negotiators pressed their case, governed by 'fears of invasion of Canadian sovereignty by the US' and a desire to regularize the North Atlantic partnerships. From the Canadian perspective, the more nations involved the better, and there was even talk in Ottawa of admitting non-Atlantic Commonwealth dominions. Escott Reid, the deputy Under Secretary of State for External Affairs, whose vision of a treaty was the most generous, also insisted that it should transcend purely military arrangements and encompass social and economic issues as well, producing a 'spiritual mobilization' of the Western democracies.[33] Reid was unable to gain complete support for his views even in Canadian circles, but the final treaty did pay lip-service to a Canadian insistence on what Reid later described as 'provisions on economic and social co-operation and on the promotion of democracy.'[34] From the perspective of the United States, however, what mattered were the Treaty's military and security provisions, particularly the centralization of command under what inevitably had to be an American general. The regular meeting of the North Atlantic Council, for which Canadians and others had held such high hopes, quickly turned into a perfunctory diplomatic event.[35] Though Canada may not have had much choice, it had created and joined an American-controlled alliance. Perhaps symbolically, the United States Marine Band that serenaded the Washington signing ceremony for the North Atlantic Treaty in April 1949 played 'It Ain't Necessarily So' and 'I Got Plenty of Nothin'' from Gershwin's *Porgy and Bess*. Pearson found the choice of selections 'regrettable', but they aptly summarized how Canada would eventually regard its handiwork.[36]

✐ The Search for Middle-Power Status

By the time of the establishment of NATO in 1949 the Cold War had widened out of Europe into Asia, where the pro-Western National Government of China had plainly been superseded by a Communist government headed by Chou En-lai. The Communists had made great gains in many parts of Asia in the period between the defeat of Japan and the re-establishment of 'legitimate'—often European colonial—governments, usually by becoming the spokesmen for national aspirations. They had established regimes through partition in places like Indochina and Korea. The United States always saw these Communist governments as mere extensions of international Communism emanating from the USSR, ignoring what often seemed to other observers—including Canadians—as the Communists' fundamentally nationalistic as well as Marxist aspirations. The US refused to recognize any of these governments as legitimate, or to seat them in the United Nations. Canada was on the verge of some form of recognition of the People's Republic of China in 1950—despite American objections—when North Korea invaded American-controlled South Korea.

The Korean crisis provided a serious challenge to Canada's international aspirations. The Americans took advantage of a Soviet boycott of the Security Council of the United Nations to invoke universal collective security. The Council recommended that its member nations assist the Republic of Korea militarily, thus supporting unilateral American intervention already taken by order of President Harry S Truman. The Canadian government was in a quandary. It had not yet really re-established its military forces after post-war demobilization, and had never been enthusiastic about American insistence on the principle of automatic collective security. A collective UN response to most international crises certainly seemed unlikely. But the Americans expected Canadian support for the UN forces under General Douglas MacArthur, and public opinion in Canada agreed. The Canadian government offered three destroyers, calling such aid 'no mere token'. One American official allegedly commented, 'Okay, let's call it three tokens.'[37] Canada continued to drag its heels while it desperately sought volunteers for a 'Canadian Army Special Force' composed of over 10,000 men, more than 3,000 from Quebec. Eventually 20,000 Canadians served in Korea, with 1,557 casualties and 312 fatalities.[38]

While Canada recruited and trained its troops, events in Korea took a series of startling turns. The allied army—mainly Americans and South Koreans, assisted by a single British brigade—commanded by MacArthur, broke out of a defensive position and headed north across the 38th Parallel to the Yalu River. There they unexpectedly met Chinese 'volunteers', who pushed the allies southward. The contending forces surged back and forth across the 38th Parallel for months. To bring the war to a quick end, MacArthur advocated the use of nuclear weapons if necessary. As a result he was ordered home by President Truman, delivering the famous 'Old Soldiers Never Die' address to the American Congress. Canada had always favoured an armistice, on the grounds that the United Nations had made its point about aggression, and Chinese intervention only strengthened the case. As Canadian diplomats scurried about seeking ways to peace, Canadian-American relations became badly strained. The key show of strength came over an American UN resolution condemning the Chinese as aggressors, and in the end—despite statements of reservations—Canada voted for it. Canada continued private disagreements with the United States about the eventual peace settlement, but always ended up supporting the Americans.

Korea offered many lessons to Canadian policy-makers, but its chief effect was to add further pressure on the nation to build up its military forces and rearm them appropriately. By 1953 the defence budget stood at nearly 2 billion dollars, up tenfold since 1947. Public opinion in the 1950s consistently supported rearmament, and there were precious few internal critics of the policy in those years. Opposition to C.D. Howe's Defence Production Bill of 1951—which gave the Governor-in-Council extraordinary powers 'to control and regulate the production, processing, distribution, acquisition, disposition, or use of materials, or the supply or use of services deemed essential for war purposes'—was directed more to Howe's arrogance than to the principle, and the bill passed easily after some unseemly exchanges in the House of Commons.[39]

The policy-makers at External Affairs did their best to give Canada the semblance of an autonomous international presence, chiefly through the development of a Canadian 'peacekeeping' role in Indochina and the Middle East. Most of that function involved small numbers of Canadian soldiers acting for supervisory agencies set up internationally to monitor local conditions in particularly troubled corners of the world, such as Cyprus and Indochina. The nation's standing as a peacekeeper reached its high point in 1957, when External Affairs Minister Lester B. Pearson won the Nobel Prize for Peace for his proposal to the United Nations General Assembly—which was passed and implemented—that a UN Emergency Force be created to supervise the end of hostilities during the complex Suez crisis of 1956. Engaging in ingenious international negotiations to permit Britain and France to back out of an impossible situation resulting from their ill-conceived invasion of Egypt to protect the Suez Canal, Pearson certainly deserved this tribute. That he had the wholehearted support and approval of the United States for his efforts was not an unimportant factor in his success, although the British and French were equally grateful for the Canadian initiative, which could be seen as being in Canada's best interests because it was so necessary to maintaining the North Atlantic Alliance and the cause of world peace.

Canada had earned its place among the 'middle powers'—an epithet that became popular with Canadian international-relations specialists, as it flattered the nation's pretensions. Pearson's triumphant negotiations occurred at the tail end of the Liberal Party's twenty-year dominance of federal government and of External Affairs. And after Suez, Canada's status as a middle power came increasingly into question. Both the world and the Canadian-American relationship gradually changed after 1957.

✐ The Retreat from Internationalism

Part of the gradual change in Canada's place in the world was a result of technology. When, in 1953, the USSR added a hydrogen bomb to its nuclear arsenal, Canadians became even more conscious than before that their nation

John and Olive Diefenbaker. Metropolitan Toronto Library Board.

sat uneasily in the middle of any bomber flight-plans of the two nuclear giants and adjacent to many military targets in the United States. Everyone's attention naturally turned to air defence. Canada expanded the RCAF, and began development of the famed CF-105 (the Avro 'Arrow'). The United States pushed for increased electronic surveillance in the Arctic, and in 1955 Canada agreed to allow the Americans to construct at their expense a series of northern radar posts called the Distant Early Warning (or DEW) Line. The Americans also began pressing for an integrated bilateral air-defence system, the North American Air Defence Command (NORAD), which was agreed to by the Diefenbaker government soon after it took office in 1957.

The first prototype Avro Arrow during the roll-out ceremony at Malton, Ontario, 4 October 1957. Department of National Defence.

John Diefenbaker (1895-1979) was simultaneously a Cold Warrior and a Canadian nationalist, holding both positions with unquestioned moral fervour and integrity. Unfortunately they were mutually contradictory, and the Diefenbaker governments of 1957-63 never succeeded in sorting them out. As a result, Diefenbaker found himself involved in an ongoing series of inconsistencies, particularly involving Canadian-American defence arrangements. His administration simultaneously 'sold out' the big principles to the Americans and balked over the unpleasant consequences and details. Diefenbaker was thoroughly disliked by American President John F. Kennedy, who referred to the 'Chief' as one of the few men he had ever totally despised.

Three related issues—the decision to scrap the Avro Arrow, the acceptance of American Bomarc missiles on Canadian soil, and the government's reaction to the Cuban missile crisis of 1962—illustrate the sorry tale. When Diefenbaker terminated the Avro Arrow project early in 1959, he did so for sound fiscal reasons. The plane had no prospective international market and would be inordinately expensive to make only for Canadian needs. But the Prime Minister explained his decision in terms of changing military technology and strategy. An aircraft to intercept bombers would soon be obsolete, said Dief, and what Canada needed were missiles, obtainable from the Friendly Giant. (Canada also still needed fighters, however, and bought some very old F-101 Voodoos from the United States.) By surrendering Canada's principal technological breakthrough into big military rearmament, in return for an agreement whereby parts of equipment purchased by Canada from the American defence industry would be assembled in Canada, Diefenbaker further integrated the two nations. The Bomarc-B missile was armed with a nuclear warhead, but Canada had a non-nuclear policy. Diefenbaker thus refused to allow the Bomarcs to be properly armed, erroneously insisting that they could be equipped with non-nuclear warheads. The question came to a head in 1962, after President Kennedy confronted the USSR over the installation of Russian missile bases in Cuba. As Soviet ships carrying the missiles cruised westward towards Cuba and Kennedy threatened war if they did not turn back, NORAD automatically ordered DEFCON 3, the state of readiness just short of war. Neither Diefenbaker nor his ministers were consulted about this decision by the Americans. The Prime Minister was furious that a megalomaniac American president could, in effect, push the button that decided Canada's future. In the end Nikita Kruschev backed down in the fearsome game of nuclear chicken.

But Cuba changed Canadian public opinion, which had been tending against nuclear armament. The crisis provoked considerable media discussion of the government's prevarications and inconsistencies over nuclear and defence policy. NATO made quite clear that Canada was part of the nuclear system, and Liberal leader Lester Pearson announced that the Liberals would stand by the nation's nuclear commitments even if the government that had made them would not. There was obviously no point in housing nuclear weapons on Canadian soil in a state of readiness if they could not be instantly deployed in the event of crisis. Such defence blunders certainly did Diefenbaker no good in the 1962 election, and by January 1963 they had reduced his cabinet to conflicting factions. The minority government fell shortly afterwards. Traditional Canadian nationalism as practised by John Diefenbaker was simply not compatible with the missile age.

The returning Liberals—who regained power in 1963 under Pearson—spent much of the 1960s attempting to implement the integration of Canada's armed forces, chiefly on the grounds that duplication of resources and command structures was an expensive luxury the nation could not afford. A unified Canadian military would be both leaner and meaner, capable of remaining within budget figures that the nation could afford. The country and its politicians, however, both continued their schizophrenic attitudes towards the Canadian military and its foreign obligations. Genuine Canadian neutrality in international affairs would cost even more than the American

Lester B. Pearson
during the federal
election campaign of
1963. Photograph by
Duncan Cameron.
National Archives of
Canada, C-31796.

and NATO alliances, and so everyone pretended that Canada could hold the line on defence spending and still honour its commitments through military rationalization.

Despite Prime Minister Pearson's high profile as a successful world diplomat, his governments were not distinguished for their triumphs in the international arena. In fairness to Pearson, the world was changing in ways not sympathetic to Canada's self-proclaimed position as a middle power. After 1960 the United Nations General Assembly opened its doors to dozens of Third World countries, many of them recently emerged from colonial status and often quite hostile to Western democracies. The new complexities of politics and expectations at the Assembly, and in the various collateral UN organizations, worked against a highly developed and industrialized nation such as Canada—populated chiefly by descendants of white Western Europeans—which also happened to be a junior partner of the United States.

Canadian diplomats found themselves in the embarrassing position of defending in UN bodies the country's internal policy—particularly towards native peoples—against criticisms of racism and insensitivity to minority rights. Canada was not as bad as South Africa, but its record on human rights was not an easy one to explain. At the same time, the success of the European Economic Community (established in 1958) made Western European nations more important international players, while Japan had succeeded in restoring its industrial position. As a result, Canadian influence among the world's developed countries was greatly reduced.

Not only the configuration of world politics had altered by the 1960s. So too had the policy of the United States—and therefore its attitudes towards Canada. President Kennedy and his successor Lyndon B. Johnson were actually more hard-bitten and confrontational Cold Warriors than their predecessors in Washington. President Eisenhower had been extremely embarrassed in 1960 when the Russians shot down an American U-2 spy plane and captured its pilot, Francis Gary Powers. Kennedy authorized dirty tricks by the CIA in foreign countries without the slightest suggestion of apology when they were exposed. His only regret about the abortive 1961 Bay of Pigs invasion of Cuba by US-backed Cuban exiles, for example, was that it had failed. Most importantly, both Kennedy and Johnson allowed their governments to become ever more deeply involved in the quagmire of Indochina.

Like Korea, Indochina had been partitioned into Communist and non-Communist states after the Second World War. When the French government proved incapable of retaining its colonial control against armed 'insurgents' from the Democratic Republic of Vietnam (North Vietnam, governed by Ho Chi Minh), Canada in 1954 became involved in attempts at international control as one of three members, with Poland and India, of a commission.[40] Canada was actually eager to participate, as part of its middle-power role in world affairs. The 1954 commission set the pattern for the next twenty years: one Iron Curtain nation, one Western ally of the United States, one neutral power, with votes often going against Canada. From the outset Canada had deceived itself into believing that it had a free hand to carry out its mandate without either upsetting the Americans or appearing to act merely as a lackey of the United States. As the American administrations gradually escalated both US involvement and the shooting war in Vietnam after 1963, Canada's position became increasingly anomalous, both on the commission and outside it. Pearson was still trying to mediate in April 1965 when he used the occasion of a speech in Philadelphia to suggest that the American government might pause in its bombing of North Vietnam to see if a negotiated settlement was possible. He was soon shown the error of his ways in no uncertain terms when, in a private meeting with Lyndon Johnson shortly thereafter, the American president shook Pearson by his lapels and criticized Canadian presumptuousness with Texan profanity. (Pearson never quite recovered from the assault.) Vietnam certainly contributed to a new Canadian mood in the later 1960s, both in Ottawa and on the main streets of the country. Canadians now sought to distance themselves from the policies of the 'Ugly Americans'—although not by open withdrawal from the American defence umbrella.

After Pierre Elliott Trudeau (b. 1919) succeeded Pearson as Prime Minister in April 1968, an undeclared and never co-ordinated policy of retreat from middle-power pretensions was accelerated. Trudeau had long been critical of Canada's foreign and defence policies. Soon after his accession to office he initiated formal reviews, which the Departments of National Defence and External Affairs found most threatening. The Prime Minister was particularly eager to ask 'fundamental questions', such as whether there really was a Russian threat, or 'Will the US sacrifice Europe and NATO before blowing up the world?'[41] The bureaucrats were not eager to answer such questions, nor were several of his cabinet colleagues. Trudeau had a reputation as an internationalist, but he disliked the military, and ultimately proved much more concerned with domestic matters than external ones. He did shake up the military and foreign-policy bureaucracies, but the result was less rather than more. For Trudeau, protection of the sovereignty of Canadian territory was far more important than international peacekeeping. Defence budgets were cut, and active Canadian involvement in NATO was pared to the lowest limits of allied acceptability. The best-known action by the Canadian military was in occupying Quebec during the October Crisis of 1970. In 1973 Canada did send a large military mission to Vietnam to serve on a revised International Commission for Control and Supervision—essentially to oversee the American withdrawal from that troubled corner of the world. But the commission was not able to act effectively, and the Trudeau government ordered the Canadian personnel home in mid-1973. Canada was no longer a self-defined middle power, and had no clear conception of its place or role in world affairs.

chapter nine

Prosperity and Growth, 1946-1972

In April 1958 the long-awaited final Report of the Royal Commission on Canada's Economic Prospects—the Gordon Commission—was made available to the public. The opening sentence announced its major concerns: 'What will be Canada's economic potentialities over the next twenty-five years and what must we to do if they are to be fully realized?' The Report began by admitting the difficulties of 'fortune-telling' and disclaiming total accuracy or consistency. It maintained that its forecasting had sought to achieve scientific quality. No doubt the sheer audacity of attempting to look a full quarter-century forward was possible only in the optimistic air of the 1950s. Most of the Commission's prognostications were based on projecting existing trends into the future, and it was on the whole bullish:

> The promise of the economic future as we foresee it is one to command enthusiasm. An atomic war would blast it. A deep depression would blight it. But failing either of those catastrophes, which we believe it should not be beyond the wit of man to avoid, the next two or three decades should bring great prosperity for Canadians.[1]

The Commission saw some existing and potential problems, including the extent of foreign ownership of Canadian industry, but prospects were generally very promising. Predicting great increases in both the size of the nation's labour force and its productivity, the Report envisaged a 1980 national income three times as large of that of 1955.

Royal commissions are notorious in Canada as the graveyards of prospective change and innovation. But whatever their impact on public policy, their findings—and the considerable evidence on which they are based—constitute a wonderful source for the historian because they reveal the conventional thinking on the subject of enquiry at the time of investigation. The guiding assumptions made by the Gordon Commission tell us much about the overall climate of opinion, economic and non-economic, of its day. The Commission assumed that nuclear war could be avoided, for example, chiefly because its occurrence would be so devastating as to be unthinkable. It pointed out that a single 'old-fashioned' hydrogen bomb 'could contaminate with radioactive fallout an elliptical area 200 miles or more in length, stretching, for example, along Lake Ontario from Hamilton to Kingston or along the St. Lawrence from Cornwall to Quebec.'[2] It also assumed that defence spending by Canada would continue to be high, since it foresaw no end to the Cold War.

The Commission did not contemplate a major depression and held full employment to be the indisputable goal of government, requiring a 'deliberate intervention' by the central government that it regarded as both necessary and efficacious. Reflecting the gradual, rather than cataclysmic, inflation of the time, it assumed 'no change either in the general price level or in price relationships', explaining that such matters could not be forecast. It recognized technology as a mixed blessing, but associated its chaos with war and argued that its peacetime possibilities were unending. Indeed, many of the Commission's forecasts were based on its assumption that technological development would continue unabated and, in peacetime terms, was fundamentally positive. Perhaps most important of all, the Commission assumed a continuation and even acceleration of existing trends in most aspects of Canadian life. Its chairman would later boast that most of its forecasts were accurate and that many of its recommendations were ultimately accepted by government.[3] In all its optimism—that nuclear war could be averted, that economies could be centrally managed, that technology promised an unambiguously better life—the Royal Commission on Canada's Economic Prospects reflected mainstream Canadian thinking before the early 1970s.

⊱ *The Affluent Society*

The post-Second World War era, particularly up to the early seventies, was a period of unparalleled economic growth and prosperity for Canada. It was not an age of unremitting advance, of course, for there were peaks and valleys representing economic booms and slowdowns, and even the occasional recession. But overall, Canadian production and consumption moved upward constantly, employment rose almost continuously (except in 1945, 1954, and 1958), inflation was steady but almost never excessive, and interest rates behaved themselves by seldom rising into double-digit figures. Almost all aspects of planning in both the public and private sectors were based on assumptions of constant growth, and such thinking seemed to work. Between 1946 and the early 1970s, per-capita income doubled. Even allowing for inflation, this meant that the Canadian standard of living had risen substantially. Unemployment remained reasonably low, never increasing to over 7.5 per cent of the total work force until 1976, and typically running well below it, despite the constant addition of new workers who nearly doubled the ranks of the employed in the quarter-century after the end of the war. There were major booms in the later 1940s and again in the 1960s, both fuelled by export sales and investment in domestic physical plant.

The economy in this quarter-century was of course not perfect, but both government and the vast majority of the Canadian people could be forgiven for believing that there were no limits to growth, that depressions such as the one that hit Canada in the 1930s were disasters of the past, that standards of living could continue to rise. Both politicians and economists argued that governments could now manage economies, and could correct for negative movements soon after they began to be experienced. The operative economic wisdom was Keynesianism, named after the English economist John Maynard Keynes, whose writings provided much of the theoretical underpinnings for the school. The Tremblay Commission on constitutional problems (1953) well characterized Keynesian thinking when it observed:

> The objective envisaged was the maintenance of economic stability and full employment. . . . Both expenditures and investments, by individuals as well as by companies, should, therefore, be encouraged. Moreover, the government should take a part in this, and co-operate in stabilizing the economy and in ensuring full employment by its own expenditures and investments. This would demand from it an appropriate fiscal and monetary policy, as well as a programme of carefully planned public works. . . . The new policy necessarily entailed a considered number of social security measures regarded as indispensable for the correction of variations in the economic cycle.[4]

The resulting general pattern of affluence, however, was neither solely attributable to government planning nor distinctive to Canada: it was general across the Western industrial world. It started, in part, with the rebuilding of the war-torn economies of Europe and Asia, but continued on its own momentum after those systems had been put back into operation. Some particulars of this age of affluence must be considered.

Foreign trade had always been an important component of the Canadian economy, and these years were no exception. The volume of both imports and exports increased. Indeed, after 1950 Canada began to run a trading deficit, mainly because prosperity meant that Canadians collectively chose to consume more than they produced, and financed growth both by borrowing capital from abroad and by encouraging a good deal of direct foreign investment, chiefly from the United States. The outstanding development of the period was without doubt the entrenchment of Canada's integration into the American trading market and the corresponding decline of Britain as a trading partner. In 1946 Britain received 26% of Canadian exports and provided 7.5% of imports; the United States took 38% of exports and supplied 75% of imports. By the early 1970s the Americans were still supplying over 70% of imports and Britain less than 5%. The shift resulted from the relative decline of Britain as an industrial power, joined after 1965 by a relatively open North American border in automobiles and parts. At the same time the Communist countries (especially Russia and China), the European Common Market, and Japan all became important trading partners. Sales of wheat to Russia and China were supplemented by sales of raw materials to much of the remainder of the industrialized world.

The second most important change was in the relative importance of various sectors of the domestic economy. Manufacturing and construction became marginally less important over the twenty-six year period, starting at just over 30% of national output in 1946, rising to over 35% by the early 1950s, then gradually declining to under 30% by the early 1970s. Agriculture's share of the GNP declined almost continually throughout the period, while mining held virtually steady and by 1970 was often slightly more significant than agriculture. The real growth industry was in the public sector, particularly in public administration and service, both as a producer of GNP and as an employer. On the latter front, 1946 saw just over 15% of Canadians employed in the public sector, while by the early 1970s that figure was close to 35%. Many of the public-service employees were highly educated white-collar workers, and the rapid increase in this sector not only helped change the occupational structure of Canadian employment but provided jobs for many of the constantly growing number of graduates of Canadian universities. In 1946 less than 40% of Canadians were white-collar workers, about the same percentage as blue-collar ones, with the remainder in farming and various extractive industries. By 1972 over 60% of Canadians held white-collar jobs, with an attendant great decline in the percentage of farmers. Not all the increase in white-collar work was in public service: there was a steadily growing need for skilled workers in almost every sector of the economy.

Throughout the period the Canadian government set the value of the Canadian dollar in terms of the American dollar. In 1946 the exchange rate was $1.10 Canadian for $1.00 American, and then it was at par until 1949. In 1950 the government floated the dollar, and in 1962 officially set it at $0.925 American, where it remained until 1970, after which it again floated. Throughout this period there was no relationship between the Canadian dollar and any base metal, including gold. While the Canadian government stocked gold in its vaults for exchange purposes, the dollar's value was always based on some combination of what the government said it was worth (expressed in American dollars) and what the world thought it was worth.

The dollar floated because too many people thought there was a difference between these two values, and it was too difficult for the government to maintain its official value. The Bank of Canada controlled Canadian foreign exchange and Canadian domestic banking, the latter through interest rates and the ratios between deposits and credit. Not until 1954 were banks allowed to move into consumer credit and mortgage loans, and before 1967 they were limited to a maximum of 6% interest. Consumer credit really opened up after 1967, when interest-rate restrictions were removed and the banks began to issue plastic credit cards in profusion. Canada's monetary policy increased the supply of money in circulation substantially faster than the GNP was rising, thus contributing to inflation. This result was partly an international phenomenon: a gentle increase in prices was regarded by most economists of the time as an inevitable by-product of the economic growth that characterized the period.

In most years Canadian inflation ran well under 10%, which became a sort of magic figure above which everyone suddenly became concerned. But although 'double-digit' inflation did not hit Canada until 1974, the cumulative effect of gradual increases in prices meant that the 'cost of living' rose fairly dramatically over the period, with the government constantly revising the years used to represent the base, thus disguising the cumulative extent of post-war inflation.

On the whole the price index doubled between 1945 and 1970 and would double again during the seventies, when double-digit inflation became a reality. Constant inflation was a factor against which, or with which, Canadians perennially struggled—complainingly. At the same time inflation tended to encourage consumer credit, since loans would be paid back in constant dollars that were in reality worth less than when borrowed.

Natural Resources

In the resource-extraction sector of the economy several developments occurred that helped it to maintain a fairly steady profile. In 1946 only about 10 per cent of Canada's petroleum needs were being met by domestic production. But the untapped potential was enormous, and in 1947 Imperial Oil brought in the major oil field at Leduc, in southern Alberta. Most of the expertise in oil exploration was American—Americans were more willing to risk venture capital in seeking and drilling new wells. In 1956, for example, more than 1,200 firms, most of them American-financed, were involved in western-Canadian oil and gas. The Alberta oil industry was rapidly taken over by multinational firms, and by the early 1970s seven such firms controlled more than half the Canadian oil business and took in 90 per cent of petroleum revenues. One of the chief uses for Canadian oil after 1945 was in a rapidly expanding petrochemical industry, which grew to provide synthetic products for the Canadian consumer, especially plastics and fabrics. Although the government had produced synthetic rubber at Sarnia in 1942, the first private plant was not established in Canada—at Sarnia— until 1947.[5] But despite the location of most major oil wells in Alberta, petrochemical processing in Canada mainly occurred in Ontario and Quebec. The oil was carried eastward by pipelines, and Interprovincial Pipe Line sent oil from Edmonton to Wisconsin in 1950, then on to Sarnia in 1952. Before the international oil crisis of the early 1970s, this arrangement seemed quite satisfactory.

Another major resource was natural gas. Pipelines were the only way to get the gas from the West into the major centres of population and industry. Westcoast Transmission built the first one, to Vancouver, and tried desperately to extend it into the United States, an operation requiring American approval that was not immediately forthcoming. Unlike Westcoast Transmission's Frank McMahon (1902-86, a native British Columbian), Trans-Canada Pipe Line's Clint Murchison (a Texan) advocated the construction of a transcontinental pipeline on Canadian territory rather than integration into the American market. Not surprisingly, the Canadian government—chiefly in the person of the Minister of Trade and Commerce, C.D. Howe—supported the all-Canadian scheme for political reasons. Howe's insistence on a Crown corporation to construct part of the line, and on government loans for the remainder, led to the fierce debate in the House of Commons in 1956 that would eventually bring down the Liberal government.

Potash was found in Saskatchewan during the Second World War while drilling for oil, and it began to be exploited on a large scale in the later 1950s. By 1970 the province was producing considerably more potash than the international market required, and the provincial government moved in to control production. Saskatchewan by this time was producing nearly half the world's supply of potash. Despite the limitations of the world market, potash was potentially more important as a resource than uranium, the other mineral—found in few other places in the world—that Canada had in abundance. The Eldorado mine in the Northwest Territories was at one time the only producer in Canada, and Canadian uranium had been the basis of the wartime Manhattan Project at Los Alamos, New Mexico, that produced the atomic bomb. After the war, when many thought that the peaceful use of atomic energy would greatly increase—to supply an alternate source of energy to hydroelectricity and fossil fuels—private industry discovered many new mines. By 1955 the Canadian uranium industry had moved into large-scale production, under government regulation, despite the difficulty of finding ore of commercial grade. Over-supply had become the basic problem, since the mineral could be sold only under government licence to a few major purchasers, most particularly the United States government. After 1958 the Canadian government allowed mines to sell anywhere on the world market, once they had fulfilled their military contracts to the major atomic powers of the United States and Great Britain. But the peaceful use of atomic energy failed to catch on to the extent predicted by the optimists of the forties and early fifties, chiefly because of the expenditures necessary to build and operate a nuclear reactor that offered any degree of safety. The Canadian uranium industry ultimately failed to expand beyond its 1958 capacity.

The burning of fossil fuels and the production of nuclear power were the growth areas of the energy industry until the early 1970s. In 1950 hydroelectric generation accounted for well over 90% of Canadian electrical capacity, but it slipped to less than 60% by the mid-1970s. The problem was essentially cost. The exceedingly low international price of oil, combined with the expense of transmitting power from large remote sites to population centres, discouraged hydroelectric development in Canada. Nuclear-power generation was developed by the federal government through Atomic Energy of Canada Ltd (AECL), established in 1952, which eventually produced the CANDU (Canada Deuterium-Uranium) reactor after several serious accidents at its research facilities at Chalk River, Ontario, that released significant amounts of radiation. In this period experts insisted that nuclear accidents, particularly the meltdown of a reactor core, were extremely unlikely. At the same time no serious attention was given to the disposal of the ever-increasing amounts of long-life nuclear wastes that were being accumulated and were being stored at reactor sites or buried nearby.

Indeed, environmental concerns were not seen as critical in any part of Canadian industry before the late 1960s, when the Canadian public first became dimly aware of the dangers of various forms of 'pollution', a word that had just come into common usage. Petrochemical plants dumped waste into surrounding rivers, paper-processing plants dumped poisonous mercury into water-systems. Solid industrial waste was simply buried, often being used as landfill to create new housing estates near large urban centres. Many inland rivers and lakes, particularly in the industrial regions of central Canada, deteriorated into veritable cesspools of industrial waste and human sewage, filled with toxic materials, eating up available oxygen and spawning plant and weed growth. Acid rain, while increasing continually, went almost unrecognized as an international problem. Farmers dumped chemical fertilizers and weed-killers onto their soil with no thought for tomorrow, defiling the underground aquifers that provided much of the continent's water supply. Increased productivity at lower cost was the goal, and the handful of Canadians concerned with environmental pollution were often regarded as part of a lunatic fringe of troublemakers, bringing to mind the Luddites who had attempted to break up machines in industrializing Britain at the beginning of the nineteenth century.

The Royal Commission on Canada's Economic Prospects—which, as we have seen, attempted from the vantage-point of 1956 to forecast Canada's economic potentialities and problems over the ensuing twenty-five years—

discussed the environment strictly from the perspective of rational resource management. The word 'pollution' was simply not in its vocabulary. Its discussion of effluent from the integrated pulpmills of the West Coast is revealing:

> ...considering a higher stage of manufacture, some 50 per cent of the raw material is lost in the waste liquor effluent from sulphite pumping. This waste has been referred to as 'a rich storehouse of chemicals.' Technically, so it is; but with present knowledge—and foreign tariffs on imports of chemicals— domestic demand imposes modest limits on the extent to which the store-house can yet be tapped. Nevertheless, increased utilization of the raw material and greater by-product diversification are in the shape of things to come. The benefits could be very substantial.[6]

From the standpoint of the 1950s the trouble with such waste was not that it was poisonous, but that it could not be profitably utilized.

✄ *Secondary Industry*

Despite the gradual decline in relative importance of manufacturing as an employer in Canada, most Canadians continued to regard industrial development as the key to a healthy economy. Central Canada, especially Ontario, was the chief growth area. During the war the Canadian government had attempted to spread manufacturing around a bit; but with the peace, Ontario resumed its place as the bell-wether of Canadian industry. That province produced over 50% of total manufacturing value added in the nation, reaching its highest level—54.1%—in 1971. Moreover, in many industries Ontario had more than its share of production, dominating most of the manufacturing of durable goods and big-ticket consumer items. In 1957, for example, Ontario turned out 98.8% of Canada's motor vehicles, 90.7% of its heavy electrical goods, 90% of its agricultural implements, and 80.7% of its major household appliances. In most industries Ontario workers were considerably more productive in terms of net value added by employee, and Ontario plants were significantly larger than those in the remainder of the nation both in value of production and in number of employees. Not surprisingly, the average size of industrial plants in Ontario continued to grow, from 32.5 employees per establishment in 1939 to double that number by the early 1970s. Ontario plants employed increasing numbers of the province's population, growing from 319,000 in 1939, to 598,000 in 1946, to 822,000 in 1972. The internal structure of Ontario's manufacturing sector did not change much in terms of the importance of primary and secondary production, or in the rank of major industries. What did change considerably was management structure. In 1946 less than 40% of Ontario manufacturing companies were incorporated, rising in 1957 to over 85%, whose corporations employed 99% of workers. Equally important, the extent of foreign ownership had increased substantially, encouraged by all levels of government. Most manufacturing development occurred in the regions of southern Ontario that had been long established as industrial centres.[7]

One important component of the manufacturing boom of post-war Canada resulted from the re-emergence of a posture of military readiness in Canada after the Germans and Japanese had surrendered. For the Canadian government, as well as for most Canadians, the end of the Second World War was virtually indistinguishable from the start of the Third World War—in which the enemy was not European fascism and Japanese militarism but Communist expansion. The new confrontation quickly became known as the 'Cold War', a phrase popularized, if not coined, by Winston Churchill in 1946—meaning increased federal expenditures on what was euphemistically called 'defence'. The Canadian government had managed to concentrate on peacetime reconstruction between 1945 and 1948, but increased international tensions and American pressures led Canada itself to initiate a new alliance, described by External Affairs Minister Lester B. Pearson as providing 'the basis for the organization of an overwhelming preponderance of force—military, economic and moral—over the Soviet Union and a sufficient degree of unity to ensure that this preponderance of force may be so used as to guarantee that the free nations will not be defeated one by one.'[8] The result was the North Atlantic Treaty Organization (NATO) of 1949. Between NATO pressures and the conflict in Korea, Canada's armed forces were greatly increased in 1950, and five billion dollars were set aside for rearmament, much of it to be spent on military hardware.

American military manufacturers were more than willing to subcontract parts of Canadian orders to their branch-plants, but Canada had a natural ambition to produce home-grown equipment. That desire was more difficult to fulfil, as the sad tale of the Avro Arrow would demonstrate. A.V. Roe Canada had developed an all-Canadian supersonic fighter plane at Malton, Ontario, that was brilliantly designed for Canadian needs and conditions, but was insufficiently specialized to meet the requirements of larger air forces, particularly the American one. A.V. Roe had considerable success with the Avro CF-100 Canuck, the first jet-fighter designed and built in Canada, first flown in 1950 and used extensively by NATO for ten years. The Arrow, like the CF-100, was an all-purpose fighter, with advanced fire-control and missile systems; but with the reduction of international orders it became very expensive. Moreover, its very complexity made it unsuitable for military reservists to fly, and even the RCAF had cut back on its proposed orders. The decision of the Diefenbaker government to scrap it in 1959 was very unpopular at the time—and after, particularly in 1961 when the government was forced to purchase American aircraft (with subcontracting) to handle northern defence.

The boom of the post-war years certainly had encouraged the growth of American direct investment in Canada, and the rise of the multinational corporation—usually with headquarters in the United States and a branch operation in Canada. By 1950 more than three-quarters of total foreign investment in the country was American, mainly through branch subsidiaries functioning in Canada. The chief areas of American investment were in mining, manufacturing, and petroleum. By 1968 foreign-owned companies controlled over 60% of assets in Canadian mining, nearly 80% of the oil and gas industry, and almost 60% of Canadian manufacturing. In terms of the last, American ownership was especially prevalent in the highly profitable consumer area, in which production flourished on the backs of American technology and American promotion of both goods and brand-names. American advertising and cultural values created the consumer demand on a continental basis, and Canadian subsidiaries fulfilled it within the Canadian market. Not until 1957, however, did American investment and the growth of multinationals become an important public issue. Most Canadians were happy to take advantage of the American technology and the jobs that resulted. Canadian branches were for the most part run by Canadians, and the extent of American penetration in some areas of the economy—such as transportation, communication, public utilities, finance, and construction—was relatively negligible.

✐ The Public Enterprises

Alongside the rise of the American multinationals came the growth of a Canadian public-enterprise system. This was most evident in the rapid development of Crown corporations: created by both federal and provincial governments, totally owned and financed by them, but with management structures modelled on private corporations and usually administered on a hands-off basis. The extent of the direct responsibility to government of Crown corporations was never entirely clear. The Federal Administrations Act of 1951 insisted that they were 'ultimately accountable, through a minister, to Parliament, for the conduct of affairs', but matters have never been that simple for either level of government. In terms of ultimate policy, Crown corporations have reflected the will of the governments that control the appointment of their upper management and the parliamentary allocations that supported their expansion. But on a daily basis they were given a virtually free hand. Many Canadians often doubted whether a Crown corporation paid much attention to the needs of the public, even though it was accountable to government in the end. Most Crown corporations were created to provide important services that could not be profitably offered by private enterprise, and there was therefore a tendency for public enterprise—almost by definition—to be called into existence whenever the private sector refused or failed to become involved. Increasingly governments propped up unprofitable industries—that could not, for political reasons, be disbanded—through the creation of Crown corporations to operate them. The

CCF/NDP Saskatchewan government employed the Crown corporation frequently from the time of its election in 1944, and the Quebec government became attracted to it in the 1960s. In 1962 the Social Credit government of British Columbia, under Premier W.A.C. Bennett (1900-79), found a convenient way to go into debt without formally running a deficit by financing huge hydroelectric expansion in British Columbia through a Crown corporation—BC Hydro—while Bennett insisted that his government had balanced its budget.

The first Crown corporation had been created in the Province of Canada in 1841 to build a canal network, and much of the initial development of large Crown corporations was in transportation and communication. The Canadian National Railways was founded in the early 1920s to resolve the troubled finances of much of the country's rail system, and the Canadian Broadcasting Corporation was created in 1936 to produce a national radio system. Trans-Canada Airlines began in 1937 as a subsidiary of the CNR, expanded rapidly as both a national and an international carrier, and was renamed Air Canada in 1965. Under C. D. Howe, TCA was used to develop a post-war aviation industry in Canada, particularly Canadair Limited at Cartierville, Quebec, which created the North Star airplane. During the Second World War the government had expanded and extended the use of the Crown corporation, particularly into manufacturing. After the war most of these enterprises were sold back to the private sector—an early example of privatization before the term was coined.

One of the largest public enterprises of the 1950s, the St Lawrence Seaway, was constructed and operated through a Crown corporation. It was developed with reluctant American co-operation—the United States did not regard it as necessary or profitable—but it completed almost two hundred years of development of the inland waterways of eastern Canada, linking the lakehead cities of Lake Superior with the Gulf of St Lawrence by means of a series of new canals and locks. The opening ceremonies—attended by Prime Minister John Diefenbaker, Queen Elizabeth II, and President Dwight D. Eisenhower—on 26 June 1959 are perhaps best remembered for Eisenhower's halting attempt to speak a sentence in French to the assembled crowd.

Unlike the Seaway, the Trans-Canada Highway was not associated with a Crown corporation. But its completion in 1962 marked the achievement of another major public transportation development undertaken by the federal and provincial governments. Distinguished by federal involvement on a cost-sharing basis—since most highway construction fell to the responsibility of provincial and municipal governments—it was the most visible of the efforts of Canadian governments to accommodate the demands of the motoring public and the business community for improved roads. Between 1946 and 1966 the number of motor vehicles in Canada nearly quadrupled to seven million, and the amount of paved highway outside urban areas expanded from less than 20,000 miles to nearly 100,000. Even so, much rural mileage

The Iroquois dam, which controls the outflow of water from Lake Ontario in the St Lawrence Seaway, May 1959. It spans the area between Point Rockway in the United States and Iroquois Point in Canada. Chris Lund. National Archives of Canada, PA-142854.

remained unpaved, and when the Trans-Canada Highway was officially opened in 1962, nearly half its 4,849 miles were still gravel-covered. Nevertheless, road construction and improvement were major developments of the post-war period, with expenditures increasing from $103 million in 1946 to over two billion dollars annually by the early 1970s. Not only were highways laid down in rural districts, but urban centres were criss-crossed with multi-lane expressways and interchanges. By the late 1960s the destruction of urban housing for road development had become a major political issue in most of Canada's larger cities.

For many rural Canadians the other great public development of the post-war period, besides highway construction, was the extension of electricity into all but the most remote corners of the country. Although most provincial electricity-generating systems had been an amalgam of municipal, provincial, and private ownerships, many provinces consolidated electric utilities

During construction of the Seaway over 500 dwellings were moved to the newly created towns of Ingleside and Long Sault. Ontario Hydro.

in provincial Crown corporations after the war in order to extend services into rural districts. The British Columbia Power Commission was created in 1945 to expand service, and by 1962 most of the province was served by the BC Hydro and Power Authority. Similarly, Hydro-Québec, initially created in 1944, became a major factor in the province under resources minister René Lévesque in the early 1960s, extending to the entire province in 1963. Initially organized to improve domestic service, the great Crown-corporation electrical utilities quickly became major players in public enterprise, creating massive hydroelectric projects to supply not only their own provinces, but American customers as well. The creation of Hydro-Québec was a major statement of the Quebec government of the time, which viewed such nationalization as an important part of repatriating the province's economy. In most other provinces, of course, the organization of major provincial utilities carried no such heavy ideological freight.

The Rise of Organized Labour

An increased role for organized labour accompanied other economic trends of the affluent society. Union membership increased and unions were organized in a number of new industries. The strike increasingly became the major union weapon in battles, first for recognition and then for improved working conditions. Organized labour was to some extent hampered by divisions within its own ranks, including some nasty ideological splits—such as those between Marxists and non-Marxists. On the other hand, great gains were made by labour organizers among women, French Canadians, and public-service employees. Not all unions or union members supported the CCF/NDP, but the association between labour and Canada's third party was sufficiently cosy to permit the two major parties to castigate the CCF/NDP as both leftist and labourist, criticisms that effectively confined it to a continuing minority role. At the same time, organized labour increasingly came to be seen as a counterforce to the Canadian capitalistic-enterprise system that had dominated the nation since before Confederation.

The Second World War marked a major turning-point for Canadian labour. It had fought any number of bitter strikes during the Depression in a search for recognition of an unfettered right to bargain collectively with employers, but had received precious little support from either level of government. The percentage of union members in the total civilian labour force actually declined slightly between 1929 and 1939, to 7.7% in the latter year, although as a percentage of non-agricultural paid workers it had risen from 12.6% to 17.3% during that period. Throughout the war, however, the federal government had decided to co-opt labour into the war effort, and both it and the provinces began the slow process of altering labour legislation to recognize and protect the rights to organization and collective bargaining. The key breakthrough came in 1944 when the federal government, by wartime Order-in-Council, introduced PCO 1003, which combined older Canadian labour principles of investigating disputes before allowing strikes or lockouts with recently adopted American principles (in the 1935 National Labour Relations Act, also known as the Wagner Act) of compulsory recognition and bargaining.[9] By 1946, 17.1% of all workers and 27.9% of non-agricultural workers belonged to unions.[10] With bargaining rights achieved, labour unions went on to hammer out working relationships with most of Canada's traditional industries, emphasizing what amounted to closed shops in many of them. Working conditions (including a reduction in hours and days of work), as well as wages, were negotiated. In 1956 the two largest Canadian umbrella organizations for labour—the Trades and Labour Congress of Canada and the Canadian Congress of Labour—merged into one consolidated body called the Canadian Labour Congress (CLC), as had their American counterparts, the American Federation of Labour and the Congress of Industrial Organization. Thus internal jurisdictional disputes at the top of the labour organizations were reduced.

The process of coming to terms with employers was hardly a painless one. In 1946-7, as soon as the wartime emergency had ended, major strikes occurred in almost all industries. Throughout the 1950s there were never fewer than 159 strikes per year across Canada, involving between 49,000 and

112,000 workers annually. Some of the strikes became both nationally known and symbolically important, either for particular industries or for regions. For example, the great Asbestos Strike that broke out in the town of Asbestos near Sherbrooke, Quebec, in February 1949 polarized the province and closed most of its asbestos mines for four months. This strike marked the beginning of the end for Maurice Duplessis's Union Nationale. It had supported the anglophone employers in their refusal to grant a first contract to the unions of the Confédération des Travailleurs Catholiques du Canada (CTCC), which had organized the industry under the secretary-general Jean Marchand (1918-88). There were two key points about this strike. The first was that working conditions, particularly the constant dust and its danger to health, were demonstrably appalling and caught public attention. The second was that the union involved was a Catholic one, and had the support not only of the traditional left in Quebec but also of priests, professionals, and intellectuals within the province. The ardent support of the strikers by Monseigneur Joseph Charbonneau (1892-1959), the archbishop of Montreal—who announced that 'When the working class is the victim of a conspiracy, it is the duty of the Church to intervene'—ultimately led to his mysterious retirement from office and his move to British Columbia.[11] Although the CTCC lost the strike, it continued to grow under Marchand's leadership through the 1950s.

Perhaps the most prominent strike of the fifties was the Inco strike in Sudbury in 1958. Here a union affiliated with the International Union of Mine, Mill and Smelter Workers was beaten by a large multinational corporation—the International Nickel Company of Canada—which refused to budge. After several months of stalemate the workers' wives themselves organized to call for civic intervention to end the strike, claiming that the union leadership was not listening to their husbands. In good 1950s fashion the interest of families took precedence over other priorities, and the strikers capitulated. Nevertheless, Inco strikes at Sudbury became a standard part of the labour picture in the sixties and seventies, and the workers finally won a 261-day marathon in 1978-9.[12]

Not all union battles were against employers. There were innumerable jurisdictional disputes between unions, particularly those formed in one industrial sector seeking to organize in new industries. In the period before 1960, however, many of the critical internal battles resulted from an extension of the Cold War into the labour movement. The Communist Party had long been one of the mainstays of labour militancy in Canada, but after 1945 the issue of 'communist domination' of crucial unions gained force from the international situation, from another round of 'red-hunting' in both the United States and Canada, and from the difficulties the Canadian Communist Party (and its supporters) had in freeing themselves from Stalinism. One highly publicized struggle occurred in 1950 in British Columbia, within the International Woodworkers of America (IWA). There the CCF and the

Following the settlement of the strike at Asbestos, Quebec, which involved 2,000 miners, Johns-Manville Company workers leave the company's plant for the first time in four-and-a-half months. Canapress Photo Service.

CLC, assisted by public opinion and the provincial government, managed to drive out the Communist leadership of the union.

The forces of anti-Communism were prepared to use any weapons at their disposal. The Canadian Seamen's Union (CSU) and its Communist leaders were replaced (with government connivance) by the American-based Seafarers' International Union (SIU) headed by Hal Banks, whose tactics and connections were both associated with American gangsterism of the worst sort. Seamen were a rough lot at best, but Banks introduced new standards of intimidation and corruption into Canadian unionism.[13] The Steelworkers and the United Automobile Workers were also 'purged' (or 'cleansed') of Communist links.[14]

In the 1960s 'Commie-bashing' was succeeded as the principal internal conflict of the labour movement by debates between so-called 'international unionism' and Canadian nationalists. This issue merged into others, particularly discontent among younger workers with the traditional nature of union leadership and organization. The older union leaders concentrated on improving immediate working conditions and wages through collective bargaining, and were not much interested in a broader struggle for reform, except through the union movement's close relationship with the CCF/NDP. There were many wildcat strikes against the old leaders. The issues were not always clear to contemporary observers. One comment on a strike at Stelco in Hamilton observed that the action was well orchestrated, 'but neither the union nor the company could identify those behind it', adding 'some attributed it to young hotheads, others to communists and still others to a group of Canadian autonomists within the union.'[15] Younger workers often reacted against local branches of international (i.e. American-dominated) unions that were seen as collaborators with American multinational corporations in both the 'sell-out' of Canada and the maintenance of the 'military industrial complex'. By the later 1960s, within the ranks of many Canadian unions, there were general expressions of discontent with American domination of international unions. The Americans took more money out of the country in dues than they returned in assistance; they failed to organize outside traditional industrial sectors; they often supported American military adventurism abroad; and finally, they did not understand Canada and treated Canadian members with contempt—so went the complaints. Withdrawal from international unionism began seriously around 1970, and would increase in volume over the next few years as wholly Canadian unions grew in numbers and membership.

The numbers of organized industries and union members in Canada both rose steadily from the end of the war to the early 1970s. The major gains were among the traditional white-collar employees of the service sector, including teachers, health-care workers, civil servants, and even sales clerks. In 1945 only 86,000 of 711,000 union members were in the service sector, and fewer than 50,000 of these worked under some kind of collective agreement. Banks and department stores proved extremely difficult to organize: a well-known attempt in 1951 to organize Eaton's, the third largest employer in Canada, failed by 800 of 9,000 votes cast. But a major breakthrough for public-sector unionism came at the end of the 1950s, when the postal employees organized and began demanding rights of collective bargaining. In 1963 the Canadian Union of Public Employees (CUPE) was organized, and in 1967 thousands of civil servants repudiated staff associations and formed the Public Service Alliance of Canada. Outside the civil service, but within the public sector, unionization was particularly marked in the teaching and health-care professions. Strikes by postal workers, teachers, and even policemen irritated large segments of the Canadian public and would eventually lead to a reaction against the policy of allowing strikes in the public sector.

Related to the growth in union organization in the service sector, both public and private, was a substantial expansion in the number of women union members. In 1945 Canadian unions reported just under 60,000 female members, or 9.9% of the total union membership, although in 1943 more than 250,000 women had been employed in strategic industries that tended to be heavily unionized.[16] On Prince Edward Island there were but five female union members in three locals. On the whole, these small numbers reflected the fact that after the war women tended to work in occupations that were unorganized, and of course there was a structural discrimination against women in the work force. The expansion in public- and service-sector organization in the 1960s greatly increased the number and proportion of women in the labour movement, although in 1972 women still represented only about one-quarter of union members. Women brought new issues—such as day-care, maternity leave, and sexual harassment, as well as equal pay for equal work—to the bargaining table.

By the early 1970s Canadian labour had grown in power and militancy, and the succeeding years would witness a considerable backlash against its pretensions.

✐ Science and Technology

For the most part the Canadian public did not perceive any fundamental conflict between public and private enterprise throughout the post-war period. According to conventional economic wisdom of the day, modern capitalistic states had 'mixed' economies that seemed to function quite adequately. Governments did some things that private enterprise could or would not undertake, and entered other arenas that seemed particularly suited to public management. One area that had been carved out by the public sector, however, was scientific research and development. The story of Canadian science policy after the Second World War encapsulates many of the trends and developments we have been discussing, including a fascinating internal debate within the scientific community over the question of pure versus applied research that had many other resonances across the broad spectrum of the Canadian economy.

Throughout the nineteenth century the Canadian government had supported various aspects of scientific activity in the name of economic practicality, providing a degree of government control substantially beyond that of most other nations. The first federal attempt at co-ordination of scientific activity was the Canadian Conservation Commission, formed in 1909 to advise on policy for Canadian natural resources.[17] As usual, war led both to greater efforts and to rationalization, and in 1917 the National Research Council (NRC) was created as an advisory agency to the Privy Council. In 1932 it began to create its own laboratories (which employed 300 scientists and staff in 1939) and was given a significant boost by the Second World War, when military needs dictated that top-secret research be undertaken by the

Aerial view of the Chalk River Nuclear Laboratories, 1959. Atomic Energy of Canada Limited.

government itself. Hundreds of research teams worked on military projects, making important contributions to the development of radar, the anti-G[ravity] suit, the atomic bomb, and the de-icing of propellers in flight. The largest single project after the atomic-energy one was a crash program to construct a man-made iceberg 2,000 feet by 300 feet, which could be anchored in the Atlantic Ocean to provide a fuelling stop for aircraft. 'Project Habakkuk' never became operational, but it and other projects accustomed scientists to team research on specific endeavours. None of the many Canadian scientific breakthroughs of the war ever made the transition to peace-time profits, however, partly because the plants utilizing them were rapidly shut down after 1945.

The NRC survived the war, and managed both to influence university research and to assist private enterprise with industrial research. It continued to expand its laboratory facilities, and by 1959 its total personnel numbered 2,400. Its nuclear laboratories at Chalk River, Ontario, were taken over by Atomic Energy of Canada, a Crown corporation created for this purpose in 1952. Much of the NRC's research still had military implications, or was expected to 'yield results of immediate practical value', presumably for private industry. Canadian industry generally borrowed heavily from American technology, since many research-oriented economic enterprises were run by American multinational corporations.[18] The NRC was also an active supporter of univerity scientific research in an era of great university expansion. University scientists tended to prefer 'pure' to 'applied' research, and to think of themselves as part of a great international scientific community rather than as Canadian scientists. By the early 1960s, as a delayed reaction to Russia's space achievement with Sputnik in 1957 and the subsequent worldwide debate over the merits of Western versus Soviet science, it was discovered that Canada lagged behind other industrialized nations in its investment in scientific, and particularly industrial, research.

Two aspects of Canada's efforts on behalf of science were especially criticized. One was that Canada spent a far smaller proportion of its science dollars on the development side of research and development than did other nations, such as the United States and the USSR. The second was that industry in Canada contributed a far smaller share of scientific activity (and the public sector a far greater one) than any other Western industrialized country. In 1959, for example, industry was responsible for only 39% of scientific research, as opposed to 58% in Britain and 78% in the United States. (By this time the federal government's outlays on scientific activity were in excess of $200 million per year.)[19] Other figures were equally striking. Between 1957 and 1961, for instance, 95% of all Canadian patents involved foreign applicants, nearly 70% of them American.[20] These percentages were far higher than for other industrialized countries.

In 1963 the Royal Commission on Government Organization (the Glassco Commission), as part of its overall study of the federal bureaucracy, reported on science policy and science organization.[21] It was very critical of existing science policy in Canada, noting that there was virtually no government supervision of the NRC except by the Treasury Board, and it charged that the lack of private-sector research was the responsibility of the NRC itself. Instead of supporting industrial research as a 'primary goal', argued the Commission, the NRC had relegated it to 'little more than a minor distraction—a desirable but rather difficult task, and certainly of less pressing urgency than other items on the program.' This report had two results: the creation in 1964 of a Science Secretariat in the office of the Privy Council, and in 1966 the parliamentary establishment of the Science Council of Canada 'to define and determine feasible long term objectives for science in Canada, to suggest appropriate paths for reaching them and to consider the responsibilities of the various segments of the industrial, academic and government communities in this field.'[22] Nonetheless, in 1968 Prime Minister Trudeau acknowledged that our science effort was still deplorably backward in development and in industrial contribution. The situation proved exceedingly difficult to change: encouraging the private sector to increase its role was not enough.

As in most areas, government involvement in scientific research in Canada had grown virtually unheralded in the press. Few realized in the 1960s how many government departments had research roles, or what the issues of scientific policy really were. Canadians knew that the nation lagged behind somehow in scientific activity, but did not appreciate the nature of the lag. There was no shortfall in public expenditure on scientific research. The problems were that publicly supported scientists preferred not to serve the industrial sector directly, and that Canadian industry did not feel a sufficient need to encourage co-operation with the scientists or to initiate its own research. Whether or not Canadian science should become a handmaiden of industry was not a question ever discussed at the political level, although the scientists (especially in the universities) had some strong feelings about the matter. The approved political line was that public financial support for science could be justified only in economic terms. Nobel prizes were nice, but the creation of dominant new technologies was even nicer.

The controversy over basic versus applied research was a particularly complex one. While it was true that many scientists, especially in the universities, were not concerned about applying their findings—or interested in asking questions that might lead to applications—it was equally true that criticism of 'pure' research ignored the possibility of major technological breakthroughs that could create new products and industries rather than simply refine existing processes to save money. The obvious example, of course, was the revolution in computers that began in the post-war era. Canadian scientists co-operated with American counterparts to produce the IBM 101 electronic statistical machine in time for it to analyse the 1951 Canadian census data. But the new technology became American, and Canadians were not in the front lines of the microchip revolution of later years.[23] As international competitive advantages came increasingly to depend on 'R & D', the failure of Canadian industry to spend money on it became more critical. In 1965 only 356 of 6,367 scientists and engineers employed by Canadian industry were engaged in basic research; and in 1962, expenditure on R & D as a proportion of sales averaged 0.7% by all Canadian manufacturers, as opposed to 2% by American ones.[24] Many critics claimed that the result was continued Canadian dependence in an age of increasingly complex technology.

The Contentious Economic Issues

The expansion of the public-enterprise and public-service economy at both federal and provincial levels—or its counterpart in science and technology—was not in itself a major political issue in Canada. Most Canadians accepted increased government involvement in the economy, approving public enterprise anchored by the great Crown corporations, increased public expenditure in the administration of various social-service programs, and expenditures on intellectual and scientific activities. The contentious issues were somewhat different: the perpetuation of regional and occupational economic disparities; the related question of the relationship between federal and provincial public activity; and, after 1957, the problem of foreign ownership.

Occupational and Regional Disparities

Not all sectors of the Canadian economy (and not all Canadian people) benefited equally from the affluence of the period 1946 to 1972. There were occupational disparities and regional disparities, with inevitably some overlap between the two. The most obvious occupational weakness in the Canadian economy was in the agricultural sector. Part of the problem was the same as it had been after the First World War. Canadian farmers who could not meet demand during the Second World War could hardly expect the same conditions to prevail after the war, although government policy attempted to cushion the blow by its retention of the Canadian Wheat Board as the sole Canadian marketing agency. Hence the willingness to sell Canadian wheat to the USSR and China in the early 1960s. But other factors also affected Canadian agriculture. Increased mechanization and use of fertilizers meant that fewer farmers were needed to produce larger crops, at the same time that market agriculture became ever more capital-intensive. Moreover, marginal lands continued to become less economic, while overall agricultural production (both in Canada and abroad) continued to increase steadily. Rises in productivity produced the sluggish prices that characterized the period; most increases in food costs to the consumer were caused by non-agricultural factors, such as transportation and processing, rather than by an increased return to the farmer. There was, however, a relative decrease in the cost; and since food represented the largest single item in the typical Canadian family's budget, this reduction encouraged other consumer spending while totally frustrating the farmer.

Other traditional food-oriented sectors of the economy also suffered, particularly the fishing industry, which found itself competing with large mechanized trawlers operated by foreigners within waters fished by Canadians. The fishery had long been in decline, and the admission of Newfoundland to Confederation in 1949 only increased the number of Canadian fishermen in serious difficulty. Significantly, larger fishing vessels in the Canadian fleet multiplied fivefold between 1959 and 1974, thanks chiefly to government programs to aid fishermen, and the result was an overcapacity to fish that—added to international pressures on fish stocks in Canadian waters—produced a crisis for Canadian fishermen. Until the 1970s those who argued against overfishing were largely ignored, and the fishery was one more area of Canadian development in the post-war period in which growth was encouraged without much concern for eventual consequences. Fish stocks were somewhat better managed in British Columbia than in the Atlantic region. On the west coast the fishing fleet became more independent in its operation, while the Atlantic region saw increasing numbers of large

trawlers owned by major fish-processing companies. Whatever their ownership, trawlers with freezing and refrigeration facilities had seriously depleted
the resource by the early 1970s; and while the government introduced quota
systems in some branches of the fishery, it was unable to control the larger
situation. Fishermen tended to decrease their dependence on fishing, supple-
menting their earnings with unemployment compensation for much of the
year in large portions of the Atlantic region.

   The importance of regional disparities was widely recognized, both politically and economically, throughout this period. The most significantly disadvantaged area was held to be the Atlantic region—the Maritime provinces
plus Newfoundland, which after 1949 dragged regional economic indicators
that were relatively flat even lower. The per-capita average income in the
region was persistently more than 30 per cent below the figures for the other
provinces, and a much larger proportion of the population than elsewhere
worked in marginal primary-resource extraction. Although most economists
held that lower levels of capital investment were the key to the lag in
economic growth in the region, substantially increasing capital investment
was, of course, a different matter from identifying the slow rate of growth as a
problem.

   There was a tendency outside the Atlantic region (and often within it) to
'blame the victim' for economic problems. The Gordon Commission in
1957, for example, followed its comments on comparative-income statistics
by observing that such data were not necessarily 'a true reflection of the real
standards of living in different parts of Canada.' It added: '. . .many people in
the Atlantic region would not exchange on any terms their more peaceful
way of life and the comparative ease and quiet that goes with it for the noise
and bustle and the tenseness which one associates with living in large
metropolitan areas like Montreal, Toronto and Vancouver.'[25] By implication
the region's inhabitants could balance off tranquillity against poverty. The
commissioners were incapable of understanding why such an attitude would
raise hackles in the region, though in fairness such a view of the Atlantic
provinces—that they were backward but contented—was commonly promoted by the region's own publicity and its cultural voices. Nevertheless, a
careful listener to the songs of Stompin' Tom Connors or Stan Rogers in the
next two decades would detect both a celebration of the independence and
carefree lifestyle of the ordinary Maritimer and a wistful, occasionally angry,
plaint that life might have been easier.

   Related to the view that the people of the Atlantic region had deliberately
traded Mammon for satisfaction—the classic urban view of the rural
dweller—was one that saw subsistence farmers, fishermen, and loggers with
relatively low incomes as to a large extent responsible for their own fate,
because they refused to abandon these traditional extractive employments for
others more remunerative. Indeed, the government of Newfoundland
undertook as a principal part of its modernization policy the removal of

traditional fisherfolk from the isolated outports of the province, and experienced much opposition in the process. In the fifties and sixties many people from the region did leave for other employment in other provinces, although Maritimers complained bitterly when the Gordon Commission suggested that 'generous assistance should be given to those people [from the region] who might wish to move to other parts of Canada where there may be greater opportunities.'[26] Newspapers blasted its report as 'the second rape of the Acadians'. Nonetheless, 'Newfie' jokes became common in the larger cities of central and western Canada, and not all those treated as objects of derision were from the Rock. The westward migration became the theme of fiction and of Don Shebib's film *Goin' Down the Road* (1970), which followed the sad descent of two young Cape Bretoners in Ontario into crime and ultimate disaster.

The Atlantic region seemed distinctive for its economic laggardness over the long haul, while northern Canada, equally disadvantaged in the present, was regarded as still essentially undeveloped and full of potential. In 1957 and 1958 John Diefenbaker stirred the emotions of many Canadians with his 'Vision of the North'—though neither he nor anyone else on the national scene had any comparable dream for Atlantic Canada. Not until the 1970s did neo-Marxist economic theory contribute the term and the concept of 'underdevelopment' to explain the situation of Canada's peripheries, seeing their condition as a direct product of the successful development of the economic centre of the nation. But if the peripheries were unaware of the explanatory term as applied to themselves, they plainly enough understood the problem of regional disadvantage and sought through the federal system to gain compensation.

Federal-Provincial Economic Conflict

The question of economic disparities among the provinces was basic to any understanding of the ongoing battles over constitutional matters after the Second World War. The Canadian government had greatly centralized economic policy during the course of the war, understandably arguing that the emergency demanded federal control. On the taxation front the federal government not only greatly increased its revenue but even took over some fields of taxation hitherto regarded as provincial prerogatives. Canada 'shared' its revenue with the provinces, which were on the whole happy to be relieved from the burden of debt carried over from the 1930s, and quietly began to balance their budgets. During the wartime years the provinces spent only a fraction of the central government's expenditure—only $200 million as against $4-and-a-half billion in 1944, for example. After the war the federal government insisted that only it could provide the policies to master the economy. By and large the poorer provinces were happy to go along with such a notion, which proved quite unacceptable to the larger and more dynamic provinces: Ontario, Quebec, British Columbia, and Alberta. They quickly reasserted dormant concepts of provincial rights at the Dominion-Provincial Conference on Reconstruction that opened in Ottawa in August 1945. The result was the scrapping of the emergency powers and the adoption of a complex system of tax-sharing under the guise of 'tax rentals', in which the provinces received grants and subsidies in return for not exercising their taxation powers. Ontario and Quebec refused to go along with the arrangement, but the remaining provinces (and later Newfoundland) did—at least for the moment.

The ensuing years saw the re-emergence of considerable tension between the federal government and the provinces over finances and economic development. The key period was probably the 1950s and early 1960s, when provinces greatly expanded their social services, and their civil services as well. In time, the confrontations were no longer between highly trained and skilled Ottawa mandarins and petty provincial politicians but between conflicting teams of specialists, each with its own agenda. No province was happy. The poorer provinces wanted a greater share of revenue through increased equalization payments, while the wealthier provinces (led by Ontario) opposed such schemes and demanded greater autonomy for development of their own resources. Quebec's position was particularly difficult to accommodate, since it sought to control various programs that the remaining nine provinces were willing to leave in the hands of the federal government. Moreover, Quebec had a much more general and detailed historical case to support its position.

A Royal Commission of Inquiry on Constitutional Problems (the Tremblay Commission), established by Quebec in 1953, was still able to offer a traditional and conservative French-Canadian nationalist position on these matters. The Commission's Report, submitted in 1956, argued a compact theory of Confederation. It saw the need for the protection of Quebec distinctiveness almost exclusively in cultural terms: 'Because of the religion, culture and the history of the majority of its population, the Province of Quebec is not a province like the others.'[27] It also offered a view, which would become more fashionable a decade later, of Canada as a bicultural nation.* But the Report's most interesting sections, from our present perspective, made an unfavourable analysis of what it called 'the new federalism,...a system characterized by the predominant place which the central government occupies (or seeks to occupy) in the life of the Canadian community, mainly on the grounds of national defence, social welfare and security, economic stability and the fiscal system.'[28] Quebec objected particularly to federal control of social and economic policy, seeking to direct such

---

*It could be argued that the bilingualism and biculturalism policies of the federal government in the 1960s were responding to a somewhat outdated French-Canadian analysis of federalism that emphasized cultural rather than economic autonomy.

matters itself. If its goal was biculturalism, its means were older fiscal arrangements. The 'new federalism' came to prominence only after 1940, and Quebec openly sought a return to the pre-1940 period, concentrating its financial recommendations on different formulas of tax sharing and fiscal equalization. Although the focus and particular emphasis of Quebec's constitutional position would alter over the ensuing decades, the general historical outline on which that position was based would not change very much.

Questions such as control of off-shore oil resources, which emerged as an issue in 1961 in British Columbia and made its way eastward, also continued to bedevil dominion-provincial relations. So did the problem of the international development of the power potential of the Columbia River basin, where the federal government and that of W.A.C. Bennett took opposite sides over the resulting sale of power to the US.* During the 1960s the debate on the Canadian constitution concentrated on somewhat different themes, chiefly bilingualism/biculturalism and a satisfactory means of repatriating the British North America Act from the British Parliament. But fundamental to the debate was the fact that few provinces wished to surrender to the federal government control over economic development, particularly as more and more provinces found they had bonanza resources (such as oil and gas) to protect. Indeed, one of the principal characteristics of the constitutional conflicts of the 1960s was the disparity between their apparent focus on cultural and political autonomy and the growing concern of the provinces with economic issues.

Foreign Investment

The underlying economic aspects of federal-provincial relations seldom made the newspaper headlines (or perhaps more importantly after the introduction of television, the top spot on the national TV news). The average taxpayer did not fully understand about equalization payments or oil pricing. He or she might not have appreciated the technicalities of foreign investment either, but by the late 1950s every Canadian knew that the issue was an important one for Canada. Before 1957 the nation had for decades paid virtually no attention to foreign (especially American) direct investment in its industry and resources. As late as 1956, a well-reviewed textbook in Canadian economic history discussed foreign investment in Canada chiefly as 'one of the mainsprings of progress', without much distinction between its direct and indirect strategies.[29] The man responsible for publicizing the problem was Walter Gordon (1906-87), a partner in a leading Toronto accounting firm who occasionally did work for the government. A more unlikely

---

*In 1961 the Columbia River Treaty was signed by Canada and the United States for the co-operative development of the Columbia River. The federal government initially opposed the terms of the sale, agreed to by British Columbia, of power benefits to the US, and the treaty did not come into effect until 1964.

candidate for economic prophet was at first glance hard to imagine. A soft-spoken man not known for his charisma, Gordon lacked the liberal-arts educational background of most mandarins, and had been best known for his chairmanship of the Royal Commission on Administrative Classifications in the Public Service of 1946 and his part in the reorganization and bureaucratic rationalization of the Canadian Department of National Defence in 1949. Although acquainted with many of Ottawa's top civil servants, including Mike Pearson, Gordon was a Liberal Party outsider who had for years chafed under C. D. Howe's economic czardom, which was so friendly to American business enterprise. He had refused a junior portfolio in the St Laurent ministry in 1954, after much deliberation and a conversation with Howe in which he had wondered aloud what the elder man's response would be if a new minister questioned one of his policies in cabinet. Howe, astonished, shouted: 'You'd do *what*, young man?'[30] By 1955 Gordon was advocating a royal commission to investigate Canada's economic future, and was himself subsequently appointed its chairman.

The Commission consisted of Gordon and four colleagues, as well as a research staff of 24 full-time and fifteen part-time members, most of them academic economists. The roster read like a Who's Who of Canadian economists of the day. One of its senior staff members was Simon Reisman (b. 1919), then at the Department of Finance. It began its work in the spring of 1955, started public hearings in November of that year, and finished its deliberations, including the study of 330 separate briefs, within eighteen months. Writing the final report would take longer, and it did not actually appear until April 1958 (although dated November 1957), well after John Diefenbaker's Tories had come to power in a minority government. With a federal election in the offing as the Commission's work was concluded at the end of 1956, it issued a preliminary report in December of that year that was made public a month later with considerable press coverage and controversy. C. D. Howe was extremely angry at the commission's conclusions, St Laurent was equally hostile, and Gordon (with others) lamented the Liberal Party's inability 'to accept the conclusions as a broad blueprint for the future', which he argued might have avoided the party's defeat in 1957.[31] A new approach to foreign investment was the most controversial 'conclusion' drawn by the Report. Walter Gordon was not the first member of the Liberal Party who had tried to shift it to the left, nor was he alone at the time.

The general assumptions and optimistic conclusions of the Gordon Report, discussed at the beginning of this chapter, were not seriously challenged at the time of its release in 1958. The discussion of foreign investment in Canada constituted only a part of one chapter out of twenty, although the topic received more emphasis in the preliminary release in December 1956. Most of the text set forth the current situation, which it pointed out had become more extreme since the war with the decline of British investment. The Report admitted that Canada needed external capital for development,

The Royal Commission on Canada's Economic Prospects, 1955. Left to right: A.E. (Dal) Grauer, Omer Lussier, Walter Gordon, Douglas LePan, Ray Gushue, and Andrew Stewart. National Archives of Canada.

but emphasized that since the war United States investment had more than doubled, chiefly through the retention and reinvestment of earnings by companies already controlled by American interests. It observed the concentration of American investment in secondary manufacturing and resource industries and quoted from one of its commissioned studies: 'No other nation as highly industrialized as Canada has such a large proportion of industry controlled by non-resident concerns.'[32] Only a few pages were devoted to 'the dangers...in the present situation' and to the potential conflicts between Canadian interests and foreign ownership. The Commission admitted that precise evidence was not easy to obtain, and that most foreign-controlled companies were good corporate citizens. Concerns were expressed in speculative rather than documentary fashion, and the Report went no further than to recommend that such companies employ Canadian senior personnel, make full disclosure of their Canadian operations, include independent Canadians on their boards of directors, and sell appreciable amounts of their equity stock to Canadians. Such a program was hardly very radical. The Commission did not, of course, invent the concern about foreign investment, for this ran through many of the briefs submitted to it.[33]

By the time the final Report of the Gordon Commission was issued, the Diefenbaker government was able to consign it to official limbo. Although the new Prime Minister probably concurred with its chairman's suspicions about the multinationals, he rightly regarded Gordon as a card-carrying Liberal. The community of professional economists initially greeted the Report with mixed reviews, many complaining that insufficient data were available to support even the mildest of strictures about foreign investment. But in the later 1960s the issue of American ownership began feeding into a renewed upsurge of nationalism and anti-Americanism, as well as into the New Left movement centred in the universities, which provided such a strong voice in the New Democratic Party in the latter part of the decade. Radical younger scholars such as Mel Watkins (b. 1932)—who headed the Task Force on the Structure of Canadian Industry, and in February 1968 released its report entitled *Foreign Ownership and the Structure of Canadian Industry* (the 'Watkins Report')—wanted to go farther than Walter Gordon had envisaged ten years earlier. Critiques of American multinationals merged in the later 1960s into a widespread Canadian hostility to the policies of the United States, especially in Vietnam, as well as into the concerns of those years over maintenance of a distinctive Canadian identity.[34] Public opinion shifted considerably between 1964 and 1972 over the question of further investment of US capital in Canada. According to a 1964 Gallup Poll, only 46% of Canadians thought there was enough American investment, and 33% wanted more. By 1972, 67% said 'Enough Now' and only 22% wanted more.[35]

By the early 1970s the Canadian economy had enjoyed an unprecedented quarter-century of growth and prosperity. Its problems and dilemmas did not suddenly emerge full-blown after 1972, however. There was a continual undercurrent of dissatisfaction throughout the period, although much of it came to popular attention only in the mid-1960s, when critics of the status quo found new vehicles, strategies, and ideologies for bringing discontent into the public arena. Many argued that economic questions could not be divorced from social, political, and constitutional ones; and the result, as we shall see, was a period of much questioning of prevailing policy. As the saying went, if you weren't part of the solution, you were part of the problem.

chapter ten

The Travails of Canadian Unity, 1945-1970

At 2:40 p.m. on 5 October 1970, Mitchell Sharp (b. 1911), Minister for External Affairs, rose from his seat on the front benches to read a brief statement in the House of Commons. He began: 'Mr. Speaker, I regret to have to inform the House that Mr. James Richard Cross, Senior Trade Commissioner of the British Trade Commission in Montreal, was abducted from his home early this morning by armed men. . . . The reasons for this act have not been conclusively established.' By the time of Sharp's public announcement, the governments in Ottawa and Quebec knew that the kidnapping had been carried out by the Front de libération du Québec (FLQ) as an act of political terrorism. The demands for saving the life of this 'representative of the ancient racist and colonialist British system'—the initial communiqué did not mention his return—included the release from prison of FLQ members; a 'voluntary tax' of $500,000 in gold bullion; the identity of the informer who had led police to the last FLQ cell; and both the broadcasting and newspaper publication of their communiqué, which included a lengthy statement of their political position. Thus began the 'October Crisis', a series of well-publicized events that involved the subsequent kidnapping and murder of a Quebec cabinet minister and the declaration by the federal government of a 'state of apprehended insurrection' under the War Measures Act. Canada had apparently joined the world of political terrorism and violence.

Prime Minister Trudeau arrives at the Church of Notre-Dame, Montreal, on 20 October 1970 for the funeral of the Honourable Pierre Laporte. A cell of the FLQ had seized Laporte on 10 October, and his body was found on the 17th at St Hubert airport in the trunk of a car. His murder justified to the federal government the imposition of the War Measures Act. National Archives of Canada, PA-113490.

Despite occasional bombs in mailboxes, not taken very seriously, Canadians had spent most of the 1960s as bemused observers of the era's most obvious discontents. The decade had probably been no more violent than any other in recent history, but the period had included both seemingly senseless assassinations of political leaders (John F. and Robert Kennedy and Martin Luther King in the United States) and deliberate acts of terrorism. Nor was it clear that foreign governments were themselves much different from those with whom they dealt. Canadians who later sat horrified in front of their televisions while terrorists held Jewish athletes for political purposes at the Munich Summer Olympics of 1972 had been equally astonished by police violence against student demonstrators at the Democratic National Convention in Chicago in 1968, in the Paris student riots that same summer, and by the firing on demonstrators by the National Guard at Kent State University in 1970. Many Canadians were convinced that their country had escaped the

n 3 December 1970 a well-protected motorcade carried James Cross (who had been kidnapped by the
LQ on 5 October) and his kidnappers to the site of Expo 67, where Cuban diplomats supervised an
change of the hostage for the kidnappers—who went into self-imposed exile in Cuba. CP Photo,
PT 32-24-9.

worst of wanton violence and terrorism because, as Mordecai Richler had
put it in 1967, 'we *are* nicer'.[1]

All the worst features of everybody else's 1960s were suddenly encapsulated in one set of events in Canada in October 1970. The October Crisis on
one level certainly fulfilled the ambitions of the terrorists of drawing 'the
attention of the world to the fate of French-speaking Québécois', particularly
English-speaking Canadians outside Quebec. As the drama unfolded, and
commentators attempted to explain its origins and nuances, the remainder of
Canada was brought to appreciate that while the FLQ's terrorist tactics were
not supported by most Quebeckers, the movement for political independence
they espoused had become more than a sideshow for both Quebec and
Canada. Perhaps equally important, Canadians everywhere discovered that
their own governments were no more capable of dealing with radical discontent than were those of other nations. The invocation of the War Measures

Act, with its suspension of civil liberties and questionable repression of dissent in Quebec, proved in the long run more controversial than the actions that had touched it off. Prime Minister Trudeau's television interview on 13 October, after the kidnapping of Pierre Laporte (1921-70) and before the proclamation of apprehended insurrection, caused national debate, especially with regard to the following notorious exchange:

> TRUDEAU: Yes, well there are a lot of bleeding hearts around who just don't like to see people with helmets and guns. All I can say is, go on and bleed, but it is more important to keep law and order in the society than to be worried about weak-kneed people who don't like the looks of. . .INTERVIEWER: At any cost? How far would you go with that? How far would you extend that? TRUDEAU: Well, just watch me.[2]

As historian John Saywell put it: 'Whatever the future of the FLQ, the October crisis was a turning point in Canadian history.'[3] From it there would be no turning back.

The Post-War Political Culture

The Liberal Hegemony in Ottawa

The period between the end of the Second World War and the early 1970s was part of a longer era from 1935 to 1979 in which federal politics (and the administration of government) in Canada were dominated by the Liberal Party. Except for a six-year hiatus between 1957 and 1963, when the Progressive Conservative Party under John Diefenbaker ran the nation, the Liberals were in power during post-war prosperity—and beyond. Both the party and political observers came to view Liberal government as natural and inevitable, considering the Liberals to be Canada's 'government party'. Liberal hegemony was based on a number of factors, some of which seemed so immutable that a permanent change in the national political tendency was nearly unthinkable. The Liberals might frequently fail to win a majority, but would continue to govern so long as they were the largest single party in the House of Commons. Only very occasionally could the opposing PCs hope to construct a majority themselves, and then only on the basis of a general rejection of the Liberals by the national electorate.[4]

The nature of the Canadian electoral system—particularly the 'first past the post' method of determining victorious members of Parliament—combined with the continued presence of other political parties beyond the two major ones to reduce to inconsequence the relationship between the popular vote and the strength of the party in the House of Commons that had won enough seats to form a government. True political mandates were difficult to find in such electoral results. The Liberals never won more than fifty per cent of the popular vote in any election in this period, although they came close to it in 1949 and 1953, and only the Diefenbaker government of 1958 was elected by more than fifty per cent of actual votes cast. The correlation between popular vote and number of seats could be quite low for both major and minor parties: the system tended to translate any edge in the popular vote for a major party into considerably larger numbers of seats, and to dissipate votes for other parties. Third parties were much better off if their support was confined to a few districts and not spread widely across the country, a fact that gave some clout to the Créditiste followers of Réal Caouette (1917-76) in the 1960s and advantaged Social Credit over the CCF/NDP. In 1953, for example, the Liberals had 48.8% of the popular vote to 31% for the PCs, 11.3% for the CCF, and 5.4% for the Social Credit Party. These percentages translated into 171 Liberal seats, 51 PC, 23 CCF, and 15 Social Credit.[5]

The Liberals held a number of advantages in the pursuit of continued federal power, of which two were absolutely critical. Above all was the ongoing support of Quebec, which held one of the largest blocks of seats in the House of Commons. Support from francophone Quebec had come to the Liberals in the 1890s, was solidified during the conscription crisis of the Great War, and was further confirmed by Mackenzie King's management of that same issue during the Second World War. The Liberals did not lose a federal election in Quebec between 1896 and 1958, usually winning over 75 per cent of the available seats. To triumph nationally without Quebec support, an opposition party needed to win the vast majority of seats in the remainder of the country, including Ontario (in which the two major parties were always more evenly matched than in other regions). Such a Tory victory as occurred in 1957 could produce only a minority government. The Diefenbaker sweep of 1958 was the exception that proved the rule. In all other elections the Liberals were able to persuade Quebec's francophone voters that the other parties were unsympathetic to French Canada. The apparent Liberal stranglehold on Quebec had its impact on the other parties, particularly in terms of the choice of leaders and in electoral strategies. During this period, neither the Progressive Conservatives nor the CCF/NDP ever seriously considered a leader from Quebec, much less a French Canadian. Nor did the other parties make much of an effort to campaign in French Canada, except possibly in 1958. The Liberal Party, therefore, continued its historic collaboration with francophone Quebec, and this association tended to polarize Canadian federal politics. The Liberals also did well with other francophone groups, particularly the Acadians in New Brunswick.

But the Liberal political advantage was not confined to support from francophones, as the elections of the 1960s would demonstrate. While national political parties in Canada needed to appeal to a vast spectrum of voters across the nation in order to win power, only the Liberals consistently succeeded in this appeal, chiefly by staking out their political ground outside French Canada slightly to the left of centre. Mackenzie King had specialized in adopting the most popular goals of the welfare state, often lifting them shamelessly from the platform of the CCF—a practice his successors continued. One newspaper in 1963 could describe the Liberal party as 'a coalition in the Canadian tradition that embraces people of all classes and regions built around a programme and the solution of issues rather than a person', while maintaining that the Progressive Conservatives were 'built around the personality of Mr. Diefenbaker.'[6] Equally to the point, when the Liberals failed to obtain a clear-cut parliamentary majority in the elections of 1963 and 1965, they were kept in power by the third parties. The Diefenbaker Tories, during their 1962-3 minority government, were unable to agree upon a legislative program that could win third-party approval, while the Liberals were always flexible enough to be able to accommodate third-party issues.

There were, of course, other factors in continued Liberal success besides the party's general support from French Canada and its assumption of the moderate left-of-centre position on the political spectrum. Many involved luck as much as skill, although the Liberal opportunism and instinct for power made its contribution. For example, the Liberal Party should have been in serious trouble in 1968, when the PCs finally substituted for John Diefenbaker a credible and apparently sympathetic national leader in the person of Robert Stanfield (b. 1914) of Nova Scotia. Stanfield's unquestioned integrity and good sense seemed to match him well against Prime Minister Lester Pearson. The Progressive Conservative Party had a few carefully worked-out policies, including a guaranteed annual income, designed to capture some of the left-centre ground. But in December 1967 Pearson announced his retirement.

At the leadership convention in April 1968 Pierre Elliott Trudeau, recently arrived in Ottawa and currently Minister of Justice, was elected to be his successor. Not only was Trudeau, a thoroughly bilingual French Canadian, likely to appeal in Quebec, but he was able to convince the electorate that he was far more of a reformer than either his electoral pronouncements or subsequent policies would indicate. The federal election on 25 June 1968 was the first one fought largely in the arena of the media, particularly through television, and only the Liberals had a leader who was able to project a positive and charismatic personality on the tube. Part of Trudeau's success was his ability, at the height of the sixties' ferment, to appeal to urban and women voters as a swinging 'instant pop hero', the 'Bob Dylan of the North'. The Liberal candidates grasped Trudeau's coat-tails and won a resounding victory. As Dalton Camp (b. 1920), the architect of Stanfield's leadership victory and 1968 campaign, ruefully admitted: 'When all goes well, you are . . . courted by good luck. The sun beamed down on Trudeau. The rain poured down on Stanfield.'[7] To which the Liberal strategists might have cynically responded: 'You make your own luck by your choice of candidate.'

The Liberal Party had alternated its leaders, all of whom became prime ministers of Canada, between French Canadians and Anglo Canadians.

Pierre Elliott Trudeau, Justice Minister, with Prime Minister Pearson at the Federal-Provincial Conference of February 1968. National Archives of Canada, C-25001.

Between 1887 and 1984—virtually a century—it was led by only five men: Laurier (1887-1919), Mackenzie King (1919-48), Louis St Laurent (1948-58), Lester B. Pearson (1958-68), and Pierre Elliott Trudeau (1968-84). Their longevity as leaders was greatly assisted by the party's ability to remain in office. The Liberals preferred to turn for its leaders to urbane, well-educated men from the professional middle classes oriented to federal government and politics. Each had his own expertise. King was a professional labour consultant and negotiator who had studied economics at Chicago and Harvard and had written a well-known book entitled *Industry and Humanity* (1918). St Laurent was a former law professor at Laval who became a highly successful corporation lawyer and president of the Canadian Bar Association. Pearson had begun as a history professor at the University of Toronto before joining External Affairs as a mandarin, to become a professional diplomat. Trudeau was educated at the Université de Montréal, Harvard, and the London School of Economics, and was serving as a law professor at the U de M when he was elected to Parliament in 1965. None of these men had earned a doctorate, but all held appointments that in our own time would probably require such a degree.

The Conservative Party had gone through a good many more leaders, many of whom never actually managed to govern the nation. From John A. Macdonald's death in 1891 to Brian Mulroney's election as leader in 1983, the Conservatives were led federally by fourteen men. Only Robert Borden and John Diefenbaker lasted for more than ten years. From 1945 to 1972 the Conservative Party (renamed the Progressive Conservative Party in 1942) was headed by John Bracken (1942-48), George Drew (1948-56), Diefenbaker (1956-67), and Robert Stanfield (1967-76). Apart from Diefenbaker, the other three had been popular and successful provincial premiers with little federal administrative experience. Diefenbaker's federal experience, of course, was as an Opposition spokesman in the House of Commons, in which he had served since 1940. Except for Bracken, who had been a professor of field husbandry at the University of Saskatchewn before becoming head of the Manitoba Agricultural College in 1920, they were all small-town lawyers prior to their full-time entrance into politics and government. All were regarded as being to the left of their parties, and both Bracken and Stanfield had a significant influence in bringing PC policy towards a national centre in terms of both regional and economic issues. Diefenbaker was *sui generis*, a brilliant if old-fashioned public orator and a genuine western populist. All the PC leaders had strong sympathies for the ordinary under-privileged Canadian, although only Diefenbaker had the public presence to be able to convince the electorate of his concerns. Significantly, none of these men spoke French very comfortably, and Diefenbaker's electoral victories in Quebec were largely achieved without his campaigning presence in the province.

Countervailing Liberal Hegemony

The post-war federal dominance of the Liberals as the party of government was mediated by a number of countervailing factors in Canadian politics. The Americans had provided checks and balances within their central government—the Senate, the Supreme Court— that were not available within the Canadian parliamentary system of responsible government. By both British and Canadian precedents, Parliament (especially the House of Commons) was supreme. So long as the government in power held a majority in the Commons, it had the legal and technical ability to do pretty much as it wanted. Nevertheless, there were some clear limitations on this theoretical omnipotence.

One limitation that applied to any government was the increased size and scope of the apparatus of bureaucracy, including the mandarinate and, especially, the civil service. As we have already seen, government at all levels became Canada's single largest employer, a fact that had substantial implications. From 46,000 employees in 1939 and 116,000 in 1946, twenty years later the federal government had grown to 228,000 employees. But both provincial and municipal employment grew even faster after the war, the provinces employing 50,000 in 1946 and 257,000 by 1966, the municipalities 56,000 in 1946 and 224,000 in 1966.[8] The scope of bureaucracy had political implications as well as economic ones. The larger it got, the harder it was to manage. A host of popular commentators, and the press, attacked governments at all levels for mismanagement and waste, but as one commentator pointed out:

> It is true that the initial motive for reforms may be the outsider's simple-minded belief that gigantic savings can be effected. But once set an investigation afoot and the economy motive gets quickly overlaid with the more subtle and difficult problems of improved service and efficiency.[9]

A Royal Commission on Government Organization—created by the Diefenbaker government in 1960 to improve efficiency and economy in the departments and agencies of the federal government, and chaired by J. Grant Glassco (1905-68)—found itself unable either to recommend or to effect major changes in the bureaucracy, particularly in terms of downscaling the scope of operations. All governments, including federal Liberal ones, increasingly found themselves trapped by the actions of their predecessors and by the difficulties of dismantling systems once created.

The pipeline under construction in Alberta. Photograph copyright Alain Cornu, Publiphoto.

Another important limitation was the force of public opinion. Federal politicians took their chances when they attempted policies that were well in advance of what the country found acceptable, but they ran even greater risks when they crossed an unwritten boundary of fair play in the use of their power, particularly in the legislature. The Liberals under St Laurent were defeated in the 1957 election for many reasons, but one of the most critical was a public sense that they had become too 'arrogant'. John Diefenbaker made great mileage from the abuse of the rights of Parliament in the notorious pipeline debate in May 1956. Trans Canada Pipelines Ltd, controlled by American financial interests, was building a pipeline to take surplus natural gas for export from Alberta to Montreal, and the Liberal government wanted the project completed before the next election. In April the company announced that it needed another $80 million by 7 June to complete the line from Alberta to Winnipeg. When C.D. Howe introduced a bill on 13 May to authorize the pipeline and the loan, it was attacked; but the government threatened closure if it was not passed (which it was on 1 June). The event became a symbol of Liberal contempt for the democratic process. Re-elect the Liberals, challenged Diefenbaker, but 'don't ask the opposition to stand up for your rights, because there will be no rights left.'[10] The Canadian public over the years consistently demonstrated that it would tolerate quite a lot from its politicians and political parties before it became persuaded of systematic abuse of power, and the risk of earning such public disapproval has always helped to curb excesses, particularly for governments with large majorities.

Opposition in Parliament was another factor that to some extent affected the way in which Liberal dominance was played out and became limited politically. The elections of 1957, 1962, 1963, and 1965 all returned minority governments, which meant that the government had to pay more attention to third parties. Minority governments suggested the unhappiness of large chunks of the electorate with the two principal parties. In fact, a substantial proportion of the federal electorate did not vote for either the Liberals or the Conservatives.

Percentage of Third-Party Vote in Federal Elections, 1945-1968

YEAR	1945	1949	1953	1957	1958	1962	1963	1965	1968
PERCENTAGE	32.7	20.8	20.2	20.1	12.8	25.5	25.5	27.4	23.1

Source: Tables in J. Murray Beck, *Pendulum of Power: Canada's Federal Elections* (Scarborough, 1968), *passim*.

In the post-war period the two principal third parties were the CCF/NDP and the Social Credit/Créditistes.

The Co-Operative Commonwealth Federation (CCF) had emerged from the war with high hopes, gaining 15.6% of the popular vote and 28 Members of Parliament in the 1945 federal election. Its popularity decreased in the

The 1948 national convention of the CCF in Winnipeg. Left to right: M.J. Coldwell, the leader; Frank (F.R.) Scott, the national chairman; and Tommy Douglas, then premier of Saskatchewan. In the background is a photograph of J.S. Woodsworth, the first leader. National Archives of Canada, PA-185737.

ensuing elections, however, and in 1958 it was reduced to 8 MPs and 9.5% of the popular vote. This erosion of support came about chiefly because the CCF was mistakenly thought by some to be associated with international Communism, and was regarded by much of the Canadian public as being both too radical and too doctrinaire. It failed to achieve any electoral success east of Ontario, in either Quebec or the Atlantic region, and had difficulty in presenting itself as a truly national alternative to the two major parties. After the 1958 defeat, the CCF remobilized through an alliance with organized labour (the Canadian Labour Congress), and in 1961 became the New Democratic Party under the leadership of former Saskatchewan Premier T.C. (Tommy) Douglas. As the NDP, the party did better in the sixties. It drew 13.5% of the popular vote and 19 seats in 1962, 13.1% and 17 seats in 1963, 17.9% and 21 seats in 1965, and 17.0% and 22 seats in 1968. But it continued to do poorly in Quebec and the East, and its admitted association with organized labour replaced its former alleged association with Communism as the principal explanation for its failure to make a real national breakthrough.

Although the NDP was unable to increase its national base of support, as a voice on the left it exercised considerable influence in the election campaigns of the 1960s, and real power during the minority governments of Pearson. In the 1963 campaign, for example, Douglas advocated income redistribution and improved social services, including universal medicare. These policies were far more specific than Pearson's made-in-America 'war on poverty', and they were translated into legislative commitments by the Liberals when faced with a minority situation in 1963. The CCF/NDP also had considerable success at the provincial level in this period, forming governments in Saskatchewan (1944-64, 1971-82), British Columbia (1972-5), and Manitoba (1969-77), and providing official opposition in these and other provinces. It was the Saskatchewan NDP government that pioneered the introduction of medicare in 1962, fighting it through to acceptance against considerable opposition from the province's doctors.

The CCF/NDP was not the only important third party on the federal scene. The other was the federal Social Credit Party, which had begun life as an effort by Alberta's Social Credit movement to introduce its ideas on the national level: in the election of 1935 Alberta elected 15 Social Credit MPs (with nearly 50% of the popular vote). After the war the party won some seats in Alberta and British Columbia and achieved more prominence in the early sixties, when it was led by Robert Thompson (b. 1914) with the assistance of Réal Caouette in Quebec. The Social Credit party of the sixties had two wings, one western and a more heavily supported Quebec one. In the 1962 election, for example, 26 of the 30 Social Credit MPs elected were from Quebec. After the 1963 election Caouette broke from Thompson to form his own Ralliement des créditistes, which elected 9 MPs in 1965 and 14 in 1968. Social Credit's appeal was particularly strong in rural and small-town areas, where its combination of federalism and economic reform—based on hostility to both traditional capitalism and public enterprise—was attractive.

Along with the NDP, the Social Credit Party between 1962 and 1988 garnered enough votes (and parliamentary seats) to prevent either of the two major parties from achieving majority status and firm control of the House of Commons. Although many observers bemoaned the absence of stable government in the sixties, a sizeable number argued that minority status kept governments on their toes and more responsive to the people. Certainly the governments of Lester Pearson, while constantly teetering on the edge of defeat in the Commons (and even going over it on occasion), were among the most energetic and innovative ones that Canada has experienced in this century. The Pearson governments had to deal simultaneously with the problems of national unity and increased social welfare, and did so.

While public opinion—expressed at elections—did have some force, as did third parties, a more important limiting factor on Liberal dominance was undoubtedly the historic division of power between the federal and provincial governments, and the ensuing constitutional debates. Canadian voters had long sensed that the really effective opposition to a federal majority was to be found at the provincial level, and most successful provincial governments employed 'Ottawa bashing' as an essential part of their political arsenal, since the electorate frequently voted for quite different parties at the federal level.

Provincial Politics and Federal-Provincial Relations

Few provinces after 1945 experienced the alternations of the traditional two-party system. In most, one party controlled the government even more continuously and strongly than did the federal Liberals. Except in the Atlantic region, however—where there was a long-standing electoral tradition of attempting to keep provincial and federal governments of the same party— the dominant provincial party was not Liberal. The Liberal success in Newfoundland and New Brunswick was a product chiefly of local dynamics. In Newfoundland, Joey Smallwood (1900-91) parleyed strong Liberal support for confederation with Canada into an unbroken tenure as premier from 1949 to 1971. In New Brunswick, Liberal control had been broken in 1951-60 by the Tories, but the traditional alliance between the province's Acadian minority and the Liberals was cemented by Louis Robichaud (b. 1925) in 1960. Nova Scotia was run continuously by the Tories, while Prince Edward Island had one of the few truly viable two-party political systems in the country, perhaps made possible by the small size of the province. In Quebec the Liberals under Jean Lesage (1912-80) did break through the long control of the Union Nationale in 1960, but west of Quebec provincial Liberals held little ground. Ontario continued in the grip of the 'Big Blue Machine' that controlled the province throughout the post-war period, while Alberta (1935-72) and British Columbia (1952-72) were governed by Social Credit. The only provincial Liberal government west of Quebec between 1945 and 1972 was that of Ross Thatcher (1917-71) in Saskatchewan (1964-71); but his government was one of the most vociferous critics of federal Liberalism under Pearson and Trudeau. So, wherever federal Liberalism drew its strength, it was not from provincial parties and organizations. By the early 1970s the only provincial governments controlled by the Liberals were in Prince Edward Island and Quebec. Certainly Pierre Trudeau's conception of Liberalism did not accord with that of Robert Bourassa (b. 1933), who succeeded Jean Lesage in 1970, and the two leaders (along with their governments) were continually at loggerheads.

The disagreements of the Saskatchewan and Quebec Liberals with the federal Liberals suggest that party affiliation meant little in the ongoing controversies between the Dominion and its provinces. Such conflict, which had literally been built into Confederation by the nature of the British North

America Act, had never been resolved. The Dominion of Canada had been created as a federal state, with a central government in Ottawa and local governments in the provinces. While the intention of the leading Fathers of Confederation had been to produce a strong central government and weak provincial ones, they had been forced by the insistence of the provinces—particularly, but not only, Quebec—to maintain separate identities for the constituent parts of the federation. Separate provincial identities were specifically guaranteed through an explicit division of powers between the federal and provincial governments in sections 91 and 92 of the British North America Act of 1867. The division thus created, reflecting the state of political thinking of the 1860s, gave the federal arm the authority to produce a viable national economy, and the provinces the power to protect what were at the time regarded as local and cultural concerns. Some of the provincial powers, such as those over education, were acquired because the provinces demanded them. Others, such as the powers over the health and welfare of provincial inhabitants, were not regarded by the Fathers as critical for a national government. (Lighthouses and post-offices were more important than public medical care in the 1860s.) Over time the division of powers had made the provinces responsible, in whole or in part, for many of the expensive aspects of government, including health, education, and welfare—while limiting their ability to raise a commensurate revenue. Many important aspects came to be shared between governments, while it became clear that the BNA Act's division of powers, in sections 91 and 92, was dated, ambiguous, and hence contentious.

Like most constitutional documents, the BNA Act had not been written to stand by itself. It was intended to be enshrouded in a larger context of precedent, almost all of which was British and/or British Imperial, and there was a system included in the Constitution for adjudicating disputes over boundaries. The concept of unwritten precedent, very British in nature, did provide a considerable element of constitutional flexibility. For example, the entire system of political parties and leaders—including Prime Ministers, Premiers, Privy Councils, and Cabinets—that enabled the governments of both Canada and its provinces to function, was never once mentioned in the BNA Act: it was one of the unwritten conventions of the Constitution. The official powers of the Governor-General were listed very precisely, but the document never stated that he exercised them only on advice from his Privy Councillors. Precedents, both those brought into Confederation and those evolved within it, allowed for the survival of the Canadian Constitution. Pierre Trudeau himself observed, in 1961, that the Constitution was 'the eighth oldest written Constitution, the second oldest one of a federal nature, and the oldest which combined federalism with the principles of responsible government.'[11] But despite the miracle of longevity, the BNA Act had been constantly strained. Then as now, critics of the existing system stressed its tensions, while its defenders concentrated on its capacity for survival.

One of the principal problems was in the arrangements within the BNA Act for settling disputes over its interpretation. The Act provided for a judicature modelled on British arrangements, with a general court of appeal or Supreme Court at the top. However, this court, established in 1875, was not always the court of final decision, particularly on constitutional matters. Until 1949 constitutional issues could still be appealed to a British imperial court, the Judicial Committee of the Privy Council of the United Kingdom, which in the years after Confederation had interpreted the Canadian Constitution in ways distinctly favourable to the provinces. Even with the elimination of this example of continued colonialism, amendment of the British North America Act was extremely difficult. Amending procedures were not described in the Act itself, and ultimately could be achieved only by an act of the British Parliament. By the mid-twentieth century, when the Judicial Committee's authority was removed, Canadian political leaders had worked out a variety of informal non-judicial means for resolving constitutional questions, particularly those involving federal and provincial matters. One of the most important informalities, sanctioned by pragmatic precedent, was the federal-provincial conference.

While meetings between federal and provincial governments had been an ongoing feature of Canadian political life since Confederation, organized and systematic conferences between the feds and all their provincial counterparts—particularly on a first-ministers basis—was a feature regularized only after the Second World War. As we have seen, King's Liberals led the way, calling a Dominion-Provincial Conference on Reconstruction in August 1945, when the federal government had a comprehensive program for an extended welfare state based on the tax system and the economic policy of a strong central government, and sought the co-operation of the provinces to implement its plans. What was required was agreement that Ottawa could keep the emergency powers it had acquired to fight the war. The major provinces, led by Ontario and Quebec, were not enthusiastic. The conference adjourned for 'study', and finally met again in April 1946, when Quebec and Ontario in tandem simultaneously denounced centralization while insisting on provincial autonomy. In the wake of this meeting, the federal government offered a 'tax rental' scheme to the provinces, whereby it would collect certain taxes (on incomes, corporations, and successions to estates) and distribute payments to the provinces. Ontario and Quebec went for their own schemes, but the remaining provinces (and Newfoundland in 1949) accepted tax rental.

This Conference on Reconstruction was important in several respects. First, it demonstrated that even under the best of circumstances—with a program of acknowledged public popularity and advantage—the provinces were not prepared to surrender their autonomy to Ottawa. Second, it created an institution that, in the course of time, would become entrenched. Subsequent federal-provincial conferences would be summoned on an increasingly regular basis, initially to deal with financial matters, but gradually to address constitutional matters as well. It was at the dominion-provincial conference of July 1960, called by Prime Minister Diefenbaker to discuss tax sharing, that the question of repatriation of the BNA Act (i.e. its amendment in Canada without recourse to the British Parliament) was put on the table by Premier Jean Lesage and responded to by Diefenbaker with instructions to his Minister of Justice, E. Davie Fulton (b. 1916), to meet subsequently with the attorneys general of the provinces on the question. A whole series of federal-provincial conferences—on pensions, financial arrangements, constitutional issues—followed in the 1960s, and became part of the accepted political practice of the nation.[12] Such meetings publicized the difficulties of achieving national unity in the face of opposition from Quebec (and usually at least one other province) to whatever reform or change was on the agenda.

Another whole dimension was added to the post-war constitutional morass through John Diefenbaker's insistence on the introduction of a Canadian Bill of Rights. The Americans had produced a bill of rights for their constitution (the first ten amendments) as part of the process of ratification. But the Canadian founding fathers did not follow the American lead, chiefly because the British constitutional tradition was that Parliament should be supreme, and the courts automatically protective against abuse of power. Like the British constitution, the BNA Act had enshrined minority rights—chiefly in terms of education, religion, and language—but had displayed little interest in the rights of the individual that were so crucial to the American understanding of democracy. The introduction of the notion of spelling out rights—for individuals or collective groups—was a potentially profound change in the Canadian Constitution.* Diefenbaker's Bill for the Recognition and Protection of Human Rights and Fundamental Freedoms, fulfilling campaign promises made in 1957 and 1958, was passed in 1960. As it was limited to the federal level, and the rights it enshrined could be overridden by national emergencies, it had little immediate impact: a full ten years went by before the Canadian Supreme Court heard a case based upon it. But its implications for constitutional reform—particularly when combined with the growth in the 1960s in demands from minority groups for formal recognition and equal protection and treatment under the law—were considerable.

Over the course of the post-war period Canadians discovered that the problems of their Constitution were greater than mere disputes over sections 91 and 92 of the BNA Act, or even the larger questions of dominion-provincial relations. They ought also to have become aware that neither

---

*As the United States so well demonstrated in the 1950s and 1960s, 'civil rights' cases, decided by the courts instead of the legislatures, could produce major revisions in the fabric of the nation's legal and social systems.

constitutional nor federal-provincial problems were the product simply of the presence of Quebec in Confederation. Nevertheless, the issue of Quebec became inextricably bound up with federal-provincial tensions. Constitutional reform—for better or worse—came to be seen as the panacea for what seemed to ail the nation. A host of interpreters came forward to provide the rest of Canada with the answer to that seemingly unanswerable question: What does Quebec really want?

French Canada After the War

The Ferment of the Forties and Fifties

The scope of social and economic change in French Canada, beginning in 1939, went largely unheralded in the remainder of the country until the 1960s, when the Front de libération du Québec (FLQ, founded in 1963) began placing bombs in mailboxes to call attention to its critique of Quebec's 'colonial' status. Most English-speaking Canadians refused to take the FLQ campaign very seriously, thus contributing to what would eventually become the October Crisis. There was (and is) nothing unusual about this blithe ignorance and complacency on the part of the majority in Canada; as a way of dramatizing issues, full-scale terrorist violence was occurring around the world. In English-speaking Canada, the popular press was fascinated by Maurice Duplessis and his Union Nationale, which mixed heavy-handed attacks on civil liberties and trade unions with farsighted public works and sound legislation, ignoring the underlying social changes and debates occurring within Quebec. For many English-speaking Canadians, Quebec remained a priest-ridden rural society inhabited by a simple people. One of the most common pejoratives thrown against French Canadians—'Pepsis'— was an especially curious and perhaps revealing one. In the thirties and forties it referred to Quebec's unfashionable preference for Pepsi Cola (which offered twelve rather than six ounces of drink for the same price: 'twice as much for a nickel too') over Coca Cola. That unfashionable consumer behaviour in relation to one of the major symbols of North American popular culture should have branded the province in this way no doubt said more about English Canada that it did about Quebec. The suggestion was clearly that the province was somehow backward in other areas besides. But as *Le Devoir* pointed out in 1954, the socio-economic change that was taking place in Quebec was literally unparallelled in any other industrialized country.[13]

That Quebec had been lagging in the socio-economic terms of modern industrialism made its rapid catch-up both more sensational and more unsettling. Certainly by the 1950s that province was no longer behind the remainder of Canada in most social and economic indicators, although it was not fully autonomous. Hindsight can play a variety of tricks on its practitioners, usually leading one to fasten on those aspects of the past that point to the future. But it can also lead to overemphasizing the chaos of the past in comparison with the relative order of a later time. Most Canadian commentators outside Quebec who were cognizant of the province's transformation assumed that the continued electoral success of Duplessis and the Union Nationale represented some sort of political bewilderment on the part of French Canadians. Thus they emphasized confusion before 1960, and saw the Quiet Revolution of Jean Lesage as producing some direction and order out of the chaotic ferment of the earlier period. Outside Quebec there was also an unspoken assumption, going back to the eighteenth century, that social and economic modernization would produce French-Canadian assimilation into the majority society in North America.

Neither of the standard assumptions about Quebec's modernization—that it meant short-term confusion and would lead to long-term assimilation—was particularly valid. The socio-economic transformation was accompanied by a series of profound ideological shifts within Quebec society that shook its foundations to the very core. The patterns of that development were relatively comprehensible to anyone familiar with what was happening elsewhere in developing societies. Traditional forms of defensive nationalism, including the power and authority of the Roman Catholic Church, were eventually swept away by a new secular form of nationalism that had become fully articulated in the years before the demise of Maurice Duplessis. The main opposition to this new nationalism came less from the old nationalism, which repressed ideas but could not really compete for people's minds, than from a renewed current of nineteenth-century European liberalism adapted to twentieth-century Quebec conditions. In the 1960s these two competing ideological currents would find popular labels in Quebec as 'separatism' and 'federalism'.[14]

The New Nationalism

The new nationalism in Quebec was profoundly different from the old in its intellectual assumptions, although the two nationalisms could frequently sound very similar in rhetorical manifestos. In the first place, while often espousing Catholic values, the new nationalism was profoundly anti-clerical in its opposition to the entrenched role of the Church in Quebec society. In the second place, it had no desire to return to a Golden Age of agricultural ruralism, but instead accepted the industrial and urban realities of modern Quebec. It insisted that Quebec nationalism had to be based on the aspirations of the newly emerging French-Canadian working class, which meant that nationalists had to take the lead in the battle for socio-economic change. While scorning international socialism because it would not pay sufficient attention to the particular cultural dimensions of French Canada, the new nationalists pre-empted much of the vocabulary and economic analysis of Marxism, including the essential concept of proletarian class solidarity. In their insistence on nationalism they were hardly traditional Marxists, but the post-war world saw many examples of similar movements directed at reconciling Marxist analysis with national decolonization. The new nationalists—particularly the younger, more militant ones—were able to find intellectual allies and models everywhere. The external neo-Marxism most commonly cited came from the French ex-colonial world or from Latin America. Quebec's new nationalism could and did fit easily into the North American 'New Left' movement and critique of the 1960s.[15]

The new nationalists had also long insisted that the key to their program was an active and modern state. Gérard Filion (b. 1909)—publisher of *Le Devoir* and one of the most prominent of these new nationalists—wrote in 1960:

> . . .there are a certain number of accomplishments that only a modern state can fulfil, especially when it has the responsibility of seeing to the common good of an under-developed community. A system of natural resource exploitation, a policy of energy utilization, the protection of manpower, the participation of nationals at all levels of business and industry, the control over certain large areas of public service, respect for language and culture in the making of social choices and in public relations, these are some of the many functions that a state which recognizes its responsibilities and is convinced that it is there to govern and not to be tossed about should not hesitate in undertaking.[16]

The homogeneous secular state represented the highest articulation of the nation, and was the best means of liberating humanity. For the new nationalists, traditionalist forces in Quebec had historically collaborated with forces in Canada to keep French Canadians in their place. Not until the 1960s was the new nationalism openly separatist, but such a posture was always inherent in its position.

The chief opposition to the new nationalism being developed in Montreal came from a tiny but influential group of small-'l' liberal intellectuals centred on the journal *Cité libre* (1950-66), which was founded—by Pierre Elliott Trudeau and Gérard Pelletier (b. 1919), among others—at the height of Duplessis's stranglehold on the province, to which it was a reaction. These liberals were as revisionist in spirit as the new nationalists, but simultaneously suspicious of what they regarded as simplistic ideology and committed to the secular rationalism of the new social sciences. As Trudeau wrote in an oft-quoted statement:

> We want to bear witness to the Christian and French fact in America. Agreed; but we must also throw everything else overboard. We must systematically question all political categories bequeathed to us by the intervening generation. The strategy of resistance is no longer useful for the growth and maturation of the City. The time has arrived for us to borrow from architecture the discipline called 'functional,' to cast aside the thousands of past prejudices which encumber the present, and to build for the new man. Overthrow all totems, transgress all taboos. Better still, consider them as dead ends. Without passion, let us be intelligent.[17]

Trudeau's group was even more anti-clerical than the new nationalists, perhaps because its members still believed in the need for a revitalized Catholic humanism, and thus criticized the Church from within. It was equally critical of traditional French-Canadian nationalism, which it regarded as outdated, inadequate, and oppressive, preferring instead to locate French Canada within an open multicultural and multinational state and society. Not only traditional nationalism but all nationalism was unprogressive, undemocratic, and unmodern. *Cité libre* insisted, moreover, that it was possible to be 'leftist' without being Marxist. The result was that its vision of the state was quite different from that of the new nationalists. Both groups could agree on an active state, but the new nationalists were more inclined to see it as a liberating embodiment of French-Canadian collectivities, while the *Cité libre* people wanted interventionism expressed more in terms of regulation and control.

By the mid-1960s the differences between the new nationalists and the *Cité libre* group would turn out to be major ones, and separatism was at the heart of the disagreement. Agreeing that a more imaginative and flexible Canadian federalism was necessary to meet the challenge of separatism, Pierre Trudeau and Gérard Pelletier joined Jean Marchand in becoming Liberals in 1965 (they came to be called the three 'Wise Men') and successfully standing for election to Parliament. But earlier—at the end of the 1950s—the two groups appeared to have arrived at similar conclusions. Traditional nationalism in Quebec had led nowhere. The dead hand of the Church had to be removed from any remaining positions of dominance. And a modern state, secular and interventionist in nature, was needed to complete Quebec's transformation.

The Quiet Revolution

The ground was well prepared for the famous 'Quiet Revolution' of the 1960s in Quebec. The structural changes in French-Canadian society had already taken place. Quebec by 1960 was a secularizing, urbanized, and industrialized region little different in many respects from its central-Canadian neighbour, Ontario. At the end of the fifties traditional French-Canadian nationalism in church and state, symbolized by the Union Nationale, still seemed to prevail. But the critique of tradition had already been elaborated and the program of reform for Quebec was well articulated. All that remained was to fit together the government of Quebec and popular aspirations together. That task was begun by the provincial Liberal Party led by Jean Lesage, which defeated the Union Nationale and came to power in 1960. As usually happens in such political turnovers, the Liberals did not win the 1960 Quebec election so much as the Union Nationale lost it. The death, after '100 days' as premier, of Paul Sauvé (1906-60), Duplessis's successor, and the inability of the Union Nationale to find either a high-profile leader (who remembers Antonio Barette?) or candidates, did not help a party that was more out of step with the province than analysts realized. The Liberals had a collection of well-educated stars, including television commentator René Lévesque (1922-87), and keeping their strong egos together would be one of Lesage's major problems as premier. The party promised clean government and progressive policies, but did not mention the changes in education and hydroelectricity that would come to symbolize its success. Indeed, not even the leading Liberal theorists in 1960 realized just how ready Quebec was for change, or how easily the traditional institutions and ways would crumble once they were confronted by an activist government composed of people from Quebec's new middle and professional classes.

The first major step came over hydroelectricity. The tradition that had to be overcome was the long-standing Quebec fear, well nurtured for decades by the Union Nationale, of anything resembling economic statism (or 'socialism' or 'Communism'). *Anti-étatisme* in Quebec was not quite the same thing as anti-activity, and under Duplessis the provincial government had spent a good deal of money on public services, including many hydro-electric projects to assist rural electrification. What the minister of natural resources, René Lévesque, proposed on 12 February 1962, without consulting his colleagues, was the enforced government takeover of all existing private hydroelectric companies into a massive Hydro-Quebec (initially created in 1944). Hydroelectricity was a good place to fight the battle of nationalization, partly because electrical generation and supply was a public enterprise right across North America, partly because it touched directly the pocketbook of the rural Quebecker who was most likely to oppose state action. Lévesque acted unilaterally because he sensed the value of the pre-emptive strike on his divided colleagues. Despite a famous '*Jamais!*' from Premier Lesage, nationalization (of hydroelectricity or other enterprises) was quickly accepted by the Liberal cabinet as a winning campaign issue, and the Liberals took it to the province in 1962 with the slogan '*Maîtres chez nous*'. Led by Lesage and a compelling Lévesque, the Liberals managed to turn Hydro-Quebec into a symbol of the economic liberation of Quebec from its colonial status, thus co-opting the new nationalism with a vengeance. Buying out the privately owned electrical utilities cost over $600 million, but this was only the beginning of the Liberal expenditures on public enterprise, which tripled the provincial budget in the early 1960s and saw a provincial-government involvement in almost every economic and industrial activity in the province. The second Lesage administration (1962-6), unlike the first, was unabashedly nationalistic and statist.

The other great symbolic victory of Lesage's Quiet Revolution was the secularization and modernization of Quebec's educational system. Since before Confederation it had been in the hands of the Catholic Church, which staffed it chiefly with priests and nuns teaching a curriculum that had been very slow to change from the nineteenth-century classical one. By 1960 the Church itself was in trouble, not just in Quebec but around the world. So it was perhaps not surprising that the first telling shots in the campaign against its control of Quebec education were fired by a Catholic cleric, Brother Jean-Paul Desbiens (b. 1927), who published in 1960 the bestselling *Les Insolences de Frère Untel* (*The Impertinences of Brother Anonymous*, 1962), based on a series of letters he had written to *Le Devoir* in 1959. Orchestrated by the editor of the paper, André Laurendeau (1912-68)—probably the leading mainstream spokesman for the new nationalism in Quebec—the 'Frère Untel' debate boiled in the province for over a year.[18]

Frère Untel (literally, Brother So and So) attacked Quebec education not from the progressive left, but from an élitist new nationalist stance. He equated the deterioration of French-Canadian culture with the success of an anglicizing North American popular culture, and popularized the idea that *joual*, the everyday slang of Quebec, was the product of British colonization. In a chapter entitled 'The Language of Defeat', he wrote:

> Our pupils speak joual, because they think joual, because they live joual, like everybody around here. Living joual means rock'n roll, hot dogs, parties, running around in cars. All our civilization is joual. Efforts on the level of language don't accomplish anything, these competitions, campaigns for better French, congresses, all that stuff. We must act on the level of civilization. . . .[19]

In a nice piece of rhetorical simplification Frère Untel blamed Quebec's cultural failings on *joual*, and then found 'the only possible explanation for this lamentable failure' in the system of education, which was 'a flop'. Its chief problem was a sterility resulting from the authoritarian control of the Church. As a result of his *Le Devoir* letters, Desbiens was ordered by the Church to cease all public activity and was the subject of an official letter of condemnation by the Sacred Congregation of Religious Orders before being banished to Rome.[20] The Church's actions were too late, of course, and only turned Desbiens into a martyr to freedom of speech.

The spate of responses to Frère Untel, many of them in the form of letters to the editors of newspapers, demonstrated that he had struck a chord in the province. Lesage himself responded with a provincial commission of enquiry into education, chaired by the vice-rector of Laval University, Monseigneur Alphonse-Marie Parent. The commission's hearings produced a battery of complaints and indictments against the Quebec system, most of which the commission endorsed in its 1963 report. The Parent Commission called not only for modernization along North American lines, but for administration by a unitary secular authority. Armed with this endorsement, the Lesage government in 1964 passed Bill 60, which for the first time placed education in Quebec under provincial administration. Quebec education was thereafter rapidly brought up to national standards. The Lesage government also sensed the importance of Frère Untel's call for the preservation and extension of French-Canadian culture and the French language. It had already created a cultural affairs ministry in 1961, which was presiding happily with grants and other forms of support over a veritable explosion of French-Canadian art and writing in the 1960s for which it was not directly responsible.

The ministry of cultural affairs in many ways typified the Quiet Revolution. The Lesage government was not so much the agent of change in Quebec as its *animateur*. As such it was the beneficiary of years of preparation by others. The Liberals identified some of the key problems, and liberated the new-found aspirations of Quebec. What many English-speaking Canadians forget is that the Lesage Liberals were defeated in 1966 by a rejuvenated Union Nationale under Daniel Johnson (1915-68)—chiefly, as we shall see, because they had failed to follow the logic of the revolution, over which they had presided, to its separatistic conclusion.

Quebec and the Nation

Between 1945 and 1972 Quebec succeeded in achieving virtual autonomy within the structure of Canadian Confederation. This result was not codified in formal constitutional terms, nor did it have a catchy name, but it was clearly present in practical terms. Quebec did not have the full symbols of sovereignty, such as an independent armed force and foreign policy, but by 1970 it was an active player on the international stage and was also in full control of its own internal affairs. The extent of the practical freedom of action Quebec had achieved was disguised by the demands of many vociferous elements for more explicit formulations of independence, and by a singular refusal on the part of English-speaking Canadians to recognize the political and constitutional realities within Quebec. Since almost all anglophones, at both the federal and provincial levels, spoke and behaved as if Quebec had yet to achieve autonomy, no one was really prepared to argue that it had already done so. Much of the constitutional agonizing of the post-1972 period would be about a *fait accompli*.

Three fundamental factors explain Quebec's achievement, however unacknowledged, during this period. In the first place most Canadians, and certainly most Canadian politicians—especially within the federal Liberal party—genuinely believed that Quebec was different and had some sort of special status within Confederation. Even those, perhaps especially those, who argued most strenuously against the various component parts of special status (such as the compact theory, or the 'two nations' concept) did so from some notion of Quebec's linguistic, cultural, and historic distinctiveness, as the writings of Quebec-based 'federalists' such as Pierre Elliott Trudeau made abundantly plain.[21] In 1954 Louis St Laurent had observed that Quebec could not become a province like any other. Only a relative handful of English-speaking Canadians were willing to speak out on behalf of a racially and linguistically undifferentiated Confederation (although more may have silently believed in one). Such arguments were easily dismissable as out of date, or 'racist', or worse. In the second place, it was clear that few Québécois were happy with the province's situation in Canada, either historic or present, and an increasingly larger number advocated extreme solutions. Even fewer Canadians were able to conceive of a nation without Quebec, and so it became essential to respond at least to the province's legitimate demands and aspirations. 'What does Quebec want?' began the jacket blurb of one English-Canadian paperback published in 1964. The blurb continued: 'Its grievances are desperate enough to threaten Confederation. English Canada, jolted from a state of comfortable indifference, is now forced to see and understand the plight of the Québécois.'[22] Quebec was unhappy, and most of English-speaking Canada was prepared to be sympathetic, at least to a point. That matters went further than many had anticipated was a product of the third factor: the support that Quebec's particular constitutional initiatives were able to attract from some of the remaining provinces of Canada, particularly Ontario, Alberta, and British Columbia. The political alliances between Quebec and other provinces against the federal government were constantly shifting in principles and particulars, but they were formidable.

Quebec's movement towards autonomy did not begin with the Quiet Revolution. Indeed, more than one expert has argued that the 'constitutional *coup d'état*' was delivered not by Jean Lesage or his successors but by Maurice Duplessis, who in 1954 forced Ottawa to accept Quebec's separate collection of income tax outside the tax rental system.[23] Prime Minister St Laurent had drawn back from any serious efforts to repatriate the Constitution, and that question would emerge as significant only after the Lesage victory. The Lesage Liberals had characterized Duplessis's constitutional policy as a negative one of 'defending our own', and offered instead 'positive autonomy' as 'the vision of our people'. At the 1960 dominion-provincial conference Lesage called for action on the repatriation business, and it was put back on the agenda.

The Lesage government made three distinct moves in the early 1960s as far as its declared ambition of autonomy was concerned. One was to continue the Duplessis policy of opting out of centralized financial arrangements, chiefly from various shared-cost programs. After 1960 opting-out could be done without financial disadvantage, another federal concession to Quebec. The province successfully insisted on mounting its own versions of all the major social-welfare programs, including unemployment compensation, pensions, and medicare. At another level Quebec refused to agree to proposed formal amendments to the BNA Act—such as the so-called 'Fulton-Favreau' formula—because it was not satisfied that enough provisions had been 'entrenched' in the document to ensure that amendment of key elements would be possible only with unanimous consent of the provinces. Fulton had offered to entrench all existing provincial powers, as well as language, education, and the amending procedure itself. Quebec wanted unemployment insurance as well. It rejected Fulton in 1961 and Fulton-Favreau in 1965, when further concessions had been made to Quebec and pension schemes provided an additional issue. On a third front, Lesage's government made tentative but increasingly ambitious moves into the international arena, establishing direct diplomatic links with francophone nations abroad that were not mediated through Ottawa's External Affairs department, though they were subsequently formally ratified by the federal government. On educational and cultural issues Lesage's Quebec dealt independently and bilaterally with France and other nations. Daniel Johnson and the Union Nationale were prepared to go even further.

The Nation and Quebec

The federal government, particularly the minority ministries of Lester Pearson, attempted to respond in a variety of ways to what was obviously a more feisty Quebec. One was 'co-operative federalism', a concept exemplified in a series of agreements (1963-5) between Ottawa and the provinces that accepted the need for greater consultation and flexibility. Ostensibly designed to deal with federal-provincial rather than Ottawa-Quebec tensions, co-operative federalism reflected Pearson's own inclinations as a mediator and conciliator. If everyone truly tried to get along better they could do so, and the federal government was prepared to make concessions as evidence of its good faith. This strategy eventually ran aground because, as one political scientist put it, 'Quebec's demands for autonomy appeared to be insatiable.'[24] Related to, but independent of, co-operative federalism were two other federal strategies under Pearson. One dealt with symbols of sovereignty and the other with language and culture. The former would attract a good deal more contemporary attention than the latter; indeed, Canadians proved that they could really get quite excited about flags, national anthems, and anniversary celebrations.

Since 1867 the Canadian national flag had been Britain's Union Jack, although many English-speaking Canadians would have sworn in a court of law that it was the Red Ensign. In either case the flag was a holdover from the days of the British Empire, symbolic of Canada's colonial status. Various efforts at reform had proved unsuccessful, but in 1963 Pearson raised the issue again, and several designs were vociferously debated in Parliament in June 1964. Diefenbaker's Tories preferred a version of the Red Ensign, while Pearson and the NDP wanted something with maple leaves. The result was a special committee that recommended the present flag, and it was adopted after closure later in 1964, the issue having opened serious fissures in the Progressive Conservative Party, with several Quebec MPs openly breaking with Diefenbaker.[25] The Baby Boomers took to the new flag almost instantly, however, and Confederation Year (1967) was utilized to promote it generally, and extremely successfully. Before 1967 Canada did not have an indigenous national anthem. For many English-speaking Canadians 'God Save the Queen' was good enough, although subject to the same strictures as the Union Jack. Others were quite fond of 'The Maple Leaf Forever', with its swinging tune, but its sentiment could not possibly be accepted by French

The first hoisting of the Canadian flag in Ottawa, in February 1965. Prime Minister Lester Pearson and Governor-General Georges Vanier are on the left. Photo Features Ltd, Ottawa.

Canadians ('In days of yore, from Britain's shore, Wolfe, the dauntless hero, came...'). 'O Canada' had the merit of having been written as '*Chant nationale*' by the composer Calixa Lavallée (1842-91) and Adolphe-Basile Routhier (1839-1920) for a viceregal occasion in Quebec City in June 1880. The familiar English words were written by R. Stanley Weir (1856-1926) in 1908. In 1967 Parliament approved 'O Canada' as the country's official national anthem, just in time for the Centennial celebrations. Most Canadians initially sang it self-consciously, if at all, at public occasions and sporting events.

The Centennial Year bash was a bipartisan extravaganza. Plans for the 100th anniversary of Confederation had begun under John Diefenbaker and continued under Pearson. Substantial amounts of money were spent by Ottawa (some of it naturally filtered through the provinces and municipalities) on public buildings as Centennial monuments, such as the National Arts Centre in Ottawa (which opened in June 1969). There was a national train that toured the country, and various other manifestations, including a catchy birthday song by Bobby Gimby ('Can-a-da, We Love You'). The centrepiece of the Centennial, however, was the Canadian Universal and International Exhibition at Montreal, familiarly known as Expo 67, which had as its theme Man and His World (Terre des Hommes) and the participation of some 120 governments. Canadians surprised themselves and the world by surmounting a multitude of organizational complexities to create what many said was the greatest world's fair ever. Its magnificent displays in many buildings of architectural distinction (Buckminster Fuller's geodesic dome for the American Pavilion and Moshe Safdie's Habitat '67, an experimental housing project, were among the most talked-about), its World Arts Festival, and its excellent services and staff, attracted 50 million paid admissions. Though cost overruns and construction abuses were the stuff of legend, tourist revenues generated by Expo were almost double the official $283 million cost, and all problems were easily dismissed in the euphoria and pride of having produced an undisputed world-scale triumph.[26]

During Expo an event occurred—brief, sensational, and unexpected—that shares an almost equal place in the history of the period. The occasion was the visit of the French President Charles De Gaulle. From the outset Ottawa and Quebec jostled over all aspects of De Gaulle's appearance, with protocol officers much in evidence. On 23 July he arrived on board a French naval vessel at Quebec and a day later stood on the balcony of a Montreal hotel with open arms, receiving the tumultuous applause of half a million Quebeckers. It was an emotional moment. The General spoke of his cherished memories, especially the Liberation of France in 1944. Then he concluded, before the huge crowd and a live television audience of millions more: '*Vive Montréal! Vive le Québec! Vive le Québec libre!*' Whether De Gaulle had deliberately insulted the Canadian government and people (the official Pearson response) or had merely spoken of Quebec's efforts to affirm

The Canadian Pavilion at Expo 67, dominated by a huge inverted pyramid (the Katimavik, an Inuit word for 'meeting place').The dome alongside it was clad with rows of enlarged photographs of Canada, and the show-space in the foreground featured continuous entertainment by choirs, dancers, folksingers, and other performers and musicians from across the country.

its distinct identity (the Daniel Johnson position) was irrelevant. His exclamations were vociferously cheered, and the nation had been given yet another reminder of its deep division.

The final policy initiative of the Pearson Liberals was the concept of 'equal partnership', the right of both French-speaking and English-speaking Canadians to participate equally in the institutions that controlled their present and future. This concept, along with the notions of cultural dualism and 'two founding races', was enshrined in the Order-in-Council that in 1963 set up the Royal Commission on Bilingualism and Biculturalism. The Commission's terms of reference called for it 'to inquire into and report upon the existing state of bilingualism and biculturalism in Canada and to recommend what steps should be taken to develop the Canadian Confederation on the basis of an equal partnership between the two founding races, taking into account the contribution made by the other ethnic groups to the cultural enrichment of Canada and the measures that should be taken to safeguard that contribution.'[27] Chaired by André Laurendeau and Davidson Dunton (b. 1912), president of Carleton University, the Commission was plainly a

One of the most popular features of Expo 67, the mini-rail. Sometimes intersecting itself, it traversed the entire site.The American Pavilion, Buckminster Fuller's geodesic dome, is in the background.

President De Gaulle of France on the balcony of the Hôtel de Ville in Montreal on 24 July 1967 after he had uttered the resounding words:'*Vive le Québec libre!*'. Canapress Photo Service.

response to the growing problems of Quebec and was instructed to recommend ways of facilitating Canada's cultural dualism.

Two obvious points about the work of the Commission and its eventual recommendations must be emphasized. The first is that its terms of reference stated almost all the assumptions about duality that appeared in its conclusion, which simply legitimized them in appropriate academic language. Second, the Commission neither disputed those terms of reference nor attempted to widen them. More than most royal commissions, therefore, it served as a clear facilitator of articulated public policy rather than as an instrument for the thorough examination and analysis of cherished beliefs. This distinction is important, for the B and B Commission discovered in the course of its hearings and investigations a good deal of evidence that might have suggested the very real limitations of its terms of reference. If it had paid more attention to that evidence in formulating its eventual recommendations, it might well have saved the nation a good deal of subsequent agony.

The major problem, of course, was that a cultural dualism based on the concept of two founding peoples flew in the face of much of the nation's historical reality. In its final report the Commission evaded the fact that 'two founding races' did not include Canada's native populations. In its 'General Introduction' to 'The Key Words of the Terms of Reference', the Commission alluded to the problem of the native peoples, stating that it would not examine it because 'Our terms of reference contain no allusion to Canada's native populations.' It appreciated that native people were not included among either the 'founding races' or 'other ethnic groups', but did not draw the logical conclusion. In its volume on 'Other Ethnic Groups', the Commission began with a potted history that opened with the statement: 'Canada, a vast territory inhabited in the beginning by Indians and Eskimos, was first colonized by the French, beginning early in the 17th century, and then by the British.' In a footnote after the word 'Eskimos', the commission added: 'Since the terms of reference contain no mention of Indians and Eskimos, we have not studied the question of Canada's native population.'[28] Instead it contented itself with an introductory 'reminder' to 'the proper authorities that everything possible must be done to help the native populations preserve their cultural heritage, which is part of the patrimony of all Canadians.'[29]

When the Commission moved its public hearings outside the central-Canadian corridor, it heard from hundreds of groups and thousands of individual Canadians, many of whom expressed doubts about its terms of reference. Most of the criticism came from spokesmen for ethnic communities that were not part of the cultural duality. The Commission was thus forced to devote an entire volume of its report to 'The Cultural Contribution of the Other Ethnic Groups'. The embarrassments caused by native peoples could be avoided through bureaucratic sleight-of-hand, but those caused by other ethnic groups were more complicated. The Commission dealt with them by denying ethnic validity as a 'third force' in Canadian society. Other ethnic groups were too disparate, and it was clear

...that this 'third force' does not exist in Canada in any political sense, and is simply based on statistical compilations. All the available evidence indicates that those of other languages and cultures are more or less integrated with the Francophone and Anglophone communities, where they should find opportunities for self-fulfillment and equality of status. It is within these two societies that their cultural distinctiveness should find a climate of respect and encouragement to survive.[30]

Other ethnic communities were to be seen as cultural groups, argued the Commission, rather than as a basic structural element equal to the French or the British. As more than one scholar pointed out in essays submitted at the time, however, there were serious doubts about the existence of an English-Canadian culture equivalent to that of French Canada. This question is one to which we shall return.

In the end—as the Commission recognized both in its opening remarks and in its recommendations—its principle concerns had to be language and bilingualism. Most Canadians were prepared to accept that the nation should implement equality for the two languages it declared official, and it was perhaps unfortunate that the Commission strayed into other areas (such as the definition and implications of culture), and failed to challenge more directly some of the assumptions underlying its terms of reference. Its first recommendation was implemented by the Official Languages Act of 1969, which declared French and English to be official languages with equal status in all institutions under federal jurisdiction. Most other recommendations, particularly those about language education, involved provincial co-operation and were more difficult to bring about, although many were implemented in whole or in part. They also created much subsequent controversy.

Francophones Outside Quebec

Quebec often behaved and argued as if it were synonymous with French Canada, although there were hundreds of thousands of French-speaking Canadians living outside the province. The need to provide continuing sustenance and protection for this outlying population was a principal argument of the federalist position within Quebec, and francophones outside that province were naturally fervent federalists. Only in New Brunswick were francophones—the Acadians—sufficiently concentrated geographically, and sufficiently numerous, to regard themselves as a distinct people. While they had been gradually developing and consolidating their distinctive position within New Brunswick, the 1960s saw a renaissance of Acadian culture and a new sense of political awareness. A contributing factor was the presence of Louis Robichaud, the first Acadian elected premier of the province (1960-70); but more important were the general agitations over French rights and a growing awareness among New Brunswick politicians that the Acadians were a powerful political force in the province who needed to be wooed. Robichaud's defeat in 1970 by the Tories of Richard Hatfield (1931-91) owed much to Hatfield's recognition that Acadian interests had to be served. Thus both New Brunswick parties supported bilingualism, French-language education (including a university at Moncton), and the institutional infrastructure of Acadian culture in the province.[31]

Outside New Brunswick, and to a much lesser extent Ontario (where French-speakers were numerous but not so geographically concentrated), French Canadians mainly in the West began the Sixties as a linguistic and cultural population very much on the decline. The Quebec agitation and the response of the federal government, especially its bilingualism and bicultural-ism policies, would have some spillover effect for these outlying franco-phones, almost all of whom were fluently bilingual. Not only did they gain advantages in obtaining federal employment in their regions, but their educational and cultural facilities came to receive a good deal of financial assistance from the federal government in one form or another.

To the extent that the Pearson government had intended to use bilingual-ism and biculturalism as a means of defusing the explosive situation in Quebec—as opposed merely to finding a new, more appropriate, federal language policy that had positive benefits outside Quebec—the B and B Commission was an abject failure. By the time bilingualism was formally adopted in 1969, Quebec had passed well beyond the stage of being satisfied by its implications. In the wake of the defeat of the Lesage government in 1966, all Quebec politicians and parties moved—with what appeared to be public opinion—towards a more militant view of autonomy. In 1960 the only significant party espousing open separatism was the Rassemblement pour l'indépendance nationale (RIN). But in 1968 the Parti Québécois was formed, with its platform of political independence and economic connec-tion with Canada (sovereignty association) quickly drawing much support.[32] Moreover, even while the B and B Commission was conducting its enquiries, events in Quebec were rapidly advancing, and other forces in Canadian society were emerging to render obsolescent an obsession with language rights within the cultural context of a French-English dual society. To these other forces we must now turn.

The Emergence of New Forces in Canadian Politics

Although Quebec received the lion's share of press coverage and public discussion during the 1960s, it was not the only minority in Canadian society demanding recognition and full equality. The 1960s saw a number of other groups emerge with articulated positions and demands, including native peoples, blacks, women, and homosexuals. To some extent all these minori-ties shared a common sense of liberation and raised consciousness during the heady days of the 1960s, as well as some common models and rhetoric. The several black movements in the United States, especially civil rights and black power, were generally influential, and it was no accident that almost every minority, including French Canada, found itself compared at some point with American blacks.[33] While on one level other emerging minorities could hardly avoid sympathizing with French Canada, on another level the argu-ments and aspirations of Quebec conflicted rather seriously with those of other groups. It was partly the usual story of the fate of minorities within minorities, but there were also some other fundamental issues. Perhaps the most important was the need of the other minorities to employ federal power to control and influence provincial action. A brief examination of the growth of some of the other leading minority-rights movements illustrates the complexities of the problem of simultaneously serving Quebec and everyone else.[34]

Native Peoples

As with so many other long-standing questions in Canada, that of Canada's native peoples moved into a new activist phase in the 1960s. Native activism built on its own accumulated traditions of constructing organizations to speak for Indian and Inuit concerns, but it was also able to take advantage of American models and Canadian federal policy, such as the 1960 Canadian Bill of Rights. Just as critically, the search for new sources of raw materials for exploitation in the Canadian North threatened native peoples' way of life and forced them into the political mainstream. By the end of the decade an emerging native militancy met head-on a government attempt to rethink both the situation of natives and their relationship to the federal government.

Before 1960 regional and provincial organizations had gradually developed across Canada to represent the interests of the native peoples, often in response to particular situations or to organized investigations and commis-sions on either the provincial or federal level. Thus the Depression called into existence the Native Brotherhood of British Columbia in 1931, and a strike gave rise to the Pacific Coast Native Fisherman's Association in 1936, which merged with the former in 1942. A large number of Saskatchewan Indian groups merged into the Federation of Saskatchewan Indians at the end of the 1950s. National organizations were slower to take hold. An effort originating in British Columbia in 1943 to create a national organization, called the North American Indian Brotherhood, was not successful, partly because Andrew Paull (1892-1959), the organization's founder, was seen to be linked too closely with Roman Catholic Indians. Finally in 1961 the National Indian Council was formed 'to promote unity among Indian people, the betterment of people of Indian ancestry in Canada, and to create a better understanding of Indian and non-Indian relationship.'[35] The National Indian Council was organized chiefly by urbanized Indians who hoped to combine the concerns of status and non-status Indians, including Métis. In 1968 political incompatiblity led to the dissolution of the National Indian Council and the formation of two new groups: the Canadian Métis Society, which in 1970 renamed itself the Native Council of Canada, representing Métis and non-status Indians, and the National Indian Brotherhood, which would become the Assembly of First Nations, representing status Indians.

Before the late 1960s the process of consciousness-raising with regard to native issues was slow; then a sudden shift occurred, particularly among native peoples themselves, that is still ongoing. In 1966 one government report complained of the difficulty of ascertaining Indian opinion.[36] As late as 1971 one study, 'The Indian in Canadian Historical Writing', found that Indians, particularly in survey textbooks, were regarded as inferior beings who deserved what they got from Europeans and generally were treated more as 'obstacles to be overcome' in Canada than as integral parts of historical development.[37] The real explosion of Canadian academic interest in native peoples would not come until the 1970s, and Canadian popular awareness of natives would occur at the same time, less because of the academics than because the natives themselves had discovered political and legal ways to fight for their rights that drew attention to their situation. 'Aboriginal rights' as a concept existed in the 1960s, but had not yet produced the landmark court actions of later periods.[38]

One of the real catalysts for native consciousness was the publication in 1969 of a 'White Paper' on federal policy under Indian Affairs Minister Jean Chrétien (b. 1934).[39] As one Indian leader at the time observed: 'No single action by any Government since Confederation has aroused such a violent reaction from Indian people.'[40] The White Paper dealt with all aspects of Indian policy, but its principal recommendations were threefold: the abolition of the Indian Act (and the Department of Indian Affairs), which would mean an end to status Indians; the transfer of Indian lands out of Crown trust into the hands of the Indian people; and the devolution of responsibility for Indians to the provinces.[41] The White Paper touched off bitter criticism in all quarters, and it produced the first popular manifesto for Canadian natives in Harold Cardinal's *The Unjust Society: The Tragedy of Canada's Indians* (1969), which argued for the re-establishment of special rights within the strengthened contexts of treaties and the Indian Act.

The White Paper, in broad outline, was consistent with federal policy towards all minorities, including French Canadians, at the end of the 1960s. It called for the advancement of the individual rights of Indians rather than the collective rights of native peoples:

> The Government believes that its policies must lead to the full, free and non-discriminatory participation of the Indian people in Canadian society. Such a goal requires a break with the past. It requires that the Indian people's role of dependence be replaced by a role of equal status, opportunity and responsibility, a role they can share with all other Canadians.[42]

The White Paper insisted that treaties between the Crown and Indians only produced 'limited and minimal promises' that had been greatly exceeded in terms of the 'economic, educational, health and welfare needs of the Indian people' by subsequent government policies. Allowing Indians full access to Canadian social services (many of which were provincially administered) would mark an advance over existing paternalism. The government seemed

In this photograph from June 1970 Harold Cardinal, president of the Indian Association of Alberta—who was in a delegation of some 200 native people representing most provinces—is telling Prime Minister Trudeau (left, with back to camera) and cabinet members that Indian treaties should be handed over for settlement to a 'truly impartial claims commission'. Canapress Photo Service.

surprised that Indians responded so negatively to the White Paper, conveniently ignoring its implications for the concepts of treaty rights and aboriginal rights. Prime Minister Trudeau defended the policy as an enlightened one, noting that 'the time is now to decide whether the Indians will be a race apart in Canada or whether they will be Canadians of full status.' He added: 'It's inconceivable, I think, that in a given society one section of the society have a treaty with the other section of the society. We must all be equal under the law.'[43]

Harold Cardinal (b. 1945), a member of Alberta's Sucker Creek band, had been elected in 1968 president of the Indian Association of Alberta—and had read widely in the American rhetorical literature of the 1960s. He condemned the 1969 White Paper as a 'thinly disguised programme of extermination through assimilation', adding that the federal government, 'instead of acknowledging its legal and moral responsibilities to the Indians of Canada and honouring the treaties that the Indians signed in good faith, now proposes to wash its hands of Indians entirely passing the buck to the provincial governments.' Cardinal coined the term 'the Buckskin Curtain' to refer to the separation between European and Indian in Canada, noting that while 'Canadian urbanites have walked blisters on their feet and fat off their rumps to raise money for underdeveloped countries outside Canada', Canadians generally did not 'give a damn' about the plight of their own native people. He criticized 'Uncle Tomahawks' among his own people who continually apologized for being Indian, and noted with some irony that Indians who wore their normal clothing ran the risk of being confused with hippies. Cardinal also complained of the Canadian government's 'two founding peoples' concept, which did not recognize 'the role played by the Indian even before the founding of a nation-state known as Canada.' He pointedly denied that Indians were separatists, arguing that they merely wanted their treaty and aboriginal rights recognized so that they could take their place 'with the other cultural identities of Canada'. As Cardinal and other Indian spokesmen made quite plain in 1969, Indians did not want to be abandoned to the provinces. And they were less critical of Quebec's position than insistent that they too needed what Cardinal called 'a valid, lasting Indian identity'.[44]

Blacks

By the late 1960s there were an estimated 60,000 to 100,000 blacks in Canada. No one knew for certain, since accurate numbers would require a racial question on the census form. Many of those blacks were descendants of the two major strands of early black immigration to Canada, the Loyalists in Nova Scotia and the Underground Railway in southwestern Ontario. Canadian blacks faced a variety of discriminatory realities, both subtle and open, that located them on the margins of their society. They had learned to survive partly by stoically enduring their lot with little complaint and protest, partly by merging with the white community wherever possible. Except for a history of discreet oppression and the support of their churches, which tended to provide local leadership, there was little in their lives that could be identified as a distinctive heritage.

But during the 1960s Canadian blacks, like other minority groups, underwent a transformation. The various black movements in the United States had a considerable impact in raising black consciousness in Canada. The very use of the designation 'black' to replace the more traditional and heavily freighted 'Negro' was significant, and was accompanied by an increasing sense of racial pride and identity. Some militancy came from the United States as well, but probably more important in increasing black willingness to protest discrimination were Canadian immigration trends of the Sixties, when substantial numbers of decolonized Caribbean and African blacks settled in Canada. Many of these new arrivals were highly skilled and educated professionals who were not accustomed to racism, however subtle. The most publicized incident of protest occurred at Sir George Williams (now Concordia) University in Montreal in January 1969, and is discussed in the next chapter.

Women

Like other groups that discovered a new voice in the 1960s, Canadian women had been quietly preparing for their emergence (or re-emergence) for many years. Whether or not one took a patient view of the lengthy period from the enfranchisement of women to the blossoming of 'women's lib' in the later sixties—and most modern feminists understandably did not—some things had changed, and some political experience had been acquired, particularly within the province of Quebec. The Committee on Equality for Women, which organized in 1966 to lobby for a Royal Commission on the Status of Women, consisted of experienced leaders from 32 existing women's organizations united by their feminism. Their first delegation to Ottawa was ignored, and Laura Sabia (b. 1916)— president of the Canadian Federation of University Women and leader of the call for a national investigation— responded with a classic Sixties threat: she would lead a women's protest march on the capital. The Pearson government behaved equally characteristically. Although it was not convinced that women had many grievances, it agreed to have an investigation 'to inquire and report upon the status of women in Canada, and to recommend what steps might be taken by the Federal Government to ensure for women equal opportunities with men in all aspects of Canadian society.'[45] Unlike its contemporary B and B Commission, which literally spelled out its recommendations in its terms of reference, the Royal Commission on the Status of Women, established in 1967, had a much more open-ended mandate—chiefly because the government had no preconceived position beyond a vague commitment to equality for everybody. The Commission examined areas under provincial as well as federal jurisdiction and made its recommendations based on four operating assumptions: the right of women to choose to be employed outside the home; the obligations of parents and society to care for children; the special responsibilities of society to women because of maternity; and, perhaps most controversially, the need for positive action to overcome entrenched patterns of discrimination. It provided the program that would occupy mainstream feminism for decades to come.

Virtually simultaneous with the investigations of this royal commission was the emergence of the movement usually known as 'women's liberation'. This articulate and militant branch of feminism had begun in the United States as an offshoot of the student movement of the sixties, a product of the failure of male student leaders to take women in their own ranks, or at large, sufficiently seriously. Women's liberation shared its rhetoric with all Leftist movements of decolonization. '[Woman] realizes in her subconscious what [Herbert] Marcuse says,' went one manifesto: 'Free election of masters does not abolish the masters or the slaves.'[46] Not surprisingly, the liberationists found their organizing principles in issues of sexuality, particularly in the concept that 'woman's body is used as a commodity or medium of exchange.'[47] Liberation would come only when women could control their own bodies, especially in sexual terms. Thus birth control and abortion became two of the central political issues, along with other matters such as day-care and equal pay for equal work. Such concerns brought feminists into conflict with what became known as 'male chauvinism' at all levels of society.

Despite the affinities of women's liberation with the same decolonization theory that was employed by French-Canadian radical separatists, feminists in Quebec and English Canada did not always see eye to eye. The FLQ had little to say on women's issues. But the Front pour la libération des femmes of Quebec refused to join the 1970 Abortion Caravan in its 'On to Ottawa' journey, on the grounds that such protest legitimized federalism. And Quebec society apparently supported its politicians in a general hostility to abortion on demand. At the beginning of the 1970s the women's movement generally stood poised on the edge of what appeared to be yet another 'New Day'.

Homosexuals and Lesbians: The Rise of 'Gay Power'

The minority perhaps most akin to the women's liberationists was that composed of homosexuals and lesbians. Like the libbers, the 'gays' (a term they much preferred to other, more pejorative ones) focused their political attention on sexuality, particularly on the sex offences enshrined in the Canadian Criminal Code. After Confederation, Canada had taken over most of the English statutes relating to sex offences, introducing Victorian notions and definitions of 'unnatural' deviancy from approved heterosexuality in marriage. The Canadian Parliament did make some subsequent changes in the legislation, sharpening concepts of homosexuality and homosexual behaviour as criminal. Thus the term 'unnatural' was replaced by 'against morality' to cover a broad range of deviant behaviour when male offences such as 'indecent assault' (1886) and 'gross indecency' (1892) were added to the Criminal Code.[48]

Given its perceived criminal nature, as well as the social stigma attached to it, both male and female homosexual behaviour was a distinctly underground business in Canada, and it is impossible to estimate its prevalence. References to such behaviour were common in sociological texts about the impoverished and criminal classes, which were thought to be riddled with homosexuality. But it was never considered to be generally prevalent before the 1960s. Homosexuality had been among the medical grounds on which both males and females could be rejected for military service in both world wars, but it is impossible to pinpoint this factor among the reasons why the Navy, for example, rejected 10,734 men and 775 women between 1939 and 1945. Certainly many recruits discovered their sexual inclination through their wartime experience in the military.

The era after 1945 was one of rampant heterosexuality. Canadians joined Americans in being shocked by the findings of American biologist Alfred Kinsey that homosexual practices were regular and widespread among both males and females, although the number of full-fledged homosexuals was relatively small. The idea that heterosexuals could have and execute same-gender urges was fairly revolutionary, as was the context in which sexual deviation was put in the post-war years. It was no longer so much a criminal act as a medical 'disorder' or a 'character weakness'. Thanks to the espionage and loyalty debates in the United States and Britain, homosexuals were automatically regarded as security risks because of their vulnerability to subversion, and in the 1950s the RCMP produced a special investigative unit called A-3 to identify those in government—finding a good many reported cases in Ottawa. In 1959 the federal government commissioned research to ascertain whether all homosexuals represented potential security risks, which led to the development of the notorious, if ineffectual, 'fruit machine' to detect homosexuals within the civil service.[49]* In 1952 the Canadian immigration act was amended to deny admission to homosexuals (defined as 'a status or a type of person', not in terms of particular behaviour) as possible subversives. In any event, by the 1950s there were clearly defined homosexual communities and networks in most major Canadian cities, as police raids and actions against private clubs and bath-houses demonstrated.

Criminal-code amendment, relating to sexual offences as well as other crimes, began in Canada in the 1940s. In theory the revisions were intended to sharpen the law, but in terms of sexual activity the reformers often expanded its coverage. Nevertheless, the law increasingly had to recognize new gender categories, and Canadian society gradually became more aware of the need for distinctions between gender and sexual orientation, and of the simultaneous blurring of such distinctions. The most publicized examples of blurring were the trans-sexual ('sex change') operations, beginning with

---

*The 'fruit machine' was apparently believed to do this by recording the eye movements of people viewing a series of images, some of which were pornographic.

Christine Jorgensen, that received much attention, especially in the tabloid newspapers. By the late 1950s more 'advanced' legal and medical thinking had come to recognize the value of a process of decriminalization of homosexual activity, at least between consenting males. The decade of the sixties would see the expansion of this view, in part because of public lobbying by a number of gay and lesbian organizations, such as the Association for Social Knowledge (1964), that emerged in this period. There was also an increasing number of gay newspapers and journals. Like other minority groups, gays and lesbians began to concentrate on creating a positive rather than a destructive self-identity, such as the 'gay is good' campaign begun in 1968. Finally, in 1969 Parliament decriminalized sexual offences between consenting adults, making a distinction between public and private sex. Although the 1969 revisions to the Criminal Code did not legalize homosexuality and lesbianism, they did have a considerable effect on the gay community. It was now possible (if still courageous) to acknowledge one's homosexuality, and the ranks of openly practising gays were greatly expanded. It was also possible to become more aggressive in support of homosexual rights, and the first gay-liberation organizations were formed in Vancouver, Montreal, Toronto, and Ottawa in 1970 and 1971. These groups led the way in advocating the protection of sexual orientation in any human-rights legislation adopted by the government.

By the early 1970s gay rights had joined women's and aboriginal rights at the forefront of new demands for constitutional reform and political change. The political and constitutional agenda of Canada no longer included only such matters as extending the welfare state, satisfying Quebec, or redefining the federal-provincial relationship. It now had to encompass a variety of organized and articulate collective minorities—of which native peoples, blacks, women, and gays were only the most vocal—demanding that their equality in law and practice must also be served. For the 1970s the larger political issues would become, as historian John Saywell put it, 'a re-examination of fundamental attitudes, beliefs and values', challenging 'less the existence of the nation-state than the nature of the society within it.'[50] Canadian society had itself been profoundly altered during the quarter-century after 1945, and to those changes we now turn.

chapter eleven

The New Suburban Society, 1946-1972

In September 1952 the Canadian Broadcasting Corporation opened the nation's first two television stations in Toronto and Montreal, and over the next two years it extended its television coverage into seven other major metropolitan areas. Television was hardly a new technology. The British and Americans both had experimental television stations operating before the war, and the Americans had begun introducing comprehensive television broadcasting, with national network organization, in 1946. By 1952 *I Love Lucy*, American television's first nationally popular hit show, had been running for over a year. At the time of the introduction of television broadcasting in Canada only 146,000 Canadians owned television receivers (or 'sets' as they are usually called), tuning to American border stations and using increasingly elaborate antenna systems to draw in distant signals. Most Canadians thus missed entirely the first generation of American television programming, broadcast almost exclusively live from the studio, and were able to tune in only as US television moved from live to filmed programs and from New York to Hollywood. But if Canada got a slightly late start into life with the tube, it rapidly caught up. By December 1954 there were nine stations and 1,200,000 sets; by June 1955 there were twenty-six stations and 1,400,000 sets; and by December 1957 there were forty-four stations and nearly three million sets. The rate of set proliferation had been almost twice that of the United States, and the market for new ones was virtually saturated within five years.[1]

Television's popularity has been an international phenomenon unaffected by national circumstances and socio-economic conditions. Nevertheless, for Canadian society in the post-war years television was the perfect technology, for it fitted so well into the overall social and cultural dynamics of the time. Perhaps more than the automobile, or even the detached bungalow on its carefully manicured plot of green grass, television symbolized the aspirations and lifestyle of the new suburban generation of Canadians. Unlike other leisure-time activities that required leaving the home, it was a completely domesticated entertainment package that drew Canadian families *into* the home. Until the late 1960s most Canadian television sets were located in the livingroom. Particularly on weekend evenings in the winter, the only sign of life on entire blocks of residential neighbourhoods was the flickering dull glow of black-and-white television sets coming from otherwise darkened houses. The family could even entertain friends who were interested in the same popular programs. Some of what people watched was Canadian-produced, but most of it came from the Hollywood Dream Factory. Despite the Saturday-evening popularity of 'Hockey Night in Canada', which was first telecast in 1952, television drew Canadians into the seductive world of American popular culture. Everyone watched television, but perhaps none were more influenced by it than the young, whose perceptions and reading abilities were greatly affected by their being transfixed by an endless array of images, many of which celebrated suburban life.[2]

Suburbanization was not a monolithic phenomenon in post-war Canada. After the war the serious housing shortage—there had been little new domestic building since the 1920s—and a spate of young couples starting their lives together led the government, through the Canada Mortgage and Housing Corporation (CMHC), to promote suburban development, offering very cheap mortgages. The suburbs were built quickly by companies that had gained expertise during the war, and were often developed around schools. The municipalities then had to link these new communities to each other, and to the city, through roads and other forms of infrastructure. Suburbia was a physical place of detached and semi-detached houses with yards and lawns around the outskirts of a city, but it was also a rather complex constellation of expectations and values centred on the home, the family, and continued economic affluence.

The Demographic Factors of Post-War Canada

The Baby Boom

Canadians emerged from the Second World War with virtually twenty years of disruption, deprivation, and deferral of expectations behind them. Normal expectations for family life had been interrupted in a variety of ways. Particularly during the Depression, marriage and birth rates had decreased, while the average age at marriage had risen. Both marriage rates and average age at marriage represent social tendencies that change very slowly only over long periods, so that relatively small increases or decreases are very significant. The Canadian marriage rate, which had been under 8 per thousand during the Depression, jumped to 10.8 per thousand in 1939 (as the prospect of war encouraged people to decide to get married), and remained over 9 per thousand until 1952, when it began a steady decline to well under 8 per thousand by 1966. Between 1967 and 1972 it rose again, reaching a high of 9.2 per thousand in 1972. The marriage rate leapt upwards in the ranks of the young, doubling between 1937 and 1954 for girls between 15 and 19.[3] The average age of bridegrooms fell in 1940 and 1941 to under 29 years, ran at 28+ between 1946 and 1956, then at 27+ until 1967. It dropped briefly to 26+ in 1967 and 1968, and then rose back to 27+. Over the longer period from 1921 to 1972, however, the drop in the average age of bridegrooms was nearly four years. The average age of brides was more constant, running at 25+ between 1935 and 1956, and thereafter at 24+, although the age of brides at first marriage fell by three years (from 25.4 to 22) between 1941 and 1961.[4]

A number of small statistical variations combined with a constantly growing population attributable to natural increase and immigration (and, during the war, the perceived danger of deferral) to increase the total number of Canadian marriages. In 1938, for example, 90,709 marriages took place in Canada, while the figure was 125,797 in 1940 and 130,786 in 1942. By 1945 the number of marriages declined to 111,376, but in 1946 it jumped suddenly to 137,398, hovered between 124,000 and 132,000 from 1947 to 1964, and then began gradually increasing to 200,470 in 1972.

Despite a constantly accelerating divorce rate (which went from 6.8 per 100,000 in 1931 to 26.6 in 1942 and to 54.8 in 1967, the last year before the introduction of federal legislation, then leapt to 200.6 by 1973), there were obviously many more family units being formed each year during and after the war than before. Combined with a much higher birth rate and post-war immigration, the result was the 'Baby Boom'. Several points need to be made about this extraordinary demographic phenomenon. One is that it was not caused solely by higher fertility rates, although these did increase substantially between 1941 and the early 1960s. Birth rates rose partly because of earlier marriages, partly because of decisions to have children earlier, partly because of willingness and ability to have more than two children. And all these factors linked up with the suburban mentality of the post-war period, sustained by mothers who remained at home. Further declines in infant mortality rates, to the point where only slightly more than one per cent of infants who survived birth failed to live to age one, had some impact, as did better health-care facilities for older children. Another point is that the boom was an international phenomenon in the Western industrialized world, although it began earlier in North America than in most of the nations of war-torn Europe, and lasted a bit longer as well. Finally, the fertility-rate component of the increase was very much an aberration from generally declining birth rates that had been experienced in Canada and elsewhere in the 'developed' nations since the last quarter of the nineteenth century. Nevertheless, the number of Canadian children below the age of 14 increased dramatically in each census period after 1941, until it levelled out in 1966.

Number of children under 14 in Canada (by sex and age group, in thousands) 1941-1966

YEAR	M0-5	F0-5	M6-10	F6-10	M11-14	F11-14
1941	534	518	529	517	556	545
1951	879	843	714	684	575	556
1956	1012	972	920	887	732	703
1961	1154	1102	1064	1016	948	908
1966	1129	1069	1173	1128	1071	1022

Source: Canadian census data.

Total Canadian Population of Children by Sex and Total Children Under 14 by Sex, 1941-1966

YEAR	MALE	FEMALE	MALE	FEMALE	TOTAL
	ALL AGES		UNDER 14		UNDER 14
1941	5,901,000	5,606,000	1,619,000	1,580,000	3,199,000
1951	7,089,000	6,921,000	2,168,000	2,083,000	4,251,000
1956	8,152,000	7,929,000	2,664,000	2,562,000	5,216,000
1961	9,219,000	9,019,000	3,166,000	3,026,000	6,192,000
1966	10,054,000	9.961,000	3,373,000	3,219,000	6,592,000

Source: Canadian census data.

This substantial total increase in numbers of children, rather than simply higher birth rates, represented the Baby Boom. These children had to be housed, taken through the educational system, and eventually brought into the work force, providing a substantial set of problems for the Canadian society and economy.

The Baby Boomers went through each stage of life in what were often called 'waves'—demographers would call them cohorts—which in terms of sheer numbers put heavy pressure on facilities to deal with them. The process was most observable in education. The Baby Boom was a principal component of a period of rapid population growth for the nation. When birth rates began falling after 1960, Canadian population experts began to worry that the significantly lower rates might not even allow for population replacement. This concern was felt deeply in Quebec, which had recorded 95,000 births in 1942 out of a population of 3,400,000, and the same number of births in 1967 in a population that had nearly doubled. Demographers joined French Canadians generally in fearing the cumulative effects of the change for the 'French Fact' in Canada. But times had been good between 1951 and 1961, when annual rates of Canadian population growth reached an average of 2.7 per cent. Babies, of course, were not the only reason for the sudden expansion of the Canadian population after the Second World War.

Immigration

Another major factor in population increase was immigration. After the relatively low levels of the interwar years, immigration to Canada shot up suddenly after the war. Between 1946 and 1972 more than 3.5 million 'New Canadians' arrived in the country, an average of about 135,000 per year. Even after emigration from Canada to other nations is subtracted (since people, especially recent arrivals, also *left* the country in substantial numbers), the net gain was well in excess of two million. Proportionate to total population, these figures were not as significant as the earlier influxes of immigration to Canada before Confederation and before the First World War, and were less than those for Australia in this period. They were nonetheless impressive. Certainly in terms of the relative population bases, Canada was far more a magnet for immigrants than the United States, where immigration was even more closely controlled. Net migration accounted for about 20 per cent of Canadian population growth in this period.

In general the patterns of immigration responded to both external and internal events. War brides and war refugees came in large numbers immediately after the war, British subjects in profusion during the Suez crisis, and Hungarians after the abortive Hungarian revolt of 1956. Throughout the forties and fifties most immigrants came from Europe, reflecting Canadian preferential recruitment and treatment as well as the war-ravaged state of European economies. As late as 1960 only the United States interrupted a European monopoly on the list of the ten leading sources of immigrants, which was headed by Italy. Beginning in the early sixties changes in Canadian immigration policy for the first time admitted larger numbers of non-European immigrants, and by 1973 Hong Kong, Jamaica, India, the Philippines, and Trinidad numbered among the ten leading sources. While a shift to Third World sources had begun, it had not yet made an appreciable impact on the overall ethnic composition of the Canadian people.

Canadian immigration policy has always been driven principally by internal economic rather than humanitarian considerations. Even when Canada has admitted refugees under special dispensations, it has typically attempted to select those candidates that best fitted the nation's economic needs. The principal exceptions to this rule were the war brides of the immediate post-war period, but they were regarded as relatives of Canadian nationals with special claims, not in either economic or humanitarian terms. In the period before 1960 Canada experienced a serious shortage of younger adults for the expanding economy, and healthy young immigrants would have filled the requirement admirably, yet before 1962 Canada did not welcome them. Canadian policy was influenced by a general perception, best expressed by Mackenzie King's 1947 statement on Canadian immigration, that no more immigrants should be accepted than could be absorbed into the present Canadian population in both economic and racial terms. King's euphemism for race or ethnicity was 'the present character of our population.' He was mindful of public opinion among both founding peoples, for Quebec had its own concerns over immigration, chiefly that French-speaking immigration to Quebec had always been small, and large numbers of non-francophones would dilute French-Canadian culture in that province. Canada did broaden its categories of 'sponsored relatives' after the war, and in 1951 agreed to allow a handful of immigrants from India, Pakistan, and Ceylon; but such concessions merely emphasized how restricted its immigration policy generally was.

Canada had long been under pressure from the international community to adopt a less racially restrictive immigration policy, which it was largely able to ignore in the years before 1945 when it did not regard itself as a significant player in the world arena. New international pretensions and a growth of public concern with human rights (especially following passage of Diefenbaker's Bill of Rights) led to the formal removal of racial bars from Canadian immigration policy in 1962. Five years later, in 1967, the Pearson government managed to combine Canada's principal concern—attracting suitable immigrants to fill economic needs—with a racially non-discriminatory policy through the introduction of the 'points system' of immigration selection. This procedure focused on the education and skills of the applicant, thus shifting the nature of selection criteria from race or sponsorship to special training. Since the number of applications for immigration was greatly influenced by the availability of information and local processing services for applicants, Canada could continue to some extent to control unwanted immigrants through the enthusiasm of its recruitment activities in any nation, particularly in the Third World. In any event, while a Third World engineer or doctor might gain ready admission after 1967, a Third World peasant was unlikely to have the requisite qualifications. Nevertheless, the door had been pushed ajar more than a mere crack, even if it was not opened totally.

Post-1945 immigration chiefly affected the cities. It was not well distributed across the nation either, with nearly 85 per cent of the immigrants settling in the three provinces of Ontario, Quebec, and British Columbia and very few heading for the Atlantic region. The newcomers tended to settle in the central cores of cities, and by 1971 urban areas with more than 100,000 population had received nearly three-quarters of the recent immigrants. Toronto, in the process, became a non-British city and Montreal received thousands of non-French- (and non-English-) speakers.

Mortality

A final factor in population growth was a further decline in the death rate and a corresponding increase in the median age of death. In 1946 males could expect on average to live to 63.1 years, and females to 65.3. By 1971 this life expectancy had grown to 68.5 for males and 74.7 for females. But these relatively modest increases disguised the more important point that few Canadians were dying before the age of 40 and ever-increasing proportions were living well beyond the already high averages. Deaths from communicable diseases had been well reduced for the population as a whole by 1946, and expanded government health-care service for native peoples would make significant inroads into their patterns of death as well. The result was that for Canadians overall the principal causes of death were reduced to four: cardiovascular and renal diseases, cancer, and accidents. The first three causes increased in incidence with age and had always been 'diseases of the old', while accidental death was less discriminatory. Accidents nevertheless had greatly increased as a cause of death between the earlier part of the century and the 1970s, chiefly because of the toll taken by the automobile, which became the principal weapon with which Canadians killed their fellows. Moreover, sharp increases in traffic accidents involving young (especially male) drivers helped reduce overall life expectancy from avoidable causes far more than either heart disease or cancer.

The reductions in mortality rates were to a great extent a consequence of the new universally available social-welfare legislation that was introduced into Canada during and after the Second World War and provided an appreciably more accessible health-care system for the less affluent. Family allowances, unemployment compensation, old-age pensions, and medical/hospital care together added up to a higher standard of living—always an essential ingredient of lower mortality—for most Canadians. Longer life expectancy brought with it new problems, particularly in the form of increasing numbers of older people who would have to be looked after well beyond the age of normal work. The full implications of caring for the older generation (not until later in the 1970s were they called 'senior citizens')— which would include not only increased nursing facilities but the payment of old-age pensions far longer than the actuaries could have contemplated in the 1940s—had not yet struck the vast majority of Canadians. Only 'reactionaries' wondered whether the economy could afford to extend a helping hand to all Canadians.

Native Peoples

As in earlier periods, major differentials existed between the Canadian population as a whole and certain elements of it, especially native peoples. Improvements in their medical care, which began when responsibility for it was transferred in 1945 from Indian Affairs to the Department of National Health and Welfare, closed gaps but did not eliminate them. Infant mortality rates among native peoples were greatly reduced during the first twenty-eight days of life, but continued to be four to five times the national average for the remainder of the first year. A shift in causes of death from infectious to chronic diseases also occurred, but Indian and Inuit mortality rates still ran at more than twice the national average; and the incidence of death from accidental causes and suicide only increased over this period. Accidental and violent death was third on the list of killers for all Canadians but first for native peoples, and automobile accidents were not a major factor in Indian and Inuit communities. Alcohol probably *was* a major factor, less from long-term effects than from accidents and violence, neither of which could be dealt with effectively by improved medical service. Native people drank for the same reasons that other socio-culturally dislocated and economically disadvantaged people around the world did: out of frustration and to escape. While most infectious diseases were virtually eradicated in southern Canada, they continued to be killers in the northern regions, although at a lower rate; tuberculosis especially proved amenable to improved health care. Although increased medical attention was bringing some traditional problems under control, greater contact with the outside world introduced a host of new ones, ranging from obesity to tooth decay to ingestion of liquid solvents. Attacking native problems through health care proved to have its distinct limits.[5] Exposure to modern problems occurred in different forms on reserves and off them, but by the mid-1960s there was the beginning of a noticeable movement of Indians to Canada's urban centres.

While demographic characteristics of the native population lagged fifty to one hundred years behind those of the remainder of Canada, lingering in the developmental rather than advancing to the mature industrial stage, soaring birth rates more than double the national average and reduced mortality rates combined to produce a mini population explosion. The number of registered Indians grew from 136,407 in 1949 to 224,236 by 1966, with an annual growth rate peaking in the later 1950s at just under four per cent. Indian population growth was well in excess of national rates. Counting non-status Indians was more problematic, but by 1972 they were probably in excess of half a million, and expanding rapidly.

Ethnicity and Language

A quarter-century of immigration after the war had wrought some changes in the ethnic composition of the Canadian population, although the new immigration policies had not yet produced the noticeable changes of the

1970s and 1980s. In 1941 just under half (49.6%) of the Canadian population claimed origin in one of the four nations of the British Isles, with just over 30% of French background and just over 20% from other nations—almost entirely European. The most substantial population of non-European origin was the native peoples. By 1971 the British component had dropped to 44.6%, the French to 28.6%, and the 'Others' had climbed to 26.7%. While Canadians who originated in several of the European nations had markedly increased in numbers between 1941 and 1971, the most striking change was among those of Italian origin, who had increased from 112,000 in 1941 to 730,000 in 1971. Most Italians were concentrated in southwestern Ontario, especially in and around Toronto. Other readily observable increases among less-traditional sources occurred among Portuguese and Filipinos, who settled chiefly in industrial and urban Ontario. In the first census (1971) after the official acceptance of the principle of the 'two founding peoples' of Canada, both those groups saw their proportion of the total population eroded slightly. French Canada found the downward trends extremely ominous.

Immigrants of non-European origins complained frequently about the subtleties of Canadian racism and discrimination, and they were often joined in their criticisms by people of different skin coloration who had maintained a Canadian presence for centuries, such as natives and blacks. This combination of voices indicated that the problem was not simply in the nature of being a newcomer. Ironically enough, the racial group that experienced the least difficulty were the Japanese, who had been so badly treated during the war. This may be explained not only by Canadian guilt, but also by the fact that, as a result of their wartime experience, younger Canadian-born Japanese were determined to assimilate, and did so with striking success. The extent of Canadian racism would become a public issue only in the later 1960s, but complaints of discrimination were not confined to the recognizably different. In 1965 Canadian sociologist John Porter published a significant academic study entitled *The Vertical Mosaic*, in which he documented as fact what many Canadians had long instinctively known: Canadian élites were disproportionately dominated by people of British background.[6] French Canada took such information as further evidence of its disadvantaged status in Confederation.

Other disparities soon came to light. In 1967 the final report of the Royal Commission on Bilingualism and Biculturalism documented significant differences in income and occupational status among Canadians of various origins. It pointed out that 'Canadian men of British origin earned on average nearly $1,000 more in 1961 than those of French origin', and found most other ethnic groups (except the Jews) well below the British-Canadian average. As far as occupational discrepancies were concerned, the report again found 'substantial' differences between those of French and British origin, particularly at the professional and managerial levels, where the differences were actually widening. Equally striking discrepancies could, of course, be found for other ethnic groups.[7] Much of the data for such arguments were drawn from readily available Canadian census material, which was now being collected and analysed in detail for the first time by Canadian social scientists.

Yet another ethnicity issue was that of language: specifically, the usage and protection of French. In a study entitled *Languages in Conflict*, first published in 1967, Richard Joy observed:

> An extremely significant finding of the 1961 Census was that only 31% of the population claimed to be able to speak French, even after taking into account all those for whom it was merely a second or a third language; this was hardly more than the 30% who reported their ethnic origin as being French. In sharp contrast, 80% of the population could speak English, almost double the number classed by the Census as being of British origin.[8]

Joy went on to demonstrate that the problem was not that most Canadians of non-French origin, including 95 per cent of recent immigrants, preferred to speak English rather than French as a first language, but that the use of French was becoming increasingly confined to Quebec and parts of New Brunswick; its use was declining rapidly in northern Ontario and the West, where there had previously been very concentrated French-speaking pockets of population. While such findings may seem obvious from the perspective of the 1990s, they were regarded at the time as highly significant, particularly as they substantiated or anticipated the results of the B and B Commission, which published other findings between 1967 and 1970. Though most non-English-speaking ethnic groups in Canada were concerned about the loss of language and the culture associated with it, the situation for francophones was freighted with political significance. Linguistic ghettoization and national socio-economic disadvantage together were held to have produced a powerful incentive for legitimate protest from French Canada, especially Quebec. The growth of separatism in Quebec was probably more a result of developments within that province than of the limitations of French language and culture elsewhere in Canada, but clearly important issues were connected with language usage.

Urbanization, Suburbanization, and Rural Depopulation

In overall terms the trends for urban and rural residency established in the early years of the century continued through the period 1946 to 1972. Urban population steadily increased, both absolutely and as a proportion of the total, while the numbers of rural inhabitants remained relatively constant. Within the rural population, however, a massive decrease occurred in the number of farm residents, from 3,117,000 in 1941 to 1,420,000 in 1971. This national trend was most evident in provinces still dominated by agriculture: Prince Edward Island, Manitoba, and Saskatchewan. On PEI, for example, the number of farms declined from 12,230 in 1941 to 4,543 in 1971, with the number of farm operators decreasing commensurately. Although there was no single cause, the continued inability of the farmer to make a decent financial return on his or her labour and investment was undoubtedly one of the prime factors. Canadian farms became bigger and more mechanized in an attempt to compensate for low rates of return per acre, and many farm families gave up and got out when the older generation still left on the farm died. Farm land anywhere near cities became uneconomic to retain for farming, and by 1971 most of Canada's finest agricultural land—in the Fraser Valley in British Columbia and in southwestern Ontario—had been sold to speculators or cut into hobby farm plots. Combined with low rates of return, the lure of the brighter lights of places with greater population density was extremely strong, particularly for those in the stage of family and career formation. Many former farm families discovered they did not have to move to enjoy brighter lights, for the outskirts of cities were now expanding into rural areas.

While Canadian cities certainly grew significantly in size, little of that population growth occurred in the downtown areas or the traditional residential sections. The trend in the downtown core was just the reverse. Rising land prices made it uneconomic for land there to be used residentially except for high-rise apartment blocks, which were less profitable uses of space than comparable office blocks and thus emerged only on the fringes of the downtown. Building upwards, the core of the business district produced those breathtaking skylines we have come to associate with the modern city. Gradually, beginning in the 1960s, they came to be dominated by buildings that showed vast expanses of tinted plate glass to the world, as the International Style of architecture made its way to Canada. One of the country's most famous monuments in this style is a complex of rectangular towers of black steel and dark bronze-tinted glass, the Toronto-Dominion Centre (1963-9) in Toronto, designed by the German-American architect Mies van der Rohe. Within the world of faceless skyscrapers would come two fascinating developments. One was the virtual evacuation of downtown areas after working hours. The other was the tendency of the daytime inhabitants to spend the entire day inside their office complexes, which usually contained extensive underground malls providing all necessary services.

As might have been expected, the only real development strategies for Canadian cities in this period were those dominated by greed, the market, and some unspecified and almost wistful belief that progress was inevitable and would triumph in the end. City development, like most aspects of Canadian life, had been put on hold by the Depression and the war. There was a sense among architects, planners, and developers that making new things happen was positive, even at the cost of losing links with the city's (mostly Victorian) past. The result was the destruction of many wonderful old buildings in order to make way for new ones that were often undistinguished. Such a trade-off was made in Toronto when the city's first skyscraper, the majestic Temple Building of 1895 at Richmond and Bay

Streets, was demolished in 1970 to be replaced by two bland towers without any public character at all.* In Montreal there was much more indiscriminate destruction. For example, the handsome Georgian-style Prince of Wales Terrace of eight attached dwellings — commissioned by Sir George Simpson and finished in 1860 — was demolished in 1971, to be replaced by the ungainly juxtaposition of a tall hotel and a banal six-storey building to house a department of McGill University. Admittedly, Canadian cities did not go so far with their bulldozers as the urban-renewal projects in the United States and Great Britain, where hundreds of square miles of slum dwellings were razed with little idea of sensitive replacement. While many communities were threatened, in general Canadian destruction was piecemeal rather than wholesale. For example, eleven blocks adjacent to Vancouver's Chinatown disappeared in 1960, but Chinatown itself was preserved. One entire locality, however, *was* demolished: Africville, an old working-class black district in Halifax, was razed in 1965, and has been much mourned since.

After the Second World War urban development around the Western world was dominated everywhere by an impatience to demolish (and relocate) old slums and ghettos, and in North America by a preference for suburbs. Many of the slum tenements of older cities were in the last stages of deterioration, inhabited by recent immigrants and the permanently disadvantaged; brand-new apartment blocks or bungalows seemed a considerable improvement. Not until the early 1960s — perhaps beginning with the publication of Jane Jacobs' influential *The Death and Life of Great American Cities* (1961) — was the case made publicly that any urban renewal that destroyed existing organic neighbourhoods and communities in the process was retrogressive. Academics thereafter joined some politicians, young professionals, and citizens' groups in insisting that any city planning that ignored the needs of people and neighbourhoods invited damaging consequences.

Toronto probably went furthest in its rush to modernize because of the extent of its metropolitan growth. The model planned suburb of Don Mills was developed in the early 1950s; the city was associated with twelve suburban municipalities in 1953 to form Metropolitan Toronto. In 1954 the Yonge Street subway was opened; in 1964 it was extended by the east-west Bloor line. Toronto also built a series of bypass highways — the 401, the Gardiner Expressway, the Don Valley Parkway — to enable people to get quickly from one end of the metropolitan area to another. While not quite in the same league with Los Angeles, Toronto nevertheless was moving in the same direction towards a freeway culture. With the ring-roads done, the planners began conceiving the inevitable inner-city connectors, such as the Spadina Expressway, which would give every resident ready access to the freeway system. But there were two problems. One was that superhighways created

---

*One such threatened demolition, that of Toronto's Old City Hall, was stopped in the 1960s as a result of a public outcry.

Don Mills Plaza, Toronto, *c.* 1954, designed initially by John B. Parkin Associates. It is surrounded by Don Mills Road (left), Lawrence Avenue East (bottom), and The Donway. A suburb northeast of Toronto, Don Mills was conceived as an innovative planned community that promoted comfort and convenience as ideals. Don Mills Plaza, at its centre, included — and still includes — a department store (Eaton's) and supermarket, a post office, and a complex of retail stores, restaurants, and various services. In the lower right is the public library on Lawrence East. (The curling rink at the top has been removed.) These facilities service outlying neighbourhoods, divided into quadrants, that contain schools and single-family dwellings, row houses, and apartments that originally never exceeded a moderate height. Lockwood Survey Corporation Limited, Toronto. Photograph courtesy Andrew S. Dyke.

new traffic as quickly as they relieved old bottlenecks; by 1972 bypass highways like the 401 were multi-laned traffic jams of bumper-to-bumper vehicles, at first during rush hours and eventually for almost the entire day. Improving connections between the city and its outskirts only prompted more people to move away or use the roads more frequently. The other problem was that freeways constructed in populated areas could be built only by tearing down existing housing and devastating neighbourhoods. A protracted Toronto opposition finally managed to stop construction of the

This photograph from the early 1950s captures the residential aspect of Don Mills, a suburb of Toronto, which was based on an American garden-city concept of the time. Various dwellings (attached, semi-detached, single-family, and apartments) were placed in a park-like environment in which pedestrian walkways were separated from roads. Courtesy Andrew S. Dyke.

projected Spadina Expressway in 1971, which brought to a symbolic end the period of unrestricted and unplanned expansion in the city. In Vancouver at about the same time, proposals to extend the Trans-Canada Highway into the city's centre, virtually demolishing many neighbourhoods—including the traditional Chinatown district—were fought to a standstill. By the later 1960s citizens' coalitions were at work in every Canadian city, attempting to control the developers who influenced most city councils and departments.

Urban development was orderly by comparison with what happened beyond existing settlement. New suburbs were created—usually where there were no zoning bylaws—by fast-talking developers who managed to convince rural municipal councils that population growth meant jobs (rather than new taxes and a totally changed community character). The principal attraction of the new suburbs was a lower cost per square foot of house, which meant that land costs had to be kept down by not providing amenities (especially costly sewers) in advance. The ubiquitous septic tank (and the exceptionally green grass that grew above it) became the symbol of the true suburban bungalow. Leaving trees up in a developing subdivision cost more in building costs than felling them. So down came trees, although a few developers were willing to keep them around in return for a premium price for the lot. But in most suburban developments, planting new trees and shrubs (often in areas that had only recently been heavily forested) was the first outdoor task of the new homeowner. Drawing up for any new block only a handful of floorplans—with roughly identical floor areas and number of bedrooms, and maximum mortgageable value—also saved money and made marketing easier. The number of amenities depended on price, and most builders were interested in the mass market at the lower end of the scale. The result was residential segregation based not on race or ethnicity but on number of children and ability to make mortgage payments.

No developer regarded the suburban creation of infrastructure—schools, hospitals, shopping centres, connecting roads—as part of his planning responsibility, and many buyers of the 1950s and 1960s would have shied away from any development whose community structure was predetermined. The trick was to sell houses to recent parents or the newly affluent—often the same people. The typical first-time suburban buyers were a young couple with two children, attracted to the suburb partly by a love of green grass and space, but mostly by cost. Marketing techniques tried to attract buyers by giving fantasy names to the developments themselves (Richmond Acres, Wilcox Lake, Beverly Hills) or to streets in them (Shady Lane, Sanctuary Drive, Paradise Crescent), but most newspaper advertisements concentrated on the price and down-payment required. Few buyers did much research into the surrounding amenities, most being influenced chiefly by internal house space and price. According to one informant in the sixties:

> We chose this house because of the price. It was the best we saw for the money. We drove around on Sunday afternoons looking for a place and found this one. We wanted something out of the city—a good place to bring up children. . . . We may have come a little far out—I would prefer a place in closer, you know; what everybody wants: a place that has the advantage of both, all the conveniences of the city and plenty of room and good country air besides. That seems impossible around Toronto, except for a good price, and so it is impossible for us now.[9]

Few suburbanites had any idea that they were the advance guard of a new Canadian lifestyle. Fewer still had any real idea of what their living conditions would be, particularly those who were moving to developments lacking sewers, libraries, cultural facilities, shopping, and urban transit. They had not deliberately abandoned the amenities of the city so much as they had been forced by the need for space to move beyond them. Their adjustment to new conditions became part of the major socio-cultural movement of the time.

The suburbs of the post-war period have acquired more than a bit of bad press, becoming exemplars of a vast identikit wasteland of intellectual vacuity, cultural sterility, and social conformity—Pete Seeger's 'little boxes'. They could be and sometimes were all those things, of course; but they were also the spawning ground of much of the revolt and rebellion of the 1960s. Part of the problem of understanding suburbs was the assumption of this era (and later) that they could be best represented diagramatically by concentric circles drawn from the urban centre or core to the agrarian periphery. In the thinking of central-place theory (in the 1960s called 'metropolitanism' and in the 1980s called 'heartland-hinterland'), suburbs were the amenity-less satellites of cities rather than a distinct territory of their own. But suburbia was not so much the simple projection of urban society as an imaginative re-creation of the ideal world of aspiring middle-class Canadians with the adaptations required for new social conditions (including the Little League, the barbecue, and the shopping mall—suburban adaptations all). While for many who moved to the suburbs the ultimate re-creation was never achieved, for most it had not been envisioned in the first place. 'What was sought in the suburbs, by the vast majority who settled there,' wrote S.D. Clark in 1966, 'was a home, not a new social world. . . . When the new social world developed, its development was a consequence of seeking a home, not the reverse.'[10] Nevertheless, in incremental ways a new socio-cultural world was in the making.

The New Suburban Society

The beginnings of the modern suburb can be found in eighteenth-century London, evolving gradually as 'the collective creation of the bourgeois élite.'[11] Suburbanization began as an English phenomenon, extending to North America in the nineteenth century. Europe and Latin America, by contrast, remained committed to their central cities, as any visitor to Paris or Buenos Aires quickly realizes. By the twentieth century the United States had become the international centre of suburbanization. Canada lagged behind the Americans, as in so many other matters, and at least before 1945 had never pursued the middle-class suburb with the singlemindedness of its southern neighbours.[12] Although there were many examples of Canadian suburbs before the Second World War—such as Westmount in Montreal, Lawrence Park in Toronto, Crescentwood in Winnipeg, and Shaughnessy Heights in Vancouver—they were not normally as separated from the urban centre as their American counterparts.

Suburbia had always been less a geographical place than a mental and emotional space. It was characterized by an emphasis on home and family, by a separation of the workplace from the domestic situation. The result was a domesticization of values that was new to Canada after the Second World War mainly in its general comprehensiveness. Early generations of Canadians had confined tendencies to complete domesticity to the upper and upper-middle classes; but after 1945 the trend cut well into the ranks of the lower-middles, and the traditional working classes as well, democratizing a hitherto élite preserve.[13] Suburbia not only was highly traditional in its gender roles, but it had a tendency to emphasize the role of the female as child-bearer and nurturer that was almost retrogressive. In its consumer orientation, however, and in its child-centredness, it added new ingredients to the older mix.

As might be expected, the resurgence of traditional domestic values was accompanied by a revival of Christian commitment, at least in terms of formal church membership and attendance. All the usual indices of revival, from attendance figures to enrolment in seminaries, increased in Canada after the Second World War for both Protestants and Catholics. There was no evidence that the deep-rooted problems of modern Christianity— including its identification with an outmoded morality and its reliance upon belief systems that were being challenged by secular thought—profoundly altered church membership and attendance. The religious upturn of post-war Canada, like the Baby Boom, was a temporary blip in long-term trends. Not surprisingly, much of the vitality of Christianity appeared to be in the prospering suburbs. As one observer has commented, '. . .between 1945 and 1966 the United Church [of Canada] erected 1,500 new churches and church halls, and 600 new manses—many of them handsome rambling broadloomed ranch houses.'[14]

Suburban houses became 'homes', easily the most expensive physical object possessed by their family-owners. So much time and emotional energy were devoted by some Canadian suburbanites to their house that it often seemed to possess them. The house focused the life of the nuclear family while at the same time permitting individual members to have their own private space, with each child having his or her own bedroom. A large 'recreation' or 'family' room in the basement provided a place for the children to play and for everyone to get together. (The kitchen, a traditional gathering spot, was now often too small for this purpose.) The replacement of coal with oil and gas furnaces governed by thermostats and the introduction of automatic hot-water heating and air-conditioning insulated the inhabitants from an earlier world in which domesticity required hard work and constant vigilance. Now air temperature could almost be taken for granted— no mean accomplishment in the harsh Canadian climate. Those suburbanites who worried about 'getting soft' assuaged their concerns with summer camping-trips and roughing it at the cottage.

Life in suburbia depended on a clear understanding of family roles. Husbands were the breadwinners, often working far away from the home, while their wives were responsible for its daily functioning. After the war, most Canadian women had chosen to remain out of the work-force in order to enjoy marriage and child-rearing. They were reinforced in their decisions by advertising and articles in the women's journals exalting the roles of housewife and mother. At the same time that many women made 'careers' as housewives and mothers, the sociologists of Crestwood Heights: A North American Suburb (1956)—a study based on Forest Hill Village, a wealthy residential area in Toronto— found a good deal of ambivalence over this decision and the values underlying it:

> The career of the woman in Crestwood Heights, compared with that of the man, contains many anomalies. Ideally, the man follows a continuous, if loop- ing, spiral of development; the woman must pursue two goals and integrate them into one. The first goal has to do with a job, the second with matrimony and motherhood. The second, for the woman, is realized at the expense of the first; the man's two goals combine, since matrimony is expected to strengthen him for his work, and at it.[15]

Even younger women away at university were confused. One confessed to an interviewer:

> Why I want to work—because I hope to express my personality through struggle and achievement. Why I want to get married—because my real role in society is that of wife and mother. If I don't get married, I will feel insecure—I will have no clearly defined role in society. I will probably sacrifice career to marriage if the opportunity comes because the rewards of marriage are obvious, those of a career uncertain. In a way I envy those girls who only want to get married. They don't have to equate two conflicting desires.[16]

This conflict was certainly not unknown to many women living in suburbia who had to find ways of dealing with their ambivalence.

Central to any suburban household were its children, around whose upbringing the lives of the parents increasingly revolved. The baby-boom generation of children were brought up in a child-centred environment, particularly in the home. Older standards of discipline and toughness in the parent-child relationship were replaced by permissiveness. New child-rear- ing attitudes were influenced by all sorts of factors, but found their popular expression in *The Pocket Book of Baby and Child Care* by Benjamin Spock, MD, which outsold the Bible in Canada in the years after the war. Many Canadian and American mothers referred to Spock as 'God'. Canada had its own semi-official child-care manual, *The Canadian Mother and Child*, by Ernest Couture, MD—director of the Division of Child and Maternal Health of the Department of National Health and Welfare—which was distributed free by doctors to pregnant women. It was a forbidding and austere grey- covered book, filled with slightly out-of-date photographs and written in a prim, no-nonsense style. Couture's advice to fathers was typical. They needed to accompany their wives on first visits to the doctor at the beginning of pregnancy; to understand what prenatal and postnatal care meant; and to adopt an attitude that was 'patient, kind, and forebearing' during pregnancy, for women suffered from mood changes they were 'quite unable to control'.[17] He also stressed cleanliness and good sanitation for the home: 'Plumbing and drainage should be kept in good condition. Nothing is more destructive to a home, and to health, than leaky pipes and drains.'[18] Small wonder Canadian parents, at least in English-speaking Canada, preferred the folksy, conversational approach of the American expert to the bleak advice of the Canadian.

The triumph in Anglo Canada of Dr Spock over Dr Couture says a good deal about American versus Canadian style in the realm of culture. The Canadian approach was firmly élitist, with useful information produced at the top and trickled down to the potential 'client'. The American approach was frankly democratic and commercial, with useful information mass-marketed to the 'consumer'. Spock's book was one of the earliest mass-marketed paperbacks, sold over the counter at drug stores and supermarkets. In its pages the reader could find continual reassurance. Use your common sense, said Doctor Spock, for almost anything reasonable is okay. 'TRUST YOURSELF' was his first injunction. The good doctor came down fairly hard against the use of coercion—for example, in toilet training: 'Practically all those children who regularly go on soiling after 2 are those whose mothers have made a big issue about it and those who have become frightened by painful movements.'[19]

While Spock seldom was categorical about any child-rearing strategy— adopting a non-prescriptive position on breast-feeding versus bottle-feeding, for example—he was certainly not, in early editions, enthusiastic about working mothers:

> The important thing for a mother to realize is that the younger the child the more necessary it is for him to have a steady, loving person taking care of him. In most cases, the mother is the best one to give him this feeling of 'belonging,' safely and surely. She doesn't quit on the job, she doesn't turn against him, she isn't indifferent to him, she takes care of him always in the same familiar house. If the mother realizes clearly how vital this kind of care is to a small child, it may make it easier for her to decide that the extra money she might earn, or the satisfaction she might receive from an outside job, is not so important after all.[20]

At the same time, Spock had more encouraging words for fathers than did Couture, emphasizing that 'You can be a warm father and a real man at the same time' and noting that it was 'fine' for Dad to give bottles or change diapers 'occasionally'.

In opposing over-structured child-rearing practices, Spock may well have gone too far. But the post-war Canadian mother came to rely on his commonsensical advice. He explained that children passed through stages, and that once parents recognized what stage their child had reached, they could appreciate that seemingly incomprehensible behaviour and problems were quite common. Spock's chapter on the adolescent, 'Puberty Development', dealt with the sexual maturing of children, emphasized their awkwardness, and pointed out that most girls reached puberty two years ahead of boys. A full page was devoted to 'Skin troubles in adolescence', particularly the pimples that the patent medicine folks labelled 'teen-age acne'. Spock was for washing the skin and against squeezing, which probably helps explain the folk wisdom of the era about those ubiquitous pimples.

The permissively raised Spock generation and the new affluence combined to produce large numbers of adolescents with considerable spending power. In English-speaking Canada teenagers became avid consumers—a recognizable market for fast food, popular music, acne medicine, and clothing fads. Melinda McCracken has explained that '. . .to be a real teenager you had to drink Cokes, eat hamburgers [known as nips in Winnipeg, because the local Salisbury House chain, started in the thirties by R. M. Erwin, an American, sold them as such], French fries [known in Winnipeg as chips, in the English tradition], go to the Dairy Queen, listen to the Top Forty and neck.'[21] The authors of *Crestwood Heights* found a central theme for their study in the 'difficulties experienced by the child in living up to the expectations of both parents and the school for "responsibility" and "independence" ', adding that the problems were only amplified 'in an environment which largely eliminates necessity for striving in this direction.'[22] They labelled the ages sixteen to nineteen 'Dependent Independence'. For the new term 'teenager', an English-language neologism, there is no equivalent in French. ('Adolescence'—used in both English and French—does not carry the same cultural freight.) French Canada has never had a 'teenage problem', but rather a '*problème de jeunes*'—*les jeunes* being not so alienated from their elders as anglophone teenagers were.

In the autobiographical *Nègres blancs d'Amérique* (1968)/ *White Niggers of America* (1971), the radical Québécois Pierre Vallières (b. 1938)—who was jailed on charges connected with his FLQ activities and wrote his book in prison— suggests that men like his father had their own suburban fantasies:

'If only Madeleine [Vallières' mother] can agree to it,' he said to himself. He was marshalling his arguments and silently preparing his case. 'We'll be at peace. The children will have all the room they need to play. We'll be masters in our own house. There will be no more stairs to go up and down. . . .Pierre won't hang around the alleys and sheds any more. . . .The owner was prepared to stretch the payments out over many years. . . .Life would become easier. . . .He would enlarge the house. A few years from now, Madeleine and the 'little ones' would have peace and comfort.[23]

And so in 1945 the Vallières family moved to Longueuil-Annexe: 'the largest of an infinite number of little islands of houses spring up here, there, and everywhere out of the immense fields which in the space of a few years were to be transformed into a vast mushroom city.'[24]

↰↰↰↰ Education

The school and the university took on new meaning for Canadians after the Second World War. Not only did parents become more concerned about what was happening within the educational system itself, they also had to see that appropriate facilities (both teachers and buildings) were available for their children. The rapid expansion of Canadian education was a product of two overlapping trends. One, of course, was the Baby Boom. The other was an alliance between the educational system and parents that pressed constantly for the democratization of access to education for all students. Canadians had long accepted the concept of universal education in the primary grades. Education for all was extended in the 1940s and 1950s to secondary levels through the raising of school-leaving age to 16 and the creation of new facilities, and universal access to universities was afforded in the 1960s. Politicians, educational administrators, and parents alike came to agree that improved education was necessary if the younger generation was to cope with an ever more complex economy and society.

Educators talked about instilling a sense of social responsibility in their charges, while parents were more attracted to the practical benefits of education in providing future employment and a better life for their children. At the same time, an increasing horde of youngsters had to be taken through the first years of schooling. The results in the 1960s were enormous pressure on education budgets and increasing demand for the production of more—and better—teachers. School authorities attempted to ease some of their problems by consolidating rural education through use of the ubiquitous yellow school bus, a process that went on until the early 1970s. Teachers acquired more formal credentials, became better paid, and organized themselves into a powerful professional lobby, often unionized. While most provinces confronted their educational problems through provincial boards of education that assumed schooling was a public matter, Quebec and Newfoundland struggled to reform denominational school systems that were holdovers from far less complicated times. In any event, education and its developments served as a mirror for the society as a whole, as trends that began in the middle-class suburbs gradually took hold across the nation.[25]

Elementary school enrolment was the first to increase immediately after the war—a result of the large number of births in the wartime period following years of declining birth rates: the average size of first-grade classes doubled between 1945 and 1965.[26] It was not long before secondary-school enrolments too began to rise. But not until the middle-fifties was a serious educational crisis perceived, for in the decade after the war classes in existing schools simply got larger while only a few more teachers were hired to deal with the added numbers. Finally, the problems of overcrowding were too obvious to ignore. Population shifts to the suburbs, combined with larger numbers of pupils, and heavier demand for a better education for a higher proportion of Canadians, made a real difference. The Baby Boom provided one level of pressure on the system, at least until 1966, but it was only part of the push for expansion. Canadian educators began to press hard for the extension of universal education, at least through the high-school level, with the campaign reaching full fruition by the later 1950s. The new insistence on a high-school education for all represented a profound social revolution and was arguably necessary, given the increased complexity of technology requiring skilled workers in modern industrial Canada.[27] Curiously, however, Canada lagged badly in terms of vocational and practical education, preferring instead to force the vast majority of its students into traditional academic endeavours. Much of the case for expanded education was imported from the United States, but it was increasingly accepted by Canadian parents and taxpayers—particularly after 1957, when the Russians put Sputnik into orbit and inadvertently gave rise to a concerted campaign for educational reform throughout North America.

As late as 1960 the number of children kept in school beyond Grade 6 or 7 showed substantial provincial variation, as did other major variables. In British Columbia, half of all possible candidates got through Grade 12, while in Newfoundland only 2% graduated. Ontario retained 41% from Grade 2 to Grade 11, which was double the rate for Quebec. In general, the retention rate before 1960 declined systematically as one moved from the Pacific Coast to the Atlantic.[28] The Sixties were spent in attempting to achieve approximate national equality in terms of retention, with considerable success. By 1970 over 90% of children of high-school age were enrolled in such schools, most of them graduating. Canadians, ever forgetful of their past, do not appreciate how recent the shift to the universal High School Diploma has been. But it was the swing to universality at ever-increasing levels of education, more than the sheer numbers produced by the Baby Boom, that profoundly altered Canadian education.

The most telling argument for parents to keep children in school beyond school-leaving age was one based on the enhancement of human capital. Statistics were constantly trotted out to prove that it paid to go to school, showing a correlation between lifetime income and years of schooling. Every penny spent on education was an investment. The result was a major shift in Canadian expenditure on education. Public spending rose from 2.5% of the Gross National Product in 1950 to 9% in 1970—a percentage that represented eight billion dollars.[29] It also represented nearly 20% of all taxes levied by all three levels of government (federal, provincial, municipal).[30] Between 1950 and 1970 school enrolment nearly tripled, exerting profound strains on government budgets and teacher-training facilities. As with relief expenditures during the Depression, Canadian municipalities were in the front line when it came to financing educational expansion, although the federal government did increase its funding over the period. By 1970 one-third of Canada's total population was in school, and teaching was easily the nation's most numerous occupation. And teachers organized, into both professional organizations and labour unions; in the late 1960s there were some well-publicized work stoppages, particularly in Ontario.

In 1956 the authors of *Crestwood Heights* observed that the flagship suburban community they had studied was 'literally, built around its schools', with the 'massive centrality of the schools' representing 'the most immediate physical impact on any outside observer coming into the Heights.'[31] Crestwood Heights was also an early exemplar of the new style of education, 'aimed primarily at preparing pupils for a middle-class vocation in a highly-industrialized culture.'[32] By 1970, this style had overtaken the entire nation, merging into the general movement of suburbanization.

The 'progressive' ideals of Deweyism, which had taken hold before the war, now triumphed everywhere in Canada. No longer were children in school to learn facts by rote. The development of the 'whole child' was in vogue everywhere, and education now emphasized socialization and co-operation, to prepare children for their roles in a more sophisticated techno-logical society. The new system contained its own internal contradictions, of course, attempting to meet the needs both of the child and of society. As the authors of *Living and Learning*, an influential Ontario report on the aims and objectives of education, explained in 1968:

> The good school fosters a continuing desire to learn. It helps the individual pupil to feel secure and adequate within himself, encourages him to manage his own affairs, and helps him gain a measure of social competence. It gives all pupils an understanding of man and his world, encourages them to adopt positive attitudes toward change, and accustoms them to solving problems and overcoming difficulties. The good curriculum helps young people to acquire a purpose in life. It prepares them for the world of work and leisure. . . .[33]

Living and Learning was the product of a commission co-chaired by Mr Justice Emmett M. Hall and Lloyd Dennis, a former school principal. It recom-mended continuous inter-disciplinary education attuned to the needs of individual students; the abolition of grades, exams, failure; streaming by ability or competence; centralized curricula; and liberal electives and pupil participation in choice of content. Many of its recommendations were accepted by the Ontario Ministry of Education, radically changing the school system in that province—and reaching farther afield.

In 1946 the typical teacher had enjoyed a year or two at a teacher-training college; but by 1970 this autonomous institution had virtually disappeared into the university. School boards across the country required that newly hired teachers have university degrees that combined educational skills with subject-area background. Such teachers were therefore 'professionals', as their predecessors had never been. Not all Canadians were convinced that enhanced education and professionalization had improved what went on in the classroom, particularly in view of the complete triumph of the principles of progressivism. Thrown out with the strap were provincial examinations and any tests that might evaluate the achievement of traditional skills. Instead—as the Hall-Dennis Report stressed—came 'the right to learn, to play, to laugh, to dream, to dissent, to reach upward, and to be himself.'[34]

The educational spiral was, of course, continuous and in some ways vicious. The need for more and supposedly better-educated teachers com-bined with the general extension of the principle of universality to produce a demand for higher levels of university education. The same arguments used for high-school universality were simply extended to the universities, with

The academic quadrangle at Simon Fraser University. The two levels are supported by massive columns so that the quadrangle is open on all sides. Classrooms are in the lower level and faculty offices and lounges in the upper. SFU-87096-16.

increased enrolments justified chiefly in economic terms.[35] For governments, the gains were to be general; for parents, they were individual. At first substantial increases in university enrolments were met chiefly by existing facilities and teaching staffs, as the university student population doubled between 1945-6 and 1948, and then nearly doubled again by 1963.

By the later 1950s existing facilities could no longer contain the human growth. Established universities began building programs and a number of new universities were founded. In some cases existing colleges were given independence—for example, Victoria College (of UBC) became the University of Victoria (1963) and United College (of the University of Manitoba) the University of Winnipeg (1967)—but others were new institutions: Carleton (1957), Trent (1964-8), Brock (1964), Simon Fraser (1965), and York (1965).* The largest university in Canada, the University of Toronto,

---

*York University was affiliated with the U of T from 1959 until it became independent in 1965.

expanded with two suburban campuses, Scarborough College (1964) and Erindale College (1966), and three colleges on the downtown campus: Massey (1960-3), a superb complex designed by Ron Thom (1923-86) for the use of scholars and graduate students; New (1962); and Innis (1964). There was much competition among the new universities for architectural distinction—and perhaps only Simon Fraser, designed by Arthur Erickson (b. 1924), and Trent, designed by Ron Thom, were truly impressive. In retrospect, what is most striking about these creations of the fifties and sixties is their almost universal adoption of pre-stressed concrete as the preferred building material and an extraordinary similarity of vision (or lack of it) across the nation. Most universities quite appropriately built or expanded on suburban sites, usually attempting to dominate the landscape in one way or another. Given the amount of space available, high-rise buildings were less required than desired—almost every campus (suburban or urban) had its high-rise office complex.

If new or expanding universities competed architecturally, they also competed for faculty. The Canadian higher educational system had not looked ahead in the forties and fifties, totally failing to expand its graduate training facilities to meet its undergraduate pretensions. The result was that when the Baby Boomers hit the universities in the 1960s, it was far easier to construct buildings than it was to build faculties. Canada recruited over 20,000 new university faculty members in the 1960s, most of them from the United States, Britain, and elsewhere in the Commonwealth. These new teachers quickly geared up to produce a generation of graduate students who were not always trained in a Canadian context. Indeed, there was some backlash within the universities against this massive intrusion of foreign teaching staff, chiefly for its importation of non-Canadian approaches and general ignorance of Canadian society. Few economics departments, for example, discussed the Canadian economy in any but advanced and specialized courses. The movement for Canadian Studies grew as a consequence, attempting to force departments, particularly in the social sciences and humanities, to introduce Canadian content.

As with so much else in the post-war period, the expansion of the educational system in the fifties and sixties occurred without appropriate planning or thinking, in an environment of unprecedented population growth, a revolutionary shift in expectations, and a general level of economic prosperity. Few were prepared to counsel a gradualist approach, or to warn of impending disaster when either the money or the new students ran out. By 1970 the demographic revolution had ended, and its demise had begun working its way through the schools. The result was obvious. The system began turning out large numbers of teachers (for all levels of education) at the very time the profession had begun contracting. Jobs became increasingly hard to find. Only the earliest of the Baby Boomers found employment prospects encouraging when they came out of the educational system. For later generations, scrambling became the name of the game.

Profound and even revolutionary changes in educational systems were put in force before the early 1970s with a minimum of public debate, much less deep political division and disagreement. The writings of a few critics of progressivism, such as Hilda Neatby's *So Little for the Mind* (1953), seemed too old-fashioned to make much impression on a society that was impatient for an improved standard of living—which it tended, rightly or wrongly, to associate with educational expansion. Neatby's work did stir up some discussion in the academy, but not much in ministries of education. In Quebec, as we have seen, Frère Untel was able to combine an élitist condemnation of the culture of *joual*—that rich brew of anglicisms, obscenities, blasphemy, and non-standard syntax—with an attack on the unprogressive educational system of the province. His criticisms achieved far greater popularity than those of Professor Neatby. Outside Quebec (and to a lesser extent Newfoundland), one of the outstanding characteristics of the post-war educational revolution was the relative absence of systematic public opposition. Part of the reason for the lack of controversy was the unwillingness of Canadians to challenge the 'experts' in education, a point observed by the authors of *Crestwood Heights* in 1956. 'The school,' they wrote, 'supported by the human relations experts and their institutions, has largely replaced the church as an ideological source.'[36]

Extreme educational reform and change were implemented in most provinces with a minimum of objection. Only after the deeds had been done did people begin to question their validity. Thus a school consolidation program that was described by one educator as 'the most complete and socially significant transition to occur in Prince Edward Island since the Second World War'—it wiped out, virtually overnight, the small wooden schoolhouse, one of the most significant elements of village life and local identification on the Island—was implemented in the later 1960s and early 1970s without any significant local opposition. Only after centralization in PEI had been effectively completed, and had not brought about the advantages of cost efficiency and improved educational access claimed by its proponents, did parents and communities organize to object to it.[37] Other parts of the country were equally slow to object to the general trend of rural-school consolidation.

In Quebec the political aspects of educational change focused on the refusal or inability of a traditionally oriented system, run by ecclesiastics, to respond to the new educational expectations of an increasingly industrialized and urbanized society. Educational reform in Quebec became inextricably bound up with the 'Quiet Revolution'. In Newfoundland, the Smallwood government used educational opportunity as a principal argument in support of its policy of depopulating isolated outports and modernizing the province's society. Most of the political objection was not to educational reform itself, but to the underlying changes for which it served as harbinger. In the end, Canada had brought about profound social change through education with very little political controversy.

The Radical Sixties

The usual picture of Canada in the quarter-century after the end of the Second World War presents a naive, optimistic, traditional, politically apathetic, and thoroughly complacent society suddenly, after 1960, questioning virtually all its values and overturning a good many of them. The impetus for such radicalism came largely from the United States. Such a view is reasonably accurate, but several important qualifications need to be emphasized at the outset. One is that there was more ferment under the surface in 1950s Canada than is usually recognized; few 'revolutions' are truly sudden, and that of the 1960s was no exception. In many respects 1960 simply marked a shift to the public stage of ideas and behaviour that until then had been strictly private. Moreover, although the Sixties on one level involved a generational reaction by the maturing Baby Boomers against their suburban parents, this decade's upheaval grew out of the same romantic optimism and sense of general economic prosperity that had characterized the decade preceding. As is so often the case, confrontation occurred more because many (including the younger generation) became impatient with the slow speed of change than because they wished to alter its ultimate implications or even direction. The Sixties' upheaval was a distinctly middle-class or bourgeois movement, particularly in Canada, and was mounted on the rising expectations created by economic affluence. Finally, while American developments were extremely influential, Canadians did raise their home-grown concerns. Moreover, one of the chief reasons that Canadians were able to take over so much of the American vocabulary and issues was that they shared US critics' profound suspicions of the American system and establishment. American social critics of the Sixties struck a respondent chord in Canadians, who had often had similar feelings about the United States.

The Sixties were a complex period of currents and countercurrents. Even analysis of the major movements can do little more than scratch the surface. Nevertheless, any discussion of the Sixties must consider at least two of the period's most striking developments: a broad societal shift towards liberalization and the appearance of a youth-centred counterculture that scorned anyone over thirty. Sixties rhetoric was able to find a venue and outlet on TV, and the reformers were the first ever to have access to universally available colour television. Only a few contemporaries were able to get beneath the rhetoric, however, to attempt to come to terms with the substance of the critique.

The Emancipation of Manners

The Sixties have often been credited with (or blamed for) a moral revolution, in which the traditional values of our Victorian ancestors were overturned virtually overnight. But firmly held moral beliefs probably do not collapse quite so rapidly as the developments of this decade might suggest. Rather, a moral belief system that was already in a state of deterioration, and was out-of-step with what people actually did in their daily lives, was finally questioned publicly and proved incapable of surviving widespread scrutiny. The temporary upsurge of formal Christianity in the post-war period collapsed, and the churches found themselves deeply divided internally, at the same time that most Canadians were drawing away from organized religion. The crisis was simultaneously over the fundamental theological doctrines of Christianity—many of which had been developed in the first days of the church and had long been under attack—and over Christianity's social policy. But whether support for Christianity declined because its doctrines were not credible or its actions were considered irrelevant, the bottom fell out of Canada's principal belief structure. Again, the process of deterioration had been a long one, and had only been temporarily disguised by a revival of traditionalism immediately after the Second World War.[38] If there was an apparent moral collapse—the culmination of a very long process—it was more likely that fundamental morality was unchanged, while a previous Canadian reticence to talk about it and to question some of its Victorian manifestations had led to a general alienation from the church. The shift was probably less in morals than in manners. Moreover, the change was an international one—and went much further elsewhere in the highly industrialized world. By comparison with Europe or California, Canadian manners appear now to have remained relatively stable.

The liberation of manners occurred on several levels in the 1960s, but some of these were particularly visible. The old taboos against sexual explicitness, obscenity, and graphic violence in the media virtually disappeared. Although television attempted to maintain some kind of distinction between the movie theatre and the livingroom, TV news undermined that self-restraint, particularly with regard to violence. The Sixties were probably not a more violent period than any other, but constant television coverage of its most brutal features, increasingly in 'living' colour, brought such events to everyone's attention. The memories of almost anyone who lived through the period include a veritable kaleidescope of violent images: the assassinations of John Kennedy, his brother Robert, and Martin Luther King; the Paris student riots of 1968; battle scenes in Vietnam. Canadians liked to believe that most violence happened outside Canada, especially in the United States. In 1970 the Guess Who, a Canadian Rock group, had an extremely popular hit in 'American Woman', which pursued one of the most common Canadian metaphors of the time: identifying Canada's relationship with the United States in sexual terms.

As for sexuality, it became explicit in all sorts of ways. Canadians began to talk and write openly about sexual intercourse, contraception, abortion, pre-marital sex, and homosexuality. In place of the winks and nudges that had always accompanied certain 'unmentionable' topics, a refreshing frankness was accepted. Many of the issues of sexuality revolved around women's desire (hardly new) to control their own bodies and reproductive functions. The rapid spread in the use of 'Enovid', the oral contraceptive known as 'the pill' after its introduction in 1960, was part of the new development. The pill seemed to offer an easier and more secure method of controlling conception than previous ones, and its use became quite general before some of its side-effects came to light. One of its advantages was that the woman herself was responsible for its proper administration. The birth rate had begun declining in 1959, before the pill, and would probably have followed a similar course without it. Nevertheless, the pill became a symbol of a new sexual freedom for women that gradually worked its way into the media. By the middle sixties popular women's magazines that had previously preached marriage and domesticity were now featuring lead articles on the possibility (if not desirability) of pre-marital sex and marital affairs, options formerly regarded as male prerogatives.

Language, at least as the media used it, was equally liberated. Canadian writers—whether in fiction, poetry, drama, or film—had always used a sanitized and unrealistic version of spoken French or English. Earle Birney's comic war novel *Turvey* (1949) suggested the use of profanities by Canadian soldiers by means of the traditional dashes in the text. But in everyday life many ordinary Canadians relied heavily not only on swear-words but on a rich vocabulary of slang that could be found in few standard dictionaries. In French Canada the equivalent was *joual*. While earlier writers like Gabrielle Roy had suggested the presence of *joual*, later writers such as Michel Tremblay (b. 1942), in his play *Les Belles-Soeurs*, actually used it. Tremblay's play was written in 1965 but was not produced until 1968, chiefly because of concerns about its language. His later plays added sexually explicit themes, including transvestism and homosexuality. By 1970 both language and subjects previously considered taboo could be heard, read, and seen by Canadians across the country.

The state played its own part in the reformation of manners in the 1960s. Pierre Elliott Trudeau achieved the reputation that helped make him Prime Minister by presiding over a reformist Department of Justice in 1967-8. He became associated with the federal reform of divorce in 1968, as well as with amendments to Canada's criminal code dealing with abortion and homosexuality (both in 1969). Trudeau was Prime Minister in 1969 when a royal commission was appointed to investigate the non-medical use of drugs. While its report, published in 1970, did not openly advocate the legalization of so-called 'soft drugs', such as marijuana, its general arguments about the relationship of law and morality were symptomatic of the period. The commission insisted that the state had the right to limit the availability of harmful substances through the criminal code, but at the same time maintained that it was not necessarily 'appropriate to use the criminal law to enforce morality, regardless of the potential for harm to the individual or society.'[39]

The concept that it was not the function of the state to enforce morality, particularly any morality not held universally by all Canadians, informed many of the other legal reforms of the later 1960s. Divorce reform was not opposed by many major elements of Canadian society. A number of Roman Catholic bishops, in a brief to a special joint committee of the legislature on divorce, stated in 1967:

> It will be up to the legislator to apply his principles to the concrete and often complicated realities of social and political life and to find a way to make these principles operative for the common good. He should not stand idly by waiting for the Church to tell him what to do in the political order. . . . The norm of his action as a legislator is not primarily the good of any religious group but the good of all society.[40]

Such liberated thought not only paved the way for a thorough-going reform of federal divorce legislation—making divorce easier and quicker to obtain—but brought about an amendment to the Criminal Code in 1969 that made abortions legal if they were carried out by physicians in proper facilities, and following a certification by a special panel of doctors that 'the continuation of the pregnancy of such female person would or would be likely to endanger her life or health.' The Criminal Code was also amended in 1969 to exempt from prosecution for 'indecent actions' by consenting couples over the age of 21 who performed such acts in private.

This reformation of manners, if not morals—including the twin concepts that the state had no place in the bedrooms of the nation (a view first enunciated by Trudeau) and that individuals were entitled to make their own decisions—was largely completed in principle by 1969. Since that time, Canada has witnessed a resurgence of demands for state intervention in areas where liberalization is seen to have had adverse consequences. Thus many women's groups have come to advocate stricter legislation on obscenity and indecency, particularly in the media, in order to protect women and children from sexual abuse.

The Counter-Culture

One of the most obvious manifestations of the ferment of the Sixties was the rebellious reaction of the young Baby Boomers against the values of their parents, a movement that has come to be known as the 'counter-culture'. Although they had their own home-grown concerns, Canadian rebels of the decade took much of the style and content of their protest from the United States, where the inconsistencies between the rhetoric of optimistic middle-class affluence, on the one hand, and reality on the other, were even more apparent than they were in Canada. As in the United States, youthful rebellion in Canada had two wings, never mutually exclusive: a highly politicized movement of active revolution, centred in the universities, and a less overtly political one of self-reformation, centred on the 'hippie'. Student activists and hippies were often the same people, and even when different personnel were involved, the culture was the same, anchored by sex, dope, and rock 'n' roll. The participants in the two Canadian branches of youthful protest also had in common distinctly middle-class backgrounds, for this movement was not one of the disinherited.

The spiritual home of the Sixties counterculture, in Canada and everywhere else in the world, was the United States. Americans had gone farther than anyone else both in suburbanization and in universalizing education, and their rapidly expanding university campuses provided the ideal spawning ground for youthful rebellion. They had also generated, in the civil-rights movement, a protest crusade that served as a model for subsequent agitation. Civil rights as a public concern focused attention on the rhetorical contradictions of mainstream American society that preached equality while denying it to blacks, and mobilized youthful idealism. The civil-rights movement also demonstrated the techniques of the protest march and civil disobedience, as well as the symbolic value of popular song. When some blacks left the movement, convinced that only violence could truly alter the status quo, they provided further models for urban guerilla activity. In itself, the public concern for civil rights was an important element in the education of the Sixties generation. Nevertheless, what really touched off the revolt of American youth was the war in Vietnam.

Even in retrospect, the extent to which Vietnam dominated the period is not clear, largely because that war was the perfect symbol for the Sixties generation of everything that was wrong with mainstream American society. Vietnam was certainly the wrong war for the Sixties. It required America's young to fight overseas in a conflict with which they had no sympathy. Indeed, it was difficult for American youth not to identify with the enemy, who were struggling for national liberation against a modern example of the worst features of imperialism. Vietnam was equally exportable as a symbol of American Evil, for it represented everything that the rest of the world hated about the United States, particularly its arrogant assumption that it could do anything it pleased overseas. Vietnam was central to the Canadian counterculture in a variety of ways and provided more than a mere symbol. Hostility to American policy in Vietnam was the central feature of a collection of opinions about the United States by Canadian writers edited by Al Purdy: *The New Romans: Candid Canadian Opinions of the U.S.* (1967). But it also connected young Canadians with the burgeoning American movements of protest. Many Canadian university faculty members recruited during the decade were Americans, most of them recent graduate students who were critical of American policy. They were joined in their sympathies by an uncounted number of American draft-dodgers—perhaps as many as 100,000 at the height of the Vietnam war, the majority of whom sought refuge in communities of university students or hippies in Canada.

Post-war society in North America—a product of capitalist prosperity—was full of imperfections that included a failure to allow everyone to share in the affluence and a largely unquestioned emphasis on material possessions. The Baby Boomers had been exhorted in their schools and homes to think for themselves, but they were really able to do so only after they had reached university age. By that time they felt alienated from the mainstream society that had nurtured them, because—some said— their parents had not really provided them with a value system in which to believe. Perhaps it is inevitable that a younger generation will rebel against their parents; but in this case the search for alternatives was complicated by the fact that the parents themselves were not very clear about their values, apart from material success. Any rebellion against the materialism of the capitalist society was bound to turn to the alternative ideology of socialism—although, as the young liked to emphasize, their parents would have denied that capitalistic materialism was simply a competing ideology. The youthful reaction was to advocate an eclectic kind of socialism—Marxist-influenced, democratically oriented, and idealistically verging on romanticism—usually referred to as the 'New Left'. The movement was much better at explaining what was wrong with the existing system than at proposing workable alternatives; it had no example of a large-scale society that operated successfully (or even unsuccessfully) on its principles. Nevertheless, Canadian student activists rose to positions of power in their universities, and produced several national organizations, such as the Student Union for Peace Action (SUPA, 1965). Student radicalism was never dominant in most Canadian universities, although it flourished at a famous few, such as Simon Fraser in 1969-70, York University, and the Université de Montréal.[41]

Perhaps the best-known student protest in Canada occurred in February 1969, when the Computer Centre at Sir George Williams University (now Concordia) in Montreal was occupied for two weeks to protest racial intolerance and 'the military, imperialistic ambitions of Canada in the West Indies.'[42] The student protesters completed their occupation on 11 February by smashing the computers and causing damage to the university's equipment and records, estimated in the millions of dollars, thus attracting the attention of Canadians everywhere. Ninety 'occupiers' were arrested, including 41 blacks, many of whom came from the Caribbean. The episode was a classic example of student radicalism.

Student activism was not the same in Quebec as in the remainder of Canada. While Quebec's young were no more alienated than their anglophone counterparts, their anger was directed less against parents or their community than against the external colonial oppression of English Canada as expressed in Canadian federalism. English-speaking Canadian students spoke of 'the student as nigger' (a conceit imported from the United States), but French-Canadian students compared their entire society with blacks. Only in Quebec could blacks protest as they did at Sir George Williams, since only in that province was there a well-developed notion of colonialism, summarized in Pierre Vallières's *Nègres blancs d'Amérique*. Radical Quebec students were able to serve as the vanguard of a related series of movements

Debris on MacKay Street, Montreal, after the Sir George Williams University riot, 11 February 1969. National Archives of Canada PA-139986.

of protest and reform, support for which cut across the age structure of Quebec society. They were not totally isolated from the mainstream, as their counterparts in English Canada were.

What did radicalized students in Canada in the Sixties believe? It is probably better to describe the ideology's component parts, rather than to search for a system. Their Marxism was typically an over-simplification, often derived from other commentators such as Herbert Marcuse or Chairman Mao. In the first place the students were persuaded that action and theory could not be divorced—the well-known concept that 'if you're not part of the solution you're part of the problem.' They also held that reform from within the existing system was impossible, since the system would either repress or co-opt any such efforts. They rejected study of the past as outworn 'historicism'. Only the present moment (and perhaps the future) was 'relevant'. Most believed that they, as university students, could be the vanguard of a 'new working class'. They were no more sympathetic to communism than to capitalism, however, which helps explain why the Canadian philosopher George Grant (1918-91), who criticized both *isms* from a humanist

Tory perspective, was one of their leading Canadian heroes. Many of the less extreme student activists joined the so-called 'Waffle' movement, which attempted between 1969 and 1972 to radicalize the New Democratic Party in the direction of economic nationalism and social reform.

'The bureaucratic forms of organization shared by communism and capitalism', wrote one American activist, 'were embodiments of insult to the ideals of individualism, spontaneity, mutual trust and generosity that are the dominant themes of the new sensibility.'[43] These were the ideals of the hippies, who accordingly dropped out. Earlier generations of middle-class Canadians had struggled dutifully up the ladder of success, and later ones would strive even harder, but the Sixties' Baby Boomers were an aberration in their lack of traditional ambition or direction. They were their parents' children, however, in their search for personal self-fulfilment by any possible means. For some the quest led to vulgarized versions of Eastern mystical religions. For others it led to communes close to nature. For the vast majority it meant experimentation with hallucinogenic drugs, particularly cannabis, and a sexual freedom bordering on promiscuity that seemed to be danger-free at a time when sexually transmitted disease could be easily treated with antibiotics. Such experiments, together with a revolution in popular music, were the core of the Sixties, for participants and observers alike. Rock music was almost impossible to define, incorporating as it did so many musical styles ranging from black 'rhythm and blues' to traditional folk music to Indian *ragas* and medieval Gregorian chant. For the young, Rock served as a symbol that both united them and separated them from older generations.

It is impossible to identify a precise moment when the bubble of the Sixties burst. Many of the characteristics and tendencies of the period continued in fragmented fashion into the following decades. But at the end of the Sixties the idealistic thrust of the era received a series of shocks when American student activists were violently suppressed (Chicago, 1968; Kent State, 1970). At the same time their central rallying point—American involvement in Vietnam—was gradually removed. In Canada, the founding of the Parti Québécois in 1968 provided a place within the system for many Quebec student activists. Two years later the October Crisis had a profound impact, demonstrating both how far some activists were prepared to go in the use of violence, and how far the Canadian state was prepared to go in suppressing it. The purging of the 'Waffle' movement from the Ontario NDP in 1972 perhaps completed the process of neutralizing activism in English Canada.

Some observers explained the collapse of the Sixties movements of young people simply in terms of their getting older and requiring jobs. Perhaps. In any event, by 1972 only memories of the 'good old days' remained for most of the Sixties generation. Not only had the bloom disappeared from the affluent optimism of the post-war period, but new circumstances and conditions had accumulated to produce a host of new reactions against it, in which all Canadians had to share.

chapter twelve

Canadian Culture, 1945-1972

The 28th of September 1972 is one of those rare days of the past when a great many Canadians, at least those over the age of eight at the time, know where they were and what they were doing. Most were ensconced somewhere in front of television sets, which even factories, offices, shops, and schools right across the country had hastily installed. The largest television audience ever assembled in Canada was glued to the tube, while others listened on radio, mesmerized by an unofficial sporting event, played for no historic trophy or recognized world title: the eighth and last game of the Canada-Russia hockey series. The first seven games had been played to a virtual standstill, Canada winning only one and drawing one of the first four games played on home ice, and then winning two of the first three played in Moscow. This final game was equally close. The Russians took an early lead, the Canadians fought back, and Paul Henderson of the Toronto Maple Leafs scored the game- (and series-) winning goal with 34 seconds remaining in regulation time. Canadian National Honour in Canada's National Game was vindicated—if only barely. Given the country's pre-series expectations of an easy victory by its finest professional players, who had never previously been allowed to compete against the Russians, the victory could also be interpreted as a defeat, in so far as Canada's assumptions about its hockey pre-eminence were shattered.

In the long run the 1972 series would completely alter the way Canadians played hockey and lead to reform of the rough style of play, the so-called 'goon' tactics that they, and indeed all players in the NHL, practised. At the time, more than one observer asked how Canada could place its collective self-image at the mercy of a handful of professional athletes, most of whom collected their regular pay cheques from foreign employers. The contest *was* important to the country's self-image, however, though few then or now would see it in cultural terms. But sport in general was a part of culture — popular culture — and hockey was an integral component of both the Canadian National Culture and the national psyche. Moreover, after 1945 hockey had shared many of the same problems and changes as other elements of culture in Canada. Considering the priority Canadians gave to hockey, the wonder was that Canadian governments had not made more effort to make it a part of deliberate cultural policy.

Culture in Canada and Canadian culture (the two were not quite synonymous) emerged after the Second World War as major concerns for governments at all levels and for the private sector as well. Culture had not entirely been ignored before 1945, but it had always taken a back seat to political and economic matters, with Canada's performance (or lack of it) explained chiefly in terms of priorities; culture was a luxury, went the argument, that would come with political and economic maturity. Such maturity was now at hand. Four parallel and not necessarily related developments affecting culture occurred after 1945. One involved attempts at both federal and provincial levels to articulate and implement public cultural policy. The second was an explosion of artistic activity and cultural industry that carried with it a significant rise not only in quantity and quality but also in the number of people who earned their living in the production or support of culture. Third, the outcome of the combination of public policy and cultural explosion was quite contradictory, for while in fields of 'serious' culture Canada did develop a national profile, at the same time production of culture became diffused far more widely across the nation and cultural centralism was reduced. Another shift was a greatly expanded conception of what sorts of activity might be accepted as 'culture', along with some new aesthetic approaches in painting, music, and literature that redefined — or were unconcerned with — what might be regarded as pleasing. But with all these changes a clear theoretical understanding of the meaning of 'culture' did not emerge anywhere, and popular culture (such as hockey) did not really become integrated into anybody's cultural policy.

The Meanings of Culture

Neither before 1945 nor at any time in the post-war period did Canadians fully appreciate how many complexities were wrapped up in the term 'culture'. It was used to apply to a variety of phenomena, and much of what often seemed confusing was really a product of semantic difficulties. Some contemporaries recognized the problem of terminological ambiguities, which one government commission described as the 'general uncertainty of ideas respecting one of the major premises of socio-political thought in Canada'.[1] While Canadians commonly used the word 'culture' to refer to very different things without ever sorting out the complexities, they did appreciate that culture was a complicated business. In its several guises it was the central subject of four federal royal commissions: on the arts, letters and sciences (the Massey Commission, 1949); on radio and television broadcasting (the Fowler Commission, 1955); on magazine publishing (the O'Leary Commission, 1961); and on bilingualism and biculturalism (the Laurendeau-Dunton Commission, 1963, also called the B and B Commission). It was also the subject of the crucial opening chapter of the Report of the Quebec Royal Commission of Inquiry on Constitutional Problems (the Tremblay Commission, 1953). The disparate subjects of these commissions suggest that culture was virtually all-embracing. It was also freighted with political implications.

As the topics of the royal commissions indicate, Canadians in the post-war period really dealt with three very different meanings of culture. One was in a broad sense humanistic, referring to the creative and intellectual aspects of civilization as manifested through such institutions as art galleries, museums, and libraries. Artistic productivity and its artifacts (books, music, paintings) were interchangeably regarded as 'culture'. The Massey Commission concentrated on these aspects. A second meaning of culture was an anthropological one explored by the Tremblay and Laurendeau-Dunton Commissions. It was defined by the latter as:

> ...a way of being, thinking and feeling. It is a driving force animating a significant group of individuals united by a common tongue, and sharing the same customs, habits, and experiences.[2]

But Laurendeau-Dunton also used the word culture in the humanistic sense when talking about other ethnic groups and the 'cultural enrichment of Canada'. It briefly indicated its awareness of the confusion in the opening pages of its report, but permitted it to stand. Thus Laurendeau-Dunton used culture in one way when it talked about 'biculturalism', and in a quite different sense when it spoke about 'multiculturalism'.

There was a third dimension of culture, however, in the form of popular or mass or folk culture. Nobody quite understood, in this period, how to deal conceptually with popular culture. For most intellectuals it was the vulgarized other side of humanistic culture, mere trash for the marketplace. The Fowler Commission did not explicitly use the term 'culture' in relation to the radio and television broadcasting it was investigating, although it was precisely in the context of culture that such broadcasting most needed to be placed. The problem was particularly acute in terms of the relationship between popular culture in the intellectual/aesthetic sense and in the anthropological sense. Put simply, what was the effect of television advertising, of fast food, of the American sitcoms, or of American involvement in professional hockey on Canadians' lives? The Tremblay Commission had some awareness of this issue, for while it distinguished between the 'culture of the élite' and 'a common culture which is that of the mass',[3] it found that 'between the common culture and the culture of the élite, there is . . .such inter-dependence and constant inter action that the problem of culture remains a single one.' It also maintained that mass culture was 'the culture of origin' and that élite influences were assimilated to it.

Some critics attempted to distinguish between a popular culture that was dispensed by the 'media' (itself a new term of the post-war period, covering radio, television, and big-circulation journalism) and a popular culture that was intrinsic to the lives of ordinary people. The chief international guru of 'media' culture was the Canadian scholar Marshall McLuhan (1911-80). His first book, *The Mechanical Bride: Folklore of Industrial Man* (1951), examined comic strips, advertisements, and other promotional imagery of the American press to convey some insights into how 'many thousands of the best-trained individual minds have made it a full-time business to get inside the collective public mind'. Three years later, in the journal *Explorations: Studies in Culture and Communications* (1953-9), founded by Edmund Carpenter (b. 1922)—and itself one of the cultural landmarks of the fifties—McLuhan wrote an article entitled 'Notes on the Media as Art Forms':

> The use of the term 'mass media' has been unfortunate. All media, especially languages, are mass media so far at least as their range in space and time is concerned. If by 'mass media' is meant a mechanized mode of a previous communication channel, then printing is the first of the mass media. Press, telegraph, wireless, telephone, gramophone, movie, radio, TV, are mutations of the mechanization of writing, speech, gesture. Insofar as mechanization introduces the 'mass' dimension, it may refer to a collective effort in the use of the medium, to larger audiences or to instantaneity of reception. Again, all of these factors may create a difficulty of 'feedback' or lack of rapport between 'speaker' and audience. There has been very little discussion of any of these questions, thanks to the gratuitous assumption that communication is a matter of transmission of information, message or idea. This assumption blinds people to the aspect of communication as participation in a common situation. And it leads to ignoring the *form* of communication as the basic art situation which is more significant than the information or idea 'transmitted'.[4]

His later catch-phrase, 'the medium is the message', echoed through the 1960s (and is still heard).*

The distinction between media culture and received popular culture could be seen in popular music. Some songs became well known only through the

---

*It first appeared in book form in McLuhan's *Understanding Media:The Extensions of Man* (1964), in which he discussed how life and culture were being shaped by the new electronic communications technologies.

Marshall McLuhan, *c*. 1946.

media, while folksongs became known as part of a cultural heritage; to put it another way, some music was performed to the audience, while other music was performed by that audience itself. The modes of passive spectating and active performance became differentiated. The production of folk culture received a substantial boost from the Royal Commission on Bilingualism and Biculturalism, which saw it as part of the cultural contribution of immigrants to Canada, and from the subsequent introduction of official multiculturalism in 1971.

Canada was hardly alone in discovering that culture in its various manifestations was a contentious matter in the post-war world, but no nation had more problems with culture.* Nor did any nation have a greater need for conscious cultural policy on the part of government. Canada faced several

---

*It is perhaps symptomatic that Canada, which had not been distinguished for its production of abstract theorizing, actually generated two major theorizers who were at the cutting edge of thinking about culture change: Harold Adams Innis (1894-1952) and Marshall McLuhan. Innis's *Empire and Communications* (1950), which examined 'the roles of different media with reference to civilizations' and contrasted the civilizations, had a great influence on McLuhan's *Gutenberg Galaxy: The Making of Typographic Man* (1962).

obvious cultural difficulties, and some less obvious ones as well. It was a nation without a single unifying language and with at least two of what people after 1945 increasingly called 'founding cultures'. Moreover, although the word looks the same in both languages, French- and English-speaking Canadians often meant something quite different when they talked about 'culture', and while nobody doubted that French Canada had a distinctive one, defining the culture of English-speaking Canada was considerably more problematic. Unlike French Canadians, who fairly happily looked to Montreal as their cultural capital, English-speaking Canadians outside Ontario (and perhaps within that province as well) resented any suggestion of the cultural dominance of Toronto. Indeed, in many cultural senses that city's claim to pre-eminence declined after the war. For historic reasons, most of the 'other ethnics' whose culture was held by Laurendeau–Dunton to be so enriching resided in English-speaking Canada and were associated with it. While Canada lacked anything resembling a homogeneous national culture at either the humanistic or anthropological level, it was at the same time more than most nations exposed to external cultural influences, particularly from its behemoth neighbour to the south, the United States, which purveyed first to Canada, and then to the world, a profound influence on popular culture. If nations insulated from the Americans by geography and history could be strongly affected by American popular culture, the situation for Canada—geographically contiguous and historically closely connected—was alarming, at least for those who worried about the integrity of Canadian culture. Certainly every one of the royal commissions that dealt with culture in its various guises began by rehearsing this problem.

The association of culture, in both anthropological and humanistic senses, with the nation-state was a product of the nineteenth century that continued to have powerful support in the twentieth. One of the strongest arguments for the creation of many European nation states in the nineteenth century had been the cultural and linguistic homogeneity of a particular group of people, and the very term 'nation' was associated with the possession of a common culture. The notion that language and culture should be identical with political boundaries had informed the diplomats, led by American President Woodrow Wilson, at the Versailles Peace Conference after the Great War. Such a notion was of course fundamental to Quebec nationalism. As the Tremblay Commission put it in 1956, 'the nation is a sociological entity, a community of culture which forms and renews itself down through the years by the common practice of a same general concept of life'.[5] Much of the discussion about Canadian culture revolved around the assumption that it had to be 'distinctive' in order to be truly valid. Attempting to ascertain what was distinctive about Canadian culture was about as difficult as attempting to define the characteristics that made up the Canadian Identity.[6] Nevertheless, the two quests were obviously related, and became central themes of Canada's cultural existence. Among the Canadian cultural nationalists, those from Quebec and those from English-speaking Canada often had quite different definitions of culture and typically referred to different nations. Within both Quebec and Canada, however, there were many who did not think that there could or should be a 'national genius', or that the state should attempt to encourage one.

At the same time, there was a growing international recognition that the older cultural categories and canons of taste had been extremely limited. Artists, critics, and consumers all moved simultaneously to take seriously forms and styles that had previously been regarded as frivolous. The barriers that separated high culture, popular culture, and folk culture were in some fields reduced and in others totally demolished. Leonard Cohen, a well-regarded Canadian poet and novelist, became an internationally acclaimed pop-folk songwriter and singer. Creations in the visual arts by untrained artists of the past were brought out of the cupboards where they had been kept for generations and presented to a receptive public as fresh and attractive aesthetic approaches by 'naive' artists.[7] Many contemporary artists—such as Jan Wyers (1888-1973), William Panko (1894-1948), and William Kurelek (1922-77)—deliberately cultivated a naive style with considerable public success. Indian, and especially Inuit, art was literally brought into existence by a collaboration between European-trained and traditional native artists, assisted by government. Some critics sought the true Canadian content in folk art rather than in high culture. In any event, older boundaries and canons were breached, to the pleasure of almost everyone except the traditionalists.

The Development of Cultural Policy

On the development of cultural policy after 1945 by all levels of government, one point should be emphasized: governments were not operating in a vacuum. In 1945 (or for that matter at any point in its history) Canada had considerably more cultural life and creative activity than most Canadians would have recognized at the time. One of the reasons for the failure of recognition was that cultural critics and commentators relied on highly restrictive critical canons and categories. Art critics and historians used European standards to search for the origins of high art in Canada, neglecting badly a considerable achievement in folk art and craft. In many fields, such as classical music, specialists did not even bother to investigate the Canadian past, since everyone believed that little would be found. The general assumption was that only professional artists and performers, or at least properly trained amateurs, could possibly produce useful work.[8] Much of Canada's cultural life had occurred, and in 1945 was still occurring, outside the boundaries of what critics and experts regarded as Culture with a capital 'C'. It was practised by amateurs for their own pleasure—a tradition that offered fertile ground for growth but went unchronicled. One of the effects of Canadian cultural policy after 1945 would be to encourage and support the professionalization of culture that was gathering steam.

Theatre is a case in point. Amateur theatre flourished in many parts of

Canada in the nineteenth century and, as community theatre, in the twentieth, reaching its flowering in the Little Theatre Movement, of which Hart House Theatre was the standard-bearer. The vitality of these theatres was demonstrated in competitions at the annual Dominion Drama Festival (DDF), organized in 1932. Many actors who later became professional (John Colicos, Judith Evelyn, Amelia Hall, Douglas Rain, Kate Reid, et al.) and several playwrights (including Robertson Davies, Marcel Dubé, Robert Gurik) gained experience in Little Theatre and in the DDF competitions. But beginning in the 1950s, professional theatre was established in Canada with the founding of the Crest Theatre in Toronto and the Stratford Festival, both in 1953, the Manitoba Theatre Centre (the model for regional theatre) in 1958, and the National Theatre School in 1960.

With the growth in professional theatre in the sixties and seventies, combined with the expansion of television, the DDF was changed to Theatre Canada, dropping the competitive element and showcasing amateur theatres; but it collapsed in 1978. Amateur theatre, however, never completely died out in Canada. Similarly in music, professional choirs emerged in the fifties and sixties, though countless amateur choirs continued to flourish. And to the established symphony orchestras in Quebec (1902), Toronto (1926), Vancouver (1930), and Montreal (1934) were added orchestras in other cities, including Winnipeg (1948) and Ottawa (the National Arts Centre Orchestra 1968), while many new community orchestras were organized and others managed to keep performing.

Cultural Policy Before the Massey Commission

The war had provided a focus for many cultural organizations and artists, attempting simultaneously to rally public opinion, to provide temporary escape from the crisis, and to demonstrate the values of democracy. It also provided an impetus for consolidating national organizations; the Federation of Canadian Artists, for example, was founded in 1941. As Group of Seven artist Lawren Harris, who would become its first president, had argued: 'the time has come when the artists of this country should contribute consciously and designedly to the growth of a more highly socialized democracy by forming a nation-wide and inclusive organization and by working through the organization to serve the cultural needs of the Canadian public.'[9] Representatives of sixteen major cultural organizations met in Toronto in 1944 to prepare a single brief to the House of Commons Special Committee on Reconstruction and Re-establishment, pointing out the need for public financial support for the arts in Canada. The sixteen co-operating organizations were heavily concentrated in the visual arts in English-speaking Canada—fourteen of them based in Toronto—and among the interests not represented were those of French Canada, women, popular culture, the media, and the regions.

In December 1945 many organizations (chiefly in the visual arts) formed the Canadian Arts Council—just six months after the birth of the British Arts Council. This umbrella group lobbied provincial governments to set up cultural facilities, and served as the official Canadian body for the International Olympic Committee. But it sought in vain to be accepted by the federal government as the Canadian representative to UNESCO. External Affairs minister Louis St Laurent (1882-1973) told the Council that there would be constitutional difficulties with the provinces—which were responsible for education—over setting up a national arts board under the UNESCO charter. Moreover, St Laurent argued, 'music, literature, theatre and the visual arts did not really have a wide appeal in Canada—their place having been taken by the movies, the radio and the more popular magazines.'[10] A recognition of the unlikelihood of the federal government's assisting the development of cultural life had led amateur playwright Walter Herbert in 1945 to create the Canada Foundation to grant subsidies for such activities. The Canada Foundation was to be financed from the private sector, and by 1947 had raised $45,000. Given its tax-deductible status as a charity, however, the failure of the Foundation to raise more money provided evidence of the lack of interest on the part of Canadian businessmen in Canadian culture, at least in the 1940s.

It must be emphasized, however, that by 1945 Canadian governments— particularly at the federal level with the Public Archives, the National Gallery, the National Film Board, and the Canadian Broadcasting Corporation—already had a substantial involvement in cultural activity and institutions, though the extent of their involvement and the nature of their funding were not clearly understood by either politicians or the public. In 1947 the vice-chairman of the British Arts Council, B. Ilfor Evans, was invited to tour Canada to talk about the Council, and he pointed out that the reluctance of the Dominion to support cultural agencies like the Canadian Arts Council was surprising, given the government's existing, albeit unco-ordinated, involvement in cultural affairs.[11] Perhaps part of the reason for this lack of co-ordination was that while the wartime government had fostered culture in the name of the national emergency and the highest values of Western civilization, Canadian politicians were not generally keen on state involvement in culture.

As in so many other matters, the CCF had a much more activist policy in cultural affairs than other major parties. The CCF government in Saskatchewan did not hesitate to found a provincial archive (1945) or a regional library system (1950), and in 1948 it established the first publicly authorized North American arts co-ordinating organization in the Saskatchewan Arts Board, modelled on the British Arts Council. The Social Credit government of Alberta would follow the Saskatchewan lead, demonstrating that support for the arts was not always a partisan matter. As the Arts Board was administered in Saskatchewan, however, it was quite different from its British inspiration.

The particular vision of its administrators (and the government that appointed them) and the nature of arts co-ordination in a sparsely populated Canadian province made the Saskatchewan Arts Board a grass-roots body, fostering artistic activity at the local and individual levels, rather than chiefly co-ordinating the activities of provincial and urban organizations.[12]

Louis St Laurent—who succeeded Mackenzie King as Liberal leader and Prime Minister in 1948—was told that in the 1949 election the Liberals might lose votes to the CCF from 'those Canadians who have a distinct national consciousness and feel that more should be done to encourage national culture and strengthen national feeling.'[13] He was eventually persuaded to find employment for Vincent Massey—recently high commissioner in London—by making him chairman of a commission of inquiry. The Commission's scope was described in the 1949 Speech from the Throne as including

> all government agencies relating to radio, films, television, the encouragement of the arts and sciences, research, the preservation of our national records, a national library, museums, exhibitions; relations in these fields with international organizations, and activities generally which are designed to enrich our national life, and to increase our own consciousness of our national heritage and knowledge of Canada abroad.[14]

The Canadian federal government had finally decided to look for a national cultural policy.

The Massey Commission

The Royal Commission on National Development in the Arts, Letters and Sciences, usually known after its chairman as the Massey Commission, was a landmark development of the post-war period in terms of élite culture. Like many another royal commission, the Massey was brought into existence because its time had come, though its appearance just prior to a cultural explosion does not mean that it was solely responsible for the phenomenon. While its recommendations were crucial in increasing government involvement in the arts, they were precisely the ones envisioned in the Commission's terms of reference, which in turn were a product of considerable lobbying by well-established arts groups in the private sector. Although direct public patronage of the arts through national institutions and granting agencies was enhanced by the Commission, the indirect patronage in the form of full-time employment at universities was probably an equally important factor in supporting Canadian artists. Moreover, while the Massey Commission has often been viewed as ahead of its time in its advocacy of public support for the arts, in most respects it looked backward instead of forward. It attempted to promote a vision that came straight out of the Victorian era in its separation of culture and economics, and quite failed to come to terms with the many real problems of culture in Canada in the middle of the twentieth century—such as the relationship of culture and the marketplace. It did establish most

The Massey Commission: Dr Arthur Surveyer, the Most Reverend Georges-Henri Lévesque, the Right Honourable Vincent Massey, Dr Hilda Neatby, Dr Norman A.M. Mackenzie. National Archives of Canada, C-16986.

of the agenda for federal cultural policy for at least a generation to follow, but that agenda was narrowly conceived.

The strengths and weaknesses of the Royal Commission on the Arts, Letters and Sciences were epitomized in the figure of its chairman, Vincent Massey (1887-1967), who would subsequently become Canada's first native-born governor general—an appointment that was observed by B.K. Sandwell (1876-1954), the former editor of *Saturday Night*, in the following quatrain:

ON THE APPOINTMENT OF
GOVERNOR-GENERAL VINCENT MASSEY, 1952

> Let the Old World, where rank's still vital,
> Part those who have and have not title.
> Toronto has no social classes—
> Only the Masseys and the masses.[15]

Having prospered in the Massey-Harris farm-implement firm, the Massey family were notable patrons. Vincent's grandfather, Hart Massey (1923-96), set a precedent for patronage when he endowed the building of Massey Hall

(1894) in Toronto; when he died he left the bulk of his estate—out of which the Massey Foundation was created—for philanthropic purposes. Many buildings connected with education, music, and drama were endowed. Vincent Massey himself, who had a strong interest in architecture, was much involved in the design of Hart House (1910-19) and Massey College (1960-3) in the University of Toronto. An amateur actor, he was also an organizer of the Dominion Drama Festival. He attended the University of Toronto and then Balliol College, Oxford, where he indulged an anglophilia that remained with him throughout his life. After teaching history at the University of Toronto, a stint as president of Massey-Harris, and an appointment to Mackenzie King's cabinet in 1925 (he failed to win a seat in Parliament), he entered the diplomatic service at the ambassadorial level, serving as Canadian minister in Washington (1926-30) and as High Commissioner in Great Britain (1935-46).

In England, Massey consorted with the aristocracy and cultivated a reputation as a connoisseur and collector of art, particularly English painting. He was a trustee of the National Gallery of Canada, advising it on the acquisition of old masters. More importantly, through the Massey Foundation he had assembled a splendid collection of modern English painting that he presented in 1946 to the National Gallery of Canada. As a trustee (and chairman) of the National Gallery in London he served on several important British cultural committees.[16] Massey was a cultivated amateur, a British-style 'gentleman of leisure', and a patron, and both his cultural style and his aesthetic tastes were reflected in the Massey Report. His closest connections to the world of popular culture came through his own interest in contemporary drama and in the career of his famous actor-brother Raymond. As governor-general (1952-9) he would be something of a paradox: in many ways staunchly Canadian, and the first Canadian to hold that office, he invested it with trappings that suggested an excessive reverence for Buckingham Palace rather than what was expected at Ottawa's Rideau Hall in the middle of the twentieth century.

Assembling a committee of like-minded individuals—including Hilda Neatby (1904-75), professor of history at the University of Saskatchewan, later the author of the controversial *So Little for the Mind*—Massey led his forces into a whirlwind of action that was carefully catalogued in his final report:

> ...we have held public hearings in sixteen cities in the ten provinces. We have travelled nearly 10,000 miles, over 1,800 of these by air. In all, the Commission has held 224 meetings, 114 of these in public session. We have received 462 briefs, in the presentation of which over 1,200 witnesses appeared before us. The briefs included sub-missions from 13 Federal Government institutions, 7 Provincial Governments, 87 national organizations, 262 local bodies and 35 private commercial radio stations.[17]

As both these statistics and the Commission's terms of reference demonstrate, there already was an active cultural life in Canada, with lobbying organizations eager to step into a new era.

Given its mandate to articulate a national cultural policy, in terms not only of élite culture but of radio and television broadcasting as well, the way in which the Commission approached Canadian culture was absolutely critical. In the opening chapters of its final report it indicated by discussion and omission its own predilections. It began by calling attention to the overall problem of American influence, following with a series of chapters on the media and popular culture that suggested both the intimate relationship of these matters to the United States and the difficulty the commissioners had in concentrating on them. But it disposed of these matters in 65 pages of a 515-page report and then moved on to more congenial territory in the high arts. Nevertheless, it had made its hostility to both American influence and popular culture quite apparent.

The Massey Commission Report was interested not only in élite culture itself, but in élitist ways of assisting and regulating culture. The first item of the Commission's terms of reference had required it to recommend the principles for a policy for radio and television broadcasting in Canada. Since there was no television broadcasting yet in existence, its recommendations— if adopted by the government—would set the path. With some reluctance, and chiefly to counter the Americans, the Commission recommended that a national television service be created as quickly as possible. It further recommended that direction and control of television broadcasting, as well as radio broadcasting, 'continue to be vested in the Canadian Broadcasting Corporation', and that private television broadcasting be permitted only after the CBC had achieved national programming in both French and English. The costs of television programming, which would be very high, were to be met from parliamentary grants and a licence fee on television sets. The arguments for giving a monopoly to the CBC were made chiefly in terms of the lower costs of start-up, but also 'in order to avoid excessive commercialism and to encourage Canadian content and the use of Canadian talent.'[18] The Commission plainly approved CBC's radio programming, while it condemned private radio for its excessive commercialism, its undervaluation of public taste, and its poverty of 'cultural offerings', a phrase it did not define but that clearly meant serious, uplifting, and educational content. At the same time it associated commercialism (the 'appeal to material instincts of various kinds') with Americanism, and in turn Americanism with meretricious popular culture. These connections were classic Canadian assumptions of the time, particularly among those, like Vincent Massey, who could bemoan Canada's failure to produce a 'leisured class which may be expected to produce a few men in each generation devoted to the pursuit of learning and to the revelation of truth for its own sake.'[19]

The Commission proceeded from broadcasting to other matters that fell broadly into two categories. One involved a series of recommendations to strengthen existing national cultural agencies and to create others. The

Commission was supportive of the National Film Board, the National Gallery, the National Museum, the Public Archives, the Library of Parliament, and the Historic Sites and Monuments Board of the National Parks Service. It recommended more money and enlarged functions for these agencies, as well as the institution of new museums (one for history and one for science), national botanical and zoological gardens, and a National Library. Its other thrust involved federal aid for universities and scholarship, both through direct grants to the provinces and through the extension of the concept of the National Research Council (which supported scientific research) into the humanities and social sciences. It recommended graduate scholarships and advanced Canada Fellowships, as well as other grants to artists and scholars, all to be administered by a Council for the Arts, Letters, Humanities and Social Sciences. This 'Canada Council' would not only deal with grants and fellowships, but also co-ordinate Canada's relationship with UNESCO and 'promote a knowledge of Canada abroad'. While the Commission recognized the importance of the press and publishing to Canada and especially to Canadian culture—it called the content of the periodical press 'our closest approximation to a national literature'—it observed that it had no mandate in this area and made no recommendations on such matters. Nevertheless, it noted that 'Canadian magazines, unlike Canadian textiles or Canadian potatoes, are sheltered by no protective tariff, although the growing extent of the Canadian market has attracted the interest of American advertisers and magazines so that competition from the south has become increasingly vigorous.'[20]

In its recommendations the Massey Commission had produced a cultural agenda that would engage the federal government for the next quarter-century and beyond. Its conception of culture was unabashedly traditional, élitist, and nationalistic. What needed to be preserved and encouraged was not simply a culture of excellence, but a culture that was 'resolutely Canadian'. Finally, in its centralist philosophy the report was well suited to the inclinations of governments of the era.[21]

Cultural Policy After the Massey Commission

The various recommendations of the Massey Commission were acted on by federal governments in piecemeal fashion over the next decade. Federal assistance for universities had been instituted in 1950, the National Library was established in 1953, while branches in Natural and Human History at the National Museum of Canada were created in 1956. In March 1957, in the last days of the St Laurent government, one of the principal recommendations of the Massey Commission was finally adopted by Parliament as the Canada Council. Set up on a 'hands-off' basis with an endowment fund created out of windfall succession duties to finance its operations and an autonomous board of directors appointed by the government, the Council had an initial annual budget of $1.5 million to cover all the expenses of supporting the arts, humanities, and social sciences. It began making two sorts of grants, one to individual artists and scholars and the other to cultural organizations, and its assistance was limited largely to élite forms of culture and to the more professional organizations and individuals. It was understood at the time that governments could pursue national aims through policies of protectionism or of subsidies (bounties) to producers. The Canadian government in 1957 chose subsidies, and the system would achieve considerable success, although the financial costs would quickly exceed the endowment and prove potentially bottomless.

The Massey Commission had also recommended a new study of broadcasting after the initial three-year trial period for television under CBC control. In 1955 a second Royal Commission on the subject was appointed, chaired by Robert Fowler (1901-80) of Montreal, which made its final report in 1957. The Fowler Commission faced a number of problems, of which the most thorny were the shift in the content of radio with the introduction of television and the prevalence of American productions on both media. Television took over all the formats developed for radio— adding sight to sound on sitcoms, game shows, and drama, for example— and turned radio into a transmitter chiefly of news and recorded music. A detailed program analysis commissioned by the Fowler Commission easily documented the change. The largest music category had become 'Popular and Dance', chiefly from recordings. While CBC radio and Radio Canada continued to broadcast some live music, the independent radio stations in both languages relied on recordings for over 98 per cent of their popular and dance programming. The study was unable to identify the 'nationality of source for any sound radio programs', but most popular recordings of the time were clearly American in origin.[22]

Similar results were found for television programming, particularly in the prime-time entertainment slots and especially in English-speaking Canada. Analyst Dallas W. Smythe found that 48.5% of total program output on all Canadian television stations was produced in Canada, 47.9% in the United States, and only 3.6% in other countries. French-language stations drew only 8.4% of their programming from the United States, producing 80.5% at home. But in English Canada the programming was 53.1% American, and the situation was even worse when categories of programs were considered. Canadians produced nearly all the programming in fine arts, dance, and 'serious' music; more than half of 'serious' drama; all the 'serious' children's programs; and most sports. But in the more popular categories—domestic drama, comedy, western and crime, romantic, musical comedy, and even total children's shows (including cartoons)—prime-time programming for English Canada came mainly from the United States.[23] One of the major effects of the shift from radio to television was to raise costs of production.

The CBC had been able to compete better with the Americans in prime-time entertainment during the radio era, when production costs of shows like 'Jake and the Kid' or 'Anthology' were relatively low. But by the mid-1950s, Hollywood was producing most American programming on film for the American networks and was able to sell its shows to Canadian stations at a fraction of the cost of Canadian production. Moreover, public viewing habits were even less Canadian than Smythe's programming data suggested. Many major Canadian cities were within reach of American television stations (some deliberately placed on the border) and Canadians in Toronto, Montreal, and Vancouver could and did watch American programs on those channels as well as on Canadian ones.

The problems, as the Fowler Commission saw them, were serious:

> No other country is similarly helped and embarrassed by the close proximity of the United States. Much that is good and valuable can come from this closeness; there is an increasingly rich fare of programs on both radio and television available at relatively low cost from the United States. Much of this we cannot hope to duplicate and we would be poorer if we did not have it available as part of our total program supply. But as a nation we cannot accept, in these powerful and persuasive media, the natural and complete flow of another's culture without danger to our national identity. Can we resist the tidal wave of American cultural activity? Can we retain a Canadian identity, art and culture—a Canadian nationhood?. . .We may want, and may be better to have, a different system— something distinctively Canadian and not a copy of a system that may be good for Americans but may not be the best for us.[24]

The Commission enunciated the standard Canadian wisdom of the era when it responded to American integration by insisting that 'The Canadian answer, irrespective of party or race, has been uniformly the same for nearly a century. We are prepared, by measures of assistance, financial aid and conscious stimulation, to compensate for our disabilities of geography, sparse population and vast distances, and we have accepted this as a legitimate role of government in Canada.' While such a policy would be expensive, the Commission argued, the 'fact is that for Canada there is no choice,' at least if the financial cost could be kept 'within reason'.[25]

To subsidies and protectionism the Fowler Commission added a third cultural strategy: regulated competition within a 'mixed system of public and private ownership'. While it accepted that the Federal Treasury should support the CBC, it argued that expansion of broadcasting hours and geographical coverage (particularly for television) should also be met by private enterprise, which implied a second television network. Rather than permitting the CBC to continue to control broadcasting, it recommended the creation of an independent regulatory agency. Such a board had been suggested by the private broadcasters to deal with their own activities, but the Commission instead opted for a single regulatory agency called the Board of

Broadcast Governors (BBG), which would monitor all aspects of broadcasting performance, including program content, whether on public or privately owned stations.

The Diefenbaker government translated the Commission's recommendation into its Broadcasting Act of 1958, giving the new Board responsibility for regulating 'the activities of public and private broadcasting stations in Canada and the relationship between them,...ensuring the continued existence and efficient operation of a national broadcasting system.' The BBG was also given a mandate to promote and ensure 'the greater use of Canadian talent by broadcasting stations', so that the service would be 'basically Canadian in content and character.'[26] After public hearings in 1959, the Board introduced 'Canadian content' regulations for television, a sort of quota system, to become effective 1 April 1961. However, the definition of Canadian content was so broad as to be operationally meaningless, and it applied only to television. A more significant action by the BBG was its licensing of new stations, including those that would constitute a second Canadian television network (CTV), which began operations in 1961. These private stations were allowed to confine their 'Canadian content' to certain categories of programming (sports, news, children's shows, and other less-expensive programs) shown mainly out of prime time. The CTV network thus became even more dependent on American production than the CBC.

Ostensibly committed to principles of Canadian nationalism, the Diefenbaker government in 1961 took up the challenge—left dangling by the Massey Commission—of investigating the problems of Canadian magazine publishing. Under the chairmanship of Ottawa journalist Grattan O'Leary (1889-1976), a Royal Commission was created to investigate the abuse of Canadian hospitality by American popular magazines, chiefly *Time* and *Reader's Digest*, which had special editions for the Canadian market carrying Canadian advertising. This practice was cultural branch-planting with a vengeance, and the O'Leary Commission tried for a solution within the realm of the relatively unused strategy in the nationalist arsenal: protectionism. It recommended that any foreign periodical containing advertising directed specifically at the Canadian market be denied entry into the country; and, conversely, that any advertiser's expenses in such a periodical be ineligible for tax exemptions. The Diefenbaker government accepted the principal recommendations, but allowed *Time* and *Reader's Digest* special exemptions. It also failed to generate legislation, thus producing a controversy that would continue long after Diefenbaker had fallen from power.

By 1961, therefore, the federal government had not only implemented most of the Massey Report's major recommendations, but had experimented with all the possible strategies of a national cultural policy, ranging from subsidies (the Canada Council) to protectionism (periodical policy), to regulated competition (the BBG). Of these policies, subsidies unquestionably worked best, and the Canada Council became a major success story, providing 'serious' Canadian artists, writers, scholars, and cultural organizations with a degree of support that was the envy of much of the Western world. As we shall see, the government was also prepared by 1961 to offer subsidies in other cultural areas, including sport. The main problem, of course, was that subsidies were expensive and created expectations that were hard to meet—even where high culture alone was concerned—in an era of major expansion of cultural activity. By 1964, within only a few years of its creation, the Canada Council was spending beyond its original endowment, and the Pearson government determined to fund the additional expenses out of annual parliamentary grants, which came to cover an increasing proportion of the Council's expenditures. In the process the Council lost its independence of public control, at least over general policy.

At the same time that the federal government was defining and expanding a national cultural policy, devoted chiefly to fostering a distinctive Canadian identity in the face of the ubiquitous Americans, provinces and municipalities also became involved in cultural affairs in direct and indirect ways. The arts became a growth area everywhere for a variety of reasons. Cities and provinces, anxious to promote tourism and equally concerned to overcome the foreign misconception of Canada as the home of little besides ice and snow, built museums and auditoriums, often in conjunction with various anniversary celebrations. Quebec established its own ministry of culture in 1961 to promote the province's culture within the larger Canadian matrix. According to the government of Jean Lesage, 'It is by our culture rather than by numbers that we will prevail...that our French presence in North American can assert itself.'[27] The chief new developments in cultural policy throughout most of the 1960s occurred below the national level and went relatively unheralded—though all levels of government greatly increased their expenditure on arts and culture, particularly in the context of the Centennial celebrations of 1967.

In 1968-9 the 'new broom' of the Trudeau administration produced some technical adjustments to the existing federal system of cultural policy. It studied sport and fitness and produced a landmark report. The Social Sciences and Humanities Research Council was hived off from the Canada Council in 1968. The Broadcasting Act of 1968 replaced the BBG with the Canadian Radio-Television Commission (CRTC), which would regulate all broadcasting without having to deal with the CBC Board of Governors. The CRTC continued to experiment with regulation, particularly in the form of Canadian-content quotas. The 1968 legislation insisted that Canadian broadcasting must be run by and owned by Canadians, and in 1970 the CRTC redefined its content rules so that sixty per cent of all television programming (in prime time as well as overall) had to be Canadian in origin, and thirty per cent of all music played on radio had to have some Canadian involvement. The rules encouraged new Canadian production, and Canadian music and musicians, although in television it led chiefly to clones of cheap and out-dated American formats. The CRTC also began to be concerned about a form of broadcasting that had previously been ignored: the Community Antenna Systems (i.e. cable television). Cable TV had initially been developed in Canada to make it possible for remote areas to receive Canadian transmissions; but its market success had come in the early 1960s in urban regions, where it permitted viewers to receive distant American stations for one monthly fee. By 1968 cable was providing strong competition; however, the CRTC would not succeed in bringing it under regulation until the 1970s.

A final addition to Canadian cultural policy came in the later 1960s with the government's discovery of folk culture, particularly within the ethnic communities of Canada. Though the Royal Commission on Bilingualism and Biculturalism was briefed to find ways of promoting the ideal of bilingualism throughout Canada, the Commission had another mandate on which it reported in *The Cultural Contribution of Other Ethnic Groups* (1969). It recognized the richness of ethnic cultures and led in 1971 to a new federal policy of multiculturalism, in 1972 to a separate minister, and in 1973 to a Multiculturalism Directorate in the office of the Secretary of State. In this context the concern of the B and B Commission, and of subsequent federal policy, was less to preserve cultures in the anthropological sense than to maintain the 'cultural heritage' of ethnic groups—music, dance, costumes and foods. Quite independently of government policy, in 1970 Winnipeg organized the first large-scale multicultural festival in Canada as part of Manitoba's Centennial celebrations. 'Folklorama' rapidly became a major tourist attraction, and ethnic culture in general became another way to promote Canada abroad.

Much of the ethnic folk culture of the sixties was associated with relatively recent immigrants—but not all. There was a resurgence of interest in traditional folk culture in many provinces, notably in Quebec and the Atlantic region, especially Newfoundland. To some extent the interest was part of the counter-culture's rejection of industrial capitalism and its search for rural, pre-industrial roots. In Newfoundland this movement had the additional political edge of celebrating the culture of the outports, which were under heavy pressure from the government of Premier Smallwood to modernize. The only full-fledged university folklore department in Canada—at Memorial University in St John's—studied Newfoundland song, legends, and language. This interest in folk culture was simultaneously progressive in its acceptance of diversity, conservative in its celebration of pre-modern traditions, and nationalistic in its search for historic justifications of separate cultures.[28] At the same time, much of the tradition of folk culture 'recovered' by the folklorists—such as Inuit art or Haida totemic sculpture—was really 'invented' in its new self-consciousness, as artists were not only encouraged but in some cases even taught to work in older forms.

Cultural policy in Canada until 1970 was characterized by only the most imprecise considerations of financial cost. For the most part cultural agencies were expected to keep costs manageable by avoiding the arena of popular culture, where, most commentators agreed, Canadians could not afford to compete with Americans. Within the realm of 'serious' culture Canadian governments at all levels were prepared to spend large amounts of money to raise culture to international standards, and to a considerable extent they succeeded. Whether the culture that resulted was Canadian Culture was, of course, another matter.

∼∼∼∼ The Culture of the Élite

The term 'Culture of the Élite' comes from the 1954 Tremblay Report, which postulated an interesting, though not entirely unusual, relationship between high culture and the 'common culture which is that of the mass'. Unlike many cultural commentators before the 1960s, the Tremblay Commission assumed that the common culture—'made up of knowledge, means of expression, and values blended into a tradition of life'—was the fundamental base culture. At the same time, however, it was élite culture that produced 'a civilization highly representative of humanity's greatest ideals.' For the Tremblay Commission,

> The level of the common culture tends all the more to elevate itself to the extent that an active elite, through its works, specific action and general influence, incites it to surpass itself. In return, there is all the more chance of the elite increasing in quality and number as the level of the common culture itself becomes more elevated.[29]

While this mutually beneficial dynamic was somewhat unusual, the notion that élite culture represented the highest ideals of humanity was standard thinking before the 1960s, when many cultural theories were made to stand on their head.

For most Canadians, including those who were not participants in élite culture, its production and consumption were synonymous with culture itself. While the Tremblay Commission could postulate a symbiotic relationship between mass culture and élite culture, the typical Canadian recognized only élite culture as proper culture, either consigning mass culture to a much lower level or ignoring it entirely. As fund-raisers for the institutions of élite culture fully recognized, Canadian businessmen who had not been raised in its milieu often tended to hold it in very high esteem. Supporting élite culture became a major mark of status for an increasingly affluent and sophisticated society, and there were those who argued that by 1970 certain forms of élite culture (symphony orchestras, ballet, art museums, and opera, for example) had in the process become so democratized as to have shifted over into the realm of popular culture. Whether or not such democratization made élite culture less élite, in some areas it exerted pressures against new

forms—such as atonal music—that were also limitations on its Canadianization, particularly at the level of artistic creation. Many contemporary Canadian artists were ignored by the public as too avant-garde, while millions of
dollars were spent on productions of nineteenth-century Italian opera.

The Literary Scene in English Canada

There has never been any dearth of Canadian writers, and after the war their
books continued to be published in ever-growing numbers. Some novels
earned both critical acclaim and commercial success, as well as enduring
respect, and their authors were beginning 'to "create" Canada in the way
that Hawthorne, a century earlier, helped to create New England.'[30] W.O.
Mitchell's memorable novel of a Saskatchewan boyhood, *Who Has Seen the
Wind*, was published in 1947. In 1951 alone there appeared Morley Callaghan's *The Loved and the Lost*; Hugh MacLennan's *Each Man's Son*; *The
Nymph and the Lamp* by Thomas Raddall, who had achieved an earlier
success with three historical romances; and the first of Robertson Davies'
three satirical Salterton novels, *Tempest-tost*. Ethel Wilson's *The Equations of
Love* and Ernest Buckler's *The Mountain and the Valley* were published in
1952. As a token of a future distinguished career, the 23-year-old Mordecai
Richler's *The Acrobats* was published in England, with little Canadian notice,
in 1954. Four well-known novels appeared in 1959: Hugh MacLennan's *The
Watch That Ends the Night*, Sheila Watson's experimental *The Double Hook*,
Richler's *The Apprenticeship of Duddy Kravitz*, and *The Luck of Ginger Coffey*
by the Belfast-born novelist Brian Moore, who was then living in Montreal—where he wrote his classic *The Lonely Passion of Judith Hearne*
(1953)— and had become a Canadian citizen. But in spite of these successes
the market for, and interest in, works of literature by Canadian writers was
not strong, though a few houses—among them the Ryerson Press; McClelland & Stewart; Macmillan Canada; Clarke, Irwin; and (for poetry) Oxford
University Press—continued to publish them.

Apart from a group of forties poets in Montreal—including F.R. Scott,
A.J.M. Smith (1902-80), A.M. Klein, Patrick Anderson (1915-79), Louis
Dudek (b. 1918), Irving Layton (b. 1912), P.K. Page (b. 1916), and Miriam
Waddington (b. 1917)—there was almost no sense of a literary community in
English Canada. This absence was first noticed by F.R.Scott, whose attempts
to organize a gathering of writers in 1946 did not bear fruit until a three-day
Canadian Writers' Conference was held at Queen's University in July 1955.
In bringing together some hundred delegates—poets, novelists, publishers,
editors, critics, librarians, and interested members of the public—this Kings-
ton Conference was a milestone. Its thrust can be observed in *Writing in
Canada* (1956)—edited by the poet and scholar George Whalley (1915-
83)—which divided the papers into three sections: 'The Writer', 'The
Writer's Media', and 'The Writer and the Public'. Though no problems were
solved, an attempt to bring about a literary community had begun.

Mordecai Richler, *c.* 1990.
Photograph copyright
P. Andrews, Publiphoto.

At the time of the 1955 Writers' Conference, *Northern Review* (1945-56) was the leading literary magazine. But in 1956 its editor, John Sutherland, died, and Robert Weaver (b. 1921) founded *The Tamarack Review* (1956-82), which featured stories, poems, interviews, essays, and reviews. *Tamarack* published the early, sometimes the first, work of several leading Canadian writers: Timothy Findley (b. 1930), Jay Macpherson (b. 1931)— both of whom appeared in the first issue—Alice Munro (b. 1931), Mordecai Richler (b. 1931), Hugh Hood (b. 1928), and others. The second issue contained Alice Munro's well-known story 'Thanks for the Ride' and an interview (by Nathan Cohen) with Mordecai Richler, who was living in London, England. Some of Richler's remarks indicate the lassitude of Canadian publishers where fiction by young writers was concerned:

> I have had one experience with a Canadian publisher. When *The Acrobats* had been accepted here I was in Canada, and André Deutsch wrote to me to visit the Canadian distributor. I spent a day in Toronto and went to visit him. And the first question this man who distributes books for—well, a dozen very reputable publishers—the first question he asked me about my novel was 'Is it a thick book?' Because Canadians like thick books. The second question he asked was

Margaret Laurence in the
1960s.

are there any Communists in it and is it anti-Canadian? The whole thing was
ridiculous. The system of publishing in Canada and the system of awards is just
a joke.[31]

However, *The Apprenticeship of Duddy Kravitz* met with great success and
established Richler as a major writer. Duddy Kravitz entered Canadian
folklore. Richler was not the first Canadian novelist to mine the rich vein of
ethnicity, particularly Jewish, but he was the first to mythologize the urban
ghetto, its inhabitants and way of life. In 1966 he confessed: 'No matter how
long I continue to live abroad, I do feel forever rooted in Montreal's St
Urbain Street. This was my time, my place, and I have elected to get it exactly
right.'[32] *St. Urbain's Horseman*, arguably his best novel, was published in 1971.
    Margaret Laurence (1926-89) was another major new novelist of the
period. Having lived with her husband in Somalia and Ghana from 1950 to
1957, she was living in Vancouver when her African novel *This Side Jordan*
(1960) appeared. Soon afterward she completed the first of her four
Manawaka novels, which brought her international acclaim. *The Stone Angel*
(1961), *A Jest of God* (1966), *The Fire-Dwellers* (1969), and *The Diviners*
(1974) could be read on many levels and were easily the most richly textured

W.O. Mitchell, Robertson Davies, and (*above*) Timothy Findlay and Margaret Atwood in 1988, when all four writers were about to have new books published. Courtesy *Maclean's*.

fiction ever produced by a Canadian writer. The mythical prairie town of Manawaka was itself a strongly conceived and living entity, linking some powerful female protagonists struggling against its hypocritical Scots-Canadian constrictions and their own past. Noting that she was not much aware that her 'so-called Canadian writing' was essentially Canadian, Laurence commented that 'this seems a good thing to me, for it suggests that one has been writing out of a background so closely known that no explanatory tags are necessary.'[33]

Further west two other novelists were beginning their long and successful publishing careers: Rudy Wiebe (b. 1934) of Edmonton with *Peace Shall Destroy Many* (1962) and American-born Audrey Thomas (b. 1935) of Vancouver with *Mrs Blood* (1970). The Toronto poet Margaret Atwood (b. 1939) launched a career as a novelist of international importance with *The*

Edible Woman (1969) and *Surfacing* (1972). And Robertson Davies (b. 1913) took a new direction in his writing of fiction with his masterpiece *Fifth Business* (1970)—followed by *The Manticore* (1972) and *World of Wonders* (1975), making up the Deptford trilogy—which put him in the company of the leading novelists outside Canada.

The genre of short stories is a relatively old, and respected, tradition in Canadian literature and in this period Mavis Gallant (b. 1922), with *The Other Paris* (1956) and *My Heart is Broken* (1964), and Alice Munro with *Dance of the Happy Shades* (1968) and *Lives of Girls and Women* (1971), established the basis for their present international standing among the best writers of short stories in English.

With a much smaller readership than fiction commanded, poetry not only held its own but acquired a substantial audience. Irving Layton, Earle Birney (b. 1904), Al Purdy (b. 1918), Margaret Atwood, Michael Ondaatje, and Leonard Cohen gained a public that in some respects put them on the same plane of popularity as their fellow writers of fiction. Margaret Atwood followed *The Circle Game* (1966) with *The Animals in That Country* (1968), *The Journals of Susanna Moodie*, and *Procedures for Underground* (both 1970). Michael Ondaatje (b. 1943) published his first collection, *The Dainty Monsters*, in 1967, and his celebrated *The Collected Works of Billy the Kid* in 1970. Layton, Purdy, and Birney were sent on reading tours by their publisher, McClelland and Stewart, and became almost as adept in performance as in writing.

Performance of a different kind took over the career of Leonard Cohen (b. 1934), who straddled the worlds of high and pop culture when he set some of his poems to music, wrote new songs, and sang them to his own guitar accompaniment. He published his first book of poetry, *Let Us Compare Mythologies*, in 1956 at the age of 22. It was followed in the sixties by two novels, including his classic *Beautiful Losers* (1966), and by several poetry collections that were exceptionally appealing to the younger generation in their imagery and themes. In 1968, the year he refused a Governor General's Award for his *Selected Poems*, his first record album, *Songs of Leonard Cohen*, appeared, soon to be followed by *Songs from a Room* (1969). A few of his songs had already been performed by Joan Baez and Judy Collins, but Cohen's own chanting baritone was the perfect vehicle for popularizing them. By 1970 he was competing successfully with other pop poet-singers like Bob Dylan and Donovan Leitch, and such songs as 'Suzanne', 'The Master Song', 'It Seems So Long Ago, Nancy', and 'Bird on a Wire' entered the counterculture. Cohen captured youth's scorn for hypocrisy, and his songs counselled survival by withdrawing from the contests of life into a private world of the spirit, not in triumph but in endurance through ceremony and self-understanding—powerful messages for the Woodstock generation. Ironically, while Cohen's songs were far less identifiably Canadian than the prose of his fellow novelists, his sense of self-deprecation and self-abnegation was probably deeply rooted in his Canadian persona.

Earle Birney, E.J. Pratt, Irving Layton, and Leonard Cohen on Bloor Street West, Toronto, in the 1950s.

Concurrently with all this new writing the subject of Canadian literature came to be considered in terms of its history and long-neglected books. McClelland and Stewart's enduring New Canadian Library series began in 1958, offering mainly reprints of novels but also some brief critical studies of individual authors. *Canadian Literature*, 'the first review devoted only to the study of Canadian writers and writing', was founded in 1959 by George Woodcock (b. 1912). The *Literary History of Canada* was published by the University of Toronto Press in 1965. At the beginning of his 'Conclusion' to this work, a classic essay on the literature, Northrop Frye (1912-91) wrote:

> The book is a tribute to the maturity of Canadian literary scholarship and criticism, whatever one thinks of the literature. Its authors have completely outgrown the view that evaluation is the end of criticism, instead of its inciden-
> tal by-product. Had evaluation been their guiding principle, this book would, if

Northrop Frye in 1960. The
United Church of Canada/
Victoria University Archives,
Toronto (91.161 P805).

written at all, have been only a huge debunking project, leaving Canadian literature a poor naked *alouette* plucked of every feather of decency and dignity. True, the book gives evidence, on practically every one of its eight hundred odd pages, that what is really remarkable is not how little but how much good writing has been produced in Canada.

And at the end:

> For present and future writers in Canada and their readers, what is important in Canadian literature, beyond the merits of individual works in it, is the inheritance of the entire enterprise. The writers featured in this book have identified the habits and attitudes of the country, as Fraser and Mackenzie have identified its rivers. They have also left an imaginative legacy of dignity and of high courage.[34]

By 1970 virtually every Canadian university offered an undergraduate course in Canadian literature, and a critical canon had more or less been established, which naturally emphasized the 'distinctively Canadian' qualities of Canadian writing. Without the new breed of scholarly critics who were prepared to take Canadian writing seriously—as well as the subsidies that helped sustain author, critic, and journals—that writing would probably have developed much more slowly. Before the 1950s precious few scholars and critics in Canada were prepared to devote much attention to writing in their own country. The change was doubtless symbiotic, with both the writing and the critical approach improving and reinforcing one another simultaneously. One leading critic, George Woodcock, insisted on not 'getting caught in the trap of a narrow nationalism', maintaining that 'the study of Canadian literature is merely the study of writers who happen to live and work in Canada.'[35] But inevitably the bias of Canadian literary scholarship and criticism was in favour of those who, in one way or another, interpreted the Canadian identity. Northrop Frye stated in a 1959 review of poetry that 'the centre of reality is wherever one happens to be, and its circumference is whatever one's imagination can make sense of.'[36] According to this logic, a Canadian-based writer would have to reflect Canada somehow. For many critics the challenge was to reveal quintessential Canadian-ness in the imaginative element of the literature. Some critical writing, however, showed more imagination than the fiction. Notable in this regard was Margaret Atwood's *Survival: A Thematic Guide to Canadian Literature* (1972), which made the great leap from literary themes to the collective persona in positing the central image of Canada (and Canadian literature) as survival within the context of victimization. Seeing literature as 'a map, a geography of the mind', she examined the map of Canadian literature in a way that excited widespread interest, and much discussion that included disagreement. *Survival* was a watershed book, after which the terrain of the literature became relatively familiar and compelling, readers multiplied, and new writers proliferated.

In his 'Conclusion' to the *Literary History*'s Second Edition of 1976, Northrop Frye noted 'the colossal verbal explosion that has taken place in Canada since 1960.' It was this growth, as well as the nationalistic climate that developed before and after Centennial Year, 1967, that encouraged small publishing enterprises to form across the country, making Toronto less of a power-base for all future English-language publishing. In 1967 alone Talonbooks (Vancouver), Hurtig Publishers (Edmonton), House of Anansi (Toronto), and Tundra Books (Montreal) were founded; other small presses included Breakwater (St John's), Harvest House (Montreal), Oberon (Ottawa), Turnstone (Winnipeg), Fifth House (Saskatoon), NeWest (Edmonton), and Sono Nis (Victoria). While small presses spread publishing activity across the country, Toronto inevitably gave birth to more of them than any other city (Coach House, Anansi, New Press, James Lorimer, Lester and Orpen). In the meantime a financial crisis was occurring in certain established Toronto houses. The oldest, the Ryerson Press, supported by the United Church of Canada, was so much in debt that it was sold in 1970 to the American firm McGraw-Hill. And the Ontario government, just as it appointed a Royal Commission on Book Publishing (1970), at the same time rescued McClelland and Stewart from an American take-over.

Despite the fact that the federal government established a policy of giving support to Canadian-controlled publishing firms, through such agencies as the Canadian Book Publishing Development Program and the Canada

Council—as did provincial governments in various ways; the Ontario Arts Council is only one example of a provincial funding agency—Canadian publishing was in a chronically precarious state. The relatively small market for English-language books, the enormous volume of American and British as well as Canadian books available, the dominance of foreign-owned publishers, and the policy of full return of unsold books put Canadian-owned publishers at a competitive disadvantage—though this did not discourage many more small publishers from setting up business throughout the seventies and eighties as more and more Canadian writers produced publishable work. Publishers in Quebec experienced less difficulty then those in the rest of Canada, despite the small market: apparently the people of Quebec were more willing to read about themselves.

The Québécois Novel

The beginning of our period was also a turning-point in French-Canadian fiction, marking an end to the century-old tradition of the *roman de la fidélité*—novels that had safeguarded the survival of the French-Canadian people by celebrating their customs, traditions, and faith. In 1945 *Le Survenant* by Germaine Guèvremont (1893-1968) cast one of the final blows against this tradition. That year, and the year before, two well-known novels made the break complete by having urban settings and being about under-privileged workers: Roger Lemelin's *Au pied de la pente douce* (1944) and Gabrielle Roy's *Bonheur d'occasion* (1945). All three novels were published in English translation—as *The Outlander*, *The Town Below*, and *The Tin Flute* respectively—and were widely read in English Canada, as were the succeeding books of Roy and Lemelin (1919-92). Another important novel of the period was *Poussière sur la ville* (1953) by André Langevin (b. 1927)—translated as *Dust Over the City*—set in the asbestos-mining town of Thetford Mines, Quebec. But the sensation of the fifties was *La Belle Bête* (1959) by the twenty-year-old Marie-Claire Blais (b. 1939), which astonished the reading public—even in its English edition, *Mad Shadows*—and scandalized the clergy for its portrayal of characters representing various kinds of moral and physical ugliness, and for its powerful, impressionistic scenes of betrayal, disfigurement, pyromania, murder, and suicide. With this novel Blais began a long and prolific career.*

The effect of the Quiet Revolution on Quebec fiction was considerable, though in fact the influence was reciprocal: one fuelled the other. The

---

*Blais was 'discovered' outside Quebec by the American critic Edmund Wilson, who later discussed her first four books in his *O Canada: An American's Notes on American Culture* (1964). Observing that Blais showed herself 'incapable of allowing life in French Canada to appear in a genial light or to seem to embody any sort of ideal', Wilson describes her as 'a true "phenomenon"; she may possibly be a genius.'

Marie-Claire Blais, *c.* 1959.
Wheler-Scott Ltd.

literary transformation that began in this decade and continued through the seventies and eighties—the anger and violence of language and subject matter, radical changes in syntax and formal structure—not only mirrored but fostered the spirit of liberation and the new goals of Quebec society. And this work was no longer called French-Canadian but Québécois fiction. The journal *parti pris* (1963-8), founded just after the first wave of FLQ bombings with an *indépendantiste* and a Marxist perspective, published in January 1965 a special issue entitled *Pour une littérature québécoise*—giving a name, which was quickly adopted, to the current and future works of francophone writers in Quebec. That issue also promoted the use of *joual* in creative writing. The poet Paul Chamberland (b. 1939), one of the founding editors, wrote: '. . .my language must be shaken to its very foundations through the disfigurement inherent in our common speech, and in the lives of all of us.'

Exemplifying the new *texte national* in fiction were novels by Jacques Godbout (b. 1933), Hubert Aquin (1929-77), Claude Jasmin (b. 1930), and Jacques Ferron (1921-85): Godbout's *L'Aquarium* (1962), *Le Couteau sur la table* (1965)/*Knife on the Table*, and *Salut Galarneau!* (1967)/*Hail Galarneau!*; Aquin's first novel *Prochain épisode* (1965, translated with the same title), which was proclaimed the great novel of Quebec's 'revolutionary' period; Jasmin's *Éthel et le terroriste* (1964)/*Ethel and the Terrorist*; and Ferron's *Les*

Paul-Émile Borduas, *c.* 1958, a
still from the film *Paul-Émile
Borduas.* L'Office National du
Film.

Confitures de coings (1972)/*Quince Jam*, in which a leading character is a cruel parody of F.R. Scott (who had a long friendship with Ferron that ended when Scott backed the War Measures Act of 1970). These few novels, however, are only a token of the flowering that took place in Québécois fiction, which today includes a large body of brilliant and innovative works.[37]

Painting: The Ascendancy of Non-objective Art

The Quiet Revolution of the 1960s also had an interesting connection with the painting community of Montreal over a decade earlier. After the war there was a strong reaction, in Canada and elsewhere, among young painters against figurative painting and even the modernist painters of France. This took the form of abstraction and had its first expression, during the war, in the Surrealist paintings of several young Montreal artists, whose teachers were Alfred Pellan at the École des beaux-arts and Paul-Émile Borduas at the École du Meuble. As early as 1942 Borduas had said that what was required was a kind of stream-of-consciousness — an 'automatic painting that permits the plastic expression of images, of memories assimilated by the artist and which make up the sum of his psychic and intellectual being.'[38] He attracted a group of young painters — including his own students Marcel Barbeau (b. 1925) and Jean-Paul Riopelle (b. 1923), as well as Pierre Gauvreau (b. 1922) and Fernand Leduc (b. 1916) from the École des beaux-arts. This group came to be called *Les Automatistes*, a name given to them after a small group show in an apartment on Sherbrooke Street West in February–March 1947 that included a Borduas canvas, *Automatisme 1.47* (also known as *Sous le vent de l'île*), a classic Surrealist painting that is now in the National Gallery of Canada. Before the end of the year Borduas struck out against all the religious and political inhibitions that constrained his creative life by writing perhaps the most important manifesto of modern Quebec, *Refus global*. Four hundred copies were put on sale in August 1948.

Written in late 1947 and signed by fifteen members of his group, *Refus global* is a rambling series of passionate, almost poetic utterances attacking virtually everything in Quebec society at the time. Borduas described the province where he was born as 'a colony trapped within the slippery walls of fear, the customary refuge of the vanquished', condemned the restrictive powers of the Church, and called for both the artist's personal liberation and a social revolution:

> Break permanently with the customs of society, dissociate yourself from its utilitarian values. Refuse to live knowingly beneath the level of our spiritual and physical potential. Refuse to close your eyes to the vices, the frauds perpetrated under the guise of learning, favour, or gratitude. Refuse to live in the isolation of the artistic ghetto, a place fortified but too easily shunted aside. Refuse to be silent—make of us what you please, but you must understand us—refuse glory, honours (the first compromise): stigmata of malice, unawareness, servility. Refuse to serve, to be made use of for such ends. Refuse every INTENTION, pernicious weapon of REASON. Down with them both, to second place!
>
> MAKE WAY FOR MAGIC! MAKE WAY FOR OBJECTIVE MYSTERIES!
> MAKE WAY FOR LOVE!
> MAKE WAY FOR NECESSITIES!
>
> . . .The self-seeking action remains with its author—it is stillborn. Passionate acts take wing by their own energy. We cheerfully take the entire responsibility for tomorrow. . . .In the meantime, without rest or cessation, in a community of feeling with those who thirst for a better existence, without fear of a long deferment, in the face of encouragement or persecution, we will pursue in joy our desperate need for liberation.[39]

The next month Borduas was fired from the École du Meuble on the instruction of Paul Sauvé, minister of social welfare and youth (and Duplessis's successor as premier in 1959). In 1953 Borduas moved to New York, where he was influenced by American Abstract Expressionists, and began his famous series of black-and-white paintings. In 1955 he moved to Paris, where his steady application to painting was rewarded by growing international recognition through numerous one-man shows. He died in 1960, too soon to witness the cultural liberation he had advocated, never realizing that he would become a hero of the 1960s counterculture, or that with his *Refus global* modern Quebec began.

Automatisme gradually dissolved after *Refus global*, as its exponents moved on geographically and conceptually. Some young painters were not satisfied with the combination of spontaneity and traditional spatial perspectives advocated by Borduas. Led by Fernand Leduc, they produced a manifesto in 1955—signed *Les Plasticiens*—that was not inflammatory, like *Refus global*, but it too insisted on artistic freedom and acknowledged the importance of Borduas. It said that they were drawn to 'plastic qualities: tone, texture, forms, lines, and the final unity between elements'.[40] They came increasingly to appreciate the importance of structure in their painting, insisting that abstractionism constituted a more objective version of reality by probing beneath the superficial. When a famous 'Art abstrait' show was held in Montreal in 1959, the *Plasticiens* disappeared and a new group became prominent, with Guido Molinari (b. 1933) and Claude Tousignant (b. 1932) eventually joining the ranks of the leading painters of the country. Abstractionism was no longer regarded as particularly *avant-garde*, but had become part of the mainstream, not only in Quebec but in Canada generally.

In the 1940s the rest of the country—even Toronto, though Borduas exhibited there frequently—was isolated from all the energy and innovative work of the French-Canadian painters in Montreal. But on the west coast one painter was attracted by non-objective art. Scottish-born Jock (J.W.G.) Macdonald (1897-1960) came to Canada in 1926 to head the design department of the Vancouver School of Decorative and Applied Arts, and in 1930 took up painting. He soon began experimenting with automatic painting and was encouraged by Lawren Harris, who moved to Vancouver in 1940. In 1947—the year Macdonald exhibited thirty-six of his abstracts at the San Francisco Museum of Art—he moved to Toronto to teach drawing and painting at the Ontario College of Art. There he became the mentor of William Ronald (b. 1926), encouraging him to study for six weeks with the great teacher Hans Hofmann in New York. Ronald was captivated by the Abstract Expressionism of the New York painters.

In 1953 Ronald persuaded the Robert Simpson Company in Toronto—where he had worked for a time in the display department—to host an 'Abstracts at Home' exhibition, which included the work of six painters besides himself: Kazuo Nakamura (b. 1926), Alexandra Luke (1901-67), Ray Mead (b. 1921), Oscar Cahén (1916-56), Jack Bush (1909-77), and Tom Hodgson (b. 1924). Out of this exhibition a group was formed—with the addition of Jock Macdonald, Hortense Gordon (1887-1961), Walter Yarwood (b. 1917), and Harold Town (1924-90)—called Painters Eleven, and they had an opening show at the prestigious Roberts Gallery in Toronto. The initial reaction was uncomprehending and cool, or indifferent. But many other exhibitions followed—including one at New York's Riverside Museum in 1956—and in spite of internal wranglings, Painters Eleven

Painters Eleven, 1957. Only nine painters are in this photograph, taken for the catalogue of a show at the Park Gallery, Toronto, in November 1957: William Ronald, the founder, had resigned on 17 August, and Oscar Cahén died in an accident the previous year. *Seated*: Tom Hodgson, Alexandra Luke (above), Kazuo Nakamura, Hortense Gordon, Jack Bush. *Standing*: Harold Town, Jock Macdonald, Walter Yarwood, Ray Mead. The two canvases are by Cahén. Photograph by Peter Croydon courtesy The Robert McLaughlin Gallery, Oshawa.

continued for seven years, acceptance was achieved, and four members went on to greater glory. Jack Bush achieved international recognition. Harold Town had a long career as a protean artist—a brilliant draughtsman and graphic designer who worked not only as an abstract impressionist but also as a printmaker, collage artist, and sculptor. William Ronald had a highly successful one-man show at the Kootz Gallery in New York in 1957 (the year he resigned from Painters Eleven) that was followed by four more; he became an American citizen in 1963. And Jock Macdonald, Ronald's teacher, was given in April 1960 a retrospective exhibition at the Art Gallery of Ontario—the first living Canadian outside of the Group of Seven to be paid this honour. He died of a heart attack in December, just two months after Painters Eleven was formally dissolved.[41]

Ballet, Opera, Theatre

In the rapid development of the performing arts in Canada after the Second World War we can see one major shift in the nature of culture in Canada. Canada ended the war with an amateur tradition in the performing arts, but by 1970 had achieved a full-fledged professional system operating from coast to coast. In the process institutions of performance had diffused all across Canada.

A ballet club in Winnipeg—started in 1938 by two English dance teachers, Gweneth Lloyd (b. 1901) and Betty Farrally (b. 1915)—developed in 1941 into the Winnipeg Ballet, which in 1953 was named the Royal Winnipeg Ballet, the first ballet company in the Commonwealth to be granted a royal charter. Under the directorship of Saskatchewan-born Arnold Spohr (b. 1928), it went on to receive international acclaim, employing distinguished choreographers—including the Canadians Brian Macdonald (b. 1928) and Norbert Vesak (b. 1936)—and creating a major star in Evelyn Hart (b. 1956). In 1950 the English dancer and choreographer Celia Franca (b. 1921) was brought to Canada by some Toronto ballet enthusiasts to form a national company, and the next year the National Ballet of Canada was born (and in 1959 the National Ballet School). Expansion and expertise in the great classical ballets made it possible for the National to hold its seasons in Toronto's O'Keefe Centre, and to attract the collaboration of the world-famous dancers Rudolf Nureyev (who staged his celebrated version of *The Sleeping Beauty* for the National in 1972) and Erik Bruhn (who would be artistic director from 1983 until his death in 1986). In Montreal a ballet company founded by the Latvian-born Ludmilla Chiriaeff (b. 1924) became in 1958 Les Grands Ballets Canadiens, which since 1959 has maintained a strong profile, particularly in modern dance, and tours the world.

Opera was always part of Canada's musical life. In the nineteenth century, for example, famous singers gave recitals in the main cities; touring companies visited, and opera associations formed briefly in Montreal and Toronto. Today there are opera associations in Vancouver, Calgary, Edmonton, Winnipeg, Hamilton, and Quebec City. The company with the longest season and the largest budget is the Canadian Opera Company (COC), which grew out of the Opera Festival of the Royal Conservatory Opera Company (1950) and was formed in Toronto in 1958. As with all new opera companies, the favourite operas were the staples and it was not until the 1980s that the COC strayed into Janáček and Berg; but in Centennial Year, 1967, it produced a Canadian opera, *Louis Riel*, by Harry Somers (b. 1925), to critical appreciation.

The gradual spread of artistic activity across English Canada was particularly notable in regional or 'alternative' theatre, which pursued a more experimental course than mainstream theatre. In 1958 the Manitoba Theatre Centre was formed—as an amalgamation of the Winnipeg Little Theatre and

Theatre 77, co-founded by John Hirsch (1930-89) and Tom Hendry (b. 1929)—becoming professional in the early sixties. Other new regional theatres that followed were the Neptune (Halifax) and the Vancouver Playhouse, founded in 1963; the Citadel (Edmonton, 1965); the Globe (Regina, 1966); the Saidye Bronfman Centre (Montreal, 1967); Theatre New Brunswick (Fredericton) and Theatre Calgary, both founded in 1968; Centaur (Montreal, 1969); Toronto Arts Productions at the St Lawrence Centre (1970); Theatre London, Sudbury Theatre, Theatre NorthWest (Thunder Bay) and the Bastion in Victoria—all founded in 1971. In Quebec, with its centralized culture, theatres proliferated in Montreal: Théâtre du Rideau Vert (1948), Théâtre du Nouveau Monde (1951), Théâtre de Quat'Sous (1955), the Comédie-Canadienne (1958) of Gratien Gélinas (b. 1909), La Poudrière (1958), Théâtre Populaire du Québec (1963), and Théâtre d'Aujourd'hui (1968). In the sixties and seventies there also developed many small 'alternate' theatres specializing in innovation and new genres such as documentary drama and collective creations. The first alternate theatre in English Canada was Toronto Workshop Productions, founded in 1959 by George Luscombe (b. 1926); others that followed in that city included Theatre Passe Muraille (1968), Factory Theatre (1970), and Tarragon (1971). Elsewhere in the country there were Theatre 3 (Edmonton, 1970), Tamahnous (Vancouver, 1971), 25th Street Theatre (Saskatoon, 1971), and the Mummer's Troupe (St John's, 1972).

In this period English-Canadian plays were not often produced—or, apparently, desired—though in 1967 George Ryga's *The Ecstasy of Rita Joe* at the Vancouver Playhouse, *Lulu Street* by Ann Henry (b. 1914) at the Manitoba Theatre Centre, and *Colours in the Dark* by James Reaney (b. 1926) at the Avon Theatre of the Stratford Festival all received successful productions. It was not until 1972 and after that such prominent English-Canadian playwrights as Carol Bolt (b. 1941), David Freeman (b. 1947), David French (b. 1939), David Fennario (b. 1947), Larry Fineberg (b. 1945), Michael Cook (b. 1933), and Erika Ritter (b. 1948) first had their plays produced.[42]

Contemporary drama by Québécois playwrights had a much earlier start and a stronger following, beginning with Gratien Gélinas's *Tit-Coq*, which was first produced at Montreal's Monument National theatre in May 1948. Ten years later Gélinas founded the Comédie-Canadienne, which produced eleven Quebec plays between 1958 and 1961, including works by Marcel Dubé (b. 1930), Françoise Loranger (b. 1913), and Félix Leclerc (1914-88). Other important playwrights who helped to create the energetic climate of Quebec theatre were Jacques Languirand (b. 1931), Jacques Ferron (1921-85), Robert Gurik (b. 1932), Guy Dufresne (b. 1915), Jean Barbeau (b. 1943), and of course Michel Tremblay.

It came as a surprise to many Canadians that outside of Toronto and Montreal it was possible to create stable institutions for the performing arts, and world-class facilities such as the Jubilee Auditoriums in Edmonton and

Calgary (1955), Vancouver's Queen Elizabeth Theatre (1959), the Confederation Centre in Charlottetown and the Playhouse in Fredericton (both 1964), Edmonton's Citadel Theatre (1965), the Arts and Culture Centre in St John's (1967), and the National Arts Centre in Ottawa (1969). Winnipeg, for example—a middle-sized, geographically isolated urban centre with no particular tradition of cultural patronage—by 1970 was supporting a fully professional symphony orchestra; the Royal Winnipeg Ballet and other dance companies; an opera association mounting several works each year; the Manitoba Theatre Centre, an acclaimed model for regional theatre, whose impressive mainstage opened in 1970; an active art gallery; and a major concert hall. Thanks to various centennials, similar facilities and institutions were available in every major urban centre across Canada. By 1970 no important Canadian city or region was without its own professional theatre company, art gallery, and symphony orchestra. Created with substantial public monies in the form of block grants from all levels of government, new institutions initially relied heavily on recent immigrants to Canada for professional expertise, and as had been hoped, many of these professionals became teachers and sponsors of spin-off activities. It was not long before highly qualified younger Canadians were ready to step into these companies and organizations, and a substantial local audience had been developed. In music and theatre one of the secrets of public success was the introduction of annual subscription campaigns: unlike audiences in New York, London, and Paris, where tickets were sold only for individual events, not for series, patrons in Canada's regional centres were asked to buy blocks of tickets to guarantee an audience in advance.

Scholarship, and the Curious Case of Canadian History

Canadian scholarship, like other areas of élite culture, expanded and was strengthened in the post-war era, particularly beginning in the 1960s, when a combination of grants from the Canada Council and the Social Sciences and Humanities Research Council of Canada (SSHRC), and an increase in the number of Canadian universities, vastly added to the numbers both of academics and of those doing research. Canadian scholarship grew not only in volume but in content, achieving international recognition in many disciplines. In literature the first two books of Northrop Frye, *Fearful Symmetry: A Study of William Blake* (1947) and *Anatomy of Criticism: Four Essays* (1957), established his international reputation as a scholar and critic. In philosophy leading writers were Charles De Koninck (1906-65), author of *The Hollow Universe* (1964); George Grant (1918-90), author of *Philosophy in the Mass Age* (1959); Francis Sparshott (b. 1926), author of *An Enquiry into Goodness and Related Concepts* (1958) and *The Structure of Aesthetics* (1963); and Fernand Dumont (b. 1927), author of *Le Lieu de l'homme* (1968) and *La Dialectique de l'objet économique* (1970). In chemistry the German-born Walter Herzberg (b. 1904), of the National Research Council, was the author

of numerous publications and won the Nobel Prize in 1971 for his contribution 'to the knowledge of electronic structure and geometry of molecules,
particularly free radicals'.

The arrival in the 1960s of so many Ph.D.s on the staffs of Canadian
universities—mainly, but not solely, from American graduate schools—gave
Canadian scholarship a new flavour that was simultaneously American and
international in nature. The increase in activity was especially noticeable in
the humanities and social sciences; the sciences, which had for many years
basked in government generosity, particularly extensive research monies,
were far less immediately affected.

One field that had great difficulty in coming to terms with the rapidly
changing world of scholarship was Canadian history, which had arguably
been the premier humanistic discipline before the 1960s. Canadian historians
had served as the effectual arbiters of, and spokesmen for, Canadian nationalism (or in the case of Quebec historians, Quebec nationalism)—not merely
within the academy, but within the political arena as well. Since the 1920s the
writing of Canadian history in English Canada, and the training of graduate
apprentices to continue that writing, was dominated by the University of
Toronto. That institution controlled not only graduate training but the
Canadian Historical Review and the University of Toronto Press, founded in
1901, which was virtually the only Canadian academic publisher in English
of non-commercial monographs. Even those historians who were not closely
associated with Toronto shared in its general view of the nature and shape of
the Canadian historical experience.

For most historians of Canada working within the English-speaking tradition, Canadian History was National History. Confederation served as the
break between colonial beginnings and the fulfilment of national destiny.
The focus was political/constitutional and unremittingly progressive—the
country was settled; adopted representative government; turned representative government into responsible government, and responsible government
into a union of the provinces; and with union continued to move towards full
nationhood. The direction was well suggested by the title of a popular history
of Canada, *From Colony to Nation* (1948) by Arthur Lower (1889-1988), a
historian who had taught at Wesley College, Winnipeg, and was teaching at
Queen's University when this book was published. The post-Confederation
perspective—on the development of, and debates about, national policy—
was centred on Ottawa. Not only was Ottawa the focus of the post-
Confederation perspective, but as the home of the Public Archives of Canada
it was also the principle place where historians did their research. Perhaps not
surprisingly, this unofficial fraternity helped to confirm the Ottawa-centric
paradigm of national development. Quebec, of course, had its own paradigm,
equally nationalistic and political.

For much of this period the world inhabited by historians of Canada was a
cosy, friendly, and largely masculine one. In English-speaking Canada most

historians shared similar small-town or rural Protestant Ontario back-grounds—sons of the manse were conspicuous in the generation that was still dominant in the early 1960s. Works published in a single year were few enough that they could be read by all. Historiographical controversy was kept to a minimum by the consensus tradition of the politics studied, through informal principles of territoriality and the conviviality that held sway in the Public Archives and at the annual Learned Societies meetings. As most of these historians were men, the history they wrote was profoundly male-centered, oriented around politics, war, and public service, and discussed within a progressive chronology. Popular topics were the era of Confedera-tion and the Fathers of Confederation, with major award-winning biogra-phies of John A. Macdonald (two volumes) and George Brown (the first of two volumes)—by Donald Creighton (1902-79) and J.M.S. Careless (b. 1919) respectively, both of the University of Toronto—appearing in the 1950s.[43] These highly respected historians were secure in their epistemology, believing that truth was not only definable but attainable, and that historical objectivity, while perhaps not entirely possible, was still a goal worth pursuing.

This tidy world came under seige on all fronts during the decade of the sixties, though it would not collapse until the 1970s. The University of Toronto was unable to supply enough graduate students in Canadian history to maintain its intellectual dominance, as other universities went into the graduate business themselves (the total number of graduate students more than tripled in the decade after 1966). The result was a process of diffusion and regionalization, much as occurred in other areas of culture. By and large, Canadian history was not directly invaded by non-Canadians so much as it was undermined by the other influences to which graduate students in Canadian history were exposed in their non-Canadian seminars. In truth, Canadian history as it was currently being taught and written was profoundly out of step with what was happening in the rest of the world, where non-political dimensions and new ways of examining them had been discovered and elaborated. Moreover, as the old political consensus reflected in the traditional historiography was undermined by a whole new set of issues that had never before been examined, more international and socially concerned approaches to the teaching of history made increasingly compelling sense.

Younger historians of Canada began asking new questions about race, class, ethnicity, and gender that emerged out of the political turmoil of the late 1960s, and about the glaring neglect in traditional historiography of Indians, women, the working-classes, and racial minorities. To these changes in perspective, historians of Quebec added their own, often influenced by the 'annales' school of French historical analysis. Requiring new methodologies and new theories, the new research and writing in Canadian social and economic history asked implicitly whether the old paradigm of nation-building was flexible enough to provide a framework for integrating what was being discovered. By 1970 it was becoming increasingly clear that it was not, although mainstream Canadian historians had no idea how to make up for the shortfall. They tended to fall back on adding new material as additional chapters to textbooks that continued to focus on the nation and the problems of nation-building. Those holding to a concept of a national history would not give up easily.

By the early 1970s the writing of Canadian history had altered substantially, as had the milieu in which it was being written. Moving away from the biographical and narrative approach to history, it became more specialized and concentrated. Young historians were quite indifferent to such large, nebulous topics as the national character, preferring to study various areas of history from a feminist perspective, examine regional history, or explore subjects pertaining to specific fields such as labour, industry, or medicine. Like many other branches of élite culture, Canadian history had experienced both a geographical and a thematic diffusion. The traditional synthesizing way of looking at the past had been breached, but there was no new vision to replace it. Moreover, the extent of the problem was disguised, because Canadian history continued to be popular. Enrolments and attendance figures ran high, and few wanted to fix what did not yet appear to be broken.

Popular Culture

The post-war years were also critical ones for popular culture in Canada. While governments wrestled with aspects of a cultural policy intended to protect Canadian culture and the Canadian identity from 'foreign' (i.e. American) influence, their focus before 1960 was almost entirely on high culture. Few Canadians appreciated that Americans were making a cosmic shift in cultural terms, particularly in the development of institutions of popular culture that could be exported. The secret of American post-war success was an extraordinarily prosperous home economy, based partly on the extension of technological innovation into nearly every American household. Many of these new consumer goods, such as television sets and high-fidelity equipment, required the development of related cultural products— TV programs, recordings—to make the new gadgets essential to every family, and the American entertainment industry was clearly up to the challenge. Hollywood suffered initially under the impact of the shift to home entertainment, but by the end of the 1950s it had captured control of American television production and was well on its way to dominating popular music as well. All aspects of American popular culture, particularly sports, were systematically brought into the web of the entertainment industry. The effect on Canada would be profound.

While Canadians had long been susceptible to American popular culture in the form of print, film, and radio, they were now being literally inundated with new technologies whose influence was far more pervasive. To some

extent the readiness of Canadians to accept the new technological innova-
tions and the American culture they purveyed was a product of positive
attraction. As Melinda McCracken has pointed out in her autobiographical
account of teenage life in Winnipeg in the 1950s, '...everything American
was so desirable. America appeared to be the source of all good things, things
that were magical and ingenious and fun.'[44] American popular culture had
virtually no competition from the remainder of the world until the mid-
1960s, when the 'British invasion' of the Beatles and Carnaby Street struck
North America—and the American entertainment industry soon co-opted
it. Canadians could distinguish foreign from domestic high culture, but
could not do so with popular culture. Moreover, Canada's traditional leadership tended to disdain popular culture as degraded or irrelevant.

In his influential *The Canadian Identity*, written at the close of the fifties
and published in 1961, the Manitoba historian W.L. Morton (1908-80)
observed that it did not

> ...greatly matter that Americans and Canadians share the same popular culture;
> after reading the same comic strips, and the same periodicals, Canadians remain
> as distinct as they ever were. What differentiates the two people are things far
> deeper than the mass culture of North America, which both countries share and
> both created.[45]

Morton's comment was illuminating in several respects. In his reference to
comic strips and periodicals, he demonstrated how out-of-date he was.
Thinking no doubt of the O'Leary Commission on magazine publishing—
and dismissing it as trivial—Morton obviously shared the government's
limited conception of culture while remaining hopelessly unaware of the
action of the fifties. In a similar way, while Harold Innis in *The Bias of
Communication* (1951) clearly identified the relationship between technology
and culture, he also totally failed to comprehend the importance of the new
media of his day. For Innis, radio (rather than television) illustrated his
argument. Not until McLuhan's *The Gutenberg Galaxy* would a Canadian
thinker seriously attempt to comprehend the developments of the past few
years. McLuhan doubtless overstated the case in arguing that print, the
technology that had dominated modern history, had become obsolescent
(though he qualified this in one of his letters by saying 'obsolescence never
meant the end of anything'). But at least he understood the implications of
the electronic age.

If most Canadian commentators lagged at least a generation behind Americans in their understanding of the technology of popular culture, they also
tended to underestimate its pervasiveness. Again, McLuhan made the cosmic
leap in his aphorism 'the medium is the message'—an insight that was
criticized for all the wrong reasons. Most commentators before 1960 would
have agreed with W.L. Morton that of course there was an American-
dominated mass culture—but Canadian distinctiveness resided elsewhere. A
concentration on popular culture as significant would simply not have been

Canadian, since popular culture was American: one sought the Canadian Identity in other places, chiefly in Élite Culture. This factor helps account for the difficulty of *finding* the Canadian identity. But it also helps explain much of the passivity with which Canadians accepted what was happening in such aspects of their popular culture as film and hockey.

The sixties did bring a somewhat new government attitude to popular culture, at least in the sense that a willingness gradually emerged to bring segments of it under the umbrella of government policy. The politicians were not often clear that what they were doing was expanding Canada's cultural policies, nor did they appear to understand any relationship between culture and other factors, such as technology or industry. But they did begin acting.

Canadian Film in the Post-war Era

The tale of the Canadian film industry in the years immediately after the war offers an excellent introduction to the problems facing Canada in the context of popular culture. Film was one of the few arenas of popular culture that the federal government of the immediate post-war era attempted to enter in a policy sense. Unfortunately, the government did so in the wrong way for the wrong reasons, and its attempted intervention failed miserably.

Since the 1920s American film corporations had dominated the motion picture business in Canada. Not only did they produce most of the films Canadians wanted to see, but to make certain that Canadians saw them they also controlled distribution. In 1951 over eighty per cent of feature-film distribution in Canada was in the hands of Canadian subsidiaries of Hollywood's largest studios, including 20th Century-Fox, Paramount, Columbia, and Warner Brothers. Hollywood-owned theatre outlets (Famous Players and Odeon) held two-thirds of Canadian commercial cinemas, chiefly in the prime locations.[46] Not surprisingly, Canada had an unfavourable balance of payments in terms of motion pictures. At the end of 1947, when a general currency flow to the United States threatened the Canadian dollar and various restrictions were placed on American imports, there was talk of imposing a quota system for American films in the name of austerity.[47]

C. D. Howe, the Minister of Trade and Commerce in charge of international trade (including motion-picture imports), saw the problem largely in economic terms, although others hoped to use the currency crisis to begin a Canadian film industry. M. J. Coldwell (1888-1974), leader of the CCF, proposed that 'Canada should set up the protective tariff restricting the amount of money that could be taken out each year by the American distributors to ensure that a portion of the film profits made in Canada each year would be used to stimulate a Canadian film industry.'[48] This suggestion was classic 'National Policy'. Ross McLean, Commissioner of the National Film Board from 1945 to 1950, recommended both that American companies be required to use part of their revenue to make films in Canada for international audiences, and that American distribution companies be 'induced' to distribute short subjects produced by Canadian film-makers, including the NFB. That organization was the logical place to turn for Canadian production—which was part of the problem. During the critical period of government negotiation with Hollywood in 1947-8, the NFB was experiencing another American import known as 'Communist witch hunting'. John Grierson's former secretary had been named by Igor Gouzenko as a Soviet spy, and the entire Board was under investigation for Communist sympathies.[49]

As for Hollywood, it saw the dangers to itself clearly enough. J. J. Fitzgibbons, president of Famous Players, put the case succinctly in a letter to the head of 20th Century-Fox:

> There are people in Canada—as in every other country where American films are released—who insist upon American companies building studios all over the world and scattering their production activities in an uneconomic fashion. If we are to avoid extreme pressure for expensive and expansive studio operations in Canada, then we must demonstrate to the Canadian government our capacity really to do a job for the Dominion.[50]

And they did. In a whirlwind of activity such as only Hollywood could unleash, ranging from celebrity luncheons to visiting Hollywood starlets, the movie moguls persuaded the Canadian government that, rather than a quota system, it would make more sense to use Hollywood's control of film to Canada's advantage. What Hollywood offered was to publicize Canada in its movies, thus encouraging tourist travel in the Dominion and improving the balance of payments. They offered more newsreel coverage, promised to screen more NFB films, and agreed to 'undertake a program designed to insure proper selection of product.' This last point was significant, for as a result of discussions with Canadian officials the moguls (who were no fools when their own economic interests were at stake) decided that a principal Canadian concern was, as the president of the Motion Picture Association of America put it, 'to avoid dollar expenditure by Canada for gangster films or other pictures of a low-toned nature.'[51] In other words, the Canadian government resented losing precious dollars for kitsch.

Thus the Canadian Co-operation Project (CCP), a Hollywood press agent's dream, was born. While little actually happened, somebody got paid for a number of years documenting that something did happen. One of the few immediate beneficiaries of American concern was flood-inundated southern Manitoba in 1950, which received even more newsreel coverage than the photogenic disaster might otherwise have induced, and as a result actually collected more money in disaster relief than the administrators could figure out how to spend.[52] Whether such disaster coverage brought in tourist dollars was another question. In 1952 the official Project report, while admitting that 'the amount of Canadian material shown in US newsreels during 1951 showed ten fewer sequences than last year', added that 'the material used was of a highly significant nature and included fewer items dealing with unfortunate floods, fires and airplane accidents.' Moreover, through the newsreels, '1,500,000,000 audience impressions about Canada were brought to US theatre audiences.'[53]

The other major accomplishment of the CCP was in the words of Blake Owensmith, its man in Hollywood—to 'get in what we called hidden advertising—in other words a plug for Canada without being too obvious.' These tourist lures were actually reprinted in the 1952 report. The 'plugs' from the dialogue of a film entitled *This is Dynamite* were typical:

- I'll refresh your memory. In 1932 Peter Manzinates was a produce dealer who refused to pay the organization. He went to Canada and never came back. . . .
- Maybe the guy liked to travel.
- March, 1932. You took a leave of absence from the police force. Gone three weeks. . . .
- A vacation.
- Did you like Canada?
- Didn't go there.
- You and Jimmy Kchop went to Canada. You took Manzinates to Canada and murdered him.
- I never went to Canada. I don't know Manzinates, I never heard of Jimmy Kchop.[54]

Four (count 'em) Canadian references, multiplied by the theatre audience to give millions of 'audience impressions' of Canada. In a later interview Owensmith offered 'as a perfect example of what we tried to do over the years' the change in the dialogue of *New York Confidential*:

The script read, 'They caught Louis Engleday in Detroit.' We thought that was a very good chance to put in a plug for Canada, so we changed the dialogue to read, 'They caught Louis Engleday on his way to Canada.' This was a very good example because it flowed in and didn't seem forced and it got our plug over.[55]

Whether the idea of Canada as a haven for gangsters, any more than newsreel footage of floods and fires, improved tourist revenue is an unanswerable question.

Blake Owensmith eventually moved on from the CCP to become producer of *Sergeant Preston of the Yukon* for television, a series he insisted 'was a hell of a good promotional scheme; unwittingly they were selling Canada.' And so, in Hollywood terms, they were. No matter that the series promoted a variety of erroneous or outdated stereotypes about Mounties, the Canadian climate, and the Yukon goldrush. For the movie types, all publicity was grist for the mill.

As for Canadian film-making, it stuck with high-quality educational short subjects on Canadian films until the early sixties, and began making feature-length films only when it appeared likely that the industry would succumb totally to television. These included William Davidson's *Now That April's Here* (1958), an adaptation of four of Morley Callaghan's short stories; Don Haldane's *The Drylanders* (1963); *Nobody Waved Goodbye* (1964) and *The Ernie*

A still from *Mon Oncle Antoine* (1971) — with Jacques Gagnon (Benoît) and Jean Duceppe (Antoine) — directed by Claude Jutra (1930-86). After more than two decades, it is arguably the finest film ever made in Canada. *National Film Board of Canada.*

Game (1967), both directed by Don Owen; Peter Pearson's *The Best Damn Fiddler from Calabogie to Kaladar* (1969); Don Shebib's *Goin' Down the Road* (1970); Paul Almond's *Isabel* (1968), *Act of the Heart* (1970), and *Journey* (1972), all starring the Canadian actress Geneviève Bujold (b. 1942); Harvey Hart's *Fortune and Men's Eyes* (1971); Peter Carter's *The Rowdyman* (1971), written by and starring Gordon Pinsent (b. 1930); Claude Jutra's *Mon Oncle Antoine* (1971); and William Fruet's *Wedding in White* (1972).[56]

Hockey

Nothing could be more quintessentially Canadian than hockey. But that sport entered the post-war period in the hands of the American entertainment industry, and the situation never really altered. The main function of hockey in Canada had become supplying players for the professional teams, which almost without exception were located in large American cities. In 1950, only at the National Hockey League (NHL) level did Canadian teams have any real representation (two of six teams, in Toronto and Montreal). At the minor-league level only Vancouver had a professional team. But in the two decades after 1950 two major developments hit the game: in the fifties international hockey gathered steam, and in the sixties the NHL expanded. Between these two developments Canadian governments finally stirred to action with a public policy.

Hockey had been played internationally—even at the Winter Olympics— for many years, but in the early 1950s several European countries, particularly Russia and Czechoslovakia, decided to go into the sport in a big way. Over the years Canada had occasionally participated in international tournaments, but never on a serious basis; the Canadian teams won easily when they bothered to compete. But in 1954 the USSR decided to send a national team to the international ice-hockey championships in Stockholm. The Canadian Amateur Hockey Association (CAHA) managed to scrape up a senior team from a Toronto suburb—the East York Lyndhursts—which had experienced trouble beating teams like the Ravina Ki-Y Flyers in its own league. Though the Lyndhursts were not great, they were the best team willing to pay their own way to play the Russians, Swedes, Finns, and Czechs, all of whom were heavily subsidized by their governments and regarded as instruments of national policy. Most Canadians agreed that the Lyndhursts should be good enough—for Canadians had invented the game, hadn't they? The Lyndhursts were indeed good enough to make the finals, when they were clobbered by the Soviet Union 7-2. The defeat electrified Canada, which had been so blasé about the game that no Canadian sportswriter had taken the trouble to attend. The Canadian government responded to editorials and public outcries by declaring firmly that it had no intention of interfering in, much less spending money on, hockey.[57]

The Stockholm defeat put the world tournament on the sports schedule for Canadians. Throughout the fifties the CAHA sent teams—local senior amateur teams, but better than East York— which managed to win most of the time. The Penticton Vees revenged the 1954 defeat in 1955 with a 5-0 win over the Russians; the Whitby Dunlops beat the Soviets 4-2 in Oslo in 1958; and the Belleville McFarlands defeated the Russians 3-1 in Prague in 1959. But these teams still had to finance their own way to Europe, and at best they were only semi-professional. Canadians told themselves that the pros could wipe the upstarts out. But the Europeans were improving rapidly, and Canada did little before 1961 to alter its own style of hockey to meet the growing challenge.

Two problems needed to be met. The first was the organization of Canadian amateur hockey, designed chiefly to provide players for the professionals. Most talented young players turned professional, making them technically ineligible for international hockey. As later developments showed, the pro/amateur distinction was less critical than the fact that American employers were not willing to lose their best players to a Canadian national team. The North American professional hockey schedule was not organized around the world tournament, which occurred at the same time as the financially remunerative playoffs leading to the Stanley Cup. Second, the

North American game of hockey had over the years developed differently from the international game, although both had started from roughly the same Canadian rule book. The unsophisticated American audiences liked their hockey gladiatorial; they preferred hockey to be a contact sport, like American football. The Europeans preferred to model their version on soccer—the rink was much larger, body-checking was definitely limited, and the emphasis was on finesse and fast skating. Canadians trained for the professionally oriented techniques of bodily mayhem found it difficult to play by international rules. Having acquired European reputations as goons and bullies, Canadian teams spent most of their game time in Europe playing shorthanded because of penalties. The Canadians complained about the bad refereeing, and it was true that they were being penalized for activities that were not only allowed but encouraged at home. One Canadian TV commentator at the 1972 Canada-Russia series was notorious for his failure to understand the differences in the games and for openly advocating more extensive body contact as the best way to counter skilful skating and passing.

In 1961 the federal government finally took some initiative on the problem of sport in Canada, including hockey, attacking indirectly the amateur aspect of the hockey problem. Bill C-131, intended 'to encourage, promote and develop fitness and amateur sport in Canada', passed both Houses of Parliament unanimously in September of that year. Much of its bipartisan political support was a result of public outcry over Canada's poor performance in international competitions, and was more the product of the Cold War than anything else. Speaking about amateur sports in September 1961, the Opposition leader Lester Pearson (who had played lacrosse and hockey while he was at Oxford), said:

> ...all the publicity attached to international sport and the fact that certain societies, particularly the communist societies, use international sport, as they use everything else, for the advancement of prestige and political purposes, it is a matter of some consequence that we in Canada should do what we can to develop and regain the prestige we once had, to a greater extent than we now have in international competition.[58]

Although the Act was deliberately vague, it allowed the government to subsidize amateur coaches and teams, particularly in national and international competitions. In 1968 the National Advisory Council, set up under the Act to recommend policy and its implementation, was shunted to one side in favour of professional bureaucrats within the ministry of National Health and Welfare. In that same year Trudeau promised in the election campaign a new study of sport in Canada, and the *Report of the Task Force on Sports for Canadians*, containing recommendations that shaped the agenda of federal policy on sport for the next two decades, was published in 1969.

From hockey's perspective, the most important government action had come before the completion of the Task Force report, when Hockey Canada was organized to deal with problems at the international level, including the organization of national teams (which had been created in the mid-sixties) and negotiations with the NHL for professional players. Hockey Canada, which made possible the 1972 Canada-Russia hockey series, was a belated political response to the major developments in the world of professional hockey. Among these was the expansion in 1967 of the NHL, which had determined to expand because its Board of Directors (also the team owners) recognized there was more money to be made from hockey than was presently being realized. Other professional sports leagues in the United States, such as those in baseball and football, had already expanded to new cities with new facilities. Sports events were exciting and photogenic, and with television's insatiable demand for programming American networks bid against each other to gain exclusive coverage.

While television may not have been the sole factor behind hockey expansion, it clearly controlled the nature of that expansion, which ignored Canadian applicants to the NHL, such as Vancouver, in favour of American centres such as St Louis, where there was no hockey tradition whatsoever. American TV viewers would not watch professional sports played by 'foreign' teams in foreign leagues, as various attempts in the sixties to package Canadian Football League games for television had plainly demonstrated. Despite public concern in Canada, no level of government wanted to tackle the corporate aspect of sport, and NHL expansion provoked little political response—except for Hockey Canada, which dealt only with contractual matters involving players and national teams. In 1969, however, the American sports moguls showed that their attitude was not blindly chauvinistic when the National Baseball League granted a franchise to a Montreal team, the Expos, giving the signal that if their markets were big enough Canadians could play in the American Big Leagues.

Hockey developed, in the post-war period, in ways remarkably similar to those of other cultural sectors in Canada. By the early 1970s hockey had been drawn into the net of government policy and still had not resolved the question of whether excellence and Canadian-ness were truly compatible. As for high culture, by the early seventies it shared with other aspects of Canadian experience—politics, the economy, society—a sense of existing on some kind of precipice, about to free-fall into new and unknown territory. What directions the fall would take were anybody's guess, although increasingly there were mutterings about 'the limits of growth'. After 1972 Canadians would explore together the implications of a world in which not all things were possible.

chapter thirteen

The Collapse of Liberal Federalism

In May 1986 Michael Wilson (b. 1937), the federal Minister of Finance, labelled as 'not acceptable' a review committee's recommendation that Canada Post be allowed a period of grace until 1990 before becoming financially self-supporting. His statement symbolized the new political thinking of the post-1972 period. An earlier federalism, which viewed the Canadian Post Office as a universally accessible national service, had shifted to an insistence solely on its 'financial self-sufficiency'.[1]

From the first Post Office Act of 1867, the Canadian government had emphasized the need for a cheap, accessible, and efficient postal system. In 1884 one politician summarized the overall attitude well when he argued in a House of Commons debate that 'Post Offices are not established for the purpose of providing a revenue, but for the convenience of the people,' adding that post offices, like public works, could be viewed from the standpoint 'that the general business of the country will be promoted by them'.[2] Although the system was greatly expanded before the First World War, it turned surpluses regularly, if not annually, between 1900 and 1958. They resulted from two factors: the extent to which the Canadian postal service dominated Canadian communications, and the government's accounting practices, which charged costs of land, buildings, and furnishings to Public Works rather than to the Post Office. In the 1960s the postal service became unionized and no longer ran at a profit, but no one was yet threatening to dismantle it.

Not until the early 1980s did many commentators become concerned about the Post Office's 'deficit', which was made substantially larger by recent government accounting practices that no longer buried postal costs under other departments. The deficit was regarded as shocking by those Canadians, chiefly businessmen, who no longer had to rely exclusively on the mail to conduct their business, and increasingly saw the government postal service less as an essential public service than as a commercial operation competing with other delivery systems. Much of the competition had developed in response to the interruption of mail delivery by a series of crippling postal strikes in 1965, 1968, 1975, and 1981 (with another one in August 1991!), and by the general deterioration of service, some of which was connected with attempts by the Post Office itself to reduce its deficit. In 1980 the federal minister responsible for the Post Office, André Ouellet, threw his support behind the central recommendation of a 1978 study group that a Crown postal corporation be established, to 'give Canada Post the independence to function in the marketplace in a way that is not possible now.' By 1985 another review committee insisted that the continuing operating deficit of Canada Post had to be eliminated quickly, emphasizing that Canadians were prepared to accept far longer delivery goals (which had already increased from one day after posting in 1962 to four days coast-to-coast in 1985), and higher costs, in return for some standard of reliability.[3] Although much older than the many other universally accessible national services created in the affluent period following the war, the postal system—like them—also had been sheltered by the pre-1972 consensus, and was shattered by its collapse.

The Collapse of Federal Liberalism/Nationalism

Until the early 1970s the post-war period had been for most Canadians an era of affluence and optimism, and of a nationalism based on the assumption of a strong central federal government. These relatively upbeat characteristics had been achieved by policies dominated by twentieth-century small-l 'liberalism'—a delicate balancing act that accepted an economic system based on private enterprise and corporate capitalism, while also attempting to provide a social-welfare net for the nation's citizens. Not all the resulting policies were influenced by Keynesian economics, but many of them were, and the whole system was well integrated by Keynesian assumptions. Such policies were the operative ones not merely for governments in Canada, but for governments throughout the Western industrialized world. All major Canadian political parties, at all levels of government— ranging provincially from the Socreds of the West to the separatists of Quebec—were essentially exponents of liberalism with a small 'l'.

If the political consensus sought by all democratic governments in this period was initially dominated by liberal economic assumptions, the division over the constitutional framework in which this liberalism was to work increasingly produced conflict in Canada. For much of the period before 1970, the Liberal Party had combined liberal economics with a constitution-centralized federalism-nationalism; and though the Progressive Conservatives, in their six years of power between 1957 and 1963, had demonstrated different emphases, even it had not seriously considered overturning the broad framework. As we have seen, the Liberal consensus increasingly came under attack in the 1960s. It began seriously unravelling in the 1970s, and was in tatters by the 1980s.

The Canadian political arena seemed incapable of dealing with both economic problems and constitutional problems simultaneously, at the same level of intensity, and so the period after 1972 saw an alternation of focus between the Constitution and the economy. The two questions were not entirely divorced, of course, for one of the major arguments of the federalists was that only strong national policies could deal with the problems of the economy—and with the demands of minorities not geographically embodied in provinces and regions. Moreover, while constitutional matters were almost totally under the control of Canadians, economic ones were largely world-oriented. After the election of a Tory government under Brian Mulroney in 1984, both nationalism and federalism were jettisoned for Free Trade and Meech Lake, while the principles of liberal economics were replaced by privatization, claw-backs, and deregulation.

No single event or factor can possibly be isolated as responsible for the collapse of federal liberalism-nationalism in Canada. Instead, a cumulation of what Marxist analysts would call 'contradictions'—matters that simply could not be resolved within the context of either consensus or liberalism—would eventually defy attempts at management, or policies of hopeful neglect. They would come together at centre-stage to produce a series of what the media liked to call 'crises'. Many of the pressures were really not of Canada's own making, but part of world-wide trends over which no Canadian government had much control. Increasingly both politicians and public came to feel that all political responses were defensive reactions to unmanageable situations, and all policies were merely band-aids placed over festering wounds. Public trust in the nation's political leaders declined, as the consensus disintegrated and was not really replaced. Cynicism became entrenched at the core of the Canadian national psyche. To some imponderable extent the increase of cynicism, and the gradual emergence of ever more unalloyed self-interest as the mainspring of human motivation, contributed to the deterioration of the old consensus. The Second World War had been fought on the basic principles of the deferral of expectations and the need for national sacrifice for the greatest good of the greatest number—a classic liberal position. Canadians, whether as private individuals or as voting citizens, became after 1945, and especially after 1970, less and less willing to buy such arguments. They became ever more prepared to accept the calls of leaders who, by implication or open statement, opposed either waiting or sharing.

In 1973 a cease-fire agreement allowed the United States to withdraw from Vietnam, and the process of national disillusionment continued into the Watergate Affair, in which an apparently successful President was eventually forced to resign, on 9 August 1974, rather than risk removal from office by impeachment for years of cheating and lying to the public. In Canada, Vietnam had been less important than the fact that the October Crisis had brought to the fore the Parti Québécois, which succeeded in getting seven candidates elected in 1970.

On 6 October 1973 the Arabs and Israelis went to war, as they had done from time to time for many years. On this occasion, however, events in the Middle East had an immediate impact on the world. The Arab oil exporters (who dominated the world market) embargoed shipments of oil to nations supporting Israel, including Canada. Shortly thereafter, the Organization of Petroleum Exporting Countries (OPEC), which for thirteen years had been a toothless cartel, managed to agree on another even more substantial price rise than the modest one announced before the Yom Kippur War. The price of oil per barrel more than tripled in 1973, and all Western industrial nations were suddenly brought to recognize how much their economic prosperity had depended on a constant supply of cheap oil.

Perhaps more than any other single commodity of the post-war era, oil symbolized the economics of the age of affluence, as well as its North American contradictions. It was cheap oil that made possible the development of the large, powerful, and comfortable automobile—the 'Yank Tanks', as they were called in Canada before they became the 'Detroit Dinosaurs'—that sat in every suburban driveway and clogged every freeway. Those freeways, of course, had been paved with materials conjured out of petroleum derivatives. The manufacture and sale of instantly obsolescent gas-guzzling automobiles, as well as the construction of roads that connected thousands of new suburban developments, were major components of post-war economic prosperity in both the United States and Canada. Some saw the car as a symbol of post-war America; others saw it as a sex symbol—but either way, a 20-horsepower electric engine could hardly provide the desired potency. The typical Detroit automobile not only consumed gas and oil as if there was no tomorrow, but discharged harmful hydrocarbons that were a principal component of the air pollution that was increasingly affecting all North Americans' health. Detroit engineering had never been renowned for its flexibility, and it proved very slow to respond to a new need for fuel efficiency brought by significantly higher oil prices. By the time it had done so and moved to smaller vehicles, the Japanese had taken command of the North American automobile market, a fact that strongly suggested a new world trading order.

If petroleum—literally as well as symbolically—fuelled the contradictions of the North American economy, it also exposed Canadians to a number of problems that were distinctly their own. Many of these matters had already been newsworthy before OPEC pulled the plug, but they seemed more urgent and apparent as the nation searched for a viable energy policy. The Canadian petroleum industry, located chiefly in Alberta, was almost entirely owned and operated by multinational corporations, most—though not all—of them American-based. Oil, indeed, was one of those industrial arenas that most obviously epitomized the problems of foreign ownership that were addressed by a series of governments and task forces in the sixties and early seventies. Moreover, although the petroleum still in the ground not tied up by the multinationals was a Crown resource, provincial governments controlled it, not the federal state. When the problems of jurisdiction over offshore oil were added to the provincial control of oil as an internal natural resource, the result was a key item of potential dispute in federal–provincial relations. Most of the consumption of oil in Canada occurred in the industrialized East, while most of the raw material was in the resource-based West—a discrepancy that exacerbated regional tensions. Finally, increased petroleum prices had a ripple effect throughout the Canadian and world economies, raising an already steady inflation to new highs—this at a time when Canadian labour unions had recently succeeded in establishing themselves in many key industries, especially in the public sector. Having achieved full recognition of collective bargaining, union organizers next moved for improved working conditions and higher wages beyond the cost-of-living inflation facing their members. OPEC's price increases, with promises of more to follow, thus affected Canada in several critical areas: foreign ownership, federal–provincial relations, regional conflicts, and labour relations.

Virtually the only long-standing problem that oil did not seem to affect directly was the French-Canada/Quebec one, although it certainly did so indirectly. On 29 October 1973, only a bare three weeks after the first shots of the Yom Kippur War, Quebeckers went to the polls to elect a new provincial government. From the outset of the contest between the Liberals of Robert Bourassa and the Parti Québécois headed by René Lévesque the chief issue had been the desirability of a separate Quebec, and both parties had worked to polarize the electorate on this simple issue. The result, on the surface, was a resounding victory for the Liberals: 1,600,000 votes (54.8 per cent of the total vote cast) to 897,000 for the PQ, and 102 seats in the legislature to 6 for the PQ and 2 for the Créditistes. Nevertheless, the Péquistes had improved their performance over the 1970 election in almost every riding, and did exceptionally well among younger voters in Montreal. Post-election studies suggested that a majority of Liberal supporters had favoured federalism and a majority of PQ supporters independence for Quebec.[4] While no other province was quite prepared to join the PQ in the front lines of the quest for a totally new constitutional arrangement for Canada, resource-rich provinces like Alberta certainly supported new guarantees of constitutional autonomy for the provinces.

The relationship between Quebec separatism and Canada's economic problems after 1973 did not lie so much in positive as in negative polarities. In

1976 the PQ won a somewhat unexpected victory—which was not necessarily to be interpreted as a mandate for separatism or sovereignty association, though one of its pre-election platforms was the promise of a referendum on sovereignty association. When the referendum was held in May 1980 the *Nons*— those opposed to negotiating for sovereignty association—won 60 per cent to 40 per cent. The PQ, however, were re-elected the next year. Especially after the referendum, the federal government of Pierre Elliott Trudeau turned its energy from the economy to the constitution. Trudeau himself was not only a federalist Quebecker but a constitutional lawyer far more comfortable with the intricacies of the British North America Act than with oil-price equalization or economic planning. Oil and the Constitution were scarcely the only issues after 1973, but they were certainly front and centre for many years, and the various attempts to resolve the problems they posed (as well as the ones they ignored) precipitated the deterioration of the traditional consensus.

The Shape of Federal Politics

The scene in Ottawa divides into two periods, broken in 1984. During most of the first period the Liberals under Trudeau clung tenaciously to power in a series of very close elections (1972, 1974, 1979, 1980), although they were replaced in office briefly, in 1979, by a minority Tory administration headed by Joe Clark. This period could best be characterized as one of gradual Liberal disintegration, accompanied by the unravelling of the small-l liberal consensus of the post-war era. In 1984 the Tories under Brian Mulroney swept to power in the most decisive election since 1945, exceeding even the Diefenbaker sweep of 1958 in percentage of popular vote and number of seats. As with most decisive electoral shifts in Canada, the one in 1984 involved a massive reorientation of votes in Quebec and Ontario. The change in Quebec was particularly critical, although it still is not clear whether Quebec had made the sort of permanent move it did in 1896 and reconfirmed after 1918.

The Liberals

Whether Mulroney's Tories actually represented a different vision that could serve as the basis for an alternative consensus was, and is, an open question. Certainly they sought the consensual centre, which public-opinion polls and voting behaviour suggested had become dubious about many of the assumptions of the old federal liberalism. But there was no clear evidence that a new political paradigm was emerging from the shards of the old liberal one. Instead, the events of the late eighties and beyond strongly suggested that Mulroney, like Diefenbaker a generation earlier, had no true alternative to offer and was simply perplexed by the chaos of disintegration. As the keepers of the most unadulterated version of federalist-nationalist liberalism, the New Democrats were hardly in a position to offer much help in any reorientation of the paradigm. On more than one occasion in the 1970s (especially in the minority government of 1972-4) they had forced the Liberals to remain true to the liberal nationalist position, but they could neither replace the Liberals as the other major national party nor provide new alternatives. As of 1992, political analysts were still waiting to see whether anything positive and coherent would emerge from the unquestioned collapse in Canada of post-war liberal nationalism, or whether another international economic crisis or constitutional confrontation might indeed help to reinvigorate it.

The fortunes of the federal Liberal Party between 1968 and 1984 became increasingly associated with Pierre Elliott Trudeau, its leader for most of that period.[5] The identification was partly due to television's relentless search for visual images and Trudeau's brilliant mastery of the medium. But it was also a result of Trudeau's own political and administrative style; increasingly, he operated as a loner and did not encourage strong professional politicians to emerge around him. Some analysts also talked about the emergence of a new presidential-style politics in Canada, and, as we shall see, there were some strong American influences appearing. But Trudeau's 'arrogance'—the term most often used to describe his behaviour—was personal, not political. As a French Canadian who had always firmly opposed Quebec separatism, he had little scope for manoeuvre as public opinion polarized in that province. As an equally strong federalist, he had as little time for western expressions of provincial or regional autonomy as for Quebec's. A central-Canadian intellectualized urbanite, he could not empathize with the problems of either the Atlantic region or western Canada. The East never deserted him—indeed, his worst performance in Atlantic Canada was against Stanfield in 1968—but the West gradually abandoned the Liberals, Trudeau, *and* Canadian federalism. By 1980 'western alienation' had reduced the number of Liberal MPs west of Ontario to two (both from Manitoba). Never a fervent party man, Trudeau did not cultivate the grass roots, and the powerful Liberal political organizations that had existed before 1970 were allowed to wither away in most provinces, surfacing when federal patronage was to be dispensed but not at federal election time.

Trudeau disturbed many Canadians with occasional forthrightness ('Just watch me'), vulgarity bordering on obscenity (one four-letter word in the House of Commons was transcribed as 'fuddle duddle'; a raised-finger gesture to a western crowd appeared in newspapers across the nation), and unconventionality (he married, separated from, and divorced Margaret Sinclair while in office, dating other women after the separation in 1977 and fathering a child out of wedlock in 1991). Perhaps most damaging of all was an increasing tendency to treat almost everyone (members of his own caucus, the opposition, reporters, the voters) as ill-informed and irrational. Trudeau's public persona oscillated between that of an affable 'swinger' and that of a university professor faced with a particularly stupid class.

Trudeau had announced his intention of retiring to private life late in

Justice Minister John Turner and Prime Minister Trudeau fielding questions following the constitutional conference in Victoria, June 1971. Canapress Photo Services, Toronto.

1979, following the Liberals' unexpected electoral defeat by Joe Clark's Progressive Conservatives.[6] But the Clark minority government fell before Trudeau's replacement could be chosen, and the Liberal caucus persuaded Trudeau to lead the party into the unexpected election of 1980, which returned one of the largest Liberal majorities of the post-war period. Remaining in power for four more years, which made him one of the longest-serving prime ministers in Canadian history and easily the veteran among contemporary world leaders, Trudeau again declared his intention of resigning in 1984 and this time made it stick. John Turner (b. 1929) had for years before 1984 been touted as the logical successor to Trudeau, and a Liberal leadership convention chose him on 16 June. Turner became Prime Minister two weeks later, and on 9 July dissolved Parliament for the fateful 1984 election.

John Turner was born in England, came to Canada as a child with his mother and stepfather, and was educated at the University of British Columbia, Oxford, and the University of Paris. Thoroughly bilingual, he had entered Parliament in 1962, representing an English-speaking constituency in Montreal (he later moved to an Ottawa one), and first entered the cabinet, under Pearson, in 1965. He had run against Trudeau for the leadership in 1968 and remained in the government as one of its most powerful ministers until September 1975, when he quit the cabinet and then left politics until he was chosen to succeed Trudeau.

Turner had a difficult decision to make over the question of an election.

The polls indicated that the Liberals were in serious trouble. Turner's alternatives were to run as a fresh face, on the momentum of the publicity surrounding his selection as leader, or to remain in office a few months and attempt to make some headway with the existing government. He chose the former option, then compromised it by making a number of appointments in order to accommodate members of the Trudeau team. And he took no new policies into the election campaign, which he had to fight in the face not only of Trudeau's mounting unpopularity and the general deterioration of liberal nationalism, but of a well-orchestrated campaign by the Progressive Conservatives. To the surprise of almost everyone, Turner turned out to have a singularly inept media presence, particularly on television. Never really perceived by the voters as a fresh face, he went down to a disastrous defeat. While the weak Liberal showing of 1984—the party was reduced to 40 seats in Ottawa—was hardly unexpected, more was hoped for in 1988 than Turner and the Liberal campaign were able to deliver. The Liberals did even worse in Quebec in 1988 than in 1984, and not much better in the West or the Atlantic region; only a resurgence in Ontario prevented another utter disaster. Turner was viewed as a lame duck almost from the announcement of the results at the polls. Shortly thereafter he declared his intention to step down as Liberal leader, although a leadership convention was not held until the summer of 1990, when Jean Chrétien was selected after a lacklustre campaign.

Like Turner, Jean Chrétien (b. 1934) was a veteran of the Pearson and Trudeau cabinets. Unlike Turner, he had remained in politics and the government throughout the Trudeau years, serving loyally in a number of portfolios, including the difficult finance post. He had finished second to Turner in 1984, and for some time had been the frontrunner to succeed him. Chrétien had many strengths. He was a proven campaigner, particularly in French Canada, and his down-to-earth persona and speaking style worked exceptionally well in both French and English. Never flashy, he was a loyal party man and understood the importance of the local Liberal organizations, which he had assisted and cultivated for many years. His leadership opponents had done their best to label him 'Yesterday's Man', and indeed Chrétien stood foursquare for all the traditional values of federal liberal nationalism, most of which he had helped to implement over his long career in Ottawa. Chrétien might have been beaten by a leadership candidate who was able to present convincingly either a new vision or a new style to the delegates, but neither Sheila Copps nor Paul Martin Jr was the charismatic fresh new face that Trudeau had been in 1968.

The Progressive Conservatives

As for the Progressive Conservatives, Robert Stanfield served as leader through three successive defeats at the hands of the Trudeau Liberals, and finally retired in 1976; he was perhaps the best federal leader of the century who never became prime minister. His strengths—the three c's of common

Robert Stanfield—the former
premier of Nova Scotia—in
1967, when he was appointed
national leader of the
Progressive Conservative Party.
Photograph by John de Visser.

sense, compassion, and consensus-making—would have served him extremely well if he could have persuaded the voters to elect a majority of his
party to Parliament. Unfortunately, the Canadian electorate found him much
too low-key and uncompelling. In his best chance, the election campaign of
1974, he had called for wage and price controls, which Prime Minister
Trudeau continually ridiculed—although he turned to them himself soon
after his electoral victory. Stanfield spoke French badly and his party never
did well in Quebec during his leadership. The Tory weakness in Quebec was
the product of many more factors than Stanfield's French, of course, but he
was never able to mount a credible campaign in Quebec: his party won only
4 seats there in 1968, 2 in 1972, and 3 in 1974.

Stanfield was succeeded as Tory leader by Joe (Charles Joseph) Clark (b.
1939), one of the few federal leaders of this century who had no adult
occupation other than that of politician. He had been a student politician at
the University of Alberta, and subsequently worked for the PCs in Alberta
and Ottawa until his election to Parliament in 1972. He persevered to
improve his French, which became more than passable, if occasionally awkward. He unexpectedly emerged as the compromise 'progressive' candidate
at the 1976 leadership convention, defeating among others Brian Mulroney,
who was easily the leading PC in Quebec despite never having held public
office. For many Canadians Clark was 'Joe Who?' The PCs had not made
much showing in Quebec since the Diefenbaker years, and by the time of

Joe Clark speaking at the Progressive Conservative leadership convention in 1976, which he won. He was Prime Minister from May 1979, when the Conservatives won a minority government, until December of that year, when the government fell on a vote of non-confidence over the budget. Photograph by John de Visser.

Clark had virtually written the province off. The unpopularity of Trudeau's Liberals was well demonstrated in the 1979 election, when Clark's Tories received 136 seats to 114 for the Liberals, and formed a minority govern-ment. The 1979 election, however, also illustrated the limitations of serious campaigning only in English-speaking Canada. The Tories won only 2 seats in Quebec to the Liberals' 67; anything resembling the electoral trend in most of the remaining provinces would have given Clark a clear-cut majority.

Despite his government's precarious minority status, Clark attempted to govern Canada as if he had a majority. He believed that the other parties (especially the NDP) would not wish to fight another election too quickly, and thought that if his government was forced to another election prema-turely, it could win its majority as Diefenbaker had in 1958. Clark quickly came up against one of the other verities of Canadian politics apart from the Quebec Fact: the NDP could keep the Liberals in power (as it had in 1963-5 and 1972-4) but would not support a Tory government, particularly one committed to the privatization of Petro-Canada and to balanced budgets. Moreover, Clark's public image did not improve in office. He received much criticism for wanting to implement his campaign promise of moving the

Brian Mulroney in 1983, the year he became leader of the Progressive Conservative Party, MP for Central Nova, and leader of the Opposition. He became Prime Minister the following year. Photograph by Ed McGibbon. National Archives of Canada, PA-146485.

Canadian Embassy in Israel from Jerusalem to Tel Aviv. Like American President Gerald Ford a few years earlier, Clark appeared on television as a bit of an unco-ordinated oaf, continually out of his depth. In December 1979 his government was defeated on a motion of non-confidence on John Crosbie's budget, involving gasoline pricing, and was then beaten by a resurgent Pierre Trudeau in the ensuing election.[7]

As Leader of the Opposition, Clark played a constructive role in the constitutional reforms of the early 1980s, but neither the public nor his party demonstrated any confidence in him. Eventually he called a leadership convention in June 1983, and on the fourth ballot was replaced as PC leader by 'the Boy from Baie Comeau', Brian Mulroney (b. 1939). If Joe Clark had never been anything but a politician, Mulroney entered politics at the highest level without ever having held public office, although he had been active in the backrooms for years. Unlike Clark, whose public utterances were unpolished and delivered in a boyish tenor (he took elocution lessons to lower his voice), Mulroney was not only slick in presentation and perfectly bilingual, but the possessor of one of the deepest and most mellifluous voices in Canadian public affairs. He was an experienced labour lawyer and corporate executive, proud of the fact that he had closed his company's mine at

Schefferville, Quebec, with a minimum of public reaction. Trained as a professional conciliator, Mulroney understood about keeping promises vague and making deals. He also appreciated the need for Tory success in Quebec, and as his major leadership plank had promised the party a breakthrough in that key province. In the 1984 election he successfully captured the centre of the Canadian political spectrum, which was considerably less liberal and interventionist than it had been twenty years earlier.

Mulroney's Tories promised that they would not dismantle the existing social-welfare state, although the likelihood of continuing equal access for all Canadians seemed dubious given PC insistence on 'fiscal responsibility'. The Tories were equally committed to better relations between Canada and the United States, which meant less insistence on economic nationalism; and to improved relations between Ottawa and the provinces (especially, but not only, Quebec), which meant surrendering federal power to the provinces. Once in office with an enormous majority, including 58 seats from Quebec, Mulroney succeeded in 1987 in negotiating a Free Trade Agreement with the United States and the Meech Lake constitutional accord with the provinces. His party was returned to office easily in 1988, with a smaller but still impressive majority, with 63 of its 169 seats from Quebec.

The New Democratic Party

Throughout this period the New Democratic Party remained a constant third force. Its continuity was exemplified by the steadiness of its popular vote in federal elections, which ran between fifteen and twenty per cent, and by the steadiness of its policies, which were unquestionably federalist, nationalist, and liberal. The party had purged its socialist wing, the Waffle, in the early seventies, in order to remain in the centre of the political spectrum; but it continued to be unable to make significant inroads in either Atlantic Canada or Quebec to establish a truly national presence. None of its leaders managed to establish credibility in Quebec. The NDP was always the biggest loser when the popular vote was translated into parliamentary seats, particularly in eastern Canada. In 1988, for example, it won nearly half a million votes in Quebec, but absolutely no seats. The party occasionally had influence beyond its number of MPs, however, especially during the Trudeau minority government of 1972-4 and the Clark minority government of 1979-80. In the first case, the NDP pushed the Liberals towards policies it regarded as more satisfactory, while in the second case its refusal to support the PCs led to the Clark government's demise.

From 1971 to 1975 the NDP was led by David Lewis (1909-81). The son of Russian immigrants to Canada, he graduated from McGill University, was a Rhodes scholar, and practised law in Ottawa until in 1936 he began his association with the CCF as its national secretary. Lewis was also an active member of the League for Social Reconstruction. He had played a major role during the 1950s in fighting Communist influence in Canada's labour

David Lewis, *c.* 1966. Becoming leader of the NDP in 1971, Lewis and his party held the balance of power in the Liberal minority government from 1972 to 1974, when Lewis was defeated in the federal election of that year. National Archives of Canada, PA-185722.

unions, and was a major figure in the creation of the NDP. His selection in 1971 as leader, succeeding Tommy Douglas, came after a bitter fight with the Waffle, the ultra-nationalist caucus within the NDP established by university professors Mel Watkins and James Laxer, who was Lewis's chief contender for the leadership. In his first election campaign as leader in 1972, Lewis coined the phrase 'corporate welfare bums' to refer to the many tax advantages enjoyed by Canadian business, and led the NDP to a position in the Commons that enabled them to hold the balance of power in the minority Liberal government until 1974. In that year he and his party paid for their collaboration with the Liberals when the NDP won only 16 seats (its lowest total ever) and Lewis himself was defeated in his Toronto riding.

David Lewis was succeeded in 1975 by Ed Broadbent (b. 1936), a former political-science professor at York University who had built up a considerable constituency in his home town of Oshawa, Ontario. Despite his inability to improve the party's overall position in a series of elections, Broadbent was an increasingly popular leader. The only serious challenge to his position came in the early eighties, when many party faithful objected to his positive stand on Trudeau's constitutional repatriation formula. Broadbent and his NDP benefited from the relative abandonment of traditional economic ground by the Trudeau and Turner Liberals in several elections, notably in 1980 and 1984. For most of the Turner years the NDP kept federal liberal nationalism alive in Ottawa, and Broadbent was frequently regarded in public-opinion polls as the most trustworthy political leader in Ottawa. This ringing public endorsement for the man never did translate into significant party gains, however, and Broadbent retired in 1990, to be replaced by Audrey McLaughlin (b. 1936), a former social worker representing the Yukon Territory in Parliament. Like both her predecessors and her leading competitors for the leadership, McLaughlin spoke halting French and was hardly likely to appeal in Quebec. Her selection as the first female party leader in Canada, however, marked the NDP as yet again in advance of the other parties, for feminist issues were part of the unresolved agenda of Canadian politics entering the 1990s.

The Americanization of Canadian Politics?

Many observers had begun complaining, as early as the selection of Trudeau as Liberal leader in 1968, that Canadian politics was becoming increasingly a triumph of style over substance, of image over policies, of executive prime minister over party caucus and Parliament—all characterizations typically associated with American politics. Many of the charges—both of Americanization and of a noticeable drop in the intellectual content of Canadian politics—came from people who did not understand the past. Style and image had always mattered in Canadian politics, as the careers of Sir John A. Macdonald, Sir Wilfrid Laurier, and Mackenzie King attested. Strong prime ministers had always dominated party caucuses and even Parliaments. Canadian politicians had always quite willingly adapted to new technologies, particularly on the campaign trail. But the Americans, international leaders in both popular politics and popular culture, were usually in the vanguard of the exploitation of new technology to political ends, and Canada typically lagged behind. Moreover, the Americans had developed constitutional mechanisms that were much more responsive to the popular will than the Canadian parliamentary system, which was based on British democratic principles that never included much direct reference to the people.

Canadian political parties plainly copied their careful management of leadership conventions from the Americans, particularly in using these events in the best interests of the television public rather than of the delegates. By the 1970s it would have been unthinkable to choose a party leader except in the full glare of the television cameras. Parties came to see the leadership convention as one way to monopolize a few days of Canadian network transmission and to provide a launching platform for a new leader. The Liberals had won an election in 1968 partly on the strength of the publicity accompanying a leadership convention, although it failed to work for them again in 1984. Even more evident than the imitation of the Americans by the politicians, however, was the cloning of American television presentation by the Canadian television networks at these periodic rituals. Despite the introduction of televised parliamentary debates, most Canadians still got much of their political information from American-style TV news.

Whether the American 'presidential style' had a significant influence in Canada is somewhat less clear. Television not only encouraged the public to perceive the President (or Prime Minister) as the embodiment of the entire government, but made it essential that the chief executive perform well on TV. (The Americans took this conjunction to its logical conclusion when they elected a professional actor as their President.) Certainly Pierre Trudeau and Brian Mulroney both benefited from their ability to project on TV. A more obvious example of American influence was the suggestion that the Canadian Senate be made 'Triple E': equal, elected, and effective. The idea of electing senators and giving them a positive role in the legislative process is profoundly American, and would unquestionably disrupt the Canadian political tradition of British-style responsible government. Because Senate reform along these lines would encourage an unstable relationship between the legislative and executive branches, it would no doubt eventually require that the Prime Minister be elected independently of Parliament.

The 1980 referendum in Quebec to measure the extent of public support for sovereignty-association was often regarded as an American innovation. It was true that the United States had made frequent use of the referendum, which was one of the principal populist reforms introduced into American politics in the early years of the century. But the device was not unknown in Canadian politics. The federal government had employed the referendum in 1898 (prohibition) and 1942 (conscription)—although in the latter case it was called a plebiscite—and Newfoundland held several referendums in connection with its unification with Canada.

In many ways the most important new political weapon of the post-1970 period was the computer, particularly when it was harnessed to the older device of the public-opinion poll. The computer not only permitted political campaigns to target potential supporters for special attention, but it also made possible the sophisticated projection of public opinion in terms of policy alternatives. Using the computer and the polls, politicians were now able to gain regular feedback about whether or not their policies would be popularly accepted. Like the software, most of the polling techniques were taken from contemporary market research, largely American, and the central assumption was that political policies could be sold to the electorate as soft drinks were. In the 1984 election campaign the Mulroney Tories pioneered in the sophisticated application of computerized marketing, obviously quite successfully. Once in power, the Mulroney government allegedly used similar techniques to market free trade and Meech Lake to the Canadian public.

The Federal Civil Service

By the end of the 1960s the federal government employed 200,000 in its public service. That number grew by 37 per cent during the first half of the seventies, reaching 273,000 by 1976. This figure actually disguised the real extent of staffing activity within the public service, for between 1970 and 1976 there were 241,000 new appointments made to the service and 438,000 appointments within it.[8] Under Trudeau the government had made a serious effort to rationalize and control the civil-service bureaucracy. The result was initially a greatly increased prime ministerial staff, headed first by Marc Lalonde (b. 1929) and then by Michael Pitfield (b. 1937)—who was the source of many of the complaints about encroaching presidential style. Ultimately an entirely new level of bureaucrats emerged whose task was to use contemporary systems analysis to plan, rationalize, and staff. Nine cabinet committees were created in the early seventies to assist in the process, recruiting new super-bureaucrats who were young, male, and university-trained in public administration. They were attracted to Ottawa by the obvious opportunities for involvement in power politics.[9]

By the mid-1970s the federal service was exhibiting many characteristics that would become more entrenched over the succeeding years. There were very high rates of turnover, often leading to instability, and increasing tendencies towards centralization in Ottawa-Hull, particularly in senior-management positions. By 1976, 70 per cent of senior managers were in the national capital. (One result was that Ottawa-Hull consistently had the country's highest average income per family.) The federal public service had always discriminated against women at the upper levels, a tendency that became even more pronounced after 1976, a year when half the male civil servants were managers and over 90 per cent of the females were non-managers. No agency was more male-dominated than the Privy Council Office itself. The managers were also relatively young, and the federal bureaucracy came to resemble other professional bodies of the post-1970 period in its inability to recruit new members into its upper ranks because of the large numbers already incumbent there. When the size of the bureaucracy was finally in practice frozen in the early 1980s, it was an aging, male-dominated hierarchical structure that was almost totally unresponsive to outside directives or official policy statements. Instead of serving as the instrument of centralized federal policy, the federal bureaucracy had become a symbol of its stagnation.

The Provinces, the Constitution, and the Charter of Rights

The Shape of Provincial Politics

Traditional political theory and political analysis in Canada did not before 1970 devote much attention to the provinces or the political parties that had emerged to govern them. Canada's political scientists, like most other Canadian intellectuals, were for the most part committed centralists who concentrated on the national arena. Thus the first edition (1963) of a very popular collection of university-level readings on Canadian politics, Hugh Thorburn's *Party Politics in Canada*, paid almost no attention to the provincial scene. Subsequent editions, however, trace the increasing importance of the provinces, while in the latest editions the provinces appear as significant as the federal government.

Most of the important long-term trends in provincial politics continued after 1970. The provinces, even more than the country, failed to generate truly viable two-party or multi-party systems. Instead, most provinces operated through a single dominant party (often outside the two major federal

Prime Minister Pierre Elliott Trudeau and Robert Bourassa, the newly elected premier of Quebec, at the federal-provincial conference in Ottawa, September 1970. Photograph by Duncan Cameron. National Archives of Canada, PA-117468.

parties) that remained in office in election after election, producing what C.B. Macpherson described for Alberta as a 'quasi-party' system.[10] A single dominant party, Macpherson argued, satisfied voters and mediated local conflict by insisting that the important battle was not internal but against external forces often symbolized by the Canadian federal government. Certainly conflict with Ottawa had been an endemic feature of provincial politics and government since Confederation. Offers to outbash the opposition in Ottawa were standard fare in provincial elections, particularly highly contested ones. Party identification with the government in Ottawa was always extremely dangerous when provincial-rights issues were on the table.

The 1970s were particularly hard on dominant parties in the provinces. Four long-dominant provincial parties went down to defeat in the seventies: the Liberals in Newfoundland and Quebec, and the Socreds in Alberta and British Columbia. It was never clear whether the coincidence of these defeats was part of a much larger political shift, the product of changing economic circumstances, or mere accident. In Alberta, Ernest Manning had retired in 1968 after twenty-five years as Socred premier, and it was his successor, Harry Strom, who lost the 1971 election. But in Newfoundland and British

Columbia voters plainly rejected two of the grand old men of Canadian politics, each of whom had dominated his province politically for decades. Liberal Joey Smallwood, Newfoundland premier since 1949, finally left office early in 1972 after an electoral defeat a few months earlier at the hands of Frank Moores' Tories. W.A.C. Bennett, premier of British Columbia since 1952, was electorally defeated by the NDP under Dave Barrett (b. 1930) in 1972. Smallwood and Bennett both eventually stepped down as leaders, the latter to be replaced by his son William. In any case, 'Yesterday Men' were ultimately replaced by younger leaders—such as Peter Lougheed (b. 1928) in Alberta, Brian Peckford (b. 1942) in Newfoundland, Bill Bennett (b. 1932) in British Columbia—whose sense of federal-provincial relations was not conditioned by depression, war, or post-war prosperity, and who were completely ruthless in their pursuit of their own province's interests.

Dominion-Provincial Relations

The 1970s Throughout the seventies federal-provincial relations were dominated by oil, Quebec, and attempts at constitutional reform. In 1971 the Trudeau administration made yet another effort to reach agreement on a formula for constitutional repatriation that would satisfy Quebec's aspirations. The federal government offered to the newly elected Robert Bourassa a package of reform that included some constitutional rights to be entrenched in a charter, and an amending formula that gave Ontario and Quebec a perpetual veto. Bourassa insisted that the provinces would have to control social policy, and the federal government succeeded in persuading the have-not provinces that such a situation might well jeopardize national programs, which made them less than enthusiastic. In the end, a final agreement was not reached at the premiers' conference held in Victoria in June 1971. The participants were given ten days to concur with the tentative understanding (which did not really provide a special status for Quebec)—or, as Prime Minister Trudeau put it, 'That is the end of the matter.' Premier Bourassa faced a storm of protest and criticism of the arrangement when he returned to Quebec, and he refused to sign on until he saw the final text, which could hardly have been expected within the ten days he allowed it. Three points are worth emphasizing about the 1971 constitutional negotiations: first, entrenching rights in a charter was regarded as one way to reassure those who feared losing the British requirement of an Act of Parliament to change the Constitution; second, Quebec did not achieve a sufficiently distinctive place in Confederation under this agreement to suit the province's demands; and finally, only Quebec and Ontario were given perpetual vetoes (other provinces could together mount a veto using complicated co-operative formulas). The question of constitutional reform was thus dropped in 1971, and was not picked up until 1980, by which time much had changed for both Canada and its provinces.

At the same time, oil and the whole question of resource management were subjects of continual tension between some of the provinces (led by Alberta) and the federal government during the seventies. When OPEC pulled the plug in 1973, Alberta had been Ottawa's chief provincial opponent over resource management, as Quebec had been over social programs. As oil prices continued to increase, making new sources (such as tar sands or offshore fields) financially viable, and prices of other resources rose constantly, more provinces recognized the advantages of provincial autonomy. Traditional 'have-not' provinces—like Newfoundland, Nova Scotia, and Saskatchewan—joined the resource-rich provinces of Alberta and British Columbia, and the simply rich provinces of Ontario and Quebec, in discovering the evils of national policy. Only PEI, Manitoba, and New Brunswick were left to view their provincial self-interest as best served by a strong central government. By 1980 the rich provinces, often led by hard-headed businessmen who insisted that they put balance sheets ahead of sentiment, were ready to help dismantle the post-war arrangement of Ottawa centralization.

The Parti Québécois and the Constitution   The occasion for a new round of constitutional discussions was provided by the Parti Québécois, not through its electoral victory of 1976 but through its referendum on sovereignty-association of 1980. The PQ victory came as a shock to English-speaking Canada, although it was really quite predictable given the situation in Quebec. The Bourassa government had been badly shaken by charges of scandal and corruption on top of its seeming inability to deal expeditiously with either the separatists or Pierre Trudeau. It had lost considerable face when the Canadian Airline Pilots Association produced a national strike in June 1976, ostensibly over safety but really over bilingualism, which only the federal government could resolve. Rumours of cost overruns and construction disasters in the preparations for the 1976 summer Olympics in Montreal had been rife for years. Bourassa's government was not directly involved in the problems, which were the primary responsibility of Jean Drapeau's Montreal government. But Drapeau was a Liberal ally, Bourassa had waffled over stepping into the crisis, and the province took over Olympic construction only at the last minute. Many Montreal residents blamed the Olympic disaster on both Drapeau and Bourassa, the latter for failing to control the former.[11] There were similar concerns over the control of James Bay hydroelectric development, but in the summer of 1976 these were not so immediately apparent in Montreal as was the Olympic fiasco. A resurgent Union Nationale won many of the non-PQ votes, as the electorate simultaneously rejected Bourassa's Liberals and supported Lévesque's PQ.

Issues are never tidy in any election, and there was no evidence to suggest that the PQ, despite its resounding victory, had received any mandate for its well-publicized objective for constitutional reform, which it called 'sovereignty-association'. The Péquistes had insisted that they would not act unilaterally on separation without a provincial referendum, so it was possible to support the reformist social-democratic zeal of the PQ without signing on to its extremist constitutional position. English-speaking Canada, however, responded to the Quebec election by assuming that separatism had triumphed in Quebec and that the nation had to be saved at any cost. Had Lévesque sought to renegotiate the constitutional issues in 1976 or 1977, he would probably have been offered some sort of two-nations construct. But the PQ was committed both to internal reform within Quebec and to a democratic approach to separation.

In office Lévesque's PQ successfully pursued a policy of economic and linguistic nationalism. Its most controversial legislation was Bill 101, which went well beyond an earlier piece of Bourassa legislation, known as Bill 22, in turning Quebec into a unilingual francophone province. Bill 101 made it necessary for most Quebeckers, regardless of their background or preference, to be educated in French-language schools. Only those temporarily resident in Quebec or whose parents had been educated in English-speaking schools in Quebec were exempted. The Bill also insisted that French was the only legal medium of business and government, requiring the elimination of almost all English-language signs in the province. In 1979 the Quebec government produced a White Paper detailing what it meant by 'sovereignty-association'. It wanted 'a free, proud and adult national existence', but in the context of a series of joint Quebec-Canada institutions, including a court of justice and a monetary authority. A totally independent Quebec, it insisted, would still have access to Canada and its economy. Outside the ranks of the converted, the scheme seemed far too lopsided in Quebec's favour, and it must be emphasized that the province had no agreement with Canada on the subject: the proposal was a unilateral Quebec initiative.

As had been promised, there was a referendum, eventually scheduled for 20 May 1980. Referendums are notoriously tricky political instruments, in which there is often much encouragement to vote 'no' regardless of the nature of the disagreement with the positive side. Certainly the non-francophones in Quebec (who represented less than 20 per cent of the population), although vehemently opposed to a 'yes' vote, were not numerous enough by themselves to reject sovereignty-association. But in the end almost 60% of the province's voters and even a bare majority (52%) of its francophones voted 'Non', a fairly decisive result, although it did still leave 40.5% of the Quebec population, and just under half of its francophones, in favour of sovereignty-association. Nevertheless, Quebec had publicly rejected separation from Canada, and the nation responded by breathing a collective sigh of relief and calling for a new federalism.

The First Round of Constitutional Revisions   Ever since the PQ victory in 1976, Canadians had discussed and debated both national unity and constitutional change. There were more than enough proposals for reform floating around

the country, many of which surfaced in the travelling road-show (known as the Task Force on National Unity) sent across Canada in 1978. Out of the flurry of activity and the myriad suggestions, a number of points were clear. One was that many Canadians—including a fair proportion of academics and lawyers—were prepared to make relatively major alterations in the British North America Act that served as the nation's constitution. A second was that the vast majority of anglophone Canadians not only did not wish Quebec to separate from Canada and become independent, but were prepared to make substantial concessions to keep Quebec within Confederation. A third point, perhaps the least well understood by the public, was that the anglophone provinces of Canada—led by the western provinces of Alberta, British Columbia, and Saskatchewan, and supported strongly by Nova Scotia and Newfoundland—had developed their own agenda for constitutional reform. These provinces had long-standing regional grievances against Ottawa's centralizing federalism, which they regarded as operating almost exclusively in the interests of Ontario and Quebec. They were quite prepared to take advantage of Quebec's moves towards greater autonomy, particularly if these pressures reduced Quebec's influence within Confederation and allowed for constitutional change in the best interests of other provinces besides Quebec. What the other provinces chiefly wanted was unrestricted control over their own natural resources and a reform of some of Ottawa's governing institutions, notably the Senate and the Supreme Court, to reflect regional interests. The Trudeau government had seemed on the verge of conceding much of the provincial program when it was defeated in 1979, and the Clark government had not had time to deal with the issue when it too failed at the polls.

The opportunity presented to Prime Minister Trudeau by the neutralizing effect of the Quebec referendum, as he called a first ministers' conference for early June 1980, was simultaneously real and dangerous. From the federalist perspective it was necessary to deal with Quebec's aspirations without conceding too much to the other provinces, none of which was controlled by a Liberal government and all of which wanted their own versions of change. The federal government's most consistent ally was Ontario, which confirmed the regional charge that it had been the chief beneficiary of the old federalism by opposing most aspects of decentralizing reform. Quebec was hardly

(*Top*) Claude Ryan (b. 1925), formerly editor of *Le Devoir*, was chosen in 1978 to succeed Robert Bourassa as leader of the Quebec Liberal Party and he campaigned vigorously for the *Non* side in the 1980 referendum on Quebec sovereignty-association. (After his party was defeated in the 1981 election, he resigned as leader in the fall of 1982.) National Archives of Canada, PA-141501.

◀ (*Bottom*) René Lévesque in May 1980—sitting in front of the poster of the *Oui* campaign, which he had supported—after a referendum on the future of the province of Quebec, which had rejected (by a majority of 59 per cent) the sovereignty-association that had been proposed. Courtesy Sygma, Paris.

prepared to take the lead in the new round of discussions, nor could it be churlish about them. Its best strategy was to allow the anglophone provinces to initiate the dismantling of Confederation; and indeed, one of the principal characteristics of this round of constitutional discussion was that Quebec's concerns were not perceived to be central factors. General consensus was developed on economic issues, balancing provincial resource control against federal economic planning. But other questions remained difficult to resolve. Ottawa wanted to entrench a charter of rights in any constitutional document, chiefly to guarantee francophone linguistic rights across the nation, but the majority of the provinces (including Quebec) objected to such a charter as threatening their own rights. The provinces, for their part, wanted an amending formula that allowed all provinces both the right of veto and the right to opt out of any amendments that they regarded as threatening their powers. This round of discussions broke down in September 1980, and as Prime Minister Trudeau had been threatening for months, Ottawa prepared to take unilateral action.

Politically the federal constitutional package developed in Ottawa was carefully calculated. As an ardent federalist, a trained constitutional lawyer, and an exponent of *realpolitik*, Pierre Trudeau was clearly in his element. The new proposal called for the elimination of recourse to the British Parliament for amendment of the British North America Act ('repatriation'). It contained a charter of rights plus a number of qualifications on their applicability. The inclusion of the rights of other minorities prevented the French Canadians from being treated as a distinctive case. The package also provided for a new method of amendment, through national referendum initiated by Ottawa, in case of provincial obstructionism. The Trudeau government was prepared to pass the package in the federal Parliament and send it to Britain for approval without recourse to either the Supreme Court of Canada or the provinces, although it clearly infringed on the 'right' of the provinces to consent to constitutional change. Not surprisingly, the federal NDP supported this position, leaving the Progressive Conservative minority in Parliament to oppose it and voice the objections of nearly all the provinces except (again not surprisingly) Ontario. Parliamentary amendments dealt with some of the least sellable features of the original proposal, and introduced some new wrinkles, including the specific affirmation of 'aboriginal and treaty rights of the aboriginal peoples of Canada'. The Liberal government had neatly set in opposition two sets of rights, one the human rights protected in the entrenched charter and the other the provincial rights ignored in both the amending process and the charter itself. Eight of the provinces (excluding Ontario and New Brunswick)—often called unsympathetically in the media 'the Gang of Eight'—organized as the leading opponents of unilateral repatriation, although Quebec and the English-speaking premiers had quite different interests on many issues.

The first major hurdle for the federal initiative was the Supreme Court of

Canada, to which constitutional opinions from several provincial courts had gone on appeal. If the federal government won in the Supreme Court, it would make fairly untenable the provincial claim that the package was unconstitutional. While the Court deliberated the questions before it, René Lévesque and the PQ won a resounding electoral victory in Quebec. The win did not, of course, resolve the deep contradiction that the PQ represented as a separatist party committed to non-separatist action, but it did reactivate Quebec on constitutional matters. Although the British government had refused to deal officially with the provincial premiers (much as had been the case in 1867, when Nova Scotia sent Joseph Howe to London), Canada's native peoples set up their own lobbying office in London as the Office of First Nations of Canada. They had some claim to direct treaty connections with the British Crown, and a decent legal case.

The Supreme Court of Canada handed down its ruling on 28 September 1981. Many Canadians had a good deal of difficulty in comprehending both the process and the decision, since neither the constitutional nor the political role of the Canadian Supreme Court was as clearly understood as that of its American equivalent. As one constitutional expert commented, the decision was in legal terms 'complex and baffling and technically unsatisfactory.'[12] In political terms, such complexity was doubtless exactly what the Court had intended. Essentially, by a decision of 7 to 2, it declared the federal patriation process legal, since custom could not be enforced in courts. It then opined, by a decision of 6 to 3, that federal patriation was unconventional. Since most of the legal arguments against the process revolved around violations of constitutional 'convention' (or custom), these two opinions were mutually contradictory, although in law Ottawa had won. What the politicians could make of a result that said, in effect, that the federal package of repatriation was strictly speaking legal but at the same time improper was another matter.

In the end the nine English-speaking premiers, including seven members of the Gang of Eight, worked out a deal with Prime Minister Trudeau on 5 November 1981. Trudeau made considerable concessions to his original formulations—abandoning, for example, the provision for a referendum. Ontario joined Quebec in agreeing to drop its right of veto in favour of a complex formula that ensured that either one or the other (but not both) would have to agree to an amendment, which represented less a loss for Ottawa than for the central provinces, especially Quebec. At the same time, up to three provinces that had refused to concur with any constitutional change had the right to remain outside of its provisions until choosing to opt in—a considerable move from Trudeau's earlier positions. Trudeau's greatest concessions, however, were made on the Charter of Rights, particularly the so-called 'notwithstanding' clause, which allowed any province to opt out of clauses in the charter covering fundamental freedoms and legal and equality rights, although not other categories of rights, including language rights. There was disagreement over the intention of the negotiations regarding native peoples, resulting in a temporary omission of the clause guaranteeing Indian treaty rights that had to be subsequently restored by Parliament. As for the definition of those rights themselves, there was to be a constitutional conference to identify them. The final compromise satisfied the nine English-speaking premiers and certainly theoretically strengthened the rights of the provinces to opt out of the charter on critical issues, including both native rights and women's rights, using the 'notwithstanding' clause. Perhaps understandably, both women's groups and native groups vowed to fight on in opposition to the revised constitutional package. As for Quebec, it had lost nothing except much of its self-perceived distinctive status in Confederation. That loss would prove fairly important, however, for Quebec would consistently refuse to accept the constitutional reforms on the grounds that one of Canada's two 'national wills' had not been consulted. That position would lead to another attempt at provincial unanimity at Meech Lake in 1987.

The revised constitutional package passed the Canadian Parliament in December 1981 and the British Parliament early in 1982. The latter had resolutely refused to become involved in the various protests against the new package, surrendering its role as a court of last resort against unconstitutional actions within Canada. Canadians did not at the time entirely appreciate what had happened constitutionally, or what the changes would mean. The principle of patriation had been purchased at considerable expense by the Trudeau government. It was true that the Charter of Rights reflected the principle that collective and individual rights transcending the existent British North America Act (and its conception of relevant players) had to be carefully guarded. But in place of the earlier British constitutional notion that the legislature (federal and provincial) was the source of protection, the Charter established the American constitutional notion that the court system needed to ensure fundamental rights against the legislature and the government responsible to it. And in place of the earlier concept that Parliament (especially the federal one) was supreme, it introduced a whole new series of formal checks and balances limiting parliamentary supremacy.

The new Constitution not only gave new powers to the provinces, which were traditional political units, but it also recognized new and rather more amorphous political units in the Charter of Rights, which was somewhat less concerned than the American Bill of Rights to define the individual rights of Canadians, and somewhat more concerned to delineate their collective rights. Thus, in addition to providing equality before the law for individuals facing discrimination 'based on race, national or ethnic origin, colour, religion, sex, age or mental or physical disability' (section 15.1), the Charter also specifically permitted in section 15.2, 'any law, program or activity that has as its object the amelioration of conditions of disadvantaged individuals or groups', including (but not limiting itself to) those disadvantaged by the factors of discrimination mentioned in section 15.1. In addition, aboriginal and treaty rights of the aboriginal people—although carefully not defined—

Queen Elizabeth signing the Canadian Constitution in April 1982. Attending her are André Ouellet, President of the Privy Council, and Gerald Regan, Secretary of State; Prime Minister Trudeau; and Michael Pitfield and Michael Kirby, Clerk and Deputy Clerk of the Privy Council respectively. Canapress Photo Service, Toronto.

were entrenched, as were sexual equality and multiculturalism. Although at first glance these Charter provisions seemed to represent the ultimate triumph of liberalism, in several respects they negated it. In the first place, the liberal Charter provisions were balanced by the increased power given to the provinces to control their own resources and to call their own shots about the applicability of the Charter and any constitutional amendments. In the second place, the constitutional introduction of a whole series of new collectivities provided further complications for an already overloaded political process, which in the end helped to limit the liberal impulse itself. Finally, the well-publicized antics of the politicians over the constitution contributed to a further reduction in the esteem in which those politicians were held by the Canadian public.

Constitutional Revision: Round Two   The 1982 Charter, with its explicit and implicit recognitions of both collective and individual rights, was hardly the last word on the subject. An ongoing body of case law would have to be developed in the courts, especially the Supreme Court of Canada, which became the ultimate arbiter to interpret the vague terminology of the Charter. Governments, however, could have dealt in more specific terms with some of the recognized collectivities, such as women and aboriginal people. The earlier understanding that existing aboriginal rights would be spelled out in more detail was never really acted upon seriously, although the Liberal government had some concrete proposals in hand when it was defeated in 1984. As for women's rights, a few cosmetic changes were made administratively or legislatively. But throughout the 1980s the key issue of abortion remained unresolved. The Charter was simply a wild card exercised by the Supreme Court of Canada on behalf of a woman's right to abortion through its clause in section 7 concerning the 'life, liberty and security of the person'. For women, as for aboriginal people, the court system proved more open to change than the parliamentary system.

In 1987 the Mulroney government fastened on one of the loose ends of the 1982 constitutional process: the refusal of Quebec to accept the 1982 Constitution. By this time René Lévesque had retired,* and his party had been defeated at the polls (in December 1985) by the Liberals under a rehabilitated Robert Bourassa, who proved an exception to the rule that politicians could not return from devastating electoral defeats. Once again in power, Bourassa offered to compromise, and Mulroney summoned a new 'Gang of Ten' to a closed-door session on 30 April 1987 at Meech Lake, where a revised constitutional arrangement acceptable to Quebec was worked out. While Quebec was to be constitutionally recognized as a 'distinct society' and given further concessions, including a veto over most amendments to the constitution, there were also inducements to the other provinces, which would share with Quebec several of the most important new features of autonomy. All provinces would be compensated by the federal government for programs they refused to join, and each province was given a veto over future amending. There was to be regular discussion of Senate reform, although no particular formula was agreed upon. Nevertheless, there was a consensus among participants that the federal Parliament, and the legislatures of all ten provinces, would have to approve the agreement by early June 1990, the lengthy time-frame allowed for public hearings and feedback—or the arrangement was dead.

The three years permitted between the Meech Lake meeting and the requirement of unanimous acceptance by the various legislatures later created difficulties. While the Mulroney government understandably insisted that no changes could be made in the agreement until it had been approved,

---

*Lévesque resigned in June 1985 and was succeeded as PQ leader by Pierre-Marc Johnson (b. 1946); he in turn resigned in November 1987, a week after Lévesque's death, and was succeeded by Jacques Parizeau (b. 1930).

The 'Gang of Ten'—the ten provincial premiers—meeting at Meech Lake in April 1987. On Prime Minister Mulroney's left are Robert Bourassa (Quebec), Richard Hatfield (New Brunswick), William Van der Zalm (British Columbia), Grant Devine (Saskatchewan), and Brian Peckford (Newfoundland). On the Prime Minister's right are David Peterson (Ontario), John Buchanan (Nova Scotia), Howard Pawley (Manitoba), Joseph Ghiz (Prince Edward Island), and Donald Getty (Alberta). Photograph by P. Andrews, courtesy Publiphoto.

not every provincial government felt bound by the particular terms of a controversial understanding accepted by whoever happened to be its premier in April 1987. The subsequent public debate made clear that not all Canadians agreed with what was perceived to be a further dismantling of the federal government's authority in favour not merely of Quebec, but of all the provinces. The poorer 'have-not' provinces—led by Manitoba, New Brunswick, and eventually Newfoundland—were particularly concerned that few new federal programs would be successfully mounted if the richer provinces had the option of receiving federal funds for their own versions. Other collectivities, such as aboriginal people and women, worried that their rights were being bartered away to the provinces. Across the country suggested revisions sprouted up almost like grass, many of them offering structural panaceas, such as a reformed and more effective Senate. As the deadline for acceptance loomed, only Manitoba and Newfoundland held out, the latter having rescinded an earlier legislative endorsement after Brian Peck-ford's Tories were defeated by the Liberals under Clyde Wells (b. 1937). Prime Minister Mulroney tried the time-honoured tactics of the labour negotiator on the premiers, calling them into closed-door sessions, on the eve of the deadline, designed to shame them into support. This tactic appeared to work. But in the subsequent sessions of the Manitoba legislature, Indian leader Elijah Harper (b. 1949) refused to give the unanimous consent neces-sary to beat the deadline. Since Manitoba was not going to approve, Newfoundland's Wells backed off a previous commitment to supply his province's legislative endorsement. In the end, the two provinces refused their endorsement and Meech Lake failed.*

In the post-mortems a number of points stood out. One was that after 1987 the popular support for Brian Mulroney (and the federal PC party) and Meech Lake had declined together. Quebec understandably interpreted the mounting hostility to Meech Lake in English-speaking Canada as directed specifically against the 'distinct society'. The cause was not helped when a number of Conservatives, including a prominent cabinet minister, resigned from the caucus in the spring of 1990 in order to take independent separatist positions. But the fact was that most Canadians appeared to be prepared to allow Quebec almost total autonomy; what was objected to was the exten-sion of much of that autonomy to the other provinces—which would in effect balkanize the nation. Symbolically, Elijah Harper's action called atten-tion to a related problem: Meech Lake's potential incompatibility with the collective rights recognized by the Canadian Charter. During the summer of 1990 the failure of Meech Lake was followed by an extremely volatile confrontation between natives in Quebec, led by the Mohawks of Oka, and the Bourassa government. Bourassa responded to the crisis by calling in the federal armed forces (as had been done in the October Crisis of 1970).

Whether the crushing defeat in early September 1990 of one of the main supporters of Meech Lake, Premier David Peterson of Ontario, by the NDP led by Bob Rae (b. 1948), was another straw in the wind was debatable. Certainly the achievement by the NDP (for the first time) of power in Ontario—still the most liberal, centralist, and nationalist of Canada's political parties—suggested that the steady collapse of those principles might be coming to an end. Subsequent 1991 victories by the NDP in British Colum-bia and Saskatchewan provided further confirmation that the electorate had mixed feelings about conservative rhetoric.

---

*The Meech Lake Accord died when it was not ratified by the deadline of 23 June 1990; a month previously (21 May) several Conservatives, led by Lucien Bouchard (b. 1938), the Minister of the Environment, left the government to form the pro-independence Bloc Québécois.

The Economy and Its Issues in the 1970s

The 'Economic Crisis'

The so-called 'economic crisis' of the mid-seventies did not come upon Canada overnight, and it ought not to have been unexpected. At the same time, the measurable components of the crisis did not square well with the liberal economics (*pace* Keynes) that had dominated Canadian thinking since the Second World War. Runaway inflation, high interest rates, high levels of unemployment, and substantial poverty—all highly visible economic indicators—were supposed to be things of the past, and in any event ought not all to be occurring simultaneously. In traditional economics, unemployment and poverty represented an economic downturn, even a recession or depression. Nobody wanted a depression, but the system ought to have been self-correcting, with inflation and interest rates falling in response to the economic slowdown. Instead, some aspects of the economy were behaving as if they were overheated, while others were giving quite contrary signals.

The reasons for the contradictory economic signals were not easy to explain to the Canadian public, particularly since the experts themselves were not agreed on an interpretation. Several realities were, or ought to have been, eminently clear. One was that the manufacturing economies of the remainder of the industrialized (and industrializing) world had not only recovered from the devastation of the Second World War, but had modernized and jumped ahead of a laggard Canada, which was unable to compete either internationally or in its own domestic market. While there were many factors in Canada's manufacturing decline relative to its competitors, a key point was output per worker, which was one of the lowest around and was responsible for substantially higher costs per unit. Some Canadians blamed the decline on foreign ownership, others on the lack of research and development. For some years, beginning in the 1960s, Canada had protected its domestic market and industries with higher tariffs and import quotas, but such responses only made it more difficult to sell Canadian goods in the world market. Canada was now manufacturing in a far more competitive and cut-throat world than ever before.

At the same time that Canadian manufacturing—notably in traditional sectors such as steel, automobiles, textiles, and shoes—was in serious trouble, Canada seemed unable to take full advantage of what many thought ought to have been its principal economic advantage: access to cheap energy and raw materials. Here, of course, what was in the best interests of the manufacturing industries was not in the best interests of the possessors and producers of those raw materials. The international cost of many raw materials shot up markedly in the early 1970s, creating a boom in the resource sector of the Canadian economy just as the manufacturing sector was becoming increasingly flat. The federal government tried to balance matters out a bit—as with its complicated multi-tiered pricing system for petroleum—but it only succeeded in incurring the wrath of the producers (led by the Alberta government) without receiving the gratitude of consumers. Higher prices for gas, oil and coal not only enraged consumers in central Canada, but also encouraged producers to sell abroad.

The Resource Sector and Its Problems

To make matters worse, not all sectors of Canada's resource economy benefited equally from international inflation. On the whole, the price of raw foodstuffs—either internationally or domestically—did not increase commensurately with that of other materials. The price of wheat more than doubled during the early seventies, to the benefit of western farmers, but the price of oil rose from $2.00 to $30.00 per barrel and the price of breakfast cereal more than tripled. Through a complicated system of protectionism and subsidization, federal and provincial governments succeeded during the seventies in insulating both the Canadian farmer and the Canadian consumer from the worst effects of the pricing problems, but they remained unresolved. The price of food in Canada remained comparatively low, costing a lower percentage of family income in 1980 than it had in 1970. Despite quotas and marketing boards, the Canadian farmer continued to produce more than the market could consume, especially when that market was also being supplied by American farmers who could produce at even lower costs. No Canadian doubted that farmers were part of the backbone of Canadian society, or that—despite the temporary prosperity provided by wheat production in the early 1970s—the agricultural system, along with Canadian society, was in serious trouble. Nevertheless, government assistance for the farmer was a solution preferred to higher food prices. Not all farmers would be supported, however.

In early June 1986 the leading bureaucrat in Agriculture Canada created an uproar in Parliament by admitting in an interview that the federal government intended to resolve the Canadian 'farm problems' by encouraging thousands of marginal farmers to leave the business. 'To me, the basic dilemma of the next three years will be to ease, assist and support the transition without installing terribly uneconomic devices,' he said. 'I think 15 to 20 percent [fewer farmers] is not unrealistic. The period is another matter.'[13] Rural depopulation was hardly a new phenomenon in Canada, and programs to eliminate from the primary sector uneconomic producers, such as fishermen, went back many years. But to state openly and baldly that there were too many farmers was not only to play with political dynamite, but to provide a graphic illustration of how much the nation had changed since Confederation, which had been partly brought about to allow Canada to open a new agricultural West.

Although the Opposition in Parliament wanted to be told how the 'one-in-five' farmer to be eliminated would be chosen, there was no mystery about who was most vulnerable: younger entrant farmers were at maximum risk, although any farmer heavily in debt was in trouble. In the early 1970s young entrants particularly had responded, with the usual optimism of the agricultural community, to the higher grain prices created by crop failures in the USSR, India, and Argentina, and to windfall oil profits in many Third World countries. They had bought land at inflated prices and financed its purchase, and the acquisition of equipment, with borrowed money. In the early 1980s a combination of high inflation and falling commodity prices produced disaster for many in the farm community, despite heavy subsidies. The downward turn in the cycle of the eighties was a short-term factor in the farm crisis. Perhaps the most important long-term ingredient was the cost of farm land, which was driven up by non-agricultural causes. In Ontario, for example, land prices averaged $795 an acre—obviously much higher in prime areas—even after the bottom had dropped out of a speculative market in 1984, and good wheat land in the West was worth nearly $1,000 an acre. Those who did not inherit their land began farming deeply in debt, which only buoyant prices could alleviate.

But the farmer's dilemma during the seventies and eighties was not as apparent as the fisherman's. Not only were fish stocks being constantly depleted by overfishing on the part of both domestic and international fleets, but the price of fish was not entirely dependent on supply, for fish was in competition with other foods. Luxury items such as lobster could sustain greater price increases, but their market was limited at best. Were the price of fish to get distinctly out of line with wheat, beef, or chicken, the market could stop consuming entirely. Canadian fishermen demanded protection for their fish stocks, while repeated government investigations indicated that there were too many Canadian fishermen as well as too much international fishing in Canadian waters, especially off the eastern coasts. Many fishermen and their families compensated for inadequate earnings by collecting unemployment compensation (made possible by changes in the Unemployment Insurance Act of 1971), and by working in other jobs much of the year. But these strategies offered no permanent solution.

A more promising way of dealing with the difficulties experienced by Atlantic fishermen was to provide them with alternative forms of employment. Under the Trudeau government of 1968-72, regional economic development and the correction of long-standing regional economic disparities had assumed a high priority. The result was a number of federal programs, spearheaded by the creation of the Department of Regional Economic Expansion (DREE), which pumped large sums of money into the Atlantic region. Unfortunately, regional development turned into a contest between the federal government and the provinces, partly because Ottawa needed justifications for expanded centralization to keep Quebec and the West from getting out of control. Nor was job creation a panacea for regional disparities. In the Atlantic region, for example, while new jobs were created in the early

1970s at rates above the national average, the regional rate of unemployment grew more rapidly than that of job creation, chiefly because of population growth fuelled by the promise of new jobs.

The Trudeau Government and Economic Policy: The Early Years, 1968-1973

The first Trudeau government had been concerned with what the Prime Minister had called 'the Just Society'—relating the performance of the Canadian economy to the needs of Canadian society. If that government had 'discovered' the structural realities of regional economic disparities, it also drew attention to the structure of poverty in Canada. The two issues were not unrelated. The key document was a report of a special Senate Committee on Poverty (appointed late in 1968) entitled *Poverty in Canada*, which first appeared in November 1971 and was reprinted several times over the ensuing months. In many respects this report represented the high point of official liberal thinking in Canada. It recognized that not all Canadians had shared equally in the prosperity of the fifties and sixties. It not only insisted that Canada had the highest rate of unemployment among industrially advanced nations, but that such unemployment, instead of being randomly distributed, was centred on a small minority of the labour force in certain economic sectors and in certain regions. Canadian poverty had become structural, in effect perpetuating itself despite the welfare system. Indeed, the report maintained that the operation of the welfare system helped continue poverty. While the committee recognized that single mothers were an important component of the impoverished, it did not give special attention to their problems beyond calling for improved day-care facilities. Its radical conclusion was to call for a guaranteed annual income for all Canadians and incorporation of 'the right to an adequate standard of living for all Canadians into the *Canadian Bill of Rights*.'[14] Such a call was doubtless Utopian, though the social inadequacies of the existing welfare system were well documented in the report.

In 1972 the Canadian electorate decided that the Trudeau government did not deserve a majority, electing 109 Liberal, 107 Tory, and 31 NDP MPs. Trudeau continued to govern with the support of David Lewis's NDP. The Just Society was put on the back-burner during much of Trudeau's minority government, chiefly because of the oil crisis, which forced a concentration on the economy itself. While the Foreign Investment Review Agency was put in place to deal with the problem of foreign ownership in Canada, the OPEC action put oil and its successor, inflation, at centre stage. The government's complex oil policy was intended to use federal power to equalize oil prices across the country and to create a new national energy policy based in part on a federally owned petroleum company to be called Petro-Canada. As might have been expected, Canadians had difficulty understanding the complications of the intersection of international and domestic economic problems. In 1974 the Trudeau Liberals again went to the polls. Robert Stanfield's PCs wanted to deal with an escalating double-digit inflation by introducing wage and price controls, a policy the Prime Minister pooh-poohed from coast to coast. To Stanfield's disappointment, voters in the summer of 1974 were not persuaded of the need for controls, and Trudeau won a resounding (and fairly surprising) victory that almost demolished the NDP.

The unholy trinity of obvious economic problems—double-digit inflation, interest rates, and unemployment—continued unabated. Canadians sought a reassuring way of comprehending the difficulties, for the notion that the country could not compete internationally was too painful to be seriously contemplated. There were several potential scapegoats at hand. The bankers could have been blamed for the interest rates, or the businessmen for the unemployment. Instead the country chose to fasten on the most visible and immediate of the trinity of indicators—inflation—and on a single factor to explain it. Polls taken in 1975 indicated that Canadians believed the chief culprits responsible for inflation were over-powerful labour unions demanding unreasonable wage settlements.

The triumph of organized labour in Canada occurred after the Second World War and especially after 1960, when it grew in total membership, in its percentage of the work force, and in its penetration of new industries, particularly in the public sector. Labour unions sought to protect their members from the effects of the new economic situation, particularly by demanding high wage settlements and opposing management efforts to rationalize and modernize their work forces through the traditional mechanisms of the layoff or firing of redundant workers. Strikes in many industries—including a much-publicized postal strike in the summer of 1975—made the demands of labour appear unreasonable. The 'posties' not only disrupted a public service that Canadians had long taken for granted, but won a substantial wage increase and a significantly shorter work week in the process. There was apparently little public sympathy for such public-sector employees as the postal workers, though their wages had systematically fallen behind those of the private sector, and their civil-service managers appeared incapable of dealing fairly with them. When policemen, firemen, nurses, and teachers began taking similar steps, Canadians became alarmed. Not only were key public services threatened with interruption, but wage settlements in the public sector would have to be financed either with higher taxes or with deficit spending.

The Growth of Government Spending

It must be remembered that the traditional Keynesian system—in which deficits were not a significant problem—had become conventional wisdom because it offered alternative economic theories to those of the Great Depression, which had been so obviously inadequate and unacceptable. Though political leaders in the thirties had balanced budgets, a great many people suffered. According to Keynes, balancing budgets was exactly the wrong thing to do in times of depression. Instead, governments needed to spend money in order to stimulate the economy, correcting the deficits of bad times by creating higher revenues and, by extension, good times. Some liberal economists held that deficits never did have to be retired although the age-old problem with public deficits is that they really represent government debt that has to be maintained through interest payments. High interest rates, such as those of the early 1970s, made the government debt much more expensive to service, and the economic problems of the period set into motion a number of automatic mechanisms, built into the welfare state's safety net, that greatly increased public expenditures. When particular government programs of the day were added to automatic spending, the result was such a rapid increase in deficits that they too became a public issue.

Two competing theories were developed to explain the growth of government spending. One saw increased spending as natural, inevitable, and incremental, the product of a modern economy and society that had new demands and expectations. The other was rooted in the self-interest of collective decision-making, and has usually been called the 'public-choice' theory. It argued that the self-interest of politicians for popularity and of civil servants for larger budgets coincided to produce constant pressure on budgets. Public-choice theory lies at the heart of the British television series 'Yes, Minister' (later 'Yes, Prime Minister') that was widely enjoyed in Canada.[15] It is far more cynical then the incremental interpretation, and further substantiates the suspicion, harboured by many Canadians, of their political leaders.

Most Canadians recognized that they could not run their own households forever on the spending principles of the government, and a host of more conservative economists now appeared to confirm such an understanding. The rise of conservative economics in Canada could be seen in several places. One was the establishment of organizations such as the Fraser Institute of Vancouver (1974), which supported the publication and dissemination of conservative economic views by respectable economists and academicians. The other was the rise of departments and faculties of business and management at Canadian universities, a development that really took wing in the early 1970s. The establishment or expansion of these faculties was partly a response to the alleged failure of departments of economics (often dominated by the liberal Keynesians or even Marxists) to serve the needs of Canadian business and industry.

Trudeau's Economic Policy

The net result of these developments was the about-turn executed by Prime Minister Trudeau on wage and price controls, as well as on public-service unions. The government's tinkering with policies of voluntary restraint is associated with Finance Minister John Turner, whose May 1974 budget was defeated, forcing an election. He resigned in September 1975 and left politics the next year. On Thanksgiving Day 1975—a day chosen to catch the largest number of Canadians at home—Trudeau announced in Parliament and on national television that mandatory controls were necessary on any private corporation with more than 500 employees and on every public civil servant employed by the federal government. Increases would be held to 10% in the first year, 8% in the second, and 6% in the third year of the program. Provincial—even NDP—governments accepted the policy. The Anti-Inflation Board limited wages more than prices, but the Canadian public appeared to approve, as it did of a far more confrontational government policy towards its public-service unions.

The economic crisis of the mid-seventies, brought about when the policies and principles of thirty years of prosperity all seemed to collapse together, marked a period when new initiatives were required from governments and populace alike. Some members of the Canadian public sensed the deep-rooted nature of the problem, but most preferred to take refuge in scapegoat tactics, blaming labour unions for something that was everybody's responsibility. Like the public, Pierre Trudeau's federal Liberals talked about the need for structural reform of the economy, but they were satisfied with band-aid solutions. Trudeau himself spoke of the need to consume less, but did nothing to facilitate such a development. The crisis period passed without significant economic alterations at either the public or the private level; and with the PQ victory in late 1976, the constitutional problems posed by Quebec were considered by the Trudeau government to be more compelling than the economic crisis. It continued—like all other governments in Canada and around the world—to spend more than it collected in taxes and revenue, seemingly without much concern for the future.

The Economy in the 1980s

The eighties were spared economic crises such as those of 1973-5 until the very end of the decade. The Canadian economy, however, settled down to rates of unemployment, inflation, interest charges, housing costs, and taxation that would previously have been regarded as disastrous. Throughout the eighties the annual seasonally adjusted unemployment rate never went below 7.5 per cent, and remained in double figures between 1982 and 1985. Inflation dropped below double figures in 1982, but consumer prices continued to increase steadily throughout the remainder of the decade, at rates ranging from a low of 4% (1985) to a high of 5.8% (1983). Interest rates dropped from 1981 highs close to 20% for prime borrowers, but the 'prime' fell under 10% only in 1987 and increased again substantially in 1989 and 1990. Taxes as a percentage of personal income ran at 18.9% in 1980 and 22.0% in 1990; in no intervening year was there anything but a small annual increase.[16]

Canadians quickly became accustomed to the new situation, and stoically

Unemployment Rates, 1981-1990

Year	Unemployment	Female	Male	Under 25
1981	7.5	8.3	7.0	13.2
1982	11.0	10.9	11.0	18.7
1983	11.8	11.6	12.0	19.8
1984	11.2	11.3	11.2	17.8
1985	10.5	10.7	10.3	16.4
1986	9.5	9.8	9.3	15.1
1987	8.8	9.3	8.5	13.7
1988	7.8	8.3	7.4	12.0
1989	7.5	7.9	7.3	11.3
1990	7.9	7.9	7.9	12.5

Source: Minister of Industry, Science and Technology, *Canadian Economic Observer: Historical Statistical Supplement, 1990/91* (Ottawa, 1991), p. 36.

took even the worst of times in stride. An economic slowdown that started in 1980, and by 1983 saw unemployment climb to 11.8% of the total work-force (19.8% in the under 25s), received minimal attention from the media, perhaps because of the great public debate over the Constitution. There were no major new public initiatives for dealing with the economy and its problems in this recession. The social-welfare net clicked in automatically, and while more Canadian families fell below the poverty line, few actually starved—or demonstrated in the streets. Canadians became more conscious that jobs were harder to get and to keep. The young, in increasingly large numbers, responded to the new situation by going on to higher education, insisting on taking courses that promised some immediate economic payout. But they did not become radicalized in any serious way—perhaps they were too busy working to keep up the payments on their credit cards.

If the early seventies had witnessed a round of doomsayers arguing that Canada, along with the rest of the Western world, was mortgaging its future, those Cassandras hadn't 'seen nothin' yet'. The 1980s—despite the decline in the Keynesian ethic of twentieth-century liberalism and a growth of private enterprise (confusingly, nineteenth-century liberalism)—set new records for living literally beyond one's means among everyone from the government in Ottawa to first-year university students. West Edmonton Mall—at the time of its completion in 1986, the world's largest—could be seen as a symbol for this consuming society. The total debt of the federal government grew from $100 billion in 1981 to $380 billion in 1990, which on a per-capita basis was an increase from $4,140 to $14,317 per Canadian in only ten years. (In 1970 the per-capita figure was a mere $795.60.) There had not been a budget surplus since the fiscal year 1972-3. Among developed nations only Italy—

Part of West Edmonton Mall. Built in three phases from 1981 to 1986 and a prime tourist attraction, it is located some nine kilometres west of Edmonton's centre. It is a huge complex of department stores, shops, restaurants, recreation areas, amusements, and services that also includes a luxury hotel. Photograph courtesy West Edmonton Mall.

always regarded as the sick country of post-war Europe—had a worse record of debt management.

At the same time, the Canadian consumer debt more than doubled from $46 billion to $101 billion in the eighties, increasing in small but steady stages from 18.7% of post-tax personal income to 21.5%. Much of that debt, of course, was incurred through the medium of plastic credit cards, issued in profusion by banks, credit unions, stores, and just about every other business imaginable. In the last year of the decade the number of bank credit-card transactions alone increased from just over 100 billion to over 150 billion. Residential mortgage debt nearly tripled (from $88 billion to $237 billion) and as a percentage of post-tax personal income grew from 35.4% to 50.2%. Over ten years Canadian personal consumer debt (including mortgages) had increased from 54.1% of disposable personal income to 71.7%, despite a larger tax bite and truly debilitating interest rates, which for individuals never dropped into single digits over the entire decade. Personal savings rates declined constantly over the 1980s, and personal consumption rates increased considerably in excess of inflation. Given the amount of deficit financing, it was surprising that only two major financial institutions (the Northlands and

Canadian Commercial Banks in Alberta) collapsed, although there were reports that several of the chartered banks were in some difficulty because of loans made to Third World nations.*

Both the housing industry (nearly 2 million new housing starts) and the automobile industry (nearly 10 million new cars and over 7.5 million trucks) boomed for most of the decade, as did manufacturers of big-ticket consumer items like furniture and household appliances. Many of the popular automobile bumper stickers dealt with consumer spending, perhaps the most ubiquitous reading: 'We're spending our children's inheritance.' As always, Canadian secondary manufacturing relied on the domestic market (which was going ever deeper into debt) for its prosperity. In 1981 nearly 60 per cent of the value of Canada's exports was in primary and resource commodities, and that figure did not change appreciably over the decade, declining slightly towards the end of the period because of the softness of the international resource market. Despite the generally overheated nature of the Canadian economy—perhaps because of it—not all Canadian corporations flourished. The early eighties saw three well-publicized corporate busts: Massey-Ferguson, the farm-equipment manufacturers; Canadair Limited; and Dome Petroleum. The first two succumbed to better-managed international competition, the last to a rapidly acquired debt-load with chartered banks that represented a substantial proportion of its capital.

The Triumph of the Private Enterprise Mentality

While one business watchword of the eighties was 'better management practices'—necessary if Canadian corporations were to compete in the dog-eat-dog world of international business—there were also some contradictory trends, such as the growth in the mystique of the swashbuckling entrepreneur. The complexities of the era were reflected in the titles of two popular books for business readers: *In Search of Excellence* and *The Money-Rustlers*. The favoured entrepreneurialism took two basic forms. One involved manipulating billions of dollars of borrowed money (in an age of easy access to credit at all levels) as a mega-speculator on the international level. Robert Campeau (b. 1923), perhaps the most notorious speculator, had begun as an Ottawa contractor and flourished in the dizzy world of real-estate development from the sixties to the eighties, along with Albert, Paul, and Ralph Reichmann (Olympia & York) and E.P. Taylor (Cadillac-Fairview). Campeau eventually moved into the American market, obtaining a number of merchandising corporations (including Saks Fifth Avenue and Bloomingdale's) on his way to

---

*In March 1992 it emerged that some of the chartered banks' diciest loans—made in 1990—were to a Canadian corporation, Olympia & York Developments Ltd, for the construction of a major new office complex in the Docklands area of London.

eventual collapse. The other favoured entrepreneur was the small business-man, who became one of the darlings of government in the latter 1980s.

It would be foolish to suggest that the resurgence in the 1980s of a Private Enterprise mentality, at the political as well as popular level, was a distinctly Canadian phenomenon. The Mulroney Tories were slightly belated partici-pants in a world-wide trend that was characteristic of the decade. It had begun in Britain with the election of Margaret Thatcher in 1979 and continued in the United States with the triumph of Ronald Reagan at the polls in 1980. (Even the Russians would get into the act, with Mikhail Gorbachev proving the most committed private-enterpriser of the lot.) In the 1984 election campaign, Brian Mulroney had sought the political centre, one commentator arguing that he promised 'what amounts to Liberalism with a Fresh Face.'[17] But his party had strong support from the Canadian business community, which wanted to see the deficit and tax reform, as well as a reduction in the government's direct involvement in the economy, move to the top of Ottawa's agenda.

In power the Tories found balancing the budget a difficult political task, although they managed to reduce the growth-rate of the deficit. Mulroney's first administration emphasized closer attention to spending rather than major budget cuts—and the beginning of privatization, such as the selling of the assets of the Canada Development Investment Corporation (CDIC). The government backed away, however, from an open confrontation with the principle of universality of welfare services, and chose instead to concentrate on increasing revenue through greater economic prosperity. The main vehi-cle for prosperity was to be a new economic relationship with Canada's largest trading partner, the United States. The eventual 'Free Trade Agree-ment'—negotiated in secret during 1986 and 1987—ran to 3,000 pages of legal language and would take years to work out in detail. Tariffs would gradually be removed, although Canadians would discover to their surprise that tariffs were not the levy responsible for most of the unaccountable disparity between what goods cost in American and Canadian shops. They were equally surprised to find that 'free trade' did not apply to ordinary people shopping in the United States and returning with purchases to Canada.

The most important principle of the Free Trade Agreement was that discrimination on the basis of nationality would be eliminated. The resulting national debate over the deal was characterized by much heat and very little light. Not even the economic experts could safely predict the ultimate effects of the treaty, although most favoured it in principle. Critics complained that the Canadian negotiators had traded access to the American market for Canadian resources (including energy) in return for continental economic integration. But most of that integration had already occurred in previous arrangements, and only a small percentage of total Canadian-American trade was actually affected by the treaty. The strongest nationalist argument against the agreement was that Canada would no longer have complete control of its own social policies, since many of them could be interpreted as unfair subsidies that breached the national treatment rule. But the most telling criticism that could have been advanced against free trade was that it would *not* revolutionize Canadian-American economic relations; that in fact it was merely a cosmetic overhaul of the existing continental arrangement. A government seeking accomplishments suitable for an election campaign had oversold it to the Canadian electorate.

The election in 1988 was held before ratification of either the Free Trade Agreement or the Meech Lake Accord, so that the victorious Tories were not hampered either by the public's eventual recognition that the former would make little real positive difference in their lives, or by the controversy that would surround the latter. In its second term, the Mulroney government ran into many more problems than in its first. As we have seen, it failed miserably with Meech Lake, and then ran into stubborn opposition over tax reform. Characteristically, the Tories concentrated on change in business taxation instead of attacking the structure of the personal income tax system. They decided to replace lost tariffs and other existing levies with a single across-the-board nine per cent value-added tax (called the Goods and Services Tax, or GST) imposed at the cash register. Not surprisingly, the provinces resolutely refused to eliminate their sales taxes in favour of the new federal levy, which would be paid by the consumer and administered by businessmen—who, despite the added paperwork involved, were virtually the only supporters of the scheme. Finance Minister Michael Wilson responded to business pressure by reluctantly agreeing to reduce the amount of the tax from nine to seven per cent, but neither he nor the government was really prepared for the extent of public opposition that emerged as the date for implementation came closer and the need to pass appropriate legislation became urgent. As with other of its policies, such as Meech Lake and free trade, the Mulroney government had allowed a long lead time between setting the policy and its ultimate ratification. The intention here was to allow the government to make minor last-minute concessions (such as the reduction to seven per cent) and disarm the opposition. As Meech Lake had demonstrated, however, not until the actual deadline for ratification approached did opposition really crystallize, and then the government was in serious trouble.

The Mulroney government had assumed that its overwhelming majority in the Commons would ensure passage of the GST, whatever the public or the Liberal-controlled Senate felt. Michael Wilson's department began the process of instructing businessmen on the intricacies of the tax and its collection before the requisite legislation had received final legislative approval. The Liberal majority in the Senate dug in its heels, encouraged by public-opinion polls indicating that a vast majority of Canadians were dead set against the GST. With the threat of deadlock looming between the two houses of Parliament, the Tories implemented the ultimate threat that had been held for years over all upper houses operating within the parliamentary system when they challenged the power of the House of Commons. Eight new senators were swiftly appointed in late September 1990, giving the Tories a majority in both houses. Such an action was in broadest terms constitutional, although court cases were initiated over technical details. But whether it was politically wise was another matter, since the government would inevitably be charged with 'arrogance', and the measure at issue was clearly so unpopular that the 'thwarting the will of the people' argument about opposition in the Senate could hardly be invoked except with the utmost cynicism. What was clear was that any Senate reform that did not jettison the parliamentary system of placing government responsibility in the House of Commons would offer no protection against a majority government's enforcing its will. Less clear was whether the indisputable unpopularity of the Mulroney government had anything to do with its Private Enterprise philosophy and policies, or was merely a product of bad tactics. Canadian prime ministers create governments that in some ways reflect their own personalities. Mulroney and *his* government had in common secretiveness, abortive manipulativeness, and ultimate heavyhandedness.

Canada and the World

In the 1960s Canada's external relations fell into disarray and never did recover. The problem was basically simple. Canada's economic activity entitled it to major-league status, but its close relationship with the United States had made it a minor-league subsidiary. Its image abroad was as perplexing as its policies. On the one hand it continued its habit of preaching from on high to nations that did not regard themselves as morally inferior and relished the opportunity to catch Canada out in hypocritical moral contradictions. On the other hand Canada continued to be one of the most favoured destinations of immigrants around the world—which suggested that it was doing something right.

Whatever the Department of External Affairs was or was not doing, Canadians themselves had become citizens of the world in a way that would have been unthinkable to previous generations. Relatively cheap plane tickets to anywhere in the world had by the early 1970s become an accepted part of life, so that kids in the 1960s could travel the world, carrying backpacks festooned with the new Canadian flag and sleeping in youth hostels. Now their parents followed them, staying in hotels that were just like those at home. Almost every Canadian family had at least one member with photographs of a major overseas expedition, and memories to go with them. Cheap foreign travel worked both ways, and as many Canadian immigrant families entertained relatives at home as travelled abroad to visit kinfolk. Added to this, the substantial shifts in the origins of immigrants beginning in the sixties made Canada an increasingly cosmopolitan place to live. Canadians drank less beer and more wine (much of it imported). They ate in restaurants with exotic cuisines, cooked similar food at home, and insisted on its availability in their supermarkets.

At the same time that Canadians were enlarging their horizons, however, their government was attempting to pull back from the international role given it by Lester Pearson, first as Minister of External Affairs and then as Prime Minister. Pierre Trudeau favoured such a retreat, partly because he regarded domestic matters as more critical, partly because the world had changed and he fancied himself a realist. In his first administration Trudeau had tried to reorient Canadian foreign policy, with limited success, when he initiated a foreign-policy review that was independent of External Affairs. This produced remarkably few new insights and avoided the thorniest of all questions: Canada's relationship with the United States. His major success had been to reduce Canada's military commitment to NATO, and to reduce generally the size of the Canadian military presence. Unilateral disarmament was no more seriously considered than was military expansion. In 1972 the government produced a policy document on Canadian–American relations that advocated a 'Third Option'. Instead of the status quo (option one), or even closer relations with the United States (option two), it recommended option three: less dependence on the Americans. But if Canada moved away from the Americans, where would it go? The obvious answer was to Europe, which was growing stronger day by day through the European Economic Community and was increasingly visualizing itself as a third world force in distinction to the Americans and the Russians. The trouble was that Canada had waited too long, and become too closely identified with the United States. Closer ties with European nations might have been forged in the days before the Common Market and European resurgence, but during that period Canada had backed the American horse, and could not change its bet now.

The fizzle of the European initiative left Canada little option, after 1975, but to return to closer ties with the United States. By this time the Americans had succeeded in disengaging themselves from their manifestly unpopular war in Vietnam and, despite the disaster of Watergate, were back in favour with Canada. If Canadians travelled everywhere around the world, they also travelled most often to the United States, particularly in the winter. Canadians continued their love-hate relationship with the Americans, but after the mid-seventies a Canada fully independent of American pressures was not often mooted as a serious possibility in circles of power.

Apart from the perennial concern over trade figures, and the occasional international conference attended by the Prime Minister, Canada's relations outside North American assumed a very low profile during the eighties. Some attempt was made to gain political mileage from Prime Minister Trudeau's increasing international stature, particularly in comparison with that of Joe Clark; but while Trudeau always performed well at international events his heart was seldom in them. Canadians seemed to understand instinctively that Canada was not a major world player and expected very little from foreign-policy initiatives. The negotiation and acceptance of the Free Trade Agreement with the Americans, of course, signalled to everyone that Canada was even more closely bound to the United States.

The key international events impinging on Canada in the 1980s were ones over which the nation had absolutely no control. The first was 'glasnost', the process of liberation from repressive Communism in the Soviet Union, associated with Mikhail Gorbachev. The Soviet regime had been gradually opening up for decades. *Détente* between the USSR and the US had been achieved in the early 1970s, greatly altering the old Cold War antagonisms and alliances. But no one was prepared for the rapid changes of the later 1980s, as the Russians made clear that they were no longer prepared to prop up unpopular governments in Eastern Europe and wanted to shift their own internal priorities in what could only be described as capitalistic and democratic directions. The most obvious symbol of collapse was the razing of the Berlin Wall—which was demolished, along with the government of East Germany, in November 1989, clearing the way for German reunification in late 1990. It was still too soon to celebrate the death of Communism, but clearly many of the old assumptions of international trade and diplomacy were up for grabs at the end of the 1980s. Certainly Canada's principal formal link with Europe—the North Atlantic Treaty Organization—was under considerable challenge as the Russians offered to disarm and the Warsaw Pact disintegrated.

A reduction of tension in Europe did not necessarily mean that the world had been saved for democracy. As if to demonstrate the fragility of international peace, in the summer of 1990 the Iraqi army invaded Kuwait, one of the small independent and oil-rich principalities on the Persian Gulf. The world witnessed not only a *coup d'état* in terms of the occupation itself, but the unusual spectacle of American-Russian co-operation at the United Nations, and elsewhere, in opposition to Saddam Hussein's move. With Russian approval, President George Bush sent American forces to the Persian Gulf with the object of preventing Iraq from taking over more oil states and, eventually, forcing the Iraqis out of Kuwait by military means. Canada contributed three ancient destroyers to the international force assembling in the Gulf in opposition to Iraq—another 'three tokens'—although in fairness, the vessels were the best the Canadian forces could muster. The Iraqi takeover of Kuwait naturally caused the price of oil to increase almost instantly from $20 a barrel—a stable price throughout the 1980s—to $35.

The price of oil brings us back full circle to the early 1970s. Whether this price increase and more to follow would force Canadians in the 1990s to rethink their lifestyles and their economy—as in the end they had not been required to do in the 1970s—was another matter. While many of Canada's worst economic problems were caused by international developments beyond the nation's control, and others could be resolved only by collective rethinking and behaviour, Canadians understandably preferred to focus on government policy. In so doing they may instinctively have recognized a basic flaw in the Private Enterprise mentality: the assumption that the invisible hand of the market actually worked to everyone's advantage. In hard times, few wanted to chance the benevolence of that invisible hand.

Society and Culture in an Age of Retrenchment, Confusion, and Diffusion, 1972-1990

On 28 May 1971 a seventeen-year-old black teenager named Sandford Seale left a church-hall dance in Sydney, Nova Scotia, to make his way home before a midnight curfew. Walking through Wentworth Park at about 11:40 p.m., he met another seventeen-year-old, Donald Marshall, Jr. Sometime between then and midnight Sandy Seale was fatally stabbed, dying in hospital about twenty hours later. Although Donald Marshall had called the ambulance and reported to police that he and Seale had been assaulted by two older men (whom he described in considerable detail), the police investigation quickly focused on Marshall himself, who had a reputation as an Indian 'troublemaker'. Witnesses were persuaded that Marshall had been the assailant, alternative evidence was ignored, and the young Micmac was arrested and charged with murder on 4 June. Like the Sydney police, the Crown prosecutor ignored a file full of conflicting evidence and testimony. Defence counsel, although well-paid and competent criminal lawyers, did not bother to ask the Crown to disclose its case or the contradictions in it. Compounding matters, the trial judge limited the cross-examination of important witnesses and refused to permit other important testimony in Marshall's favour to be heard. Not surprisingly, Marshall was convicted and sentenced to life imprisonment.

Within days of the Marshall conviction the Sydney Police Department was presented with evidence that not Donald Marshall but Roy Ebsary (who fit the description of the man Marshall said had attacked Seale) had committed

Donald Marshall in 1982 after
he had been released from
prison following eleven years
of confinement. Canapress
Photo Service.

the murder. A cursory police investigation of the new testimony was conducted, but neither its existence nor its inconclusive results were communicated to Marshall's lawyers before they appealed the conviction. For its part, the appeal did not properly represent the extent of the court's interference with the defence, and the junior counsel who researched the appeal in the Halifax office of the Department of Attorney General, while he recognized judicial error, did not pursue the question because defence counsel had not raised it. The appeal was thus summarily rejected.

Marshall's case was re-examined at least three more times while he was in prison. On the third such occasion, in 1982, Marshall was interviewed in Dorchester Penitentiary by RCMP investigators after testimony that Ebsary had boasted about stabbing young Seale. Marshall provided new details that indicated he and Seale had been involved in attempted robbery when the stabbing occurred. The RCMP reinvestigation would in the long run lead to Marshall's release and acquittal, but in the short run it totally failed to evaluate the behaviour of the Sydney Police Department in the original investigation. Finally, on 29 July 1982, the Nova Scotia Court of Appeal permitted an application for bail for Donald Marshall and he was released. Because he had never admitted culpability and was released on bail rather than paroled, the institutional structure of the system provided Marshall with absolutely no assistance or counselling as he emerged from eleven years of confinement.

Donald Marshall's lawyer in 1982 insisted that Marshall be acquitted rather than pardoned, and the Nova Scotia Court of Appeal decided on a procedure that literally forced Marshall to prove his innocence. It heard the evidence of seven witnesses in early December 1982 and re-examined older files and transcripts. On 10 May 1983 it reversed Marshall's 1971 conviction and entered a verdict of acquittal. The appeal court insisted that 'no reasonable jury could', on the evidence before it, find Donald Marshall Jr, guilty of the murder of Sandy Seale. The court had been asked to deal only with the conviction. But it went on in its ruling to comment that 'any miscarriage of justice is...more apparent than real', and insisted that Marshall's 'untruthfulness through this whole affair contributed in large measure to his conviction', thus introducing an element of reluctance in its judgement while at the same time absolving the Nova Scotia justice system of responsibility for his conviction and imprisonment. Moreover, the Court of Appeal's unnecessary comments, particularly its acceptance of his 1982 statement regarding the attempted robbery, obviously did not fully exonerate Marshall. As a subsequent royal commission observed: 'Having concluded that Marshall was involved in a robbery attempt, the Court then took it upon itself to blame him for not confessing to this criminal offence—one with which he had not been charged—in order to win his freedom on another charge, of which he was not guilty.'[1]

The case did not end with Marshall's acquittal. Concerned citizens asked the government of Nova Scotia in 1983 to institute a public inquiry into the affair, but the request was rejected without serious consideration by the Deputy Attorney General. On a number of occasions the Nova Scotia Attorney General's Department subsequently refused to assist Marshall and his lawyers in obtaining the information and evidence they required to gain compensation, and worked actively to keep the compensation figure as low as possible. As a result, Marshall was awarded some $270,000 to drop all claims he might have against the government, a figure substantially lower than he might otherwise have received. After three trials, Roy Ebsary was finally convicted of Sandy Seale's death and sentenced to three years in prison; in 1986 his sentence was reduced by the Court of Appeal to one year. Finally, on 28 October 1986 the Nova Scotia government appointed a royal commission to examine the Marshall case. It heard 67 witnesses over 36 days in Sydney, beginning in September 1987, and another 52 witnesses during 53 days of public testimony in Halifax. The public hearings produced nearly 17,000 pages of transcript evidence, and the commission launched its own research program into race and the criminal-justice system in Nova Scotia, which resulted in a number of major documents and studies.

The final report of the commission, released late in 1989, concluded:

The criminal justice system failed Donald Marshall, Jr. at virtually every turn from his arrest and wrongful conviction for murder in 1971 up to, and even beyond, his acquittal by the Court of Appeal in 1983. The tragedy of the failure is compounded by evidence that this miscarriage of justice could—and should—have been prevented, or at least corrected quickly, if those involved in the system had carried out their duties in a professional and/or competent manner. That they did not is due, in part at least, to the fact that Donald Marshall, Jr. is a Native.[2]

The 'Marshall case' had dragged on for nearly twenty years. It did not end even with the royal commission report of 1989, which was criticized for pulling its punches about the extent of the 'cover-up' by provincial police officials and civil servants. The chairman of the commission, the chief justice of Newfoundland, had also been associated (although never personally involved) with another bureaucratic cover-up in his own province, connected with sexual abuse at the Mount Cashel orphanage. Above all, the Marshall case demonstrated that the judicial system of Nova Scotia not only operated against visible minorities, but was entirely capable of ignoring abuse until evidence of its existence became overwhelming. The sadly consistent findings of other public enquiries across the nation—including the Aboriginal Justice Inquiry in Manitoba (1991)—suggested that the Canadian judicial system itself had become abusive.

The older verities that had so painfully been constructed, particularly since 1939, appeared to be falling apart. For pessimists, much of life in post-1972 Canada appeared to be in a state of disintegration and collapse, while optimists spoke of diffusion and reorientation. If Canadian society seemed often to be in disarray, so in its own way did Canadian culture. Canada was no longer in a period of building a national consensus, but seemed instead in the process of demolishing one.

⟿⟿ Abuse and Self-Indulgence

Canadian society in the seventies and eighties appeared to oscillate—some would say it vacillated, others that it staggered—between abuse (often violent) of others and extreme self-indulgence. While superficially the two tendencies seemed quite disparate, they really represented the two extremes of a continuum that suggested the unsettled and even decadent nature of life in the era. As the Italian Marxist Antonio Gramsci had put it more than half a century earlier in another context: 'The old is dying and yet the new cannot be born. In this interregnum, a variety of morbid symptoms appear.' Abuse of others and self-indulgence were both the products of alienation. They were also linked to the power of the media, which in the one case publicized what had long been occurring beneath the surface, and in the other produced new consumer fads, fashions, and even needs.

Whether abuse actually increased in incidence became a hotly debated topic among both experts and the public. The general professional consensus was that it probably had not greatly altered in extent. What had certainly changed, of course, was the attention paid to abuse (by society's institutions and by the media) and thus the likelihood of its being reported to somebody.

Pressures by collective minorities to achieve genuinely equal treatment for their members—under the Canadian Charter of Rights—played an important role here as well. Racial and sexual abuses that might have gone unrecognized in previous generations were now openly publicized, if not resolved. In 1990 a schoolteacher in Alberta was removed from the classroom, after a controversial trial, for teaching racial hatred; another teacher was removed in 1991 in New Brunswick for similar reasons, but without trial. A series of incidents across the nation, including the Donald Marshall case, demonstrated that both the social-service and legal systems, as visible minorities had always claimed, were loaded against them and rife with racism. In 1991 Manitoba's Aboriginal Justice Inquiry was extremely critical of the police and the courts in that province. Priests and teaching brothers in Newfoundland were accused and convicted of sexual abuses against children. In the later 1980s hundreds of Canadians—many of them raised in institutions such as orphanages and boarding schools—complained publicly that they had been sexually abused by teachers and other authority figures. Sexual abuse of children, often incestuous in nature, was increasingly brought to light, sometimes by authors confronting experiences of childhood abuse in painful memoirs. Wife-beating—for decades the most common domestic crime on the police blotter—greatly increased in incidence and public concern. On 6 December 1989 a lone gunman, apparently a misogynist, killed fourteen female engineering students at the École Polytechnique in Montreal. This horrifying event occurred near the close of a year in which, according to one estimate, over 32,000 Canadian women had been raped.

Not surprisingly, much of the abuse was directed against the less powerful—children, women, aboriginal people, and visible minorities—by traditional authority figures ranging from fathers to pastors to teachers to policemen. On one level it was possible to take solace in the fact that such malign behaviour was now being recognized and addressed. On another it was possible to argue that what had changed was not authority behaviour but society's willingness to tolerate its worst extremities. But on yet a third level both the extent of the abuse and the undermining of authority to which it contributed were distressing. Canadians could no longer believe, as before, that they were all 'good guys' living in the 'Peaceable Kingdom'. Nor could they believe in the inherent beneficence of fathers, priests and ministers, teachers, doctors, policemen—or the entire judicial system. The revelations of the post-1972 period, particularly the 1980s, could only contribute to a growing national mood of sullen cynicism with regard to authority—which was hardly appeased by the behaviour of the politicians discussed in the previous chapter.

Another striking characteristic of Canadian society since the early 1970s, observed by many commentators, was the strong aura of personal self-absorption—called 'narcissism' by the American historian Christopher Lasch in *The Culture of Narcissism: American Life in an Age of Diminishing*

Expectations. Several factors helped account for this tendency on both sides of the border, including the economic situation of the post-Keynesian period, with its overheated short-term speculation, fundamental lack of optimism, and ultimate sense of the limits of growth. Opportunity did not exactly disappear—indeed, in the boom period of the 1980s it seemed to flourish— but its pursuit had to be quite ruthless and single-minded. Another factor was the Baby Boom, which meant that in the 1960s a much larger cohort of individuals had entered an expanding job market, dominated by relatively small numbers of 'Depression babies', and they progressed together through the seventies and eighties.

In many professions and occupations, entry-level employment became increasingly difficult to obtain as expansion ceased in the 1970s. At every career step the promotion lane was clogged by large numbers of relatively equally qualified individuals. Job prospects were further limited in most fields owing to the fact that most employees could now expect to live to retirement age, while mandatory retirement at age 65 was struck down by courts in several provinces as discriminatory practice. Younger Canadians responded to the challenges of finding an occupation by seeking further educational credentials and enrolling in courses in a continuing (but soon exhausted) series of temporarily underdeveloped but financially remunerative profes- sions, such as accountancy, pharmacy, and computer programming. Those who succeeded in making their way to the top rewarded themselves with luxuries and expensive toys. Others, stuck in the middle, had to settle for more affordable comforts. But the impoverished—including those dominant categories, single mothers, the aged, and aboriginal people—had little access to any kind of pleasure that was not physically harmful. Smoking, for example, became a class-influenced indulgence, far more in evidence at the bottom of the social scale than at the top.* The visible gulf between the poor and the remainder of society thus widened in a variety of ways.

Employment opportunity was not the only kind to shrink in the 1970s and 1980s, and the job market was not the only place where singleminded pursuit of goals was essential. For many, however, the problem was to find some fulfilling (or even time-consuming) goals worth pursuing. There seemed to be so little to cling to in the present world. The traditional indicators of 'instability'—marital breakdown, divorce, suicide, rape, crime—all appeared to be on the rise, and some new ones, such as large-scale sexual abuse of children, raised their ugly heads publicly for the first time. In 1974 a study had found that suicide had become Canada's fifth-ranked cause of 'early death' (i.e. death between the ages of 1 and 70), at a time when the annual rate of suicide per 100,000 Canadians was 11.9. By 1983 that rate had jumped to 15.1 and was still rising. In 1984 the National Task Force on

---

*And in 1992 Canada became the first country in the world to have more women than men smokers.

Suicide in Canada indicated that the causes were 'complex and multifactorial', but noted that 'inter-provincial studies appear to show that there has been a change in the contemporary fabric of society with lessened self-restraints and lowered morals (anomie). This coincides with a period of expanding economy, greater affluence as a whole, high-technology industrialization and increased unemployment.'[3] A similar explanation could have been advanced for many of Canada's 'morbidities'.

Another set of rising statistics related to criminal activity, particularly involving crimes of violence against the person. Between 1972 and 1987 the number of criminal-code offences reported in Canada rose from 1,192,984 to 2,955,510. The increase in these statistics, as in most others, was fairly constant, reflecting in part a growing population. However, the rates of increase were quite different for crimes against property and crimes of violence against people. For example, from 1982 to 1987 crimes against property increased 0.1 per cent, while crimes of violence increased 30.1 per cent. Complete data on the nature of violent crimes are available only through 1982, because changes in the Criminal Code in 1983 made it illegal to publish detailed statistics on sexual offences. Nevertheless, data for 1971-82 suggest that in all categories of violent offences, rates had increased dramatically, especially for crimes of sexual violence. Per 100,000 population, the rate for rape offences in 1971-82 jumped from 5.7 to 10.2 and for assault from 391.4 to 511.1. Homicide rates rose from 2.2/100,000 in 1972 to 2.7/100,000 in 1982. The slowest rate of increase occurred in indecent assault upon men. Victimization rates also displayed gender differences. Men were twice as likely as women to be victims of robbery or assault, slightly less likely to be victims of personal theft, and less than one-sixth as likely to be victims of sexual assault.[4]

The number of divorces in Canada was 32,389 in 1972 and 86,985 in 1987, representing a divorce rate of 649/100,000 among married women aged 15 years and over in 1972, and 1372.2/100,000 in 1987. The increase had been fairly constant, with a slight fall in 1984 and 1985 (perhaps reflecting economic conditions) and a compensating increase in 1986. While the proportion of those divorces involving couples without dependent children grew from 44.2 per cent in 1972 to 54.6 per cent in 1986, the absolute number of dissolved marriages involving dependent children grew from 15,546 in 1972 to 34,576 in 1986. By 1986 it was estimated that at least half of all Canadian children born after 1980 would at some point experience a broken home. Though not all marital separations and divorces left deep permanent scars on the children, all were at least temporarily traumatic and disruptive.

Ironically enough, legal protection for victims meant that adequate and accurate long-term data on crimes affecting women and children became difficult to obtain in the later 1980s. What Canada had instead was a series of well-publicized incidents that involved abuse of a wide range of victims. Perhaps the most shocking revelations came from Newfoundland, where a provincial inquiry in 1989 brought to light evidence of sexual abuse of children that had been ignored by the province's social service workers and covered up by its police and civil servants.[5] Few had been willing to blow the whistle on either the Christian brothers who ran Mount Cashel orphanage or the province's Catholic priests; and when the whole sordid business became public knowledge, the faithful turned against their Church with a vengeance, producing a veritable crisis of belief in that province.

In some ways traditional religion in Canada remained curiously unchanged during this period—though it seemed to be providing neither moral guidance nor solace for Canadians, especially among the young. In the 1981 census, over 90% of Canadians offered a religious affiliation to the census-takers, in almost all cases that of their parents. Nearly half (47.3%) described themselves as Roman Catholic, 41.2% as Protestant, and only 7.3% claimed to have 'No Religion'. Only Alberta and British Columbia had more than 10% of their people in the 'No Religion' category, at 11.5% and 20.5% respectively. Few Canadians displayed interest in any of the 'new' or alternative religious systems publicized during the 1960s: in the 1980s the country contained only 700 Scientologists, 450 Hare Krishnas, perhaps 600 Moonies, and 250 Children of God.[6] Protestant sectarianism of the evangelical or pentecostal variety made some gains, particularly in suburbia, but few inroads among members of the major institutional churches. Third World immigration did not greatly increase the percentages of other religions (non-Christian and non-Jewish) among the Canadian population, partly because many of the newcomers themselves came from Judeo-Christian backgrounds. At the same time, declaring a religious affiliation to a census-taker did not say very much about the state of religion in the country.

The percentage of Canadians who regularly attended religious services declined precipitously. The question 'Did you yourself happen to go to church or synagogue in the last seven days?' elicited the following responses: The fall-off began earlier with Protestants, but affected Catholics beginning in the late sixties and early seventies. Those Catholics who continued to attend Mass overwhelmingly approved the changes instituted by Pope John

Service Attendance, 1946 to 1986 (in percentages)

	1946	1965	1986
Roman Catholics	83	83	43
Protestants	60	32	27
All Canada	67	55	35

Source: Reginald W. Bibby, *Fragmented Gods: The Poverty and Potential of Religion in Canada* (Toronto, 1987), p. 17.

XXIII, but most non-practising Catholics complained about either what the Church was doing or what it had not yet done. The situation was particularly bad in Quebec. In that province 88% of Catholics in 1965 had attended Mass at least twice a month; that percentage was down to 38% in 1985. Figures for divorce, abortion, and the overall birth-rate indicated that most Québécois did not pay much attention to the teachings of their Church. According to the surveys most Canadians continued to believe in God, in the divinity of Christ, and in the standard belief system of Christianity. But while nearly two-thirds asserted belief in some sort of life after death, very few had any specific notion of what that belief meant.

In almost every religious denomination the young were less committed and knowledgeable than their elders, with the greatest discrepancies between young and old among Quebec Catholics. Secularization was growing, and while it did not alter traditional affiliations, it did greatly reduce the numbers of Canadians for whom traditional religion provided real meaning.[7] More to the point, nothing really had replaced the traditional churches in providing a sense of meaning. In one survey less than one-third of those who were asked 'How sure are you that you have found the answer to the meaning of life?' answered that they had any certainty at all.[8] Writers were already sensitive to the problem, and this *Angst* was one of the principle themes of Canadian fiction after 1972.

One can understand why nostalgia flourished for bygone periods of sup-posedly greater stability—for example, the 1950s. More leisure time pro-duced more need to fill it. In the 1980s those who were ambitious invested much of their leisure time in furthering their career prospects. Participation rates in sport activity and culture-making increased from their 1960s low-point, when spectatorism had reached its height, but many Canadians had little involvement in the outside world that was not directly connected with themselves. Even athletic activity was often justified in terms of health and longevity rather than community improvement. Sexual adventurism dwin-dled markedly in the 1980s, as the increasing incidence of AIDS, well publicized as a sexually transmitted disease, forced many out of the 'meet market' bars and back into the home. Television became one of the narcotics of the age, although the availability and use of drugs continued to increase steadily. Alcohol abuse continued unabated, along with substance abuse of many descriptions, including gasoline sniffing—and the use of steroids by athletes became common. Canada's most notorious drug abuser was the Olympic sprinter Ben Johnson (b. 1961), whose Gold Medal at Seoul in 1988 was ignominiously stripped from him for the use of steroids he initially denied but eventually admitted at another well-publicized public enquiry. The growing utilization of drugs of all kinds provided a link between abuse of others and extreme self-indulgence, demonstrating that people could abuse themselves as well as their fellow human beings.

The most dangerous drug of all was tobacco. Adults, especially those over forty, quit cigarettes in their concern for better health, and Canadians led the world in stopping smoking during the late 1980s, with a per-capita decrease in tobacco consumption of nearly thirty per cent between 1984 and 1990. Yet as late as 1986 nearly half a million Canadians under the age of nineteen annually smoked over $260 million worth of cigarettes a year, undeterred by prices often in excess of $4.00 per pack—rising to over $6.00 by 1990—and young smokers proved most resistant to the overall trend. The greatest increase of smokers in Canada occurred among those under fourteen, who were apparently immune to evidence of the addictive dangers of tobacco presented to them in school and on television. One calculation revealed that tobacco would ultimately kill eight times as many fifteen year-olds as automobile accidents, suicide, murder, AIDS, and drug abuse combined. But although few Canadians would begin smoking after age nineteen, the anti-smoking campaign—ostensibly aided by prohibitions against tobacco advertising and by enormous consumer taxes on the products—was fighting a losing battle. Young Canadians continued to abuse their bodies and minds with tobacco and other addictive products of all descriptions.[9]

While the trends of the late twentieth century were largely negative, there were occasional bright spots. Three of them were named Fox, Fonyo, and Hansen. Terry Fox (1958-81), having lost a leg to cancer, originated the 'Marathon of Hope', in which he would run across Canada with one artificial leg to raise money for, and public awareness of, cancer research. Fox began in St John's, Newfoundland, on 12 April 1980 and ended at Thunder Bay on 1 September when tests revealed further cancer. In the process, he inspired the world as well as Canada and the money he initially raised has increased substantially in annual commemorative runs since his death. Like Fox, Steve Fonyo (b. 1965) ran with an artificial leg. He finished his cross-country run 29 May 1985, also raising millions for cancer research. Rick Hansen (b. 1957) was a friend of Fox whose 'Man in Motion' tour around the world in a self-propelled wheelchair began on 21 March 1985 and ended on 22 May 1987. All three athletes raised public awareness of the courage and capabilities of the physically disabled. They also encouraged other young Canadians to look beyond themselves.

Social Trends

In many respects there was little that was surprising or unpredicted in the post-1970 period. The most obvious trend was the way in which the Baby Boom generation worked collectively through life's stages, creating dominant (and changing) trends in every decade. By 1990 the first of the Baby Boomers were beginning to contemplate retirement, and the problems of an aging Canada started to become more apparent, although they received considerably less public attention than the emergence in the 1980s of the new killer disease, AIDS. But both geriatrics and AIDS were far more commonly

Terry Fox running in northern Ontario in the summer of 1980. Canapress Photo Service.

publicized and understood than were the ongoing health problems of Canada's aboriginal minorities. Canada's population continued to grow in size, the distribution of that population continued its westward movement, and the origins of Canada's immigrants were almost entirely in the Third World.[10] Poverty continued to be the most immediate problem for all too many Canadians, although it too had a low profile.

The Baby Boomers

The post-1970 decades, in many senses, have been dominated by the Baby Boom generation as it has moved through life. As we have seen, until 1970 the Baby Boomers had their chief impact on the educational system, but thereafter their influence has been felt in almost every aspect of Canadian society. Canada had 2 million teenagers in 1960, and over 3 million by 1975. The Baby Boomers, who hit the school systems in the 1950s and the universities in the 1960s, appeared in full force on the job market in the seventies and eighties and would thereafter reduce in number, thus theoretically lowering the entry-level pressure on employment. Not only did Baby Boomers put pressure on the employment system by their sheer numbers, but they were also far better qualified educationally than previous generations, and the qualifications and expectations for females were little different than for males. Unsurprisingly, not all were able to get the jobs for which they had prepared, particularly since both teaching and government employment had peaked in terms of numbers by the time the Boomers reached the market, and changing concepts about aging and retirement kept many older employees in the work force.

The largest cohort of Baby Boomers began their working lives in the 1970s, reaching mid-career in the 1980s. That fertility rates fell even further than forecasters had predicted was a result of the coincidence of a number of factors. Young women beginning careers were less willing to interrupt them to bear children and rear them. Moreover, the tightness of the job market combined with the increased consumer needs of the Boom generation to produce more childless working couples—the notorious DINK (Double Income, No Kids) families. The demands of parenting reduced what was regarded as the ideal number of children to two or one, and the increasing number of broken homes in the post-war years made adults fear both divorce *and* its effects on any children. In the later 1980s there was a slight resurgence of childbearing in some sectors of the population, as childless women of the Baby Boom generation discovered that their biological clocks would soon run down, though birth rates were consistently lower in Quebec than elsewhere in Canada.

By the 1980s the Baby Boomers were having a noticeable effect on housing, particularly in Toronto and Vancouver, which had attracted so many newcomers after 1970. In the early eighties the Boomers had become well enough established in their lives and careers that home ownership—especially of detached bungalows with green lawns—was now regarded as essential. Given the difficulties of building enough new detached housing within easy commuting distance of cities, the real-estate market inevitably took off during the decade and affected prices in surrounding districts. Thus in Scarborough, Ontario, the price of a typical three-bedroom detached bungalow rose from $71,700 in 1979 to $255,000 in 1989, while in Burnaby, British Columbia, similar accommodation rose from $76,500 to $215,000 in the same period.[11] The upward spiral was finally broken nationally by the depression of 1990. Prices could never return to previous figures, and even after the inevitable bust it was estimated that in the cities of premium-priced housing, less than a quarter of those seeking to purchase their first house could qualify for a mortgage.

The emergence of several sizeable groups with money to spend on nice things—'My Tastes Are Simple', read one popular bumper sticker, 'I Like the Best'—often because of double incomes and an absence of children, encouraged various advertising ploys. Aging Baby Boomers whose children had left home were one such population segment. Yuppies (young urban professionals—the acronym developed about 1984) were another. Many aging Boomers and Yuppies were also DINKS, although the term was usually used to refer to young careerist couples. Marketing strategies included slick consumer magazines distributed free to homes in targeted neighbourhoods with the appropriate demographics. Articles on various aspects of affluent lifestyles—home (re)decorating, gourmet foods, luxury travel—were some of the subjects featured. Advertisements were for such desirables as European cars. Focusing on carefully targeted audiences became a feature of market research and advertising campaigns in the 1980s. With the warning in their ears that the days of profitable consumer mass-marketing were numbered, advertisers and retailers sought a market 'niche' by offering goods and services for those who could afford them; such policies would prove disastrous when the economy slowed down in the 1990s.

The needs of those reaching mid-career and middle age were of especial interest. One of the most prevalent effects of aging is on vision. For those with normal eyesight, vision only begins deteriorating over the age of 40, although the deterioration is then fairly extensive, particularly at short range. One could thus safely predict an increased demand for eye-glasses, which suddenly became available in a wide variety of styles, some at luxury prices. But there was also a market for a host of other less essential products ranging from expensive books to special computer keyboards for those too vain to admit their problems with vision. Predictably, golf—which required no physical fitness and could be played by moneyed people of any age and state of health—became the growth sport of the later eighties. Finally, the Boomers continued their fascination with the pop and rock music of the fifties and sixties, when they were adolescents, and the musical-nostalgia industry thrived. Radio stations that had for decades tried to appeal to the kids suddenly shifted their programming to 'The Golden Oldies' in a blatant effort to capture the largest single audience segment: middle-aged Baby Boomers.

The Predictable Crisis: The Aging of Canada

The progressive aging of the Canadian population—the 'process whereby a population is made up increasingly of older age groups'[12]—was neither a new development of the post-1970 period nor a distinctly Canadian one. If the Canadian population had been consistently living longer for nearly one hundred years, this was a world-wide phenomenon generally associated with countries in a stage of advanced industrial development. In terms of aging, Canada was not, by the 1970s, as far down the road as many other industrialized countries of Europe, nor was it likely to catch up. It has been established that by the year 2000 the percentage of Canada's population over 65 will still not have reached Sweden's percentage in 1965 or that of the United States in

1935.[13] Indeed, because of the Baby Boom and immigration, the percentage of the Canadian population over 65 had not altered dramatically over the entire century, increasing only from 5 per cent in 1901 to 9.7 per cent by 1981. What was new was the attention being given to the problem of aging and the elderly, especially after 1976, when the Science Council of Canada published *Perceptions 2: Implications of the Changing Age Structure of the Canadian Population*. The emerging conception of a 'crisis' was primarily connected with what seemed to be the increased costs associated with the elderly in the welfare states of Europe.

While the numbers of elderly grew, change also occurred in the proportion of the population under age 14—from nearly 20% in 1901 to less than 13% by 1976—a function more of declining fertility rates than of declining death rates. What had altered in Canada, therefore, was not only the total number of people over 65, but their relationship to those presumed to be still in the labour force. While such measures as 'dependency ratios' are not perfect ways of depicting demographic trends, they are both suggestive and illustrative because they indicate the pressures on institutions and facilities in the social arena. When the proportion of the Canadian population over 18 and under 65—younger children and older people being theoretically assumed not to be productive members of the work force—at the turn of the century is compared with the present, it is evident that there has been remarkably little change. The proportions of the traditional working-age population and their dependants remained relatively stable over this century. But while the number of children has declined, the number of the aged has increased, resulting in a great alteration in the meaning of dependency. In 1911 the dependency ratio for the elderly (the proportion of elderly to the proportion theoretically productive) was 8.8:100. By 1983 it was 18:100; and if birth rates do not alter, one prediction is for a dependency ratio of 52:100 by 2031: in other words, 52 people over age 65 for every 100 between 18 and 64. Of course not all of the increased 'elderly' will be dependent and non-productive; but in terms of sheer numbers many more will be so.

Population aging means that Canada's social responsibilities are increasingly shifting from providing for the young to providing for the elderly, a change that still requires a good deal of conceptual and physical reorientation. The shift may produce a much higher demand for health-care facilities, for example, than for day-care services, but only if it continues to be presumed that the very young are cared for in the home and the very old outside it. The higher demand on health care for the elderly may be perceived to be a constantly escalating expense, but only because society has never attempted to calculate the cost of caring for the young at home in the same way it calculates the cost of hospitals and nursing homes. When one considers actual public expenditures on the young and the old, it appears to cost only one-third as much to provide schools as senior health-care. But if the total expenditure on child-rearing is taken into account, the young cost substantially more than the old. Many experts have predicted major conflict 'between groups which have catered to the needs of or benefited from a youthful population and those whose interests lie with the elderly.'[14] This struggle—expressed as a contest for funding between education and health care in the various provinces—was apparent by the later 1980s.

As for pension plans, their actuarial basis was threatened in the 1980s because they were always founded on the notion that the working generation supports the retired one. Many governments, moreover, raided their own pension funds for ongoing expenses, and were forced to replenish them through current levies. One study argued that by the year 2021 the funds required for public pensions will be three and one-half times greater than in 1976, given the continuation of the 1976 level of payments. Without a high level of pension support (and reform of the system to provide adequate pensions for segments of the population, such as women, not constantly employed throughout their working lives), the elderly—especially elderly women, who constitute a disproportionate number of the old because they outlive men by nearly a decade—would become an even larger proportion of Canadians below the so-called poverty line. In 1986, for example, 46.1 per cent of unattached females over the age of 65 were living below the poverty line.[15]

Researchers continue to argue over the medical implications of increased life expectancy. Many insist that improved health care prolongs life more than it improves its quality. Others have maintained that there will be an eventual 'compression of morbidity', in which improved diet and exercise in their earlier years will mean that the elderly will be subject to fewer disabilities associated with old age. All these arguments, however, can only be tested over time. Meanwhile the Canadian health-care system has been very slow to respond to the new conditions. Although Canadians have been more inclined to institutionalize their elderly than most European nations, in 1986 only nine per cent of Canada's elderly were able to be accommodated in nursing homes, and far too many were staying in hospitals awaiting admission to underfunded chronic-care facilities. The trend to 'home care' of the elderly has been extremely limited, and has not developed the sorts of supportive mechanisms necessary to enable it to replace public institutionalization. In most provinces funding for home-care assistance for the elderly remains considerably less stable than funding for chronic-care facilities, for example. It has been extremely difficult to persuade Canadians that the same energy should be expended on the dependent old, whose lives have run their course, as on the dependent young, whose lives remain before them. Moreover, increasing numbers of Canadians find themselves 'sandwiched' between the generations requiring care, with youngsters and oldsters competing for limited financial and emotional resources.

Although the emergence of the problem of the elderly was quite predictable, Canada was very tardy in facing it seriously and by 1990 still had not come to terms with many of its implications. Except in certain limited areas, such as retirement housing, the elderly have still not been perceived by most

Canadian businesses as a separate market with distinctive needs. Given our capitalist system, it could well be argued that until the nation's businessmen understand about the aged, nothing much will change. At the same time, most experts are persuaded that there need be no crisis in Canada over the aging of the population, since total dependency ratios will continue to fall until the twenty-first century. But while the nation may have a period of grace to work out new relationships, it will have to do better than it had done by 1990 if it is to make the transition from caring for the young to caring for the old.

The Unanticipated Crisis: AIDS   The demographic aging of the Canadian population was a condition that could have been predicted from long-term trends. Nothing, however, could have prepared Canadians for the onslaught of the acquired immune deficiency syndrome, commonly known as AIDS, which burst on the scene in the early 1980s. Since the mid-nineteenth century, communicable disease had proved the most susceptible to advances in medical science. Tuberculosis, pneumonia, diphtheria, scarlet fever, influenza, smallpox, and typhoid—all major killers and all with potential for becoming epidemic—were eliminated from the list of serious communicable diseases. Even polio had been conquered through vaccination. The first case of AIDS in Canada probably occurred in Montreal in 1978, but went undiagnosed because nobody knew what to look for. Not until 1981 did the Center for Disease Control of the United States Public Health Service begin receiving enough reports of cases that a world-wide epidemic of an immunodeficiency disease caused by an infectious virus was recognized. In 1982 the Laboratory Centre for Disease Control in Ottawa began tracking the disease in Canada, although not until 1983 did the Institut Pasteur in France claim to have isolated one of the new viruses involved.[16]

There are three major means of transmitting the immunodeficiency viruses (HIV) that are believed to cause AIDS: through sexual contact, through parenteral means (such as blood transfusions or contaminated needles and syringes), and through perinatal transmission (from an infected mother to an infant). The majority of cases reported in Canada (and the United States) have involved homosexual men, but increasing numbers of heterosexuals have contracted the disease. As of this writing there is no cure for anyone who has contracted HIV, and avoidance of transmission is not only the best but the only strategy. Most of those unfortunate individuals infected with HIV through the receipt of blood products were haemophiliacs continually at risk in a period when the dangers were not clearly understood. HIV-antibody screening procedures were not routinely introduced in Canadian blood banks until 1985, but since then the risk of such transmission has been almost totally eliminated in this country. Unfortunately needle contamination and unsafe blood transfusion remain common causes of transmission in many other countries of the world.

Although the belief—commonly held in the earlier 1980s— that AIDS was caused only by certain homosexual practices was soon discredited, the disease was still connected with promiscuous sexuality of all kinds. This relationship was unavoidable, given the nature of the campaign mounted by Canadian authorities to prevent its spread. It has been difficult to compile data on the present and future extent of AIDS in Canada, partly because of its associations with promiscuity and homosexuality, and partly because it has not been possible to measure the extent to which the general population has been infected. Present evidence suggests that about one-third of HIV-infected persons will develop AIDS within seven years, and there are some suggestions that certain lifestyles increase risk. But whether all HIV-infected persons will eventually develop AIDS is not clear. Estimates in 1987 revealed that 30,000 Canadians were HIV-infected, and over 1,300 cases of AIDS had been reported. The per-person annual hospital costs of AIDS patients varied in 1987 from $50,000 in Vancouver to $75,000 in Quebec, excluding the costs of drugs before hospitalization, and the total direct cost of HIV infection in 1987 was estimated at $150 million.

Because AIDS is mainly a sexually transmitted disease, with a high incidence among homosexuals and the sexually adventurous, it became a favourite target for moralists in the 1980s. Many concerns were expressed over the decade that AIDS would encourage a judgemental response from Canadians to both homosexuality and sexual freedom, but they were not borne out in the available survey literature. While surveys indicate that relatively few Canadians were morally judgemental, they also demonstrated much ignorance about AIDS and its prevention. Moreover, Canadians responded far less vigorously to the fear of infection than one might have expected, given the media attention AIDS had received. In one recent (1989) Canadian study, for example, 63% of those questioned knew that sexual intercourse was the most common way of becoming infected with AIDS, and about half identified homosexuals as the most likely people to become infected. Virtually 90% knew that the best prevention was safe sex, with 40.5% regarding condoms as 'very effective', while 77.5% and 81.0% regarded not having intercourse and having sex with one partner in a long-term relationship respectively as 'very effective' means of prevention. At the same time, however, only 54% of male and 41% of female respondents had changed their sexual behaviour because of the risk of AIDS infection; truly safe sex was far from the Canadian norm. Not only did large numbers of respondents practise no caution, but the study suggested a tendency, particularly among males, for people with more knowledge to take more risks.[17]

Abortion

Undoubtedly the most heavily contested health-care issue of the seventies and eighties was neither AIDS nor Aging, but Abortion. Never an unequivocally feminist issue, abortion had a tendency to divide women in ways that

Dr Henry Morgentaler in Toronto after he had been granted a stay of proceedings on abortion-related charges in September 1986. Morgentaler and Dr Nikki Colodny, on his right, had been arrested at their homes earlier in the day. Canapress Photo Service.

day-care or equal pay did not. At the same time, pro and anti positions on the issue of abortion on demand became inextricably interwoven with larger feminist questions. By and large, militant feminists were pro-abortion, while the anti-abortion faction was often composed of women who still believed that their place was in the home. Ironically, the individual who galvanized these positions was not a woman but Henry Morgentaler (b. 1923), a Polish-Canadian Jewish doctor who had survived the Holocaust and made the provision of therapeutic abortions his life's work.

While Canadian abortion law was liberalized in 1969, when abortions performed by doctors in hospitals were permitted if a committee of physicians decided that the pregnancy would endanger life or health, Dr Morgentaler went well beyond these conditions, carrying out abortions in private Montreal clinics. In 1973 he revealed that he had performed over 5000 abortions, and as a result was charged in Quebec under Article 251 of the Criminal Code and found not guilty by a jury. He was imprisoned after the Quebec Court of Appeal overturned the jury verdict in 1974, but two further trials in Quebec led to acquittal, the juries in both cases apparently accepting his arguments that his actions were necessary because the law denied women equal access to abortion.[18] Attacks on Morgantaler shifted to other cities as he deliberately expanded his clinics. He and two colleagues were again acquitted in Toronto in 1984 of conspiring to procure a miscarriage, and upon appeal by Ontario the Supreme Court of Canada in 1988 declared the abortion law in conflict with the Charter of Rights. It held at that time that 'forcing a woman, by threat of criminal sanction, to carry a fetus to term. . .is a profound interference with a woman's body and thus an infringement of security of the person.'

The arguments of the anti-abortion faction came to centre on the rights of the fetus, an issue further complicated by new developments in reproductive technology. The ethical consequences of such scientific techniques as in-vitro fertilization and genetic engineering were not thoroughly aired, and there was little public consensus about them. Equally worrying was the fact that scientific advances were being made under conditions that showed precious little concern for either ethical or feminist concerns. In any event, by the late 1980s abortion had become such a divisive issue that Parliament proved quite incapable of new legislation on the matter: a free vote on a bill to put abortion back into the Criminal Code failed in early 1991 after a tie. Meanwhile the incidence of therapeutic abortions in Canada had stabilized in the early 1980s. The rate of abortion had increased steadily from the 1969 liberalization to 1980, when it peaked at 10.7 per 1,000 females. By 1987 the rate had become fairly constant at 9.7 per thousand and showed every sign of remaining there.[19]

Canada's Native Peoples

In 1990 there were some 450,000 status Indians in Canada. Two-thirds of them lived on 2,300 reserves in 596 registered bands, and the remainder resided chiefly in larger southern cities such as Winnipeg. The numbers of non-status Indians and Métis are harder to estimate, but probably total at least 500,000 across Canada. Despite increased levels of media attention, governmental expenditure, and native self-consciousness, the demographic realities of native life—while improving—continued through the seventies and eighties to recall conditions in nations generally regarded as the most backward on the planet.

Between 1980 and 1985 infant mortality among Canadian Indians ran at nearly three times the overall national average, at 19.6 deaths per 1,000 live births versus 7.9 per 1,000 in the population as a whole. Among the Cree-Ojibwa in northwestern Ontario, overall mortality rates in the early 1980s were twice the national average. Although infectious diseases among the Cree-Ojibwa accounted for only a small proportion of deaths, a native person was more than four times as likely as an ordinary Canadian to die from them. Other diseases associated with industrialization, such as diabetes, increased markedly after 1950, suggesting that some Indians had 'caught up' with the worst features of civilization. Tuberculosis rates on prairie reserves in the 1970s ran at 161 per 100,000, while comparable figures in the African nation of Tanzania were only 50 per 100,000. Native life-expectancy continued to be ten years less on average than the overall Canadian figure, reaching an average of 66 years by 1990.

Indian death rates from accidents and violence continued well above the national average, and the percentage of natives who died from such causes was on the increase. In 1964, for example, 22% of Indian deaths resulted from accidents and violence, while by 1990 the figure was up to 35% (the national figure was 5%). Natives were more than four times more likely to be murdered than were Canadians as a whole. In the Sioux Lookout area of northwestern Ontario, only in the categories of accidental falls and motor-vehicle accidents were natives no more likely than other Canadians to experience accidental or violent death. In most categories, such as house fires and drowning, native rates far outdistanced Canadian figures. Native suicide rates, especially among young men, ran well above national norms and reached epidemic proportions in some communities. In one Alberta community of Cree reserves made relatively wealthy by oil, the suicide rate in the early 1980s ran over eighty times the national average. Alcohol and substance abuse too continued to be serious problems. Levels of smoking remained higher than national norms, and gasoline sniffing became 'a favourite form of mood alteration among socially deprived children' throughout the Canadian North.[20]

Particularly after 1945 substantial improvements in many categories of native health had been brought about by developing new ways of delivering health care to native peoples, particularly in remote locations. Whether those health services were a matter of treaty right or of humanitarian generosity was for long a contentious issue, with the Department of National Health and Welfare (which in 1945 assumed responsibility for Indian health care from Indian Affairs) often insisting that it did not provide these services 'as a matter of Indian right'. With the arrival of the principle of provincially supported medical treatment in the 1960s, the question moved from federal benefits to the federal provision of benefits beyond ordinary universality. After 1970, however, the introduction of the principle of universality into Canadian medical care softened much of this discussion over rights, at the same time that it led to a shifting of much health-care responsibility from the federal government to the provinces.

Nevertheless, the native peoples continued to lag badly behind the average Canadian in terms of health status. As early as 1973 some experts were warning that Indian health care could not be considered in isolation from either other factors of native existence or the overall context of Canadian development.[21] By end of the 1980s the experts were insisting that limits had been reached in improving native health through concentration on health-care systems. In 1988, for example, one scholar asserted categorically that 'present-day Indian health services in the remote subarctic are comparable to those received by most Canadians and, in many respects, are superior in terms of the accessibility to and availability of basic services.'[22] The result, he maintained, was 'a situation where a high-quality health-care system is found in a region that rates very poorly in terms of its health status.' The gap was no longer a matter of health service, but of a lower standard of living and socio-economic development. Attacking these larger social problems would obviously be much more difficult than improving health care, particularly since native activists had never contested the dynamics of health care as vigorously as they did other governmental policies, such as education.

Population Growth and Shifts

Many of the developments in Canada's population growth after 1971 merely perpetuated long-term trends, and most others had been predicted. The total population of the country continued to expand from 21,568,311 in 1971 to 25,923,300 in 1988, although the rate of growth—which had peaked at 2.8% in 1956—continued to slow thereafter, reaching less than 1 (.08)% in 1986. The population of Canada's cities kept growing faster than that of the country as a whole, with the average growth rate of its twenty-five largest metropolitan areas in 1986 at 5.9% (as compared with .08% for the entire country). Most of the largest increases came in suburban sections. The fastest-growing metropolitan area was Saskatoon, partly reflecting the continuing depopulation of prairie farms. The regional distribution of Canada's population also continued to shift westward. In 1971 the Atlantic provinces contained 9.54% and they, plus Quebec, represented 37.5% of the total

Immigrant Arrivals by Continent of Last Residence, 1972 and 1987

REGION	1972	1987
Europe	51,293	8,547
Africa	8,308	8,501
Australasia	2,148	753
North & Central America [including the Caribbean]	31,836	26,067
South America	11,057	10,801
Oceania	787	1,074
Asia	23,325	67,337
	122,006	152,098

Source: *Canada Year Book 1989* (Ottawa, 1989).

Canadian population. By 1988 the Atlantic provinces had fallen to just under 9% of the total, and they plus Quebec were only 34.5% of the total. The big provincial gainers were Alberta and British Columbia, up from 17.7% of the total in 1971 to 20.8% in 1988. Preliminary results from the 1991 Census indicate that Quebec's share of the total Canadian population had fallen from 29 per cent in 1971 to just over 25 per cent in 1991.

While the Canadian population continued to drift off the farms, westward, and into the cities, it also became increasingly dependent for its growth on immigration, which continued its shift away from the highly industrialized preferred nations of western Europe that had represented Canada's earlier sources of newcomers.

The new immigrants, largely from Third World areas, continued to prefer urban destinations in Ontario and the West, eschewing Atlantic Canada and Quebec. They also brought new cultures and new languages into Canada's cities, providing new social problems in the process.

Poverty and the Limits of the Welfare State

Poverty, like death, was omnipresent in Canada in the 1970s and 1980s. According to official sources poverty's incidence decreased over the era, although some experts disagreed. In 1969 nearly one-quarter of all Canadians (4,851,000) lived below the poverty line, while in 1986 that figure had officially declined to 14.9% (3,689,000). There was, of course, a direct correlation between the behaviour of the economy and the poverty statistics. The recession of the early eighties put nearly a million Canadians back on the poverty rolls, and the prosperity of the later eighties temporarily took them off again. The depth and extent of the economic collapse of 1990 would control the figures for the opening years of the decade, but the trend was likely to be upward. The federal government proclaimed proudly a substantial reduction in poverty among the nation's senior citizens, which it credited to the Guaranteed Income Supplement for the low-income elderly and the full operation of the Canada and Quebec Pension Plans. But it also admitted that certain groups were 'particularly vulnerable to poverty'. Such vulnerability cut across lines of age, gender, race, and region.[23]

The so-called 'feminization of poverty' was one long-term trend that stabilized during the 1980s. But it hardly went away. Families led by women were over four times as likely to be poor as families headed by males, and women ran a higher risk of poverty than men in almost all categories, although with considerable variation. In 1986 women comprised 71.7 per cent of seniors below the poverty line. Single mothers with children were five times as likely to be poor as mothers in two-parent families. Single native mothers were even worse off. In 1980 the average income for all native single parents was $4,000 less than for all Canadian single female parents.[24] Poverty had not only age and gender characteristics. The average family income for all natives hovered around the poverty line throughout the period. Residents of certain provinces, notably Newfoundland, were more likely to be poor. The lower the level of education of a family head, the greater the chance of falling below the poverty line.

Although it was possible to argue that the state had reduced the number of poor in Canada through various social-welfare programs, it was clear that government policy had not in any sense redistributed income. One government publication in 1988 admitted that official data for raw income demonstrated that it was 'distributed in a highly unequal and regressive manner, and there has been little progress in redistributing income over the last thirty-five years.'[25] Families in the top income group had six times the share of total income of the poor. On the other hand, the gap between rich and poor was to some extent reduced by government transfer programs and income taxes, although there was considerable debate over their impact, particularly the direction they would take during the 1980s. By the early 1970s the basic blocks of the Canadian version of the welfare state were all in place, but as one commentator put it in 1987, 'The social role of the Canadian state is a comparatively modest one, representing a restrained response to the social insecurities of industrial life.'[26] Although Canadian spending on social programs came to equal that in the United States in terms of amounts per capita of Gross National Product, at the point that cut-backs began to be seriously debated it had not reached levels of per-capita expenditures in many European countries.

Pressure for continual expansion of the welfare state came from many directions before 1980, one scholar has noted, because income security became 'an instrument for sustaining or enhancing the *political* power of the federal government' since it was the 'only direct, beneficial link between Ottawa and the public.'[27] After 1980, however, contrary tendencies became apparent and eventually dominant. Canada's unsolved economic and social problems continued to produce demands for expansion of income security. But with the erosion of government revenue and intense international competition, the federal government came increasingly to focus on restraint and privatization. The latter tendency was part of an international movement that assigned responsibility for national economic and social decline to welfare-state expenditure.[28] As of this writing, no major element of the existing welfare net has actually been eliminated, and there was even improvement in increased pension benefits for the elderly. But the government cumulatively reduced the universality of the system of family benefits through the so-called 'claw-back', by which the income-tax system took back benefits (such as Family Allowance) paid to Canadians with higher incomes. In unemployment compensation, revised regulations increased the waiting period and made it more difficult to use unemployment funds as income supplements in seasonal industries. The notorious GST was a thoroughly regressive tax that hit harder at lower-income than higher-income families, despite the income supplements paid to the poorest Canadians. One of the major points of universality, of course, was that it had prevented governments from deciding arbitrarily on where to draw the line, as well as obviating the urge to distinguish the 'deserving' from the 'undeserving' among those classes that it chose to assist. Universality also was a less ambiguous way of expressing social rights.

When other factors were added to the mix—such as constitutional problems and international trade agreements (the United States tends to view Canadian social-assistance programs as indistinguishable from government subsidization of economic enterprise, which runs contrary to the Free Trade Agreement)—it appeared unlikely that the Canadian welfare state could do anything but continue to contract through the 1990s. Canadian politicians will probably not choose obviously Draconian solutions, preferring instead to implement gradual reductions in welfare through cumulative regulations and complex taxation measures limiting eligibility. Since Canada had never attempted to go so far in its welfare measures as other smaller developed nations like Sweden or Switzerland, a weakening of the Canadian welfare net would not be quite so painful as it would be in those countries; but indications were that it would be painful enough.[29] Moreover, in all the talk of cutbacks the greatest irony of government policy towards social welfare remained alive. The government of Brian Mulroney, which reduced social programs and increased taxation in order to lower the deficit, had no trouble finding funds to support its military co-operation in the war against Iraq. The Riddle of Social Justice remained unsolved.

Canadian Culture

After 1972 Canadians discovered that culture had not only moral, intellectual, and aesthetic dimensions, but powerful economic implications as well. Canadian bureaucrats began to talk about 'cultural industries' instead of culture alone, measuring jobs and spin-off as well as uplift. At about the same time, governments began to discover how much money they had been putting into various aspects of culture since the halcyon days of the fifties and sixties, and an additional debate over cultural policy focused on how both to limit and supplement the vast public expenditures on activities ranging from university research to art happenings. Not only limitation but pay-off became issues. Canadian cultural policy was hotly debated, particularly since the politicians sought to use cultural policy to other ends besides enhancing arts and culture—notably after 1970 in the area of 'multiculturalism'. Popular culture (including sports) became more frequently recognized as a legitimate and important element of the overall cultural picture because the always artificial distinction between commercial and non-commercial culture had now been partially overcome by the inclusion of cultural enterprise in the economy. At the same time the schism between francophone and anglophone cultures was constantly widening, and all levels of government continued to jostle for advantages. The result was a strong sense of diffusion and decentralization—some would say regionalization (although not merely geography was involved) of what had once been perceived as a monolithic cultural establishment and enterprise. Such developments parallelled and reinforced the retreat of centralist/liberal nationalism in the political and constitutional arena—as well as contributing to the sense that Canadian society was coming apart.

The Business of Culture; or, The Rise of the Cultural Industries

The 1972 *Canada Yearbook* had no separate sections (or even index entries) for the Arts or Culture. By the 1990 edition, however, Culture had its own lengthy entry, which began:

> Culture plays a significant role in Canada's economy, providing jobs and contributing to national income and growth. In 1985, the cultural labour force was estimated at 307,000. The cultural sector is the fourth largest employer in Canada—three times larger than the forestry sector and equal to the agricultural sector. Cultural revenues totalled about $10 billion, placing the cultural industries on a par with the metals and mining industry. The cultural industries' direct and indirect effect on Canada's economy is estimated between $15 billion and $20 billion.[30]

This statement represented the end product of several decades of a shifting analysis of the significance of culture in Canada. As we have seen, the Massey Commission in 1951 had viewed culture almost exclusively in moral and aesthetic terms. For the next thirty years there was no similar effort by the federal government to provide an overview of cultural policy, chiefly because the French-English split made such an enterprise politically dangerous. By 1982, when the Federal Cultural Policy Review Committee (not a royal commission), chaired by Louis Applebaum and Jacques Hébert—often contracted to 'Applebert'—made its report, the term 'cultural industry' was well established, although it was still chiefly used to refer to what were once called 'the media'.[31] One of Applebert's major recommendations was for the systematic collection of statistics on culture in Canada. By the mid-1980s critics of government intervention in the cultural arena, such as Steven Globerman and George Woodcock, recognized that the concept of the cultural industry was potentially very elastic, and not confined to the media.[32]

Finally, in 1985 Statistics Canada produced a compendium entitled *Arts and Culture: A Statistical Profile*, which responded to the Applebert request by presenting cultural statistics on a national scale and attempting to calculate the economic importance of culture-related activities. This report estimated that in 1982 culture's share of the Gross Domestic Product was $8 billion, calculated that there were 280,000 Canadian arts-related jobs in the 1981 census, and insisted that arts jobs were growing at a faster rate than the total labour force in all provinces. The economic impact of culture depended on how one defined it. *Arts and Culture* adopted an 'arts-related' definition, but the 1986 Task Force on Funding in the Arts quickly pointed out the limitations of that definition, which did 'not represent the economic support provided by numerous sectors of allied artistic and cultural activity, such as consumer expenditures on leisure materials of a cultural nature for the home, capital cost expenditures on arts and culture infrastructure, and outlays in certain commercial arts and culture sectors.'[33] This Task Force calculated the economic dimensions of the overall cultural sector at $12 billion (rather than $8 billion) in 1981, insisting that if one added 'arts related' jobs to those in the arts industries, then the 'total number of Canadians who can be seen as working in arts-and-culture-related jobs' in 1981 was 415,000, or 3.5 per cent of the total labour force. If it had added some proportion of the education sector—particularly the component of higher education, where many creative artists were employed and which was responsible for cultural education in Canada—the figure would have been even higher.

Several interesting observations could be made about the emerging Economy of Culture in Canada. One was that the level of public support for the arts industries was substantial: $4.6 billion in 1986, for example, of which the federal government's share was $2.5 billion. Government spending on arts-related culture nonetheless represented only about 2 per cent of the total of government expenditure on all levels. If one added some percentage of the more than $6 billion spent on higher education by Canadian governments (which financed more than 90 per cent of higher education in the nation), both total expenditures and government proportion went higher. One could view such figures either as representing an alarming proportion of cultural expenditure—dangerous to the independence of the artist and the autonomy of the market, as some vociferous critics saw them—or as a minuscule investment in a major economic sector, as a series of government commissions considered them in the 1970s and 1980s.[34] It was by now clear that one of the new arenas of expertise in Canadian Culture, and in the Canadian bureaucracy, was that of 'cultural policy'.

Whatever position one took on government involvement and expenditure, the fact was that little of the money trickled down to the primary producer, the creative artist—the writer, painter, actor, composer, *et al.* In this sense Canadian Culture had much in common with that other economic sector of similar size, Agriculture, where the farmer's returns were minuscule by comparison with the total value of the sector. Government surveys of artists from 1978 to 1984 indicated that very few Canadians made a living from the sale of their works or talents and most held other employment, often in teaching. Less than 20% of 3,500 visual artists earned more than $5,000 from the sale of their works in 1977 and just over 25% of 3,100 writers in 1978 earned $5,000 from writing. Writers and visual artists, of course, were the indigenous producers of Canadian work. Figures for the performing arts (where the works were not necessarily Canadian) were slightly better, with 57.1% of actors and directors reporting incomes over $5,000 in 1979, and just under 70% of musicians earning more than $5,000 in 1982. The fact that a relatively large number of Canadians even conceived of making a living—

however inadequate—as professional artists certainly distinguished the post-1970 period from former times.

Still, what continued to be striking about the Cultural Economy was how few primary producers were really involved. They not only did badly financially, but represented only a small fraction of the total 'industry', much of which had little to do with intellectual or aesthetic values of any sort, indigenous or not. To include a construction worker in Montreal helping to build an arts complex was to push the cultural umbrella to the point of absurdity. Out of an 'arts-and-culture-related' work-force of over half a million Canadians, there were probably fewer than 10,000 making any serious effort to produce original creative work, which says a good deal about the problem of Canadian Culture in the late twentieth century.

Cultural Policy and Its Complexities

The very notion of 'cultural policy' would have astounded earlier generations of Canadian politicians and civil servants, but it had gradually become a central feature of government planning at both the federal and provincial levels. Despite the broadening of the concept of the Economy of Culture, however, there continued to be much confusion over the meaning of culture. As a result, different agencies of government planned different aspects of cultural policy, recognizing neither the existence of other initiatives nor the potential contradictions inherent in the situation. The policy of Multiculturalism offers perhaps the best illustration of the possible confusions.

As we have seen, Multiculturalism was born in a haze of semantic confusion over the meaning of the word 'culture'. The B and B Commission had recognized the need to preserve ethnic culture in Canada, but had not realized that 'ethnic culture' and 'founding culture' are quite different, and by more than a mere matter of degree. Those who accepted and promulgated Multiculturalism glossed over both the possible contradiction between official Biculturalism and official Multiculturalism and the problem of reconciling the notion of a National Culture with Multiculturalism. The latter was certainly possible, but only by equating the two; while suiting ethnic and regional interests, however, this was an utterly disastrous concept for centralist nationalism in Canada.

The Multiculturalism program that emanated from the Secretary of State's office in Ottawa became one of the federal government's most successful cultural subsidization operations, although none of the various commissions, committees, and task forces that ostensibly dealt with Canadian cultural policy appeared aware of its existence. The program subsidized publication ventures such as the *Generations* series of the *History of Canada's Peoples* and also provided grants for all manner of ethnic group activity. Canadian ethnic groups tended to be regionally rather than nationally based, and so supporting their artistic and heritage pretensions produced cultural diffusion on several levels: geographic, linguistic, and artistic. Critics of the policy and the program were doubtless quite right when they said that the whole operation was only intended to be cosmetic, not truly reformist, but the various governments that bought into Multiculturalism, particularly at the federal level, may have got more than the politicians at least had bargained for in the vehemence of resurgent ethnic consciousness.

Education

Though a major revolution appeared to be brewing in Canadian education in the 1960s, in the end very little actually changed. Fourteen major provincial enquiries on education had been initiated between 1960 and 1973—at least one in every province and two each in Alberta, New Brunswick, Ontario, and Prince Edward Island. The resulting reports called for sweeping and expensive change, but very little was altered. There were a number of problems. One was that the commissions' claim that 'investment in human resources' would pay off for Canadians demonstrated a faith—not shared by all educators—in the miraculous ability of education to improve society. Another was that the per-capita level of Canadian expenditures on education—one of the highest in the world in terms of percentage of GNP—could only with difficulty be perpetuated in the changed economic climate of the post-1972 period, particularly as the Baby Boomers passed through the expanded system and left it contracting.[35]

Despite the attention and many well-publicized recommendations, the only substantial pedagogical change deliberately introduced into the pre-university educational system in the entire period of reform was what one authority described as the 'transformation of the high school from a screening institution to a holding basin.'[36] This change had many ramifications after 1972. It was associated with an almost across-the-nation elimination of the strict and traditional academic standards of the provincially administered examination, simultaneously giving teachers more flexibility and freedom to design their own courses while removing the opportunity to monitor what students had been taught. The universities soon began complaining that the students they were accepting were less literate and less numerate than in previous years.

Efforts, particularly by provincial education departments, began as early as the mid-1970s to restore 'standards' through curriculum reform. Almost without exception, such initiatives as the reintroduction of a 'core curriculum' failed to produce much noticeable improvement. Part of the problem was that the younger generation, brought up on television, was not an easy one to teach in traditional subjects. Not only did they read and write less, but television had led them to expect learning to be both instant and fun. The culprit was not so much *Sesame Street* as the entire philosophy of educational television, which emphasized slickly prepackaged knowledge rather than actual discovery or constant practice to improve skills. Most children had probably always hated drilling and repetition, and the disciplinary revolution of the 1950s and 1960s left the system with very little muscle to enforce such unpopular activities. The democratization of high-school education meant that students came from all social backgrounds with great variation in their intellectual capacities and interests. Critics attacked the tendency to teach to the lowest common denominator and let someone else separate the sheep from the goats. By the mid-1980s many middle-class parents had decided to do their own separating, and there was almost a stampede into expensive private schools that advertised 'standards' and stressed academic achievement.

The relative absence of academic discrimination at the secondary-school level inevitably spilled over into the universities and became part of the malaise of higher education, which was in turn part of the malaise of education generally. While secondary-school democratization was the chief product of reform, this was offset by systematic cuts after 1972 in the funding of education at all levels as a percentage of the Gross Domestic Product (GDP) and as a proportion of personal income. In 1987-8 education expenditure had dropped to 7.1% of GDP from a high of 8.6% in 1970-1, and to 8.4% of personal income from 9.8% in 1977-8.[37] The international Organization of Economic Cooperation and Development in 1976 reported with some surprise that 'Canadian education policy may be one of the least "politicized" in the world', adding that changes were made pragmatically and that the Canadian system excluded most opportunities for conflict.[38] The absence of politicization was apparent in the fact that Canadian voters in most provinces were not much interested in making education a public issue. Public-opinion polls indicated that Canadians put quality education high on their list of priorities, but they refused to translate this feeling into political pressure on governments for increased funding. Educators at all levels felt blocked and frustrated, for it was difficult to demonstrate that budget cuts were damaging to what happened in the classroom.

The one general exception to the rule about the non-politicization of education came, as might have been expected, in Quebec. Here the issue was not so much funding as overall educational policy, focusing on language of instruction. Not until 1969 had Quebec formally accepted the right of parents to have children educated in either French or English, when passage of Bill 63 ('An act to promote the French language in Quebec') required English-speaking students to have a working knowledge of French and immigrants to enrol their children in French-language schools. Protests from francophone Quebec over Bill 63—they considered it too weak—led in 1974 to Bill 22, which made French the official language of civic administration and services, and of the workplace. But it also replaced 'language of choice' with a more restrictive policy for English-speaking schools, confining entrance to those already knowledgeable in the language. Another issue was the education of new immigrants to Quebec and especially Montreal, most of whom chose to be educated in English rather than French schools. Under the Parti Québécois, Bill 101 in 1977 made French the official language of the province. The opportunity for newcomers to Quebec to choose English-language education was greatly reduced: only those children whose parents or siblings had been educated in English in Quebec could enter English schools. By the end of the seventies this Draconian policy had certainly reduced enrolments in anglophone schools, and was taken by many English-speaking Quebeckers as a virtual declaration of war against their continued presence in the province.[39] At this point many anglophone Canadians outside Quebec lost patience with the Québécois quest to be '*maîtres chez nous*'.

In the rest of Canada, budgetary cuts (or failures to keep pace with inflation) at the pre-university levels could be associated to some extent with shrinking school populations. This relationship was not so evident at the university level, where enrolments steadily increased after the mid-1970s despite the disappearance of the largest cohort of Baby Boomers from the system. More of the young continued into higher education, and the universities began attracting larger numbers of 'mature' students. At the university level governments spent less and expected more. The cuts affected all areas of university life, including maintenance of buildings and grounds, but were mainly absorbed by hiring freezes, which meant essentially that the faculty hired in the earlier period of expansion—chiefly young, white, and male—grew old together. By 1985 the age and sex profile of the Canadian professorate looked like this:

University Teachers: 1985

AGE	MALE	FEMALE	
65+	332	44	
60-4	2039	312	
55-9	3183	526	
50-4	4539	603	
45-9	5848	932	
40-4	6246	1271	
35-9	4284	1209	
30-4	2200	811	
25-9	476	254	
under 25	16	25	
	29,166	5,978	Total: 35,144

Source: *Education in Canada: A Statistical Review for 1985-6* (Ottawa, 1986), p. 221.

Such figures offer a perfect example of a blocked profession, with a big bulge (that would move upward annually) in the 40-to-50 age category, a decreasing number of new entries, and little opportunity to correct existing imbalances in such categories as the male-female ratio.

The concern over the Americanization of the university teaching profession died away after 1971 and was replaced by other issues. The report of the Commission on Canadian Studies (1975) insisted that not Americans but Canadians were responsible for the weak representation of Canadian content in the curriculum. Apart from the obvious aging of the professorate, the big staffing issue of the post-1971 period was the role of women. In 1985 only 17 per cent of university teachers were female, despite a student population that was almost evenly balanced. Too many of that percentage were employed on annual or part-time contracts, and even those in tenured positions were paid substantially less for their services than their male equivalents. Although by the 1980s virtually half (and in some fields and some universities more than half) of the undergraduate population was female, and more than half of all first degrees were awarded to women, figures slipped off at the graduate level. In 1985 only 26.4 per cent of doctorates in Canada were awarded to women. One could take heart from such a figure, which almost tripled the 9.3 per cent of 1971, but there was obviously a long way to go. Members of the academy could not dispute the data, but disagreed about the remedy. The big debate was whether such imbalances ought to be corrected by positive policies, such as intervening in the hiring process—which went against the grain of most academic thinking.

Despite the valiant efforts of Thomas Symons and his Commission (1972-74), there were real limits to the extent of Canadianization that could be achieved in the university curriculum. In *To Know Ourselves: The Report of the Commission on Canadian Studies* (1975), Symons and his small team of collaborators attempted to identify the extent of Canadian content in the overall university curriculum, concluding that there were many fields in which more could be done. The Commission was quite unhappy that thousands of graduates were being produced who were scientific illiterates, and even more upset that many graduating in the sciences had no understanding of Canada, much less the ways in which scientific research could contribute to that understanding. Many of the Commission's informants went further, insisting that science teaching from American-produced textbooks in Canada led almost inevitably to 'reading and thinking like an American.'[40] The various Symons reports did help to increase Canadian content in some disciplines already disposed in that direction, notably the social sciences, but produced no great upsurge across the universities.

After 1972 public concern was continually expressed over Canada's record in producing scientists and engineers—those occupations regarded as essential to industrial growth and development in the modern world. The fact was, however, that Canada was doing more than most industrialized nations about training in scientific and technological areas—behind only the United Kingdom in the percentage of graduates in science and technology. By the late 1980s Canada was producing three times as many engineering and science graduates per head of population as West Germany, and fifty per cent more than Japan.[11]

In the humanities there was evidence, in the later 1980s, that student interest was higher than ever. But this preference was seldom reflected in the allocations for research support by the federal government, or in the internal priorities of university administrations. Faculties of Humanities felt threatened, not only by their inability to communicate to policy-makers that both the perspectives and the skills acquired within the humanities were at least as vital to the nation as technology, but also by substantial 'post-modernist' intellectual shifts within their own ranks that weakened the confidence of many of their members. The key changes revolved around standards of objectivity and truth. Until the late 1960s humanists had generally believed that truth and objectivity—while difficult, and perhaps impossible, to obtain in non-scientific work—were nonetheless goals worth striving for. The post-1972 period saw international challenges to these aspirations in virtually every area of humanistic study, and by 1990 the quest for some generally valid standard of objective truth had been abandoned almost everywhere within the humanities; such a quest was even under attack in several of the scientific disciplines.

The principal culprit in the perceived failure of truth was language, a means of communication that was increasingly viewed as heavily and inescapably freighted with the cultural assumptions of those who employed it. Without a neutral (and neutered) language with which to communicate, it was impossible to make statements that were anything other than reflections of the individual's own cultural background. A variety of critical theories sprang up—deconstructionism and hermeneutics were two of the best publicized—all of which shared a philosophical hostility to any concept of an Objective Truth, while offering their own way of looking at the world. Without a shared means of validation, however, humanistic research tended to divide up into hotly contested theoretical camps resembling sixteenth-century Protestant sects. The more impossible the validation process, the louder seemed the insistence on the exclusive validity of one's own non-objective approach. The result of the collapse of Truth, and the appearance of often arcane theories to replace it, was to drive a still deeper wedge—previously bridged by the critic—between the creative producer of art/culture and the audience.

Culture: Its Audience, and the Problem of Canadian Content

Whatever the major conceptual shift in Canada regarding the meaning of Culture, which had come to incorporate popular culture—now perceived as a separate (and lively) economic sector—little was changed about the question of Canadian content, except that things got worse. Many continued to bemoan the difficulty Canadians experienced in finding examples of their own culture amidst the vast Arts and Culture edifice, and there were attempted solutions aplenty. As one government document put it in 1987, despite 'a steady build-up of creative organizations' that made Canada 'now comparable to. . .other developed countries', the reality was 'that the fundamental structural dilemma affecting Canada's cultural industries has worsened.'[42] The statistics were revealing. In book publishing, for example, titles published in Canada in 1984 (mainly written by Canadian authors) accounted for only 25 per cent of books sold, while imported titles represented the remainder. Nearly half the books sold to Canadians went directly from foreign sources to the reader. In 1983 revenues earned from Canadian films counted for less than 1 per cent of the revenue generated within Canada in that year. Twelve foreign-controlled firms in 1984 had 89 per cent of the sound-recording market in Canada, mostly for non-Canadian records.

There was much evidence that most Canadians supported the principle of government assistance for Canadian cultural activities. The question was whether the public would take advantage of the cultural production it thus subsidized. A Gallup Poll in 1980 demonstrated that two-thirds of Canadians approved of a CRTC policy insisting that television programming exhibit at least fifty-per-cent Canadian content. But Canadians did not necessarily choose to watch such programs. For example, in one week in 1986 the top seven TV shows in English-speaking Canada were all American, and the leading regularly produced Canadian program was the CBC National News, at number 13. The situation was very different in French Canada, however, where all top seven shows were locally produced. Great hope was held out in the 1980s for satellite and cable technology, which certainly improved access to broadcasting for many Canadians, but did little for Canadian production. The disparity between abstract commitment to Canadian culture and the desire to experience it became truly dangerous when arguments for public support were expressed in economic terms. If government subsidies for the CBC became connected with ratings, for example, the CBC would be in serious trouble—at least in English-speaking Canada. Although public appreciation for culture grew substantially in the seventies and eighties, the average Canadian still seemed unable to comprehend that a true Canadian culture demanded not only the indigenous creative production of a body of Canadian work, but public appreciation and support of that work. The gap between the Canadian artist and his/her audience was a product of many factors.

In concert music there was a continual blurring, throughout much of this period, of the lines between performance and production, so that a Beethoven symphony performed by a Canadian orchestra, broadcast on the CBC, was defined as acceptable Canadian content—although the performance was indistinguishable, in a general sense, from that of any non-Canadian orchestra. Canadian symphony orchestras continued to import their conductors from abroad.* While those conductors often made statements of commitment to the performance of Canadian music, such promises were never intended to produce any substantial changes in the repertoire, which was basically European in origin because this is what audiences wanted. Canadian composers such as Murray Adaskin, John Beckwith, Gabriel Charpentier, Jean Coulthard, S.C. Eckhardt-Gramatté, Serge Garant, Srul Irving Glick, Pierre Mercure, Oskar Morawetz, Barbara Pentland, Clermont Pépin, R. Murray Schafer, Harry Somers, and John Weinzweig had to contend with the fact that not only had international performance and recognition eluded them; but when their works were infrequently performed by Canadian orchestras, their contemporary, sometimes dissonant, sounds and forms found little receptivity from Canadian audiences attuned to the classical tradition. Beginning in the eighties, however, this situation changed to some extent. Partly because of the CBC's perennial championship of Canadian composers, the programming of Canadian works no longer sent waves of displeasure and boredom through a subscription audience, and more of them were being heard. They have even been enjoyed, and R. Murray Schafer, among others, now has an international reputation. Furthermore, a whole new generation of composers has appeared.

In the eighties also a great upsurge of musical activity across the country meant that gifted young musicians could pursue careers—as soloists or as members of chamber groups—to a great extent in Canada alone, with occasional forays south of the border and abroad. Canadian musicians have always been subject to the stern dictum that they had to be tested and acclaimed in one of the musical centres of the world before being given major status at home. Considering the country's relatively small population, it is astonishing that so many artists trained in Canada have gone on since the fifties to have brilliant international careers: Maureen Forrester, Judith Forst, Paul Frey, Ben Heppner, Lois Marshall, Alan Monk, Louis Quilico, Gino Quilico, Catherine Robbin, Léopold Simoneau, Teresa Stratas, Jon Vickers, Edith Wiens (opera and concert singers); the late Glenn Gould, Angela Hewitt, André Laplante, Louis Lortie (pianists); Kenneth Gilbert (harpsichordist); James Campbell (clarinetist); Robert Aitken (flutist). In the field of popular music there are Bryan Adams, Bruce Cockburn, k.d. lang, Gordon Lightfoot, Joni Mitchell, Anne Murray, Oscar Peterson, Robbie Robertson,

---

*Exceptions to this rule were the brilliant Canadian-born musician Sir Ernest MacMillan (1893-1973), who conducted the Toronto Symphony Orchestra from 1931 to 1956; Mario Bernardi (b. 1930), who was the first conductor of the National Arts Centre Orchestra (1968-82) and became music director of the Calgary Philharmonic in 1984; and Boris Brott (b. 1944), who was made music director of the Hamilton Philharmonic in 1969.

and Neil Young; and in Quebec Céline Dion, the late Félix Leclerc, Monique Leyrac, and Gilles Vigneault. An international status for these artists meant that they could live anywhere, and it is perhaps remarkable that most of them remained committed to Canada.

Cultural Diffusion

Government support for High Culture aided the further development of a respectable Canadian showing in many of the traditional areas, particularly in literature and painting. The cultures of Quebec and Acadia were particularly lively, and artists there continued to be highly politicized. Canadians writers, both in English and French, were regularly nominated for (and occasionally won) international literary prizes, and the major journals in both England and France began recognizing—somewhat to their surprise—that Canada and Quebec/Acadia were no longer merely distant and imitative colonies of the mother country. But as Canadian High Culture achieved international recognition, it also continued a process of diffusion that produced tensions between what came to be labelled 'national' and 'regional' culture, both in Canada as a whole and in the linguistic dualities of French and English. Neither the pretensions to, nor the realities of, centralism went away. Nevertheless, three aspects of cultural diffusion are perhaps worth emphasizing: the decentralization of cultural presentation; the rise of feminism; and the emergence to recognition of the so-called 'third cultures' of Canada.

Before the later sixties, one of the major problems faced by Canadian artists, particularly those working outside broad international currents, was to receive any kind of public exposure outside Toronto and Montreal. The small presses and galleries that cropped up across the country in the sixties and seventies became possible for several reasons. One was the allocation of new provincial funding for the arts, chiefly from the revenues of publicly authorized gambling activities, such as lotteries and bingo. Another was the emergence of local cultural entrepreneurs, and pressure from writers and painters, who sometimes took the lead in organizing presses and galleries. For example, in 1975 a group of Manitoba writers, disenchanted with the prevailing critical standards of what some of them regarded as the 'eastern establishment', founded Turnstone Press in Winnipeg. Finally there was now a large enough market for culture in such second-tier cities as Halifax, Quebec, Winnipeg, and Edmonton to justify more local production and presentation.

Almost inevitably the new publishers and galleries tended to stress local themes and settings, partly because the owners and the creative people involved saw themselves in the regional context, and partly because the local market was perceived to require a product with which it could identify. Turnstone's first publication was W.D. Valgardson's *In the Gutting Shed* (1976), a collection of poems that featured a strong association with the commercial fishery of the Manitoba interlake region. Two years later the press achieved its first 'success' when it published Robert Kroetsch's *Seed Catalogue* (1977), poems grounded in prairie experience. In response to the reiterated question 'How do you grow a poet?' Kroetsch wrote:

> This is a prairie road.
> This road is the shortest distance
> between nowhere and nowhere.
> This road is a poem.
>
> Just two miles up the road
> you'll find a porcupine
> dead in the ditch. It was
> trying to cross the road.[43]

By the early 1980s Turnstone had become a major regional publisher, and some of its books had received nominations for national and international awards.

One of the accompaniments of political regionalization was a growing sense of cultural regionalism, which was particularly strong in those marginal and peripheral places that had for so long been neglected by the dominant centre. British Columbia, Atlantic Canada, the Prairies, and Acadia had always had strong regional cultures—to which central Canada (Ontario, and to a lesser extent Quebec) had paid little attention. From the perspective of those geographical peripheries, Quebec appeared very much part of the centre, even more so when to geographical marginality was added cultural marginality. The Massey Commission's treatment of the regions and regional culture had been, like that of most government commissions on the arts, shameful. It had recognized Quebec grudgingly, but no other region. What was new was not regional culture itself, but the opportunity for artists to find outlets for their work in local presses and galleries. It was no longer necessary to work in channels that were nationally or internationally acceptable; and to the surprise of many, strong regional accents often won more favour in the outside world than the bland North Americanism of the forties and fifties. It appeared as though the very concept of a Canadian National Culture was an artificial construct, impossible for most Canadian artists to realize in a nation made up of regions.

Another major element of the diffusion of High Culture came from conscious feminism, which initially was based on the growing body of theory produced around the world—usually associated with some analysis of historical patriarchy. 'Feminism', one exponent wrote recently, 'has moved us away from the totalizing discourse of humanism, which assumes the right to speak *for* everyone in naming the world, and has become the catalyst across our culture moving us out of the Modernist era, denouncing the humanist subject as white and male.'[44] If the Canadian creative establishment could be geographically associated with central Canada, it could also be associated with male domination. In English-language literature the feminist author who perhaps most immediately comes to mind is Margaret Atwood, who has

Antonine Maillet. Photograph
copyright P. Roussel, Publiphoto.

brilliantly taken up the feminist debate on personal relations in her novels,
stories, and poetry:

> *you fit into me*
> *like a hook into an eye*
>
> *a fish hook*
> *an open eye*

This is the epigraph to one of Atwood's well-known books of poetry, *Power
Politics* (1971), the title expressing a conflict that informs all her writing,
though her concerns range far beyond those of women specifically. Her
voice—wry, controlled, elliptical, prosaic—is very distinctive, but stylisti-
cally her writing is well within the mainstream of accessibility.

The many feminist writers in Quebec have been much more adventurous,
having transcended the bounds of literary conventions in their formal experimentation—such as combining poetry, prose, and unconventional forms of
layout and narrative—and collectively shaken up the institutionalized patriarchy in Quebec. Among these audacious, original writers are Louky Bersi-
anik, Nicole Brossard, Madeleine Gagnon, Jovette Marchessault, and
Yolande Villemaire.[45]

Much better known in English Canada is the Acadian writer Antonine

Maillet (b. 1929), who first achieved prominence across the country when her one-woman show *La Sagouine* (1971), based on sixteen monologues, was unforgettably acted in both French and English by Viola Léger. The title character (a talkative, clear-headed, long-suffering old charwoman, the wife of an Acadian fisherman who recalls her past); the language (a salty, rough version of sixteenth-century French); and the Acadian folk heritage implicit in it—are all typical of most of Maillet's work, including her celebrated novel *Pélagie-la-Charrette* (1979). Translated as *Pélagie:The Return to a Homeland*, it is about an Acadian woman who, in a ten-year picaresque journey, makes her way back from expulsion in the southern American colonies to her native soil. For this novel Maillet became the first non-French-born writer to win the prestigious Prix Goncourt.

There was a growing recognition of other cultures at work in Canada besides French and English, particularly after 1972, whan multiculturalism policy (and expenditure) made a big difference. In the post-war period, especially after the mid-1960s, Canada received a number of Eastern European literary exiles who continued to write in their native languages. Canada's Ukrainian presses, which go back into the nineteenth century, have been joined in modern times by those of other nations and languages, and some have received subsidies from Departments of Multiculturalism. The most famous European press here was founded by Josef Škvorecký (b. 1924), who was already a well-known writer in Czechoslovakia when he immigrated in 1968, with his wife Zdena Salivarova, to teach at the University of Toronto. He has since become an internationally acclaimed novelist through the publication of English translations of his works. In 1971 he and his wife founded the Czech publishing firm Sixty Eight—named after the year of the Soviet invasion of Czechoslovakia, which was also the year they came to Canada—making Toronto a major publishing centre in the Czech language. Its contribution to the underground life of the country after 1971 was inestimable; but happily the need for the publishing house ceased to exist with the overthrow of Communist rule in Czechoslovakia.

Among Canada's native peoples, beginning in the 1950s the art of the Inuit, and the painting and writing of Indians, gradually developed into an explosion of creativity. Inuit sculptures and prints are highly sought after by collectors. Among many distinguished Inuit artists are the sculptors Vital Makpaaq (1922-78); John Pangnark (1920-80); and Qaqaq (b. 1928) and Kiugak (b. 1933) Ashoona, sons of Ashoona Pitseolak (1907-83), who was one of many outstanding graphic artists that included Kenojuak Ashevak (b. 1927)—who created the famous print *The Enchanted Owl*—and Jessie Oonark (1906-85), who became famous for her inspired and brilliantly coloured wall hangings. Indian painters—including Norval Morrisseau (b. 1932) and Jackson Beardy (1944-1984)—have reached wide audiences through exhibitions and prints of their work; and numerous Indian writers are being published. The native sensibility and vision, at long last, are now being revealed by natives for non-natives.

Popular Culture

In the post-seventies it was the perception of many Canadian intellectuals and creative artists (the people who worried most about culture) that American popular culture had become even more ubiquitous and dominant—though such matters are largely subjective and impossible to measure quantitatively. 'Increasingly,' said Canadian playwright John Gray in 1986, 'American mass culture is being seen by Canadians as "normal" culture, and Canadian mass culture as "abnormal" culture.'[46] It certainly was documentable that the so-called 'cultural industries' of Canada relied increasingly on product created elsewhere, chiefly in the United States. It was equally documentable that the Canadian public, if forced momentarily to consider the question, would in public-opinion polls allow that there was entirely too much American influence in Canada. But at the same time, the Canadian love affair with American popular culture continued unabated. Only in francophone Canada was there any serious evidence of resistance, particularly in Quebec, where the arts and entertainment were sustained by much local creativity and public enthusiasm.

The situation in professional sports is perhaps illustrative.[47] The Canadian Football League—despite, or perhaps because of, continual public protection from a series of Canadian governments against increasing domination by American coaches and quarterbacks—began a slow decline in popularity that would not be arrested. In 1987 the Montreal Alouettes ceased operations just as the season was beginning, and the CFL's television contract was not renewed. Although Canadian-trained players were increasingly assigned important positions, touchdowns were usually scored by highly paid American specialists, most of whom would have preferred to play in the National Football League across the border. The CFL and most of its teams did little to encourage local loyalty in an increasingly competitive entertainment market. For most Canadians the CFL did not offer Canadian but minor-league football. On the other hand, were the CFL to collapse and the Americans to expand into Canada, only the major markets of Toronto, Montreal, and possibly Vancouver could expect to be awarded franchises—as happened with both professional hockey and baseball.

Although hockey was far more popular in Canada than in the United States, the National Hockey League had expanded in 1967 only into American cities failed. Reluctantly the League's board of governors responded to Canadian public opinion and added a franchise in Vancouver in 1970; but it was prepared to go no further, insisting that no other Canadian city could support a team. The result was the creation of an alternative league, the World Hockey Association, in which a number of Canadian cities— including Winnipeg, Calgary, Edmonton, and Quebec—held successful franchises. The WHA collapsed in 1979, not because the Canadian teams were unprofitable, but because American-based teams in Kansas City and other American cities failed. The NHL then allowed four new franchises in WHA

Seconds before this photograph was taken, Mario Lemieux of the Pittsburgh Penguins scored the winning goal for Canada—assisted by Wayne Gretzky (on the left) of the Edmonton Oilers—against the Soviet Union in the 1987 Canada Cup hockey tournament. Photograph by Doug MacLellan, courtesy the Hockey Hall of Fame, Toronto.

cities, including three Canadian ones: Edmonton, Quebec, and Winnipeg. The Atlanta Flames were subsequently moved to Calgary, and in a round of expansion in 1990 a team was accepted in Ottawa. Hockey standards, which had declined during the expansions of the seventies, recovered in the eighties as the game acquired new pools of talent and new skills, chiefly in Europe. Nevertheless, the hockey moguls continued to regard Canadian franchises as marginal, despite their continued profitability, and the smaller cities of Winnipeg and Quebec lived under the constant threat that their teams would head south to centres of hockey enthusiasm in Florida, California, and Texas. The 'Great One' himself, Wayne Gretzky (b. 1961) of the Edmonton Oilers, was sold by his team's owner to the Los Angeles Kings, integrating nicely into the Entertainment Capital of the World.

Most of the players in the Canadian Football League—if not the offensive stars—were Canadians, and Canadians continued to dominate the National

The Skydome, Toronto, before the start of a baseball game in the first week of June 1989, shortly after it opened. Photograph by Norm Betts, courtesy Canada Wide Feature Services Limited and the Toronto *Sun*.

Hockey League, despite the increased numbers of American and European players. Canadian baseball, on the other hand, was played almost entirely with imported Americans. Canada's two teams, the Montreal Expos (1969) and the Toronto Blue Jays (1977), both performed well on the field in the 1980s, although neither could win a League championship. But Toronto finally reached the World Series, which it won against the Atlanta Braves in October 1992. The Blue Jays were winners at the box office even before they moved into a state-of-the-art domed stadium in 1989. The Toronto Sky-dome became the architectural wonder of its age. The domes in Toronto and Montreal ended one complaint of Americans playing in Canada, the climate, but made it clear that only cities that could afford such facilities could expect franchises. Moreover, Canadian teams operated under at least one severe disadvantage: many American players had clauses in their contracts prevent-ing them from having to play in Canada, where they would be paid in 'funny money' and taxed at a much higher rate than at home. American baseball officials continued to view Canadian cities as the back of beyond, refusing to entertain the possibility of minor-league expansion to Winnipeg, for exam-ple, because of 'transportation difficulties' and the cost of living. Despite the attitude of some of the players and their families—one player's wife com-plained of living in Montreal because of the absence of familiar fast-food outlets—Canadians got much more excited about baseball in the 1980s and early 1990s than about football or even hockey, thus paralleling the American experience. The exception was in French Canada, especially Montreal, where the Canadiens reigned supreme and attendance for baseball in the Olympic Stadium precipitously declined. The Expos were far more popular elsewhere in the country, through television exposure, than in their home town.

Similar stories could be repeated in many other areas of popular culture in Canada. 'Canadian artists have moved to the fringe of their own country,' said John Gray. 'Thus, in the video rental shop I frequent, the films of Claude Jutra are classified as "foreign" films. And in the record store, "Canadian" records have a special bin, along with Ukrainian dances and Flamenco guitarists.'[48] The endemic problem, well phrased by a government report in 1987, was a paradox: 'Although Canadian consumption of cultural products represents a substantial market, Canadian cultural industries generally exist in a state of financial weakness and vulnerability, unable to become self-financ-ing from market revenues.'[49] As critics of this 'cultural industry' approach had already pointed out, once culture was measured in economic terms, it could easily be found wanting. The experience of the CBC here was instructive.

In the complex world of the late 1980s even the Canadian Broadcasting Corporation—that previously sacrosanct institution of national unity and culture—proved its vulnerability to market forces and political pressures. Most of the CBC's problems revolved around its television rather than radio operations, the latter being generally regarded as among the best and most

effective in the world. Unfortunately, the federal government, which provided the funding for the CBC, was unable to control where cuts would be
made when funds were reduced, and the Corporation continually reduced its
funding for radio. Certainly television broadcasting in Canada after 1972 was
changed enormously by new technologies, including expanded cable networks and satellite communications. CBC television had many difficulties
with these changes, chiefly an inability to decide clearly on its priorities so as
'to maintain a vigorous Canadian presence within a broadcasting system that
is so plentifully supplied with popular foreign programming,' as the Applebert committee had put it.[50]

The Corporation's dilemmas involved cruel and perhaps impossible
choices. The 1980 cultural policy commission had insisted that 'what Canadians need from the CBC is an alternative to private broadcasting,'[51] but
based its arguments on the assumption that the CBC would continue to be
fully funded by Parliament, and could indeed cease competing for commercial advertising. But broadcasting was expensive—the CBC received nearly
$600 million from Parliament in 1981/2, for example—and it represented an
obvious place to cut expenditures whenever any government was looking for
ways to save money. The perceived need to remain competitive with private
broadcasting prevented the Corporation from truly seeking alternative
routes. The result was a CBC television programming, particularly in English, that came closer to duplicating CTV than the Public Broadcasting
Service in the US.

As well as being torn between providing commercial success or alternative
service, the CBC found itself caught in other cruel dilemmas. One was the
question of regional service, particularly outside Quebec, which had its own
system in Radio-Canada. Clearly the regions were the likely place to seek
out alternative Canadian programming, but the devolution of television
production proved an impossibility for an entrenched bureaucracy as centralist and nationalistic in its sensibilities as that of the Canadian Broadcasting
Corporation. As the budget cuts came, the CBC inevitably decided to inflict
them on regional rather than central broadcasting and production facilities,
thus further reducing its capacity for fulfilling its mandate. Like the nation it
sought to represent, as the 1990s began the CBC found itself in serious
trouble, perhaps even on the verge of collapse.

After 1970 Culture had become not only a major economic sector in
Canada, but a central arena of political disagreement. In early 1991, when the
Quebec government of Robert Bourassa finally responded to the collapse of
Meech Lake, it listed immigration, health and manpower, and cultural
matters as the key areas in which it would demand increased powers. 'As far
as culture is concerned, yes we should be in charge,' announced Liberal
cultural-affairs minister Liza Frulla-Herbert in January 1991. 'We have to
work toward being the one and only one giving the pulse of Quebec culture.
Listen, culture belongs to Quebec.'[52] Six months later, Stephen Godfrey

wrote in *The Globe and Mail* that Montreal

> . . .is the place where culture becomes politics, and political survival becomes cultural survival. Quebec is the only province where you can see, feel and taste that commitment, and where the exhilaration of living here is tinged with regret at an inescapable conclusion. If English Canadians were as fierce about their culture—in deed as well as word—as French-Canadians are, this would be a far stronger country.[53]

No Canadian could doubt that in Quebec, culture was lively and distinctive, and was certainly better able to withstand American influence than elsewhere in Canada. Those who enjoyed the films of Claude Jutra and Denys Arcand and others were introduced to a world where the familiarly North American had acquired a quite different shape and meaning. But whether Quebec Culture was a National Culture became, in the end, a question more susceptible of political than intellectual answers.

Towards the 21st Century

It is perhaps frivolous to think of Canada's travails over the past two decades as exemplifying Murphy's Law—the 1950s name given to various aphoristic expressions of the perverseness of things, of the inherent likelihood of their going wrong and getting worse. But in the early 1990s—when the country's political constitution, as well as its economy, society, overall culture, and very *raison d'être* appeared to be unravelling before one's eyes—a whole series of Murphy's Laws seemed to be at work. Suddenly politicians and journalists (and not a few academics) were asking Canadians to consider the future of Canada by making simple choices bearing on society, culture, economics, or politics—issues that turned out to be extremely complex, contradictory, and agonizing, as the 1992 referendum well demonstrated.

Society

None of the social trends discussed in Chapter 14 have markedly altered. The Supreme Court of Canada did hand down several landmark rulings affecting women—for example on rape and abortion—without establishing a consistent position favouring women. In the case of rape trials, it ruled that the complainant's past sexual history could not in fairness be excluded from the trial, although impeaching the victim was the usual defence on the part of males accused of rape. As far as abortion was concerned, the Supreme Court on 21 March 1991 ruled, in a controversial decision, that a fetus is not a person, thus undercutting one of the major arguments of the opponents of abortion. Late in February 1992 the Court unanimously ruled that the federal government had not overstepped the Charter of Rights in declaring certain kinds of materials pornographic. Many women's groups applauded this decision, while civil-rights leaders were less enthusiastic, pointing to the dangers of censorship.

Perhaps the key question was whether Canada could become a viable multicultural nation, whether the national fabric could be made flexible enough to accommodate the Canadian Peoples as they were coming to define themselves. Those Peoples did not include merely several groups of francophones and anglophones, but the First Nations, whose roots predated European 'Discovery', as well as very recent immigrants of non-European origin, many from the Third World. The process of definition was an open-ended and dynamic one, subject to continual modification.

The traditional goal of Canadian society had always been cultural assimilation into one of the two major language groups. Polls taken in 1991 indicated that Canadians still believed that they had a duty to 'assist young newcomers' transition to their new land's culture and society', and that the desire for newcomers to fit in was particularly evident in Quebec.[1] A recent national survey on attitudes to multiculturalism (published in the *Winnipeg Free Press*, 24 December 1991) revealed that forty-six per cent of those polled agreed that people who come to Canada should change their behaviour 'to be more like us', and forty-two per cent found national unity weakened by ethnic groups' 'sticking to their old ways'. In this poll the greatest objection to ethnic newcomers came from Toronto—perhaps not surprisingly, given their numbers in that city. A full two-thirds of those polled thought that racial discrimination against 'non-whites'—which would obviously place limits on the extent of assimilation possible—was a serious problem in Canada. At the same time there was equally strong support in principle for most of the basic tenets of multiculturalism, including the recognition of diversity, the elimination of racism, and the guarantee of equal access to employment. Which side of these contradictory results represents the future remains unclear.

Culture

By the end of the 1980s public support for many of the institutions of the arts, especially outside Quebec, had peaked and begun to decline. The 1980s had witnessed a major explosion of support for the arts, with season's subscriptions and attendance at theatre, concerts, and dance reaching new highs. New organizations were formed and existing organizations balanced their books or showed modest surpluses, often for the first time in years. But by 1992 the arts were again in serious trouble. Most of those involved credited precipitous declines in attendance to the economic climate, arguing that in hard times cultural activities were the first to be reduced in the budget of a family or a government. A few more sophisticated observers added to the simple explanation of economic recession the stunning increases in the incidence of home-entertainment equipment, particularly the VCR, which was at least in part linked to the 'cocooning' instincts of the early 1990s—the tendency for people to retreat from the outside world into home and family. When Canadians turned from live performance in theatres and concert halls in their own communities to taped performance in the comfort of their own homes, they did more than merely cocoon, however. They also ceased to support Canadian artists and institutions, funnelling their money instead into the vast American entertainment empire of popular culture. The differences between Quebec and the rest of Canada in terms of the importance of culture to its way of life took on new significance. Quebec's continued support for its own cultural institutions and performers suggested a degree of vitality and commitment that might well become an important factor in larger political and constitutional negotiations, since it represented important evidence of a will to survive independently.

✒ The Economy

Canada's economic problems in the 1990s began with an international slow-down that was inevitable after the overheating of the late 1980s. When, in early 1991, the bottom finally dropped out of both the resource economy and the manufacturing sector, the consequences included reduction in consumer spending and dramatic increases in plant closures, bankruptcies, mortgage foreclosures, and rationalizations. Canadian government policy, which had emphasized both free trade and consumption taxation (the Goods and Services Tax being the prime example), was blamed by many critics for a good number of specific weaknesses in the economy.

The GST was a perfect illustration of how the government became hoist on its own petard. The tax had never been an ideal instrument of fiscal policy. In applying equally to everyone it was inequitable, hitting particularly hard those with lower incomes; and as a visible surcharge, it reminded consumers of that inequity every time it was levied. The Mulroney government had calculated that the furor over the GST would quickly die away, as it had in other nations that had introduced something similar—although most of them did not also have a Provincial Sales Tax (PST), which ranged from 7 to 12 per cent. The government obviously had not calculated on the extent to which the Canadian taxpayer would regard the GST as the straw that broke the camel's back. Nor had it realized that some taxpayers would be willing and able to take evasive action because there was a relatively easy way to avoid the GST, one available to a great many Canadians. It involved crossing the border and shopping in the United States, where prices were for the most part lower and the GST would certainly not apply. Some of the purchased goods could be brought back into Canada legally, but most had to be 'smuggled' across the border. Many Canadian shoppers were quite prepared to smuggle, perhaps reasoning that there was supposed to be free trade between the two countries. The vast increase in cross-border traffic after the introduction of the GST on 1 January 1991 would have been noticeable under any circumstances. But when it was combined with the simultaneous collapse of the Canadian retail trade under the weight of the mounting international recession, cross-border shopping suddenly appeared as a major problem.

The Canadian retail trade, however, would doubtless have collapsed without the GST. As we saw in Chapter 13, the prosperity of the late 1980s had been floated on the strength of plastic credit, and eventually consumers would reach saturation point, particularly given the 'upmarket' direction of retailers ranging from clothing stores to automobile showrooms. Conventional retail wisdom in the late 1980s had been that the Canadian consumer was becoming more sophisticated, requiring attractive design and quality materials rather than the cheapest goods. As a result many retailers had expanded into costly premises in glitzy shopping malls, justifying these moves with visions of higher mark-ups on more expensive goods. The Yuppie generation of Baby Boomers—so went the story—were prepared to pay for quality and style. The financial pages of newspapers and magazines were replete with the constantly repeated story of the Discovery of Upmarket.

By the beginning of 1992 press stories about the successes of discounters had replaced those about upmarketers. Frequenting 'flea markets' and garage sales became a new recreation among Canadians of all classes, and cocktail-party one-upmanship centred on saving rather than spending money. Many stores in the major malls were empty, and a number of Canadian retailing chains, particularly in the clothing business, had gone into receivership. In December 1991 alone, Grafton-Fraser Inc. announced that 221 of its Jack Fraser and George Richards men's-apparel stores were closing, while Ayre's Ltd said that three of its upmarket women's clothing chains would be closed. Henry Birk and Sons, the jewellers, also revealed plans to shut 12 Canadian stores, and early in 1992 People's Jewellers Ltd proposed closing 20 Canadian outlets. The number of bankruptcies among small businesses, chiefly in the retail sector, hit a new record. It was simple enough to blame cross-border shopping. The province of New Brunswick, for example, calculated that its retail shops had lost $200 million in 1991 to American merchants, while Ontario counted its losses in the billions.

To make matters worse, while Canadians clogged the border crossings and the cheap motels around American shopping malls, there was no compensating rush of American visitors into Canada. Statistics Canada calculated the net loss to Canada in 1991 at over $6 billion, with Canadians spending $10 billion in the United States and Americans only $4 billion in Canada. Quite apart from the border runners, the United States was even more attractive to Canada than usual, and record numbers of Canadians spent record amounts of money fuelling the American economy, not just in border-town shopping malls but in warm places like Florida, California, Texas, and the Sun Belt. There were so many Canadians in Florida in the winter that separate newspapers sprang up to cater to them with Canadian news unavailable through the American media, which continued to see Canada mainly as the source of bad winter weather and Wayne Gretzky.* The GST thus seemed to represent a double whammy on the Canadian economy. It not only lessened the proclivity to spend; it also symbolized an increasing tendency to transfer expenditure totally out of an economy already hard hit by international recession and free-trade adjustments.

Those who fly the highest during booms experience the greatest difficulties in the ensuing bust. The Canadian automobile industry, which had been the flagship of Ontario prosperity throughout the 1980s, suddenly began experiencing difficulties. Sales fell off dramatically, and the major manufacturers announced plant closures, layoffs, and general restructuring. National unemployment rose from an average 7.6% of the labour force in 1989 to 9.3% by December 1990 to 10.3% by December 1991. For most provinces the changes in unemployment were marginal. But in Ontario, which averaged 5.4% in 1989, a rise to double figures by mid-1991 (10.2% in July 1991) was regarded as a major disaster. Combined with a severe collapse in many housing markets—headed by a vastly overinflated one in Toronto—and falling provincial revenues, Ontario seemed in particularly rough shape.

Overall, claimed Statistics Canada, the losers in the 1991 recession were blue-collar workers, among whom unemployment rates reached 15.2 per cent. Particularly disadvantaged were older blue-collar workers. In the words of Philip Cross of Statistics Canada: 'If you lose your job and you're fifty years old, have less than a high-school education and few skills, you're toast in this economy.' While 128,000 jobs were lost in 1991 (88,000 in retail trade and manufacturing, 40,000 in construction), 113,000 new jobs were created in the public sector, mainly at the municipal level to service burgeoning welfare rolls caused by the recession. Employment among those with university degrees rose 4.1 per cent in 1991, while it declined for those at the bottom end of the educational scale.

Statistics Canada also provided evidence that the spendable income of Canadians had marginally decreased over the ten years ending in 1991, mostly owing to higher taxes. The personal tax bite rose from 19.9 per cent of total family spending in 1986 to 22.3 per cent by 1991. As one Canadian worker put it: 'The paycheques look a lot bigger, and you say "Wow", but when you detail it out there's nothing left.'[2] Understandably, financial pressures drove many married women back into the work force, and as a result they put new demands on overcrowded and underfunded day-care facilities. The economic downturn also increased the poverty gap, with the number of families living below the poverty line (and dependent on welfare income)

---

*On the Saturday morning TV line-up, Gretzky became an American cartoon 'Pro-Star', joining Bo Jackson (representing football and baseball) and Michael Jordan (representing basketball).

rising in every province, but especially in Ontario. Although the downturn cut substantially into the rate of inflation, it never totally eliminated the sorts of modest annual advances in price levels (around 4 per cent in 1991) that had been experienced since the Second World War.

As for interest rates, the prime (the rate charged by the Bank of Canada to the major chartered banks) dropped lower than it had been in decades, with mortgage rates actually plummeting under double-digit figures. By mid-1992 a one-year mortgage could be obtained for as little as 7 per cent. Federal banking policy continued to emphasize the fight against inflation, which meant that interest rates were never lowered as much as they might otherwise have been, and they were certainly kept well above American levels. Perhaps most disturbingly, the government (preoccupied with the Constitution?) refused to force the country's financial institutions to reflect fully the lowered prime rates of, for example, the Bank of Canada, especially for credit-card financing. Although overall industrial profits in Canada fell off substantially in 1991, the result was that the financial industry continued to show higher and higher profits, while complaints of gouging from consumer groups went unheeded.

An economic recession is never a good time to introduce a new visible surcharge, nor is it a propitious moment to expand free-trade negotiations internationally. How serious the recession really was (or would become) was a matter of some debate among the economists, but there seemed general agreement that—while it was probably more serious than the one of the early 1980s—it was far from being in the same league with the great economic collapse of the 1930s. Even so, given its choice, the Canadian government would probably have stayed out of the international discussions among 108 nations over GATT (the General Agreement on Trade and Tariffs), and away from talks with the United States and Mexico about a continental free-trade zone.

For a variety of reasons free trade certainly appeared considerably less attractive in 1991 than it had in 1985. In the first place, it soon became abundantly clear that the Americans really believed in free trade only on their own terms, and would invoke protectionism whenever necessary—an out-come that was foreseen by the many scorned opponents to free trade when it was being promoted by the Mulroney government. In the second place, it became equally clear that Canada and Canadians could not easily move to become competitive with the United States, not to mention Asia and a revitalized Europe. A combination of GATT revisions and American com-petition, for example, threatened those Canadian farmers who had been spared earlier disasters associated with the collapse of international markets, especially in grain. Specialized producers of such foodstuffs as eggs, turkeys, and dairy products for the domestic market, who had enjoyed both protec-tion and guaranteed price regulation through supply marketing boards, were now threatened with the elimination of such boards through international agreement, thus exposing them to American competition. These prosperous farmers responded with emotional media campaigns about the threat to the family farm (the one for dairy producers was especially poignant) rather than with detailed explanations of why they were unable to compete with the United States. Such explanations—which would have included lower human productivity, greater expectations, higher taxes, economies of scale, and a generally lower level of government support—would probably also have encapsulated the Canadian dilemma of competing internationally in the 1990s. From the vantage point of the consumer, it did not much matter where eggs came from, particularly if they were less expensive. Neither the farmers nor the retail sector made much mileage out of nationalistic arguments about voluntarily buying Canadian. Consumers continued to ignore such blandishments and went for the lowest prices.

Indeed, the economic problems facing Canada appeared likely to get only worse throughout the remaining decade of the century, whatever the immediate international situation. If Canada could not supply an essentially unprotected domestic market with competitively priced goods, in what directions could it possibly turn for economic salvation? Convincing answers to this most urgent of questions were not forthcoming. Symptomatic of the problem was the confusion of those concerned with job retraining for the unemployed. These people were under no illusions about the realities of employment options. The average Canadian would have to accept that his or her existing skills would become obsolete several times during a working lifetime, and that nobody could be guaranteed immunity from geographical relocation. But not even realistic job retraining and counselling was particularly useful when nobody knew what or where the jobs of the future would be.

A similar uncertainty hung over growing environmental problems. American studies released early in 1992, for example, indicated a level of ozone depletion far more serious than previously acknowledged, affecting most Canadian cities and likely only to worsen over the remainder of the decade. While fears of skin cancer in children allowed to play out in the sun were perhaps over-reactions, the long-term implications of the effect of chlorofluorocarbons (CFCs) and other ozone-depleting chemicals in the atmosphere were singularly unpleasant. Unfortunately most of the culprits were associated with industrial pollution and the internal combustion engine. Relief was simple but expensive—and expensive is never really simple. While Canadians in general favoured environmental reform, their support softened considerably when specific measures and costs were revealed. All evidence pointed to the fact that environmental cleanup would greatly increase taxes, and probably cost jobs by pricing Canadian products further out of the market.

Politics and the Constitution

The scene is a Winnipeg kindergarten playground in early winter. A number
of young girls are engaging in a traditional childhood activity: skipping rope.
The chanted refrain to which they skip, perhaps symptomatically of the
1990s, is taken not from the vast Ur-pool of such chants, but from an
American children's cartoon program entitled 'Tiny 'Toons'. The words,
however, are given a decidedly Canadian slant:

> We're tiny, we're toony,
> We've also lost our loonie,
> 'Cause Brian Mulroney,
> Invented GST!

Those skipping (and those watching) understand the stresses of the chant,
that hard stomp on 'Mulroney' and 'GST!'.

The depth of general cynicism about Prime Minister Mulroney was also
revealed in public-opinion polls, in which the proportion of those queried
who approved of his performance over the winter of 1991-2 hovered around
a mere fourteen per cent. Hitching a ride on the successful military coat-tails
of President George Bush—himself no paragon of popularity by the end of
1991—had done the Mulroney government no apparent good. Rumours
abounded throughout 1991 (officially denied) that Brian Mulroney wanted
desperately to be Secretary General of the United Nations, perhaps seeing
such a position as a graceful way to step out of Canadian politics. Polling
evidence suggested that only Joe Clark had any hope of leading a Progressive
Conservative government to another victory in English-speaking Canada.
Yet at the same time, only Mulroney offered the PCs any possibility of
Quebec support, without which any federal party (and perhaps Canada as a
nation) was doomed.

A new spirit of separatism emanated from Quebec in the wake of the
failure of the Meech Lake Accord, which had the unfortunate result of
persuading many Québécois that the rest of Canada did not understand their
aspirations and was not seeking to accommodate them. Meech Lake was
viewed by the Quebec press as a decisive rebuff from anglophone Canada,
and the sense of grievance did not recede much with time. At the same time,
many Quebec business leaders now claimed that they could survive separation from Canada, although it remained unclear whether such survival could
occur in a situation of complete independence or only in the environment of
sovereignty-association still advocated by the Parti Québécois, in which an
independent Quebec would continue to be plugged into the Canadian
monetary and financial systems. The federal government was not prepared to
go as far as some outside Quebec advocated—eschewing suggestions, for
example, that it restore the old pre-Confederation boundaries that would

deprive the province of most of its northland. But the feds tried to make plain to Quebec that the rest of the country would not allow a fully sovereign Quebec to have its cake and eat it too.

In terms of the world situation, which in 1991 witnessed the virtual break-up of a number of federations, including those of the USSR and Yugoslavia, under the mounting pressure of old nationalisms that had not gone away despite generations of Eastern Bloc 're-education', the Canadian situation was not a disaster area. A smaller proportion of the population in Quebec wanted full sovereignty in 1991 than sought devolution in Wales or Scotland. Neither side in Canada was seriously suggesting armed confrontation (as in Yugoslavia and Ireland). Nevertheless, the press continued to treat the constitutional issue as being in 'crisis'. Brian Mulroney and his government perpetuated the pattern of Canadian politics over the last thirty years in their seeming inability to deal simultaneously with constitutional and economic issues. Given the conceptual and practical difficulties for the Mulroney government of 'jump-starting' the Canadian economy in the face of a downturn that was both cyclical and international, its concentration on the constitutional mess was perhaps understandable. It seemed virtually impossible for the government to return to Keynesian principles and attempt to spend its way out of recession, particularly when the federal deficit was still growing.

The deficit seemed to have a life of its own, its increase fuelled by declining government revenues (despite the GST) and the automatic action of social-welfare programs, chiefly unemployment compensation. The deficits of the provincial governments rose from $4 billion in 1988 to $21 billion in 1992 as the federal government reduced transfer payments. The truly cynical insisted that the government's obvious preference for dealing with the Constitution grew from its hope that debate over such matters as the 'Triple E' Senate and the 'distinct society' clause would distract the Canadian public's attention until the economy, largely of its own volition, recovered. Since most of the economic forecasters thought 1992 would be a year of economic recovery—although there was some disagreement over how swift the rebound would be—there appeared to be some sense in the strategy.

With economic recovery and constitutional resolution—so the argument went—the demonstrably short memories of the Canadian electorate would allow the Tories to remain in power. The emergence of a taxpayer revolt, such as had occurred in other Western nations in the 1980s, was still a distinct possibility, however. Meanwhile the Mulroney government (with the increasingly popular Joe Clark as minister in charge of constitutional reconciliation) was attempting to thread its way between the Scylla of Quebec separatism and the Charybdis of voter alienation as represented, for instance, by the Reform Party of Preston Manning, which came from an increasingly disenchanted West, and the NDP victories of 1991 in British Columbia and Saskatchewan. For students of Canadian political history, there was a strong sense of *déja vu* in all these conflicting forces, however new and different the government and the media attempted to make them appear.*

The federal government spent most of 1991 attempting to figure out how to allow for 'democratic input' in the process of constitutional revision. It was clear that the Mulroney administration, whatever its parliamentary strength, was far too unpopular simply to force through new legislation with its substantial numerical majority. A system of public hearings across the country in the summer and early autumn, chaired jointly by Winnipeg MP Dorothy Dobbie and, latterly, Senator Gérald Beaudoin of Quebec, turned into a series of embarrassing fiascos, and was eventually abandoned in favour of a number of weekend conferences held in major cities from coast-to-coast early in 1992. The lists of invitees to these gatherings, a few hundred people per conference, and their agendas, could be controlled to some extent. Nobody managed (or even bothered) to explain the way in which the guest-lists had been prepared or how they were at all representative. The constitutional conferences could only partially be managed, however, and the vociferous presentations of the collective minorities—particularly native peoples and women—could not be suppressed. Indeed, the conferences provided an ideal platform for minority representatives to state their cases, and the government was obliged to alter its thinking to some extent, particularly regarding native rights and the entrenchment of social-welfare obligations. On the basis of the atmosphere created by the conference Clark was prepared to move ahead. The rhetorical excesses of the Quebec press over the inadvertent failure of Maureen Forrester to close the final conference (at Vancouver) by singing the national anthem in both languages merely served as a reminder of how little of the constitutional debate was being conducted along truly rational lines. And then the ominous anti-anti-climax: the Beaudoin-Dobbie Report on constitutional reform was released in March 1992 and was summarily rejected by both the Parti Québécois and the Quebec Liberals, with Robert Bourassa protesting its 'domineering federalism'; and even Marcel Masse, Mulroney's defence minister, saying, when asked if the Report would be sellable in Quebec:

> That's not the point—the point is not if it is sellable. . . . From my point of view it's not—it's as simple as that. The question to ask is, 'Is it possible for the government to find a better approach to meet Quebec's demands?'
>
> I believe that Quebec forms a nation, it has a will to live together, and it needs legislative powers to fashion itself. That is the reality. And it flows from everything that has been sought from Mercier to Bourassa.[3]

---

*There was an interesting division of opinion between Canadian historians and political scientists over the constitutional crisis. A large number of historians seemed persuaded that it represented nothing very distinctive and was best ignored; historian Michael Bliss of the University of Toronto led the way here by calling for a ten-year moratorium on constitutional change. Political scientists, on the other hand, appeared fascinated by the possibility of substantial constitutional experimentation and revision.

In early July 1992 a tentative agreement on a new constitutional package was negotiated by the federal government and the premiers of the nine anglophone provinces, but it was not immediately accepted by the government of Quebec. But in August all partners, including representatives of the native peoples, met at Charlottetown and agreed on a revised package. Whether the demands of Quebec could be met by constitutional reform was only one of several other problems, which included pressures by the aboriginal community to practise self-government without being denied the benefits of federal social services.

At this cliff-hanging point, the long saga (so short in terms of world history) of the people and country of Canada must end. Looking back, one sees it as an amazing story of a great experiment that created, in the northern hemisphere, a mainly thriving and beneficent country of the Western world out of accommodations that were extraordinarily struck and maintained by two peoples of European descent—called, for the sake of convenience, the English and the French—often at the expense of others.

No history of a country can have a 'happy ending'—or any real ending at all. The truism that history is in a constant state of flux was famously demonstrated some two and a half years ago in Russia and Eastern Europe. In 1992 it applied particularly to Canada, when a referendum on the new constitutional agreement, held in October, resulted in an overall 'No/*Non*' vote—with six provinces and one territory voting 'No'.

So—quite apart from the economic dislocations and other pressures emanating from both outside and inside Canada, and the change in the composition of the population that is taking place steadily as a result of immigration—political change inexorably lies ahead. As long ago as 1837/8 Lord Durham stated in his *Report*, dedicated to the young Queen Victoria, that he found that 'two races' had been 'brought into the same community, under circumstances which rendered their contact inevitably productive of collision.' A more-or-less continuous effort to deny this perception has been undertaken over the following century and a half, never more assiduously than in the last thirty years—though one has lately been conscious of ominous signs that, in Margaret Atwood's words, 'This is not a debate/but a duet/with two deaf singers' ('Two-Headed Poems').

As the moment of truth hovers, we can only wonder whether the worldwide trend towards localization will help to produce the sovereign country of Quebec, or whether a shared past and mutual economic dependency will help to bring about a workable political accommodation. This, it has become plain, is desired by virtually all Anglo-Canadians, and by a great many Québécois. But what kind of country will Canada then become?

This must remain, for the present, a great unanswered question.

Notes

Chapter One: The Completion of Confederation
[1]Quoted in George F.G. Stanley, *Louis Riel* (Toronto, 1963), p. 63.
[2]Ibid.
[3]Quoted in Hartwell Bowsfield, *Louis Riel: The Rebel and the Hero*, Canadian Lives (Toronto, 1971), p. 35.
[4]Quoted in Margaret A. Ormsby, *British Columbia: A History* (Toronto, 1958), p. 245.
[5]Ibid., p. 248.
[6]Robert G. Cail, *Land, Man, and the Law: The Disposal of Crown Lands in British Columbia 1871-1913* (Vancouver, 1974).
[7]Quoted in Frank P. MacKinnon, *The Government of Prince Edward Island* (1951), p. 136.
[8]Quoted in James Hiller, 'Confederation Defeated: The Newfoundland Election of 1869', in James Hiller and Peter Neary, eds., *Newfoundland in the Nineteenth and Twentieth Centuries* (Toronto, 1980), pp. 70-1.
[9]A.I. Bloomfield, *Patterns of Infrastructure in International Investment Before 1914* (Princeton, 1968), pp. 42-4.
[10]M. Simon, 'New British Investments in Canada 1865-1914', *Canadian Journal of Economics*, 3 (1970), p. 241.
[11]Quoted in W.T. Easterbrook and M.H. Watkins, eds., *Approaches to Canadian Economic History* (Ottawa, 1962), p. 238.
[12]*Confederation Debates in the Province of Canada*, p. 511.
[13]Quoted in Ramsay Cook, *Provincial Autonomy, Minority Rights and the Compact Theory 1867-1921* (Ottawa, 1969), p. 10.

[14]Ibid., p. 11.
[15]Ibid., p. 13.
[16]Ibid., p. 31.
[17]Ibid., p. 33.
[18]Quoted in Carl Berger, 'The True North Strong and Free', in J.M. Bumsted, ed., *Interpreting Canada's Past*, II, (Toronto, 1986), pp. 154-60.
[19]Quoted in A.W. Rasporich, 'National Awakening: Canada at Mid-Century', in J.M. Bumsted, ed., *Documentary Problems in Canadian History* (Georgetown, 1969), I, p. 225.
[20]Quoted in Moncrieff Williamson, *Robert Harris 1849-1919: An Unconventional Biography* (Toronto, 1970), p. 64.
[21]The Royal Society of Canada, *Fifty Years' Retrospect 1882-1932* (Toronto, 1932), pp. 91-2.
[22]For further discussion, see Dennis Reid, *Our Own Country Canada: Being an Account of the National Aspirations of the Principal Landscape Artists in Montreal and Toronto 1860-1890* (National Gallery of Canada, Ottawa, 1979), pp. 298ff.
[23]Quoted in Neil McDonald, 'Canadianization and the Curriculum: Setting the Stage, 1867-1890', in E.B. Titley and Peter J. Miller, eds., *Education in Canada: An Interpretation* (Calgary, 1982), p. 97.
[24]Ibid., p. 100.
[25]Dale McIntosh, *History of Music in British Columbia 1850-1950* (Victoria, 1989).
[26]Quoted in Helmut Kallmann, *A History of Music in Canada* (Toronto, 1987), pp. 137-8.
[27]Don Morrow et al., *A Concise History of Sport in Canada* (Toronto, 1989), pp. 45 ff., 109 ff.
[28]Quoted in D.N. Sprague, 'The Manitoba Land Question, 1870-1882', in J.M. Bumsted, ed., *Interpreting Canada's Past*, II, p. 4.
[29]Quoted in the *DCB*, XI, p. 746.
[30]Quoted in Bowsfield, op. cit., p. 116.
[31]Ibid., p. 121.
[32]Ibid., p. 122.
[33]Ibid., p. 153.
[34]Quoted in Barbara Robertson, *Wilfrid Laurier: The Great Conciliator*, Canadian Lives (Toronto, 1971), pp. 50-1.
[35]Quoted in Peter Li, *The Chinese in Canada* (Toronto, 1988), p. 29.
[36]Quoted in A.I. Silver, *The French-Canadian Idea of Confederation, 1864-1900* (Toronto, 1982), p. 147.

Chapter Two: The First Triumph of Industrialism, 1885-1919

[1]J.C.M. Ogelsby, *Gringos from the Far North: Essays in the History of Canadian-Latin American Relations 1866-1968* (Toronto, 1976), pp. 111-12; see also Christopher Armstrong and H.V. Nelles, *Southern Exposure: Canadian Promoters in Latin America and the Caribbean, 1896-1930* (Toronto, 1988).
[2]Quoted in Michael Bliss, 'Canadianizing American Business: The Roots of the Branch Plant', in Ian Lumsden, ed., *Close the 49th Parallel: The Americanization of Canada* (Toronto, 1972), p. 38.
[3]Ibid.

[4]Ibid., p. 30.

[5]Ibid., p. 27.

[6]Robert Armstrong, *Structure and Change: An Economic History of Quebec* (Toronto, 1984), p. 233.

[7]William L. Marr and Donald G. Paterson, *Canada: An Economic History* (Toronto, 1980), p. 384.

[8]Craig Heron, *Working in Steel: The Early Years in Canada, 1883-1935* (Toronto, 1988).

[9]Eric W. Sagar with Gerald E. Panting, *Maritime Capital: The Shipping Industry in Atlantic Canada, 1820-1914* (Montreal, 1990).

[10]Quoted in T.W. Acheson, 'The National Policy and the Industrialization of the Maritimes', in J.M. Bumsted, ed., *Interpreting Canada's Past* (Toronto, 1986), II, p. 77.

[11]Gustavus Myers, *History of Canadian Wealth* (Toronto, 1972), p. xxiii.

[12]Quoted in R.T. Naylor, *The History of Canadian Business, 1867-1914* (Toronto, 1975), I, pp. 74-5. See also his *Bankers, Bagmen and Bandits: Business and Politics in the Age of Greed* (Montreal, 1990).

[13]Naylor, op. cit., pp. 74ff.

[14]Ibid.

[15]Ibid., I, p. 103.

[16]Edward J. Chambers and Donald F. Gordon, 'Primary Products and Economic Growth,' *Journal of Political Economy*, LXXIV (1966), pp. 315-32.

[17]J. Hiller, 'The Railway and Local Politics in Newfoundland', in Peter Neary and James Hiller, eds, *Newfoundland in the 19th and 20th Centuries* (Toronto, 1980), pp. 121-55.

[18]Quoted in H.V. Nelles, *The Politics of Development: Forests, Mines & Hydro-Electric Power in Ontario, 1849-1941* (Toronto, 1974), p. 217.

[19]Ibid., p. 54.

[20]Ibid., p. 60.

[21]Ibid., p. 77.

[22]Ibid., p. 18.

[23]Ibid., p. 188.

[24]Ibid., p. 147. See also Michael Bliss, *A Living Profit: Studies in the Social History of Canadian Business, 1883-1911* (Toronto, 1974).

[25]Nelles, op. cit., p. 149.

[26]T.W. Acheson, 'The Social Origins of the Canadian Industrial Elite, 1880-85', in David S. Macmillan, ed., *Canadian Business History: Selected Studies, 1497-1971* (Toronto, 1972), pp. 144-75; 'Bourgeoisie and Petty Bourgeoisie', in Paul-André Linteau et al., *Quebec: A History 1867-1929* (Toronto, 1983), pp. 399-407.

[27]Craig Heron and Bryan Palmer, 'Through the Prism of the Strike: Industrial Conflict in Southern Ontario', *Canadian Historical Review*, 58 (December 1977), pp. 423-58.

[28]Ibid.

[29]Quoted in John Herd Thompson, *The Harvests of War: The Prairie West, 1914-1918* (Toronto, 1978), p. 67.

[30]Quoted in A.R. McCormack, *Reformers, Rebels and Revolutionaries: The Western Canadian Radical Movement, 1899-1919* (Toronto, 1977), p. 128.

[31]Quoted in Donald Avery, 'The Radical Alien and the Winnipeg General Strike of 1919', in Bumsted, ed., *Interpreting Canada's Past*, II, p. 222.
[32]Ibid., p. 227.
[33]Ibid., p. 224.
[34]Ibid.

Chapter Three: Urban Canada, 1885-1919

[1]Paul Rutherford, ed., *Saving the Canadian City: The First Phase 1880-1920* (Toronto, 1974), p. 233.
[2]Ibid., p. 76.
[3]Quoted in Judith Fingard, *The Dark Side of Life in Victorian Halifax* (Porters Lake, NS, 1989), p. 18.
[4]Stephen Leacock, *Arcadian Adventures with the Idle Rich* (London, 1914), p. 3.
[5]Alan Gowans, *Building Canada: An Architectural History of Canadian Life* (Toronto, 1966), caption to Plate 164.
[6]Quoted in Barry Potyondi, 'The Town Building Process in Minnedosa', in A.F.J. Artibise, ed., *Town and City: Aspects of Western Canadian Urban Development* (Regina, 1981), pp. 130-1.
[7]Quoted in Terry Copp, *The Anatomy of Poverty: The Condition of the Working Class in Montreal 1897-1929* (Toronto, 1974), p. 33.
[8]Gregory Kealey, *Hogtown: Working Class Toronto at the Turn of the Century* (Toronto, 1974), p. 25; see also Michael Piva, *The Condition of the Working Class in Toronto, 1900-1921* (Ottawa, 1979).
[9]Ibid., p. 22.
[10]Quoted in A.F.J. Artibise, *Winnipeg: A Social History of Urban Growth, 1874-1914* (Montreal, 1975), p. 241.
[11]Kealey, op. cit., p. 24.
[12]Patricia Roy, 'Vancouver: "Mecca of the Unemployed", 1907-1929,' in A.F.J. Artibise, ed., *Town and City*, pp. 393-414, esp. p. 402.
[13]Mariana Valverde, *The Age of Light, Soap, and Water: Moral Reform in English Canada, 1885-1925* (Toronto, 1991).
[14]G. Frank Beer, 'A Plea for City Planning Organization' (1914), in Rutherford, op. cit., p. 233.
[15]See Desmond Morton, *Mayor Howland: The Citizens' Candidate* (Toronto, 1973).
[16]C.S. Clark's *Of Toronto the Good* was reissued in the Coles Canadiana Collection in 1970. The quotation is on p. 209.
[17]James Shaver Woodsworth in *My Neighbour: A Study of City Conditions, a Plea for Social Service* (Toronto, 1972 reprint), p. 212.
[18]Quoted in Artibise, *Winnipeg*, p. 257.
[19]Ibid., p. 202.
[20]Ibid., p. 204.
[21]Quoted in Walter Van Nus, 'The Fate of the City Beautiful Movement in Canada, 1893-1930', in Gilbert A. Stelter and Alan F.J. Artibise, eds., *The Canadian City: Essays on Urban History* (Toronto, 1977), pp. 162-85 at p. 171; see also Margaret Meek, 'History of the City Beautiful Movement in Canada, 1890-1930', unpublished MA thesis, University of British Columbia, 1979.

[22]Frank Underhill, 'Commission Government in Cities (1910-11)', in Rutherford, op. cit., pp. 326-34.

[23]R.D. Waugh, 'The Reform of Municipal Government' (1916), in Rutherford, op. cit., p. 338.

[24]See Jean Sutherland Boggs, *The National Gallery of Canada* (Toronto, 1971),

[25]Eugene Benson and L.W. Conolly, eds, *The Oxford Companion to Canadian Theatre* (Toronto, 1989), pp. 558-63.

[26]Jean-Marc Larrue, *Le Théâtre à Montréal à la fin du xixe siècle* (Montreal, 1981).

[27]H. Charles Ballem, *Abegweit Dynasty: The Story of the Abegweit Amateur Athletic Association, 1899-1954* (Charlottetown, 1986).

[28]Quoted in Don Morrow et al., *A Concise History of Sport in Canada* (Toronto, 1989), pp. 172, 188.

Chapter Four: Rural Canada, 1885-1919

[1]Mary Rubio and Elizabeth Waterston, eds, *The Selected Journals of L.M. Montgomery, Volume I: 1889-1910* (Toronto, 1985), p. 235.

[2]Ibid., pp. 236-7.

[3]Wendy J. Owen, ed., *The Wheat King: The Selected Letters and Papers of A.J. Cotton, 1888-1913* (Winnipeg, 1985), p. 70.

[4]Ibid., p. 68.

[5]Quoted in R. Douglas Francis and Howard Palmer, eds, *The Prairie West: Historical Readings* (Edmonton, 1985), p. 344.

[6]Quoted in David C. Jones and Ian MacPherson, eds, *Building Beyond the Homestead: Rural History on the Prairies* (Calgary, 1985), p. 117.

[7]Quoted in Paul Voisey, *Vulcan: The Making of a Prairie Community* (Toronto, 1988) p. 158.

[8]Rubio and Waterston, op. cit., p. 177.

[9]Marjorie Griffin Cohen, *Women's Work, Markets, and Economic Development in 19th-Century Ontario* (Toronto, 1988), pp. 93-117.

[10]Quoted in Veronica Strong-Boag and Anita Fellman, eds, *Rethinking Canada: The Promise of Women's History* (Toronto, 1986) p. 99.

[11]Quoted in Gérard Bouchard, 'Family Structures and Geographic Mobility at Laterrière, 1851-1935', *Journal of Family History*, 2 (1977), pp. 364-5.

[12]Ibid., p. 365.

[13]Quoted in Jones and MacPherson, op. cit., p. 126.

[14]Rubio and Waterston, op. cit., p. 116.

[15]Paul-André Linteau et al., *Quebec: A History 1867-1929* (Toronto, 1983), p. 470.

[16]Margaret Coulby Whitridge, ed., *Lampman's Sonnets 1884-1899* (Ottawa, 1976), p. 36.

[17]Quoted in English translation by Linteau et al., op. cit., p. 286.

[18]Ernest Thompson Seton, *Wild Animals I Have Known* (New York, 1898).

[19]Charles G.D. Roberts, *The Last Barrier and Other Stories*, New Canadian Library (Toronto, 1958), p. 100.

[20]F.A. Wightman, *Our Canadian Heritage: Its Resources and Possibilities* (Toronto, 1905), p. 206.

[21]Quoted by Ian Ross Robertson in his Introduction to Andrew Macphail, *The Master's Wife*, New Canadian Library (Toronto, 1977), p. xiii.

[22]Ibid., p. xiii.

[23]J. Russell Harper, *Painting in Canada: A History: Second Edition* (Toronto, 1966), p. 204.

[24]Quoted in Edith Fowke, *Canadian Folklore*, Perspectives on Canadian Culture (Toronto, 1988), p. 17.

[25]Sarah Carter, *Lost Harvests: Prairie Indian Reserve Farmers and Government Policy* (Montreal and Kingston, 1990), p. 15.

[26]Ibid., p. 15.

[27]Ibid., p. 20.

[28]Ibid., p. 129.

[29]Charles Gordon Hewitt, *The Conservation of the Wild Life of Canada* (New York, 1921), p. 235.

[30]Bruce Hodgins et al., *Nastawgan: The Canadian North by Canoe and Snowshoe: A Collection of Historical Essays* (Toronto, 1985), p. 145.

[31]Ibid.

[32]For example, Hesketh Prichard, *Indian Joe: The Detective of the Backwoods* (1913; reprinted 1936 with an introduction by John Buchan).

[33]Quoted in Young, 'Conscription and Ontario Farmers', *Canadian Historical Review*, 53 (1972), p. 293.

[34]Ibid., p. 294.

Chapter Five: Imperialism, Racism, and Reform, 1885-1919

[1]André Siegfried, *The Race Question in Canada*, the Carlton Library (Toronto, 1966), edited and with an Introduction by Frank M. Underhill, p. 113.

[2]Quoted in John English, *The Decline of Politics: The Conservatives and the Party System, 1901-20* (Toronto, 1977), p. 74.

[3]Quoted in Gordon T. Stewart, 'Political Patronage Under Macdonald and Laurier 1878-1911', in J.M. Bumsted, ed., *Interpreting Canada's Past* (Toronto, 1986), II, p. 33.

[4]Quoted in Christopher Armstrong, 'The Mowat Heritage in Federal-Provincial Relations', in Bumsted, ed., op. cit., p. 54.

[5]Quoted in J.M. Bumsted, *Documentary Problems in Canadian History*, vol. II (Georgetown, 1969), p. 1.

[6]Quoted in C.P. Stacey, ed., *Records of the Nile Voyageurs, 1884-1885: The Canadian Voyageur Contingent in the Gordon Relief Expedition* (Toronto, 1959), p. 6.

[7]Quoted in Bumsted, *Documentary Problems*, II, p 78.

[8]Ibid., p. 76.

[9]Ibid., p. 72.

[10]Goldwin Smith, *The Political Destiny of Canada* (London, 1878), p. 130.

[11]Goldwin Smith, *Canada and the Canadian Question* (London, 1891), p. 191.

[12]Siegfried, op. cit., p. 28.

[13]John S. Ewart, *The Kingdom of Canada: Imperial Federation, the Colonial Conferences, the Alaska Boundary and Other Essays* (Toronto, 1908), p. 6.

[14]Ibid., p. 364.

[15]Ibid., p. 80.

[16]Quoted in Denis Monière, *Ideologies in Quebec: The Historical Development* (Toronto, 1981), p. 189.

[17]Ibid., p. 190.

[18]Quoted in Ramsay Cook, ed., *French-Canadian Nationalism:An Anthology* (Toronto, 1969), p. 147.

[19]Quoted in John Kendle, *The Round Table Movement and Imperial Union* (Toronto, 1975), p. 29.

[20]Quoted in Mason Wade, *The French Canadians, 1760-1945* (Toronto, 1968), I, p. 479

[21]Ibid., p. 480.

[22]Sara Jeannette Duncan, *The Imperialist*, New Canadian Library (Toronto, 1961), p. 98.

[23]George Parkin, *Imperial Federation, the Problem of National Unity* (London, 1892), p. 15.

[24]George Parkin, *The Great Dominion: Studies of Canada* (London, 1895), p. 5.

[25]Goldwin Smith, *Loyalty,Aristocracy and Jingoism* (Toronto, 1896), p. 92.

[26]Siegfried, op. cit., p. 96.

[27]Smith, *Canada and the Canadian Question*, p. 10.

[28]Quoted in Bruce Hodgins and Robert Page, eds, *Canada Since Confederation* (Georgetown, 1976), pp. 322-3.

[29]Ibid., p. 326.

[30]Quoted in Wade, op. cit., p. 509.

[31]Quoted in Cook, op. cit., p. 133.

[32]Hansard, 1906, pp. 5636-7.

[33]Siegfried, op. cit., p. 87.

[34]Robert Macdougall, *Rural Life in Canada: Its Trends and Tasks* (1913, reprinted Toronto 1973, with an introduction by Robert Craig Brown), p. 34.

[35]Based on Donald K. Pickens, *Eugenics and the Progressives* (Nashville, 1968); Angus McLaren, *Our Own Master Race: Eugenics in Canada, 1885-1945* (Toronto, 1990).

[36]Quoted in Carol Bacchi, 'Race Regeneration and Social Purity: A Study of the Social Attitudes of Canada's English-Speaking Suffragists', in Bumsted, *Interpreting Canada's Past*, II, p. 195.

[37]Quoted in W.P. Ward, *White Canada Forever: Popular Attitudes and Public Policy toward Orientals in British Columbia* (Montreal, 1978), p. 75.

[38]Patricia Roy, *A White Man's Province: British Columbia Politicians and Chinese and Japanese Immigrants 1858-1914* (Vancouver, 1989).

[39]Carol Bacchi, 'Divided Allegiances', in Linda Kealey, ed., *A Not Unreasonable Claim:Women and Reform in Canada 1880s-1920s* (Toronto, 1979), pp. 89-108.

[40]Wayne Roberts, 'Rocking the Cradle for the World', in Kealey, op. cit., pp. 15-46.

[41]Bacchi, 'Race Regeneration. . .', p. 196.

[42]Quoted in Ramsay Cook and Wendy Mitchison, eds, *The Proper Sphere: Women's Place in Canadian Society* (Toronto, 1976), pp. 230 ff.

[43]Quoted in Bumsted, *Documentary Problems*, II, p. 191.

[44]Wendy Mitchison, 'The WCTU,' in Kealey, op. cit., pp. 73, 151-68.

[45]Quoted in Kealey, op. cit., p. 73.

[46]*Le Devoir*, 5 August 1916.

[47]Quoted in John Herd Thompson, *The Harvests of War:The Prairie West, 1914-1918* (Toronto, 1978), p. 109.

[48]Ibid., p. 101.

Chapter Six: Economy, Polity, and the 'Unsolved Riddle of Social Justice', 1919-1945

[1]Alan Bowker, ed., *The Social Criticism of Stephen Leacock:The Unsolved Riddle of Social Justice and Other Essays* (Toronto, 1973), p. 74.

[2]Ibid., p. 79.

[3]Paul MacEwan, *Miners and Steelworkers: Labour in Cape Breton* (Toronto, 1976); David Frank, 'Class Conflict in the Coal Industry: Cape Breton, 1922,' in Gregory Kealey et al., eds, *Essays in Working Class History* (Toronto, 1970).

[4]W.L. Morton, *The Progressive Party of Canada* (Toronto, 1950).

[5]Quoted in David Jones, *Empire of Dust: Settling and Abandoning the Prairie Dry Belt* (Edmonton, 1987), p. 175.

[6]Ernest R. Forbes, *The Maritime Rights Movement, 1919-1927:A Study in Canadian Regionalism* (Montreal, 1979).

[7]Quoted in Ernest R. Forbes, 'The Emergence of the Campaign for Maritime Rights, 1921-2', in J.M. Bumsted, *Interpreting Canada's Past* (Toronto, 1986), II, p. 243.

[8]Susan Mann Trofimenkoff, ed., *Abbé Groulx: Variations on a Nationalist Theme* (Toronto, 1974); Trofimenkoff, *Action Française: French-Canadian Nationalism in the Twenties* (Toronto, 1975).

[9]Quoted in Mason Wade, *The French Canadians, 1760-1945* (Toronto, 1955), pp. 880, 869.

[10]Quoted in Ramsay Cook, ed., *French Canadian Nationalism:An Anthology* (Toronto, 1969), p. 193.

[11]Quoted in Wade, op. cit., p. 880.

[12]James Gray, *The Roar of the Twenties* (Toronto, 1975).

[13]Margaret A. Ormsby, *British Columbia:A History* (Toronto, 1971), p. 439.

[14]See, for example, Peter C. Newman, *The Bronfman Dynasty:The Rothschilds of the New World* (Toronto, 1978), esp. pp. 74-96.

[15]Doug Fetherling, *Gold Diggers of 1929: Canada and the Great Stock Market Crash* (Toronto, 1979).

[16]Barry Broadfoot, *Ten Lost Years 1929-1939* (Toronto, 1973), p. 6.

[17]A.E. Safarian, *The Canadian Economy in the Great Depression* (Toronto, 1959).

[18]Michael Bliss and L.M. Grayson, eds, *The Wretched of Canada: Letters to R.B. Bennett, 1930-1935* (Toronto, 1971).

[19]Bettina Bradbury, 'Municipal Unemployment and Relief in the Early Thirties: Burnaby, North Vancouver City and District, and West Vancouver', unpublished M.A. thesis, Simon Fraser University, 1974.

[20]Hansard, February 1930, p. 55.

[21]James Gray, *The Winter Years* (Toronto, 1966).

[22]J.H. Wilbur, ed., *The Bennett New Deal* (Toronto, 1968).

[23]Alvin Finkel, *Business and Social Reform in the Thirties* (Toronto, 1979).

[24]Ibid., pp. 31-2.

[25]Quoted in Alvin Finkel, 'Origins of the Welfare State in Canada', in Bumsted, *Interpreting Canada's Past*, II, pp. 294-314 at p. 298.

[26]Ibid., p. 300.

[27]John A. Irving, *The Social Credit Movement in Alberta* (Toronto, 1959); C.B. Macpherson, *Democracy in Alberta: The Theory and Practice of a Quasi-Party System*

(Toronto, 1953); John L. Finlay, *Social Credit:The English Origins* (Montreal, 1972).
[28]L.H. Thomas, ed., *William Aberhart and Social Credit in Alberta* (Toronto, 1977).
[29]Conrad Black, *Duplessis* (Toronto, 1977).
[30]Quoted in Gregory Baum, *Catholics and Canadian Socialism: Political Thought in the Thirties and Forties* (Toronto, 1980), p. 179
[31]Ibid., p. 184.
[32]Ibid.
[33]Alex Laidlaw, ed., *The Man from Margaree: Writings and Speeches of M.M. Coady* (Toronto, 1971).
[34]The Research Committee of the League for Social Reconstruction, *Social Planning for Canada* (Toronto, 1935; reissued 1975), Introduction, pp. x, ix.
[35]Michiel Horn, 'Frank Underhill's Early Drafts of the Regina Manifesto 1933', *Canadian Historical Review*, 54 (1973), pp. 393-418. See also Horn's *The League for Social Reconstruction: Intellectual Origins of the Democratic Left in Canada, 1930-1942* (Toronto, 1980), esp. pp. 36-53.
[36]Kenneth McNaught, *A Prophet in Politics:A Biography of J.S. Woodsworth* (Toronto, 1959).
[37]Quoted in Ormsby, op. cit., p. 453.
[38]S.M. Lipset, *Agrarian Socialism:The Cooperative Commonwealth Federation in Saskatchewan:A Study in Political Sociology* (Berkeley, 1968).
[39]Lita-Rose Betcherman, *The Little Band:The Clashes Between the Communists and the Political and Legal Establishments in Canada, 1928-1932* (Ottawa, 1982).
[40]Ormsby, op. cit., pp. 463-4.
[41]C.P. Stacey, *Arms, Men and Governments: The War Policies of Canada, 1939-1945* (Ottawa, 1970), p. 488.
[42]Robert Bothwell and William Kilbourn, *C.D. Howe:A Biography* (Toronto, 1979).
[43]Quoted in Robert B. Boyce, *Maturing in Hard Times: Canada's Department of Finance Through the Great Depression* (Kingston and Montreal, 1986), p. 120
[44]Leonard Marsh, *Report on Social Security for Canada* (reprinted Toronto, 1975).

Chapter Seven: Canadian Society and Culture, 1919-1945

[1]Pierre Berton, *The DionneYears* (Toronto, 1977).
[2]James G. Snell, *In the Shadow of the Law: Divorce in Canada 1900-1939* (Toronto, 1991).
[3]E. Palmer Patterson II, *The Canadian Indian: A History Since 1500* (Don Mills, 1972).
[4]A. Romaniuk and V. Piché, 'Natality Estimates for the Canadian Indian by Stable Population Models, 1900-1969', *Canadian Review of Sociology and Anthropology*, 9 (1972), pp. 1-20.
[5]Ibid., p. 19, p. 7.
[6]M.G. Hurlich, 'Historical and Recent Demography of the Algonkians of Northern Ontario', in A.T. Steegman, ed., *Boreal Forest Adaptations: The Northern Algonkian* (New York, 1983), pp. 143-99.
[7]A. Romaniuk, 'Modernization and Fertility: The Case of the James Bay Indian', *Canadian Review of Sociology and Anthropology*, 11 (1974), pp. 344-59.
[8]G. Graham-Cummings, 'Health of the Original Canadians, 1867-1967', *Medical Services Journal Canada* 23 (1967), pp. 115-66.

[9]T. Kue Young, *Health Care and Cultural Change: The Indian Experience in the Central Subarctic* (Toronto, 1988).

[10]Grey Owl, *Pilgrims of the Wild* (Toronto, 1982), p. 163.

[11]Quoted in Norah Lewis, 'Physical Perfection for Spiritual Welfare: Health Care for the Urban Child, 1900-1939', in Patricia Rooke et al., eds, *Studies in Childhood History: A Canadian Perspective* (Calgary, 1982), p. 135.

[12]Quoted in Nancy M. Sheehan, 'Indoctrination: Moral Education in the Early Prairie School House', in David Jones et al., eds, *Shaping the Schools of the Canadian West* (Calgary, 1979), p. 226.

[13]See Frank Peers, *The Politics of Canadian Broadcasting, 1920-1951* (Toronto, 1969).

[14]Margaret Prang, 'The Origins of Public Broadcasting in Canada,' *Canadian Historical Review*, 44 (1965), pp. 1-31.

[15]Gordana Lazarevich, *The Musical World of Frances James and Murray Adaskin* (Toronto, 1988), esp. pp. 34-70.

[16]Quoted in John Herd Thompson and Allen Seager, *Canada, 1922-1939: Decades of Discord* (Toronto, 1985), p. 158.

[17]Quoted in Carl F. Klinck, *Literary History of Canada* (Second edition, Toronto, 1976), II, p. 8.

[18]Mary Vipond, 'Canadian Nationalism and the Plight of Canadian Magazines in the 1920s', *Canadian Historical Review*, LVIII (March 1977), pp. 43-63.

[19]Ibid., p. 58.

[20]Pierre Berton, *Hollywood's Canada: The Americanization of our National Image* (Toronto, 1975).

[21]Don Morrow et al., *A Concise History of Sport in Canada* (Toronto, 1989), pp. 90-5.

[22]Quoted in Klinck, op. cit., p. 242.

[23]Quoted in Thompson and Seager, op. cit., p. 162.

[24]Barry Lord, *The History of Painting in Canada* (Toronto, 1974), p. 152.

[25]A.R. Allen, *The Social Passion: Religion and Social Reform in Canada, 1914-1928* (Toronto, 1971).

[26]See Claris E. Silcox, *Church Union in Canada: Its Causes and Consequences* (New York, 1933).

[27]John Webster Grant, *The Canadian Experience of Church Union* (London, 1967).

[28]William Calderwood, 'Pulpit, Press and Political Reactions to the Ku Klux Klan in Saskatchewan', in Susan Mann Trofimenkoff, ed., *The Twenties in Western Canada* (Ottawa, 1972), pp. 191-229; Patrick Kyba, 'Ballots and Burning Crosses', in Norman Ward and Duff Spafford, eds, *Politics in Saskatchewan* (Toronto, 1968), pp. 105-123.

[29]Patricia Roy, *A White Man's Province: Politicians and Chinese and Japanese Immigrants 1858-1914* (Vancouver, 1989).

[30]See also Veronica Strong-Boag, *The New Day Recalled: Lives of Girls and Women in English Canada, 1919-1939* (Toronto, 1988).

[31]Ruth Roach Pierson and Marjorie Griffin Cohen, *'They're Still Women After All': The Second World War and Canadian Womanhood* (Toronto, 1986).

[32]In general, see Norman Hillmer et al., eds, *On Guard for Thee: War, Ethnicity, and the Canadian State, 1939-45* (Ottawa, 1988).

[33]Ken Adachi, *The Enemy that Never Was* (Toronto, 1976); Ann Sunahara, *The Politics of Racism: The Uprooting of Japanese Canadians During the Second World War* (Toronto, 1981).

[34]Quoted in William R. Young, 'Academics and Social Scientists *versus* the Press: The Policies of the Bureau of Public Information and the Wartime Information Board, 1939 to 1945', *Canadian Historical Association Historical Papers*, 1978, pp. 217-40.

Chapter Eight: Canada and the World, 1919-1973

[1]J.L. Granatstein, *The Ottawa Men:The Civil Service Mandarins 1935-1957* (Toronto, 1982). See also Douglas Owram, *The Government Generation: Canadian Intellectuals and the State 1900-1945* (Toronto, 1986).

[2]Quoted in C.P. Stacey, *Canada and the Age of Conflict:A History of Canadian External Policies, Volume I: 1867-1921* (Toronto, 1977), pp. 153-4.

[3]Ibid., p. 192.

[4]Quote dated 16 April 1917 from Stacey, op. cit., p. 213.

[5]Quoted in Richard Veatch, *Canada and the League of Nations* (Toronto, 1975), p. 9.

[6]Quoted in Stacey, op. cit., p. 51.

[7]Quoted in Granatstein, op. cit., p. 37n.

[8]Ibid., p. 41.

[9]Ibid., p. 13.

[10]Quotes from C.P. Stacey, *Canada and the Age of Conflict: A History of Canadian External Policies,Volume II: 1921-1948* (Toronto, 1981), pp. 23-5.

[11]Ibid., p. 135.

[12]Ibid., p. 137.

[13]Ian Drummond, *British Economic Policy andThe Empire 1919-1939* (London, 1972); Drummond, *Imperial Economic Policy 1917-1939: Studies in Expansion and Protection* (Toronto, 1974).

[14]Stacey, op. cit., II, p. 169.

[15]Ibid., p. 173.

[16]Desmond Morton, *A Military History of Canada* (Edmonton, 1985), pp. 165-75.

[17]C.P. Stacey, *Arms, Men and Governments: The War Policies of Canada 1939-1945* (Ottawa, 1970), p. 3.

[18]Ibid., pp. 195-6.

[19]Irving Abella and Harold Troper, *None is Too Many: Canada and the Jews of Europe, 1933-1948* (Toronto, 1982), p. 18.

[20]Ibid., p. 32.

[21]Ibid., p. 46.

[22]Robert Bothwell and William Kilbourn, *C.D. Howe:A Biography* (Toronto, 1979), pp. 152-3.

[23]Quoted in John Holmes, *The Shaping of Peace: Canada and the Search for World Order, 1943-1957* (Toronto, 1979), Volume 1, p. 35.

[24]Quoted in Robert Bothwell and John English, 'Canadian Trade Policy in the Age of American Dominance and British Decline, 1943-1947', *Canadian Review of American Studies*, VIII (Spring 1977), p. 54.

[25]Ibid.

[26]C.D. Howe to Combined Policy Committee on 20 September 1949, quoted in James Eayrs, *In Defence of Canada, vol. 4: Growing Up Allied* (Toronto, 1980) p. 236.

[27]Robert Cuff and J.L. Granatstein, 'The Rise and Fall of Canadian-American Free Trade, 1947-8,' *Canadian Historical Review, LVIII* (December 1977), pp. 459-82.

[28]Quoted in Eayrs, op. cit., p. 63.

[29]Ibid.

[30]Ibid., p. 64.
[31]Document 1 in Eayrs, op. cit., pp. 369-370.
[32]Quoted in Eayrs, op. cit., p. 70.
[33]Escott Reid, *Time of Fear and Hope: The Making of The North Atlantic Treaty 1947-1949* (Toronto, 1977).
[34]Ibid., pp. 219-20.
[35]L.B. Pearson, *Diplomacy in the Nuclear Age* (Toronto, 1958).
[36]L.B. Pearson, *Mike: The Memoirs of the Rt Hon. Lester B. Pearson, II, 1948-1957* (Toronto, 1973), p. 60.
[37]Holmes, op. cit., Volume 2 (Toronto 1982), p. 145.
[38]Morton, op. cit., pp. 234-5.
[39]Donald Creighton, *The Forked Road: Canada 1939-1957* (Toronto, 1976), p. 233.
[40]James Eayrs, *In Defence of Canada, vol. 5: Indochina: Roots of Complicity* (Toronto, 1983).
[41]Quoted in J.L. Granatstein and Robert Bothwell, *Pirouette: Pierre Trudeau and Canadian Foreign Policy* (Toronto, 1990), p. 17.

Chapter Nine: Prosperity and Growth, 1946-1972
[1]Gordon Report: *Royal Commission on Canada's Economic Prospects* (Ottawa, 1958), p. 15.
[2]Ibid., p. 19.
[3]James Marsh, ed., *The Canadian Encyclopedia* (Edmonton, 1985), Second Edition, III, p. 1603.
[4]David Kwavnick, ed., *The Tremblay Report* (Toronto, 1973), pp. 183-4.
[5]Keith Chapman, 'Public Policy and the Development of the Canadian Petrochemical Industry', *British Journal of Canadian Studies*, IV, no. 1 (1989), pp. 12-34.
[6]Gordon Report, p. 209.
[7]Statistics Canada, *Manufacturing Industries of Canada, 1957*, section D (31-206), pp. 5-6. In general, see K.J. Rea, *The Prosperous Years: The Economic History of Ontario 1939-1975* (Toronto, 1985).
[8]Quoted in James G. Eayrs, *In Defence of Canada, Vol. 4: Growing Up Allied* (Toronto 1980), p. 97.
[9]H.D. Woods and Sylvia Ostry, *Labour Policy and Labour Economics in Canada* (Toronto, 1962).
[10]*Annual Report on Labour Organization in Canada for 1972* (Ottawa, 1973), pp. xxiv-xxv.
[11]Quoted in Susan Mann Trokimenkoff, *The Dream of Nation: A Social and Intellectual History of Quebec* (Toronto,1982), p. 292; see also Pierre Elliott Trudeau, ed., *La Grève de l'amiante: Un Étage de la révolution industrielle au Québec* (Montreal, 1956), translated as *The Asbestos Strike* (Toronto, 1974).
[12]Wallace Clement, *Hardrock Mining: Industrial Relations and Technological Changes at Inco* (Toronto, 1981).
[13]John Stanton, *Life and Death of a Union: The History of the Canadian Seamen's Union, 1936-1949* (Toronto, 1978).
[14]Irving Abella, *Nationalism, Communism, and Canadian Labour* (Toronto, 1973).
[15]Quoted in Bryan D. Palmer, *Working-Class Experience: The Rise and Reconstitution of Canadian Labor, 1800-1980* (Toronto, 1983), p. 281.
[16]*Annual Report on Labour Organization in Canada, 1946* (Ottawa, 1948).
[17]Trevor Levere, 'What is Canadian about Science in Canadian History?', in R.A.

Jarrell and N.R. Ball, eds, *Science, Technology, and Canadian History* (Waterloo, 1980), pp. 14-23.

[18]James Guillet, 'Nationalism and Canadian Science,' in Peter Russell, ed., *Nationalism in Canada* (Toronto, 1966), pp. 221-34.

[19]G. Bruce Doern, *Science and Politics in Canada* (Montreal and London, 1972), p. 6.

[20]C. Freeman and A. Young, *The Research and Development Efforts in Western Europe, North America and the Soviet Union* (Paris, 1965).

[21]Canada, *Royal Commission on Government Organization*, vol. 4, Report no. 23, Scientific Research and Development (Ottawa, 1963).

[22]House of Commons, *Debates*, vol. 3, 1966, p. 2849.

[23]J.J. Brown, *Ideas in Exile: A History of Canadian Invention* (Toronto, 1967), pp. 287-9.

[24]Kari Levitt, *Silent Surrender: The Multinational Corporation in Canada* (Toronto, 1970), pp. 127-135.

[25]Gordon Report, p. 403.

[26]Walter Gordon, *A Political Memoir* (Toronto, 1977), p. 64.

[27]David Kwavnick, ed., *The Tremblay Report* (Toronto, 1973), p. 45.

[28]Ibid., p. 166.

[29]W.T. Easterbrook and Hugh G.J. Aitken, *Canadian Economic History* (Toronto, 1956).

[30]Gordon, op. cit., p. 57.

[31]Gordon Report, p. 64.

[32]Ibid., p. 384, quoting Irving Brecher and S.S. Reisman, 'Canada–United States Economic Relations', a draft report prepared for the Commission.

[33]A.E. Safarian, *Foreign Ownership of Canadian Industry* (Toronto, 1966), pp. 21-2.

[34]Kari Levitt, *Silent Surrender*, illustrates the latter; for a more recent overview, see Gordon Laxer, *Open for Business: The Roots of Foreign Ownership in Canada* (Toronto, 1989).

[35]*The Gallup Report*, 19 July 1975, as cited in Robert Laxer, *Canada's Unions* (Toronto, 1976).

Chapter Ten: The Travails of Canadian Unity, 1945-1970

[1]Quoted from Mordecai Richler, 'The North American Pattern' in Al Purdy, ed., *The New Romans: Candid Canadian Opinions of the U.S.* (Edmonton, 1967), p. 15.

[2]Quoted from transcript reprinted in John Saywell, *Quebec 70: A Documentary Narrative* (Toronto, 1971), p. 73.

[3]Ibid., p. 152.

[4]Generally useful on the shape of Canadian politics is David Bell and Lorne Tepperman, *The Roots of Disunity: A Look at Canadian Political Culture* (Toronto, 1979). For the recent period, see also Richard Simeon and Ian Robinson, *State, Society, and the Development of Canadian Federalism* (Toronto, 1990), and Sylvia Bashevkin, *True Patriot Love: The Politics of Canadian Nationalism* (Toronto, 1991).

[5]On federal elections, see J. Murray Beck, *Pendulum of Power: Canada's Federal Elections* (Scarborough, Ontario, 1968).

[6]*Ottawa Citizen*, 4 April 1963.

[7]*Toronto Star*, 29 June 1968.

[8]J.E. Hodgetts and O.P. Dwivedi, 'The Growth of Government Employment in Canada', *Canadian Public Administration*, XI (1969), pp. 224-38.

[9]J.E. Hodgetts, 'The Changing Nature of the Public Service', in L.D. Musolf, ed., *The Changing Public Service* (Berkeley, 1968), pp. 7-18.

[10]*Halifax Chronicle-Herald*, 6 June 1957, quoted in Beck, op. cit., p. 297.

[11]Pierre Elliott Trudeau, 'The Practice and Theory of Federalism', in Michael Oliver, ed., *Social Purpose for Canada* (Toronto, 1961).

[12]Richard Simeon, *Federal-Provincial Diplomacy:The Making of Recent Policy in Canada* (Toronto, 1972).

[13]*Le Devoir*, 9 janvier 1954, cited in Michael D. Behiels, 'Quebec: Social Transformation and Ideological Renewal, 1940-1976', in Behiels, ed., *Quebec Since 1945* (Toronto, 1987), p. 22.

[14]Michael D. Behiels, *Prelude to Quebec's Quiet Revolution: Liberalism Versus Neo-Nationalism, 1945-1960* (Montreal and Kingston, 1985).

[15]For an example, see Pierre Vallières, *White Niggers of America* (Toronto, 1971).

[16]Quoted in Behiels, *Prelude*, p. 109.

[17]Pierre Elliott Trudeau, 'Politique fonctionnelle I,' *Cité libre* 1 (June 1950), quoted in Behiels, op. cit., p. 69.

[18]For Laurendeau, see *André Laurendeau: Witness for Quebec: Essays*, selected and translated by Philip Stratford (Toronto, 1973); Denis Monière, *André Laurendeau et le destin d'un peuple* (Montreal, 1983).

[19]Jean-Paul Desbiens, *The Impertinences of Brother Anonymous* (Toronto, 1962), p. 29.

[20]Jean-Paul Desbiens, *For Pity's Sake: The Return of Brother Anonymous* (Toronto, 1965), pp. 72ff.

[21]See Pierre Elliott Trudeau, *Federalism and the French Canadians* (Toronto, 1980).

[22]Frank Scott and Michael Oliver, eds, *Quebec States Her Case* (Toronto, 1964).

[23]The characterization is Gérard Bergeron's in 'The Québécois State Under Canadian Federalism' in Behiels, *Quebec Since 1945* p. 178.

[24]See D.V. Smiley, 'Canadian Federalism and the Resolution of Federal-Provincial Conflict', in Frederick Vaughan et al., eds, *Contemporary Issues in Canadian Politics* (Scarborough, 1970), pp. 48-66; W.R. Lederman, 'The Limitations of Co-operative Federalism,' *Canadian Bar Review*, XLV (1967).

[25]G.F.G. Stanley, *The Story of Canada's Flag: A Historical Sketch* (Toronto, 1965).

[26]Robert Fulford, *This Was Expo* (Toronto, 1968).

[27]Appendix I, *Report of the Royal Commission on Bilingualism and Biculturalism*, Vol. 4.

[28]Ibid., 4, p. 4.

[29]Ibid., 1, p. xxvii.

[30]Ibid., 4, p. 10.

[31]Jean Daigle, ed., *The Acadians of the Maritimes* (Moncton, 1982).

[32]Other works about Quebec include: Alain G. Gagnon, ed., *Quebec: State and Society* (Toronto, 1984); Denis Monière, *Ideologies in Quebec: The Historical Development* (Toronto, 1981); Dominique Clift, *Quebec: Nationalism in Crisis* (Montreal and Kingston, 1982); Léandre Bergeron, *Petit manuel d'histoire du Québec;* (translated into English as *The History of Quebec:A Patriote's Handbook*, Toronto, 1971); Herbert Guindon, *Quebec Society; Tradition, Modernity, and Nationhood* (Toronto, 1988); Marcel Rioux and Yves Martin, eds, *French-Canadian Society*, I (Toronto, 1964); Marcel Rioux, *Quebec in Question* (Toronto, 1971).

[33]For example, Vallières's *White Niggers of America*.

[34]For a contemporary discussion of minorities, see Jean Leonard Elliott, 'Minority Groups: A Canadian Perspective', in Elliott, ed., *Native Peoples* (Toronto, 1971), pp. 1-14.

[35]Quoted in E. Palmer Patterson, *The Canadian Indian: a History Since 1500* (Toronto, 1972), p. 177.

[36]H.B. Hawthorn, ed., *A Survey of the Contemporary Indians of Canada: Political, Educational Need and Policies*, I (Ottawa, 1966).

[37]James Walker, 'The Indian in Canadian Historical Writing', *CHA Historical Papers*, 1971, pp. 21-47.

[38]J. Rick Ponting and Roger Gibbins, *Out Of Irrelevance: A Socio-Political Introduction to Indian Affairs in Canada* (Toronto, 1980).

[39]*A Statement of the Government of Canada on Indian Policy* (Ottawa, 1969), tabled in the House of Commons on 25 June 1969.

[40]Quoted in Patterson, op. cit., p. 178.

[41]Derek G. Smith, ed., *Canadian Indians and the Law: Selected Documents, 1663-1972* (Ottawa, 1973); Sally M. Weaver, *Making Canadian Indian Policy: The Hidden Agenda 1968-70* (Toronto, 1981); Bradford Morse, ed., *Aboriginal Peoples and the Law: Indian, Métis, and Inuit Rights in Canada* (Ottawa, 1989).

[42]*Statement. . .on Indian Policy*, op. cit., p. 5.

[43]R.J. Macdonald, *Native Rights in Canada* (Toronto, 1970), Appendix 8.

[44]Harold Cardinal, *The Unjust Society: The Tragedy of Canada's Indians* (Edmonton, 1969), pp. 170.

[45]*Report of the Royal Commission on the Status of Women in Canada* (Ottawa, 1970), p. vii.

[46]Quoted in Myrna Kostash, *Long Way From Home: The Story of the Sixties Generation in Canada* (Toronto, 1980), p. 169.

[47]Ibid., p. 171.

[48]Gary Kinsman, *The Regulation of Desire: Sexuality in Canada* (Montreal, 1987).

[49]John Sawatsky, *Men in the Shadows: The RCMP Security Service* (Toronto, 1980), pp. 124-32.

[50]Saywell, op. cit., p. 152.

Chapter Eleven: The New Suburban Society, 1946-1972

[1]J.M. Bumsted, 'Canada and American Culture in the 1950s', in Bumsted, ed., *Interpreting Canada's Past* (Toronto, 1986), II, p. 405.

[2]Paul Rutherford, *When Television was Young: Primetime Canada 1952-1967* (Toronto, 1990).

[3]Alison Prentice, et al., *Canadian Women: A History* (Toronto, 1988), p. 311.

[4]Monica Boyd et al., 'Family: Functions, Formations, and Fertility', in Gail Cook, ed., *Opportunity for Choice: A Goal for Women in Canada* (Ottawa, 1976), p. 18.

[5]T. Kue Young, *Health Care and Cultural Change: The Indian Experience in the Central Subarctic* (Toronto, 1988).

[6]John Porter, *The Vertical Mosaic: An Analysis of Social Class and Power in Canada* (Toronto, 1965).

[7]*Canadian Royal Commission on Bilingualism and Biculturalism Report*, Book III, Part 1, Chapters 1 and 3.

[8]Richard J. Joy, *Languages in Conflict: The Canadian Experience* (reprinted Toronto, 1972), p. 9.

[9]S.D. Clark, *The Suburban Society* (Toronto, 1966), p. 68.

[10]Ibid., p. 110.

[11]Robert Fischman, *Bourgeois Utopias:The Rise and Fall of Suburbia* (New York, 1987), p. 9.

[12]Paul-André Linteau, 'Canadian Suburbanization in a North American Contest— Does the Border Make a Difference?', *Journal of Urban History* 13 (May 1987, 252-74.

[13]John C. Weaver, 'From Land Assembly to Social Maturity: The Suburban Life of Westdale (Hamilton) Ontario, 1911-1951', in G. Stelter and A. Artibise, eds, *Shaping the Urban Landscape:Aspects of the Canadian City Building Process* (Ottawa, 1982), pp. 321-55; David B. Hanna, 'Creation of an Early Victorian Suburb in Montreal', *Urban History Review*, 9 (1980), pp. 38-64.

[14]John Webster Grant, *The Church in the Canadian Era: The First Century of Confederation* (Toronto, 1972), p. 155.

[15]John R. Seeley, R. Alexander Sim, and Elizabeth W. Loosley, *Crestwood Heights:A North American Suburb* (Toronto, 1956), p. 139.

[16]Ibid., p. 148.

[17]Canada, Department of National Health and Welfare, *Canadian Mother and Child* (Ottawa, 3rd ed., 1968), pp. 35-6.

[18]Ibid., p. 37.

[19]Benjamin Spock, *The Pocket Book of Baby and Child Care*, 1948 ed., p. 195.

[20]Ibid., p. 476.

[21]Melinda McCracken, *Memories Are Made of This:What It Was Like to Grow Up in the Fifties* (Toronto, 1975), p. 72.

[22]Seeley, Sim, and Loosely, op. cit., p. 111.

[23]Pierre Vallières, *White Niggers of America* (Toronto, 1971), p. 98.

[24]Ibid., p. 100.

[25]J. Donald Wilson et al, *Canadian Education: A History* (Scarborough, 1970); C.E. Phillips, *The Development of Education in Canada* (Toronto, 1957).

[26]John Kettle, *The Big Generation* (Toronto, 1980), esp. pp. 56-89.

[27]See, for example, the arguments in C.E. Phillips, *Public Secondary Education in Canada* (Toronto, 1955).

[28]J.E. Cheal, *Investment in Canadian Youth: An Analysis of Input-Output Differences Among Canadian Provincial School Systems* (Toronto, 1963).

[29]Kettle, op. cit., p. 61.

[30]Joseph Katz, *Education in Canada* (Newton Abbot, 1974), p. 29.

[31]Seeley, Sim, and Loosely, op. cit., p. 224.

[32]Ibid., p. 226.

[33]*Living and Learning: The Report of the Provincial Committee on Aims and Objectives of Education in the School of Ontario* (Toronto, 1968), p. 75.

[34]Ibid., p. 47.

[35]Paul Axelrod, *Scholars and Dollars: Politics, Economics, and the Universities of Ontario 1945-1980* (Toronto, 1982).

[36]Seeley, Sim, and Loosely, op. cit., p. 241.

[37]Verner Smitheram, 'Development and the Debate over School Consolidation', in Smitheram et al., eds, *The Garden Transformed: Prince Edward Island, 1945-1980* (Charlottetown, 1982), pp. 177-202.

[38]Robert T. Handy, *A History of the Churches in the United States and Canada* (New York, 1977), pp. 409-27.

[39]Commission of Inquiry into the Non-Medical Use of Drugs, *Interim Report* (1970), especially pp. 503-26.

[40]*Proceedings of the Special Joint Committee of the Senate and House of Commons on Divorce*, 1967, pp. 1515-16.

[41]Myrna Kostash, *Long Way From Home: The Story of the Sixties Generation in Canada* (Toronto, 1980).

[42]Quoted in Dennis Forsythe, ed., *Let the Niggers Burn: The Sir George Williams University Affair and its Caribbean Aftermath* (Montreal, 1971), p. 9.

[43]Quoted in Kostash, op. cit., p. 250.

Chapter Twelve: Canadian Culture, 1945-1972
[1]David Kwavnick, ed., *The Tremblay Report* (Toronto, 1973), p. 8.

[2]*Report of Royal Commission on Bilingualism*, I, p. xxi.

[3]Kwavnick, op. cit., p. 12.

[4]*Explorations: Studies in Culture and Communications*, Issue 2, April 1954, p. 6.

[5]Kwavnick, op. cit., p. 14.

[6]For example, W.L. Morton, *The Canadian Identity* (Toronto, 1961), Malcolm Ross, ed., *Our Sense of Identity: A Book of Canadian Essays* (Toronto, 1954).

[7]J. Russell Harper, *People's Art: Native Art in Canada* (Ottawa, 1973); *A People's Art: Primitive, Native, Provincial, and Folk Painting in Canada* (Toronto, 1974).

[8]Julian Park, ed., *The Culture of Contemporary Canada* (Toronto, 1957).

[9]Quoted in Maria Tippett, *Making Culture: English-Canadian Institutions and the Arts Before the Massey Commission* (Toronto, 1989), p. 166.

[10]Quoted in Tippett, op. cit., p. 176.

[11]Ibid., pp. 180-1.

[12]John Archer, *Saskatchewan: A History* (Saskatoon, 1980), pp. 290-2.

[13]Quoted in Tippett, op. cit., p. 182.

[14]Quoted in Tippett, op. cit., p.184.

[15]F.R. Scott and A.J.M. Smith, eds, *The Blasted Pine: An Anthology of Satire, Invective, and Disrespectful Verse* (Toronto, 1957), p. 59.

[16]Claude Bissell, *The Imperial Canadian: Vincent Massey in Office* (Toronto, 1986).

[17]*Report of the Royal Commission on National Development in the Arts, Letters and Sciences* (Toronto, 1951), hereafter referred to as the Massey Report, p. 8. In general, see Paul Litt, *The Muses, The Masses, and the Massey Commission* (Toronto, 1992).

[18]Massey Report, p. 305.

[19]Ibid., p. 163.

[20]Ibid., p. 64.

[21]See J.M. Bumsted, 'Canada and American Culture in the the 1950s', in Bumsted, ed., *Interpreting Canada's Past* (Toronto, 1986), II, pp. 401-2.

[22]Dallas W. Smythe, 'Canadian Television and Sound Radio Programmes,' Appendix 14 to *Report of the Royal Commission on Broadcasting* (1957).

[23]Bumsted, op. cit., p. 405 (table).

[24]*Report of the Royal Commission on Broadcasting*, p, 8.

[25]Ibid., p. 10, p. 11.

[26]E. Austin Weir, *The Struggle for National Broadcasting* (Toronto/Montreal, 1965), p. 372.

[27]Quoted in Richard Handler, *Nationalism and the Politics of Culture in Quebec* (Madison, Wis., 1988), p. 103.

[28]James Overton, 'Towards a Critical Analysis of Neo-Nationalism in Newfoundland,' in R. Brym and R.J. Sacouman, eds, *Underdevelopment and Social Movements in Atlantic Canada* (Toronto, 1979), 219-249.

[29]Kwavnick, op. cit., p. 12.

[30]Hugo McPherson in 'Fiction, 1940-1960', in Carl F. Klinck, ed., *Literary History of Canada* (Toronto, 1965), p. 694.

[31]*The Tamarack Review*, Issue 2, Winter 1957, pp. 13, 17.

[32]Mordecai Richler, 'The Uncertain World', in George Woodcock ed., *The Sixties: Writers and Writing of the Decade* (Vancouver, 1969), p. 27.

[33]Margaret Laurence, 'Ten Years' Sentence', in Woodcock, op. cit., p. 9.

[34]Northrop Frye, 'Conclusion', in Klinck, op. cit., pp. 821, 849.

[35]George Woodcock in Woodcock, op. cit., p. 8.

[36]'Letters in Canada, 1959', in Northrop Frye, *The Bush Garden: Essays on the Canadian Imagination* (Toronto, 1971), p. 126.

[37]Ben-Z. Shek, *French-Canadian and Québécois Novels* (Toronto, 1991), pp. 57-8.

[38]Quoted in Ann Davis, *Frontiers of Our Dreams: Quebec Painting in the 1940's and 1950's* (Winnipeg, 1979), p. 18.

[39]Translations are from Dennis Reid, *A Concise History of Canadian Painting* (Toronto, 1988), pp. 234-5. The complete text of *Refus global* is reproduced in facsimile form in *Paul-Émile Borduas: Écrits/Writings* (Halifax, 1978), published by the Press of the Nova Scotia College of Art and Design.

[40]Quoted in Davis, op. cit., p. 35.

[41]Reid, op. cit., pp. 247-72.

[42]Eugene Benson and L.W. Conolly, eds, *The Oxford Companion to Canadian Theatre* (Toronto, 1989).

[43]For a different interpretation of the same information, see Carl Berger, *The Writing of Canadian History; Aspects of English-Canadian Historical Writing: 1900 to 1970* (Toronto, 1976; Second Edition, 1986).

[44]Melinda McCracken, *Memories Are Made of This: What It Was Like to Grow Up in the Fifties* (Toronto, 1975), p. 60.

[45]W.L. Morton, *The Canadian Identity* (Toronto, 1961), p. 81.

[46]Kirwan Cox, 'Hollywood's Empire in Canada: The Majors and the Mandarins through the Years', *Cinema Canada*, 22 (October 1975).

[47]Pierre Berton, *Hollywood's Canada: The Americanization of our National Image* (Toronto, 1975), pp. 169-170.

[48]Quoted in S.M. Crean, *Who's Afraid of Canadian Culture* (Don Mills, 1976), p. 90.

[49]Rick Salutin, 'The NFB Red Scare', *Weekend Magazine*, 23 September 1978.

[50]Quoted in Berton, op. cit., p. 172.

[51]Ibid., p. 171.

[52]J.M. Bumsted, 'Developing a Canadian Disaster Relief Policy: The 1950 Manitoba Flood', *Canadian Historical Review*, 68 (1967), pp. 347-73.

[53]Berton, op. cit., pp. 187-8.

[54]Quoted in Berton, op. cit., p. 190.

[55]Quoted in Berton, op. cit., p. 191.

[56]David Clandfield, *Canadian Film*, Perspectives on Canadian Culture (Toronto, 1987), pp. 87ff.

[57]Scott Young, *War on Ice: Canada in International Hockey* (Toronto, 1976).

[58]Quoted in Don Morrow et al., *A Concise History of Sport in Canada* (Toronto, 1989), p. 328.

Chapter Thirteen: The Collapse of Liberal Federalism
[1]Brian S. Osborne and Robert M. Pike, 'From "A Cornerstone of Canada's Social Structure" to "Financial Self-Sufficiency": The Transformation of the Canadian Postal Service, 1852-1987', *Canadian Journal of Communication*, 13 (1988), pp. 1-26.
[2]Quoted in ibid., p. 4.
[3]Government of Canada, *Report of the Review Committee on the Mandate and Productivity of Canada Post Corporation*, 2 vols (Ottawa, 1985).
[4]John Saywell, *The Rise of the Parti Québécois 1967-1976* (Toronto, 1977), pp. 72-105.
[5]Richard Gwyn, *The Northern Magus* (Toronto, 1980); Christina McCall-Newman, *Grits: An Intimate Portrait of the Liberal Party* (Toronto, 1983).
[6]Jeffrey Simpson, *Discipline of Power: the Conservative Interlude and the Liberal Restoration* (Toronto, 1980).
[7]Ibid.
[8]Nicole Morgan, *Implosion: an Analysis of the Growth of the Federal Public Service in Canada (1945-1985)* (Montreal, 1986), p. 78.
[9]Colin Campbell and George J. Szablowski, *The Superbureaucrats: Structure and Behaviour in Central Agencies* (Toronto, 1979).
[10]C.B. Macpherson, *Democracy in Alberta* (Toronto, 1973).
[11]Nick Auf der Maur, *The Billion-Dollar Game: Jean Drapeau and the 1976 Olympics* (Toronto, 1976).
[12]E. McWhinney, *Canada and the Constitution 1979-1982* (Toronto, 1982), p. 80.
[13]Quoted in Barry K. Wilson, *Farming the System: How Politicians and Producers Shape Canadian Agricultural Policy* (Saskatoon, 1990) p. 2.
[14]Senate Committee on Poverty, *Poverty in Canada* (Ottawa, 1971), p. 175.
[15]Donald Savoie, *The Politics of Public Spending in Canada* (Toronto, 1990).
[16]*Financial Post* data.
[17]Richard Gwyn, *Edmonton Journal*, 22 August 1984.

Chapter Fourteen: Society and Culture in an Age of Retrenchment. Confusion, and Diffusion, 1972-1990
[1]*Royal Commission on the Donald Marshall, Jr., Prosecution* (Halifax, 1989), I, p. 119.
[2]Ibid., 'Digest of Findings and Recommendations 1989,' p. 1.
[3]National Task Force on Suicide in Canada, *Suicide in Canada* (Ottawa, 1984), p. 9.
[4]Statistics Canada, *Crime and Enforcement Statistics* (Ottawa, 1985); Solicitor General of Canada, *Canadian Urban Victimization Survey* (Ottawa, 1981).
[5]Michael Harris, *Unholy Orders: Tragedy at Mount Cashel* (Markham, 1990).
[6]Reginald W. Bibby, *Fragmented Gods: the Poverty and Potential of Religion in Canada* (Toronto, 1987), p. 38.
[7]See also Hans Mol, *Faith and Fragility: Religion and Identity in Canada* (Burlington, Ont., 1985); Stewart Crysdale and Les Wheatcroft, *Religion in Canadian Society* (Toronto, 1976).
[8]Bibby, op. cit., p. 64.
[9]Health and Welfare Canada, *Special Study of Youth* (Ottawa, 1988).
[10]For demographic trends, see Roderic P. Beaujot and Kevin McQuillan, 'The Social Effects of Demographic Change: Canada 1851-1981,' *Journal of Canadian Studies*, 21, no. 1 (spring 1986), 57-69.
[11]1990 *Royal Lepage Survey of Canadian House Prices*.

[12]Susan A. McDaniel, *Canada's Aging Population* (Toronto and Vancouver, 1986), p. 2.

[13]L.O. Stone and S. Fletcher, *A Profile of Canada's Older Population* (Montreal, 1982), p. 7.

[14]Maureen Baker, *The Aging Canadian Population* (Ottawa, 1988), p. 23.

[15]National Council of Welfare, *Poverty Profile 1988* (Ottawa, 1988), p. 40.

[16]Royal Society of Canada, *AIDS: A Perspective for Canadians* (Ottawa, 1988), 2 vol.

[17]Michael Ornstein, *Aids in Canada: Knowledge, Behaviour, and Attitudes of Adults* (Toronto, 1989).

[18]Angus and Arlene Tigar McLaren, *The Bedroom and the State: The Changing Practices and Politics of Contraception and Abortion in Canada*, 1880-1980 (Toronto, 1986).

[19]*Women in Canada: a Statistical Report* (2nd ed., Ottawa, 1990), p. 144.

[20]T. Kue Young, *Health Care and Cultural Change: The Indian Experience in the Central Subarctic* (Toronto, 1988); Geoffrey York, *The Dispossessed: Life and Death in Native Canada* (Toronto, 1988).

[21]Robin F. Badgley, 'Social Policy and Indian Health Services in Canada,' *Anthropological Quarterly*, 46 (1973), 150-9.

[22]Young, op. cit., p. 126.

[23]Ian Adams et al., *The Real Poverty Report* (Toronto, 1971).

[24]Pamela White, *Native Women: a Statistical Overview* (Ottawa, 1985), p. 25.

[25]National Council of Welfare, *Poverty Profile 1988* (Ottawa, 1988), p. 105.

[26]Keith G. Banting, 'The Welfare State and Inequality in the 1980s,' *Canadian Review of Sociology and Anthropology*, 24(3), 1987, p. 311.

[27]Keith G. Banting, *The Welfare State and Canadian Federalism* (2nd ed., Montreal and London, 1987), p. 177. See also Banting, ed., *The State and Economic Interests* (Toronto,]986), especially Andrew Martin, 'The Politics of Employment and Welfare: National Policies and International Dependence,' pp. 157-242.

[28]Allan Moscovitch, 'The Welfare State since 1975', *Journal of Canadian Studies*, 21, 2 (Summer 1986), pp. 77-95.

[29]In general, see Thomas O. Hueglin, 'The Politics of Fragmentation in An Age of Scarcity: A Synthetic View and Critical Analysis of Welfare State Crisis,' *Canadian Journal of Political Science*, 20 (1987), pp. 235-64.

[30]*Canada Year Book 1990* (Ottawa, 1990).

[31]*Report of The Federal Cultural Policy Review Committee* (Ottawa, 1982); Paul Audley, *Canada's Cultural Industries: Broadcasting, Publishing, Records and Film* (Toronto, 1984).

[32]Steven Globerman, *Cultural Regulation in Canada* (Montreal, 1983); George Woodcock, *Strange Bedfellows: the State and the Arts in Canada* (Vancouver, 1985).

[33]*Funding of the Arts in Canada to the Year 2000: the Report of the Task Force on Funding of the Arts* (Ottawa, 1986), p. 26.

[34]Ibid.

[35]J. Donald Wilson, 'From the Swinging Sixties to the Sobering Seventies,' in E. Brian Titley and Peter J. Miller, eds, *Education in Canada: an Interpretation* (Calgary, 1982), p. 197.

[36]Ibid., p. 200.

[37]*Education in Canada: A Statistical Review for 1988-9* (Ottawa, 1990), p. 215.

[38]Organization for Economic Co-operation and Development, *Reviews of National Policies for Education: Canada* (Paris, 1976).

[39]Roger Magnuson, *A Brief History of Quebec Education* (Montreal, 1980).

[40] *The Symons Report* (Toronto, 1977), p. 106.
[41] *Bulletin of the Canadian Federation for the Humanities*, XIII (4), Autumn 1990, pp. 1-3.
[42] Government of Canada, Department of Communications, *Canadian Cultural Industries:Vital Links* (Ottawa, 1987).
[43] Robert Kroetsch, *Seed Catalogue* (Winnipeg, 1977), p. 26.
[44] Theresa de Lauretis, 'Introduction', *Canadian Woman Studies*, 11 (Spring 1990), p. 5.
[45] Ben-Z. Shek, *French-Canadian and Québécois Novels* (Toronto, 1991), pp. 86-99.
[46] Quoted in Audley, op. cit., p. 21.
[47] In general, see Don Morrow et al., *A Concise History of Sport in Canada* (Toronto, 1989).
[48] Audley, op. cit., p. 21.
[49] Ibid.
[50] *Report of the Federal Cultural Policy Review Committee* (Ottawa, 1982) p. 270.
[51] Ibid., p. 273.
[52] CP, reported in the *Winnipeg Free Press*, 25 Jan. 1991.
[53] Stephen Godfrey, *The Globe and Mail*, June 15, 1991, p. C1.

Epilogue
[1] *Globe and Mail*, Toronto, 12 July 1991, p. A3.
[2] *Winnipeg Free Press*, 21 February 1991, p. A18.
[3] *Globe and Mail*, Toronto, 11 March 1992.

Suggestions for Further Reading

These brief bibliographies relating to each chapter are not intended to be compre-hensive: they provide merely an introduction to the complex literature. For general works covering more than one chapter, see the General Bibliography beginning on page 559.

Chapter One: The Completion of Confederation
For the first Riel rebellion, W.L. Morton, ed., *Alexander Begg's Red River Journal: and Other Papers Relative to the Red River Resistance of 1869-1870* (Toronto, 1956), and his edition of *Manitoba: the Birth of a Province* (reprinted Winnipeg, 1986); George F.G. Stanley, *Louis Riel* (Toronto, 1963); and Hartwell Bowsfield, *Louis Riel: The Rebel and the Hero*, Canadian Lives (Toronto, 1971). For British Columbia, Margaret A. Ormsby, *British Columbia: A History* (Toronto, 1958) and D.B. Smith, ed., *The Reminiscences of Doctor John Sebastian Helmcken* (Vancouver, 1975). For the Métis, D.N. Sprague, *Canada and the Métis, 1869-1885* (Waterloo, 1988), and Thomas Flanagan, *Métis Lands in Manitoba* (Calgary, 1991). On cultural nationalism, Dennis Reid, *'Our Own Country Canada': Being an Account of the National Aspirations of the Principal Landscape Artists in Montreal and Toronto 1860-1890* (Ottawa, 1979); and Suzanne Zeller, *Inventing Canada: Early Victorian Science and the Idea of a Transcontinen-tal Nation* (Toronto, 1987). On racism, which was hardly confined to the west coast but was only most obvious to contemporaries there, see Patricia Roy, *A White Man's Province: British Columbia Politicians and Chinese and Japanese Immigrants, 1858-1914* (Vancouver, 1989).

Chapter Two: The First Triumph of Industrialism, 1885-1919
On Canadians in Latin America, see H.V. Nelles and Christopher Armstrong, *Southern Exposure: Canadian Promoters in Latin and America and the Caribbean, 1896-*

1930 (Toronto, 1988). On the Canadian Northern, T.D. Regehr, *The Canadian Northern Railway: Pioneer Road of the Northern Prairies 1895-1918* (Toronto, 1976). For the period in general, Peter B. Waite, *Canada 1874-1896: Arduous Destiny* (Toronto, 1971); Robert Craig Brown, *Canada, 1896-1921: A Nation Transformed* (Toronto, 1974); Paul-André Linteau *et al.*, *Quebec; A History 1867-1929* (Toronto, 1929). On the 'National Policy', J.H. Dales, *The Protective Tariff in Canada's Development* (Toronto, 1966). On foreign investment, William L. Marr and D.G. Paterson, *Canada, an Economic History* (Toronto, 1980), and Paterson's *British Direct Investment in Canada, 1890-1914* (Toronto, 1976). On Canadian businessmen, J.M. Bliss, *A Living Profit: Studies in the Social History of Canadian Business, 1883-1911* (Toronto, 1974); Gustavus Myers, *A History of Canadian Wealth* (1914, reprinted NY, 1968). On industrialization, Craig Heron, *Working in Steel: The Early Years in Canada, 1883-1935* (Toronto, 1988). For shipping, Eric Sager with Gerald Panting, *Maritime Capital: The Shipping Industry in Atlantic Canada, 1820-1914* (Montreal, 1990). On banking, R.T. Naylor, *Bankers, Bagmen and Bandits: Business and Politics in the Age of Greed* (Montreal, 1990); Ronald Rudin, *Banking en français: The French Banks of Quebec, 1835-1925* (Toronto, 1985). On western agriculture and settlement, W.A. Mackintosh and W.L.G. Joerg, eds., *Canadian Frontiers of Settlement*, 9 vols (reprinted NY, 1974); David Jones, *Empire of Dust: Settling and Abandoning the Prairie Dry Belt* (Edmonton, 1987); David Jones and Ian MacPherson, eds., *Building Beyond the Homestead: Rural History on the Prairies* (Calgary, 1985); David Breen, *The Canadian Prairie West and the Ranching Frontier 1876-1924* (Toronto, 1983). On mining, D.M. Le Bourdais, *Metals and Men: The Story of Canadian Mining* (Toronto, 1957); Pierre Berton, *The Golden Trail: The Story of the Klondike Rush* (Toronto, 1954); Morris Zaslow, *Reading the Rocks: The Story of the Geological Survey of Canada, 1842-1972* (Toronto, 1975). On forestry, A.R.M. Lower, *The North American Assault on the Canadian Forest* (Toronto, 1938). For the CPR, Pierre Berton, *The Last Spike: The Great Railway 1881-1885* (Toronto, 1971) and *The National Dream: The Great Railway, 1871-1881* (Toronto, 1970). On electricity, Clarence Hogue *et al.*, *Québec: un siècle d'électricité* (Montreal, 1979); Merrill Denison, *The People's Power: The History of Ontario Hydro* (Toronto, 1960). On development, H.V. Nelles, *The Politics of Development: Forests, Mines and Hydro-Electric Power in Ontario, 1849-1941* (Toronto, 1974); Bruce Hodgins and Jamie Benidickson, *The Temagami Experience: Recreation, Resources, and Aboriginal Rights in the Northern Ontario Wilderness* (Toronto, 1989). For labour, A.R. McCormack, *Reformers, Rebels, and Revolutionaries: The Western Canadian Radical Movement, 1899-1919* (Toronto, 1977); Robert Babcock, *Gompers in Canada: A Study in American Continentalism before the First World War* (Toronto, 1974). On the Great War, see Michael Bliss, *A Canadian Millionaire: The Life and Business Times of Sir Joseph Flavelle, bart., 1858-1939* (Toronto, 1978); John H. Thompson, *The Harvests of War: The Prairie West, 1914-1918* (Toronto, 1978). On the Winnipeg General Strike, David Bercuson, *Confrontation at Winnipeg: Labour, Industrial Relations, and the General Strike* (Montreal, 1974).

Chapter Three: Urban Canada, 1885-1919

Urban reform is considered in Paul Rutherford, ed., *Saving the Canadian City, the First Phase 1880-1920: An Anthology of Early Articles on Urban Reform* (Toronto, 1974), and Harold Kaplan, *Reform, Planning, and City Politics: Montreal, Toronto, Winnipeg* (Toronto, 1982). For the cities themselves and their living conditions, see, for example, Judith Fingard, *The Dark Side of Life in Victorian Halifax* (Porters Lake, NS, 1989); Terry Copp, *The Anatomy of Poverty: The Condition of the Working Class in Montreal 1897-1929* (Toronto, 1974); Paul-André Linteau, *The Promoters' City: Building the Industrial Town of Maisonneuve, 1883-1918* (Toronto, 1985); Michael Piva, *The Condition of the Working Class in Toronto, 1900-1921* (Ottawa, 1979); Alan Artibise, *Winnipeg: A Social History of Urban Growth, 1874-1914* (Montreal, 1975); H.J.M. Johnston, *The Voyage of the Komagata Maru: The Sikh Challenge to Canada's Colour Bar* (Delhi, 1979); Working Lives Collective, *Working Lives: Vancouver 1886-1986* (Vancouver, 1985); Alan F.J. Artibise, ed., *Town and City: Aspects of Western Canadian Urban Development* (Regina, 1981). For J.S. Woodsworth, see Allen Mills, *Fool for Christ: The Political Thought of J. S. Woodsworth* (Toronto, 1991). For children and reform, Neil Sutherland, *Children in English-Canadian Society: Framing the Twentieth-century Consensus* (Toronto, 1976). The social gospel and the relationship between religion and reform are considered in Ramsay Cook, *The Regenerators: Social Criticism in Late Victorian English Canada* (Toronto, 1985); Richard Allen, ed., *The Social Gospel in Canada: Papers of the Interdisciplinary Conference on the Social Gospel in Canada, March 21-24 1973* (Ottawa, 1975). On western reform, see James Gray, *Booze: The Impact of Whisky on the Prairie West* (Toronto, 1972) and his *Red Lights on the Prairies* (Toronto, 1971). For Stephen Leacock, Alan Bowker, ed., *The Social Criticism of Stephen Leacock* (Toronto, 1973). For women and reform, Linda Kealey, ed., *A Not Unreasonable Claim: Women and Reform in Canada, 1880s-1920s* (Toronto, 1979). On museums, Archie F. Key, *Beyond Four Walls: The Origin and Development of Canadian Museums* (Toronto, 1973). On the theatre, Murray D. Edwards, *A Stage in Our Past: English-Language Theatre in Eastern Canada from the 1790s to 1914* (Toronto, 1968); F.R. Stuart, *The History of Prairie Theatre* (Toronto, 1984); Jean-Marc Larrue, *Le Théâtre à Montréal à la fin du XIXe siècle* (Montreal, 1981); Eugene Benson and L.W. Conolly, eds, *The Oxford Companion to Canadian Theatre* (Toronto, 1989).

Chapter Four: Rural Canada, 1885-1919

On Lucy Maud Montgomery, see Mary Rubio and Elizabeth Waterston, eds, *The Selected Journals of L.M. Montgomery* (2 vols, Toronto, 1985, 1988). On western agrarian conditions, see, for example, Doug Owram, *Promise of Eden: The Canadian Expansionist Movement and the Idea of the West, 1856-1900* (Toronto, 1980); Wendy J. Owen, ed., *The Wheat King: The Selected Letters and Papers of A.J. Cotton, 1888-1913* (Winnipeg, 1985); Paul L. Voisey, *Vulcan: The Making of a Prairie Community* (Toronto, 1988); John Ryan, *Mixed Farming near Carman, Manitoba* (Toronto, 1968). For the Okanagan and Kootenay regions, see R.M. Middleton, ed., *The Journal of Lady Aberdeen: The Okanagan Valley in the Nineties* (Victoria, n.d.); R. Cole Harris and Elizabeth Phillips, eds, *Letters from Windermere, 1912-1914* (Vancouver, 1984). For Quebec, Serge Courbille and Normand Séguin, *Rural Life in Nineteenth-Century Quebec* (Ottawa, 1989); Normand Séguin, *La Conquête du sol au XIXe siècle* (Trois-Rivières, 1977); R. Hardy and Normand Séguin, *Forêt et société en Maurice, 1830-1930* (Montreal, 1984). On child emigration, see G. Joy Parr, *Labouring Children: British Immigrant Apprentices to Canada, 1869-1924* (London, 1980); Kenneth Bagnell, *The Little Immigrants: The Orphans Who Came to Canada* (Toronto, 1980). On patriarchy, Dick Harrison, *Unnamed Country: The Struggle for a Canadian Prairie Fiction* (Edmonton, 1977); Andrew Macphail, *The Master's Wife* (Toronto, 1977). For Charles G.D. Roberts, see Laurel Boone, ed., *The Collected Letters of Charles G.D. Roberts* (Fredericton, 1989). For Ernest Thompson Seton, see Betty Keller, *Black*

Wolf: The Life of Ernest Thompson Seton (Vancouver, 1984); H. Allen Anderson, *The Chief: Ernest Thompson Seton and the Changing West* (College Station, Texas, 1986). For Ralph Connor, see Charles Gordon, *Postcript to Adventure: The Autobiography of Ralph Connor* (Toronto, 1975). On folklore, see Edith Fowke, *Folklore of Canada* (Toronto, 1976); *Canadian Folklore* (Toronto, 1988); *Hommage à Marius Barbeau* (Montreal, 1947). On the north, Bruce Hodgins and Margaret Hobbs, eds., *Nastawgan: The Canadian North by Canoe and Snowshoe: A Collection of Historical Essays* (Toronto, 1985). On the Group of Seven, Peter Mellen, *The Group of Seven* (Toronto, 1981). On Indian farming, Sarah Carter, *Lost Harvests: Prairie Indian Reserve Farmers and Government Policy* (Montreal, 1990). One contemporary view of the rural crisis is outlined in John MacDougall, *Rural Life in Canada: its Trend and Tasks* (Toronto, 1913, reprinted Toronto, 1973).

Chapter Five: Imperialism, Racism, and Reform, 1885-1919

For Canadian politics in this period, see John English, *The Decline of Politics: The Conservatives and the Party System, 1901-20* (Toronto, 1977); Sir John Willison, *Sir Wilfrid Laurier and the Liberal Party: A Political History*, 2 vols (Toronto, 1903); H. Blair Neatby, *Laurier and a Liberal Quebec: A Study in Political Management* (Toronto, 1973). For Quebec, see Jean Hamelin *et al.*, *Aperçu de la politique canadienne au XIXe siècle* (Quebec, 1965); Richard Desrosiers, ed., *Le Personnel politique québécois* (Montreal, 1972); Jean-Paul Bernard, ed., *Les idéologies québécoises au 19e siècle* (Montreal, 1971). For Robert Borden, Robert Craig Brown, *Robert Laird Borden: A Biography*, 2 vols (Toronto, 1975-80). On the critical election of 1911, Paul Stevens, ed., *The 1911 General Election: A Study of Canadian Politics* (Toronto, 1970). For the Equal Rights movement in Quebec, James R. Miller, *Equal Rights: The Jesuits' Estates Act Controversy* (Montreal, 1979). On the 1885 Riel Rebellion, see G.F.G. Stanley, *The Birth of Western Canada: A History of the Riel Rebellions* (Toronto, 1936, reprinted 1961); Thomas Flanagan, *Riel and the Rebellion: 1885 Reconsidered* (Saskatoon, 1983). On imperialism, Carl Berger, *The Sense of Power: Studies in the Ideas of Canadian Imperialism, 1867-1914* (Toronto, 1970); John Kendle, *The Round Table Movement and Imperial Union* (Toronto, 1975). On the participants in the debate, see Elisabeth Wallace, *Goldwin Smith, Victorian Liberal* (Toronto, 1957); Joseph Levitt, *Henri Bourassa and the Golden Calf: The Social Program of the Nationalists of Quebec (1900-1914)* (Ottawa, 1969); Marian Fowler, *Redney: A Life of Sara Jeannette Duncan* (Toronto, 1983); Lionel Groulx, *Mes Mémoires*, 2 vols (Montreal, 1970-1). For the ideas of the suffragists, see Carol Bacchi, *Liberation Deferred? The Ideas of the English-Canadian Suffragists, 1877-1918* (Toronto, 1983). The standard work on the suffrage movement itself is Catherine Cleverdon, *The Woman Suffrage Movement in Canada* (Toronto, 1950, 1974). On women in general, see Ramsay Cook and Wendy Mitchison, *The Proper Sphere: Woman's Place in Canadian Society* (Toronto, 1976). On prohibition, see A.R. Allen, *The Social Passion: Religion and Social Reform in Canada, 1914-28* (Toronto, 1971, 1973). On the politics of the war, Elizabeth Armstrong, *The Crisis of Quebec, 1914-18* (NY, 1937); J.L. Granatstein and J.M. Hitsman, *Broken Promises: A History of Conscription in Canada* (Toronto, 1977); Daphne Read, ed., *The Great War and Canadian Society: An Oral History* (Toronto, 1978); William Roger Graham, *Arthur Meighen, a Biography*, 3 vols (Toronto, 1960-65).

Chapter Six: Economy, Polity, and the 'Unsolved Riddle of Social Justice', 1919-1945
For the Spanish influenza pandemic of 1917, see Eileen Pettigrew, *The Silent Enemy: Canada and the Deadly Flu of 1918* (Saskatoon, 1983). The best survey of the interwar period is John Herd Thompson, with Alan Seager, *Canada 1922-1939: Decades of Discord* (Toronto, 1985). On the industrial unrest, see Paul MacEwan, *Miners and Steelworkers: Labour in Cape Breton* (Toronto, 1976). On the Progressive Party, W.L. Morton, *The Progressive Party in Canada* (Toronto, 1950, reprinted 1967); W.K. Rolph, *Henry Wise Wood of Alberta* (Toronto, 1950). Maritime Rights are treated in Ernest R. Forbes, *The Maritime Rights Movement, 1919-1927: A Study in Canadian Regionalism* (Montreal, 1979). For Groulx and l'Action Française, see Susan Mann Trofimenkoff, *Action Française: French Canadian Nationalism in the Twenties* (Toronto, 1975). On the twenties in western Canada, James Gray, *The Roar of the Twenties* (1975, reprinted 1983). The Bronfman myth is extended in Peter C. Newman, *The Bronfman Dynasty: The Rothschilds of the New World* (Toronto, 1978). The stock market crash of 1929 is discussed in Doug Fetherling, *Gold Diggers of 1929: Canada and the Great Stock Market Crash* (Toronto, 1979). On the Depression economy, see A. Safarian, *The Canadian Economy in the Great Depression* (Toronto, 1959). Letters to Prime Minister Bennett are reprinted in Michael Bliss and L.M. Grayson, eds., *The Wretched of Canada: Letters to R.B. Bennett, 1930-1935* (Toronto, 1971). Oral accounts of the Depression are collected in Barry Broadfoot, *Ten Lost Years 1929-1939* (Toronto, 1973). The best memoir of the period is James Gray, *The Winter Years* (Toronto, 1966). On the Bennett New Deal, see J.R.H. Wilbur, ed., *The Bennett New Deal: Fraud or Portent* (Toronto, 1968). On business, Alvin Finkel, *Business and Social Reform in the Thirties* (Toronto, 1979). Western responses are discussed in Walter Young, *Democracy and Discontent: Progressivism, Socialism and Social Credit in the Canadian West* (Toronto, 1969). On Social Credit, see the series entitled 'Social Credit in Alberta', which includes C.B. Macpherson, *Democracy in Alberta: The Theory and Practice of a Quasi-Party System* (Toronto, 1953); David Elliott, *Bible Bill: A Biography of William Aberhart* (Edmonton, 1987); and Alvin Finkel, *The Social Credit Phenomenon in Alberta* (Toronto, 1989). On Duplessis and the Union Nationale, Conrad Black, *Duplessis* (Toronto, 1977); Denys Arcand, *Duplessis* (Montreal, 1978); Cameron Nish, ed., *Quebec in the Duplessis Era, 1935-1959: Dictatorship or Democracy* (Toronto, 1970). For the Antigonish movement, Gregory Baum, *Catholics and Canadian Socialism: Political Thought in the Thirties and Forties* (Toronto, 1980). The League for Social Reconstruction is examined in Michiel Horn, *The League for Social Reconstruction: Intellectual Origins of the Democratic Left in Canada, 1930-1942* (Toronto, 1980). On Duff Patullo and British Columbia, see Robin Fisher, *Duff Patullo of British Columbia* (Toronto, 1991). For Communism, Lita-Rose Betcherman, *The Little Band: The Clashes between the Communists and the Political and Legal Establishments in Canada, 1928-1932* (Ottawa, 1982). The On-to-Ottawa trek is examined in Victor Howard, *We Were the Salt of the Earth! A Narrative of the On to Ottawa Trek and the Regina Riot* (Regina, 1985). For the Rowell-Sirois report, see *Report of the Royal Commission on Dominion-Provincial Relations*, 3 vols (Ottawa, 1940). For the Second World War, W.A.B. Douglas and Brereton Greenhous, *Out of the Shadows: Canada in the Second World War* (Toronto, Oxford, New York, 1977); Robert Bothwell, *C.D. Howe: A Biography* (Toronto, 1979); William Kilbourn, *The Elements Combined* (Toronto, 1960); Farley Mowat, *The Regiment* (Toronto, 1955); Murray Peden, *A Thousand Shall Fall* (Stittsville, Ont., 1979); Paul Fussel, *Wartime:*

Understanding and Behaviour in the Second World War (NY, 1989). John Kendle treats John Bracken in his *John Bracken: A Political Biography* (Toronto, 1979). The literature on Mackenzie King is immense, but see especially Joy Esberey, *Knight of the Holy Spirit: A Study of William Lyon Mackenzie King* (Toronto, 1980); C.P. Stacey, *A Very Double Life: The Private World of Mackenzie King* (Toronto, 1976); Robert MacGregor Dawson, *William Lyon Mackenzie King: A Political Biography*, 3 vols (Toronto, 1958-); J.L. Granatstein, *Canada's War: The Politics of the Mackenzie King Government 1939-1945* (Toronto, 1975); Brian Nolan, *King's War: Mackenzie King and the Politics of War, 1939-45* (Toronto, 1988). On the Marsh report, see Leonard Marsh, *Report on Social Security for Canada* (Toronto, 1975).

Chapter Seven: Canadian Society and Culture, 1919-1945
The Dionne phenomenon is discussed in Pierre Berton, *The Dionne Years: A Thirties Melodrama* (Toronto, 1977). For Grey Owl, see Lovat Dickson, *Wilderness Man: The Strange Story of Grey Owl* (Toronto, 1973). On new attitudes towards children, see Patricia T. Rooke and R.L. Schnell, eds, *Studies in Childhood History: A Canadian Perspective* (Calgary, 1982); David C. Jones *et al.*, eds, *Shaping the Schools of the Canadian West* (Calgary, 1979). There is no good book in print on the automobile in Canada. On broadcasting, see Frank Peers, *The Politics of Canadian Broadcasting, 1920-1951* (Toronto, 1969). On music, consult Gordana Lazarevich, *The Musical World of Frances James and Murray Adaskin* (Toronto, 1988). On twenties nationalism, see Mary Vipond, *The Mass Media in Canada* (Toronto, 1989). For Raymond Massey, see his autobiography, *When I Was Young* (Toronto, 1976). Hollywood and Canada are the subject of Pierre Berton's *Hollywood's Canada* (Toronto, 1977). On hockey, see Brian McFarlane, *One Hundred Years of Hockey* (Toronto, 1989). Church union is considered in John W. Grant, *The Canadian Experience of Church Union* (London, 1967). The KKK is treated in Julian Sher, *White Hoods: Canada's Ku Klux Klan* (Vancouver, 1983), and given context in Susam Mann Trofimenkoff, ed., *The Twenties in Western Canada* (Ottawa, 1972). On Orientals, see W. Peter Ward, *White Canada Forever: Popular Attitudes and Public Policy toward Orientals in British Columbia* (Montreal, 1978). For Emily Carr, see Maria Tippett, *Emily Carr: A Biography* (Toronto, 1979). On women, see Veronica Strong-Boag, *The New Day Recalled: Lives of Girls and Women in English Canada, 1919-1939* (Toronto, 1988); Ruth Roach Pierson, *'They're Still Women After All': The Second World War and Canadian Womanhood* (Toronto, 1986); Beth Light and Ruth Roach Pierson, eds., *No Easy Road: Women in Canada 1920s to 1960s* (Toronto, 1990). The evacuation of the Japanese from British Columbia is the subject of many studies; see especially Ken Adachi, *The Enemy That Never Was: A History of the Japanese Canadians* (Toronto, 1976); Ann Sunahara, *The Politics of Racism: The Uprooting of Japanese Canadians during the Second World War* (Toronto, 1981). On propaganda, see Gary Evans, *John Grierson and the National Film Board: The Politics of Wartime Propaganda* (Toronto, 1984).

Chapter Eight: Canada and the World, 1919-1973
For general surveys of Canadian foreign relations, see Charles P. Stacey, *Canada and the Age of Conflict: A History of Canadian External Policies*, 2 vols (Toronto, 1977-81); G.P. deT. Glazebrook, *A History of Canadian External Relations*, 2 vols (rev. ed., Toronto, 1966); James G. Eayrs, *In Defence of Canada*, 5 vols (Toronto, 1965-). Donald

Creighton's *The Forked Road: Canada, 1939-1957* is an interesting study of a crucial period. On the mandarins, see J.L. Granatstein, *The Ottawa Men: The Civil Service Mandarins, 1935-1957* (Toronto, 1982); Douglas Owram, *The Government Generation: Canadian Intellectuals and the State, 1900-1945* (Toronto, 1986). For the League of Nations, see Richard Veatch, *Canada and the League of Nations* (Toronto, 1975). On interwar economic matters, Ian Drummond, *British Economic Policy and the Empire, 1919-1939* (London, 1972), and Drummond and Norman Hillmer, *Negotiating Freer Trade: The United Kingdom, the United States, Canada, the Trade Agreements of 1938* (Waterloo, 1989). On Canadian-American relations, Robert D. Cuff and J.L. Granatstein, *Canadian-American Relations in Wartime: From the Great War to the Cold War* (Toronto, 1975), and their *American Dollars, Canadian Prosperity: Canadian-American Economic Relations, 1945-50* (Toronto, 1978). On collective security in the thirties, see W.L. Morton, ed., *The Voice of Dafoe: A Selection of Editorials on Collective Security, 1931-1944, by John W. Dafoe* (Toronto, 1945). On the Second World War (besides those titles listed for Chapter 7), see C.P. Stacey, *Arms, Men and Governments: The War Policies of Canada, 1939-1945* (Ottawa, 1970). On the Jewish question, Irving Abella and Harold Troper, *None Is Too Many: Canada and the Jews of Europe, 1933-1948* (Toronto, 1982). On Newfoundland, Peter Neary, *Newfoundland in the North Atlantic World, 1929-1949* (Kingston, 1988). On the post-war period, see John W. Holmes, *The Shaping of Peace: Canada and the Search for World Order, 1943-1957*, 2 vols (Toronto, 1979-); James Eayrs, *Northern Approaches: Canada and the Search for Peace* (Toronto, 1961). On Gouzenko and espionage generally, see J.L. Granatstein and David Stafford, *Spy Wars: Espionage in Canada from Gouzenko to Glasnost* (Toronto, 1990). Lester Pearson's memoirs were published as *Mike: The Memoirs of the Right Honourable Lester B. Pearson*, 3 vols (Toronto, 1972-5); see also John English, *Shadow of Heaven: The Life of Lester Pearson*, vol. 1 (Toronto, 1989). The Korean business is considered in Denis Stairs, *The Diplomacy of Constraint: Canada, the Korean War, and the United States* (Toronto, 1974). The Vietnam involvement is discussed in Douglas A. Ross, *In the Interests of Peace: Canada and Vietnam 1954-1973* (Toronto, 1984), and Victor Levant, *Quiet Complicity: Canadian Involvement in the Vietnam War* (Toronto, 1986). For the Kennedy-Diefenbaker show, see Knowlton Nash, *Kennedy and Diefenbaker: Fear and Loathing Across the Undefended Border* (Toronto, 1990). On Trudeau's foreign stance, J.L. Granatstein and Robert Bothwell, *Pirouette: Pierre Trudeau and Canadian Foreign Policy* (Toronto, 1990).

Chapter Nine: Prosperity and Growth, 1946-1972

Much of this chapter is based on government statistical data reported by the Dominion Bureau of Statistics and other agencies. For the Gordon Report, see *Royal Commission on Canada's Economic Prospects* (Ottawa, 1957). For the Tremblay Report, see David Kwavnick, ed., *The Tremblay Report* (Toronto, 1973). For Ontario in this period, see K.J. Rea, *The Prosperous Years: The Economic History of Ontario, 1939-1975* (Toronto, 1985). For Quebec, Robert Armstrong, *Structure and Change: An Economic History of Quebec* (Toronto, 1984). On oil, see Ed Gould, *Oil: The History of Canada's Oil and Gas Industry* (Saanichton, B.C., 1976). For the Avro Arrow, see Murray Peden, *Fall of an Arrow* (Toronto, 1987). Foreign ownership is considered in A.E. Safarian, *Foreign Ownership of Canadian Industry* (Toronto, 1966). The public economy is dealt with by Hershel Hardin in *A Nation Unaware: The Canadian Economic*

Culture (Vancouver, 1974). On airlines, see K.M. Molson, *Pioneering in Canadian Air Transport* (Winnipeg, 1978). For the St Lawrence Seaway, William Willoughby, *The St. Lawrence Waterway: A Study in Politics and Diplomacy* (Madison, Wisconsin, 1961). For the Trans-Canada Highway, Edward McCourt, *The Road Across Canada* (Toronto, 1965). For Hydro-Quebec, Clarence Hogue, *Quebec: Un Siècle d'eléctricité* (Montreal, 1979). On labour unions, Irving Abella, *Nationalism, Communism, and Canadian Labour* (Toronto, 1973); Pierre Elliott Trudeau, *La Grève de l'amiante*, translated as *The Asbestos Strike* (Toronto, 1974); Wallace Clement, *Hardrock Mining: Industrial Relations and Technological Changes at Inco* (Toronto, 1981). Science policy is outlined in G. Bruce Doern, *Science and Politics in Canada* (Montreal, 1972). On regional disparities and underdevelopment, see Manitoba Bureau of Statistics, *Canadian Regional Economic Development: A Historical Review, 1961-1987* (Winnipeg, 1989); L.D. McCann, ed., *Heartland and Hinterland: A Geography of Canada* (Scarborough, 1987); Economic Council of Canada, *Living Together: A Study of Regional Disparities* (Ottawa, 1977); David G. Alexander, *Atlantic Canada and Confederation: Essays in Canadian Political Economy* (Toronto, 1983). For the Columbia River treaty, see Neil A. Swainson, *Conflict Over the Columbia: The Canadian Background to an Historic Treaty* (Montreal, 1979). Walter Gordon's autobiography is *A Political Memoir* (Toronto, 1977). For the Watkins report, see Task Force on the Structure of Canadian Industry, *Foreign Ownership and the Structure of Canadian Industry: Report of The Task Force* (Ottawa, 1968); Kari Levitt, *The Silent Surrender: The Multinational Corporation in Canada* (Toronto, 1989); Dave Godfrey with Mel Watkins, eds, *Gordon to Watkins to You: Documentary: The Battle for Control of Our Economy* (Toronto, 1970).

Chapter Ten: The Travails of Canadian Unity, 1945-1970

The Canadian Annual Review (Toronto, 1960-) is an invaluable guide to recent affairs. For the FLQ crisis, see John Saywell, *Quebec 70: A Documentary Narrative* (Toronto, 1971); Gérard Pelletier, *The October Crisis* (Toronto, 1971). On Canadian politics generally, see David Bell and Lorne Tepperman, *The Roots of Disunity: A Look at Canadian Political Culture* (Toronto, 1979); J.M. Beck, *Pendulum of Power: Canada's Federal Elections* (Scarborough, Ont., 1968). For the prime ministers: J.W. Pickersgill, *The Mackenzie King Record* (Toronto, 1960-70), 4 vols, especially vols 3 and 4; Dale Thomson, *Louis St. Laurent: Canadian* (Toronto, 1967); Peter C. Newman, *Renegade in Power: The Diefenbaker Years* (Toronto, 1963); Bruce Thordarson, *Lester Pearson: Diplomat and Politician* (Toronto, 1974); Richard Gwyn, *The Northern Magus: Pierre Trudeau and Canadians* (Toronto, 1980). See also Geoffrey Stevens, *Stanfield* (Toronto, 1973); Dalton Camp, *Gentlemen, Players and Politicians* (Toronto, 1970). On the civil service, see L.D. Musolf, ed., *The Changing Public Service* (Berkeley, 1968). On the CCF/NDP, Walter D. Young, *The Anatomy of a Party: The National CCF, 1932-1961* (Toronto, 1969); Desmond Morton, *NDP: The Dream of Power* (Toronto, 1974); Thomas H. McLeod, *Tommy Douglas: The Road to Jerusalem* (Edmonton, 1987). On Social Credit, Maurice Pinard, *The Rise of a Third Party: A Study in Crisis Politics* (Englewood Cliffs, NJ, 1971). For a few of the leading provincial politicians, see David Mitchell, *W.A.C.: Bennett and the Rise of British Columbia* (Vancouver, 1983); Harold Horwood, *Joey* (Don Mills, 1989); Jean Provencher, *René Lévesque: Portrait of a Québécois* (Toronto, 1975). On the Constitution, Edward McWhinney, *Quebec and the Constitution, 1960-1978* (Toronto, 1979); Richard Simeon, *Federal-Provincial Diplomacy: The Making of Recent Policy in Canada* (Toronto, 1972); Andrew D. Heard,

Canadian Constitutional Conventions: The Marriage of Law and Politics (Toronto, 1991). For Quebec, John Saywell, *The Rise of the Parti Québécois, 1967-1976* (Toronto, 1977); Michael Behiels, *Prelude to Quebec's Quiet Revolution: Liberalism versus Neo-Nationalism, 1945-1960* (Kingston, 1985), and his edition of *Quebec Since 1945: Selected Readings* (Toronto, 1987); Alain G. Gagnon, ed., *Quebec: State and Society* (Toronto, 1984); Dominique Clift, *Quebec: Nationalism in Crisis* (Montreal and Kingston, 1982); Léandre Bergeron, *Petit Manuel d'histoire du Québec* (Montreal, 1971); Herbert Guindon, *Quebec Society: Tradition, Modernity, and Nationhood* (Toronto, 1988); Pierre Vallières, *White Niggers of America* (Toronto, 1971). For Expo '67, see Robert Fulford, *Remember Expo: A Pictorial Record* (Toronto, 1968). For bilingualism and biculturalism, see the *Report of the Royal Commission on Bilingualism and Biculturalism*, 5 vols (Ottawa, 1967-70). On the collective minorities, see Jean Daigle, ed., *Acadians of the Maritimes: Thematic Studies* (Moncton, 1982); J.R. Ponting and Roger Gibbins, *Out of Irrelevance: A Socio-Political Introduction to Indian Affairs in Canada* (Toronto, 1980); Harold Cardinal, *The Unjust Society: The Tragedy of Canada's Indians* (Toronto, 1969); *Report of the Royal Commission on the Status of Women in Canada* (Ottawa, 1970); Francine Barry, *La Travail de la femme au Québec: L'Évolution de 1940 à 1970* (Montreal, 1977); Gary Kinsman, *The Regulation of Desire: Sexuality in Canada* (Montreal, 1987); James W. St. G. Walker, *Racial Discrimination in Canada: The Black Experience* (Ottawa, 1985).

Chapter Eleven: The New Suburban Society, 1946-1972

Canadian television is discussed in Paul Rutherford, *When Television Was Young: Primetime Canada 1952-1967* (Toronto, 1990). On suburbia, see Robert Fischman, *Bourgeois Utopias: The Rise and Fall of Suburbia* (NY, 1987); Kenneth T. Jackson, *Crabgrass Frontier: The Suburbanization of the United States* (NY, 1985); S.D. Clark, *The Suburban Society* (Toronto, 1966); John R. Seeley et al., *Crestwood Heights: A Study of the Culture of Suburban Life* (Toronto, 1956). On the Baby Boomers, see John Kettle, *The Big Generation* (Toronto, 1980). Immigration policy and practice are discussed in Freda Hawkins, *Canada and Immigration: Public Policy and Public Concern* (1972; rev. ed., Kingston, 1988); David Corbett, *Canada's Immigration Policy: A Critique* (Toronto, 1957); Reg Whitaker, *Double Standard: The Secret History of Canadian Immigration Policy* (Toronto, 1987). For academic views of Canadian society, see Richard Joy, *Languages in Conflict: The Canadian Experience* (Toronto, 1972); John Porter, *The Vertical Mosaic: An Analysis of Social Class and Power in Canada* (Toronto, 1965); S.D. Clark, *The Developing Canadian Community* (Toronto, 1962). For views of growing up in Canada, Melinda McCracken, *Memories Are Made of This: What It Was Like to Grow Up in the Fifties* (Toronto, 1975); Myrna Kostash, *Long Way from Home: The Story of The Sixties Generation in Canada* (Toronto, 1980). On urban reform, see Jane Jacobs, *The Death and Life of Great American Cities* (NY, 1961); David and Nadine Nowlan, *The Bad Trip: The Untold Story of the Spadina Expressway* (Toronto, 1970). For education, see *Living and Learning: The Report of the Provincial Committee on Aims and Objectives of Education in the Schools of Ontario* (Toronto, 1968); Paul Axelrod, *Scholars and Dollars: Politics, Economics, and the Universities of Ontario 1945-1980* (Toronto, 1982); Hilda Neatby, *So Little for the Mind* (Toronto, 1953); Jean-Paul Desbiens, *The Impertinences of Brother Anonymous* (Montreal, 1962); Dennis Forsythe, ed., *Let the Niggers Burn: The Sir George Williams University Affair and its Caribbean Aftermath* (Montreal, 1971).

Chapter Twelve: Canadian Culture, 1945-1972

For the 1972 Canada-Russia tourney, see Scott Young, *War on Ice: Canada in International Hockey* (Toronto, 1976). For the royal commissions on culture, consult *Report of Royal Commission on National Development in the Arts, Letters and Sciences* (Ottawa, 1949-51) and *Royal Commission Studies: A Selection of Essays Prepared for the Royal Commission on National Development in the Arts, Letters and Sciences* (Ottawa, 1951); *Report of Royal Commission on Broadcasting* (Ottawa, 1957); *Report of Royal Commission on Publications* (Ottawa, 1961). For Marshall McLuhan, see Philip Marchand, *Marshall McLuhan: The Medium and the Messenger* (Toronto, 1989); Matie Molinaro, Corinne McLuhan, and William Toye, eds., *Letters of Marshall McLuhan* (Toronto, 1987). For Harold Innis, see Graeme H. Patterson, *History and Communications: Harold Innis, Marshall McLuhan, the Interpretation of History* (Toronto, 1990). For Quebec culture, see Richard Handler, *Nationalism and the Politics of Culture in Quebec* (Madison, Wis., 1988); Gabriel Dussault *et al.*, *L'État et la culture* (Quebec, 1986). For English Canada up to the fifties, see Julian Park, ed., *The Culture of Contemporary Canada* (Toronto, 1957); Maria Tippett, *Making Culture: English-Canadian Institutions and the Arts before the Massey Commission* (Toronto, 1990). On theatre, see Betty Lee, *Love and Whisky: The Story of the Dominion Drama Festival and the Early Years of Theatre in Canada, 1606-1972* (Toronto, 1982); Eugene Benson and L.W. Conolly, *The Oxford Companion to Canadian Theatre* (Toronto, Oxford, New York, 1989). For Vincent Massey, see Claude Bissell, *The Imperial Canadian: Vincent Massey in Office* (Toronto, 1986). For folklore see Edith Fowke, *Canadian Folklore* (Toronto, 1988). On literature, see William Toye, ed., *The Oxford Companion to Canadian Literature* (Toronto, 1983); George Woodcock, ed., *The Sixties: Writers and Writing of the Decade* (Vancouver, 1969); Margaret Atwood, *Survival: A Thematic Guide to Canadian Literature* (Toronto, 1972); Ben-Z. Shek, *French-Canadian and Québécois Novels* (Toronto, 1991); Larry Shouldice, ed., *Contemporary Quebec Criticism* (Toronto, 1979); Ronald Sutherland, *Second Image: Comparative Studies in Quebec/Canadian Literature* (Toronto, 1971); John Moss, *Patterns of Isolation in English Canadian Fiction* (Toronto, 1974). On painting, see Dennis Reid, *A Concise History of Canadian Painting: Second Edition* (Toronto, 1988); Ann Davis, *Frontiers of Our Dreams: Quebec Painting in the 1940s and 1950s* (Winnipeg, 1979); Quebec Museum of Contemporary Art, *Borduas et les automatistes* (Montreal, 1971); J. Russell Harper, *Painting in Canada: A History, Second Edition* (Toronto, 1977). On ballet, see Christopher Dafoe, *Dancing Through Time: The First Fifty Years of Canada's Royal Winnipeg Ballet* (Winnipeg, 1990). For history, see Carl Berger, *The Writing of Canadian History: Aspects of English-Canadian Historical Writing, 1900-1970* (Toronto, 1976; Second Edition, 1986); Serge Gagnon, *Quebec and Its Historians: The Twentieth Century* (Montreal, 1985). On film, see Gene Walz, ed., *Flashback: People and Institutions in Canadian Film History* (Montreal, 1986); Bruce Elder, *Image and Identity: Reflections on Canadian Film and Culture* (Waterloo, 1989); David Clandfield, *Canadian Film* (Toronto, 1987); Joyce Nelson, *The Colonized Eye: Rethinking the Grierson Legend* (Toronto, 1988).

Chapter Thirteen: The Collapse of Liberal Federalism

On agriculture, see Barry K. Wilson, *Farming the System: How Politics and Farmers Shape Agricultural Policy* (Saskatoon, 1990). For oil development, see J.D. House, *The Challenge of Oil: Newfoundland's Quest for Controlled Development* (St John's, 1985); G. Bruce Doern, *The Politics of Energy: The Development and Implementation of the NEP*

(Toronto, 1985); Jim Lyon, *Dome: The Rise and Fall of the House that Jack Built* (Toronto, 1983). On the brief Clark administration, see Jeffrey Simpson, *Discipline of Power:The Conservative Interlude and the Liberal Restoration* (Toronto, 1980). Trudeau is considered in a number of works, but see especially Christina McCall-Newman, *Grits:An Intimate Portrait of The Liberal Party* (Toronto, 1982); Stephen Clarkson and Christina McCall, *Trudeau and Our Times: Volume 1: The Magnificent Obsession* (Toronto, 1990); James Laxer and Robert Laxer, *The Liberal Idea of Canada: Pierre Trudeau and the Question of Canada's Survival* (Toronto, 1977); Larry Zolf, *Just Watch Me: Remembering Pierre Trudeau* (Toronto, 1984). For Brian Mulroney, see especially Michel Gratton, *'So, What Are the Boys Saying?':An Inside Look at Brian Mulroney in Power* (Toronto, 1987); Claire Hoy, *Friends in High Places: Politics and Patronage in the Mulroney Government* (Toronto, 1987); John Sawatsky, *Mulroney: The Politics of Ambition* (Toronto, 1991). On the bureaucracy, see Nicole Morgan, *Implosion: An Analysis of the Growth of the Federal Public Service in Canada, 1945-1985* (Montreal, 1986); Colin Campbell and George J. Szablowski, *The Superbureaucrats: Structure and Behaviour in Central Agencies* (Toronto, 1979). For provincial politics, see, for example, David G. Wood, *The Lougheed Legacy* (Toronto, 1985); Robert Paine, *Ayatollahs & Turkey Trots: Political Rhetoric in the New Newfoundland* (St John's, 1981); Stan Persky, *Bennett II: The Decline and Stumbling of Social Credit Government in British Columbia, 1979-83* (Vancouver, 1983). The Montreal Olympics of 1976 are considered in Nick Auf der Maur, *The Billion-Dollar Game:Jean Drapeau and the 1976 Olympics* (Toronto, 1976), and Jack Ludwig, *Five-Ring Circus:The Montreal Olympics* (Toronto, 1976). For the PQ in power, see Graham Fraser, *René Lévesque and the Parti Québécois in Power* (Toronto, 1984); Pierre Vallières, *The Impossible Quebec* (Montreal, 1980). On the Constitution, see David Milne's *The New Canadian Constitution* Toronto, 1983), *The Canadian Constitution: From Patriation to Meech Lake* (Toronto, 1989), and his *Tug of War: Ottawa and the Provinces under Trudeau and Mulroney* (Toronto, 1986); and Edward McWhinney, *Canada and the Constitution 1979-1982* (Toronto, 1982). On Meech Lake, see Andrew Cohen, *A Deal Undone:The Making and Breaking of the Meech Lake Accord* (Vancouver, 1990). For Canada's regional economy, see O.F.G. Sitwell and N.R.M. Seigfried, *The Regional Structure of the Canadian Economy* (Toronto, 1984). On Free Trade, see John Whalley *et al.*, *Canada-United States Free Trade* (Toronto, 1985); Richard Gwyn, *The 49th Paradox: Canada in North America* (Toronto, 1985). For the budget, Donald Savoie, *The Politics of Public Spending in Canada* (Toronto, 1990). For Massey-Ferguson, Peter Cook, *Massey at the Brink:The Story of Canada's Greatest Multinational and Its Struggle to Survive* (Toronto, 1981).

Chapter Fourteen: Society and Culture in an Age of Retrenchment, Confusion, and Diffusion, 1972-1990
For the Donald Marshall case, see *Royal Commission on the Donald Marshall, Jr., Prosecution* (Halifax, 1989); Michael Harris, *Justice Denied: The Law Versus Donald Marshall* (Toronto, 1986). On Mount Cashel, consult Michael Harris, *Unholy Orders: Tragedy at Mount Cashel* (Markham, Ont., 1990). On Canada's younger generation, see Reginald W. Bibby and Donald C. Postereski, *The Emerging Generation:An Inside Look at Canada's Teenagers* (Toronto, 1985). On religion, see Reginald W. Bibby, *Fragmented Gods:The Poverty and Potential of Religion in Canada* (Toronto, 1987); Hans Mol, *Faith and Fragility: Religion and Identity in Canada* (Burlington, Ont., 1985). On

aging, Susan A. McDaniel, *Canada's Aging Population* (Toronto and Vancouver, 1986); Maureen Baker, *The Aging Canadian Population* (Ottawa, 1988). On Aids, Michael Ornstein, *Aids in Canada: Knowledge, Behaviour, and Attitudes of Adults* (Toronto, 1989). On abortion, Angus and Arlene McLaren: *The Bedroom and the State: The Changing Practices and Politics of Contraception and Abortion in Canada, 1880-1980* (Toronto, 1986). On native peoples, Geoffrey York, *The Dispossessed: Life and Death in Native Canada* (Toronto, 1988); Larry Krotz, *Indian Country: Inside Another Canada* (Toronto, 1990). On immigration, Freda Hawkins, *Canada and Immigration: Public Policy and Public Concern* (2nd ed., Kingston, 1988). On poverty, Pierre Perron and François Vaillancourt, *The Evolution of Poverty in Canada, 1970-1985* (Ottawa, 1988); Keith G. Banting, *The Welfare State and Canadian Federalism* (Montreal, 1987). On cultural policy, Steven Globerman, *Cultural Regulation in Canada* (Montreal, 1983); George Woodcock, *Strange Bedfellows: The State and the Arts in Canada* (Vancouver, 1985); Paul Audley, *Canada's Cultural Industries: Broadcasting, Publishing, Records and Film* (Toronto, 1983); *Report of the Cultural Policy Review Committee* (Ottawa, 1982). On education, E.B. Titley and Peter J. Miller, eds, *Education in Canada: An Interpretation* (Calgary, 1982). On Quebec culture, Susan Crean and Marcel Rioux, *Two Nations: An Essay on the Culture and Politics of Canada and Quebec in a World of American Pre-eminence* (Toronto, 1983); Gabriel Dussault *et al.*, *L'État et la culture* (Quebec, 1986); Richard Handler, *Nationalism and the Politics of Culture in Quebec* (Madison, Wis., 1988). On the Canadian Football League, see Robert A. Stebbins, *Canadian Football: The View from the Helmet* (London, 1987). On the CBC, see for example Herschel Hardin, *Closed Circuits: The Sellout of Canada Television* (Vancouver, 1985).

General Bibliography

There are always works that do not fit into neat chronological pigeon-holes. Readers should be aware of the riches of biographical and other information in the multi-volumed *Dictionary of Canadian Biography* (Toronto, 1966-), and of the topographical (and graphical) information provided in the *Historical Atlas of Canada*, volumes I and III of which have been published. The four-volume *Canadian Encyclopedia: Second Edition* (1988) is a useful source that embraces many fields of enquiry.

Middle-level synthesis (between the survey and the monograph) has never been one of Canadian historiography's strong suits, but there are some good works. The following represents a sampling of the most useful titles.

On Canada in the world, see R.T. Naylor, *Canada in the European Age, 1453-1919* (Vancouver, 1987). On Canadian business, Michael Bliss, *Northern Enterprise; Five Centuries of Canadian Business* (Toronto, 1987). An overall view of economic development is to be found in William L. Marr and Donald G. Paterson, *Canada: An Economic History* (Toronto, 1980). For women, see Alison Prentice et al., *Canadian Women: A History* (Toronto, 1988). On the constitution, see G.F.G. Stanley, *A Short History of the Canadian Constitution* (Toronto, 1969). On politics, see David Bell and Lorne Tepperman, *The Roots of Disunity: A Look at Canadian Political Culture* (Toronto, 1979). For Indians, see J.R. Miller, ed., *Sweet Promises: A Reader on Indian-White Relations in Canada* (Toronto, 1991). On Quebec thinking, see Denis Monière, *Ideologies in Quebec: The Historical Development* (Toronto, 1981). For education, see J. Donald Wilson et al., *Canadian Education: A History* (Scarborough, Ont., 1970). For Canadian-American relations, consult Edelgard E. Mahant and Graham Mount, *An Introduction to Canadian-American Relations* (Toronto, 1984).

Much good work has been done on provincial history, including John Chadwick, *Newfoundland: Island into Province* (Cambridge, 1967); F.W.P. Bolger, *Island into Province* (Charlottetown, 1973; Toronto, 1984); Susan Mann Trofimenkoff, *A Dream of Nation: A Social and Intellectual History of Quebec* (Toronto, 1983); Joseph Schull, *Ontario since 1867* (Toronto, 1978), and Robert Bothwell, *A Short History of Ontario* (Toronto, 1986); W.L. Morton, *Manitoba: A History* (Toronto, 1957); John Archer, *Saskatchewan: A History* (Saskatoon, 1980); Howard Palmer with Tamara Palmer, *Alberta: A New History* (Edmonton, 1990); Margaret Ormsby, *British Columbia: A History* (Toronto, 1958), and Jean Barman, *The West Beyond the West: A History of British Columbia* (Toronto, 1991).

Index